Business
Concepts

Business
Concepts

FIRST CANADIAN EDITION

William M. Pride
Texas A & M University

Robert J. Hughes
Dallas County Community College

Jack R. Kapoor
College of DuPage

Brahm Canzer
John Abbott College *and* Concordia University

Richard C. Powers
University of Toronto

Houghton Mifflin Harcourt Publishing Company
Boston   New York

FOR MY LOVING FAMILY—CAROLE, MATTHEW, AND SARAH.

—BRAHM CANZER

I WOULD LIKE TO DEDICATE THIS BOOK TO MY PARENTS, RICHARD AND MARILYNE POWERS, FOR THEIR GUIDANCE, SUPPORT, AND LOVE
THROUGHOUT MY CAREER—THEY WERE ALWAYS THERE. I WOULD ALSO LIKE TO THANK BRAHM CANZER, MY PARTNER ON THIS PROJECT.

—RICHARD POWERS

Project Manager: **Timothy Cullen**
Sponsoring Editor: **Mike Schenk**
Executive Editor: **Lisé Johnson**
Development Editor: **Glen Herbert**
Senior Project Editor: **Fred Burns**
Editorial Assistant: **Jill Clark**
Senior Marketing Manager: **David Tonen**
Art and Design Manager: **Jill Haber**
Cover Design Director: **Tony Saizon**
Senior Composition Buyer: **Chuck Dutton**
Manager of New Title Project Management: **Patricia O'Neill**

Cover credit: © Lew Lause / Superstock

Printed in the U.S.A.

Library of Congress Control Number: 2008928641

ISBN 13: 978-0-547-06816-9
ISBN 10: 0-547-06816-6

1 2 3 4 5 6 7 8 9—CRK—12 11 10 09 08

Brief Contents

Contents

CHAPTER 5

Choosing a Form of Business Ownership 136

CHAPTER 8

Creating a Flexible Organization 222

CHAPTER 9

Producing Quality Goods
and Services 250

CHAPTER 10

Attracting and Retaining the Best Employees 282

CHAPTER 11

Motivating and Satisfying Employees and Teams 312

CHAPTER 12

Building Customer Relationships Through Effective Marketing 344

CHAPTER 13

Creating and Pricing Products That Satisfy Customers 372

CHAPTER 14

Distributing and Promoting Products 410

CHAPTER 15

Using Accounting Information 454

CHAPTER 16

Mastering Financial Management 486

Preface

Change. That six-letter word says a lot about the world in which we live. Think for a moment about the remarkable changes we have seen over the last few years, and consider how those changes have affected the business environment:

* Canadian global business activity continues to grow in importance both as a contributor to job creation and overall well-being.

* The job opportunities in our economy continue to grow more in service businesses than in manufacturing.

* New telecommunications technologies link people and information in ways that, just a few decades ago, were unheard of.

These important changes along with many more that are just as important are discussed in *Business Concepts*, First Canadian Edition.

The primary impetus of this edition was to provide students and instructors with the latest information and the latest concepts in a manner that was accessible and stimulating. Our objective has been to provide students and instructors with the best book possible. We have worked hard to make sure that *Business Concepts*, First Canadian Edition, reflects the wants and needs of students and instructors.

A Team Approach: Built by Professors and Students, for Professors and Students

Over the past four years Houghton Mifflin has conducted research and focus groups with a diverse cross-section of professors and students to create a textbook that truly reflects what professors and students want and need in an educational product. Everything we have learned has been applied to create and build a brand new educational experience and product model, from the ground up, for our two very important customer bases. The structure and content of *Business Concepts* reflects the results of that research. Based within that product model, it is designed to meet the teaching needs of today's instructors as well as the learning, study, and assessment goals of today's students. Professors have also played an integral role as content advisers through their reviews, creative ideas, and contributions to this new textbook.

What Students Told Us

Students have told us many things. While price is important to them, they are just as interested in having a textbook that reflects the way they actually learn and study. As with other consumer purchases and decisions they make, they want a textbook that is of true value to them. *Business Concepts* accomplishes both of their primary goals: it provides them with a price-conscious textbook, and it presents the concepts in a way that pleases them.

Today's students are busy individuals. They go to school, they work, some have families, they have a wide variety of interests, and they are involved in many activities. They take their education very seriously. Their main goal is to master the materials so they can perform well in class, get a good grade, graduate, land a good job, and be successful.

Different students learn in different ways; some learn best by reading, some are more visually oriented, and some learn best by doing through practice and assessment. While students learn in different ways, almost all students told us the same things regarding what they want their textbook to "look like."

The ideal textbook for students:

* Gets to the point quickly

* Is easy to understand and read

* Has pedagogical materials designed to reinforce key concepts

* Is cost conscious

Students want smaller chunks of information rather than the long sections and paragraphs found in traditional textbooks. This format provides them with immediate reinforcement and allows them to assess the concepts they have just studied. They like to read materials in more bulleted formats that are easier to digest than long sections and paragraphs. They almost always pay special attention to key terms and any materials that are boldfaced or highlighted in the text. In general, they spend little time reading or looking at materials that they view as superficial, such as many of the photographs (although they want some photos for visual enhancement) and long, drawn out boxed materials. However, they do want a textbook that is visually interesting, designed in an open, friendly, and accessible way. They want integrated study and assessment materials that help them reinforce, master, and test their knowledge of key concepts.

While students learn and study in a variety of different ways, a number of students told us that they often attend class first to hear their professor lecture and to take notes. Then they go back to read the chapter after (not always before) class. They use their textbook in this fashion not only to get the information they need but also to reinforce what they have learned in class. Students told us that they study primarily by using index or flashcards that highlight key concepts and terms, by reading lecture notes, and by using the supporting book website for quizzing and testing of key concepts. They also told us that they are far more likely to purchase and use a textbook if their professor actively uses the textbook in class and tells them that they need it.

Taking What Professors and Students Told Us to Create *Business Concepts*

Business Concepts provides exactly what students want and need pedagogically in an educational product. It does this by:

* Being concise and to the point

* Presenting more content in bulleted or more succinct formats

* Highlighting and boldfacing key concepts and information

* Organizing content in more bite-size formats

* Providing a system for immediate reinforcement and assessment of materials through-out the chapter

* Creating a design that is open, user friendly, and interesting for today's students

* Eliminating or reducing traditional chapter components that students view as superficial

* Creating a product that is easier for students to read and study

* Providing students with a product they feel is valuable

* Developing a total instructional package that helps students learn and professors teach

Text Features to Spark Interest

Chapter opening vignettes, titled "**Inside Business**," bring business concepts alive for students. We introduce the theme of each chapter focusing on pertinent activities of a real organization. The decisions and activities of these and other familiar organizations not only demonstrate what companies are actually doing, but also make the materials in each chapter relevant and absorbing for students. The opening vignette is then used as a review feature, and is revisited in the **Return to Inside Business** box that appears at the end of each chapter. There is a restatement of the concept as it relates to the example given in the opening vignette.

Effective Learning Aids Map Content

Each chapter begins with clearly stated **Learning Objectives** and a concise statement of "Why this chapter matters." Students then begin the chapter with a clear understanding of the concepts to be mastered and how they will relate to their experience in the world of business. Marginal **Key Terms** are also listed at the opening of each chapter, along with page references to where the terms are defined. The learning objectives are restated through the chapter material to further highlight the key concepts for learning.

The Most Current and Relevant Information

Throughout the text, special features help relate the concepts to real-world examples. Boxed features in this edition are brief, to the point, and fun to read, reflecting themes that many instructors feel are the most important: **Your Career,**

Entrepreneurial Challenge, Examining Ethics, Business Around the World, and **BizTech,** which presents concepts related to business technology.

Tools for Success

The **Chapter Review,** organized around the chapter learning objectives, provides a review of the key concepts covered in the chapter. **Review Questions** reinforce definitions and concepts, and **Discussion Questions** promote critical thinking. End-of-chapter cases focus on recognizable organizations and allow students to further consider the real-world implications of the concepts covered in the chapter.

ACKNOWLEDGMENTS

Many talented professionals have contributed to the development of *Business Concepts*, First Canadian Edition. We are especially grateful to Glen Herbert, Debbie Underhill, David Tonen, and Tim Cullen.

As we began the process of creating this text, we asked many individuals for ideas and suggestions that would help professors teach better and help students learn more efficiently. We have incorporated those ideas and suggestions into *Business Concepts*. We can only say *thank you* for your suggestions, ideas, and support. For the generous gift of their time and for their thoughtful and useful comments and suggestions, we are indebted to:

Glenn Brophy, Nipissing University

Choon Hian Chan, Kwantlen College

Victoria Digby, Fanshawe College

Sherry Finney, Cape Breton University

Jane Forbes, Seneca College

Tim Hardie, Lakehead University

Cathy Hurley, University of New Brunswick

Robert Maher, University of New Brunswick

David McConomy, Queen's University

Valerie Micelli, Seneca College

Lisa Phillips, Douglas College

Kim Richter, Kwantlen College

Frank Shychoski, University of Saskatchewan

Patti Stoll, Seneca College

William Thurber, Brock University

Jamie Wilson, St. Clair College

Brahm Canzer
Richard C. Powers

About the Authors

BRAHM CANZER

Brahm Canzer currently teaches business management courses to John Abbott College students in Montreal. He also is an adjunct lecturer at Concordia University specializing in e-Marketing. During his teaching career he has also taught undergraduate and graduate business courses to students at Concordia, McGill, and the University of Toronto. Professor Canzer received his PhD (1995) and MBA (1976) from Concordia University in Montreal. Professor Canzer's expertise includes finding web-based opportunities and solutions, and he was among the pioneers to design and teach MBA courses online for Simon Fraser University.

RICHARD C. POWERS

After receiving his MBA and LLB from Queen's University, Rick worked as a corporate lawyer for Smith, Lyons, Torrance, Stevenson and Mayer (now Gowlings). He later served as Corporate Counsel for Honda Canada Inc. before joining The University of Toronto in 1992. Rick is currently the Assistant Dean and Executive Director, MBA Programs at The Rotman School of Management. A recipient of numerous teaching awards, Rick's areas of expertise include corporate governance, ethics, business and corporate law, and sports marketing. Rick is an Academic Director of The Directors Education Program and the Governance Essentials Program (in partnership with the Institute of Corporate Directors—ICD). He also teaches in Rotman's Executive MBA, MBA, and Executive Education Programs. In the past he has been extensively involved in both the Bachelor of Commerce and Bachelor of Business Administration programs at The University of Toronto. He is a director of several not-for-profit organizations and frequently comments on legal and governance issues in various media across Canada.

Business
Concepts

CHAPTER 1

Exploring the World of Business and Economics

Your Guide to Success in Business

Why this chapter matters
Studying business will help you to choose a career, become a successful employee, perhaps start your own business, and become a better-informed consumer and investor.

LEARNING OBJECTIVES

1. Discuss your future in the world of business.

2. Define *business* and identify potential risks and rewards.

3. Define *economics* and describe the two types of economic systems: capitalism and command economy.

4. Identify the ways to measure economic performance.

5. Outline the four types of competition.

6. Summarize the factors that affect the business environment and the challenges that Canadian businesses will encounter in the future.

Growing Global Demand for Energy Boosts Canada's Economy

Canada is among the top ten producers in the world of all energy sources (except coal) and number one in the production of hydro-electric power. Given the dramatic increases in prices for energy in recent years to more than $76 (U.S.) per barrel in 2006, from about $20 (U.S.) during the late 1990s, it should be clear why Alberta and Newfoundland and Labrador, and to a lesser degree British Columbia, Quebec, and other energy producing provinces have enjoyed strong economic growth. In 2003, energy from all sources contributed $62.8 billion to the Canadian economy—about 5.6 percent of our gross domestic product and employed over 300,000 people in the energy sector, representing about 2.5 percent of our workforce.[1]

Canadian businesses are participants in the global marketplace for energy, often in collaboration with other companies or governments, domestic and foreign. For instance, Calgary's EnCana Corporation, Canada's biggest independent oil and gas company, and ConocoPhillips Company of Houston plan to spend $10.7 billion (U.S.) to produce and upgrade 400,000 barrels a day of raw oil sands crude by 2015. Extraction of the oil from Alberta's tar sands will be handled by EnCana, while the refining of the oil into products such as gasoline, diesel, and heating oil will be managed by ConocoPhillips at their facilities at Wood River near the Mississippi River in Illinois and Borger in northern Texas. EnCana is experienced in the emerging technology of extracting oil from the Alberta tar sands by pumping steam below ground and forcing the oil to the surface. ConocoPhillips provides refining facilities and a distribution network to deliver products to customers. Together, these businesses provide employment to a variety of skilled and knowledgeable people who are part of the complex energy supply chain in North America.[2]

Canada produces about 2.4 million barrels of oil a day while the U.S. produces about 7.6 million barrels. But whereas Canada enjoys a surplus beyond its own needs, which can be exported, the U.S. is a net

continued on next page

• • •

DID YOU KNOW?

Rising global demand for more energy has driven oil exploration and development in Newfoundland and Labrador and Alberta, making these two provinces leading contributors to Canadian economic growth.

K E Y   T E R M S

free enterprise (5)	capitalism (14)	recession (22)	monopolistic competition (25)
cultural (or workplace) diversity (7)	invisible hand (14)	depression (22)	product differentiation (25)
business (10)	market economy (14)	monetary policies (22)	oligopoly (25)
profit (11)	mixed economy (15)	fiscal policy (22)	monopoly (26)
stakeholders (12)	consumer products (16)	federal deficit (23)	natural monopoly (26)
economics (13)	command economy (18)	national debt (23)	standard of living (27)
economy (13)	productivity (19)	competition (23)	barter (27)
microeconomics (13)	gross domestic product (GDP) (20)	perfect (or pure) competition (24)	domestic system (27)
macroeconomics (13)	inflation (21)	supply (24)	factory system (28)
factors of production (13)	deflation (21)	demand (24)	specialization (28)
entrepreneur (14)	business cycle (21)	market price (25)	e-business (29)

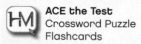
ACE the Test
Crossword Puzzle
Flashcards

importer. Much of that energy comes from the highly volatile Middle East, where supply disruption is a concern. Saudi Arabia produces 9.5 million barrels of the roughly 80 million barrels of oil produced each day around the world.[3] However, transportation to customers in the U.S. is far more problematic than from Canada. Therefore, countries like the U.S., whose economies are heavy consumers of energy, will likely continue to seek out more secure sources of supply and alternative energy sources such as gas, hydro-electric, coal, solar, wind, etc.

Just why is energy so valuable? Energy is necessary for virtually any modern economic development. Without energy, production, transportation, and communication would be limited to primitive levels of performance. Modern factories need electricity to run machinery for efficient production of goods and vehicles need fuel to transport materials to production centres and then on to customers. In essence, the demand for energy is directly related to the level of economic activity in any country. These days, China and India are leading the world in economic development and represent much of the growing demand for energy. From footwear production to customer service call centres, these two economic giants, with about one third of the world's population, are expected to continue to lead demand for more resources as their economies grow. As a result, countries like Canada will benefit as we help supply not only our own energy needs, but also the rising global demand for energy.

Business is unquestionably one of the most powerful and ubiquitous social institutions affecting the way we Canadians live today. Business activity in one way or another touches us all. For instance, each one of us is a consumer of products and services that businesses produce—such as energy. Some of us are employees who produce these products and services and others are perhaps the investors and owners of the businesses.

Canadian businesses that prosper in our communities share their prosperity with employees, investors and consumers through the payment of salaries and wages, dividends, and the creation of a wider variety of products and services from which consumers can choose. Furthermore, prosperous Canadian communities contribute tax dollars to our governments to help pay for social infrastructures such as public education and health services that contribute to the quality of life we enjoy. In short, we are all inextricably linked together through business activity and rely on the mechanisms of our economic system to effectively and fairly distribute wealth, employment, and the products and services we both need and want.

Just how does all this business exchange between people work? How is it all organized? How do we get the products and services we want and need and how is it that some people and businesses enjoy greater success in this scheme than others? What key relationships and associations are there that can help explain and predict business activity, job opportunities, and investment success? This business textbook will address all of these questions as well as fundamental business concepts, vocabulary, and strategic thinking.

Regardless of which career you eventually select for yourself, knowledge of business and business thinking is necessary because, quite simply, there is very little that happens in life that does not have something to do with business. Whether you are determined to pursue more advanced business courses later or are simply seeking an overview of business to complement your program of study now, an understanding of business will be an invaluable contribution to your education.

Business Is Dynamic

Like all the social sciences, business is a dynamic phenomenon. A student can only attempt to learn about business by calling a temporary "time-out," and then examining the details of the moment. But as surely as the sun rises each day, change will enter the situation under study and things will not remain the same for long. As with all living systems, change is a given. So, we will call a time-out and examine where Canadian business is today. Furthermore, we will try to explain just how we got here and suggest where we are likely to find ourselves in the future.

Canadian business is not something that has evolved in isolation. Our story is heavily influenced by world events, great inventions, migration of people, and relationships with global partners, most notably United States and the European nations. One major change that has transformed the way Canadian business will function in the foreseeable future was the signing of the Free Trade Agreement with the United States, in 1989, and, subsequently, the North American Free Trade Agreement or NAFTA with United States and Mexico, in 1994. Canadians have recently entered a new world of business in which many of the old rules for behaviour have been replaced by new ones and the strategies for success have dramatically changed.

Today, more than ever before, Canadian business must compete in the North American and global marketplace. Small branch plants that previously supplied only the Canadian market have either been transformed into production centres of new products for the entire globe, been reduced in scale of operation, or have been closed completely. This new competitive environment presents Canadian businesses with both opportunities for growth and challenges to survival against strong American competitors who previously were hampered by trade restrictions. These trade restrictions have all but been eliminated through the NAFTA and Canadian business students will need to understand more about American and global business competitors than ever before if they are to gain a clear understanding of our future path.

In order to better understand this new North American competitive environment, we will make a point of examining and comparing ourselves to American business strategic thinking and behaviour, for the United States is our number-one competitor. So much of our business environment is in some way influenced by American firms; just think of all the American-origin consumer products we Canadians take for granted in our economy such as Coca Cola and IBM. Likewise, many Canadian firms and brands are equally well known in the U.S., such as Waterloo-based Research In Motion's Blackberry and the Toronto-based Roots clothing brand. Clearly, a greater degree of trans-North American business activity is already well underway and Canadian business students will need to understand this phenomenon better.

The system of business, in which individuals decide what to produce, how to produce it, and at what price to sell it, is called **free enterprise**. Our free-enterprise system ensures, for example, that Research In Motion can introduce new products, license their technology for other companies to use, change their prices and the method of distribution, and attempt to produce and market products in other countries. Our system also gives executives the right to manage the company, compete with other producers, and distribute earnings to stockholders who share in the success of the

free enterprise the system of business in which individuals are free to decide what to produce, how to produce it, and at what price to sell it

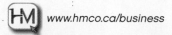

company. Finally, our system allows customers the right to choose between products produced by Research In Motion and those by competitors.

Competition among businesses is a necessary and an extremely important by-product of free enterprise. Because many individuals and groups can open businesses, there are usually many firms offering similar products. Each of the firms offering similar products must therefore try to convince any potential customer to buy its product rather than a similar item made by someone else. In other words, these firms must compete with each other for sales to potential customers. Under a free enterprise system, competition works to ensure the efficient and effective operation of business and ensures that a firm will survive only if it serves its customers well.

In this chapter we look briefly at what business is and how it got that way. First, we discuss your future in business and explore some important reasons for studying business. Second we define *business*, noting how business organizations satisfy needs and earn profits. Third, we examine how capitalism, socialism, and communism answer four basic economic questions. Fourth, our focus shifts to how the nations of the world measure economic performance and the four types of competitive situations. And fifth, we look at the events that helped shape today's business system, the current business environment, and the challenges that businesses face.

Your Future in the Changing World of Business

Learning Objective

Discuss your future in the world of business.

The key word in this heading is *changing*. A student taking business courses or an employee just starting a career must learn to deal with the multi-disciplinary complexities of our ever-changing business world. Successful students will find a greater variety of career opportunities out there for people who are willing to work hard and continue to learn and who possess the ability to adapt to change.

Whether you want to obtain part-time employment to pay education and living expenses, begin your career as a full-time employee, or start a business, always remember that it is you who must bring something to the table that makes you different from the next person. Employers in our capitalist economic system are more demanding than ever before. Ask yourself: What can I do that will make employers want to pay me a salary? What skills do I have that employers need? With these two questions in mind, we begin the next section with another basic question: Why study business?

Why Study Business?

The potential benefits of higher education are enormous. To begin with, there are economic benefits. Over their lifetimes, college and university graduates on average earn much more than high school graduates. And while lifetime earnings are substantially higher for college and university graduates, so are annual income amounts.

The nice feature of education and knowledge is that once you have it, no one can take it away. It is yours to use for a lifetime. In this section we explore what you may expect to get out of this business course and text. You will find at least four quite compelling reasons for studying business.

For Help in Choosing a Career What do you want to do with the rest of your life? Someplace, sometime, someone probably has asked you this same question. And like many people, you may find it a difficult question to answer. This business course will introduce you to a wide array of employment opportunities. In private enterprise, these range from small, local businesses owned by one individual to large companies that employ thousands of employees. There are also employment opportunities with federal, provincial, and local governments and with not-for-profit organizations such as the Red Cross and Save the Children. In addition to career information in Appendix A and on the text website, a number of additional websites provide information about career development.

One thing to remember as you think about what your ideal career might be is that a person's choice of a career ultimately is just a reflection of what he or she values and considers most important. What will give one individual personal satisfaction may not satisfy another. For example, one person might dream of a career as a corporate executive and becoming a millionaire before the age of thirty. Another might choose a career that yields more modest monetary rewards but that provides the opportunity to help others. One person may be willing to work long hours and seek additional responsibility in order to get promotions and pay raises. Someone else may prefer a less demanding job with little stress and more free time. What you choose to do with your life will be based on what you feel is most important. And the *you* is a very important part of that decision.

To Be a Successful Employee Deciding on the type of career you want is only a first step. To get a job in your chosen field and to be successful at it, you will have to develop a plan, or road map, that ensures that you have the skills and knowledge the job requires. You will be expected to have both the technical skills needed to accomplish a specific task and the ability to work well with many types of people in a culturally diverse work force. **Cultural** (or **workplace**) **diversity** refers to the differences among people in a work force owing to race, ethnicity, and gender. These skills, together with a working knowledge of the Canadian business environment and an appreciation for a culturally diverse workplace, can give you an inside edge when you are interviewing with a prospective employer.

Don't underestimate your part in making your dream a reality. It will take hard work, dedication, perseverance, and time management to achieve your goals. Communication skills are also important. Today, most employers are looking for employees who can compose a business letter and get it in a proper form. They also want employees who can talk with customers and use e-mail to communicate with people within and outside the organization. Employers also will be interested in any work experience you may have had in cooperative work/school programs, during summer vacations, or in part-time jobs during the school year. These things can make a difference when it is time to apply for the job you really want.

To Start Your Own Business Some people prefer to work for themselves, and they open their own businesses. To be successful, business owners must possess many

UJING THE INTERNET

To find out the details about a specific career, expected growth in an industry, training and other qualifications, and earnings, visit the Human Resources and Social Development Canada resource centre located at www.hrsdc.gc.ca/en/home.shtml and the special youth services centre at http://www.youth.gc.ca/.

cultural (or **workplace**) **diversity** differences among people in a work force owing to race, ethnicity, and gender

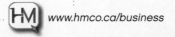
www.hmco.ca/business

of the same skills that successful employees have. And they must be willing to work hard and put in long hours.

It also helps if your small business can provide a product or service that customers want. For example, Mark Cuban started a small Internet company called Broadcast .com that provided hundreds of live and on-demand audio and video programs ranging from rap music to sporting events to business events over the Internet. When Cuban sold Broadcast.com to Yahoo! Inc., he became a billionaire. Today he is an expert on how the Internet will affect society in the future and believes that there is a real need for all companies, not just technology companies, to provide something that their customers want. If they don't do that, their company could very well fail.

Unfortunately, many small businesses fail; most estimates suggest that perhaps 70 percent of them fail within the first five years. Typical reasons for business failures include poor management, undercapitalization (not enough money), poor business location, poor customer service, and lack of a proper business plan. The material in Chapter 6 and selected topics and examples throughout this text will help you to decide whether you want to open your own business. This material also will help you to overcome many of these problems.

To Become a Better Informed Consumer and Investor The world of business surrounds us. You cannot buy a home, a new Grand Prix from the local Pontiac dealer, a Black & Decker sander at a Canadian Tire store, a pair of jeans at the Gap, or a hot dog from a street vendor without entering into a business transaction. Because you no doubt will engage in business transactions almost every day of your life, one very good reason for studying business is to become a more fully informed consumer. Many people also rely on a basic understanding of business to help them to invest for the future. It is important to learn the basics about the economy and business, stocks, mutual funds, and other alternatives before investing your money. And while this is an obvious conclusion, just dreaming of being rich doesn't make it happen. In fact, like many facets of life, it takes planning and determination to establish the type of investment program that will help you to accomplish your financial goals.

Special Note to Students

It is important to begin reading this text with one thing in mind: *This business course does not have to be difficult.* In fact, *learning about business and how you can be involved as an employee, business owner, consumer, or investor can be fun!*

We have done everything possible to eliminate the problems that students encounter in a typical class. All the features in each chapter have been evaluated and recommended by instructors with years of teaching experience. In addition, business students were asked to critique each chapter component. Based on this feedback, the text includes the following features:

* *Your Guide to Success in Business* is placed at the beginning of each chapter and provides learning objectives, key terms, and helpful suggestions for mastering chapter content.

* *An Opening Case* highlights how successful companies do business on a day-to-day basis.

* *Margin notes* are used throughout the text to reinforce both learning objectives and key terms.

* *Boxed features* highlight career information, starting a business, ethical behaviour, global issues, and the impact of technology on business today.

* *Spotlight* features highlight interesting facts about business and society and often provide a real-world example of an important concept within a chapter.

* *End-of-chapter materials* provide questions about the opening case, a chapter summary, review and discussion questions, and two cases. The last section of every chapter is entitled Building Skills for Career Success and includes exercises devoted to exploring the Internet, building team skills, and researching different careers.

In addition to the text, a number of student supplements will help you to explore the world of business. We are especially proud of the website that accompanies this edition. There, you will find online study aids, including interactive study tools, practice tests, audio reviews for each chapter, flashcards, and other resources. If you want to take a look at the Internet support materials available for this edition of *Business,*

1. Make an Internet connection and go to **www.hmco.ca/business.**

2. Choose one of the topics and click.

As authors, we want you to be successful. We know that your time is valuable and that your schedule is crowded with many activities. We also appreciate the fact that textbooks are expensive. Therefore, we want you to use this text and get the most out of your investment. In order to help you get off to a good start, a number of suggestions for developing effective study skills and using this text are provided in Table 1.1.

1. ***Prepare before you go to class.***	Early preparation is the key to success in many of life's activities. Certainly, early preparation can help you to participate in class, ask questions, and improve your performance on exams.
2. ***Read the chapter.***	Although it may seem like an obvious suggestion, many students never take the time to really read the material. Find a quiet space where there are no distractions, and invest enough time to become a "content expert."
3. ***Underline or highlight important concepts.***	Make this text yours. Don't be afraid to write on the pages of your text. It is much easier to review material if you have identified important concepts.
4. ***Take notes.***	While reading, take the time to jot down important points and summarize concepts in your own words. Also, take notes in class.
5. ***Apply the concepts.***	Learning is always easier if you can apply the content to your real-life situation. Think about how you could use the material either now or in the future.
6. ***Practise critical thinking.***	Test the material in the text. Do the concepts make sense? To build critical-thinking skills, answer the questions that accompany the cases at the end of each chapter. Also, many of the exercises in the Building Skills for Career Success require critical thinking.
7. ***Prepare for exams.***	Allow enough time to review the material before exams. Check out the summary and review questions at the end of the chapter. Then use the resources on the text website.

Table 1.1

Seven Ways to Use This Text and Its Resources

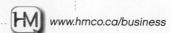

Why not take a look at these suggestions and use them to help you succeed in this course and earn a higher grade.

Business: A Definition

business the organized effort of individuals to produce and sell, for a profit, the goods and services that satisfy society's needs

Business is the organized effort of individuals to produce and sell, for a profit, the goods and services that satisfy society's needs. The general term *business* refers to all such efforts within a society (as in "Canadian business") or within an industry (as in "the steel business"). However, *a business* is a particular organization, such as WestJet Airline Limited or Roots Canada Limited. To be successful, a business must perform three activities. It must be organized. It must satisfy needs. And it must earn a profit.

The Organized Effort of Individuals

For a business to be organized, it must combine four kinds of resources: material, human, financial, and informational. *Material* resources include the raw materials used in manufacturing processes, as well as buildings and machinery. For example, Roots Canada Limited needs wool, thread, zippers, and other raw materials to produce the clothing products it sells worldwide. In addition, this Toronto-based company needs human, financial, and informational resources. *Human* resources are the people who furnish their labour to the business in return for wages. The *financial* resource is the money required to pay employees, purchase materials, and generally keep the business operating. And *information* is the resource that tells the managers of the business how effectively the other resources are being combined and used (see Figure 1.1).

Figure 1.1

Combining Resources

A business must combine all four resources effectively to be successful.

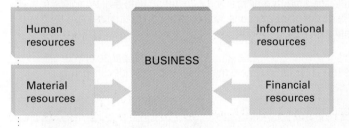

Today, businesses usually are organized as one of three specific types. *Manufacturing businesses* process various materials into tangible goods, such as delivery trucks or towels. Intel, for example, produces computer chips that, in turn, are sold to companies that manufacture computers. *Service businesses* produce services, such as haircuts, legal advice, or tax preparation. And some firms, called *marketing intermediaries*, buy products from manufacturers and then resell them. Research In Motion Limited is a manufacturer that produces communications equipment among other things. These products may be sold to a marketing intermediary, such as Best Buy or Future Shop, which then resells the manufactured goods to consumers.

Satisfying Needs

The ultimate objective of every firm must be to satisfy the needs of its customers. People generally do not buy goods and services simply to own them; they buy products and services to satisfy particular needs. Some of us may feel that the need for transportation is best satisfied by an air-conditioned BMW with stereo CD player, automatic transmission, power seats and windows, and remote-control side mirrors. Others may believe that a Ford Focus with a stick shift will do just fine. Both products are available to those who want them, along with a wide variety of other products that satisfy the need for transportation.

When firms lose sight of their customers' needs, they are likely to find the going rough. However, when businesses understand their customers' needs and work to satisfy those needs, they are usually successful. Back in 1962, Sam Walton opened his first discount store in Rogers, Arkansas. Although the original store was quite different from the Wal-Mart Superstores you see today, the basic ideas of providing customer service and offering goods that satisfied needs at low prices are part of the reason why this firm has grown to become the largest retailer in the world. Today, Wal-Mart provides its products and services to more than 176 million customers each week and has more than 3,800 retail stores in the United States and over 2,600 retail stores in nine different countries including 278 in Canada employing more than 70,000 Canadians.[4]

Low carbs and diet drinks can equal fat profits

Many restaurant owners have found that one way to improve sales and profits is to meet the needs of diet-conscious consumers.

Business Profit

A business receives money (sales revenue) from its customers in exchange for goods or services. It also must pay out money to cover the expenses involved in doing business. If the firm's sales revenues are greater than its expenses, it has earned a profit. More specifically, as shown in Figure 1.2, **profit** is what remains after all business expenses have been deducted from sales revenue. A negative profit, which results when a firm's expenses are greater than its sales revenue, is called a *loss*. A business cannot continue to operate at a loss for an indefinite period of time. Management and employees must find some way to increase sales revenues and/or reduce expenses in order to return to profitability. In some cases, the pursuit of profits is so important that some

profit what remains after all business expenses have been deducted from sales revenue

> **Figure 1.2**
>
> **The Relationship Between Sales Revenue and Profit**
>
> Profit is what remains after all business expenses have been deducted from sales revenue.

Sales revenue	
Expenses	Profit

corporate executives, including those from such corporations as Nortel, Enron, WorldCom, and Adelphia Communications have fudged their profit figures to avoid disappointing shareholders, directors, Wall Street and Bay Street analysts, lenders, and other stakeholders. The term **stakeholders** is used to describe all the different people or groups of people who are affected by the policies, decisions, and activities of an organization.

The profit earned by a business becomes the property of its owners. Thus, in one sense, profit is the reward business owners receive for producing goods and services that consumers want. Profit is also the payment that business owners receive for assuming the considerable risks of ownership. One of these is the risk of not being paid. Everyone else—employees, suppliers, and lenders—must be paid before the owners. A second risk that owners undertake is the risk of losing whatever they have invested into the business. A business that cannot earn a profit is very likely to fail, in which case the owners lose whatever money, effort, and time they have invested.

To satisfy society's needs and make a profit, a business must operate within the parameters of a nation's economic system. In the next section we define economics and describe two different types of economic systems.

BIZ TECH

Different Paths to E-Profits

Three of the world's largest high-tech firms have pursued different paths to profits.

Amazon. Founded as an online bookstore, Amazon.com was unprofitable in the early years but today rings up $9 billion annually selling everything from diamonds to DVDs. Offering free shipping on purchases of $25 or more cuts into profits but encourages repeat business. Amazon also charges a commission when other merchants make a sale through its site—much like eBay.

eBay. eBay pioneered online auctions in 1995 and was profitable from the start. Why? Because it doesn't actually own what it sells but does receive a commission on every transaction. Now more than 150 million people worldwide use eBay to buy and sell all kinds of goods and services. The firm recently bought Skype, a company that specializes in online telephone communications.

Google. This well-known search site opened for business in 1998 and was profitable by the end of 2001. Google makes most of its money selling advertising links alongside search results. With services such as Froogle shopping search and Google Earth maps—plus new technologies—Google wants to attract more users and keep them on Google sites for as long as possible.

Types of Economic Systems

Learning Objective

Define *economics* and describe the two types of economic systems: capitalism and command economy.

Economics is the study of how wealth is created and distributed. By *wealth*, we mean "anything of value," including the products produced and sold by business. *How wealth is distributed* simply means "who gets what." Experts often use economics to explain the choices we make and how those choices change as we cope with the demands of everyday life. In simple terms, individuals, businesses, governments, and society must make decisions that reflect what is important to each group at a particular time. For example, you want to take a weekend trip to some exotic vacation spot, and you also want to begin an investment program. Because of your financial resources, though, you cannot do both. You must decide what is most important. Individuals, along with business firms, governments, and, to some extent, society, must deal with scarcity when making important decisions. In this case, *scarcity* means "lack of resources"—money, time, natural resources, and so on—that are needed to satisfy a want or need. The decisions that individuals, business firms, government, and society make and the way in which people deal with the creation and distribution of wealth determine the kind of economic system, or **economy**, that a nation has.

Today, experts often study economics from two different perspectives: microeconomics and macroeconomics. **Microeconomics** is the study of the decisions made by individuals and businesses. Microeconomics, for example, examines how the prices of homes affect the number of homes built and sold. On the other hand, **macroeconomics** is the study of the national economy and the global economy. Macroeconomics examines the economic effect of taxes, government spending, interest rates, and similar factors on a nation and society.

Over the years, the economic systems of the world have differed in essentially two ways: (1) the ownership of the factors of production and (2) how they answer four basic economic questions that direct a nation's economic activity. **Factors of production** are the resources used to produce goods and services. There are four such factors:

* *Land and natural resources*—elements in their natural state that can be used in the production process to make appliances, automobiles, and other products. Typical examples include crude oil, timber, minerals, land, water, and even air.

* *Labour*—the time and effort that we use to produce goods and services. It includes human resources such as managers and employees.

* *Capital*—the facilities, equipment, machines, and money used in the operation of organizations. While most people think of capital as just money, it also can be the manufacturing equipment on a Ford automobile assembly line or a computer used in the corporate offices.

* *Entrepreneurship*—the resources that organize land, labour, and capital. It is the willingness to take risks and the knowledge and ability to use the other factors of

economics the study of how wealth is created and distributed

economy the way in which people deal with the creation and distribution of wealth

microeconomics the study of the decisions made by individuals and businesses

macroeconomics the study of the national economy and the global economy

factors of production resources used to produce goods and services

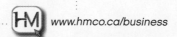

production efficiently. An **entrepreneur** is a person who risks his or her time, effort, and money to start and operate a business.

A nation's economic system significantly affects all the economic activities of its citizens and organizations. This far-reaching impact becomes more apparent when we consider that a country's economic system determines how the factors of production are used to meet the needs of society. Today, two different economic systems exist: capitalism and command economies. The way each system answers the four basic economic questions below determines a nation's economy.

1. What goods and services—and how much of each—will be produced?
2. How will these goods and services be produced?
3. For whom will these goods and services be produced?
4. Who owns and who controls the major factors of production?

Capitalism

Capitalism is an economic system in which individuals own and operate the majority of businesses that provide goods and services. Capitalism stems from the theories of the eighteenth-century Scottish economist Adam Smith. In his book *Wealth of Nations*, published in 1776, Smith argued that a society's interests are best served when the individuals within that society are allowed to pursue their own self-interest. In other words, people will work hard only if they can earn more pay or profits in the case of a business owner. According to Smith, when an individual is acting to improve his or her own fortunes, he or she indirectly promotes the good of his or her community and the people in that community. Smith went on to call this concept the "invisible hand." The **invisible hand** is a term created by Adam Smith to describe how an individual's own personal gain benefits others and a nation's economy. For example, the only way a small-business owner who produces shoes can increase personal wealth is to sell shoes to customers. To become even more prosperous, the small-business owner must hire workers to produce even more shoes. According to the invisible hand, people in the small-business owner's community not only would have shoes, but some workers also would have jobs working for the shoemaker. Thus the success of people in the community and, to some extent, the nation's economy is tied indirectly to the success of the small-business owner.

Adam Smith's capitalism is based on four fundamental issues illustrated in Figure 1.3. First, Smith argued that the creation of wealth is properly the concern of private individuals, not government. Second, private individuals must own the resources used to create wealth. Smith argued that the owners of resources should be free to determine how these resources are used and also should be free to enjoy the income, profits, and other benefits derived from the ownership of these resources. Third, Smith contended that economic freedom ensures the existence of competitive markets that allow both sellers and buyers to enter and exit as they choose. This freedom to enter or leave a market at will has given rise to the term *market economy*. A **market economy** (sometimes referred to as a *free-market economy*) is an economic system in which businesses and individuals decide what to produce and buy, and the market determines quantities sold and prices. Finally, in Smith's view, the role of government should be limited to providing defence against foreign enemies, ensuring internal order, and furnishing public works and education. With regard to the economy, government should act only as rule maker and umpire. The French term *laissez-faire* describes Smith's capitalist system and implies that there should be

Laissez-faire capitalism

Right to create wealth

Right to own private property and resources

Right to economic freedom and freedom to compete

Right to limited government intervention

Figure 1.3

Basic Assumptions for Adam Smith's Laissez-Faire Capitalism

no government interference in the economy. Loosely translated, this term means "let them do" (as they see fit).

Canada's Economic System

Our economic system is rooted in the laissez-faire capitalism of Adam Smith. However, our real-world economy is not as laissez faire as Smith would have liked because government participates as more than umpire and rule maker. Our economy is, in fact, a **mixed economy**, one that exhibits elements of both capitalism and socialism.

In a mixed economy, the four basic economic questions discussed at the beginning of this section (what, how, for whom, and who) are answered through the interaction of households, businesses, and governments. The interactions among these three groups are shown in Figure 1.4.

mixed economy an economy that exhibits elements of both capitalism and socialism

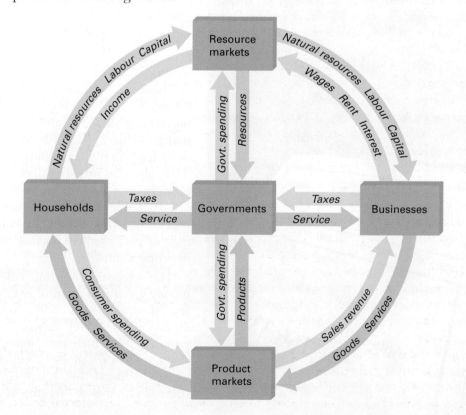

Figure 1.4

The Circular Flow in Our Mixed Economy

Our economic system is guided by the interaction of buyers and sellers, with the role of government being taken into account.

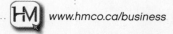

Households Households, made up of individuals, are the consumers of goods and services, as well as owners of some of the factors of production. As *resource owners*, the members of households provide businesses with labour, capital, and other resources. In return, businesses pay wages, rent, and dividends and interest that households receive as income.

As *consumers*, household members use their income to purchase the goods and services produced by business. Today, approximately 50 percent of our nation's $1.3 trillion total production consists of **consumer products**—goods and services purchased by individuals for personal consumption. (The remaining half is purchased by Canadian businesses and governments and foreign buyers of our exports.[5]) This means that consumers, as a group, are the biggest customers of Canadian business.

Businesses Like households, businesses are engaged in two different exchanges. They exchange money for natural resources, labour, and capital and use those resources to produce goods and services. Then they exchange their goods and services for sales revenue. This sales revenue, in turn, is exchanged for additional resources, which are used to produce and sell more goods and services. Thus the circular flow of Figure 1.4 is continuous.

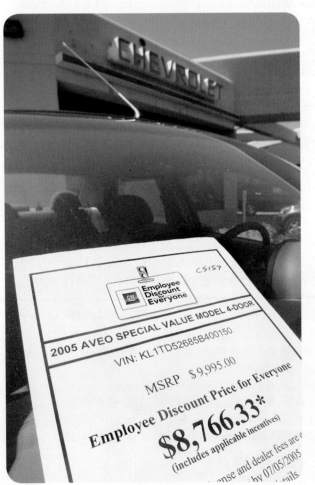

Along the way, of course, business owners would like to remove something from the circular flow in the form of profits. And households try to retain some income as savings. But are profits and savings really removed from the flow? Usually not! When the economy is running smoothly, households are willing to invest their savings in businesses. They can do so directly by buying stocks in businesses, by purchasing shares in mutual funds that purchase stocks in businesses, or by lending money to businesses. They also can invest indirectly by placing their savings in bank accounts. Banks and other financial institutions then invest these savings as part of their normal business operations.

The exception to this rule is money generated in another country. Most countries in the world do not allow money earned to be removed from their economies. In short, if you earn money, local laws usually demand that you spend it there in either new investment ex-

consumer products
goods and services purchased by individuals for personal consumption

Let's make a deal (or a market economy)

In order to increase sales and reduce inventory, General Motors uses employee discount pricing for everyone. This practical example of a market economy illustrates how businesses (who will decide what to produce) and individuals (who decide what to buy) interact with the real world.

pansion or on whatever can be bought within the country. One of the reasons that foreign investment is attracted from around the world to Canada is the freedom to convert profit earned into another currency and then repatriate it back to the country of the foreign investor. Control lies with the investor.

Although business investment is a small component of total economic spending, it is extremely important because it represents the future. Investment means building new plants and facilities to produce products for customers. Businesses will only do this if there is sufficient confidence in future customer's willingness to buy these products. After all; why else would anyone want to build the plant in the first place? If business decision makers are wrong and sales revenue do not appear as expected, losses may produce a variety of problems and eventually could even lead to bankruptcy.

The other reason that business investment is so important is its connection with employment. A new plant represents new jobs that can be thought of as permanent, as much as any job ever can be. Furthermore, these workers will contribute to the local economy by spending more, paying more taxes, and so on. In essence, business investment is the starting point of economic growth.

When business profits are distributed to business owners, these profits become household income. (Business owners are, after all, members of households.) And, as we saw, household income is retained in the circular flow as either consumer spending or invested savings. Thus business profits, too, are retained in the business system, and the circular flow is complete. How, then, does government fit in?

Governments The primary responsibility of government is to protect and promote the public welfare. Local, provincial, and federal governments discharge this responsibility through regulation and the provision of services. Government regulation of business has already been mentioned; specific regulations are discussed in detail in various chapters of this book. In addition, governments provide numerous services that are considered important and perhaps critical to our collective well-being. Among these services are national defence, police and fire protection, welfare payments and old age pension income, education, national and provincial parks, roads and highways, unemployment insurance programs, healthcare services, and research.

This list could go on and on, but the point is clear: governments are deeply involved in business life. To pay for all these services, governments collect a variety of taxes from households (such as personal income taxes and sales and property taxes) and from businesses (corporate income taxes).

Figure 1.4 shows this exchange of taxes for government services. It also shows government spending of tax dollars for resources and products required to provide these services. In other words, governments, too, return their incomes to the business system through the resource and product markets.

And governments are also often business owners on behalf of their constituents as in the case of provincial electric utility companies such as BC Hydro. Furthermore, governments can be pivotal decision makers in large-scale projects helping to share in great risk as with the Hibernia oil exploration project off the Grand Banks of Newfoundland.

Actually, with government included, our circular flow looks more like a combination of several flows. And in reality it is. The important point is that, together, the various flows make up a single unit—a complete economic system that effectively provides answers to the basic economic questions. Simply put, the system works.

Command Economies

Before we discuss how to measure a nation's economic performance, we look quickly at another economic system called a *command economy*. A **command economy** is an economic system in which the government decides what goods and services will be produced, how they will be produced, for whom available goods and services will be produced, and who owns and controls the major factors of production. The answers to all four basic economic questions are determined, at least to some degree, through centralized government planning. Today, two types of economic systems—*socialism* and *communism*—are examples of command economies.

command economy an economic system in which the government decides what goods and services will be produced, how they will be produced, for whom available goods and services will be produced, and who owns and controls the major factors of production

Socialism In a *socialist* economy, the key industries are owned and controlled by the government. Such industries usually include transportation, utilities, communications, banking, and industries producing important materials such as steel. Land, buildings, and raw materials also may be the property of the state in a socialist economy. Depending on the country, private ownership of smaller businesses is permitted to varying degrees. People usually may choose their own occupations, but many work in state-owned industries.

What to produce and how to produce it are determined in accordance with national goals, which are based on projected needs and the availability of resources. The distribution of goods and services—who gets what—is also controlled by the state to the extent that it controls taxes, rents, and wages. Among the professed aims of socialist countries are the equitable distribution of income, the elimination of poverty, and the distribution of social services (such as medical care) to all who need them. The disadvantages of socialism include increased taxation and loss of incentive and motivation for both individuals and business owners.

Communism If Adam Smith was the father of capitalism, Karl Marx was the father of communism. In his writings during the mid-nineteenth century, Marx advocated a classless society whose citizens together owned all economic resources collectively. He believed that such a society would come about as the result of a class struggle between the owners of capital and the workers they had exploited. All workers then would contribute to this *communist* society according to their ability and would receive benefits according to their need. In other words, there would be no private ownership of any economic resources or businesses; everybody would own all resources communally and government bodies would carry out decision making.

Today, the so-called communist economies found in The People's Republic of China and Cuba practise what should be better labelled as strictly controlled socialism. They even allow a bit of free enterprise here and there. The government in these countries owns almost all economic resources and the basic economic questions are answered through centralized state planning that also sets prices and wages. The needs of the state, as viewed by government decision makers generally outweigh the wishes of individual citizens. Emphasis is placed on allocating resources to produce goods and services the government views as important for the whole population, rather than on the things that individual consumers might wish.

Given recent events in Eastern Europe, China and the rest of Asia, it appears more likely that so-called communist and strongly socialist-oriented economies will be taking a closer look at more capitalistic economic alignments and the associated democratic freedoms that go along with them.

Measuring Economic Performance

Learning Objective ④

Identify the ways to measure economic performance.

Today, it is hard to turn on the radio, watch the news on television, or read the newspaper without hearing or seeing something about the economy. Consider for just a moment the following questions:

* Are Canadian workers as productive as workers in other countries?
* Is Canada's gross domestic product increasing or decreasing?
* Why is the unemployment rate important?

The information needed to answer these questions, along with the answers to other similar questions, is easily obtainable from many sources. More important, the answers to these and other questions can be used to gauge the economic health of a nation.

The Importance of Productivity in the Global Marketplace

One way to measure a nation's economic performance is to assess its productivity. **Productivity** is the average level of output per worker per hour. An increase in productivity results in economic growth because a larger number of goods and services are produced by a given labour force. When measuring the health of the nation's economy, economists often refer to the productivity rate—a measure that tracks the increase and decrease in the average level of output per worker. Productivity growth in Canada and our primary competitor the United States has increased dramatically over the last several years as investment in new technologies has enabled workers to increase production efficiency. While 2005 was Canada's best performance improvement since 2000, according to Statistics Canada, for 2005 as a whole, the average annual rate of growth in productivity for both Canadian and U.S. businesses was identical, a 2.3 percent increase.[6] And yet, before you think that all the nation's economic problems are over, consider the following questions:

productivity the average level of output per worker per hour

Question: *How does productivity growth affect the Canadian economy?*

Answer: Because of productivity growth, it now takes fewer workers to produce what was produced before. As a result, employers have reduced costs, earn more profits, and/or can sell their products for less. Finally, productivity growth helps Canadian

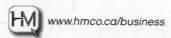

SP⊙TLIGHT

The Canadian labour force

The Canadian Labour Force

Labour force characteristics of Canadians 15 years and older

Population	26,232,500
Labour force	17,629,700
Employment	16,488,800
Full-time	13,565,100
Part-time	2,923,700
Unemployment	1,140,900
Participation rate	67.2
Unemployment rate	6.5
Employment rate	62.9
Part-time rate	17.7

Source: Statistics Canada, Labour Force Survey, October 6, 2006, http://www.statcan.ca/english/Subjects/Labour/LFS/lfs-en.htm.

business to compete more effectively with other nations in a competitive world.

Question: *How does a nation improve productivity?*

Answer: Reducing costs and enabling employees to work more efficiently are at the core of all attempts to improve productivity. For example, productivity in Canada is expected to improve dramatically as more economic activity is transferred onto the Internet, reducing costs for servicing customers and handling routine ordering functions between businesses. Encouraging customers to book their own reservations on the WestJet Airlines website (www.westjet.com/) reduces the number of customer service representatives the firm needs. Methods that can be used to increase productivity are discussed in detail in Chapter 9.

Question: *Is productivity growth always good.*

Answer: While economists always point to increased efficiency and the ability to produce goods and services for lower costs as a positive factor, at least two factors must be considered when answering this question. First, fewer workers producing more goods and services is good for employers. As mentioned above, increased productivity enables business owners to make more profit and/or sell their products for less. On the other side, increased productivity can lead to higher unemployment rates. And unemployed workers often find that employers are not hiring as many new employees because existing employees are more productive.

Key Economic Indicators That Measure a Nation's Economy

gross domestic product (GDP) the total monetary value of all goods and services produced by all people within the boundaries of a country during a one-year period

In addition to productivity, a measure called *gross domestic product* can be used to measure the economic well-being of a nation. **Gross domestic product (GDP)** is the total value of all goods and services produced by all people within the boundaries of a country during a one-year period. For example, the value of airplanes produced by employees in both a Canadian-owned Bombardier plant and automobiles in a Japanese-owned Toyota plant in Canada are included in the GDP for Canada. Canada's GDP in 2005 was about $1,371 billion[7] whereas the U.S. GDP was about ten times greater, as is usually the case, at $13,197 billion.[8]

The GDP figure facilitates comparisons between Canada and other countries because it is the standard used in international guidelines for economic accounting. It is also possible to compare the GDP for one nation at several time periods. Finally, this comparison allows observers to determine the extent to which a nation is experiencing economic growth. GDP growth rates of about 3 to 4 percent each year are generally considered economically good years for the Canadian economy since this traditionally allows for new workers entering the workforce to find employment and provides satisfactory opportunities for businesses to grow.

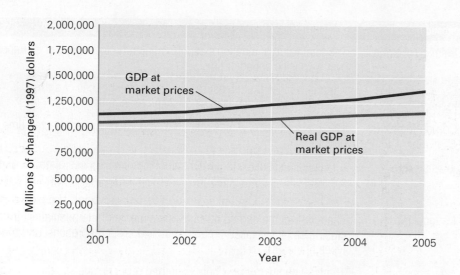

Figure 1.5

GDP in Current Dollars and in Inflation-Adjusted Dollars

The changes in GDP and *real* GDP for Canada from one year to another year can be used to measure economic growth.

Source: Statistics Canada, Real gross domestic product, expenditure-based, accessed October 19, 2006, http://www40 .statcan.ca/l01/cst01/ econ05.htm and Gross domestic product, expenditure-based http://www40.statcan .ca/l01/cst01/econ04.htm.

To make accurate comparisons of the GDP for different years, we must adjust the dollar amounts for inflation. **Inflation** is a general rise in the level of prices. (The opposite of inflation is deflation.) **Deflation** is a general decrease in the level of prices. By using inflation-adjusted figures, we are able to measure the *real* GDP for a nation. In effect, it is now possible to compare the products and services produced by a nation in constant dollars—dollars that will purchase the same amount of goods and services. Figure 1.5 depicts the GDP of Canada in current dollars and the *real* GDP in inflation-adjusted dollars. Note that between 2001 and 2005, Canada's *real* GDP grew from $1,038 billion to $1,157 billion.[9]

In addition to GDP and *real* GDP, other economic measures can be used to evaluate a nation's economy. Some additional terms that are often reported in new reports on the radio, television, or the Internet are described in Table 1.2. Like the measures for GDP, these measures can be used to compare one economic statistic over a period of time and to measure economic growth.

inflation a general rise in the level of prices

deflation a general decrease in the level of prices

The Business Cycle

All industrialized nations seek economic growth, full employment, and price stability. However, a nation's economy fluctuates rather than grows at a steady pace every year. In fact, if you were to graph the economic growth rate for a country such as Canada, it would resemble a roller-coaster ride with peaks (high points) and troughs (low points). These fluctuations generally are referred to as the **business cycle**, that is, the recurrence of periods of growth and recession in a nation's economic activity. Generally, the business cycle consists of four states: the peak (sometimes called prosperity), recession, the trough, and recovery (sometimes called *expansion*).

During the *peak period*, unemployment is low and total income is relatively high. As long as the economic outlook remains prosperous, consumers are willing to buy products and services. In fact, businesses often expand and offer new products and services during the peak period in order to take advantage of consumers' increased buying power.

business cycle the recurrence of periods of growth and recession in a nation's economic activity

Table 1.2

Common Measures Used to Evaluate a Nation's Economic Health

ECONOMIC MEASURE	DESCRIPTION
1. Balance of trade	The total value of a nation's exports minus the total value of its imports over a specific period of time.
2. Consumer price index	A monthly index that measures the changes in prices of a fixed basket of goods purchased by a typical consumer.
3. Corporate profits	The total amount of profits made by corporations over selected time periods.
4. Inflation rate	An economic statistic that tracks the increase in prices of goods and services over a period of time. This measure usually is calculated on a monthly or annual basis.
5. National income	The total income earned by various segments of the population, including employees, self-employed individuals, corporations, and other types of income.
6. New housing starts	The total number of new homes started during a specific time period.
7. Prime interest rate	The lowest interest rate that banks charge their most credit-worthy customers.
8. Producer price index	An index that measures prices at the wholesale level.
9. Unemployment rate	The percentage of a nation's labour force that is unemployed at any time.

recession two or more consecutive three-month periods of decline in a country's GDP

depression a severe recession that lasts longer than a recession

monetary policies Bank of Canada decisions that determine the size of the supply of money in the nation and the level of interest rates

fiscal policy government influence on the amount of savings and expenditures; accomplished by altering the tax structure and by changing the levels of government spending

Economists define a **recession** as two or more consecutive three-month periods of decline in a country's GDP. Because unemployment rises during a recession, total buying power declines. The pessimism that accompanies a recession often stifles both consumer and business spending. As buying power decreases, consumers tend to become more value conscious and reluctant to purchase frivolous items. In response to a recession, many businesses focus on the products and services that provide the most value to their customers. Economists define a **depression** as a severe recession that lasts longer than a recession. A depression is characterized by extremely high unemployment rates, low wages, reduced purchasing power, lack of confidence in the economy, and a general decrease in business activity.

Economists refer to the third phase of the business cycle as the *trough*. The trough of a recession or depression is the turning point when a nation's output and employment levels bottom out and reach their lowest levels. To offset the effects of recession and depression, the federal government uses both monetary and fiscal policies. **Monetary policies** are the Bank of Canada's decisions that determine the size of the supply of money in the nation and the level of interest rates. Through **fiscal policy**, the government can influence the amount of savings and expenditures by altering the tax structure and changing the levels of government spending.

Although the federal government currently spends about $200 billion each year, about $15,000 for each Canadian, the government often spends more than it receives,

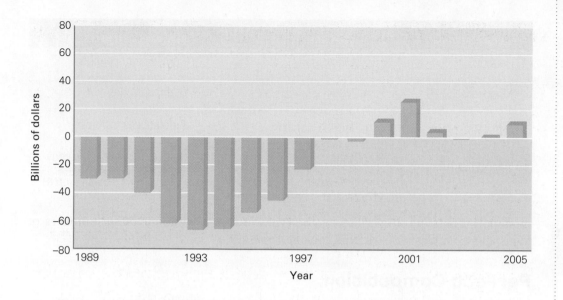

Figure 1.6

Consolidated surplus and deficit of federal, provincial, territorial, and local governments.

This graph from Statistics Canada illustrates the debts of all levels of government since 1989.

Source: Statistics Canada, CANSIM table 385-0001.

resulting in a **federal deficit**. The total of all federal deficits is called the **national debt**. Today, the national debt is about $500 billion.[10]

Some experts believe that effective use of monetary and fiscal policies can speed up recovery and reduce the amount of time the economy is in recession. *Recovery* (or *expansion*) is movement of the economy from depression or recession to prosperity. High unemployment rates decline, income increases, and both the ability and the willingness to buy rise.

federal deficit a shortfall created when the federal government spends more in a fiscal year than it receives

national debt the total of all federal deficits

Types of Competition

Learning Objective 5

Outline the four types of competition.

Our capitalist system ensures that individuals and businesses make the decisions about what to produce, how to produce it, and what price to charge for the product. Roots Canada Limited, for example, can introduce new versions of its famous clothing, license the Roots name, change their prices and method of distribution, and attempt to produce and market Roots products in other countries or over the Internet at www.roots.com. Our system also allows customers the right to choose between Roots' products and those produced by competitors.

Competition like that between Roots and other apparel manufacturers is a necessary and extremely important by-product of capitalism. Business **competition** is essentially a rivalry among businesses for sales to potential customers. In a capitalistic economy, competition also ensures that a firm will survive only if it serves its customers well by providing products and services that meet needs. Economists recognize four degrees of competition ranging from ideal, complete competition to no competition at all. These are perfect competition, monopolistic competition, oligopoly, and

competition rivalry among businesses for sales to potential customers

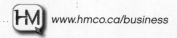

TYPE OF COMPETITION	NUMBER OF BUSINESS FIRMS OR SUPPLIERS	REAL-WORLD EXAMPLES
1. Perfect	Many	Corn, wheat, peanuts
2. Monopolistic	Many	Clothing, shoes
3. Oligopoly	Few	Automobiles, cereals
4. Monopoly	One	Software protected by copyright, local public utilities

monopoly. For a quick overview of the types of competition, including numbers of firms and examples for each type, look at Table 1.3.

Perfect Competition

Perfect (or **pure**) **competition** is the market situation in which there are many buyers and sellers of a product, and no single buyer or seller is powerful enough to affect the price of that product. Note that this definition includes several important ideas. First, we are discussing the market for a single product, say, bushels of wheat. Second, all sellers offer essentially the same product for sale. Third, all buyers and sellers know everything there is to know about the market (including, in our example, the prices that all sellers are asking for their wheat). And fourth, the overall market is not affected by the actions of any one buyer or seller.

When perfect competition exists, every seller should ask the same price that every other seller is asking. Why? Because if one seller wanted 50 cents more per bushel of wheat than all the others, that seller would not be able to sell a single bushel. Buyers could—and would—do better by purchasing wheat from the competition. On the other hand, a firm willing to sell below the going price would sell all its wheat quickly. But that seller would lose sales revenue (and profit) because buyers actually are willing to pay more. In perfect competition, then, the price of each product is determined by the actions of *all buyers and all sellers together* through the forces of supply and demand.

The Basics of Supply and Demand The **supply** of a particular product is the quantity of the product that producers are willing to sell at each of various prices. Producers are rational people, so we would expect them to offer more of a product for sale at higher prices and to offer less of the product at lower prices, as illustrated by the supply curve in Figure 1.7.

The **demand** for a particular product is the quantity that buyers are willing to purchase at each of various prices. Buyers, too, are usually rational, so we would expect them—as a group—to buy more of a product when its price is low and to buy less of the product when its price is high, as depicted by the demand curve in Figure 1.7.

The Equilibrium, or Market, Price There is always one certain price at which the demanded quantity of a product is exactly equal to the quantity of that product produced. Suppose that producers are willing to *supply* 2 million bushels of wheat at a price of $4 per bushel and that buyers are willing to *purchase* 2 million bushels at a price of $4 per bushel. In other words, supply and demand are in balance, or *in equilibrium*, at

perfect (or **pure**) **competition** the market situation in which there are many buyers and sellers of a product, and no single buyer or seller is powerful enough to affect the price of that product

supply the quantity of a product that producers are willing to sell at each of various prices

demand the quantity of a product that buyers are willing to purchase at each of various prices

the price of $4. Economists call this price the *market price*. The **market price** of any product is the price at which the quantity demanded is exactly equal to the quantity supplied. If suppliers produce 2 million bushels, then no one who is willing to pay $4 per bushel will have to go without wheat, and no producer who is willing to sell at $4 per bushel will be stuck with unsold wheat.

In theory and in the real world, market prices are affected by anything that affects supply and demand. The *demand* for wheat, for example, might change if researchers suddenly discovered that it offered a previously unknown health benefit. Then buyers would demand more wheat at every price. Or the *supply* of wheat might change if new technology permitted the production of greater quantities of wheat from the same amount of acreage. Other changes that can affect competitive prices are shifts in buyer tastes, the development of new products, fluctuations in income owing to inflation or recession, or even changes in the weather that affect the production of wheat.

Perfect competition is quite rare in today's world. Many real markets, however, are examples of monopolistic competition.

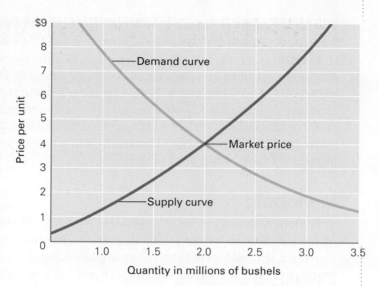

Figure 1.7

Supply Curve and Demand Curve

The intersection of a supply curve and a demand curve is called the *equilibrium,* or *market, price.* This intersection indicates a single price and quantity at which suppliers will sell products and buyers will purchase them.

market price the price at which the quantity demanded is exactly equal to the quantity supplied

Monopolistic Competition

Monopolistic competition is a market situation in which there are many buyers along with a relatively large number of sellers. The various products available in a monopolistically competitive market are very similar in nature, and they are intended to satisfy the same need. However, each seller attempts to make its product different from the others by providing unique product features, an attention-getting brand name, unique packaging, or services such as free delivery or a "lifetime" warranty.

Product differentiation is the process of developing and promoting differences between one's products and all similar products. It is a fact of life for the producers of many consumer goods, from soaps to clothing to furniture to shoes. A furniture manufacturer such as Thomasville sees what looks like a mob of competitors, all trying to chip away at its market. By differentiating each of its products from all similar products produced by competitors, Thomasville obtains some limited control over the market price of its product.

monopolistic competition a market situation in which there are many buyers along with a relatively large number of sellers who differentiate their products from the products of competitors

product differentiation the process of developing and promoting differences between one's products and all similar products

Oligopoly

An **oligopoly** is a market (or industry) situation in which there are few sellers. Generally, these sellers are quite large, and sizable investments are required to enter

oligopoly a market (or industry) in which there are few sellers

into their market. Examples of oligopolies are the automobile, car rental, cereal, and farm implement industries.

Because there are few sellers in an oligopoly, the market actions of each seller can have a strong effect on competitors' sales and prices. If General Motors, for example, reduces its automobile prices, Ford, Chrysler, Toyota, and Nissan usually do the same to retain their market shares. Product differentiation becomes the major competitive weapon; this is very evident in the advertising of the major auto manufacturers. For instance, when Toyota began offering hybrid automobiles, General Motors and Ford introduced their own hybrid models.

Monopoly

monopoly a market (or industry) with only one seller

A **monopoly** is a market (or industry) with only one seller. In a monopoly, there is no close substitute for the product or service. Because only one firm is the supplier of a product, it would seem that it has complete control over price. However, no firm can set its price at some astronomical figure just because there is no competition; the firm soon would find that it had no customers or sales revenue. Instead, the firm in a monopoly position must consider the demand for its product and set the price at the most profitable level.

natural monopoly an industry requiring huge investments in capital and within which any duplication of facilities would be wasteful and thus not in the public interest

Classic examples of monopolies in Canada are public utilities. Each utility firm operates in a **natural monopoly**, an industry that requires a huge investment in capital and within which any duplication of facilities would be wasteful. Natural monopolies are permitted to exist because the public interest is best served by their existence, but they operate under the scrutiny and control of various government agencies. While many public utilities are still classified as natural monopolies, there is increased competition. For example, there have been increased demands for consumer choice when selecting a company that provides electrical service to both homes and businesses.

A legal monopoly—sometimes referred to as a *limited monopoly*—is created when the federal government issues a copyright, patent, or trademark. Each of these exists for a specific period of time and can be used to protect the owners of written materials, ideas, or product brands from unauthorized use by competitors that have not shared in the time, effort, and expense required for their development. Because Microsoft owns the copyright on its popular Windows software, it enjoys a limited-monopoly position. Except for natural monopolies and monopolies created by copyrights, patents, and trademarks, federal competition laws prohibit both monopolies and attempts to form monopolies.

Canadian Business Today

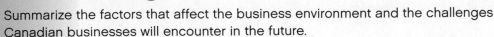

Learning Objective 6

Summarize the factors that affect the business environment and the challenges Canadian businesses will encounter in the future.

While our economic system is far from perfect, it provides Canadians with a high standard of living compared with people in other countries throughout the world.

Standard of living is a loose, subjective measure of how well off an individual or a society is mainly in terms of want satisfaction through goods and services. Also, our economic system offers solutions to many of the problems that plague society and provides opportunity for people who are willing to work and to continue learning.

To understand the current business environment and the challenges ahead, it helps to understand how business developed.

Early Business Development

Canada's business history began as part of the North American conquest by mostly British and French European interests. June 24th, 1997, marked the 500th anniversary of British trade emissary Giovanni Cabotto to the New World. Cabotto, an Italian explorer better known by his Anglicized name John Cabot, was searching for a trade route to Asia on behalf of King Henry VII of England and a group of investors. After crossing the Atlantic on the good ship *Matthew*, he established a trading depot for further travel in the welcoming harbour of St. John's, Newfoundland.

This basic story of exploration and trade is one that can be repeated about countless sites across North America. In 1534, after landing in Bonavista, Newfoundland, Jacques Cartier sailed on through the Strait of Belle Isle, which separates Newfoundland and Labrador, and then down the St. Lawrence River. He eventually landed in what would become Montreal on behalf of King Francis I of France.

The fur trade with Canada's aboriginal people led to more trade settlements along rivers and lakes, which were the primary travel routes of the day. Eventually, European settlers followed and established communities based on agriculture where possible. The first Europeans in the New World were concerned mainly with providing themselves with basic necessities—food, clothing, and shelter. Almost all families lived on farms, and the entire family worked at the business of surviving. History records that many did not fare well, succumbing to disease and starvation.

Eventually the settlers were able to produce more than they consumed. They used their surplus for trading, mainly by barter, among themselves and with the trading commercial centres, which soon became villages and later, cities. **Barter** is a system of exchange in which goods or services are traded directly for other goods and/or services without using money. As this trade increased, small-scale business enterprises began to appear.

Businesses, such as the Hudson's Bay Company, grew wealthy in this simple economy. Fish furs, and lumber, were the primary resources that fuelled Canada's economy through the mid-nineteenth century. By then, agriculture, and particularly wheat farming on the prairies, were directing expansion westward. Roads were replaced with railways, and canals were built in the east to improve transportation links between trading centres and reduce travel time and costs. Cities like Quebec City and Montreal were centres of commercial activity during this era, where trading companies, banks, and transportation businesses met and flourished. All of this economic activity helped generate the momentum for Confederation in 1867.[11]

Some people were able to use their skills and their excess time to work under the domestic system of production. The **domestic system** was a method of manufacturing in which an entrepreneur distributed raw materials to various homes, where fami-

standard of living a loose, subjective measure of how well off an individual or a society is mainly in terms of want satisfaction through goods and services

barter a system of exchange in which goods or services are traded directly for other goods and/or services without using money

domestic system a method of manufacturing in which an entrepreneur distributes raw materials to various homes, where families process them into finished goods to be offered for sale by the merchant entrepreneur

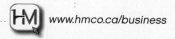 www.hmco.ca/business

lies would process them into finished goods. The merchant entrepreneur then offered the goods for sale.

Gradually, the **factory system** of manufacturing emerged, in which all the materials, machinery, and workers required to manufacture a product are assembled in one place. And a manufacturing technique called *specialization* was used to improve productivity. **Specialization** is the separation of a manufacturing process into distinct tasks and the assignment of the different tasks to different individuals.

The Twentieth Century

Industrial growth and prosperity continued well into the twentieth century, and as a newly created Canada took form, the United States had already begun to establish itself as an industrial and world power. Canada too was creating industrial and manufacturing centres of its own, albeit on a much smaller scale. Fundamental changes occurred in business ownership and management as well. No longer were the largest businesses owned by one individual; instead, ownership was in the hands of thousands of corporate shareholders who were willing to invest in—but not to operate—a business. A higher standard of living was created for most people—but it was not to last.

The Roaring Twenties ended with the sudden crash of the stock market in 1929 and the near collapse of the economy in Canada and other countries. The Great Depression that followed in the 1930s caused people to lose faith in business and its ability to satisfy the needs of society without government involvement.

The economy was on the road to recovery when World War II broke out in Europe in 1939. The need for vast quantities of war materials spurred business activity and technological development. This rapid economic pace continued after the war, and the 1950s and 1960s witnessed both increasing production and a rising standard of living.

In the mid-1970s, however, a shortage of crude oil led to a new set of problems for business. Petroleum products supply most of the energy required to produce goods and services and to transport goods around the world. As the cost of petroleum products increased, a corresponding price increase took place in the cost of energy and the cost of goods and services. The result was inflation at a rate well over 10 percent per year during the early 1980s. Business profits fell as the purchasing power of consumers was eroded by inflation and high interest rates.

By the early 1990s, unemployment numbers, inflation, and interest—all factors that affect business—were again at record lows. In turn, business took advantage of this economic prosperity to invest in information technology, cut costs, and increase flexibility and efficiency. Technological development of personal computers and connectivity through

factory system a system of manufacturing in which all the materials, machinery, and workers required to manufacture a product are assembled in one place

specialization the separation of a manufacturing process into distinct tasks and the assignment of the different tasks to different individuals

▲
Economic prosperity after World War II

Fueled by economic prosperity, Canadians bought homes, automobiles, and other consumer goods, and created an entirely new standard of living across the country.

the Internet led to the latter becoming a major force in the economy, with computer hardware, software, and Internet service providers taking advantage of the increased need for information. e-Business—a topic we will continue to explore throughout this text—became an accepted method of conducting business. **e-Business** is the organized effort of individuals to produce and sell through the Internet, for a profit, the products and services that satisfy society's needs. As further evidence of the financial health of the new economy, the stock market enjoyed the longest period of sustained economic growth in our history. Unfortunately, by the last part of the twentieth century, a larger number of business failures and declining stock values were initial signs that larger economic problems were on the way.

e-Business the organized effort of individuals to produce and sell through the Internet, for a profit, the products and services that satisfy society's needs

A New Century: 2000 and Beyond

According to many economic experts, the first few years of the twenty-first century might be characterized as the best of times and the worst of times rolled into one package. On the plus side, technology became available at an affordable price. Both individuals and businesses now could access information with the click of a button. They also could buy and sell merchandise online.

In addition to information technology, the growth of service businesses and increasing opportunities for global trade also changed the way Canadian firms do business in the twenty-first century. Because they employ over half of the Canadian workforce, service businesses are a very important component of our economy. As a result, service businesses must find ways to improve productivity and cut costs while at the same time providing jobs for an even larger portion of the workforce.

On the negative side, it is hard to watch television, surf the web, listen to the radio, or read the newspaper without hearing some news about the economy. Even though many of the economic indicators described in Table 1.2 on page 22 remain strong or show signs of improvement, there is still a certain amount of pessimism surrounding the economy.

The Current Business Environment

Before reading on, answer the following question:

In today's competitive business world, which of the following environments affects business?

a. The competitive environment

b. The global environment

c. The technological environment

d. The economic environment

e. All the above

The correct answer is "e." All the environments listed affect business today. For example, businesses operate in a *competitive environment*. As noted earlier in this chapter, competition is a basic component of capitalism. Every day business owners must figure out what makes their businesses successful and how their businesses are

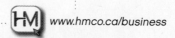

different from the competition. Often the answer is contained in the basic definition of business. Just for a moment, review the definition:

> *Business* is the organized effort of individuals to produce and sell, for a profit, the products and services that satisfy society's needs.

Note the phrase *satisfy society's needs.* Those three words say a lot about how well a successful firm competes with competitors. If you meet customer needs, then you have a better chance at success.

Related to the competitive environment is the *global environment.* Not only do Canadian businesses have to compete with other Canadian businesses, but they also must compete with businesses from all over the globe. According to global experts, China is the fastest-growing economy in the world. And China is not alone. Other countries also compete with Canadian and American firms. According to Richard Haass, president of the U.S. Council on Foreign Relations, "There will be winners and losers from globalization. We win every time we go shopping because prices are lower. Choice is greater because of globalization. But there are losers. There are people who will lose their jobs either to foreign competition or [to] technological innovation."[12]

In addition to competition and globalization, the use of technology has changed the way we do business. In fact, the *technology environment* for Canadian businesses has never been more challenging. Changes in manufacturing equipment, communication with customers, and distribution of products are all examples of how technology has changed everyday business practices. And the technology will continue to change. New technology will require businesses to spend additional money to keep abreast of an ever-changing technology environment.

In addition to the competitive, global, and technology environments, the *economic environment* always must be considered when making business decisions. While many people believe that business has unlimited resources, the truth is that managers and business owners realize that there is never enough money to fund all the activities a business might want to fund. This fact is especially important when the nation's economy takes a nosedive or an individual firm's sales revenue and profits are declining.

When you look back at the original question we asked at the beginning of this section, clearly, each different type of environment affects the way a business does *business.* As a result, there are always opportunities for improvement and challenges that must be considered.

The Challenges Ahead

There it is—the Canadian business system in brief. When it works well, it provides jobs for those who are willing to work, a standard of living that few countries can match, and many opportunities for personal advancement. However, like every other system devised by humans, it is not perfect. Our business system may give us prosperity, but it also gave us the Great Depression of the 1930s and the economic problems of the 1970s, the late 1980s, and the first part of the twenty-first century.

Obviously, the system can be improved. Certainly there are plenty of people who are willing to tell us exactly what *they* think the Canadian economy needs. But these people provide us only with conflicting opinions. Who is right and who is wrong? Even the experts cannot agree.

The experts do agree, however, that several key issues will challenge our economic system (and our nation) over the next decade. Some of the questions to be resolved include

* How can we resolve conflicts between countries throughout the world?

* How can we create a more stable economy and create new jobs?

* As a nation, how can we develop a disaster crisis management program that will help people in times of peril?

* How can we meet the challenges of managing culturally diverse workforces to address the needs of a culturally diverse marketplace?

* How can we make Canadian manufacturers more productive and more competitive with foreign producers who have lower labour costs?

* How can we preserve the benefits of competition and small businesses in our Canadian economic system?

* How can we encourage economic growth and at the same time continue to conserve natural resources, protect our environment, and meet the needs of society?

* How can we best market Canadian-made products in foreign nations?

* How can we meet the needs of two-income families, single parents, older Canadians, and the less fortunate?

The answers to these questions are anything but simple. In the past, Canadians always have been able to solve their economic problems through ingenuity and creativity. Now, as we continue the journey through the twenty-first century, we need that same ingenuity and creativity not only to solve our current problems but also to compete in the global marketplace.

According to economic experts, if we as a nation can become more competitive, we may solve many of our current domestic problems. As an added bonus, increased competitiveness also will enable us to meet the economic challenges posed by other industrialized nations of the world. The way we solve these problems will affect our own future, our children's future, and that of our nation. Within the Canadian economic and political system, the answers are ours to provide.

The Canadian business system is not perfect by any means, but it does work reasonably well. We discuss some of its problems in Chapter 2 as we examine the topics of social responsibility and business ethics.

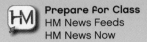

Prepare For Class
HM News Feeds
HM News Now

→ **RETURN TO INSIDE BUSINESS**

The focus of Alberta's oil and gas exploration is the development of the tar sands. Despite the technological difficulties and high costs associated with separating the oil from the mixture of soil and sand, industry engineers generally believe that there is more oil in Alberta than anywhere else in the world.

Oil located under the seabed is also a technological and costly challenge to engineers. In the summer of 1997, Hibernia's giant oil drilling platform specially built to withstand the icebergs and unforgiving Atlantic storms off the coast of Newfoundland was towed 300 kilometres southeast of St. John's and then anchored to the ocean floor. After analysis of early oil production flows in the fall, officials happily announced that the $5.8 billion dollar mega-project would prove to be more financially rewarding for its group of investors than first believed. Revised estimates of accessible oil reserves were raised by 22 percent to one billion barrels and the project would be able to run 25 years if production averaged 180,000 barrels per day as planned. Here then, was a new source of wealth for the economy of the region, and especially the province of Newfoundland and Labrador.

For the group of major investors that included Mobil Oil Canada Limited, Chevron Canada Resources Limited and Petro-Canada, a new source of oil supply was established to feed the refineries and retail distribution systems serving their customers around the world. For the governments and people of Canada and particularly, Newfoundland and Labrador, a new source of revenue, which would help stimulate other economic activity, was now clearly in place. Besides money that construction workers already earned for building the platform in Newfoundland, oil rig workers will be employed to bring oil to the surface over the life of the project. Money earned by anyone connected with Hibernia will be spent at local businesses for food, clothing and so forth. Hibernia is expected to have a major stimulative effect on the overall regional economy. In 1993, energy contributed 5 percent to Newfoundland and Labrador's economic wealth. But by 2002, this grew to almost 22 percent increasing its GDP by 16 percent over the previous year and by 2005, GDP was still changing at a double-digit rate of 10.8 percent.

In 1997, based on a projected current global market value of $20 per barrel, Hibernia contained $20 billion of wealth for its investors who shared the risk of bringing the project to life. By 2006, when oil hit $78.40 U.S. per barrel, the decision to build Hibernia must have looked pretty smart. Of course this is precisely the trickiest part of analyzing the Hibernia project. Hibernia will ship most of its output to refineries in the United States and the Caribbean and then subsequently sell the final products on world markets. If oil prices should continue to rise over the life of Hibernia, its reserves will rise in value as well. However, there is also the risk that oil prices could fall. But according to a Canadian government report published in 2006, oil prices were projected to fall to only $45 U.S. by 2010. There is no guarantee of exactly what Hibernia will pay back its owners during its productive life span. Only time will tell.

And so there lies the essence of business, albeit in this case, on a large scale. People in business make educated guesses of what they believe is likely to occur over some time period, assess the degree of risk they are prepared to take, and venture forth. If successful, retrospectively, they appear to be forward-looking and brilliant investors. If unsuccessful, judgment is less kind.

Questions:

1. Explain why you think energy prices are likely to rise, stay about the same, or fall over the next 20 years?

2. How do you think businesses and customers might respond to future price changes?

Sources: Statistics Canada, Gross domestic product, expenditure-based by province and territory, website accessed October 19, 2006, http://www40.statcan.ca/l01/cst01/econ15.htm; Eric Beauchesne, "Oil prices projected to nosedive," *National Post*, October, 05, 2006, p. FP5.

CHAPTER REVIEW

1 **Discuss your future in the world of business.**

For many years, people in business—both employees and managers—assumed that prosperity would continue. When the bubble burst, a large number of these same people then began to ask the question: What do we do now? Although this is a fair question, it is difficult to answer. Certainly, for a college or university student taking business courses or a beginning employee just starting a career, the question is even more difficult to answer. And yet there are still opportunities out there for people who are willing to work hard, continue to learn, and possess the ability to adapt to change. To be sure, employers and our capitalistic economic system are more demanding than ever before. As you begin this course, ask yourself: What can I do that will make employers want to pay me a salary? What skills do I have that employers need? The kind of career you choose ultimately will depend on your own values and what you feel is most important in life. But deciding on the kind of career you want is only a first step. To get a job in your chosen field and to be successful at it, you will have to develop a plan, or road map, that ensures that you have the necessary skills and the knowledge the job requires to become a better employee. By studying business, you also may decide to start your own business and become a better consumer and investor.

2 **Define** *business* **and identify potential risks and rewards.**

Business is the organized effort of individuals to produce and sell, for a profit, the products and services that satisfy society's needs. Four kinds of resources—material, human, financial, and informational—must be combined to start and operate a business. The three general types of businesses are manufacturers, service businesses, and marketing intermediaries. Profit is what remains after all business expenses are deducted from sales revenue. It is the payment that owners receive for assuming the risks of business—primarily the risks of not receiving payment and of losing whatever has been invested in the firm.

3 **Define** *economics* **and describe the two types of economic systems: capitalism and command economy.**

Economics is the study of how wealth is created and distributed. An economic system must answer four questions: What goods and services will be produced? How will they be produced? For whom will they be produced? Who owns and who controls the major factors of production? Capitalism (on which our economic system is based) is an economic system in which individuals own and operate the majority of businesses that provide goods and services. Capitalism stems from the theories of Adam Smith. Smith's pure laissez-faire capitalism is an economic system in which the factors of production are owned by private entities, and all individuals are free to use their resources as they see fit; prices are determined by the workings of supply and demand in competitive markets; and the economic role of government is limited to rule maker and umpire. Our economic system is a mixed economy. In the circular flow that characterizes our business system (see Figure 1.4), households and businesses exchange resources for goods and services, using money as the medium of exchange. In a similar manner, government collects taxes from businesses and households and purchases products and resources with which to provide services. In a command economy, government, rather than individuals, owns the factors of production and provides the answers to the three other economic questions. Socialist and communist economies are—at least in theory—command economies. In the real world, however, communists seem to practice a strictly controlled kind of socialism.

4 **Identify the ways to measure economic performance.**

One way to evaluate the performance of an economic system is to assess changes in productivity, which is the average level of output per worker per hour. Gross domestic product (GDP) also can be used to measure a nation's economic well-being and is the total dollar value of all goods and services produced by all people within the boundaries of a country during a one-year period. This figure facilitates comparisons between Canada and other countries because it is the standard used in international guidelines for economic accounting. It is also possible to adjust GDP for inflation and thus to measure *real* GDP. In addition to GDP, other economic indicators include a nation's balance of trade, consumer price index (CPI), corporate profits, consumer price index (CPI), inflation rate, national income, new housing starts, prime interest rate, producer price index (PPI), productivity rate, and unemployment rate. A nation's economy fluctuates rather than grows at a steady pace every year. These fluctuations generally are referred to as the business cycle. Generally, the business cycle consists of four states: the peak (sometimes referred to as prosperity), recession, the trough, and recovery. Some experts believe that effective use of monetary policy (the Bank of Canada's decisions that determine the size of the supply of money and the level of interest rates) and fiscal policies (the government's influence on the amount of savings and expenditures) can speed up recovery and even eliminate depressions for the business cycle.

5 Outline the four types of competition.

Competition is essentially a rivalry among businesses for sales to potential customers. In a capitalist economy, competition works to ensure the efficient and effective operation of business. Competition also ensures that a firm will survive only if it serves its customers well. Economists recognize four degrees of competition. Ranging from most to least competitive, the four degrees are pure competition, monopolistic competition, oligopoly, and monopoly. The factors of supply and demand generally influence the price that consumers pay producers for goods and services.

6 Summarize the factors that affect the business environment and the challenges Canadian businesses will encounter in the future.

Since its beginnings, Canadian business has been based on private ownership of property and freedom of enterprise.

From this beginning, through the Industrial Revolution of the early nineteenth century, and to the phenomenal expansion of industry in the nineteenth and early twentieth centuries, our government maintained an essentially laissez-faire attitude toward business. However, during the Great Depression of the 1930s, the federal government began to provide a number of social services to its citizens. Government's role in business has expanded considerably since that time. During the 1970s, a shortage of crude oil led to higher prices and inflation. In the 1980s, business profits fell as the consumers' purchasing power was eroded by inflation and high interest rates. By the early 1990s, the economy began to show signs of improvement and economic growth. Unemployment numbers, inflation, and interest—all factors that affect business—were then at record lows. Fueled by investment in information technology, the stock market enjoyed the longest period of sustained economic growth in our history. Increased use of the Internet and e-business now is changing the way that firms do business. Other factors that affect the way firms do business include the increasing importance of services and global trade. Unfortunately, by the last part of the 1990s, a larger number of business failures and declining stock values were initial signs that more economic problems were on the way as we entered the twenty-first century. Now more than ever before, the way a business operates is affected by the competitive environment, global environment, technological environment, and economic environment. As a result, business has a number of opportunities for improvement and challenges for the future. According to the experts, if we as a nation can become more competitive, we may solve many of our current domestic problems. As an added bonus, increased competitiveness also will enable us to meet the economic challenges posed by other industrialized nations of the world.

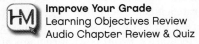

Improve Your Grade
Learning Objectives Review
Audio Chapter Review & Quiz

Review Questions

1. What reasons would you give if you were advising someone to study business?
2. Describe the four resources that must be combined to organize and operate a business. How do they differ from the economist's factors of production?
3. Describe the relationship among profit, business risk, and the satisfaction of customers' needs.
4. What are the four basic economic questions? How are they answered in a capitalist economy?
5. Explain the invisible hand of capitalism.
6. Describe the four basic assumptions required for a laissez-faire capitalist economy.
7. Why is the Canadian economy called a mixed economy?
8. Based on Figure 1.4, outline the economic interactions between business and households in our business system.
9. How does capitalism differ from socialism and communism?
10. Define gross domestic product. Why is this economic measure significant?
11. Choose three of the economic measures described in Table 1.2 and describe why these indicators are important when measuring a nation's economy.
12. What are the four steps in a typical business cycle? How are monetary and fiscal policy related to the business cycle?
13. Identify and compare the four forms of competition.
14. Explain how the equilibrium, or market, price of a product is determined.
15. Four different environments that affect business were described in Chapter 1. Choose one of the environments and explain how it affects a small electronics manufacturer located in Ontario.

Discussion Questions

1. In what ways have the economic problems that the nation has experienced in the past three years affected business firms? In what ways have these problems affected employees?
2. What factors affect a person's choice of careers?
3. Does an individual consumer really have a voice in answering the basic economic questions?
4. Is gross domestic product a reliable indicator of a nation's economic health? What might be a better indicator?
5. Discuss this statement: "Business competition encourages efficiency of production and leads to improved product quality."
6. What do you consider the most important challenges that will face people in Canada in the years ahead?

Wipro Vies to Bring Business to India

As global demand rises for technology and engineering services, Wipro, Ltd., wants to bring much of the business to Bangalore. The Indian company—which has offices across Europe, Asia, Canada, and the United States—writes software, handles back-office operations, and designs high-tech products for some of the world's largest corporations. When Fiat wanted a satellite navigation system for its Alfa Romeo sports cars, it hired Wipro. Nokia, Morgan Stanley, Cisco, Honeywell, and General Motors are among the 500 other companies that have drawn on Wipro's expertise.

Wipro is prospering from the trend toward outsourcing, in which companies reduce their costs by sending projects or jobs to countries where labour costs are lower. Skilled technology professionals in India are paid far less than their counterparts in Western Europe, Canada, and the United States. Although Wipro raises salaries regularly and offers employees stock and other benefits, "the cost advantage is still in India's favour," observes the chief marketing officer. This is why some companies hire Wipro or its main Indian competitors, Tata Consultancy Services and Infosys Technologies, to perform functions such as providing technical support to customers.

In only seven years, Wipro's annual sales have soared from $150 million to $2.4 billion. To keep up with this explosive growth, the company hires three new employees every hour of every business day. In 2002, 14,000 people were on the payroll; today, more than 50,000 are on the payroll, including several thousand who work on assignment for months at a time at customers' offices in the United States, Canada, Japan, or Europe.

By hiring Wipro to deal with operational nuts and bolts such as processing paperwork, business customers can focus on the tasks that make a difference to their customers. Florida's E-OPS, for example, is a start-up company that markets mortgage-processing services to banks. Instead of having their own employees fill out forms, make multiple copies, and send documents to different departments and organizations, banks seeking to cut costs and save time can hire E-OPS. Wipro does the actual processing, whereas E-OPS concentrates on signing new customers and meeting their needs. "It's amazing that you can run a national company with just a handful of employees, and Wipro does the rest," says the CEO of E-OPS.

As Wipro expands its menu of services, it faces tough competition not only from Indian firms but also from IBM, Accenture, and other corporations with decades of experience in working with a global customer base. Profits are healthy, and customers are satisfied, yet Wipro is constantly on the lookout for ways to improve. Not long ago, Wipro managers toured a nearby Toyota factory and came away with ideas for reconfiguring workspaces, boosting employee involvement, and more—ideas that took quality to a new level and hiked efficiency by more than 40 percent.

Wipro is also investing in new facilities for specialized services, both in India and in other countries. One of the newest is a software-development centre in Beijing's high-tech district. A senior Wipro manager points out that China is best known as the world's factory, but in the future, "there will be a shift toward the knowledge or services sector." By opening a development centre now, the company will have the time to study the foreign companies that plan to do business in China and figure out how to profit from tomorrow's opportunities. Around the world and around the clock, Wipro is pushing hard to bring more business to India.

Questions:

1. How is Wipro using the factors of production to fuel global growth?

2. What are the advantages and disadvantages of using a manufacturer like Toyota as a role model for a service business like Wipro?

3. What effect might the trend toward outsourcing have on the economy of India? What effect might this trend have on the economy of Canada and the United States?

BUILDING SKILLS FOR CAREER SUCCESS

1. Exploring the Internet

The Internet is a global network of computers that can be accessed by anyone in the world. For example, your school or firm most likely is connected to the web. You probably have private access through a commercial service provider such as Sympatico, iDirect, SBC Yahoo!, or a host of other smaller Internet service providers.

To familiarize you with the wealth of information available through the Internet and its usefulness to business students, this exercise focuses on information services available from a few popular "search engines" used to explore the web. Each of the remaining chapters in this text also contains an Internet exercise that is in some way associated with the topics covered in the chapter. After completing these exercises, not only will you be familiar with a variety of sources of business information, but you also will be better prepared to locate information you might need in the future.

To use one of these search engines, enter its *Internet address* in your web browser. The addresses of some popular search engines are

> **www.google.com**
>
> **www.msn.com**
>
> **www.yahoo.com**

Visit the text website for updates to this exercise.

Assignment

1. Examine the ways in which two search engines present categories of information on their opening screens. Which search engine was better to use in your opinion? Why?

2. Think of a business topic that you would like to know more about, for example, careers, gross domestic product, or another concept introduced in this chapter. Using your preferred search engine, explore a few articles and reports provided on your topic. Briefly summarize your findings.

2. Building Team Skills

Over the past few years, employees have been expected to function as productive team members instead of working alone. People often believe that they can work effectively in teams, but many people find working with a group of people to be a challenge. Being an effective team member requires skills that encourage other members to participate in the team endeavour.

College and university classes that function as teams are more interesting and more fun to attend, and students generally learn more about the topics in the course. If your class is to function as a team, it is important to begin building the team early in the semester. One way to begin creating a team is to learn something about each student in the class. This helps team members to feel comfortable with each other and fosters a sense of trust.

Assignment

1. Find a partner, preferably someone you do not know.

2. Each partner has two to three minutes to answer the following questions:

   a. What is your name, and where do you work?

   b. What interesting or unusual thing have you done in your life? (Do not talk about work or school; rather, focus on such things as hobbies, travel, family, and sports.)

   c. Why are you taking this course, and what do you expect to learn? (Satisfying a degree requirement is not an acceptable answer.)

3. Introduce your partner to the class. Use one to two minutes, depending on the size of the class.

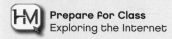

Prepare for Class
Exploring the Internet

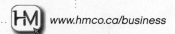

CHAPTER 2

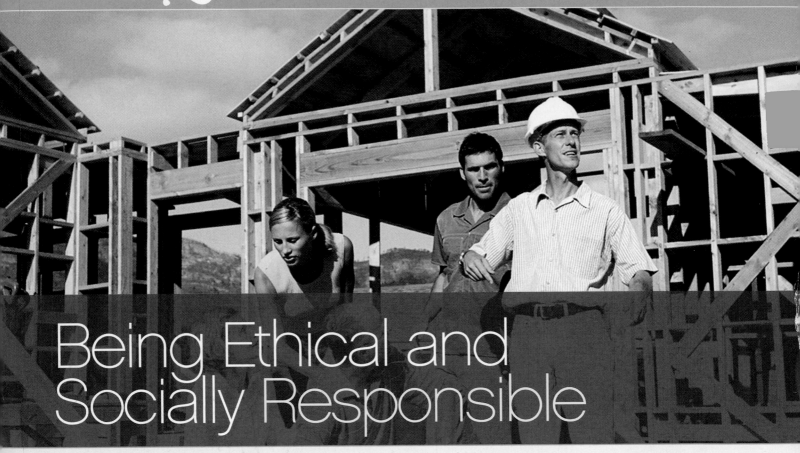

Being Ethical and Socially Responsible

Your Guide to Success in Business

Why this chapter matters
Business ethics and social responsibility are issues that have become extremely relevant to today's business world. Increasingly, corporations are developing ethics and social responsibility programs.

LEARNING OBJECTIVES

1. Understand what is meant by *business ethics*.

2. Identify ethical concerns that arise in the business world.

3. Discuss the factors affecting ethical behaviour in organizations.

4. Explain how ethical decision making can be encouraged.

5. Describe how views on social responsibility have evolved.

6. Explain the two views on the social responsibility of business.

7. List the results of the consumer movement.

8. Analyze how present employment practices may counteract past abuses.

9. Describe the major types of pollution.

10. Identify the steps toward implementing a program of social responsibility.

benefits. "Giving back to communities where we work and live is a fundamental part of Home Depot culture," says CEO Bob Nardelli.

Based on information from Christina Vance, "Store's Workers Give Back," *Bakersfield Californian*, September 21, 2005, n.p.; Jeffrey H. Birnbaum, "Stepping Up: Corporate Efforts for the Stricken Gulf Are Unprecedented," *Washington Post*, September 4, 2005, pp. F1+; "Home Depot's Net Income Rises 15%, Beats Estimates," *Los Angeles Times*, August 17, 2005, p. C3; Brian Grow, Steve Hamm, and Louise Lee, "The Debate Over Doing Good," *BusinessWeek*, August 15, 2005, p. 76; "Home Depot Lends a Helping Hand to Florida," *Industrial Distribution*, October 2004, p. 24; "Home Depot Providing 250,000 Volunteer Hours," *Home Channel News NewsFax*, September 27, 2004, p. 1; Dan Murphy, "'Good Wood' Labeling," *Christian Science Monitor*, August 23, 2001, pp. 1+; www.homedepot .com. Kathy McCormick, "Family Affair: Habitat for Humanity project honours late couple's memory," *Calgary Herald*, May 13, 2006.

Obviously, organizations like Home Depot want to be recognized as responsible corporate citizens. Such companies recognize the need to harmonize their operations with environmental demands and other vital social concerns. Not all firms, however, have taken steps to encourage a consideration of social responsibility and ethics in their decisions and day-to-day activities. Some managers still regard such business practices as a poor investment, in which the cost is not worth the return. Other managers—indeed, most managers—view the cost of these practices as a necessary business expense, similar to wages or rent.

Most managers today, like those at Home Depot, are finding ways to balance a growing agenda of socially responsible activities with the drive to generate profits. This also happens to be a good way for a company to demonstrate its values and to attract like-minded employees, customers, and stockholders. In a highly competitive business environment, an increasing number of companies are, like Home Depot, seeking to set themselves apart by developing a reputation for ethical and socially responsible behaviour. Consider the range of socially responsible thinking as set out in Home Depot's guideline to its management.

We begin this chapter by defining *business ethics* and examining ethical issues. Next, we look at the standards of behaviour in organizations and how ethical behaviour can be encouraged. We then turn to the topic of social responsibility. We compare and contrast two present-day models of social responsibility and present arguments for and against increasing the social responsibility of business. After that, we examine the major elements of the consumer movement. We discuss how social responsibility in business has affected employment practices and environmental concerns. Finally, we consider the commitment, planning, and funding that go into a firm's program of social responsibility.

Home Depot Builds a Better Community

Home Depot, the world's largest retailer of home-improvement products, is on a mission to build higher sales along with stronger communities. The chain was founded in Atlanta in 1979 and currently operates 2,000 warehouse-size stores and showrooms across North America, each is filled from floor to ceiling with thousands of items for home construction and repair. Home Depot's industry dominance and financial strength—it rings up more than $73 billion in annual sales—put real muscle behind the company's social responsibility agenda.

High on the list of worthwhile causes is affordable housing. Working with Habitat for Humanity, Rebuilding Together, and other groups, Home Depot sponsors building projects, provides money and materials, and encourages volunteers to get involved. Since 1991, it has helped construct hundreds of new homes and renovate more than 20,000 housing units for disabled and elderly residents. For example, the Leo and Goldie Sheftel Court condo project in Calgary to be built on land donated by Home Depot will house low-income families.

Another major program is Team Depot, which encourages employees in every company store and facility to donate time to community projects. Home Depot employees have volunteered to fix up parks, refurbish schools, build playgrounds, create walking trails, and help on many other local projects. After hurricanes caused flooding and severe damage throughout the U.S. Gulf Coast, Home Depot volunteers quickly joined the cleanup effort. The year before, Home Depot volunteers spruced up youth centres and helped rebuild other facilities after hurricanes tore through Florida.

In any given year, Home Depot volunteers devote two million hours to helping their communities. The company is also one of a number of corporations active in an ambitious campaign to promote volunteerism among their employees and managers. The campaign has set a goal of getting 6.4 million new volunteers within twenty-four months. Whenever Team Depot volunteers work on a local project, they look for ways to get newcomers involved—and the community

continued on next page

DID YOU KNOW?

The Home Depot, the world's largest home-improvement retailer, committed more than $9 million to the victims of hurricanes Katrina, Rita, and Wilma, and its employees donate two million hours of volunteer time to community causes each year.

K E Y   T E R M S

ethics (42)
business ethics (42)
Sarbanes-Oxley Act of 2002 (46)
code of ethics (46)
whistle-blowing (47)
social responsibility (49)

caveat emptor (51)
economic model of social responsibility (52)
socioeconomic model of social responsibility (53)
consumerism (54)

minority (58)
diversity implementation (58)
hard-to-employ (59)
pollution (59)
social audit (64)

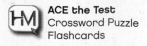

ACE the Test
Crossword Puzzle
Flashcards

THE HOME DEPOT VALUES

Excellent Customer Service: Along with our quality products, service, price and selection, we must go the extra mile to give customers knowledgeable advice about merchandise and to help them use those products to their maximum benefit.

Entrepreneurial Spirit: Home Depot associates are encouraged to initiate creative and innovative ways of serving our customers and improving the business, as well as to adopt good ideas from others.

Respect for All People: In order to remain successful, our associates must work in an environment of mutual respect, free of discrimination and harassment. Everyone has value, regardless of gender, ethnic or education background.

Building Strong Relationships: Strong relationships are built on trust, honesty and integrity. We should listen and respond to the needs of customers, associates, communities and vendors, treating them as partners.

Doing the Right Thing: We exercise good judgment by "doing the right thing" instead of just "doing things right." We strive to understand the impact of our decisions, and we accept responsibility for our actions.

Giving Back: An important part of the fabric of The Home Depot is giving part of our time, talent, energy and treasure to needs in our community and society.

Creating Shareholder Value: The investors who provide the capital necessary to allow our Company to exist need and expect a return on their investment. We are committed to providing it.

HOME DEPOT'S FOUR PRIORITY AREAS

Affordable Housing

Building and repairing houses for low-income families and helping people realize the dream of homeownership goes hand-in-hand with our business. Our commitment to developing and rehabilitating affordable housing is supported primarily through:

- Neighbourhood housing service organizations.
- Community development corporations.
- Neighbourhood revitalization groups.
- Other organizations directly involved with the creation or rehabilitation of low-income housing.

At-Risk Youth

Programs that provide children with a safe place to engage in learning activities and acquire meaningful life skills are supported, including:

- Organizations that work with young adults to teach construction techniques and the importance of working and solving problems together.
- Programs that help to develop self esteem and leadership qualities.
- Partnerships that bring young people together to participate in community service events.

Environment

Assistance is provided to non-profit organizations that direct efforts toward protecting our natural systems. Our grants program focuses on the following areas:

- Forestry and ecology.
- Green building design.
- Clean-up and recycling.
- Lead poisoning prevention.

Disaster Preparedness and Response

Associates work to educate customers on how to face emergencies—before, during and after disaster strikes. Working with relief organizations, we are able to assist our communities to:

- Prepare through clinics and awareness programs by teaching customers how to be ready for an emergency.
- Respond with needed supplies and volunteers in the wake of natural disasters and severe weather.
- Rebuild and help our neighbours return to daily life.

HOME DEPOT'S ENVIRONMENTAL PRINCIPLES

1. We are committed to improving the environment by selling products that are manufactured, packaged and labelled in a responsible manner, that take the environment into consideration, and that provide greater value to our customers.
2. We will support efforts to provide accurate, informative product labelling of environmental claims and impact.
3. We will strive to eliminate unnecessary packaging.
4. We will recycle and encourage the use of materials and products with recycled content.
5. We will conserve natural resources by using energy and water wisely and seek further opportunities to improve the resource efficiency of our stores.
6. We will comply with all environmental laws and will maintain programs and procedures to ensure compliance.
7. We are committed to minimizing environmental health and safety risk for our employees and our customers.
8. We will train our employees to enhance understanding of environmental issues and policies and to promote excellence in job performance and all environmental matters.

Figure 2.1

Defining Acceptable Behaviour: The Home Depot Values

Home Depot encourages ethical behaviour through an extensive training program and a written code of ethics and priority values.

Source: Government of Canada, Natural Resources Canada, *Corporate Social Responsibility: Lessons Learned*, http://nrcan.gc.ca/sd-dd/pubs/csr-rse/pdf/cas/hd_e.pdf, accessed on December 3, 2007.

Business Ethics Defined

Learning Objective ①

Understand what is meant by *business ethics*.

ethics the study of right and wrong and of the morality of the choices individuals make

business ethics the application of moral standards to business situations

Ethics is the study of right and wrong and of the morality of the choices individuals make. An ethical decision or action is one that is "right" according to some standard of behaviour. **Business ethics** is the application of moral standards to business situations. Recent court cases involving unethical behaviour have helped to make business ethics a matter of public concern. In one such case, Conrad Black, who once controlled *The National Post*, among other media across Canada and elsewhere through his role of CEO at Hollinger International Inc., was ousted by a shareholder revolt in 2003 after he was accused of plundering millions of dollars belonging to shareholders of Hollinger International, tax evasion, and misusing company money to bankroll his lavish lifestyle. After losing control of the firm he had built and managed, he faced criminal charges in Chicago in 2007 on charges of racketeering, wire fraud, and tax evasion. He was found guilty of mail fraud and obstruction of justice.[1] In another much-publicized case, lawsuits against tobacco companies have led to $246 billion in settlements, although there has been only one class-action lawsuit filed on behalf of all smokers. That case, *Engle* v. *R. J. Reynolds* could cost tobacco companies an estimated $500 billion.

Ethical Issues

Learning Objective ②

Identify ethical concerns that arise in the business world.

Ethical issues often arise out of a business's relationship with investors, customers, employees, creditors, or competitors. Each of these groups has specific concerns and usually exerts pressure on the organization's managers. For example, investors want management to make sensible financial decisions that will boost sales, profits, and returns on their investments. Customers expect a firm's products to be safe, reliable, and reasonably priced. Employees demand to be treated fairly in hiring, promotion, and compensation decisions. Creditors require accounts to be paid on time and the accounting information furnished by the firm to be accurate. Competitors expect the firm's competitive practices to be fair and honest. Business people face ethical issues every day, and some of these issues can be difficult to assess. Although some types of issues arise infrequently, others occur regularly. Let's take a closer look at several ethical issues.

Fairness and Honesty

Fairness and honesty in business are two important ethical concerns. Besides obeying all laws and regulations, business people are expected to refrain from knowingly deceiving, misrepresenting, or intimidating others. The consequences of failing to do so can be expensive.

In 2003, for example, the Government of Canada filed a civil lawsuit against the R.J. Reynolds and Japan Tobacco groups of companies, including JTI-Macdonald of Toronto. The government alleged that a scheme was devised and implemented to gain illicit profits from the smuggling trade in tobacco products, resulting in substantial revenue loss to the Government of Canada.[2]

Organizational Relationships

A business person may be tempted to place his or her personal welfare above the welfare of others or the welfare of the organization. For example, in late 2002, former CEO of Tyco International, Ltd., Leo Dennis Kozlowski was indicted for misappropriating $43 million in corporate funds to make philanthropic contributions in his own name, including $5 million to Seton Hall University, which named its new business-school building Kozlowski Hall. Furthermore, according to Tyco, the former CEO took $61.7 million in interest-free relocation loans without the board's permission. He allegedly used the money to finance many personal luxuries, including a $15 million yacht and a $3.9 million Renoir painting, and to throw a $2 million party for his wife's birthday.[3] Relationships with customers and coworkers often create ethical problems. Unethical behaviour in these areas includes taking credit for others' ideas or work, not meeting one's commitments in a mutual agreement, and pressuring others to behave unethically.

Conflict of Interest

Conflict of interest results when a business person takes advantage of a situation for his or her own personal interest rather than for the employer's interest. Such conflict may occur when payments and gifts make their way into business deals. A wise rule to remember is that anything given to a person that might unfairly influence that person's business decision is a bribe, and all bribes are unethical.

For example, Nortel Networks Corporation does not permit its employees, officers, and directors to accept any gifts or to serve as directors or officers of any organization that might supply goods or services to Nortel Networks. However, Nortel employees may work part time with firms that are not competitors, suppliers, or customers. At Procter & Gamble Company (P&G), all employees are obligated to act at all times solely in the best interests of the company. A conflict of interest arises when an employee has a personal relationship or financial or other interest that could interfere with this obligation or when an employee uses his or her position with the company for personal gain. P&G requires employees to disclose all potential conflicts of interest and to take prompt actions to eliminate a conflict when the company asks them to do so. Receiving gifts, entertainment, or other gratuities from people with whom P&G does business generally is not acceptable because doing so could imply an obligation on the part of the company and potentially pose a conflict of interest.

Communications

Business communications, especially advertising, can present ethical questions. False and misleading advertising is illegal and unethical, and it can infuriate customers. Sponsors of advertisements aimed at children must be especially careful to avoid

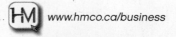

misleading messages. Advertisers of health-related products also must take precautions to guard against deception when using such descriptive terms as *organic* and *natural*. And with recent relaxation of government of Canada regulations of benefit claims for over-the-counter and non-prescription natural remedies, businesses will have to be careful to avoid charges of misrepresenting or overstating the benefits of their products.[4]

Factors Affecting Ethical Behaviour

Learning Objective ③

Discuss the factors affecting ethical behaviour in organizations.

Is it possible for an individual with strong moral values to make ethically questionable decisions in a business setting? What factors affect a person's inclination to make either ethical or unethical decisions in a business organization? Although the answers to these questions are not entirely clear, three general sets of factors do appear to influence the standards of behaviour in an organization. As shown in Figure 2.2, the sets consist of individual factors, social factors, and opportunity.

Figure 2.2

Factors That Affect the Level of Ethical Behaviour in an Organization

Source: Based on O. C. Ferrell and Larry Gresham, "A Contingency Framework for Understanding Ethical Decision Making in Marketing," *Journal of Marketing*, Summer 1985, p. 89.

LEVEL OF ETHICAL BEHAVIOUR

Individual factors | Social factors | Opportunity

Several individual factors influence the level of ethical behaviour in an organization. How much an individual knows about an issue is one factor: A decision maker with a greater amount of knowledge regarding a situation may take steps to avoid ethical problems, whereas a less-informed person may take action unknowingly that leads to an ethical quagmire. An individual's moral values and central, value-related attitudes also clearly influence his or her business behaviour. Most people join organizations to accomplish personal goals. The types of personal goals an individual aspires to and the manner in which these goals are pursued have a significant impact on that individual's behaviour in an organization. The actions of specific individuals in scandal-plagued companies such as Adelphia, Arthur Anderson, Enron, Halliburton, Qwest, and WorldCom often raise questions about individuals' personal character and integrity.

A person's behaviour in the workplace, to some degree, is determined by cultural norms, and these social factors vary from one culture to another. For example, in some countries it is acceptable and ethical for customs agents to receive gratuities for performing ordinary, legal tasks that are a part of their jobs, whereas in other countries these practices would be viewed as unethical and perhaps illegal. The actions and decisions of coworkers constitute another social factor believed to shape a person's sense of business ethics. For example, if your coworkers make long-distance telephone calls on company time and at company expense, you might view that behaviour as acceptable and ethical because everyone does it. The moral values and attitudes of "significant others"—spouses, friends, and relatives, for instance—also can affect an employee's perception of what is ethical and unethical behaviour in the workplace. Even the Internet presents new challenges for firms whose employees enjoy easy access to sites through convenient high-speed connections at work. An employee's online behaviour can be viewed as offensive to coworkers and possibly lead to lawsuits against the firm if employees engage in unethical behaviour on controversial websites not related to their job. As a result, research by Websense and the Center for Internet Studies reveals that nearly two out of three companies have disciplined employees and that nearly one out of three have fired employees for Internet misuse in the workplace.[5] Interestingly, one recent survey of employees found that most workers assume that their use of technology at work will be monitored. A large majority of employees approved of most monitoring methods such as monitoring faxes and e-mail, tracking web use, and even recording telephone calls.

Opportunity refers to the amount of freedom an organization gives an employee to behave unethically if he or she makes that choice. In some organizations, certain company policies and procedures reduce the opportunity to be unethical. For example, at some fast-food restaurants, one employee takes your order and receives your payment and another fills the order. This procedure reduces the opportunity to be unethical because the person handling the money is not dispensing the product, and the person giving out the product is not handling the money. The existence of an ethical code and the importance management places on this code are other determinants of opportunity (codes of ethics are discussed in more detail in the next section). The degree of enforcement of company policies, procedures, and ethical codes is a major force affecting opportunity. When violations are dealt with consistently and firmly, the opportunity to be unethical is reduced.

Do you make personal telephone calls on company time? Many individuals do. Although most employers limit personal calls to a few minutes, some make personal calls in excess of thirty minutes. Whether or not you use company time and equipment to make personal calls is an example of a personal ethical decision.

Now that we have considered some of the factors believed to influence the level of ethical behaviour in the workplace, let's explore what can be done to encourage ethical behaviour and to discourage unethical behaviour.

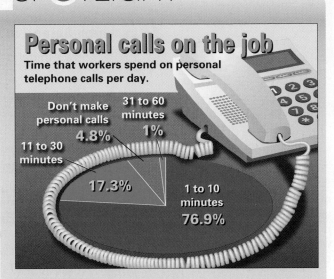

SPOTLIGHT

Personal calls on the job

Time that workers spend on personal telephone calls per day.

- Don't make personal calls **4.8%**
- 31 to 60 minutes **1%**
- 11 to 30 minutes **17.3%**
- 1 to 10 minutes **76.9%**

Source: At-A-Glance survey of 1,385 office workers. Margin of error +2.7 percentage points. O.C. Ferrell, John Fraedrich and Linda Ferrell, *Business Ethics,* 6th ed. Copyright © 2008 by Houghton Mifflin Company. Reprinted with permission of Houghton Mifflin.

Encouraging Ethical Behaviour

Learning Objective 4

Explain how ethical decision making can be encouraged.

Most authorities agree that there is room for improvement in business ethics. A more problematic question is: Can business be made more ethical in the real world? The majority opinion on this issue suggests that government, trade associations, and individual firms indeed can establish acceptable levels of ethical behaviour.

The government can encourage ethical behaviour by legislating more stringent regulations. For example, the landmark **Sarbanes-Oxley Act of 2002** provides sweeping new legal protection for those who report American corporate misconduct. The legislation was brought on by the corporate scandals such as the Martha Stewart fiasco and the collapse of Enron Corp. in 2001 that resulted in the loss of more than $60 billion U.S. in market value, almost $2.1 billion U.S. in pension plans and 5,600 jobs. Enron's collapse also caught Canadian Imperial Bank of Commerce, the Royal, and TD banks off guard, and resulted in their having to pay out of billions of dollars in liabilities related to the scandal.[6] Among other things, the law deals with corporate responsibility, conflicts of interest, and corporate accountability. However, rules require enforcement, and the unethical business person frequently seems to "slip something by" without getting caught. Increased regulation may help, but it surely cannot solve the entire ethics problem.

Trade associations can and often do provide ethical guidelines for their members. These organizations, which operate within particular industries, are in an excellent position to exert pressure on members who stoop to questionable business practices. For example, recently, a pharmaceutical trade group adopted a new set of guidelines to halt the extravagant dinners and other gifts sales representatives often give to physicians. However, enforcement and authority vary from association to association. And because trade associations exist for the benefit of their members, harsh measures may be self-defeating.

Codes of ethics that companies provide to their employees are perhaps the most effective way to encourage ethical behaviour. A **code of ethics** is a written guide to acceptable and ethical behaviour as defined by an organization; it outlines uniform policies, standards, and punishments for violations. Because employees know what is expected of them and what will happen if they violate the rules, a code of ethics goes a long way toward encouraging ethical behaviour. However, codes cannot possibly cover every situation. Companies also must create an environment in which employees recognize the importance of complying with the written code. Managers must provide direction by fostering communication, actively modelling and encouraging ethical decision making, and training employees to make ethical decisions.

During the 1980s, an increasing number of organizations created and implemented ethics codes. In a recent survey of *Fortune* 1000 firms, 93 percent of the companies that responded reported having a formal code of ethics. Some companies are now even

Sarbanes-Oxley Act of 2002 provides sweeping new legal protection for employees who report American corporate misconduct

code of ethics a guide to acceptable and ethical behaviour as defined by the organization

taking steps to strengthen their codes. For example, to strengthen its accountability, the Healthcare Financial Management Association recently revised its code to designate contact persons who handle reports of ethics violations, to clarify how its board of directors should deal with violations of business ethics, and to guarantee a fair hearing process. S. C. Johnson & Son, makers of Pledge, Drano, Windex, and many other household products, is another firm that recognizes that it must behave in ways the public perceives as ethical; its code includes expectations for employees and its commitment to consumers, the community, and society in general. As shown in Figure 2.3, included in the ethics code of electronics giant Texas Instruments are issues relating to policies and procedures; laws and regulations; relationships with customers, suppliers, and competitors; conflicts of interest; handling of proprietary information; and code enforcement.

Assigning an ethics officer who coordinates ethical conduct gives employees someone to consult if they are not sure of the right thing to do. An ethics officer meets with employees and top management to provide ethical advice, establishes and maintains an anonymous confidential service to answer questions about ethical issues, and takes action on violations of the code of ethics.

Sometimes even employees who want to act ethically may find it difficult to do so. Unethical practices can become ingrained in an organization. Employees with high personal ethics then may take a controversial step called *whistle-blowing*. **Whistle-blowing** is informing the press or government officials about unethical practices within one's organization.

Enron's Sherron S. Watkins and WorldCom's Cynthia Cooper are now well-known whistle-blowers. According to Linda Chatman Thomsen, deputy director for enforcement at the U.S. Securities and Exchange Commission, "Whistle-blowers give us an insider's perspective and have advanced our investigation immeasurably." Stephen Meagher, a former federal prosecutor who represents whistle-blowers, calls Watkins and Cooper national champions and says, "The business of whistle-blowing is booming."[7]

Whistle-blowing could have averted disaster and prevented needless deaths in the Canadian Red Cross tainted-blood supply scandal, for example. How could employees have known about life-threatening problems and not say anything? Whistle-blowing, on the other hand, can have serious repercussions for employees: Those who "blow whistles" sometimes lose their jobs. When firms set up anonymous hotlines to handle ethically questionable situations, employees actually may be more likely to engage in whistle-blowing. When firms instead create an environment that educates employees and nurtures ethical behaviour, fewer ethical problems arise, and ultimately, the need for whistle-blowing is greatly reduced.

It is difficult for an organization to develop ethics codes, policies, and procedures to deal with all relationships and every situation. When no company policy or procedures exist or apply, a quick test to determine if a behaviour is ethical is to see if others—coworkers, customers, and suppliers—approve of it. Ethical decisions always will withstand scrutiny. Openness and communication about choices often will build trust and strengthen business relationships. Table 2.1 provides some general guidelines for making ethical decisions.

whistle-blowing informing the press or government officials about unethical practices within one's organization

Figure 2.3

Defining Acceptable Behaviour: Texas Instruments' Code of Ethics

Texas Instruments encourages ethical behaviour through an extensive training program and a written code of ethics and shared values.

Source: Courtesy of Texas Instruments, www .ti.com/corp/docs/ company/citizen/ethics/ brochure/intergrity .shtml; accessed September 21, 2005. "The Values and Ethics of TI," used with permission.

TEXAS INSTRUMENTS CODE OF ETHICS

"Integrity is the foundation on which TI is built. There is no other characteristic more essential to a Tler's makeup. It has to be present at all levels. Integrity is expected of managers and individuals when they make commitments. They are expected to stand by their commitments to the best of their ability.

One of TI's greatest strengths is its values and ethics. We had some early leaders who set those values as the standard for how they lived their lives. And it is important that TI grew that way. It's something that we don't want to lose. At the same time, we must move more rapidly. But we don't want to confuse that with the fact that we're ethical and we're moral. We're very responsible, and we live up to what we say."

Tom Engibous, President and CEO
Texas Instruments, 1997

We Respect and Value People By:

Treating others as we want to be treated.

- Exercising the basic virtues of respect, dignity, kindness, courtesy and manners in all work relationships.
- Recognizing and avoiding behaviours that others may find offensive, including the manner in which we speak and relate to one another and the materials we bring into the workplace, both printed and electronically.
- Respecting the right and obligation of every Tler to resolve concerns relating to ethics questions in the course of our duties without retribution and retaliation.
- Giving all Tlers the same opportunity to have their questions, issues and situations fairly considered while understanding that being treated fairly does not always mean that we will all be treated the same.
- Trusting one another to use sound judgment in our use of TI business and information systems.
- Understanding that even though TI has the obligation to monitor its business information systems activity, we will respect privacy by prohibiting random searches of individual Tlers' communications.
- Recognizing that conduct socially and professionally acceptable in one culture and country may be viewed differently in another.

We Are Honest By:

Representing ourselves and our intentions truthfully.

- Offering full disclosure and withdrawing ourselves from discussions and decisions when our business judgment appears to be in conflict with a personal interest.
- Respecting the rights and property of others, including their intellectual property. Accepting confidential or trade secret information only after we clearly understand our obligations as defined in a nondisclosure agreement.
- Competing fairly without collusion or collaboration with competitors to divide markets, set prices, restrict production, allocate customers or otherwise restrain competition.
- Assuring that no payments or favors are offered to influence others to do something wrong.
- Keeping records that are accurate and include all payments and receipts.
- Exercising good judgment in the exchange of business courtesies, meals and entertainment by avoiding activities that could create even the appearance that our decisions could be compromised.
- Refusing to speculate in TI stock through frequent buying and selling or through other forms of speculative trading.

1. *Listen and learn.*	Recognize the problem or decision-making opportunity that confronts your company, team, or unit. Don't argue, criticize, or defend yourself—keep listening and reviewing until you are sure that you understand others.
2. *Identify the ethical issues.*	Examine how coworkers and consumers are affected by the situation or decision at hand. Examine how you feel about the situation, and attempt to understand the viewpoint of those involved in the decision or in the consequences of the decision.
3. *Create and analyze options.*	Try to put aside strong feelings such as anger or a desire for power and prestige and come up with as many alternatives as possible before developing an analysis. Ask everyone involved for ideas about which options offer the best long-term results for you and the company. Then decide which option will increase your self-respect even if, in the long run, things don't work out the way you hope?
4. *Identify the best option from your point of view.*	Consider it and test it against some established criteria, such as respect, understanding, caring, fairness, honesty, and openness.
5. *Explain your decision and resolve any differences that arise.*	This may require neutral arbitration from a trusted manager or taking "time out" to reconsider, consult, or exchange written proposals before a decision is reached.

Table 2.1

Guidelines for Making Ethical Decisions

Source: Tom Rusk with D. Patrick Miller, "Doing the Right Thing," *Sky* (Delta Airlines), August, 1993, pp. 18–22.

Social Responsibility

Social responsibility is the recognition that business activities have an impact on society and the consideration of that impact in business decision making. In the first few days after hurricane Katrina hit New Orleans, Wal-Mart delivered $20 million in cash (including $4 million to employees displaced by the storm), 100 truckloads of free merchandise, and food for 100,000 meals. The company also promised a job elsewhere for every one of its workers affected by the catastrophe. Obviously, social responsibility costs money. It is perhaps not so obvious—except in isolated cases—that social responsibility is also good business. Customers eventually find out which firms are acting responsibly and which are not. And just as easily as they cast their dollar votes for a product made by a company that is socially responsible, they can vote against the firm that is not.

Consider the following examples of organizations that are attempting to be socially responsible:

* General Mills Canada Corp. is a presenting sponsor for the 2006-07 CanWest Raise-a-Reader campaign. Raise-a-Reader—founded by CanWest Global Communications Corp.—raises funds, resources and awareness for family literacy programs across Canada. Along with its Raise-a-Reader partnership, General Mills has launched a Bite Into Books program that offers free full-length books, in both English and French, to families who buy specially marked boxes of General Mills cereals and snacks. More than four million children's books and one million adult books will be available in

social responsibility the recognition that business activities have an impact on society and the consideration of that impact in business decision making

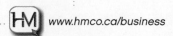

cereal packages and through a special online offer at www.BiteIntoBooks.com. The collection includes award-winning titles and best-selling authors published by Simon & Schuster Canada.[8]

* Social responsibility can take many forms—including flying lessons. Through Young Eagles, underwritten by S. C. Johnson, Phillips Petroleum, Lockheed Martin, Jaguar, and other corporations, 22,000 volunteer pilots have taken a half million youngsters on free flights designed to teach flying basics and inspire excitement about flying careers. Young Eagles is just one of the growing number of education projects undertaken by businesses building solid records as good corporate citizens.

These are just a few illustrations from the long list of companies big and small that attempt to behave in socially responsible ways. In general, people are more likely to want to work for and buy from such organizations.

The Evolution of Social Responsibility in Business

Learning Objective 5

Describe how views on social responsibility have evolved.

Business is far from perfect in many respects, but its record of social responsibility today is much better than in past decades. In fact, present demands for social responsibility have their roots in outraged reactions to the abusive business practices of the early 1900s.

During the first quarter of the twentieth century, businesses were free to operate pretty much as they chose. Government protection of workers and consumers was minimal. As a result, people either accepted what business had to offer or they did without. Working conditions often were deplorable by today's standards. The average work week in most industries exceeded sixty hours, no minimum-wage law existed, and employee benefits were almost nonexistent. Work areas were crowded and unsafe, and industrial accidents were the rule rather than the exception. To improve working conditions, employees organized and joined labour unions. During the early 1900s, however, businesses—with the help of government—were able to use court orders and brute force to defeat union attempts to improve working conditions.

During this period, consumers generally were subject to the doctrine of **caveat emptor,** a Latin phrase meaning "let the buyer beware." In other words, "what you see is what you get," and if it is not what you expected, too bad. Although victims of unscrupulous business practices could take legal action, going to court was very expensive, and consumers rarely won their cases. Moreover, no consumer groups or government agencies existed to publicize their consumers' grievances or to hold sellers accountable for their actions.

caveat emptor a Latin phrase meaning "let the buyer beware"

Prior to the 1930s, most people believed that competition and the action of the marketplace would, in time, correct abuses. Government therefore became involved in day-to-day business activities only in cases of obvious abuse of the free-market system. But the collapse of the stock market on October 29, 1929, triggered the Great Depression and years of dire economic problems for Canada and much of the world, changing this thinking forever. Although some parts of Canada suffered more than others because of differing makeup of regional and local economies, the Canadian income per capita fell an average 50 percent between 1928 and 1933. Alberta's fell more than 60 percent and Saskatchewan, where the economy was specialized and dependent on resources, fell more than 70 percent.[9]

Areas of Canada that were more dependent on the exports of resource products such as wheat, lumber, fish, and minerals suffered the most because of falling international prices and protective closing of markets to imports by trading countries. Drought conditions in 1934 and 1937 added to prairie farmers' problems. Wheat production fell from a peak 567 million bushels in 1928 to 276 million in 1934 and only 182 million in 1937, the lowest ever recorded. Farmers' incomes fell as much as 75 percent, which contributed to a chain reaction among those who depended on farmers, such as the railways.[10] Pressure mounted for the government to do something about the economy and worsening social conditions. Eventually, government became more involved

SPOTLIGHT

Top 10 Socially Responsible Canadian Corporations of 2006

RANK	COMPANY
1	Shoppers Drug Mart
2	Rothmans Inc.
3	Reitman's (Canada) Ltd.
4	Maple Leaf Foods Inc.
5	Toyota Canada
6	Home Capital Group Inc.
7	TSX Group Inc.
8	DaimlerChrysler Canada Inc.
9	Bank of Montreal
10	Transat A.T. Inc.

Source: *Corporate Knights Magazine*, page 24, accessed on October 26, 2006, http://www.corporateknights.ca/downloads/CK17.pdf. Used with permission of Corporate Knights, Inc.

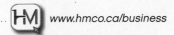

through the creation of social service programs and the making of international trade deals. These activities became the foundation for increased government involvement in dealings between business and society. As government involvement has increased, so has everyone's awareness of the social responsibility of business. Today's business owners are concerned about the return on their investment, but at the same time most of them demand ethical behaviour from employees. In addition, employees demand better working conditions, and consumers want safe, reliable products. Various advocacy groups echo these concerns and also call for careful consideration of our earth's delicate ecological balance. Managers therefore must operate in a complex business environment—one in which they are just as responsible for their managerial actions as for their actions as individual citizens. Interestingly, today's high-tech and Internet-based firms fare relatively well when it comes to environmental issues, worker conditions, the representation of minorities and women in upper management, animal testing, and charitable donations.

Two Views of Social Responsibility

Learning Objective 6

Explain the two views on the social responsibility of business.

Government regulation and public awareness are *external* forces that have increased the social responsibility of business. But business decisions are made *within* the firm— and there, social responsibility begins with the attitude of management. Two contrasting philosophies, or models, define the range of management attitudes toward social responsibility.

The Economic Model

According to the traditional concept of business, a firm exists to produce quality goods and services, earn a reasonable profit, and provide jobs. In line with this concept, the **economic model of social responsibility** holds that society will benefit most when business is left alone to produce and market profitable products that society needs. The economic model has its origins in the eighteenth century, when businesses were owned primarily by entrepreneurs or owner-managers. Competition was vigorous among small firms, and short-run profits and survival were the primary concerns.

To the manager who adopts this traditional attitude, social responsibility is someone else's job. After all, stockholders invest in a corporation to earn a return on their investment, not because the firm is socially responsible, and the firm is legally obligated to act in the economic interest of its stockholders. Moreover, profitable firms pay federal, provincial, and local taxes that are used to meet the needs of society. Thus managers who concentrate on profit believe that they fulfill their social responsibility indirectly through the taxes paid by their firms. As a result, social responsibility becomes the problem of government, environmental groups, charitable foundations, and similar organizations.

economic model of social responsibility the view that society will benefit most when business is left alone to produce and market profitable products that society needs

The Socioeconomic Model

In contrast, some managers believe that they have a responsibility not only to stock-holders but also to customers, employees, suppliers, and the general public. This broader view is referred to as the **socioeconomic model of social responsibility,** that places emphasis not only on profits but also on the impact of business decisions on society.

Recently, increasing numbers of managers and firms have adopted the socioeco-nomic model, and they have done so for at least three reasons. First, business is domi-nated by the corporate form of ownership, and the corporation is a creation of society. If a corporation does not perform as a good citizen, society can and will demand changes. Second, many firms have begun to take pride in their social responsibility records, among them Starbucks Coffee, Hewlett-Packard, Colgate-Palmolive, and Coca-Cola. Each of these companies is a winner of a Corporate Conscience Award in the areas of environmental concern, responsiveness to employees, equal opportunity, and commu-nity involvement. And of course, many other corporations are much more socially re-sponsible today than they were ten years ago. Third, many business people believe that it is in their best interest to take the initiative in this area. The alternative may be legal action brought against the firm by some special-interest group; in such a situa-tion, the firm may lose control of its activities.

socioeconomic model of social responsibility the concept that business should emphasize not only profits but also the impact of its decisions on society

The Pros and Cons of Social Responsibility

Business owners, managers, customers, and government officials have debated the pros and cons of the economic and socioeconomic models for years. Each side seems to have four major arguments to reinforce its viewpoint.

Arguments for Increased Social Responsibility Proponents of the socioeco-nomic model maintain that a business must do more than simply seek profits. To sup-port their position, they offer the following arguments:

1. Because business is a part of our society, it cannot ignore social issues.

2. Business has the technical, financial, and managerial resources needed to tackle today's complex social issues.

3. By helping resolve social issues, business can create a more stable environ-ment for long-term profitability.

4. Socially responsible decision making by firms can prevent increased gov-ernment intervention, which would force businesses to do what they fail to do voluntarily.

These arguments are based on the assumption that a business has a responsibility not only to its stockholders but also to its customers, employees, suppliers, and the general public.

Arguments Against Increased Social Responsibility Opponents of the socio-economic model argue that business should do what it does best: earn a profit by manufacturing and marketing products that people want. Those who support this po-sition argue as follows:

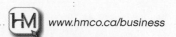

Table 2.2

A Comparison of the Economic and Socioeconomic Models of Social Responsibility as Implemented in Business

Source: Adapted from Keith Davis, William C. Frederick, and Robert L. Blomstron, *Business and Society: Concepts and Policy Issues* (New York: McGraw-Hill, 1980), p. 9. Used by permission of The McGraw-Hill Companies.

ECONOMIC MODEL PRIMARY EMPHASIS		SOCIOECONOMIC MODEL PRIMARY EMPHASIS
1. Production		1. Quality of life
2. Exploitation of natural resources		2. Conservation of natural resources
3. Internal, market-based decisions		3. Market-based decisions, with some community controls
4. Economic return (profit)	Middle ground	4. Balance of economic return and social return
5. Firm's or manager's interest		5. Firm's and community's interests
6. Minor role for government		6. Active government

1. Business managers are responsible primarily to stockholders, so management must be concerned with providing a return on owners' investments.
2. Corporate time, money, and talent should be used to maximize profits, not to solve society's problems.
3. Social problems affect society in general, so individual businesses should not be expected to solve these problems.
4. Social issues are the responsibility of government officials who are elected for that purpose and who are accountable to the voters for their decisions.

These arguments obviously are based on the assumption that the primary objective of business is to earn profits and that government and social institutions should deal with social problems.

Table 2.2 compares the economic and socioeconomic viewpoints in terms of business emphasis. Today, few firms are either purely economic or purely socioeconomic in outlook; most have chosen some middle ground between the two extremes. However, our society generally seems to want—and even to expect—some degree of social responsibility from business. Thus, within this middle ground, businesses are leaning toward the socioeconomic view. In the next several sections we look at some results of this movement in four specific areas: consumerism, employment practices, concern for the environment, and implementation of social responsibility programs.

Consumerism

Learning Objective 7

List the results of the consumer movement.

consumerism all activities undertaken to protect the rights of consumers

Consumerism consists of all activities undertaken to protect the rights of consumers. The fundamental issues pursued by the consumer movement fall into three categories: environmental protection, product performance and safety, and information disclosure. Although consumerism has been with us to some extent since the early nineteenth century, the consumer movement became stronger in the 1960s.

The Six Basic Rights of Consumers

Consumers have a right to safety, to be informed, to choose, to be heard, to consumer education, and to courteous service. These six rights are the basis of much of the consumer-oriented legislation passed during the last forty years. These rights also provide an effective outline of the objectives and accomplishments of the consumer movement.

The Right to Safety The consumers' right to safety means that the products they purchase must be safe for their intended use, must include thorough and explicit directions for proper use, and must be tested by the manufacturer to ensure product quality and reliability. There are several reasons why Canadian firms must be concerned about product safety. Federal departments such as Health Canada and Industry Canada have the power to force businesses that make or sell defective products to take corrective actions. Such actions include offering refunds, recalling defective products, issuing public warnings, and reimbursing consumers—all of which can be expensive. Businesses also should be aware that consumers and the government have been winning an increasing number of product-liability lawsuits against sellers of defective products. Moreover, the amount of the awards in these suits has been increasing steadily. For instance, 62 year-old Gerald Barnett, who had a heart attack after taking Vioxx for 31 months for pain caused by a car accident was awarded US$50-million in compensatory damages and US$1-million in punitive damages. The court found that pharmaceutical giant Merck & Co. had knowingly misrepresented or failed to disclose a material fact to the plaintiff's physicians and that doctors in the case and the plaintiff himself were not at fault. At its peak, Vioxx earned $2.5 billion a year for Merck. Merck & Co. owns Merck Frosst, one of the most important pharmaceutical companies in Canada employing 1,600 workers, including 1,100 in Montreal. When the firm was forced to stop production of Vioxx at its Montreal facilities in 2004, the ramifications were traumatic for all stakeholders. Research showed it doubled risk of heart attack and stroke after 18 months' use. Data released since then indicate the heart risks started much sooner and persisted at least a year after people stopped taking Vioxx, although Merck has disputed that. Merck has vowed to fight each Vioxx lawsuit individually, winning some and losing others, and has set aside $970 million in reserve for its legal costs, of which $285 million had been spent as of the end of 2005.[11]

Yet another major reason for improving product safety is consumers' demand for safe products. People simply will stop buying a product they believe is unsafe or unreliable.

The first concern is safety

These toys made in China were found to contain unsafe levels of lead paint. Who should be held responsible for keeping them off store shelves, importers, governments, retailers, or consumers?

The Right to Be Informed The right to be informed means that consumers must have access to complete information about a product before they buy it. Detailed information about ingredients and nutrition must be provided on food containers, information about fabrics and laundering methods must be attached to clothing, and lenders must disclose the true cost of borrowing the money they make available to customers who purchase merchandise on credit.

In addition, manufacturers must inform consumers about the potential dangers of using their products. Manufacturers that fail to provide such information can be held responsible for personal injuries suffered because of their products. For example, Maytag provides customers with a lengthy booklet that describes how they should use an automatic clothes washer. Sometimes such warnings seem excessive, but they are necessary if user injuries (and resulting lawsuits) are to be avoided.

The Right to Choose The right to choose means that consumers must have a choice of products, offered by different manufacturers and sellers, to satisfy a particular need. The government has done its part by encouraging competition through legislation. The greater the competition, the greater is the choice available to consumers.

Competition and the resulting freedom of choice provide additional benefits for customers by reducing prices. For example, when personal computers were first introduced in the early 1980s, they cost over $5,000. Thanks to intense competition and technological advancements, today personal computers can be purchased for less than $500.

The Right to Be Heard This fourth right means that someone will listen and take appropriate action when customers complain. Actually, management began to listen to consumers after World War II, when competition between businesses that manufactured and sold consumer goods increased. One way that firms could gain a competitive edge was to listen to consumers and provide the products they said they wanted and needed. Today, businesses are listening even more attentively, and many larger firms have consumer relations departments that can be contacted easily via toll-free phone numbers. Other groups listen, too. Most large cities have federal and provincial as well as business-sponsored consumer affairs offices, such as the Better Business Bureau, to act on citizens' complaints.

The Right to Consumer Education More than simply providing information through labelling and packaging, the consumer movement recognizes the need to educate people so that they are more fully informed about their rights as consumers. For instance, firms may communicate important information such as warranty extensions, explanations, and recalls of consumer products through press releases and other public relations efforts such as the website (**www.dellbatteryprogram.com**) set up to deal with Dell laptop computers' overheating battery problem.

The Right to Courteous Service The right to service, which entitles consumers to convenience, courtesy, and responsiveness from manufacturers and sellers of consumer products is part of an overall shift in business thinking and culture that recognizes the importance of maintaining positive relations with customers in order to keep them from seeking better treatment from competitors. This is especially significant for those businesses whose product offering is readily available from competitors.

Major Consumerism Forces

The major forces in consumerism are individual consumer advocates and organizations, consumer education programs, and consumer laws. Consumer advocates take it on themselves to protect the rights of consumers. They band together into consumer organizations, either independently or under government sponsorship. Some organizations, such as the Consumers' Association of Canada, operate nationally, whereas others are active at provincial and local levels. They inform and organize other consumers, raise issues, help businesses to develop consumer-oriented programs, and pressure lawmakers to enact consumer protection laws. Some consumer advocates and organizations encourage consumers to boycott products and businesses to which they have objections. Today, the consumer movement has adopted corporate-style marketing and addresses a broad range of issues. Current campaigns include efforts (1) to curtail the use of animals for testing purposes, (2) to reduce alcohol and tobacco consumption, and (3) to encourage recycling.

Educating consumers to make wiser purchasing decisions is perhaps one of the most far-reaching aspects of consumerism. Increasingly, consumer education is becoming a part of high school and adult-education programs. These programs cover many topics—for instance, what major factors should be considered when buying specific products, such as insurance, real estate, automobiles, appliances and furniture, clothes, and food; the provisions of certain consumer-protection laws; and the sources of information that can help individuals become knowledgeable consumers.

Major advances in consumerism have come through a mix of federal and provincial legislation, which take on the comprehensive title of the Consumer Protection Act for a particular province or territory. Some laws enacted are listed and described in Table 2.3. Most business people now realize that they ignore consumer issues only at their own peril. Managers know that improper handling of consumer complaints can result in lost sales, bad publicity, and lawsuits.

USING THE INTERNET

For a more exhaustive list of Canadian federal and provincial government legislation and resources available to consumers as well as guidelines for businesses, visit the Canadian Consumer Information Gateway located at http://consumerinformation.ca/.

1. The Packaging and Labelling Act requires manufacturers to disclose a variety of product information in both French and English in order to provide consumers with information about content, mass, and proper usage.

2. The Hazardous Products Act sets rules for permitted sale and distribution of hazardous products such as paint and batteries as well as restrictions on the use of some products, such as lead in gasoline fuel.

3. The Food and Drug Act controls the sale of these products because of their inherent risk to health and safety.

4. The Weights and Measures Act sets standards to assure that such things as commercial scales in food stores and the local gas pump make reasonably accurate measurements of what consumers are charged for.

5. The Textile Labelling Act regulates the labelling of clothing among other things to assure consumers of what they are buying.

Table 2.3

Examples of Consumer-protection Legislation

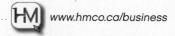

Employment Practices

Learning Objective 8

Analyze how present employment practices may counteract past abuses.

We have seen that managers who subscribe to the socioeconomic view of business's social responsibility, together with significant government legislation enacted to protect the buying public, have broadened the rights of consumers. The last four decades have seen similar progress in affirming the rights of employees to equal treatment in the workplace.

Everyone should have the opportunity to land a job for which he or she is qualified and to be rewarded on the basis of ability and performance. This is an important issue for society, and it also makes good business sense. Yet, over the years, this opportunity has been denied to members of various minority groups. A **minority** is a racial, religious, political, national, or other group regarded as different from the larger group of which it is a part and that is often singled out for unfavourable treatment.

Although laws such as the Employment Equity Act forbid discrimination in the workplace today, lower incomes and higher unemployment rates also characterize Native Canadians, handicapped persons, and women. Responsible managers have instituted a number of programs to counteract the results of discrimination.

Diversity Implementation

Diversity implementation is intended to increase the number of minority employees at all levels within an organization. The objective is to ensure that diversity is reflected within the organization in approximately the same proportion as in the surrounding community. Implementation plans encompass all areas of human resources management: recruiting, hiring, training, promotion, and pay.

Unfortunately, these kinds of programs have been plagued by two problems. The first involves quotas. In the beginning, many firms pledged to recruit and hire a certain number of minority members by a specific date. To achieve this goal, they were forced to consider only minority applicants for job openings; if they hired nonminority workers, they would be defeating their own purpose.

The second problem is that although most such programs have been reasonably successful, not all business people are in favour of diversity implementation programs. Managers not committed to these programs can "play the game" and still discriminate against workers. To help solve this problem and set an example for others to follow, the Canadian government passed the Employment Equity Act in 1986, which places an obligation on federal employers to implement employment equity by proactive means. Although subject to some criticism, there have been some improvements in women's representation since its introduction. The Canadian Human Rights Commission administers compliance by all federal jurisdictions with the Employment Equity Act and non-federal jurisdictions are the responsibility of provincial human rights commissions.

---

minority a racial, religious, political, national, or other group regarded as different from the larger group of which it is a part and that is often singled out for unfavourable treatment

diversity implementation adopting corporate practices to ensure that the diversity of the Canadian population is reflected in all levels of the organization

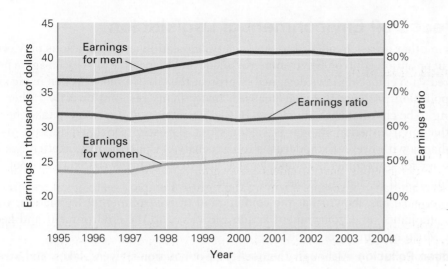

Figure 2.4

Earnings by Gender

As earnings for both men and women have grown, the gap between them remains fairly steady, with women earning about 63 percent what men earn.

Source: Statistics Canada, CANSIM, table (for fee) 202-0102. Last modified: 2006-03-28.
Source: Statistics Canada http://www40 .statcan.ca/l01/cst01/ labor01a.htm?sdi= earnings%20sex.

The threat of legal action has persuaded some corporations to amend their hiring and promotional policies, but the discrepancy between men's and women's salaries still exists, as illustrated in Figure 2.4.

Training Programs for the Hard-To-Employ

Social responsibility at some firms extends far beyond placing a help-wanted ad in the local newspaper. These firms have assumed the task of helping the **hard-to-employ,** workers with little education or vocational training and a long history of unemployment. In the past, such workers often routinely were turned down by personnel managers, even for the most menial jobs. Obviously, such workers require training; just as obviously, this training can be expensive and time-consuming. To share the costs, business and community leaders have joined together in a number of cooperative programs.

hard-to-employ workers with little education or vocational training and a long history of unemployment

Concern for the Environment

Learning Objective 9

Describe the major types of pollution.

The social consciousness of responsible business managers, the encouragement of a concerned government, and an increasing concern on the part of the public have led to major efforts to reduce environmental pollution, conserve natural resources, and reverse some of the worst effects of past negligence in this area. **Pollution** is the contamination of water, air, or land through the actions of people in an industrialized society. For several decades, environmentalists have been warning us about the dangers of industrial pollution. Unfortunately, business and government leaders either ignored the problem or were not concerned about it until pollution became a threat to life and health in Canada. Today, Canadians expect business and government leaders to take swift action to clean up our environment—and to keep it clean.

pollution the contamination of water, air, or land through the actions of people in an industrialized society

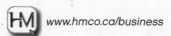

Effects of Environmental Legislation

As in other areas of concern to our society, legislation and regulations play crucial roles in pollution control. Environment Canada and respective provincial agencies are charged with enforcing laws designed to protect the environment. When made aware of a pollution problem they have caused, many firms respond directly rather than waiting to be charged with an offense. But, other owners and managers take the position that environmental standards are too strict. (Loosely translated, this means that compliance with present standards is too expensive.) Consequently, it often has been necessary for governments to take legal action to force firms to install antipollution equipment and to clean up waste storage areas.

Experience has shown that the combination of environmental legislation, voluntary compliance, and government action can clean up the environment and keep it clean. Much remains to be done.

Water Pollution Although the quality of our nation's rivers, lakes, and streams has improved significantly in recent years, many of these surface waters remain severely polluted. Currently, one of the most serious water-quality problems results from the high level of toxic pollutants found in these waters.

Among the serious threats to people posed by water pollutants are respiratory irritation, cancer, kidney and liver damage, anemia, and heart failure. Toxic pollutants also damage fish and other forms of wildlife. In fish, they cause tumours or reproductive problems; shellfish and wildlife living in or drinking from toxin-ladened waters have also suffered genetic defects.

The race to save the environment and its inhabitants

The vitality of beautiful Lake Memphremagog in Quebec's Eastern Townships is one of many lakes at risk due to the growth of blue-green algae which hurts tourism and living conditions for local residents as well.

Another serious issue is acid rain, which has contributed significantly to the deterioration of coastal waters, lakes, and marine life in eastern Canada. Acid rain forms when sulphur emitted by smokestacks in industrialized areas combines with moisture in the atmosphere to form acids that are spread by winds. The acids eventually fall to the earth in rain that finds its way into streams, rivers, and lakes. The acid-rain problem has spread rapidly in recent years, and experts fear that the situation will worsen if the United States, the source of much of the pollution, begins to burn more coal to generate electricity. The cost of this vital cleanup is high. The human costs of having ignored the problem so long may be higher still.

Air Pollution Usually, two or three factors combine to form air pollution in any given location. The first factor is large amounts of carbon monoxide and hydrocarbons emitted by motor vehicles concentrated in a relatively small area. The second is the smoke and other pollutants emitted by manufacturing facilities. These two factors can be eliminated in part through pollution-control devices on cars, trucks, and smokestacks. Add to these aviation emissions.

Aviation emissions are a potentially significant and growing percentage of greenhouse gases that contribute to global warming. Aircraft emissions are significant for several reasons. First, jet aircraft are the main source of human emissions deposited directly into the upper atmosphere, where they may have a greater warming effect than if they were released at the earth's surface. Second, carbon dioxide—the primary aircraft emission—is the main focus of international concern. For example, it survives in the atmosphere for nearly a hundred years and contributes to global warming, according to the Intergovernmental Panel on Climate Change. The carbon dioxide emissions from worldwide aviation roughly equal those of some industrialized countries. Third, carbon dioxide emissions, combined with other gases and particles emitted by jet aircraft, could have two to four times as great an effect on the atmosphere than carbon dioxide alone. Fourth, the Intergovernmental Panel recently concluded that the rise in aviation emissions owing to the growing demand for air travel would not be fully offset by reductions in emissions achieved solely through technological improvements.

A third factor that contributes to air pollution—one that cannot be changed—is the combination of weather and geography. The Toronto and Vancouver areas, for example, combine just the right weather and geographic conditions for creating dense smog—a combination of air-borne pollutants and fog.

BIZ TECH

Reduce, Reuse, Recycle Your e-waste

Electronic waste—*e-waste*—is a growing problem as technology advances and personal computers become obsolete at a rapid rate.

Tons of Trash Since the personal computer (PC) was invented in 1985, more than sixty million have been sent to landfills as North Americans trade up to newer, faster models. The U.S. National Safety Council estimates that by 2009, 136,000 PCs will be thrown away every day. Because some of the metals in PCs can leach into soil and water, e-pollution is a real concern.

Recycling Options The major computer manufacturers all offer recycling programs. For a modest fee, Hewlett-Packard, Dell, and other companies will send you a shipping label and arrange to pick up your old PC. Or nonprofits such as the National Cristina Foundation and Per Scholas may take your PC, if it's not too old. reBOOT Canada is a non-profit organization providing computer hardware, training and technical support to charities, non-profits and people with limited access to technology. Since their inception in 1996, reBOOT Canada has distributed over 60,000 pieces of computer equipment to charitable organizations across Canada. reBOOT Canada accepts donations of computer equipment from companies and individuals throughout Canada.

Find Out More For more information on e-waste and PC recycling, check Earth 911 (www.earth911 .org), the Rethink Initiative (rethink.ebay.com), or the Computer Takeback Campaign (www .computertakeback.com).

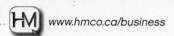
www.hmco.ca/business

How effective is air pollution control? Some authorities note that we have already seen improvement in air quality. A number of cities have cleaner air today than they did thirty years ago. But the debate about what to do is far from over. According to Environment Canada, transportation is one of the greatest sources of air pollution in Canada, particularly in urban areas where most of Canada's 18 million passenger cars are driven. The federal government's Clean Air Act of 2006 set even stricter emission limits on vehicles. But according to David Paterson, vice-president of Corporate and Environmental Affairs at General Motors, even if all new cars were made emission-free, 99 percent of Canada's smog and greenhouse gas emissions would remain. Paterson claims painting a wall with a gallon of water-based paint generates more smog than driving a new GM SUV from Toronto to Vancouver and back, and that burning a cord of wood creates more smog than a 2007 Trailblazer would driving around the circumference of the earth 37 times or 10 Chev SUVs would in their entire lifetime.

So where does air pollution come from and how can we help reduce it? Much is generated by heavy duty rail, air, and marine transportation. Operating a snowmobile for one hour produces more emissions than driving a GM vehicle for a year. Electrical generation produces 17.1 percent of all the greenhouse gas emissions and the oil, gas and coal industry contributes 20.3 percent. Real solutions will require changes in how we live, especially how we travel. Carpooling to work, using public transit, and walking instead of driving alone in our cars can make a big difference if we all do our part.[12]

Land Pollution Air and water quality may be improving, but land pollution is still a serious problem in many areas. The fundamental issues are (1) how to restore damaged or contaminated land at a reasonable cost and (2) how to protect unpolluted land from future damage.

The land pollution problem has been worsening over the past few years because modern technology has continued to produce increasing amounts of chemical and radioactive waste. Manufacturers produce millions of tons of contaminated oil, solvents, acids, and sludges each year. Service businesses, utility companies, hospitals, and other industries also dump vast amounts of waste into the environment.

Individuals in Canada also contribute to the waste-disposal problem. A shortage of landfill sites, owing to stricter regulations, makes garbage disposal a serious problem in some areas.

Incinerators help to solve the landfill-shortage problem, but they bring their own problems. They reduce the amount of garbage but leave tons of ash to be buried—ash that often has a higher concentration of toxicity than the original garbage. Other causes of land pollution include strip-mining of coal, nonselective cutting of forests, and the development of agricultural land for housing and industry.

Noise Pollution Excessive noise caused by traffic, aircraft, and machinery can do physical harm to human beings. Research has shown that people who are exposed to loud noises for long periods of time can suffer permanent hearing loss. Noise levels can be reduced by two methods. The source of noise pollution can be isolated as much as possible. (Thus many metropolitan airports are located outside the cities.) And engineers can modify machinery and equipment to reduce noise levels. If it is impossible to reduce industrial noise to acceptable levels, workers should be required to wear earplugs to guard against permanent hearing damage.

Who Should Pay for a Clean Environment?

Many business leaders offer one answer—tax money should be used to clean up the environment and to keep it clean. They reason that business is not the only source of pollution, so business should not be forced to absorb the entire cost of the cleanup. Environmentalists disagree. They believe that the cost of proper treatment and disposal of industrial wastes is an expense of doing business. In either case, consumers probably will pay a large part of the cost—either as taxes or in the form of higher prices for goods and services.

Implementing a Program of Social Responsibility

Learning Objective 10

Identify the steps toward implementing a program of social responsibility.

A firm's decision to be socially responsible is a step in the right direction—but only the first step. The firm then must develop and implement a program to reach this goal. The program will be affected by the firm's size, financial resources, past record in the area of social responsibility, and competition. Above all, however, the program must have the firm's total commitment or it will fail.

Developing a Program of Social Responsibility

An effective program for social responsibility takes time, money, and organization. In most cases, developing and implementing such a program will require four steps: securing the commitment of top executives, planning, appointing a director, and preparing a social audit.

Commitment of Top Executives Without the support of top executives, any program will soon falter and become ineffective. For example, the Boeing Company's Ethics and Business Conduct Committee is responsible for the ethics program. The committee is appointed by the Boeing board of directors, and its members include the company chairman and CEO, the president and chief operating officer, the presidents of the operating groups, and senior vice presidents. As evidence of their commitment to social responsibility, top managers should develop a policy statement that outlines key areas of concern. This statement sets a tone of positive support and later will serve as a guide for other employees as they become involved in the program.

Planning Next, a committee of managers should be appointed to plan the program. Whatever form their plan takes, it should deal with each of the issues described in the top managers' policy statement. If necessary, outside consultants can be hired to help develop the plan.

Appointment of a Director After the social responsibility plan is established, a top-level executive should be appointed to implement the organization's plan. This individual should be charged with recommending specific policies and helping individual departments to understand and live up to the social responsibilities the firm has assumed. Depending on the size of the firm, the director may require a staff to handle the program on a day-to-day basis. For example, at the Boeing Company, the director of ethics and business conduct administers the ethics and business conduct program.

The Social Audit At specified intervals, the program director should prepare a social audit for the firm. A **social audit** is a comprehensive report of what an organization has done and is doing with regard to social issues that affect it. This document provides the information the firm needs to evaluate and revise its social responsibility program. Typical subject areas include human resources, community involvement, the quality and safety of products, business practices, and efforts to reduce pollution and improve the environment. The information included in a social audit should be as accurate and as quantitative as possible, and the audit should reveal both positive and negative aspects of the program.

Today, many companies listen to concerned individuals within and outside the company. For example, the Boeing Ethics Line listens to and acts on concerns expressed by employees and others about possible violations of company policies, laws, or regulations, such as improper or unethical business practices, as well as health, safety, and environmental issues. Employees are encouraged to communicate their concerns, as well as ask questions about ethical issues. The Ethics Line is available to all Boeing employees, including Boeing subsidiaries. It is also available to concerned individuals outside the company.

Funding the Program

We have noted that social responsibility costs money. Thus, just like any other corporate undertaking, a program to improve social responsibility must be funded. Funding can come from three sources:

1. Management can pass the cost on to consumers in the form of higher prices.
2. The corporation can be forced to absorb the cost of the program if, for example, the competitive situation does not permit a price increase. In this case, the cost is treated as a business expense, and profit is reduced.
3. The government can pay for all or part of the cost through tax reductions or other incentives.

The Conference Board of Canada is a non-profit organization that government consults. It provides help to those in the business community interested in developing good, socially responsible corporate programs. The website, at http://www.conferenceboard.ca/, offers a wide variety of information on their literature, seminars, workshops, and conferences.

---

social audit a comprehensive report of what an organization has done and is doing with regard to social issues that affect it

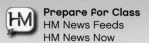

Prepare for Class
HM News Feeds
HM News Now

→ **RETURN TO INSIDE BUSINESS**

Even as Home Depot volunteers donate their time, the company donates cash and supplies through its philanthropic arm, The Home Depot Foundation. The foundation has an annual budget of about $25 million to support a variety of good causes, including disaster relief, job training, youth services, and United Way activities. After devastating hurricanes hit Florida and the Gulf Coast, the retailer donated $4.6 million in cash and suppliers to the cleanup effort.

Environmental protection is another area where Home Depot has become active. The company pledged to stop selling products made from lumber logged in endangered rainforests following a series of activist protests in the late 1990s. It also began giving preference to "certified wood"—wood products that came from nonendangered forests. With Home Depot leading the way, competitors quickly followed suit. Home Depot now requires certification from its suppliers and stocks eco-friendly substitutes so that customers have more choices.

Questions

1. Why would customers, employees, and shareholders prefer to be involved with a company such as Home Depot that wants to build stronger communities?

2. Does Home Depot's social responsibility agenda also address one or more of the basic rights of consumers? Explain your answer.

CHAPTER REVIEW

1 Understand what is meant by *business ethics*.

Ethics is the study of right and wrong and of the morality of choices. Business ethics is the application of moral standards to business situations.

2 Identify ethical concerns that arise in the business world.

In business situations, ethical issues often arise out of relationships with investors, customers, employees, creditors, or competitors. Business people should make every effort to be fair, to consider the welfare of customers and those within the firm, to avoid conflicts of interest, and to communicate honestly.

3 Discuss the factors affecting ethical behaviour in organizations.

Individual, social, and opportunity factors all affect the level of ethical behaviour in an organization. Individual factors include knowledge level, moral values and attitudes, and personal goals. Social factors include cultural norms and the actions and values of coworkers and significant others. Opportunity factors refer to the amount of leeway that exists in an organization for employees to behave unethically if they so choose.

4 Explain how ethical decision making can be encouraged.

Governments, trade associations, and individual firms all can establish definitions of ethical behaviour. Governments can pass regulations. Trade associations provide ethical guidelines for their members. Companies provide codes of ethics—written guides to acceptable and ethical behaviour as defined by an organization—and create an atmosphere in which ethical behaviour is encouraged. An ethical employee working in an unethical environment can resort to whistle-blowing to bring a questionable practice to light.

5 Describe how views on social responsibility have evolved.

In a socially responsible business, management realizes that its activities have an impact on society and considers that impact in the decision-making process. Before the 1930s, workers, consumers, and government had very little influence on business activities; as a result, business leaders gave little thought to social responsibility. All this changed with the Great Depression. Government regulations, employee demands, and consumer awareness combined to demand that businesses act in socially responsible ways.

6 Explain the two views on the social responsibility of business.

The basic premise of the economic model of social responsibility is that society benefits most when business is left alone to produce profitable goods and services. According to the socioeconomic model, business has as much responsibility to society as it has to its owners. Most managers adopt a viewpoint somewhere between these two extremes.

7 List the results of the consumer movement.

Consumerism consists of all activities undertaken to protect the rights of consumers. The consumer movement generally has demanded—and received—attention from business in the areas of product safety, product information, product choices through competition, and the resolu-

tion of complaints about products and business practices. Although concerns over consumer rights have been around to some extent since the early nineteenth century, the movement became more powerful in the 1960s. The six basic rights of consumers include the right to safety, the right to be informed, the right to choose, the right to be heard, and the rights to consumer education and courteous service.

8 Analyze how present employment practices may counteract past abuses.

Legislation and public demand have prompted some businesses to correct past abuses in employment practices—mainly with regard to minority groups. Affirmative action and training of the hard-to-employ unemployed are two types of programs that have been used successfully.

9 Describe the major types of pollution.

Industry has contributed to noise pollution and the pollution of our land and water through the dumping of wastes and to air pollution through vehicle and smokestack emissions. This contamination can be cleaned up and controlled, but the big question is: Who will pay? Present cleanup efforts are funded partly by government tax revenues, partly by business, and, in the long run, by consumers.

10 Identify the steps toward implementing a program of social responsibility.

A program to implement social responsibility in a business begins with total commitment by top management. The business should plan carefully and appoint a capable director to implement it. Social audits should be prepared periodically as a means of evaluating and revising the program. Programs may be funded through price increases, reduction of profit, or federal incentives.

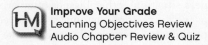

Improve Your Grade
Learning Objectives Review
Audio Chapter Review & Quiz

Review Questions

1. Why might an individual with high ethical standards act less ethically in business than in his or her personal life?
2. How would an organizational code of ethics help to ensure ethical business behaviour?
3. How and why did the Canadian business environment change after the Great Depression?
4. What are the major differences between the economic model of social responsibility and the socioeconomic model?
5. What are the arguments for and against increasing the social responsibility of business?
6. Describe and give an example of each of the six basic rights of consumers.
7. Although the population is evenly divided between males and females, why would some people consider women to be a minority with regard to employment?
8. What is the goal of affirmative action programs? How is this goal achieved?
9. Do you agree with the goal of affirmative action? Explain.
10. How do businesses contribute to each of the four forms of pollution? How can they avoid polluting the environment?
11. Our environment *can* be cleaned up and kept clean. Why haven't we simply done so?
12. Describe the steps involved in developing a social responsibility program within a large corporation.

Discussion Questions

1. When a company acts in an ethically questionable manner, what types of problems are caused for the organization and its customers?
2. How can an employee take an ethical stand regarding a business decision when his or her superior already has taken a different position?
3. Overall, would it be more profitable for a business to follow the economic model or the socioeconomic model of social responsibility?
4. Why should business take on the task of training the hard-to-employ unemployed?
5. To what extent should the blame for vehicular air pollution be shared by manufacturers, consumers, and government?
6. Why is there so much government regulation involving social responsibility issues? Should there be less?

CASE STUDY

At New Belgium Brewing, Greater Efficiency Is Blowing in the Wind

Social responsibility can help a firm differentiate itself and its brand in a competitive and crowded marketplace. For example, Dell Canada's "Plant a Tree for Me" program promotes environmental awareness and offers solutions to individual and corporate customers who are concerned about the carbon impact of electricity required to power their computers. For $2.10 per notebook and $6.30 per desktop, customers can offset the carbon emissions created to generate electricity by planting a tree through Dell Canada's non-profit partners—The Conservation Fund, Carbonfund.org (www.carbonfund.org) and Tree Canada (www.tree-arbrescanada.ca). (Source: News release, "Dell Canada Extends Environmental Leadership With 'Plant A Tree For Me' Program," August 29, 2007, http://www.treecanada.ca/news/08-29-2007.htm).

And if we were to search out a complete commitment to environmental social responsibility, perhaps a good case can be made for New Belgium Brewing of Fort Collins, Colorado. New Belgium Brewing (NBB), America's first wind-powered brewery, aims to make both a better beer and a better society.

Not only is the 80,000-square-foot facility highly automated for efficiency, but it is also designed with the environment in mind. For example, sun tubes bring daylight to areas that lack windows, which reduces the brewery's energy requirements. As another energy-saving example, the brewery's kettles have steam condensers to capture and reuse hot water again and again. The biggest energy-conservation measure is a special cooling device that reduces the need for air conditioning in warm weather. In the office section, NBB employees reuse and recycle paper and as many other supplies as possible.

Soon after opening the new brewery, the entire staff voted to convert it to wind power. In addition to saving energy and natural resources, NBB is actually transforming the methane from its waste stream into energy through the process of cogeneration. It also has found ways to cut carbon dioxide emissions and reuse brewing by-products as cattle feed. Going further, NBB donates $1 to charitable causes for every barrel of beer it sells—which translates into more than $200,000 per year.

Still, customers are most concerned with the taste of NBB's beers, which have won numerous awards and have attracted a large, loyal customer base in twelve states. In the last five years, Fat Tire's annual sales have grown from 0.9 million cases to 2.6 million cases. Many people become customers after hearing about the beer from long-time fans, and as its popularity grows, the word spreads even further. NBB does some advertising, but its budget is tiny compared with deep-pocketed rivals such as Anheuser-Busch and Miller Brewing. Instead of glitzy commercials on national television, NBB uses a low-key approach to show customers that the company is comprised of "real people making real beer."

Today, the company employs 140 people and is the sixth largest selling draft beer in America. Clearly, sales and profits are vital ingredients in NBB's long-term recipe, but they are not the only important elements. Jordan stresses that the company is not just about making beer—it is about creating what she calls "magic." Reflecting on her continued involvement in NBB, she says: "How do you support a community of people? How do you show up in the larger community? How do you strive to be a business role model? That's the part that keeps me really engaged here."

In fact, NBB has integrated social responsibility into its operations so successfully that it recently received an award from *Business Ethics* magazine. The award cited the company's "dedication to environmental excellence in every part of its innovative brewing process." Jordan, Lebesch, and all the NBB employee-owners can take pride in their efforts to build a better society as well as a better beer.

Questions:

1. What do you think Kim Jordan means when she talks about how New Belgium Brewing strives to be a "business role model," not just a beer maker?

2. Given New Belgium Brewing's emphasis on social responsibility, what would you suggest the company look at when preparing a social audit?

3. Should businesses charge more for products that are produced using more costly but environmentally friendly methods such as wind power? Should consumers pay more for products that are *not* produced using environmentally friendly methods because of the potential for costly environmental damage? Explain your answers.

BUILDING SKILLS FOR CAREER SUCCESS

1. Exploring the Internet

Socially responsible business behaviour can be as simple as donating unneeded older computers to schools, mentoring interested learners in good business practices, or supplying public speakers to talk about career opportunities. Students, as part of the public at large, perceive a great deal of information about a company, its employees, and its owners by the positive social actions taken and perhaps even more by actions not taken. Microsoft donates millions of dollars of computers and software to educational institutions every year. Some people consider this level of corporate giving to be insufficient given the scale of the wealth of the corporation. Others believe that firms have no obligation to give back any more than they wish and that recipients should be grateful. Visit the text website for updates to this exercise.

Assignment

1. Select any firm involved in high technology and the Internet such as Microsoft or IBM. Examine their website and report their corporate position on social responsibility and giving as they have stated it. What activities are they involved in? What programs do they support, and how do they support them?

2. Search the Internet for commentary on business social responsibility, form your own opinions, and then evaluate the social effort demonstrated by the firm you have selected. What more could the firm have done?

2. Building Team Skills

A firm's code of ethics outlines the kinds of behaviours expected within the organization and serves as a guideline for encouraging ethical behaviour in the workplace. It reflects the rights of the firm's workers, shareholders, and consumers.

Assignment

1. Working in a team of four, find a code of ethics for a business firm. Start the search by asking firms in your community for a copy of their codes, by visiting the library, or by searching and downloading information from the Internet.

2. Analyze the code of ethics you have chosen, and answer the following questions:

   a. What does the company's code of ethics say about the rights of its workers, shareholders, consumers, and suppliers? How does the code reflect the company's attitude toward competitors?

   b. How does this code of ethics resemble the information discussed in this chapter? How does it differ?

   c. As an employee of this company, how would you personally interpret the code of ethics? How might the code influence your behaviour within the workplace? Give several examples.

3. Researching Different Careers

Business ethics has been at the heart of many discussions over the years and continues to trouble employees and shareholders. Stories about dishonesty and wrongful behaviour in the workplace appear on a regular basis in newspapers and on the national news.

Assignment

Prepare a written report on the following:

1. Why can it be so difficult for people to do what is right?

2. What is your personal code of ethics? Prepare a code outlining what you believe is morally right. The document should include guidelines for your personal behaviour.

3. How will your code of ethics affect your decisions about

   a. The types of questions you should ask in a job interview?

   b. Selecting a company in which to work?

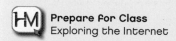

Prepare for Class
Exploring the Internet

CHAPTER 3

Exploring Global Business

Your Guide to Success in Business

Why this chapter matters
In an increasingly global culture, on some level, all business is becoming global business.

1 Explain the economic basis for international business.

2 Discuss the restrictions nations place on international trade, the objectives of these restrictions, and their results.

3 Outline the extent of international trade and identify the organizations working to foster it.

4 Define the methods by which a firm can organize for and enter into international markets.

5 Describe the various sources of export assistance.

6 Identify the institutions that help firms and nations finance international business.

With 2006 sales of US$685.5-million, net income of US$145.1-million, and market capitalization of $24 billion, RIM is continuing to grow globally, providing high-tech jobs for Canadians as it exports technological solutions around the world.

Sources: Based on information from the Research In Motion website accessed November 09, 2006; Press Release, "TrigCom and RIM introduce Blackberry in Norway," October 17, 2006, http://www.rim.com/news/press/2006/pr-17_10_2006-02.shtml; Scott Adams, "Analyst raises target for Research In Motion," *National Post*, October 31, 2006, http://www.canada.com/nationalpost/financialpost/story.html?id=1c952e83-3363-4d48-a73a-80f5841285a3&rfp=dta; Mark Evans, "RIM soars on outlook," *National Post*, September 29, 2006, http://www.canada.com/nationalpost/financialpost/story.html?id=29b3550a-804e-4a03-b6f1-fe7647f95ab8&k=34998.

Research In Motion Ltd. is just one of a growing number of Canadian companies, large and small, that are doing business with firms in other countries. Some companies sell to firms in other countries; others buy goods from around the world to import into Canada. Whether they buy or sell products across national borders, these companies are all contributing to the volume of international trade that is fuelling the global economy. The principal reason for international trade is fundamentally the same as it always has been: to exchange excess supply of domestic products for foreign ones that may not otherwise be available.

Theoretically, international trade is every bit as logical and worthwhile as, say trade between any two provinces, like Saskatchewan and New Brunswick. Yet nations tend to restrict the import of certain goods for a variety of reasons. For example, Canada's long running dispute over the export of softwood lumber into the United States has been a sore spot as Canadian lumber exports were perceived to be undercutting price levels of American producers.

Despite such restrictions, international trade has increased almost steadily since the Second World War. Many of the industrialized nations have signed trade agreements intended to eliminate problems in international business and to help less-developed nations participate in world trade. Individual firms have seized the opportunity to compete in foreign markets by exporting products and increasing foreign production, as well as by other means.

Free trade is generally perceived to be a proven strategy for building global prosperity and adding to the momentum of political freedom. Trade is an engine of economic growth. In our lifetime, trade has helped lift millions of people and whole nations out of poverty and put them on the path to prosperity.[1]

We describe international trade in this chapter in terms of modern specialization, whereby each country trades the surplus goods and services it produces most efficiently for products in short supply. We also explain the restrictions nations place on products and services from other countries and present some of the possible advantages and disadvantages of these restrictions. We then describe the extent of international trade and identify the organizations working to foster it. We describe several methods of entering international markets and the various sources of export assistance available from governments and agencies. Finally, we identify some of the institutions that provide the complex financing necessary for modern international trade.

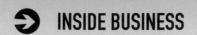

Research In Motion's Globally Popular Blackberry

If the past is any indication of the future, Waterloo, Ontario-based Research In Motion Ltd. (RIM) will continue to lead the global development, design, and distribution of mobile communications software and devices. With offices in North America, Europe, and Asia Pacific, RIM is poised to face stiff competition from innovative technology giants that include Microsoft Corp., Nokia Oyj., and Motorola Inc. Current estimates for devices like RIM's market leading seller, the Blackberry, that allow mobile access to e-mail and other communications including voice, text, and software is projected to increase ten-fold to 63 million subscribers by 2010. Much of this market is made up of business people, who realize the value of continuous global access to their e-mail and office voice-mail and computer systems through small, cost-effective mobile devices like the Blackberry. RIM's most recent introduction is the Blackberry Pearl, which looks more like a traditional cell-phone and incorporates the usual functions plus MP3 and camera technologies.

RIM's early success with the 1998 introduction of Blackberry is generally attributed to the product's reliability and the superior customer support provided by the firm to its partners around the world. To make use of a Blackberry, wireless service providers must buy into the system that RIM is selling. The individual customer buys a Blackberry but the wireless service provider must buy the software and other technology from RIM that allows these products and those that are licensed to other manufacturers by RIM to function. For example, in 2006 RIM and Norwegian communications firm TrigCom, announced a deal whereby TrigCom would offer BlackBerry service on the BlackBerry® 8700g handset, providing support for email, phone, text messaging, Internet, organizer and corporate data applications to its Norwegian customers. The BlackBerry 8700g will operate on Trigcom's GSM/GPRS, and EDGE networks. Of course this is right next door to its rival based in Finland, Nokia Oyj., which blazed the trail of global production and distribution of the early models of cellphones.

continued on next page

• • •

DID YOU KNOW?

Some analysts predict that Research In Motion's worldwide Blackberry subscriber base will jump from six million to more than 23 million by 2009?

K E Y   T E R M S

international business (73)

absolute advantage (73)

comparative advantage (73)

exporting (74)

importing (74)

balance of trade (74)

trade deficit (74)

balance of payments (74)

import duty (tariff) (76)

dumping (76)

nontariff barrier (76)

import quota (76)

embargo (76)

foreign-exchange control (76)

currency devaluation (77)

General Agreement on Tariffs and Trade (GATT) (83)

World Trade Organization (WTO) (85)

economic community (85)

licensing (89)

letter of credit (90)

bill of lading (90)

draft (90)

strategic alliance (92)

trading company (93)

countertrade (93)

multinational enterprise (93)

multilateral development bank (MDB) (97)

International Monetary Fund (IMF) (97)

ACE the Test
Crossword Puzzle
Flashcards

The Basis for International Business

Learning Objective

Explain the economic basis for international business.

International business encompasses all business activities that involve exchanges across national boundaries. Thus a firm is engaged in international business when it buys some portion of its input from or sells some portion of its output to an organization located in a foreign country.

Absolute and Comparative Advantage

Some countries are better equipped than others to produce particular goods or services. The reason may be a country's natural resources, its labour supply, or even customs or a historical accident. Such a country would be best off if it could *specialize* in the production of such products because it can produce them most efficiently. The country could use what it needed of these products and then trade the surplus for products it could not produce efficiently on its own.

Saudi Arabia thus has specialized in the production of crude oil and petroleum products; South Africa, in diamonds; and Australia, in wool. Each of these countries is said to have an absolute advantage with regard to a particular product. An **absolute advantage** is the ability to produce a specific product more efficiently than any other nation.

One country may have an absolute advantage with regard to several products, whereas another country may have no absolute advantage at all. Yet it is still worthwhile for these two countries to specialize and trade with each other. To see why this is so, imagine that you are the president of a successful manufacturing firm and that you can accurately type ninety words per minute. Your assistant can type eighty words per minute but would run the business poorly. Thus you have an absolute advantage over your assistant in both typing and managing. However, you cannot afford to type your own letters because your time is better spent in managing the business. That is, you have a **comparative advantage** in managing. A comparative advantage is the ability to produce a specific product more efficiently than any other product.

Your assistant, on the other hand, has a comparative advantage in typing because he or she can do that better than managing the business. Thus you spend your time managing, and you leave the typing to your assistant. Overall, the business is run as efficiently as possible because you are each working in accordance with your own comparative advantage.

The same is true for nations. Goods and services are produced more efficiently when each country specializes in the products for which it has a comparative advantage. Moreover, by definition, every country has a comparative advantage in *some* product. Canada has many comparative advantages—in energy, mining, research and development, high-technology industries, and grain production, for instance.

international business all business activities that involve exchanges across national boundaries

absolute advantage the ability to produce a specific product more efficiently than any other nation

comparative advantage the ability to produce a specific product more efficiently than any other product

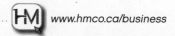

Exporting and Importing

Suppose Canada specializes in producing wheat. It then will produce a surplus of wheat, but perhaps it will have a shortage of wine. France, on the other hand, specializes in producing wine but experiences a shortage of wheat. To satisfy both needs—for wheat and for wine—the two countries should trade with each other. Canada should export wheat and import wine. France should export wine and import wheat.

Exporting is selling and shipping raw materials or products to other nations. Bombardier Inc. Canadair division, for example, exports its airplanes to a number of countries for use by their airlines. Figure 3.1 shows the top ten merchandise-exporting regions in Canada.

Importing is purchasing raw materials or products in other nations and bringing them into one's own country. Thus buyers for Sears Canada department stores may purchase rugs in India or raincoats in England and have them shipped back to Canada for resale.

Importing and exporting are the principal activities in international trade. They give rise to an important concept called the *balance of trade*. A nation's **balance of trade** is the total value of its exports *minus* the total value of its imports over some period of time. If a country imports more than it exports, its balance of trade is negative and is said to be *unfavourable*. (A negative balance of trade is unfavourable because the country must export money to pay for its excess imports.) In 2004, for example, the United States imported $1,470 billion worth of merchandise and exported $819 billion worth. It thus had a trade deficit of $651 billion. In fact, the United States has been running a growing trade deficit for more than the past 20 years, causing concern among economists who question how long this imbalance can be sustained. Much of this trade problem is due to the rising costs of imported oil—about half of America's energy needs are satisfied by imports—particularly from Alberta. A **trade deficit** is a negative balance of trade.

On the other hand, when a country exports more than it imports, it is said to have a *favourable* balance of trade. For example, Canada has consistently enjoyed a trade surplus since for more than 10 years. In 2005, exports of goods and services increased 5.2 percent to $516.4 billion in 2005, surpassing the previous record reached in 2000 ($489.0 billion). Imports also rose; 5.8 percent to $463.1 billion. The annual surplus on goods remained more or less stable at $66.7 billion, as both exports and imports rose by around $24 billion.[2] A nation's **balance of payments** is the total flow of money into a country *minus* the total flow of money out of that country over some period of time. Balance of payments therefore is a much broader concept than balance of trade. It includes imports and exports, of course. But it

exporting selling and shipping raw materials or products to other nations

importing purchasing raw materials or products in other nations and bringing them into one's own country

balance of trade the total value of a nation's exports minus the total value of its imports over some period of time

trade deficit a negative balance of trade

balance of payments the total flow of money into a country minus the total flow of money out of that country over some period of time

Figure 3.1

Share of Merchandise Exports by Canadian Region

Source: Seventh Annual Report on Canada's State of Trade, Update June 2006, Figure 4-14, http://www.dfait-maeci.gc.ca/eet/trade/sot_2006/sot-2006-en.asp#ai2. Statistics Canada information is used with the permission of Statistics Canada. Users are forbidden to copy this material and/or redisseminate the data, in an original or modified form, for commercial purposes, without the expressed permission of Statistics Canada.

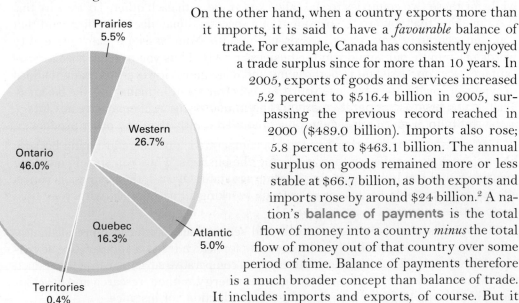

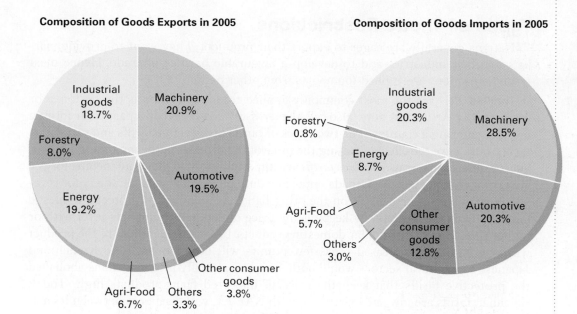

Composition of Goods Exports in 2005

Industrial goods 18.7%
Machinery 20.9%
Forestry 8.0%
Automotive 19.5%
Energy 19.2%
Agri-Food 6.7%
Others 3.3%
Other consumer goods 3.8%

Composition of Goods Imports in 2005

Industrial goods 20.3%
Machinery 28.5%
Forestry 0.8%
Energy 8.7%
Agri-Food 5.7%
Automotive 20.3%
Other consumer goods 12.8%
Others 3.0%

Figure 3.2

Composition of Canada's Exports and Imports

Trade provides a greater variety of products in each category of goods.

Source: Seventh Annual Report on Canada's State of Trade, Update June 2006, Figure 4-14, http://www.dfait-maeci.gc.ca/eet/trade/sot_2006/sot-2006-en.asp#ai2. Statistics Canada information is used with the permission of Statistics Canada. Users are forbidden to copy this material and/or redisseminate the data, in an original or modified form, for commercial purposes, without the expressed permission of Statistics Canada.

also includes investments, money spent by foreign tourists, payments by foreign governments, aid to foreign governments, and all other receipts and payments.

A continual deficit in a nation's balance of payments (a negative balance) can cause other nations to lose confidence in that nation's economy. A continual surplus may indicate that the country encourages exports but limits imports by imposing trade restrictions.

Restrictions to International Business

Learning Objective 2

Discuss the restrictions nations place on international trade, the objectives of these restrictions, and their results.

Specialization and international trade can result in the efficient production of want-satisfying goods and services on a worldwide basis. As we have noted, international business generally is increasing. Yet the nations of the world continue to erect barriers to free trade. They do so for reasons ranging from internal political and economic pressures to simple mistrust of other nations. We examine first the types of restrictions that are applied and then the arguments for and against trade restrictions.

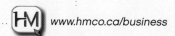

Types of Trade Restrictions

Nations generally are eager to export their products. They want to provide markets for their industries and to develop a favourable balance of trade. Hence most trade restrictions are applied to imports from other nations.

Tariffs Perhaps the most commonly applied trade restriction is the customs (or import) duty. An **import duty** (also called a **tariff**) is a tax levied on a particular foreign product entering a country. The two types of tariffs are revenue tariffs and protective tariffs; both have the effect of raising the price of the product in the importing nations, but for different reasons. *Revenue tariffs* are imposed solely to generate income for the government. For example, Canada imposes a duty on French perfume solely for revenue purposes. *Protective tariffs*, on the other hand, are imposed to protect a domestic industry from competition by keeping the price of competing imports level with or higher than the price of similar domestic products. Because fewer units of the product will be sold at the increased price, fewer units will be imported. The French and Japanese agricultural sectors would both shrink drastically if their nations abolished the protective tariffs that keep the price of imported farm products high. Today, Canadian tariffs are low and eventually, with NAFTA, will disappear between its major trading partners, the United States and Mexico.

Some countries rationalize their protectionist policies as a way of offsetting an international trade practice called *dumping*. **Dumping** is the exportation of large quantities of a product at a price lower than that of the same product in the home market. Thus dumping drives down the price of the domestic item. Recently, for example, the U.S. Department of Commerce imposed antidumping duties of 29 percent on Canadian soft lumber. After years of wrangling over the way in which Canadian producers might be receiving unfair advantage from Canadian governments by way of low fees charged for access to forests on government owned land, the dispute was settled in Canada's favour. Billions of dollars of sales were lost by Canada's forestry industry while the dispute undermined exports to the U.S.

Nontariff Barriers A **nontariff barrier** is a nontax measure imposed by a government to favour domestic over foreign suppliers. Nontariff barriers create obstacles to the marketing of foreign goods in a country and increase costs for exporters. The following are a few examples of government-imposed nontariff barriers:

* An **import quota** is a limit on the amount of a particular good that may be imported into a country during a given period of time. The limit may be set in terms of either quantity (so many tonnes of beef) or value (so many dollars' worth of shoes). Quotas might also be set on individual products imported from specific countries. Once an import quota has been reached, imports are halted until the specified time has elapsed.

* An **embargo** is a complete halt to trading with a particular nation or in a particular product. The embargo is used most often as a political weapon. At present, the United States has import embargoes against Cuba and North Korea—both as a result of extremely poor political relations.

* A **foreign-exchange control** is a restriction on the amount of a particular foreign currency that can be purchased or sold. By limiting the amount of foreign currency importers can obtain, a government limits the amount of goods importers can pur-

import duty (tariff) a tax levied on a particular foreign product entering a country

dumping exportation of large quantities of a product at a price lower than that of the same product in the home market

nontariff barrier a nontax measure imposed by a government to favour domestic over foreign suppliers

import quota a limit on the amount of a particular good that may be imported into a country during a given period of time

embargo a complete halt to trading with a particular nation or in a particular product

foreign-exchange control a restriction on the amount of a particular foreign currency that can be purchased or sold

chase with that currency. This has the effect of limiting imports from the country whose foreign exchange is being controlled.

* A nation can increase or decrease the value of its money relative to the currency of other nations. **Currency devaluation** is the reduction of the value of a nation's currency relative to the currencies of other countries.

Devaluation increases the cost of foreign goods while it decreases the cost of domestic goods to foreign firms. For example, suppose that the British pound is worth $2. Then a Canadian-made $2,000 computer can be purchased for £1,000. However, if the United Kingdom devalues the pound so that it is worth only $1, that same computer will cost £2,000. The increased cost, in pounds, will reduce the import of Canadian computers—and all foreign goods—into England.

On the other hand, before devaluation, a £500 set of English bone china will cost a Canadian $1,000. After the devaluation, the set of china will cost only $500. The decreased cost will make the china—and all English goods—much more attractive to Canadian purchasers.

Bureaucratic red tape is more subtle than the other forms of nontariff barriers. Yet it can be the most frustrating trade barrier of all. A few examples are unnecessarily restrictive application of standards and complex requirements related to product testing, labelling, and certification.

Cultural barriers can impede acceptance of products in foreign countries. When customers are unfamiliar with particular products from another country, their general perceptions of the country itself affect their attitude toward the product and help to determine whether they will buy it. Because Mexican cars have not been viewed by the world as being quality products, Volkswagen, for example, may not want to advertise that some of its models sold in North America are made in Mexico.

Reasons for Trade Restrictions

Various reasons are advanced for trade restrictions either on the import of specific products or on trade with particular countries. We have noted that political considerations usually are involved in trade embargoes. Other frequently cited reasons for restricting trade include the following:

* *To equalize a nation's balance of payments.* This may be considered necessary to restore confidence in the country's monetary system and in its ability to repay its debts.

* *To protect new or weak industries.* A new, or *infant*, industry may not be strong enough to withstand foreign competition. Temporary trade restrictions may be used to give it a chance to grow and become self-sufficient. The problem is that once an industry is protected from foreign competition, it may refuse to grow, and "temporary" trade restrictions become permanent.

* *To protect national security.* Restrictions in this category generally apply to technological products that must be kept out of the hands of potential enemies. For example, strategic and defence-related goods cannot be exported to unfriendly nations.

* *To protect the health of citizens.* Products may be embargoed because they are dangerous or unhealthy (for example, farm products contaminated with insecticides).

currency devaluation the reduction of the value of a nation's currency relative to the currencies of other countries

www.hmco.ca/business

* *To retaliate for another nation's trade restrictions.* A country whose exports are taxed by another country may respond by imposing tariffs on imports from that country.

* *To protect domestic jobs.* By restricting imports, a nation can protect jobs in domestic industries. However, protecting these jobs can be expensive.

Reasons Against Trade Restrictions

Trade restrictions have immediate and long-term economic consequences—both within the restricting nation and in world trade patterns. These include

* *Higher prices for consumers.* Higher prices may result from the imposition of tariffs or the elimination of foreign competition, as described earlier. For example, American duties charged on Canadian softwood resulted in higher prices for wood commonly used by U.S. homebuilders, and therefore, resulted in higher new home construction prices.

* *Restriction of consumers' choices.* Again, this is a direct result of the elimination of some foreign products from the marketplace and of the artificially high prices that importers must charge for products that still *are* imported.

* *Misallocation of international resources.* The protection of weak industries results in the inefficient use of limited resources. The economies of both the restricting nation and other nations eventually suffer because of this waste.

* *Loss of jobs.* The restriction of imports by one nation must lead to cutbacks—and the loss of jobs—in the export-oriented industries of other nations. Furthermore, trade protection has a significant effect on the composition of employment. Trade restrictions—whether on textiles, apparel, steel, or automobiles—benefit only a few industries while harming many others. The gains in employment accrue to the protected industries and their primary suppliers, and the losses are spread across all other industries.

The Extent of International Business

> ### Learning Objective 3
>
> Outline the extent of international trade and identify the organizations working to foster it.

Restrictions or not, international business is growing. Although the worldwide recessions of 1991 and 2001–2002 slowed the rate of growth, globalization is a reality of our time. Since the early 1980s, total trade in goods accounted for 36 percent of world gross domestic product (GDP); 23 years later, that ratio increased to 50 percent.[3] In the United States, international trade now accounts for over one-fourth of GDP but only about 10 percent when goods and services are considered together.[4] As trade barriers decrease, new competitors enter the global marketplace, creating more choices for consumers and new opportunities for job seekers. International business will grow along with the expansion of commercial use of the Internet.

The World Economic Outlook for Trade

World trade has been gaining momentum since the end of the 2000–2002 recession. Global economic growth was a satisfactory 3.5 percent in 2005 but weaker than the 4.2 percent achieved in 2004. This reduction was attributed primarily to the rising cost of oil and its damaging boost to manufacturing costs that made it more difficult for producers to pass higher prices of merchandise on to customers. In spite of rising oil prices, the value of world merchandise exports rose 13 percent in 2005, compared to 21 percent in 2004 and for the first time, world merchandise exports exceeded the $10,000 billion mark. Commercial services exports were estimated to have increased by 11 percent to $2,400 billion in 2005 surpassing the 19 percent increase in 2004. Rising oil prices however, benefitted regions such as Africa, the Middle East and Russia, which recorded strong merchandise export growth in 2005, ranging from 29 percent to 36 percent. The share of fuels and other mining products in world merchandise trade rose to 16 percent, the highest level since 1985. On the other hand, the share of agricultural products in world merchandise exports decreased to a historic low of less than 9 percent.[5]

In 2005, GDP worldwide was estimated to be $43,000 billion. The United States accounted for about 30 percent, the largest share of the global economy, with a GDP of about $12,300 billion. In comparison, Canada's GDP was about $1,100 billion.[6] Canada's economic performance has improved steadily since the end of the 2000–2002 recession producing real GDP growth rates of 2.9 percent in both 2005 and 2004. This growth was primarily driven by strong personal expenditure on goods and services, investment in residential and non-residential structures, investment in machinery and equipment, and by net exports (the difference between exports and imports). Increased demand for natural resources including energy products, contributed to Canada's record trade performance in 2005. Canada's exports of goods and services

	2000	2001	2002	2003	2004	2005
Canada	45.4	43.4	41.3	37.8	38.1	37.7
France	28.6	28.1	27.1	25.7	26.0	26.1
Germany	33.4	34.8	35.7	35.7	38.0	40.2
Italy	27.1	28.4	27.0	25.8	26.6	27.2
Japan	9.9	9.4	10.1	10.6	11.8	12.5
UK	28.0	27.4	26.2	25.5	25.2	26.1
U.S.	10.9	9.9	9.3	9.3	9.8	10.2
G7 Total	17.4	16.9	16.8	17.1	18.2	n.a.
Russia	44.1	36.9	35.2	35.2	35.0	n.a.

Table 3.1

Exports of Goods and Services as a Proportion of GDP, 2000–2005

Source: Seventh Annual Report on Canada's State of Trade, Update June 2006, Table 4.1, http://www.dfait-maeci .gc.ca/eet/trade/ sot_2006/sot-2006-en .asp#ai2. Statistics Canada information is used with the permission of Statistics Canada. Users are forbidden to copy this material and/or redisseminate the data, in an original or modified form, for commercial purposes, without the expressed permission of Statistics Canada.

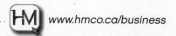

Your Career

Are You Ready for a Global Job?

ple, the homesickness. But I was learning something new every day."

Would you be successful in an international job assignment? Ask yourself:

1. How do I react to new and unfamiliar situations?
2. What strengths, skills, and knowledge do I have to offer?
3. Am I accepting of different cultures and viewpoints?
4. How will an overseas assignment help me personally and professionally?

Although some multinational corporations use English as their global business language, employees who want to work abroad may have to know the local language (or at least be able to understand basic phrases). Robyn Glennon, whose first overseas job was in Prague, sums up her experience this way: "Every day was a challenge—the language, the peo-

were equivalent to 37.7 percent of Canadian GDP in 2005. This was down somewhat from 2004 but sufficient to place Canada second among the G8 countries. Most significantly, 83.9 percent of Canada's merchandise exports—worth $365.7 billion—were destined for or through the U.S. in 2005. Only 5.7, 2.1, 1.9, and 1.6 percent of merchandise exports were bound for the EU, Japan, the U.K., and China, respectively. Merchandise imports from the U.S. were worth $258.4 billion. These statistics highlight how important U.S. trade is to Canada. In fact, Canada and the U.S. are each other's leading export and import partner.

Canada's top-five merchandise exports to the world in 2005 were mineral fuel and oil ($88 billion), motor vehicles and parts ($78.2 billion), machinery ($33.7 billion), electrical machinery and equipment ($20.5 billion), and wood ($20.3 billion). The top-five merchandise imports were motor vehicles and parts ($65.7 billion), machinery ($62.2 billion), electrical machinery and equipment ($37.6 billion), mineral fuel and oil ($35.6 billion), and plastics ($13.7 billion). Approximately 80 percent of this trade is with the United States.[7]

The International Monetary Fund (IMF), an international bank with 184 member nations, estimates that global growth in 2004 was the highest in three decades when world output increased by over 5 percent.[8] International experts expected global economic growth of 4.3 percent in 2005 and 2006, despite high oil prices and two hurricanes in the United States. At this rate of growth, world production of goods and services will double by the year 2020.

Western Europe Economies in Western Europe have been growing slowly. Only the United Kingdom enjoyed 1.9 percent economic growth in 2005 with the lowest level of unemployment in 20 years; the economies of Germany, France, and Italy all grew by less than 1.0 percent in 2005 and 1.2 percent in 2006. Recent growth in Austria, Belgium, the Netherlands, and Portugal has been slow, while growth in Greece, Ireland, and Spain has been stronger.

Mexico and South America Mexico, our trading partner with the U.S. in NAFTA, suffered its sharpest recession ever in 1995, but its growth rate in 2005 was about 4.0 percent. In general, however, the Latin American economies grew 4.1 percent in 2005 versus 5.6 percent in 2004. The economies of Argentina, Uruguay, Paraguay, Brazil, Venezuela, Ecuador, Peru, and a few other countries in that region have been sluggish owing to political, economic, and financial market problems. Future growth of about 4.0 percent is projected for the region.

Japan Japan's economy is regaining momentum. Stronger consumer demand and business investment make Japan less reliant on exports for growth. The first half of 2005 saw very strong growth, and the IMF estimated the growth at 2 percent for 2005 and 2006.

Asia The economic recovery in Asia increased significantly in 2005. For example, in China and India, the GDP increased 9.0 and 7.0 percent, respectively. Even in the hardest-hit economies in the region, Singapore and Taiwan Province of China, the recovery continued in 2005. Growth in Asia is expected to moderate somewhat to about 7.8 percent in 2005 and 7.2 percent in 2006.

China's emergence as a global economic power has been among the most dramatic economic developments of recent decades. From 1980 to 2004, China's economy averaged a real GDP growth rate of 9.5 percent and became the world's sixth-largest economy. China's total share in world trade expanded from 1 percent in 1980 to almost 6 percent in 2003. By 2004, China had become the third-largest trading nation

Table 3.2

Canada's Top 12 Net Exports in 2005 ($ in millions, customs basis)

	2002	2003	2004	2005	% CHANGE 2005/2002
Natural gas	17,661	24,262	24,474	32,281	82.8%
Passenger vehicles	32,302	27,901	31,504	29,583	−8.4%
Coniferous wood	10,201	8,306	10,866	9,776	−4.2%
Crude oil	6,009	6,629	9,052	7,990	33.0%
Newsprint	6,293	5,597	5,265	5,212	−17.2%
Vehicle transmission	7,941	5,975	4,624	4,223	−46.8%
Wood pulp	4,180	4,115	4,567	3,995	−4.4%
Paper	2,720	2,350	2,831	3,074	13.0%
Light oils (not crude)	3,298	3,408	2,891	3,021	−8.4%
Oil (not crude)	1,880	2,057	2,470	2,823	50.1%
Potassium chloride	2,375	1,922	2,169	2,758	16.2%
Aluminum alloys	2,375	2,265	2,541	2,614	10.1%

Source: Statistics Canada Seventh Annual Report on Canada's State of Trade, Update June 2006, Table A1, http://www.dfait-maeci.gc.ca/eet/trade/sot_2006/sot-2006-en.asp#ai2. Statistics Canada information is used with the permission of Statistics Canada. Users are forbidden to copy this material and/or redisseminate the data, in an original or modified form, for commercial purposes, without the expressed permission of Statistics Canada.

Table 3.3

Global Growth Remains Strong

Source: Republished with permission of International Monetary Fund, from *World Economic Outlook,* October 3, 2005, p. 263, permission conveyed through Copyright Clearance Center, Inc.

GROWTH HAS BEEN LED BY DEVELOPING COUNTRIES AND EMERGING MARKETS				
	2003	2004	Projected 2005	Projected 2006
	(annual percent change)			
World	4.0	5.1	4.3	4.3
United States	2.7	4.2	3.5	3.3
Euro area	0.7	2.0	1.2	1.8
United Kingdom	2.5	3.2	1.9	2.2
Japan	1.4	2.7	2.0	2.0
Canada	2.0	2.9	2.9	3.2
Other advanced economies	2.5	4.4	3.2	3.9
Newly industrialized Asian economies	3.1	5.6	4.0	4.7
Developing countries and emerging markets	6.5	7.3	6.4	6.1
Africa	4.6	5.3	4.5	5.9
Asia	8.1	8.2	7.8	7.2
CIS	7.9	8.4	6.0	5.7
Middle East	6.5	5.5	5.4	5.0
Western Hemisphere	2.2	5.6	4.1	3.8

This lumber is made for exporting

Canadian exports of natural resources such as lumber and other forest products provides employment and billions of dollars in business revenue. Provincial and federal governments also benefit through royalties and taxes earned on sales.

in dollar terms, behind the United States and Germany and just ahead of Japan. China's growth is estimated to be 8.2 percent in 2006.

Central and Eastern Europe and Russia After World War II, trade between North America and the communist nations of central and Eastern Europe was minimal. However, since the disintegration of the Soviet Union and the collapse of communism, trade between North America and central and Eastern Europe has expanded substantially.

The countries that made the transition from communist to market economies quickly have recorded positive growth for several years—those that did not continue to struggle. Among the nations that have enjoyed several years of positive economic growth are the member countries of the Central European Free Trade Association (CEFTA): Hungary, the Czech Republic, Poland, Slovenia, and the Republic of Slovakia. An average growth of 4.3 percent is projected for this region.

Exports and the Canadian Economy Globalization represents a huge opportunity for all countries—rich or poor. The fifteen-fold increase in trade volume over the past forty-eight years has been one of the most important factors in the rise of living standards around the world. During this time, exports have become increasingly important to the Canadian. economy. Exports represent 37.7 percent of Canada's GDP. Figure 3.3 shows the types of goods that Canada exports and Tables 3.4 and 3.5 show Canada's merchandise exports and imports with our trading partners. Note that the United States and Europe are Canada's best trading partner for exports; the U.S. Europe, and China for imports. Major Canadian exports and imports are manufactured goods, and energy.

SPOTLIGHT

Now and forever

Countries that are key trading partners with other countries tend to remain so.

Country	Number of key trading partners
United States	90
Germany	83
United Kingdom	79
Netherlands	73
France	68
Italy	65
Japan	57

Source: IMF, *Direction of Trade Statistics*, p. 20, September, 2005. Used with permission.

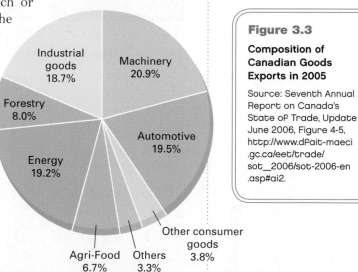

Industrial goods 18.7%
Machinery 20.9%
Forestry 8.0%
Automotive 19.5%
Energy 19.2%
Agri-Food 6.7%
Others 3.3%
Other consumer goods 3.8%

Figure 3.3

Composition of Canadian Goods Exports in 2005

Source: Seventh Annual Report on Canada's State of Trade, Update June 2006, Figure 4-5, http://www.dfait-maeci.gc.ca/eet/trade/sot_2006/sot-2006-en.asp#ai2.

The General Agreement on Tariffs and Trade and the World Trade Organization

At the end of World War II, the United States, Canada, and twenty-one other nations organized the body that came to be known as *GATT*. The **General Agreement on Tariffs and Trade (GATT)** was an international organization of 132 nations dedicated to reducing or eliminating tariffs and other barriers to world trade. These 132 nations accounted for 90 percent of the world's merchandise trade. GATT, headquartered in Geneva, Switzerland, provided a forum for tariff negotiations and a means for settling international trade disputes and problems. *Most-favoured-nation status* (MFN) was the

General Agreement on Tariffs and Trade (GATT) an international organization of 132 nations dedicated to reducing or eliminating tariffs and other barriers to world trade

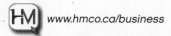

Table 3.4

Canada's Merchandise Export by Area ($ in billions)

Source: Statistics Canada. Seventh Annual Report on Canada's State of Trade, Update June 2006, Table 4.2, http://www.dfait-maeci.gc.ca/eet/trade/sot_2006/sot-2006-en.asp#ai2. Statistics Canada information is used with the permission of Statistics Canada. Users are forbidden to copy this material and/or redisseminate the data, in an original or modified form, for commercial purposes, without the expressed permission of Statistics Canada.

COUNTRY	2004	2005	SHARE IN 2005	% CHANGE 2005/2004
World	411.8	435.8	100.0	5.8
U.S.	348.1	365.7	83.9	5.1
Japan	8.6	9.1	2.1	6.6
UK	7.7	8.2	1.9	6.7
China	6.7	7.1	1.6	6.1
Mexico	3.0	3.3	0.8	8.7
Germany	2.7	3.2	0.7	21.0
Korea	2.3	2.8	0.6	23.7
France	2.4	2.5	0.6	6.5
Belgium	2.3	2.3	0.5	0.7
Netherlands	1.9	2.2	0.5	13.6
EU-25	22.8	24.7	5.7*	8.2

* Includes Germany, France, Belgium, and Netherlands

Table 3.5

Canada's Merchandise Imports by Area ($ in billions)

Source: Statistics Canada. Seventh Annual Report on Canada's State of Trade, Update June 2006, Table 4.2, http://www.dfait-maeci.gc.ca/eet/trade/sot_2006/sot-2006-en.asp#ai2 . Statistics Canada information is used with the permission of Statistics Canada. Users are forbidden to copy this material and/or redisseminate the data, in an original or modified form, for commercial purposes, without the expressed permission of Statistics Canada.

COUNTRY	2004	2005	SHARE IN 2005	% CHANGE 2005/2004
World	356.1	380.7	100.0	6.9
U.S.	209.0	215.1	56.5	2.9
China	24.1	29.5	7.8	22.4
Japan	13.5	14.8	3.9	9.4
Mexico	13.4	14.6	3.8	8.6
UK	9.7	10.4	2.7	7.7
Germany	9.4	10.3	2.7	9.0
Norway	5.0	6.1	1.6	22.3
Korea	5.8	5.4	1.4	−7.7
France	5.3	5.0	1.3	−6.4
Italy	4.6	4.6	1.2	0.1
EU-25	42.0	45.6	12.0*	8.5

* Includes Germany, France, Belgium, and Netherlands

famous principle of GATT. It meant that each GATT member nation was to be treated equally by all contracting nations. MFN therefore ensured that any tariff reductions or other trade concessions were extended automatically to all GATT members. From 1947 to 1994, the body sponsored eight rounds of negotiations to reduce trade restrictions. Three of the most fruitful were the Kennedy Round, the Tokyo Round, and the Uruguay Round.

The Kennedy Round (1964–1967) These negotiations, which began in 1964, have since become known as the *Kennedy Round*. They were aimed at reducing tariffs and other barriers to trade in both industrial and agricultural products. The participants succeeded in reducing tariffs on these products by an average of more than 35 percent. They were less successful in removing other types of trade barriers.

The Tokyo Round (1973–1979) In 1973, representatives of approximately one hundred nations gathered in Tokyo for another round of GATT negotiations. The *Tokyo Round* was completed in 1979. The participants negotiated tariff cuts of 30 to 35 percent, which were to be implemented over an eight-year period. In addition, they were able to remove or ease such nontariff barriers as import quotas, unrealistic quality standards for imports, and unnecessary red tape in customs procedures.

The Uruguay Round (1986–1993) In 1986, the *Uruguay Round* was launched to extend trade liberalization and widen the GATT treaty to include textiles, agricultural products, business services, and intellectual-property rights. This most ambitious and comprehensive global commercial agreement in history concluded overall negotiations on December 15, 1993, with delegations on hand from 109 nations. The agreement included provisions to lower tariffs by greater than one-third, to reform trade in agricultural goods, to write new rules of trade for intellectual property and services, and to strengthen the dispute-settlement process. These reforms were expected to expand the world economy by an estimated $200 billion annually.

The Uruguay Round also created the **World Trade Organization (WTO)** on January 1, 1995. The WTO was established by GATT to oversee the provisions of the Uruguay Round and resolve any resulting trade disputes. Membership in the WTO obliges 148 member nations to observe GATT rules. The WTO has judicial powers to mediate among members disputing the new rules. It incorporates trade in goods, services, and ideas and exerts more binding authority than GATT.

World Trade Organization (WTO) powerful successor to GATT that incorporates trade in goods, services, and ideas

The Doha Round (2001) On November 14, 2001, in Doha, Qatar, the WTO members agreed to further reduce trade barriers through multilateral trade negotiations over the next three years. This new round of negotiations focuses on industrial tariffs and nontariff barriers, agriculture, services, and easing trade rules. The Doha Round has set the stage for WTO members to take an important step toward significant new multilateral trade liberalization. It is a difficult task, but the rewards—lower tariffs, more choice for consumers, and further integration of developing countries into the world trading system—are sure to be worth the effort. If all global trade barriers were eliminated, approximately 500 million people could be lifted out of poverty in 15 years. Developing countries would gain about $200 billion annually in income.[9] There are encouraging signs that major developing countries are assuming an important leadership role in helping the Doha Round succeed.

International Economic Communities

The primary objective of the WTO is to remove barriers to trade on a worldwide basis. On a smaller scale, an **economic community** is an organization of nations formed to promote the free movement of resources and products among its members and to create common economic policies. A number of economic communities now exist.

economic community an organization of nations formed to promote the free movement of resources and products among its members and to create common economic policies

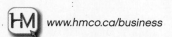

The *European Union* (EU), also known as the *European Economic Community* and the *Common Market*, was formed in 1957 by six countries—France, the Federal Republic of Germany, Italy, Belgium, the Netherlands, and Luxembourg. Its objective was freely conducted commerce among these nations and others that might later join. As shown in Figure 3.4, many more nations have since joined the EU. On May 1, 2004, the fifteen nations of the EU became the EU-25 as Cyprus, Malta, and eight Eastern European countries became members. In 2007, Romania and Bulgaria joined, and Turkey and the Balkan countries may follow later. The EU is now an economic force, with a collective economy larger than that of the United States or Japan.

Since January 2002, twelve member nations of the EU are participating in the new common currency, the euro. The euro is the single currency of the European Monetary Union nations. But three EU members, Denmark, the United Kingdom, and Sweden, still keep their own currencies.

A second community in Europe, the *European Economic Area* (EEA), became effective in January 1994. This pact consists of Iceland, Norway, and the fifteen member

Figure 3.4

The Evolving European Union

Source: Federal Reserve Bank of Dallas, *Southwest Economy*, July–August 2005, p. 12.

nations of the EU. The EEA, encompassing an area inhabited by more than 395 million people, allows for the free movement of goods throughout all seventeen countries.

The *North American Free Trade Agreement* (NAFTA) joined the United States with its first- and second-largest trading partners, Canada and Mexico. Implementation of NAFTA on January 1, 1994, created a market of over 436 million people. This market consists of Canada (population 33 million), the United States (297 million), and Mexico (106 million). Since 1994, trade among the three countries has increased more than 200 percent. Mexico's exports have increased threefold, with nearly 90 percent coming to the United States. From 1993 to 2003, U.S.–Mexico total trade increased 189 percent, from $81.4 billion to $235.5 billion.[10]

NAFTA is built on the Canadian Free Trade Agreement (FTA), signed by the United States and Canada in 1989, and on the substantial trade and investment reforms undertaken by Mexico since the mid-1980s. Initiated by the Mexican government, formal negotiations on NAFTA began among the three governments in June 1991. NAFTA will gradually eliminate all tariffs on goods produced and traded among Canada, Mexico, and the United States to provide for a totally free-trade area by 2009. Chile is expected to become the fourth member of NAFTA, but political forces may delay its entry into the agreement for several years.

The *Central American Free Trade Agreement* (CAFTA) was created in 2003 by the United States and four Central American countries—El Salvador, Guatemala, Honduras, and Nicaragua. CAFTA immediately eliminates tariffs on nearly 80 percent of U.S. exports and is expected to generate billions of dollars in increased sales of U.S. goods and farm exports.[11]

The *Association of Southeast Asian Nations* (ASEAN), with headquarters in Jakarta, Indonesia, was established in 1967 to promote political, economic, and social cooperation among its seven member countries: Indonesia, Malaysia, Philippines, Singapore, Thailand, Brunei, and Vietnam. In January 1992, ASEAN agreed to create a free-trade area known as the *ASEAN Free Trade Area* (AFTA). AFTA countries have a population of more than 550 million people, and their trade totals $750 billion.

The *Pacific Rim*, referring to countries and economies bordering the Pacific Ocean, is an informal, flexible term generally regarded as a reference to East Asia, Canada, and the United States. At a minimum, the Pacific Rim includes Canada, Japan, China, Taiwan, and the United States. It also may include Australia, Brunei, Cambodia, Hong Kong/Macau, Indonesia, Laos, North Korea, South Korea, Malaysia, New Zealand, the Pacific Islands, the Philippines, Russia (or the Commonwealth of Independent States), Singapore, Thailand, and Vietnam.

The *Commonwealth of Independent States* (CIS) was established in December 1991 by the newly independent states (NIS) as an association of eleven republics of the former Soviet Union: Russia, Ukraine, Belarus (formerly Byelorussia), Moldova (formerly Moldavia), Armenia, Azerbaijan, Uzbekistan, Turkmenistan, Tajikistan, Kazakhstan, and Kyrgystan (formerly Kirghiziya). The Baltic states did not join. Georgia maintained observer status before joining the CIS in November 1993.

In the western hemisphere, the *Caribbean Basin Initiative* (CBI) is an inter-American program led by the United States to give economic assistance and trade preferences to Caribbean and Central American countries. CBI provides duty-free access to the

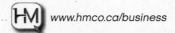

U.S. market for most products from the region and promotes private-sector development in member nations.

The *Common Market of the Southern Cone* (MERCOSUR) was established in 1991 under the Treaty of Asuncion to unite Argentina, Brazil, Paraguay, and Uruguay in a free-trade alliance; Bolivia and Chile joined as associates in 1996. The alliance represents over 230 million consumers—63 percent of South America's population, making it the third-largest trading bloc behind NAFTA and the EU. Like NAFTA, MERCOSUR promotes "the free circulation of goods, services and production factors among the countries" and established a common external tariff and commercial policy.[12]

In 1972, government leaders of Commonwealth countries in the Caribbean decided to transform the Caribbean Free Trade Association (CARIFTA) into a common market and establish the *Caribbean Community*.

The *Organization of Petroleum Exporting Countries* (OPEC) was founded in 1960 in response to reductions in the prices that oil companies were willing to pay for crude oil. The organization was conceived as a collective-bargaining unit to provide oil-producing nations with some control over oil prices.

In May 2005, the *Economic Community of West African States* (ECOWAS) approved a plan to progressively implement a common external tariff (CET). The agreement increases the number of West African countries in the CET from eight to fifteen (see Figure 3.5). The plan lowers tariffs and reduces costs for importers.[13]

Finally, the *Organization for Economic Cooperation and Development* (OECD) is a group of twenty-four industrialized market-economy countries of North America, Europe, the Far East, and the South Pacific. OECD, headquartered in Paris, was established in 1961 to promote economic development and international trade.

Figure 3.5

West African CET Members

The common external tariff (CET) simplifies the structure of tariffs, with a top bracket of 20 percent on finished goods, 10 percent on intermediate goods, 5 percent on basic necessities and raw materials, and no tariff on social goods such as medicines and publications.

Source: The U.S. Agency for International Development, "7 More West African Countries Cut Tariffs, Boost Trade Pact," *Frontlines*, September 2005, p. 13.

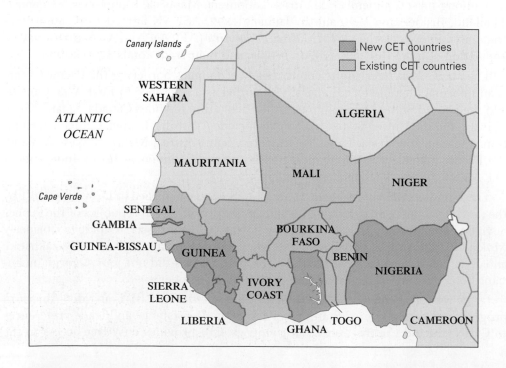

Methods of Entering International Business

Learning Objective 4

Define the methods by which a firm can organize for and enter into international markets.

A firm that has decided to enter international markets can do so in several ways. We will discuss several different methods. These different approaches require varying degrees of involvement in international business. Typically, a firm begins its international operations at the simplest level. Then, depending on its goals, it may progress to higher levels of involvement.

Licensing

Licensing is a contractual agreement in which one firm permits another to produce and market its product and use its brand name in return for a royalty or other compensation. For example, Yoplait yogourt is a French yogourt licensed for production in Canada. The Yoplait brand maintains an appealing French image, and in return, the Canadian producer pays the French firm a percentage of its income from sales of the product.

Licensing is especially advantageous for small manufacturers wanting to launch a well-known domestic brand internationally. For example, all Spalding sporting products are licensed worldwide. The licensor, the Questor Corporation, owns the Spalding name but produces no goods itself. Research In Motion Ltd. licenses its wireless communication technologies to firms around the world. The German firm of Lowenbrau has used licensing agreements, including one with Miller in the United States, to increase its beer sales worldwide without committing capital to building breweries.[14] Licensing thus provides a simple method for expanding into a foreign market with virtually no investment. On the other hand, if the licensee does not

licensing a contractual agreement in which one firm permits another to produce and market its product and use its brand name in return for a royalty or other compensation

BIZ TECH

Foreign Affairs and International Trade Canada helps Canadian companies expand and succeed internationally by promoting Canada as a dynamic place in which to invest and do business, and by negotiating and administering trade agreements, such as the Softwood Lumber Agreement of 2006.

You will find a variety of useful information related to international business and trade at the FAIT Canada website located at http://www.dfait-maeci.gc.ca/commerce/menu-en .asp. The site has links to statistics, industry analysis, trade laws, and answers to often-asked trade questions.

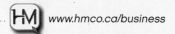

maintain the licensor's product standards, the product's image may be damaged. Another possible disadvantage is that a licensing arrangement may not provide the original producer with any foreign marketing experience.

Exporting

A firm also might manufacture its products in its home country and export them for sale in foreign markets. As with licensing, exporting can be a relatively low-risk method of entering foreign markets. Unlike licensing, however, it is not a simple method; it opens up several levels of involvement to the exporting firm.

At the most basic level, the exporting firm may sell its products outright to an *export-import merchant*, which is essentially a merchant wholesaler. The merchant assumes all the risks of product ownership, distribution, and sale. It may even purchase the goods in the producer's home country and assume responsibility for exporting the goods. An important and practical issue for domestic firms dealing with foreign customers is securing payment. This is a two-sided issue that reflects the mutual concern rightly felt by both parties to the trade deal: The exporter would like to be paid before shipping the merchandise, whereas the importer obviously would prefer to know that it has received the shipment before releasing any funds. Neither side wants to take the risk of fulfilling its part of the deal only later to discover that the other side has not. The result would lead to legal costs and complex, lengthy dealings wasteful of everyone's resources.

This mutual level of mistrust is in fact good business sense and has been around since the beginning of trade centuries ago. The solution then was as it still is today—for both parties to use a mutually trusted go-between who can ensure that the payment is held until the merchandise is in fact delivered according to the terms of the trade contract. The go-between representatives employed by the importer and exporter are still, as they were in the past, the local domestic banks involved in international business.

Here is a simplified version of how it works. After signing contracts detailing the merchandise sold and terms for its delivery, an importer will ask its local bank to issue a **letter of credit** for the amount of money needed to pay for the merchandise. The letter of credit is issued "in favour of the exporter," meaning that the funds are tied specifically to the trade contract involved. The importer's bank forwards the letter of credit to the exporter's bank, which also normally deals in international transactions.

The exporter's bank then notifies the exporter that a letter of credit has been received in its name, and the exporter can go ahead with the shipment. The carrier transporting the merchandise provides the exporter with evidence of the shipment in a document called a **bill of lading.** The exporter signs over title to the merchandise (now in transit) to its bank by delivering signed copies of the bill of lading and the letter of credit.

In exchange, the exporter issues a **draft** from the bank, which orders the importer's bank to pay for the merchandise. The draft, bill of lading, and letter of credit are sent from the exporter's bank to the importer's bank. Acceptance by the importer's bank leads to return of the draft and its sale by the exporter to its bank, meaning that the exporter receives cash and the bank assumes the risk of collecting the funds from the foreign bank. The importer is obliged to pay its bank on delivery of the merchandise, and the deal is complete.

letter of credit issued by a bank on request of an importer stating that the bank will pay an amount of money to a stated beneficiary

bill of lading document issued by a transport carrier to an exporter to prove that merchandise has been shipped

draft issued by the exporter's bank, ordering the importer's bank to pay for the merchandise, thus guaranteeing payment once accepted by the importer's bank

In most cases, the letter of credit is part of a lending arrangement between the importer and its bank, and of course, both banks earn fees for issuing of letters of credit and drafts and for handling the import-export services for their clients. Furthermore, the process incorporates the fact that both importer and exporter will have different local currencies and might even negotiate their trade in a third currency. The banks look after all the necessary exchanges. For example, the vast majority of international business is negotiated in U.S. dollars, even though the trade may be between countries other than the United States. Thus, although the importer may end up paying for the merchandise in its local currency and the exporter may receive payment in another local currency, the banks involved will exchange all necessary foreign funds in order to allow the deal to take place.

The exporting firm instead might ship its products to an *export-import agent*, who, for a commission or fee, arranges the sale of the products to foreign intermediaries. The agent is an independent firm—like other agents—that sells and may perform other marketing functions for the exporter. The exporter, however, retains title to the products during shipment and until they are sold.

An exporting firm also might establish its own *sales offices*, or *branches*, in foreign countries. These installations are international extensions of the firm's distribution system. They represent a deeper involvement in international business than the other exporting techniques we have discussed—and thus they carry a greater risk. The exporting firm maintains control over sales, and it gains both experience in and knowledge of foreign markets. Eventually, the firm also may develop its own sales force to operate in conjunction with foreign sales offices.

Joint Ventures

A *joint venture* is a partnership formed to achieve a specific goal or to operate for a specific period of time. For example, the $60 million Chin Chute Wind Power Project, located 20 kilometres southwest of Taber, is a 30-megawatt joint venture project between Acciona Wind Energy Canada Inc., Enbridge Income Fund, and Suncor Energy Products Inc. The new technology project is now operational and sending electricity to the Alberta Interconnected Electric System.[15] A joint venture with an established firm in a foreign country provides immediate market knowledge and access, reduced risk, and control over product attributes. However, joint-venture agreements established across national borders can become extremely complex. As a result, joint-venture agreements generally require a very high level of commitment from all the parties involved.

A joint venture may be used to produce and market an existing

Venturing into a joint venture

Danny Williams, Premier of Newfoundland and Labrador, addresses a news conference in St. John's in 2007 as Minister of Natural Resources Kathy Dunderdale looks on. The news was a joint venture between the provincial government and an international consortium of companies to develop Hebron offshore oil project. Estimated to be worth $6 billion, the venture could prove to be the province's most lucrative oilfield.

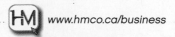

product in a foreign nation or to develop an entirely new product. Recently, for example, Archer Daniels Midland Company (ADM), one of the world's leading food processors, entered into a joint venture with Gruma SA, Mexico's largest corn flour and tortilla company. Besides a 22 percent stake in Gruma, ADM also received stakes in other joint ventures operated by Gruma. One of them will combine both companies' U.S. corn flour operations, which account for about 25 percent of the U.S. market. ADM also has a 40 percent stake in a Mexican wheat flour mill. ADM's joint venture increased its participation in the growing Mexican economy, where ADM already produces corn syrup, fructose, starch, and wheat flour.

Totally Owned Facilities

At a still deeper level of involvement in international business, a firm may develop *totally owned facilities*, that is, its own production and marketing facilities in one or more foreign nations. This *direct investment* provides complete control over operations, but it carries a greater risk than the joint venture. The firm is really establishing a subsidiary in a foreign country. Most firms do so only after they have acquired some knowledge of the host country's markets.

Direct investment can take either of two forms. In the first, the firm builds or purchases manufacturing and other facilities in the foreign country. It uses these facilities to produce its own established products and to market them in that country and perhaps in neighbouring countries. Firms such as General Motors, Union Carbide, and Colgate-Palmolive are multinational companies with worldwide manufacturing facilities. Colgate-Palmolive factories are becoming *Eurofactories*, supplying neighbouring countries as well as their own local markets. Bombardier built the Barre, Vermont, production facility in order to meet with U.S. content requirements for manufacturing 825 subway cars for New York City and in 2006 signed a contract with the Clark County Department of Aviation for new vehicles and rehabilitation of the two existing Automated People Mover (APM) shuttle systems at McCarran International Airport in Las Vegas, Nevada. The contract is valued at approximately $43 million US. It includes the supply of ten Bombardier CX-100 vehicles and upgrades to some of the electrical and mechanical equipment. The APM vehicles will be delivered between 2008 and 2009. Bombardier Transportation's facility in Pittsburgh, Pennsylvania, will be responsible for the design and supply of the ten driverless vehicles.[16] A second form of direct investment in international business is the purchase of an existing firm in a foreign country under an arrangement that allows it to operate independently of the parent company. When Sony Corporation (a Japanese firm) decided to enter the motion picture business in the United States, it chose to purchase Columbia Pictures Entertainment, Inc., rather than start a new motion-picture studio from scratch.

Strategic Alliances

strategic alliance a partnership formed to create competitive advantage on a worldwide basis

A **strategic alliance,** the newest form of international business structure, is a partnership formed to create competitive advantage on a worldwide basis. Strategic alliances are very similar to joint ventures. The number of strategic alliances is growing at an estimated rate of about 20 percent per year. In fact, in the automobile and computer industries, strategic alliances are becoming the predominant means of competing. International competition is so fierce and the costs of competing on a global basis are so high that few firms have all the resources needed to do it alone. Thus individual firms that lack the internal resources essential for international success may seek to collaborate with other companies.

An example of such an alliance is the Nortel and Microsoft agreement to co-develop the transition of traditional business phone systems into software, using a Microsoft unified communications software platform and Nortel software products to provide further advance telephony functionality. This software-centric approach will provide the easiest transition path for businesses, helping enable them to reduce the total cost of ownership and better protect current and future investments. Collaboration brings each firm's respective technical and marketing expertise to their collective benefit.[17]

Trading Companies

A **trading company** provides a link between buyers and sellers in different countries. A trading company, as its name implies, is not involved in manufacturing or owning assets related to manufacturing. It buys products in one country at the lowest price consistent with quality and sells to buyers in another country. An important function of trading companies is taking title to products and performing all the activities necessary to move the products from the domestic country to a foreign country. For example, large grain-trading companies operating out of home offices both in North America and overseas control a major portion of the world's trade in basic food commodities. These trading companies sell homogeneous agricultural commodities that can be stored and moved rapidly in response to market conditions. The best-known U.S. trading company is Sears World Trade, which specializes in consumer goods, light industrial items, and processed foods.

trading company
provides a link between buyers and sellers in different countries

Countertrade

In the early 1990s, many developing nations had major restrictions on converting domestic currency into foreign currency. Exporters therefore had to resort to barter agreements with importers. **Countertrade** is essentially an international barter transaction in which goods and services are exchanged for different goods and services. An example is Saudi Arabia's purchase of ten 747 jets from Boeing paid for in crude oil.

countertrade
an international barter transaction

Multinational Firms

A **multinational enterprise** is a firm that operates on a worldwide scale without ties to any specific nation or region. The multinational firm represents the highest level of involvement in international business. It is equally "at home" in most countries of the world. In fact, as far as the operations of the multinational enterprise are concerned, national boundaries exist only on maps. It is, however, organized under the laws of its home country.

Table 3.6 shows the ten largest foreign and U.S. public multinational companies; the ranking is based on a composite score reflecting each company's best three out of four rankings for sales, profits, assets, and market value. Table 3.7 describes the steps for entering international markets.

multinational enterprise a firm that operates on a worldwide scale without ties to any specific nation or region

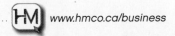

BUSINESS AROUND THE WORLD

Discount Airlines Are Flying High

Discount airlines are taking off all over the world, expanding the reach of air travel as they compete aggressively with established carriers and each other. A sample:

• Ireland: Ryanair, among the fastest-growing and most-profitable airlines on the planet, concentrates on Western European destinations.

• India: By connecting smaller cities, Air Deccan, the country's first discount airline, is fuelling a tourism boom in southern areas.

• Thailand: One-Two-Go, a subsidiary of Orient Thai Airlines, flies from Bangkok to other Thai cities and to southern China.

• Malaysia: One way that AirAsia keeps fares low is by selling food, beverages, merchandise, and other extras.

In an industry where profitability is notoriously inconsistent, how many of these airlines will still be flying in five years?

Table 3.6

The Ten Largest Multinational Corporations

Source: *Fortune* Global 500, July 25, 2005, p. 119. Copyright © 2005 Time, Inc., www.Fortune.com. All rights reserved.

2004 RANK	COMPANY	BUSINESS	COUNTRY	REVENUE ($ MILLIONS)
1	Wal-Mart Stores	General merchandiser	United States	287,989
2	BP	Energy	United Kingdom	285,059
3	ExxonMobil	Energy	United States	270,772
4	Royal Dutch/Shell Group	Energy	Netherlands/United Kingdom	268,690
5	General Motors	Automobiles	United States	193,517
6	DaimlerChrysler	Automobiles	Germany	176,687
7	Toyota Motor	Automobiles	Japan	172,616
8	Ford Motor	Automobiles	United States	172,233
9	General Electric	Electricity and electronics	United States	152,866
10	Total	Energy	France	152,609

STEP	ACTIVITY	MARKETING TASKS
1	Identify exportable products	Identify key selling features
		Identify needs that they satisfy
		Identify the selling constraints that are imposed
2	Identify key foreign markets for the products	Determine who the customers are
		Pinpoint what and when they will buy
		Establish priority, or "target," countries
3	Analyze how to sell in each priority market (methods will be affected by product characteristics and unique features of country/market)	Locate available government and private-sector resources
		Determine service and back-up sales requirements
4	Set export prices and payment terms, methods, and techniques	Establish methods of export pricing
		Establish sales terms, quotations, invoices, and conditions of sale
		Determine methods of international payments, secured and unsecured
5	Estimate resource requirements and returns	Estimate financial requirements
		Estimate human resources requirements (full- or part-time export department or operation?)
		Estimate plant production capacity
6	Establish overseas distribution Network	Determine distribution agreement and other key marketing decisions (price, repair policies, returns, territory, performance, and termination)
		Know your customer (use The Canadian Trade Commissioner Service, **www.infoexport.gc.ca**)
7	Determine shipping, traffic, and documentation procedures and requirements	Determine methods of shipment (air or ocean freight, truck, rail)
		Obtain validated export license
		Follow export-administration documentation procedures
8	Promote, sell, and be paid	Use international media, communications, advertising, trade shows, and exhibitions
		Determine the need for overseas travel
		Initiate customer follow-up procedures
9	Continuously analyze current marketing, economic, and political situations	Recognize changing factors influencing marketing strategies
		Constantly reevaluate

Table 3.7

Steps for Entering International Markets

Source: U.S. Department of Commerce, International Trade Administration, Washington, D.C.

According to the chairman of the board of Dow Chemical Company, a multinational firm of U.S. origin, "The emergence of a world economy and of the multinational corporation has been accomplished hand in hand." He sees multinational enterprises moving toward what he calls the "a national company," a firm that has no nationality but belongs to all countries. In recognition of this movement, there already have been international conferences devoted to the question of how such enterprises would be controlled.

Sources of Export Assistance

Learning Objective 5

Describe the various sources of export assistance.

Canadian corporations are encouraged and assisted by all levels of government to increase their exports. At the national level, the Department of Foreign Affairs and International Trade (DFAIT) is the primary arm of the federal government to help businesses gain access to foreign markets through market studies of target countries, and through embassy and trade commission contacts with local buyers and funding.

The Export Development Corporation (EDC) and the Canadian International Development Agency (CIDA) are just two of the better-known national organizations and programs that businesses can contact for international promotion assistance and funding opportunities.

Financing International Business

Learning Objective 6

Identify the institutions that help firms and nations finance international business.

International trade compounds the concerns of financial managers. Currency exchange rates, tariffs and foreign-exchange controls, and the tax structures of host nations all affect international operations and the flow of cash. In addition, financial managers must be concerned both with the financing of their international operations and with the means available to their customers to finance purchases.

Fortunately, along with business in general, Canada's top banks have become international in scope. Many have established branches in major cities around the world. Thus, like firms in other industries, they are able to provide their services where and when they are needed. In addition, financial assistance is available from Canadian and provincial governments and international sources.

Several of today's international financial organizations were founded many years ago to facilitate free trade and the exchange of currencies among nations. Some, such as the Inter-American Development Bank, are internationally supported and focus on developing countries. Others, such as the Export-Import Bank, are operated by one country but provide international financing.

USING THE INTERNET

Trade data, meetings, seminars, and other related information of interest to exporters is published in *CanadaExport*, the newsletter published by DFAIT and available on the Internet at http://w01.international.gc.ca/canadexport/.

The Business Development Bank of Canada

The Business Development Bank of Canada (BDC) is a financial institution wholly owned by the government of Canada. BDC plays a leadership role in delivering financial, investment, and consulting services to Canadian small businesses, with a particular focus on the technology and export sectors of the economy. You can learn more about BDC at their website www.bdc.ca.

Multilateral Development Banks

A **multilateral development bank (MDB)** is an internationally supported bank that provides loans to developing countries to help them grow. The most familiar is the World Bank, which operates worldwide. Four other MDBs operate primarily in Central and South America, Asia, Africa, and Eastern and Central Europe. All five are supported by the industrialized nations, including the United States and Canada.

The *Inter-American Development Bank* (IDB), the oldest and largest regional bank, was created in 1959 by ten Latin American countries and the United States. Forty-seven member countries—twenty-six borrowing countries in Latin America and the Caribbean and twenty-one nonborrowing countries, including the United States, Japan, Canada, sixteen European countries, and Israel—now own the bank, which is headquartered in Washington, D.C. The IDB makes loans and provides technical advice and assistance to countries.[18]

With sixty-four member nations, the *Asian Development Bank* (ADB), created in 1966 and headquartered in the Philippines, promotes economic and social progress in Asian and Pacific regions. The U.S. government is the second-largest contributor to the ADB's capital, after Japan. Recently, the ADB approved $5.4 billion for seventy-two loans in twenty-two countries; India received the largest loan of $1.5 billion, followed by China and Pakistan.[19]

The *African Development Bank* (AFDB), also known as *Banque Africaines de Developpment*, was established in 1964 with headquarters in Abidjan, Ivory Coast. Its members include fifty-three African and twenty-four non-African countries from the Americas, Europe, and Asia. The AFDB's goal is to foster the economic and social development of its African members. The bank pursues this goal through loans, research, technical assistance, and the development of trade programs.

Established in 1991 to encourage reconstruction and development in the Eastern and Central European countries, the London-based *European Bank for Reconstruction and Development* (EBRD) is owned by sixty countries and two intergovernmental institutions. Its loans are geared toward developing market-oriented economies and promoting private enterprise.[20]

The International Monetary Fund

The **International Monetary Fund (IMF)** is an international bank with 184 member nations that makes short-term loans to developing countries experiencing balance-of-payment deficits. This financing is contributed by member nations, and it must be repaid with interest. Loans are provided primarily to fund international trade.

multilateral development bank (MDB) an internationally supported bank that provides loans to developing countries to help them grow

International Monetary Fund (IMF) an international bank with 184 member nations that makes short-term loans to developing countries experiencing balance-of-payment deficits

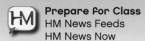

Prepare for Class
HM News Feeds
HM News Now

→ **RETURN TO INSIDE BUSINESS**

When Research In Motion Ltd. first introduced the Blackberry in 1998, it was a runaway hit with mobile business people who realized the added value of having a pager combined with the instant reception of e-mail relayed directly from their office computers. Laptops were larger, more expensive, and not readily connectable for communications purposes. The Blackberry is small, costs under $500, and allows business people to receive their e-mail virtually anywhere they might be while away from their office computers. And their connection fees were reasonably inexpensive, for the business market that

considered timely communications critical. Gradually, Blackberry added more features, such as voice communication, that allowed Blackberry to compete with cell phones. Furthermore, as more countries adopt Blackberry technology, as we describe in the chapter opening, Blackberry users will find connectivity more widely available.

Questions

1. How important do you think partnerships with telecommunications firms around the world are for Research In Motion's future success? Explain your thinking.

2. Is Blackberry competing with other hand-held devices that allow users to download MP3 files or watch video files? Explain why or why not.

CHAPTER REVIEW

1 Explain the economic basis for international business.

International business encompasses all business activities that involve exchanges across national boundaries. International trade develops when nations trade surplus products and services for those in short supply. A nation's balance of trade is the difference between the value of its exports and the value of its imports. Its balance of payments is the difference between the flow of money into and out of the nation.

2 Discuss the restrictions nations place on international trade, the objectives of these restrictions, and their results.

Despite the benefits of world trade, nations tend to use tariffs and nontariff barriers (import quotas, embargoes, and other restrictions) to limit trade. These restrictions typically are justified as being needed to protect a nation's

economy, industries, citizens, or security. They can result in the loss of jobs, higher prices, fewer choices in the marketplace, and the misallocation of resources.

3 Outline the extent of international trade and identify the organizations working to foster it.

World trade is generally increasing. The General Agreement on Tariffs and Trade (GATT) was formed to dismantle trade barriers and provide an environment in which international business can grow. Today, the World Trade Organization (WTO) and various economic communities carry on that mission.

4 Define the methods by which a firm can organize for and enter into international markets.

A firm may license a foreign firm to produce and market its products; export its products and sell them through foreign intermediaries or its own sales organization abroad; sell its exports outright to an export-import merchant; enter into a joint venture with a foreign firm; establish its own foreign subsidiaries; or it may develop into a multinational enterprise.

 Describe the various sources of export assistance.

Export services and programs of both federal and provincial government agencies can help firms compete in foreign markets and create new jobs in Canada. Sources of export assistance include Department of Foreign Affairs and International Trade (DFAIT), the Export Develop-

ment Corporation (EDC), and the Canadian International Development Agency (CIDA).

 Identify the institutions that help firms and nations finance international business.

The Export Development Corporation and the International Monetary Fund have been established to help provide financing and ultimately to increase world trade for Canadian and international firms.

HM Improve Your Grade
Learning Objectives Review
Audio Chapter Review & Quiz

Review Questions

1. Why do firms engage in international trade?
2. What is the difference between an absolute and a comparative advantage in international trade? How are both types of advantages related to the concept of specialization?
3. What is a favourable balance of trade? In what way is it "favourable"?
4. List and briefly describe the principal restrictions that may be applied to a nation's imports.
5. What reasons generally are given for imposing trade restrictions?
6. What are the general effects of import restrictions on trade?
7. Define and describe the major objectives of the World Trade Organization (WTO) and the international economic communities.
8. Which nations are the principal trading partners of Canada? What are the major Canadian imports and exports?
9. The methods of engaging in international business can be categorized as either direct or indirect. How would you classify each of the methods described in this chapter? Why?
10. In what ways is a multinational enterprise different

from a large corporation that does business in several countries?
11. List some key sources of export assistance. How can these sources be useful to small business firms?
12. In what ways do multilateral development banks and the IMF enhance international trade?

Discussion Questions

1. Canada restricts imports but, at the same time, supports the WTO and international banks whose objective is to enhance world trade. As the Prime Minister, how would you justify this contradiction to the Canadian people?
2. What effects might the devaluation of Canada's currency have on its business firms? On its consumers? On the debts it owes to other nations?
3. Should imports to Canada be curtailed? What might happen if this were done?
4. When should a firm consider expanding from strictly domestic trade to international trade? When should it consider becoming further involved in international trade? What factors might affect the firm's decisions in each case?
5. How can a firm obtain the expertise needed to produce and market its products in, for example, the EU?

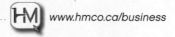

CASE STUDY

IDG Profits Globally from Local Differences

For more than four decades, International Data Group (IDG) has prospered by allowing each of its publishing, online, research, and conference businesses to find their own keys to success, nation by nation. A business idea that works spectacularly well in one country may fail miserably in another. This is why IDG's careful focus on meeting local needs—in the local language—makes all the difference in fulfilling the company's mission of spreading the computer revolution around the world.

All of IDG's businesses deal with information about technology. Its newspapers and magazines, such as *PCWorld* and *ComputerWorld,* keep business people up-to-date on technology developments. The company maintains 400 technology news websites and manages hundreds of technology conferences and exhibitions every year, such as the popular MacWorld Expo. In addition, its International Data Corporation unit specializes in researching and analyzing worldwide technology trends for business clients.

IDG's combined annual revenue from operations in eighty-five countries soon will reach $3 billion. The company is looking ahead to even higher revenue as different units expand to meet growing demand for timely technology information in Southeast Asia, China, and other areas. In each country, local interests and language preferences shape the goods and services offered by IDG's local businesses. Moreover, the company sometimes teams up with local government agencies to develop and launch new offerings. For example, it has partnered with the Ministry of Science and Technology to produce information technology conferences in Vietnam.

Unlike multinational corporations that embrace the "one size fits all" strategy, the IDG businesses in each country are expected to be entrepreneurs, investigating what their customers want and need. Top executives have given local managers the authority to make decisions based on local trends and changes. As one example, the unit in South Korea decided to introduce online services before offering magazine subscriptions because it found that most local business people rely on high-speed Internet and web-enabled cell phones to access information. IDG is not only looking at the outcome in South Korea, but it is also considering how this approach might work in other areas. Thus, in the future, IDG might decide to deliver technology news solely through wireless media in some countries rather than relying on more traditional print media.

In China, IDG is already one of the top international publishers because of its joint ventures with local companies, which publish *ComputerWorld China* and other magazines in Chinese. IDG's success here has led other U.S. publishers to seek its help in launching Chinese editions of popular U.S. consumer magazines such as *Cosmopolitan.* Having gained in-depth market knowledge and forged close ties with local businesses, IDG began investing in Chinese high-tech companies in the early 1990s. Over the years, some of these firms went bankrupt, whereas others began selling stock or became acquisition targets—vastly increasing the value of IDG's investment stake.

CEO Patrick Kenealy says that his job is to let the best ideas of IDG's businesses rise to the surface and then "help everyone share best practices." However, he and his management team recognize the potential for misinterpretation when employees from different cultures try to communicate. Because IDG's local employees speak so many languages, presentations for multinational internal audiences are made in English. Even when employees are using the same language—English—employees from the United States, Canada, United Kingdom, and Australia may not glean the same meaning from a presentation or report. This is why Gigi Wang, senior vice president of strategy, stresses that "it's not what you say that's important; it's what the listener hears."[21]

Questions:

1. What are some of the advantages and disadvantages of IDG's intense focus on meeting local needs and using the local language in every country?

2. Why do you think that IDG partners with government agencies rather than with private firms in some countries?

3. Considering that IDG's main product is information, which trade restrictions might affect its profitability?

BUILDING SKILLS FOR CAREER SUCCESS

1. Exploring the Internet

A popular question debated among firms actively involved on the Internet is whether or not there exists a truly global Internet-based customer, irrespective of any individual culture, linguistic, or nationality issues. Does this Internet-based universal customer see the Internet and products sold there in pretty much the same way? If so, then one model might fit all customers. For example, although Yahoo.com translates its web pages so that they are understood around the world, the pages look pretty much the same regardless of which international site you use. Is this good strategy, or should the sites reflect local customers differently? Visit the text website for updates to this exercise.

Assignment

1. Examine a website such as Yahoo's (**www .yahoo.com**) and its various international versions that operate in other languages around the world. Compare their similarities and differences as best you can, even if you do not understand the individual languages.

2. After making your comparison, do you now agree that there are indeed universal Internet products and customers? Explain your decision.

2. Building Team Skills

The North American Trade Agreement among the United States, Mexico, and Canada went into effect on January 1, 1994. It has made a difference in trade among the countries and has affected the lives of many people.

Assignment

1. Working in teams and using the resources of your library, investigate NAFTA. Answer the following questions:

    a. What are NAFTA's objectives?

    b. What are its benefits?

    c. What impact has NAFTA had on trade, jobs, and travel?

    d. Some Canadians were opposed to the implementation of NAFTA. What were their objections? Have any of these objections been justified?

    e. Has NAFTA influenced your life? How?

2. Summarize your answers in a written report. Your team also should be prepared to give a class presentation.

3. Researching Different Careers

Today, firms around the world need employees with special skills. In some countries such employees are not always available, and firms then must search abroad for qualified applicants. One way they can do this is through global workforce databases. As business and trade operations continue to grow globally, you may one day find yourself working in a foreign country, perhaps for a North American company doing business there or for a foreign company. In what foreign country would you like to work? What problems might you face?

Assignment

1. Choose a country in which you might like to work.

2. Research the country. The Department of Foreign Affairs and International Trade Canada website (http://www.dfait-maeci.gc.ca/) is a good place to start. Find answers to the following questions:

    a. What language is spoken in this country? Are you proficient in it? What would you need to do if you are not proficient?

    b. What are the economic, social, and legal systems like in this nation?

    c. What is its history?

    d. What are its culture and social traditions like? How might they affect your work or your living arrangements?

3. Describe what you have found out about this country in a written report. Include an assessment of whether you would want to work there and the problems you might face if you did.

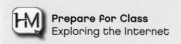
Prepare for Class
Exploring the Internet

RUNNING A BUSINESS PART 1
The Rise of Finagle A Bagel

Would bagels sell in Hong Kong? Laura Beth Trust and Alan Litchman planned to find out. Trust was in Hong Kong working in the garment manufacturing industry and Litchman was in real estate, but they were eager to start their own business. They were particularly interested in running a business where they would have direct customer contact and be able to get first-hand feedback about their products and services. And no matter what kind of business they started, it would be a family undertaking: the two entrepreneurs had recently decided to get married.

Looking around Hong Kong, Litchman and Trust noticed numerous Western-style food chains such as McDonald's, Pizza Hut, KFC, and Starbucks but no bagel places. Yet they believed that Hong Kong's sophisticated, multicultural population would welcome authentic New York–style bagels. Although both the entrepreneurs had MBA degrees from the Sloan School of Management, neither had any restaurant experience or knew how to make a bagel. Still, because they sensed a profitable opportunity and possessed solid business skills, Trust and Litchman decided to move ahead. The two incorporated a company, found a partner, and then returned to the United States to investigate the bagel business. As part of their research, they approached two knowledgeable experts for advice.

One of the bagel experts was Larry Smith, who in 1982 had co-founded a tiny cheesecake store in Boston's historic Quincy Market. When business was slow, the store began selling bagels topped with leftover cream cheese. By the late 1980s, this sideline was doing so well that Smith and his partners changed their focus from cheesecakes to bagels and changed the store's name from Julian's Cheesecakes to Finagle A Bagel. They relocated the store from a cramped 63-square-foot storefront into a more spacious 922-square-foot space in the same busy market complex. Soon so many customers were lining up for bagels that the owners began opening additional Finagle A Bagel stores around downtown Boston.

New Ownership, New Growth

By the time Trust and Litchman met Smith, he was operating six successful bagel stores, was ringing up $10 million in annual sales, and was looking for a source of capital to open more stores. Therefore, instead of helping the entrepreneurs launch a business in Hong Kong, Smith suggested that they stay and become involved in Finagle A Bagel. Because Litchman and Trust had roots in the Boston area, the opportunity to join a local bagel business was appealing both personally and professionally. Late in 1998, they bought a majority stake in Finagle A Bagel from Smith. The three owners agreed on how to divide management responsibilities and collaborated on plans for more aggressive expansion. Within a few years, Trust and Litchman completed a deal to buy the rest of the business and became the sole owners and co-presidents.

The business has grown every year since the conversion to bagels. Today, Finagle A Bagel operates twenty stores in downtown Boston and the surrounding suburbs. Because Finagle A Bagel outgrew its original production facilities, the owners recently purchased new corporate headquarters and a production centre in Newton, Massachusetts. This is where tens of thousands of bagels are prepared every day, along with enough cream cheese and cookies to supply a much larger network of stores.

Branding the Bagel

Over time, the owners have introduced a wide range of bagels, sandwiches, salads, and soups linked to the core bagel product. Bagels are baked fresh every day, and the stores receive daily deliveries of fresh salad fixings and other ingredients. Employees make each menu item to order while the customer watches. Some of the most popular offerings include a breakfast bagel pizza, salads with bagel-chip croutons, and BLT (bacon-lettuce-tomato) bagel sandwiches.

Finagle A Bagel is also boosting revenues by selling its bagels wholesale to thousands of universities, hospitals, and corporate cafeterias. In addition, it sells several varieties of bagels under the Finagle A Bagel brand to the Shaw's Market grocery chain. Shaw's has been expanding in New England through mergers and acquisitions, opening new opportunities for its bagel supplier. "As they grow, we grow with them," comments Litchman. "More importantly, it gets our name into markets where we're not. And we can track the sales and see how we're doing." If a particular Shaw's supermarket registers unusually strong bagel sales, the co-presidents will consider opening a store in or near that community.

The Bagel Economy

Although Finagle A Bagel competes with other bagel chains in and around Boston, its competition goes well beyond restaurants in that category. "You compete with a person selling a cup of coffee; you compete with a grocery store selling a salad," Litchman notes. "People only have so many 'dining dollars' and you need to convince them to spend those dining dollars in your store." Finagle A Bagel's competitive advantages are high-quality, fresh products; courteous and competent employees; and clean, attractive, and inviting restaurants.

During a recent economic recession, Boston's tourist traffic slumped temporarily, and corporate customers cut back on catering orders from Finagle A Bagel. After the company's sales revenues remained flat for about a year, they began inching up as the economy moved toward recovery. Now the business sells more than $20 million worth of bagels, soups, sandwiches, and salads every year.

Social Responsibility Through Bagels

Social responsibility is an integral part of Finagle A Bagel's operations. Rather than simply throw away unsold bagels at the end of the day, the owners donate the bagels to schools, shelters, and other nonprofit organizations. When local nonprofit groups hold fund-raising events, the co-presidents contribute bagels to feed the volunteers. Over the years, Finagle A Bagel has provided bagels to bicyclists raising money for St. Jude Children's Research Hospital, to swimmers raising money for breast cancer research, and to people building community playgrounds. Also, the co-presidents are strongly committed to being fair to their customers by offering good value and a good experience. "Something that we need to remember and instill in our people all the time," Trust emphasizes, "is that customers are coming in, and your responsibility is to give them the best that you can give them."

Even with over 320 employees, the co-presidents find that owning a business is a nonstop proposition. "Our typical day never ends," says Trust. They are constantly visiting stores, dealing with suppliers, reviewing financial results, and planning for the future. Despite all these responsibilities, this husband-and-wife entrepreneurial team enjoys applying their educational background and business experience to build a company that satisfies thousands of customers every day.

Questions

1. How has the business cycle affected Finagle A Bagel?

2. What is Finagle A Bagel doing to differentiate itself from competitors that want a share of customers' dining dollars?

3. Why would Finagle A Bagel donate bagels to local charities rather than give them away to customers or employees?

4. If you wanted to open a bagel restaurant in Hong Kong, would you license the Finagle A Bagel brand? Why or why not?

Understanding Information and e-Business

Your Guide to Success in Business

Why this chapter matters
With useful information, a manager can make more informed decisions that can improve a firm's competitive edge.

LEARNING OBJECTIVES

1. Examine how information can reduce risk when making a decision.

2. Discuss management's information requirements.

3. Outline the five functions of an information system.

4. Describe how the Internet helps employees to make decisions and communicate, assists a firm's sales force, and recruits and trains employees.

5. Analyze how computers and technology change the way information is acquired, organized, and used.

6. Explain the meaning of e-business.

7. Describe the fundamental models of e-business.

8. Understand the factors that influence an e-business plan.

9. Explore the growth trends, future opportunities, and challenges of e-business.

In the early days of the Internet, measuring and understanding visitor activity at a website was relatively simple and mirrored the research approaches traditionally developed for media such as newspapers, magazines, radio, and television. For instance, an organization's management would likely use online software to record the number of visitors to their site, the number of pages and length of time a visitor would remain at a particular page, how many pages were visited before a purchase from or a request for information might be made from the company—often called the *conversion rate*. If the researchers found that visitors were leaving the website before the critical number of pages were viewed, it might suggest a problem with the page design or some other problem that would call for management's attention. In many ways, web pages were simply thought of as pages of a magazine.

Today, many websites are much more sophisticated, complex, and, often, more difficult to gauge. Management must often measure website activity as well as the website's interactivity with mobile devices like Blackberries, MP3 players, cell phones, and so forth. For example, consider Rogers Communications Inc. media content division and its effort to measure subscriber behaviour on the Rogers Music Store website.

Rogers sells access to unlimited music downloads and ring tones to cell phone customers. To better understand customer behaviour and develop better marketing strategies, Rogers might want to know the number of downloads per month, the type of music selected, and any patterns that could be attributed to an individual subscriber. This information would allow Rogers to make content recommendations to customers, based on similar patterns demonstrated by other subscribers.[1]

Every successful business needs information. While some believe that we may be reaching an information saturation point, individuals enjoy having the information that can make life easier and more enjoyable. You, for example, can use computers or cell phones to access information about when a new Harry Potter movie is playing at a local theatre. With the help of technology, you also can obtain up-to-the-minute news, flight information for a vacation trip to British Columbia, or the latest weather forecast. Like individuals, business firms use computers and the Internet to find information about their customers, suppliers, competitors, and even new products available in the marketplace.

To improve the decision-making process, the information used by both individuals and business firms must be relevant or useful to meet a specific need. When individuals and business firms use relevant information, the result is better decisions, as illustrated below:

Relevant information → better intelligence and knowledge → better decisions

For businesses, better intelligence and knowledge that lead to better decisions are especially important because they can provide a competitive edge when compared with competitors and improve a firm's profits.

We begin this chapter by describing why employees need information. Just for a moment, assume that you graduated from school three years ago and are now working as an entry-level supervisor for an electronics firm. Consider how the answers to the following three questions could have an impact on you—the entry-level supervisor—on a daily basis.

1. How can information reduce risk when making a decision?
2. What is a management information system?
3. How do employees use an information system?

Measuring Website Activity

Within a few months of its launch in 2006, Têtes à claque—the title is a French Canadian slang expression that can loosely be translated as "a face you'd love to smack"—burst onto the Québec animation scene and became the talk of the province. The offbeat very low budget creation of Michel Beaudet and a small group of artists seemed to strike the right comedic tone with the entire population. The characters, who all have exaggerated facial features and personalities to match, follow simple skits that poke good-natured fun at familiar situations. For example, the late night television salesman hawking the "Willi Waller" potato peeler and the LCD Shovel 2007 with the built-in DVD player ". . . from the scientists at Canadian Tire" seem to resonate with audiences of both young and old. Remarkably, success was earned without any real marketing budget, as word of mouth and e-mails drove viewers to the website. Today, virtually all of Québec's French speaking population has seen the website at least once or have heard of the clay animation characters and their storylines. More remarkable still, given the lack of any serious marketing effort, is that more than 250,000 visitors get their daily dose of laughs at the website.

These audience measurements were the only numbers that Bell Canada Inc. needed to know before entering into a contract to distribute the three to four minute comedy clips to its Bell Mobility cell phone subscribers. However, most website audience measurement activity requires more complex effort in order to understand behaviour and weigh levels of success.

Rogers Communications Inc. is Canada's largest wireless voice and data communications services provider as well as Canada's largest cable television provider, offering cable television, high-speed Internet access, residential telephone services, and video retailing. Like Bell, Rogers is also looking for ways to develop its mobile customer base by offering more products and services such as program, music, games, and ring tones. In general, customer activity research is based on information gathered at websites where customers register their selections and communicate other information about their downloading preferences.

continued on next page

• • •

DID YOU KNOW?

To reach audiences, television producers are increasing delivery of podcasts, streaming video, and news broadcasts.

KEY TERMS

data (108)
information (108)
database (108)
knowledge management (109)
information technology (IT) officer (109)
management information system (MIS) (110)

data processing (113)
statistic (113)
frequency distribution (114)
arithmetic mean (114)
median (114)
mode (115)
range (115)

decision-support system (DSS) (117)
executive information system (EIS) (118)
expert system (118)
groupware (118)
collaborative learning system (118)
e-business (electronic business) (121)

outsourcing (122)
revenue stream (123)
business model (125)
business-to-business (B2B) model (125)
business-to-consumer (B2C) model (126)

ACE the Test
Crossword Puzzle
Flashcards

These questions provide the headings for the first three major sections in this chapter. In fact, a practical understanding of what information is and how an information system provides answers to important questions is the first step. The next step is to obtain the information you need. In the last part of this chapter we discuss how employees use business research methods, computers, the Internet, and software—all topics covered in this chapter—to obtain the information needed to make decisions on a daily basis. To learn more about how information can reduce risk when making decisions, read the information in the next section.

How Can Information Reduce Risk When Making a Decision?

Learning Objective ❶

Examine how information can reduce risk when making a decision.

As we noted in Chapter 1, information is one of the four major resources (along with material, human, and financial resources) managers must have to operate a business. While a successful business uses all four resources efficiently, it is information that helps managers reduce risk when making a decision.

Information and Risk

Theoretically, with accurate and complete information, there is no risk whatsoever. On the other hand, a decision made without any information is a gamble. These two extreme situations are rare in business. For the most part, business decision makers see themselves located someplace between either extreme. As illustrated in Figure 4.1, when the amount of available information is high, there is less risk; when the amount of available information is low, there is more risk.

For example, suppose that a marketing manager for Procter & Gamble responsible for the promotion of a well-known shampoo such as Pantene Pro-V has called a meeting of her department team to consider the selection of a new magazine advertisement. The company's advertising agency has submitted two new advertisements in sealed envelopes. Neither the manager nor any of her team has seen them before. Only one selection will be made for the new advertising campaign. Which advertisement should be chosen?

Without any further information available to the group, any selection is equally risky, and the team might as well make the decision by flipping a coin. If, however, team members were allowed to open the envelopes and examine the advertisements, they would have more information with which to form an opinion and make an informed recommendation. If, in addition to allowing them to examine the advertisements, the marketing manager circulated a report containing the reaction of a group of target consumers

More risk ← *Less* **Information** *More* → **Less risk**

> **Figure 4.1**
>
> **The Relationship Between Information and Risk**
>
> When the amount of available information is high, managers tend to make better decisions. On the other hand, when the amount of information is low, there is a high risk of making a poor decision.

toward each of the two advertisements, the team would have even more information with which to work. Thus information, when understood properly, produces knowledge and empowers managers and employees to make better decisions.

Information Rules

Marketing research continues to show that discounts influence almost all car buyers. Simply put, if dealers lower their prices, they will sell more cars. This relationship between buyer behaviour and price can be thought of as an *information rule* that usually will guide the marketing manager correctly. An information rule emerges when research confirms the same results each time that it studies the same or a similar set of circumstances. Because of the volume of information they receive each day and their need to make decisions on a daily basis, business people try to accumulate information rules to shorten the time they spend analyzing choices.

Information rules are the "great simplifiers" for all decision makers. Business research is continuously looking for new rules that can be put to good use and looking to discredit old ones that are no longer valid. This ongoing process is necessary because business conditions rarely stay the same for very long.

The Difference Between Data and Information

Many people use the terms *data* and *information* interchangeably, but the two differ in important ways. **Data** are numerical or verbal descriptions that usually result from some sort of measurement. (The word *data* is plural; the singular form is *datum*.) Your current wage level, the amount of last year's after-tax profit for Hewlett Packard, and the current retail prices of Honda automobiles are all data. Most people think of data as being numerical only, but they can be nonnumerical as well. A description of an individual as a "tall, athletic person with short, dark hair" certainly would qualify as data.

Information is data presented in a form that is useful for a specific purpose. Suppose that a human resources manager wants to compare the wages paid to male and female employees over a period of five years. The manager might begin with a stack of computer printouts listing every person employed by the firm, along with each employee's current and past wages. The manager would be hard pressed to make any sense of all the names and numbers. Such printouts consist of data rather than information.

Now suppose that the manager uses a computer to graph the average wages paid to men and to women in each of the five years. The result is information because the manager can use it for the purpose at hand—to compare wages paid to men with those paid to women over the five-year period. When summarized in the graph, the wage data from the printouts become information. For a manager, information presented in a practical, useful form such as a graph simplifies the decision-making process.

The average company maintains a great deal of data that can be transformed into information. Typical data include records pertaining to personnel, inventory, sales, and accounting. Often each type of data is stored in individual departments within an organization. However, the data can be used more effectively when they are organized into a database. A **database** is a single collection of data stored in one place that can be used by people throughout an organization to make decisions. Today, most compa-

data numerical or verbal descriptions that usually result from some sort of measurement

information data presented in a form that is useful for a specific purpose

database a single collection of data stored in one place that can be used by people throughout an organization to make decisions

ENTREPRENEURIAL CHALLENGE

The Rise of Craigslist

Started by Craig Newmark in 1995, Craigslist (**www.craigslist.org**) features data for everyday living, such as job openings, real estate listings, personal ads, and more. The original Craigslist focused on the San Francisco area; today, local sites are available for nearly 200 communities worldwide. How did Newmark build his information empire?

- *Standardize.* No blinking or animated ads here—just all-text, easy-to-read listings organized into categories so that users can find what they want quickly.

- *Focus on users.* Newmark spends most of his day reading users' comments, investigating their complaints, and policing the site to keep scammers out.

- *Provide value.* Businesses in selected cities, for example, pay a nominal fee to post job openings, but users have access to listings for free.

Already, Craigslist sites hold more than six million listings and generate annual revenue topping $20 million. New features are on the drawing board, and even more profits are ahead for this fast-growing business.

---

nies have several different types of databases. While databases are important, the way the data and information are used is even more important—and more valuable to the firm. As a result, management information experts now use the term **knowledge management (KM)** to describe a firm's procedures for generating, using, and sharing the data and information contained in the firm's databases. Typically, data, information, databases, and knowledge management all become important parts of a firm's management information system.

> **knowledge management** a firm's procedures for generating, using, and sharing the data and information contained in the firm's databases

What Is a Management Information System?

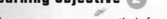

Learning Objective ❷

Discuss management's information requirements.

The purpose of an MIS (sometimes referred to as an *information technology system* or simply *IT system*) is to distribute timely and useful information from both internal and external sources to the managers and employees who need it. Today, most medium-sized to large business firms have an information technology (IT) officer. An **information technology (IT) officer** is a manager at the executive level who is responsible for ensuring that a firm has the equipment necessary to provide the information the firm's employees and managers need to make effective decisions.

> **information technology (IT) officer** a manager at the executive level who is responsible for ensuring that a firm has the equipment necessary to provide the information the firm's employees and managers need to make effective decisions

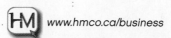

Today's typical MIS is built around a computerized system of record-keeping and communications software so that it can provide information based on a wide variety of data. After all, the goal is to provide needed information to all managers and employees.

MANAGEMENT INFORMATION SYSTEM

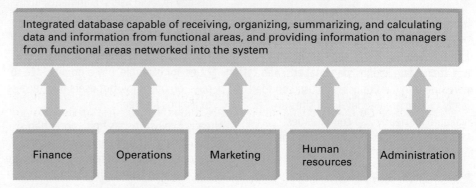

Figure 4.2

Management Information System (MIS)

After an MIS is installed, a user can get information directly from the MIS without having to go through other people in the organization.

Source: Ricky W. Griffin, *Management*, 8th ed. (Boston: Houghton Mifflin Company, 2005). Copyright © 2005 by Houghton Mifflin Company. Adapted with permission.

management information system (MIS) is a system that provides managers and employees with the information they need to perform their jobs as effectively as possible (see Figure 4.2).

Managers' Information Requirements

Managers have to plan for the future, implement their plans in the present, and evaluate results against what has been accomplished in the past. Of course, the specific types of information they need depend on their area of management.

Today many firms are organized into five areas of management: finance, operations, marketing, human resources, and administration. Managers in each of these areas need specific information in order to make decisions. For example, *financial* managers obviously are most concerned with their firm's finances. They study its debts and receivables, cash flow, future capitalization needs, financial statements, and other accounting information. Of equal importance to financial managers is information about the present state of the economy, interest rates, and predictions of business conditions in the future.

Operations managers are concerned with present and future sales levels, current inventory levels of work in process and finished goods, and the availability and cost of the resources required to produce products and services. They also must keep abreast of any innovative production technology that might be useful to the firm.

Marketing managers need to have detailed information about their firm's products and the products offered by competitors. Such information includes pricing strategies, new promotional campaigns, and products that competitors are test marketing. Information concerning the firm's customers, current and projected market share, and new and pending product legislation is also important to marketing managers.

Human resources managers must be aware of anything that pertains to the firm's employees. Key examples include current wage levels and benefits packages both within the firm and in firms that compete for valuable employees, current legislation and court decisions that affect employment practices, union activities, and the firm's plans for growth, expansion, or mergers.

Administrative managers are responsible for the overall management of the organization. Thus they are concerned with the coordination of information—just as they are concerned with the coordination of material, human, and financial resources. First, administrators must ensure that all employees have access to the information they need to do their jobs. Administrative managers must also make sure that

* information is used in a consistent manner throughout the firm,

* all managers and employees receive the skills training required to use the firm's MIS,

* money is available to update the firm's MIS when needed.

Size and Complexity of the System

An MIS must be tailored to the needs of the organization it serves. In some firms, a tendency to save on initial costs can result in a system that is too small or overly simple. Such a system generally ends up serving only one or two management levels or a single department. Managers in other departments "give up" on the system as soon as they find that it cannot process their data. Often they look elsewhere for information, process their own data, or simply do without.

Almost as bad is an MIS that is too large or too complex for the organization. Unused capacity and complexity do nothing but increase the cost of owning and operating the system. In addition, a system that is difficult to use probably will not be used at all. Obviously, much is expected of an effective MIS system. Let's examine the functions an MIS system must perform to provide the information managers need.

How Do Employees Use an Information System?

Learning Objective ③

Outline the five functions of an information system.

To provide information, an MIS must perform five specific functions. It must collect data, store the data, update the data, process the data into information, and present information to users in a practical way (see Figure 4.3).

Collecting Data

A firm's employees, with the help of an MIS system, must gather the data needed to establish the firm's *data bank*. The data bank should include all past and current data that may be useful in managing the firm. Clearly, the data entered into the system must be *relevant* to the needs of the firm's managers. And perhaps most important, the data must be *accurate*. Irrelevant data are simply

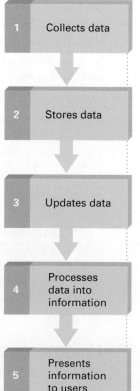

1 Collects data

2 Stores data

3 Updates data

4 Processes data into information

5 Presents information to users

Figure 4. 3

Five Management Information System Functions

Every MIS must be tailored to the organization it serves and must perform five functions.

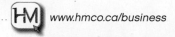

useless; inaccurate data can be disastrous. The data can be obtained from within the firm and from outside sources.

Internal Sources of Data Typically, most of the data gathered for an MIS comes from internal sources. The most common internal sources of information are managers and employees, company records and reports, and minutes of meetings. For example, past and present accounting data also can provide information about the firm's customers, creditors, and suppliers. Sales reports are a source of data on sales, pricing strategies, and the effectiveness of promotional campaigns. Human resources records are useful as a source of data on wage and benefits levels, hiring patterns, employee turnover, and other personnel variables.

Present and past production forecasts also should be included in the firm's data bank, along with data indicating how well these forecasts predicted actual events. And specific plans and management decisions—regarding capital expansion and new product development, for example—should be incorporated into the MIS system.

External Sources of Data External sources of data include customers, suppliers, bankers, trade and financial publications, industry conferences, online computer services, government sources, and firms that specialize in gathering data for organizations. For example, a marketing research company might acquire forecasts pertaining to product demand, consumer tastes, and other marketing variables. Suppliers are also an excellent source of information about the future availability and costs of raw materials and component parts. Bankers often can provide valuable economic insights and projections. And the information furnished by trade publications and industry conferences usually is concerned as much with future projections as with present conditions. Whether the source of the data is internal or external, always remember the following three cautions:

1. The cost of obtaining data from some external sources, such as marketing research firms, can be quite high.

2. Outdated or incomplete data usually yield inaccurate information.

3. Although computers generally do not make mistakes, the people who use them can make or cause errors. When data (or information) and your judgment disagree, always check the data.

Storing Data

An MIS must be capable of storing data until they are needed. Typically, the method chosen to store data depends on the size and needs of the organization. Small businesses might enter data and then store them directly on the hard drive inside an employee's computer. Generally, medium-sized to large businesses store data in a larger computer system and provide access to employees through a computer network. Today, networks take on many configurations and are designed by specialists who work with a firm's IT personnel to decide on what's best for the company.

Updating Data

Today, an MIS must be able to update stored data regularly to ensure that the information presented to managers and employees is accurate, complete, and up-to-date. The frequency with which data are updated depends on how fast they change and how often they are used. When it is vital to have current data, updating can occur as soon as new data are available. For example, Sobeys, a grocery-store chain operating under a variety of store names across Canada, has cash registers that automatically transmit data on each item sold to a central computer. The computer adjusts the store's inventory records accordingly. In some systems the computer can even be programmed to reorder items whose inventories fall below a specified level.

Data and information can also be updated according to a predetermined schedule. Data on paper documents, for instance, might be entered into a firm's data bank at certain intervals—daily, weekly, or monthly.

Processing Data

Some data are used in the form in which they are stored while other data require processing to extract, highlight, or summarize the information they contain. **Data processing** is the transformation of data into a form that is useful for a specific purpose. For verbal data, this processing consists mainly of extracting the pertinent material from storage and combining it into a report. Most business data, however, are in the form of numbers—large groups of numbers, such as daily sales totals or production costs for a specific product. Such groups of numbers are difficult to handle and to comprehend, but their contents can be summarized through the use of statistics.

data processing the transformation of data into a form that is useful for a specific purpose

Statistics as Summaries A **statistic** is a measure that summarizes a particular characteristic of an entire group of numbers. In this section we discuss the most commonly used statistics, using the data given in Figure 4.4. This figure contains only eleven items of data, which simplifies our discussion, but most business situations involve hundreds or even thousands of items. Fortunately, computers can be programmed to process such large volumes of numbers quickly.

statistic a measure that summarizes a particular characteristic of an entire group of numbers

Sky Cloud Manufacturing
Employee Salaries for April 2007

Employee	Monthly Salary
Thomas P. Ouimet	$ 3,500
Marina Ruiz	3,500
Ronald F. Washington	3,000
Sarah H. Abrams	3,000
Kathleen L. Norton	3,000
Martin C. Hess	2,800
Jane Chang	2,500
Margaret S. Fernandez	2,400
John F. O'Malley	2,000
Robert Miller	2,000
William G. Dorfmann	1,800
Total	$29,500

Figure 4.4

Statistics

Managers often examine statistics that describe trends in employee compensation.

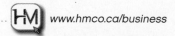

—EXAMINING ETHICS—
Screensavers That Save the World

I f you have a computer connected to the Internet, you can help save the world. How? By downloading a screensaver that allows a nonprofit group to process a small amount of data from a giant research project during your computer's free time. With tens of thousands of PCs crunching data in spare moments, scientists see the results sooner. If you volunteer your PC, your personal files won't be touched and your computer will be put to work only when it has spare processing power.

Here are a few sites that want to put your PC to work on large-scale projects:

- **grid.org** (to help find new cancer treatments)
- **folding.stanford.edu** (to help find a cure for Parkinson's or Alzheimer's)
- **setiathome.berkeley.edu** (to help search for extraterrestrial life)
- **boinc.berkeley.edu** (links to other projects such as understanding climate change)

Sources: Based on information from Courtney McCarty, "Save the World with Your Screensaver," *PC Magazine*, November 7, 2006, pp. 156+; Lee Gomes, "Wanted: Your PC's Spare Time," *Wall Street Journal*, June 19, 2006, p. R14.

frequency distribution a listing of the number of times each value appears in a set of data

Developing a frequency distribution can reduce the number of items in a set of data. A **frequency distribution** is a listing of the number of times each value appears in the set of data. The frequency distribution for the data in Figure 4.4 is as follows:

MONTHLY SALARY	FREQUENCY	MONTHLY SALARY	FREQUENCY
$3,500	2	2,400	1
3,000	3	2,000	2
2,800	1	1,800	1
2,500	1		

Measures of Size The arithmetic mean, median, and mode are statistical measures used to describe the size of numerical values in a set of data. Perhaps the most familiar statistic is the arithmetic mean, commonly called the *average*.

arithmetic mean the total of all the values in a set of data divided by the number of items

The **arithmetic mean** of a set of data is the total of all the values divided by the number of items. The sum of employee salaries given in Figure 4.4 is $29,500. The average (arithmetic mean) of employee salaries is $2,681.82 ($29,500 ÷ 11 = $2,681.82).

median the value at the exact middle of a set of data when the data are arranged in order

The **median** of a set of data is the value at the exact middle of the data when they are arranged in order. The data in Figure 4.4 are already arranged from the *highest* value to the *lowest* value. Their median thus is $2,800, which is exactly halfway between the top and bottom values.

The **mode** of a set of data is the value that appears most frequently in the set. In Figure 4.4, the $3,000 monthly salary appears three times, more often than any other salary amount appears. Thus $3,000 is the mode for this set of data.

mode the value that appears most frequently in a set of data

Although the arithmetic mean, or average, is the most commonly used statistical measure, it can be distorted by a few extremely small or large values. In this case a manager might want to rely on the median or mode, or both, to describe the values. For example, managers often use the median to describe dollar values or income levels when the arithmetic mean for the same numbers is distorted. In a similar fashion, marketers often use the mode to describe a firm's most popular product when average sales amounts for a group of products would be inaccurate or misleading.

Another characteristic of the items within a set of values is the dispersion, or spread. The simplest measure of dispersion is the **range,** which is the difference between the highest value and the lowest value in a set of data. The range of the data in Figure 4.4 is $3,500 − $1,800 = $1,700.

range the difference between the highest value and the lowest value in a set of data

Presenting Information

An MIS must be capable of presenting information in a usable form. That is, the method of presentation—reports, tables, graphs, or charts, for example—must be appropriate for the information itself and for the uses to which it will be put.

Verbal information can be presented in list or paragraph form. Employees often are asked to prepare formal business reports. A typical business report includes (1) an introduction, (2) the body of the report, (3) the conclusions, and (4) the recommendations.

The *introduction,* which sets the stage for the remainder of the report, describes the problem to be studied in the report, identifies the research techniques that were used and previews the material that will be presented in the report. The *body of the report* should objectively describe the facts that were discovered in the process of completing the report. The body also should provide a foundation for the conclusions and the recommendations. The *conclusions* are statements of fact that describe the findings contained in the report. They should be specific, practical, and based on the evidence contained in the report. The *recommendations* section presents suggestions on how the problem might be solved. Like the conclusions, the recommendations should be specific, practical, and based on the evidence.

Visual and tabular displays may be necessary in a formal business report. For example, numerical information and combinations of numerical and verbal information may be easier to understand if presented in charts and tables.

Visual Displays A *visual display* is a diagram that represents several items of information in a manner that makes comparison easier. *Graphs* are most effective for presenting information about one variable that changes with time (such as variations in sales figures for a business over a five- or ten-year period). Graphs tend to emphasize trends as well as peaks and low points in the value of the variable. Figure 4.5 illustrates examples of visual displays generated by a computer.

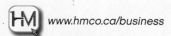

Figure 4.5

Typical Visual Displays Used in Business Presentations

Visual displays help business people to present information in a form that can be understood easily.

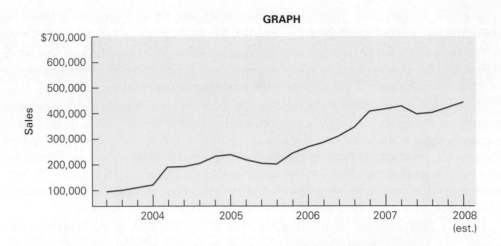

GRAPH

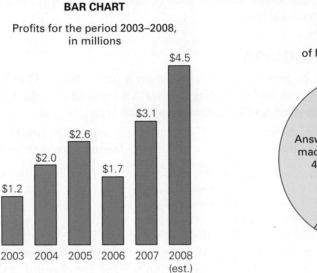

BAR CHART

Profits for the period 2003–2008, in millions

PIE CHART

Sales figures for selected products of Martin Manufacturing

In a *bar chart*, the longer the bar, the greater is the value. This type of display is useful for presenting values that are to be compared. The eye can quickly pick out the longest or shortest bar or even those that seem to be of average size.

A *pie chart* is a circle ("pie") divided into "slices," each of which represents a different item. The size of each slice shows the contribution of that item to the whole. By their nature, pie charts are most effective in displaying the relative size or importance of various items of information.

Tabular Displays A tabular display is used to present verbal or numerical information in columns and rows. It is most useful in presenting information about two or more related variables. A table, for example, can be used to illustrate the number of salespeople in each region of the country, sales for different types of products, and total sales for all products (see Table 4.1). And information that is to be manipulated—for example, to calculate loan payments—also usually is displayed in tabular form.

Tables are most useful for displaying information about two or more variables.

ALL-STAR TECHNOLOGY PROJECTED SALES			
Section of the Country	Number of Salespeople	Consumer Products	Industrial Products
Eastern territory	15	$1,500,000	$ 3,500,000
Midwestern territory	20	$2,000,000	$ 5,000,000
Western territory	10	$1,000,000	$ 4,000,000
TOTALS	45	$4,500,000	$12,500,000

Table 4.1

Typical Three-Column Table Used in Business Presentations

Tabular displays generally have less impact than visual displays. However, displaying the information that could be contained in a multicolumn table such as Table 4.1 would require several bar or pie charts.

Improving Productivity with the Help of Computers and Technology

Learning Objective 4

Describe how the Internet helps employees to make decisions and communicate, assists a firm's sales force, and recruits and trains employees.

In this section we examine several solutions to problems created when a firm or its employees use computers and the Internet. In each case a solution is always evaluated in terms of its costs and compared with the benefits a firm receives, generally referred to as a *cost/benefit analysis*. Typical areas of concern for a business include decision making, communications, sales, recruiting and training employees, and business software applications.

Making Smart Decisions

How do managers and employees sort out relevant and useful information from spam, junk mail, and useless data? Three types of applications actually can help to improve and speed the decision-making process for people at different levels within an organization. First, a **decision-support system (DSS)** is a type of computer program that provides relevant data and information to help a firm's employees make decisions. It also can be used to determine the effect of changing different variables and answer "what if" type questions. For example, a manager at a home building firm might use a DSS to determine prices for new homes built in an upscale, luxury subdivision. By entering the number of homes that will be built along with the costs associated with land, labour, materials, building permits, promotional costs, and all other costs, a DSS

decision-support system (DSS) a type of computer program that provides relevant data and information to help a firm's employees make decisions

can help to determine a base price for each new home. It is also possible to increase or decrease the building costs and determine new home prices for each set of assumptions with a DSS.

Although similar to a DSS, an **executive information system (EIS)** is a computer-based system that facilitates and supports the decision-making needs of top managers and senior executives by providing easy access to both internal and external information. With an EIS, executives can obtain information by touching a computer screen, using a mouse, or using voice recognition and simply talking to the computer. Needed data and information can be displayed in graphs, charts, and spreadsheets.

An **expert system** is a type of computer program that uses artificial intelligence to imitate a human's ability to think. An expert system uses a set of rules that analyze information supplied by the user about a particular activity or problem. Based on the information supplied, the expert system then provides recommendations or suggests specific actions in order to help make decisions. Expert systems, for example, have been used to schedule manufacturing tasks, diagnose illnesses, determine credit limits for credit card customers, and develop electronic games.

Helping Employees Communicate

One of the first business applications of computer technology was e-mail. Once software was chosen and employees trained, communications could be carried out globally within and outside a firm at any time, twenty-four hours a day, seven days a week. Today, e-mail is also used as a direct link between business and customer. When investment bank Putnam Lovell Securities, for example, sent research reports to clients by e-mail instead of printing, packaging, and shipping the reports, the firm saved over $500,000 a year.[2]

Groupware is one of the latest type of software that facilitates the management of large projects among geographically dispersed employees, as well as such group activities as problem solving and brainstorming. For example, suppose that the home office of a software development firm in a major city has been hired to prepare customized software for a client in another city. The project team leader uses groupware to establish guidelines for the project, check availability of employees around the world, give individuals specific work assignments, and set up a schedule for work completion, testing, and final installation on the client's computer. The team leader is able to monitor work progress and may intervene if asked or if problems develop. When needed, people from various locations, possessing an array of knowledge and skills, can be called to the "workspace" created on the computer system for their contribution. When the work is finally completed, it can be forwarded to the client's computer and installed.

Besides being useful in project management, groupware provides an opportunity for establishing a collaborative learning system to help solve a specific problem. A **collaborative learning system** is a work environment that allows problem-solving participation by all team members. By posting a question or problem on the groupware site, the team leader invites members, who may be located anywhere in the world, to submit messages that can help to move the group toward a solution.

---

executive information system (EIS) is a computer-based system that facilitates and supports the decision-making needs of top managers and senior executives by providing easy access to both internal and external information

expert system a type of computer program that uses artificial intelligence to imitate a human's ability to think

groupware one of the latest types of software that facilitates the management of large projects among geographically dispersed employees as well as such group activities as problem solving and brainstorming

collaborative learning system a work environment that allows problem-solving participation by all team members

Assisting the Firm's Sales Force

Internet-based software application programs sometimes referred to as *customer-relationship management* (CRM) programs focus on the special informational needs of sales personnel. For example, sales force automation programs support sales representatives with organized databases of information such as names of clients, the status of pending orders, and sales leads and opportunities, as well as any related advice or recommendations from other company personnel. Consider what happens when a sales representative for the pharmaceutical division of a company such as Johnson & Johnson is planning to visit doctors, healthcare providers, and hospitals in the Calgary area. A sales force automation software program can provide information about what the results were of the last contacts, who else in the pharmaceutical firm has interacted with the client, and previous purchases the client has made. As sales representatives complete their visits, information about what was learned should be entered into the sales force automation system as soon as possible so that everyone can use the latest information.

Recruiting and Training Employees

A common icon on most corporate websites is a link to "careers" or "employment opportunities." Firms looking for people with specialized skills can post their employee needs on their websites and reach potential candidates from around the globe. This is an extremely important method of recruiting employees for positions where labour shortages are common, and individuals with the *right* skills are in high demand.

Furthermore, software programs can help large firms to establish a database of potential employees. This is an especially important function for a firm that receives thousands of unsolicited employment applications from people all over the world. The

BIZ TECH

Log on and Learn

Just a few years ago, attending employee training meant bringing a pad and pencil to the company classroom or travelling to a special seminar. Now employees are increasingly logging on to learn. According to the American Society for Training and Development,

- Average percentage of learning hours spent in technology-based training: 29
- Average percentage of learning hours spent in classroom training: 42
- Average percentage of learning hours spent in a blend of training methods: 29

The Bank of Montreal (BMO) has invested more that $600 million in training since 1991—much of that in its Toronto-based Institute for Learning, which was opened in 1993. BMO's instructional strategy centres include not only instructor-led activities, but also online learning. For example, to handle the adoption of a new CRM system from Seibel Corp., the bank employed both conventional instruction methods and a web-based system with great success. Many companies are moving to online training because it is generally less expensive, everyone can be trained at the same time, and receives the same instruction.[3]

cost of organizing and processing this information is high, but software can reduce this expense when compared with a paper-based system. As a bonus, the software can organize data in a way most useful to the firm.

Large and midsize companies also spend a great deal of money on education and training programs for employees. By distributing information about the firm, the organization, products and services, new procedures, and general information to employees through the Internet for reading and study at convenient times and places, firms can reduce training costs dramatically. For example, new employees generally are required to attend an intensive training program in which a wide variety of information about the firm is presented in a classroom setting. Online training on a number of topics can then be used to provide additional information and keep both new and experienced employees up-to-date on the latest information about the firm's policies and its products and services. Furthermore, revision and distribution of changes to this type of information are much easier if the information is provided on the company's website.

Business Applications Software

Learning Objective 5

Analyze how computers and technology change the way information is acquired, organized, and used.

Early software typically performed a single function. Today, however, *integrated software* combines many functions in a single package. Integrated packages allow for the easy *linking* of text, numerical data, graphs, photos, and even audiovisual clips. A business report prepared using the Microsoft Office package, for instance, can include all these components.

Integration offers at least two other benefits. Once data have been entered into an application in an integrated package, the data can be used in another integrated package without having to re-enter the data. Also, once a user learns one application, it is much easier to learn another application in an integrated package. From a career

Table 4.2

Current Business Application Software Used to Improve Productivity

Word processing	Users can prepare and edit written documents and store them in the computer or on a memory device.
Desktop publishing	Users can combine text and graphics in reports, newsletters, and pamphlets in professional reports.
Accounting	Users can record routine financial transactions and prepare financial reports at the end of the accounting period.
Database management	Users can electronically store large amounts of data and transform the data into information.
Graphics	Users can display and print pictures, drawings, charts, and diagrams.
Spreadsheets	Users can organize numerical data into a grid of rows and columns.

standpoint, you should realize that firms will assume that you possess, or will possess after training, a high degree of working comfort with several of the types of software applications described in Table 4.2.

Defining e-Business

Learning Objective ⑥

Explain the meaning of e-business.

Today, many businesses use information technology to improve productivity, communicate with both customers and employees, recruit and train employees, *and* sell goods and services online. In Chapter 1 we defined *business* as the organized effort of individuals to produce and sell, for a profit, the products and services that satisfy society's needs. In a simple sense, then, **e-business**, or **electronic business**, can be defined as the organized effort of individuals to produce and sell, for a profit, the products and services that satisfy society's needs *through the facilities available on the Internet*. As you will see in the remainder of this chapter and throughout this book, e-business is transforming key business activities.

e-business (electronic business) the organized effort of individuals to produce and sell, for a profit, the products and services that satisfy society's needs through the facilities available on the Internet

Organizing e-Business Resources

As noted in Chapter 1, to be organized, a business must combine *human, material, informational*, and *financial resources*. This is true of e-business, too (see Figure 4.6), but the resources used in e-business are probably more specialized than in a typical business. For example, people who can design, create, and maintain websites are only a fraction of the specialized human resources required by e-businesses. Material resources must include specialized computers, sophisticated equipment and software,

---

Your Career

Too Much Information

Planning a job search? Don't forget to polish your online presence as well as your résumé. Many employers check to see whether job applicants have posted photos, videos, or messages on public websites, blogs, or social networking sites. This is where too much information, sometimes referred to as TMI, can work against you. If an online search turns up revealing images, confessions of illegal or questionable activities, or other details that put you in an unprofessional light, that job interview or offer could very well evaporate.

To be safe, assume that some recruiter, at some point, will try to find you on Facebook.com, Blogger, MySpace, or similar sites. "It's becoming very much a common tool," says a group marketing manager at Microsoft. "For the first time ever, you suddenly have very public information about almost any candidate." In other words, TMI (especially the wrong kind of information) can sink your career even before it begins.

Sources: Based on information from Lindsey Gerdes, "Overexposed," *BusinessWeek,* November 13, 2006, p. 12; Amy Joyce, "So Much for 'Personal' Habits," *Washington Post,* October 15, 2006, p. F1; Alan Finder, "When a Risqué Online Persona Undermines a Chance for a Job," *New York Times,* June 11, 2006, pp. A1+.

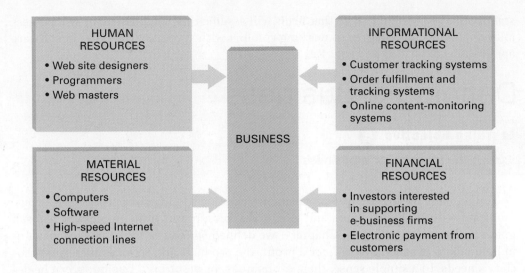

Figure 4.6

Combining e-Business Resources

While all businesses use four resources (human, material, informational, and financial), these resources typically are more specialized when used in an e-business.

outsourcing the process of finding outside vendors and suppliers to provide professional help, parts, or materials at a lower cost

and high-speed Internet connection lines. Computer programs that track the number of customers who view a firm's website are generally among the specialized informational resources required. Financial resources—the money required to start and maintain the firm and allow it to grow—usually reflect greater participation by individual entrepreneurs and investors willing to invest in a high-tech firm instead of conventional financial sources such as banks. In an effort to reduce the cost of specialized resources that are used in e-business, many firms have turned to outsourcing. **Outsourcing** is the process of finding outside vendors and suppliers to provide professional help, parts, or materials at a lower cost. For example, a firm that needs specialized software to complete a project may turn to an outside firm located in another part of Canada, the United States, India, or some Eastern European country.

Satisfying Needs Online

The Internet can be used to purchase products or services and as a source of information and interaction with other people. Today, more people use the Internet to satisfy these needs than ever before, and the number of people who use the Internet will continue to grow in the years to come

Let's consider two basic assumptions. First, the Internet has created some new customer needs that did not exist previously. Second, e-businesses can satisfy those needs, as well as more traditional ones. For example, Amazon.com gives customers anywhere in the world access to the same virtual store of books, DVDs, and CDs. And at eBay's global auction site, customers can, for a small fee, buy and sell almost anything. In each of these examples, customers can use the Internet to purchase a product or service.

Internet users also can access print media, such as newspapers and magazines, and radio and television programming at a time and place convenient to them. In addition to offering such a wide selection of content, the Internet provides the opportunity for *interaction*. In other words, communication is now an active two-way street between the online program and the viewer. CNN.com and other news-content sites encourage dialogue among viewers in chat rooms and exchanges with the writers of articles posted to the site. In contrast to the passive situation they encounter with traditional media such as television or radio, customers can respond to Internet programming by requesting more information about a product or posing specific questions, which may lead to purchasing a product or service.

Finally, the Internet allows customers to choose the content they are offered. For example, individuals can custom design daily online newspapers and magazines with articles that are of interest to them. Knowing what is of interest to a customer allows an Internet firm to direct appropriate, *smart advertising* to a specific customer. For example, someone wanting to read articles about the Toronto Blue Jays might be a potential customer for products and services related to baseball. For the advertiser, knowing that its advertisements are being directed to the most likely customers represents a better way to spend advertising dollars.

Call centres go global

When you call for technical support, the person on the other end of the phone may be in another country. The two technical support employees in this photo are located in Dakar, Senegal. Today, many firms have outsourced technical support, software development, and many other business activities to workers in nations with lower labour costs than in North America and Europe in order to reduce costs.

Creating e-Business Profit

While firms can't increase profits magically, they can increase their profits either by increasing sales revenue or by reducing expenses through a variety of e-business activities.

Increasing Sales Revenue Each source of sales revenue flowing into a firm is referred to as a **revenue stream.** One way to increase revenues is to sell merchandise on the Internet. Online merchants can reach a global customer base twenty-four hours a day, seven days a week because the opportunity to shop on the Internet is virtually unrestricted. And yet shifting revenues earned from customers inside a real store to revenues earned from those same customers online does not create any real new revenue for a firm. The goal is to find new customers and generate new sales so that total revenues are increased.

Intelligent informational systems also can help to generate sales revenue for Internet firms such as Amazon.com. Such systems store information about each customer's purchases, along with a variety of other information about the buyer's preferences.

revenue stream a source of revenue flowing into a firm

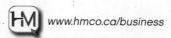

Using this information, the system can assist the customer the next time he or she visits the website. For example, if the customer has bought a Eva Avila or Ryan Malcolm CD in the past, the system might suggest CDs by similar artists who have appeared on the popular televised talent search program *Canadian Idol*.

While some customers in certain situations may not make a purchase online, the existence of the firm's website and the services and information it provides may lead to increased sales in the firm's physical stores. For example, Toyota.com can provide basic comparative information for shoppers so that they are better prepared for their visit to an automobile showroom.

In addition to selling products or services online, e-business revenue streams are created from advertising placed on web pages and subscription fees charged for access to online services and content. For example, Hoover's Online (**www.hoovers.com**), a comprehensive source for company and industry information, makes some of its online content free for anyone who visits the site, but more detailed data are available only by paid subscription. In addition, it receives revenue from companies that are called *sponsors*, who advertise their products and services on Hoover's website.

Many Internet firms that distribute news, magazine and newspaper articles, and similar content generate revenue primarily from advertising sponsors and commissions earned from sellers of products linked to the site. Online shopping malls, for example, now provide groups of related vendors of electronic equipment and computer hardware and software with a new method for selling their products and services. In many cases the vendors share online sales revenues with the site owners.

Reducing Expenses Reducing expenses is the second major way in which e-business can help to increase profitability. Providing online access to information customers want can reduce the cost of dealing with customers. For example, besides displaying seat availability and taking customer reservations on their websites, most airlines provide updated scheduling and pricing information, as well as promotional material. This reduces the costs of dealing with customers through a call centre operated by employees and of mailing brochures, which become outdated within weeks or are easily misplaced by customers. Sprint Nextel (www.sprint.com) is just one company that maintains an extensive website where potential customers can learn more about cell phone products and services and current customers can access personal account information, send e-mail questions to customer service, and purchase additional products or

Want to know something about Sprint?

To reduce the cost of staffing and operating stores, Sprint has developed an extensive website that enables customers to obtain current information and purchase the products and services that this telecommunications company offers.

services. With such extensive online services, SprintPCS does not have to maintain as many physical store locations as it would without these online services. We examine more examples of how e-business contributes to profitability throughout this chapter, especially as we focus on some of the business models for activity on the Internet.

Fundamental Models of e-Business

Learning Objective ❼
Describe the fundamental models of e-business.

One way to get a better sense of how businesses are adapting to the opportunities available on the Internet is to identify e-business models. A **business model** represents a group of common characteristics and methods of doing business to generate sales revenues and reduce expenses. Each of the models discussed below represents a primary e-business model. All the models focus on the identity of a firm's customers.

Business-to-Business (B2B) Model

Many e-businesses can be distinguished from others simply by their customer focus. For instance, some firms use the Internet mainly to conduct business with other businesses. These firms generally are referred to as having a **business-to-business, or B2B, model.** Currently, the vast majority of e-business is B2B in nature.

When examining B2B business firms, two clear types emerge. In the first type, the focus is simply on facilitating sales transactions between businesses. For example, Dell manufactures computers to specifications that customers enter on the Dell website. The vast majority of Dell's online orders are from corporate clients who are well informed about the products they need and are looking for fairly priced, high-quality computer products that will be delivered quickly. By building only what is ordered, Dell reduces storage and carrying costs and rarely is stuck with unsold inventory. By dealing directly with Dell, customers eliminate costs associated with wholesalers and retailers, thereby helping to reduce the price they pay for equipment.

A second, more complex type of B2B model involves a company and its suppliers. Today, suppliers use the Internet to bid on products and services they wish to sell to a customer, learn about the customer's rules and procedures that must be followed. For example, both General Motors and Ford. Given the potential savings, it is no wonder that many other manufacturers and their suppliers are beginning to use the same kind of B2B systems that are used by the automakers.

business model represents a group of common characteristics and methods of doing business to generate sales revenues and reduce expenses

business-to-business (B2B) model firms that conduct business with other businesses

Business-to-Consumer (B2C) Model

In contrast to the B2B model, firms such as Amazon and eBay clearly are focused on individual buyers and so are referred to as having a **business-to-consumer,** or **B2C, model.** In a B2C situation, understanding how consumers behave online is critical to a firm's success. Typically, a business firm that uses a B2C model must answer the following questions:

* Will consumers use websites merely to simplify and speed up comparison shopping?
* Will customers purchase services and products online or end up buying at a traditional retail store?
* What sorts of products and services are best suited for online consumer shopping?
* Which products and services are simply not good choices at this stage of online development?

In addition to providing round-the-clock global access to all kinds of products and services, B2C firms often make a special effort to build long-term relationships with their customers. Often firms attempt to make sure that the customer is satisfied and that problems, if any, are quickly solved. While a "little special attention" may increase the cost of doing business for a B2C firm, the customer's repeated purchases will repay the investment many times over.

Today, B2B and B2C models are the most popular business models for e-business. And yet, there are other business models that perform specialized e-business activities to generate revenues. Most of the business models described in Table 4.3 are modified versions of the B2B and B2C models.

Table 4.3

Other Business Models That Perform Specialized e-Business Activities

Although modified versions of B2B or B2C, the following business models perform specialized e-business activities to generate revenues:	
Advertising e-business model	Advertisements that are displayed on a firm's website in return for a fee. Examples include pop-up and banner advertisements on search engines and other popular Internet sites.
Brokerage e-business model	Online marketplaces where buyers and sellers are brought together to facilitate exchange of goods and services. Examples include eBay (www.ebay.com), which provides a site for buying and selling virtually anything.
Consumer-to-consumer model	Peer-to-peer software that allows individuals to share information over the Internet. Examples include Morpheus (www.morpheus.com), which allows users to exchange audio, documents, photos, or video files.
Subscription and pay-per-view e-business models	Content that is available only to users who pay a fee to gain access to a website. Examples include investment information provided by Standard & Poor's (www.standardandpoors.com) and business research provided by Forrester Research, Inc. (www.forrester.com).

Creating an e-Business Plan

Learning Objective 8

Understand the factors that influence an e-business plan.

The approach taken to creating an e-business plan will depend on whether you are establishing a new Internet business or adding an online component to an existing business. In this section we consider some important factors that affect both situations.

Starting Up a New Internet Business from Scratch

For a new Internet business, a good e-business plan should provide detailed answers to basic questions. To begin, the planners need to determine if an Internet business will meet the needs of customers. Furthermore, the planning process should provide information that can help to identify and select groups of potential buyers, direct development of the online product or service, as well as the promotion, pricing, and distribution effort. The start-up planning also should indicate whether the potential market will generate enough sales and profits to make the new venture worthwhile. The answers to these questions will determine what type of business model (B2B, B2C, or one of the specialized models described in Table 4.3) is appropriate for the new Internet business. Sometimes more than one business model is appropriate. For example, British children's author J. K. Rowling used the Internet to launch her international marketing effort for *Harry Potter and the Deathly Hallows*. Although mainly intended as a promotional effort to both bookstores and consumers, the website used both a B2B model and a B2C model. Eventually, many of these sales took place through Amazon.com and Barnesandnoble.com as customers ordered online and had the books shipped as gifts to children for their summertime reading enjoyment.

Building an Online Presence for an Existing Business

A business that already has a physical location and a customer base often looks at e-business as a way to expand sales to current customers and to add new customers who are beyond the reach of the firm's geographic location. For example, retail firms such as Radio Shack, Sears, and many others have turned to the Internet to sell more products or to lead customers to physical stores in order to purchase products or services. Both customers who are seeking the convenience of shopping online and those who are simply using the website to view a retailer's merchandise and promotions before buying in a retail store can use the firm's website to satisfy their personal shopping needs. Although developing an online presence may seem like a logical extension of what a firm already does, there are important factors that must be considered before using the Internet to sell products or services or to provide information to customers. To see how starting a new Internet business differs from building an online presence for an existing business, look at Figure 4.7.

www.hmco.ca/business

Figure 4.7

Planning for a New Internet Business or Building an Online Presence for an Existing Business

The approach taken to creating an e-business plan will depend on whether you are establishing a new Internet business or adding an online component to an existing business.

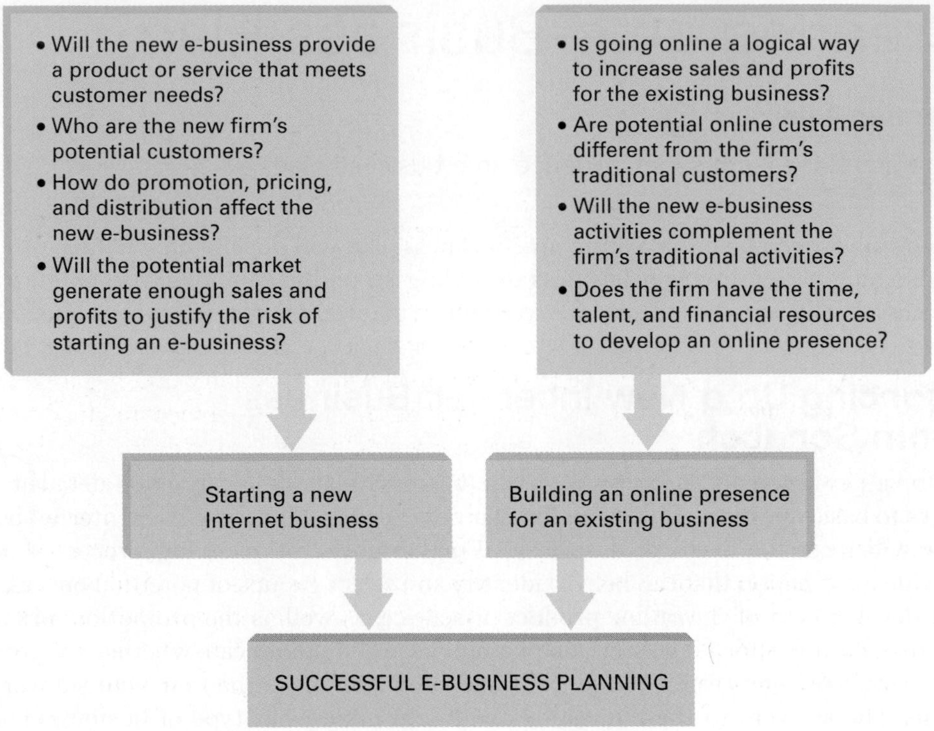

- Will the new e-business provide a product or service that meets customer needs?
- Who are the new firm's potential customers?
- How do promotion, pricing, and distribution affect the new e-business?
- Will the potential market generate enough sales and profits to justify the risk of starting an e-business?

- Is going online a logical way to increase sales and profits for the existing business?
- Are potential online customers different from the firm's traditional customers?
- Will the new e-business activities complement the firm's traditional activities?
- Does the firm have the time, talent, and financial resources to develop an online presence?

Starting a new Internet business

Building an online presence for an existing business

SUCCESSFUL E-BUSINESS PLANNING

Complexity and Time Concerns   Every business must be prepared to allow sufficient time for customers, suppliers, and staff to adapt to the new e-business methods. Online solutions such as introducing e-mail or a simple company website to help the staff to communicate better with one another, customers, and suppliers can be developed and installed quickly without undue delay, cost, or disruption of current work responsibilities. However, as the complexity of the plan increases, so too does the amount of time (and money) required to design, install, and test the new technology—and then to train the staff to use it. All this is further complicated by the need to educate customers and suppliers, who will be expected to change to a new method of placing orders, making requests for information, and other typical business activities. Internet banking, for instance, has grown in popularity, but it takes time for customers to get used to the procedures required to bank online. A strong customer-support system is critical to help customers who may be confused about the online screen options, computer and connection problems, security, and anything else with which they may need assistance.

The Future of e-Business: Growth, Opportunities, and Challenges

Learning Objective 9

Explore the growth trends, future opportunities, and challenges of e-business.

Since the beginning of commercial activity on the Internet, developments in e-business have been rapid and formidable with spectacular successes such as eBay, Google, and Yahoo!. However, the slowdown in e-business activity that began in 2000 caused a shakeout of excessive optimism in this new-business environment. By 2003, most firms involved in e-business used a more intelligent approach to development. Today, we can safely say that the long-term view held by the vast majority of analysts is that the Internet will continue to expand along with related technologies. For example, according to Forrester Research, Inc., the popularity and growth of consumer broadband access to the Internet have pushed marketers to allocate more money to advertising on-line in order to reach customers who are moving to the web and away from traditional media such as television and radio. As a result, Forrester predicts that by 2010, more than $26 billion, or about 8 percent of all advertising spending, will be online.[4]

Internet Growth Potential

To date, only a small percentage of the global population uses the Internet. Current estimates suggest that about one billion of the six billion people in the world use the web, and only about 60 percent of them are active users. Clearly, there is much more growth opportunity. An estimated 22 million of Canada's 31 million people use the Internet regularly—a high proportion that is comparable to other countries with modern communications systems. Americans comprise 20 percent of all users—the largest group online.[5] Of the almost 300 million people making up the American population, 185 million use the Internet—140 million actively. And like Canadians, more than 40 percent of Americans enjoy fast broadband access at home, suggesting future development of more online activity requiring high-speed service such as downloading entertainment content and games.[6]

Even with any future economic downturn, the Internet will continue to offer great opportunities for growth. Firms that adapt existing business models to an online

It's a small world after all.

Padmasree Warrior and Anson Chen, two Motorola executives, show off a new cell phone that has all the latest technological features at a press conference in Bangalore, India. Motorola, a leader in telecommunications, realizes that it must manufacture products for a global market: If it doesn't, a competitor will.

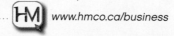

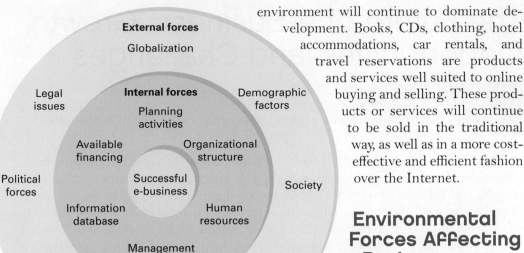

environment will continue to dominate development. Books, CDs, clothing, hotel accommodations, car rentals, and travel reservations are products and services well suited to online buying and selling. These products or services will continue to be sold in the traditional way, as well as in a more cost-effective and efficient fashion over the Internet.

Environmental Forces Affecting e-Business

Although the environmental forces at work are complex, it is useful to think of them as either internal or external forces that affect an e-business. Internal environmental forces are those that are closely associated with the actions and decisions taking place within a firm. As shown in Figure 4.8, typical internal forces include a firm's planning activities, organization structure, human resources, management decisions, information database, and available financing. For example, a shortage of skilled employees needed for a specialized project can undermine a firm's ability to sell its services to clients. Unlike the external environmental forces affecting the firm, internal forces such as this one are more likely to be under the direct control of management. In this case, management can either hire the needed staff or choose to pass over a prospective project.

In contrast, external environmental forces are factors affecting e-business planning that originate from outside the organization. These forces are unlikely to be controllable by an e-business firm. Instead, managers and employees of an e-business firm generally will react to these forces, attempting to shield the organization from any undue negative effects and finding ways to take advantage of opportunities in the ever-changing e-business environment. The primary external environmental forces affecting e-business planning include globalization, society, demographic, economic, competitive, technological, and political and legal forces.

This chapter has presented an overview of information and the fast-paced, emerging world of e-business. Throughout this book you will find more references and examples to both information and e-business as they apply to the different aspects of business, such as management, marketing, and finance. In Chapters 5 and 6 we examine issues related to forms of business ownership and special considerations surrounding small business.

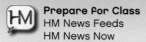

Prepare For Class
HM News Feeds
HM News Now

→ **RETURN TO INSIDE BUSINESS**

Gathering information about customer content selections that are downloaded to their mobile devices can help firms better develop strategies for marketing these products. For example, by knowing that 70 percent of customers who have downloaded one song have also downloaded another, the firm can make an intelligent suggestion to the customer who is looking for advice about which song would be most interesting to him.

Questions

1. How could this information be used to increase revenues and profits?

2. Is the investment in software to keep track of and analyze customer behaviour online really worth it? Why?

CHAPTER REVIEW

1 **Examine how information can reduce risk when making a decision.**

The more information a manager has, the less risk there is that a decision will be incorrect. Information produces knowledge and empowers managers and employees to make better decisions. Because of the volume of information they receive each day and their need to make decisions on a daily basis, business people use information rules to shorten the time spent analyzing choices. Information rules emerge when business research confirms the same results each time it studies the same or a similar set of circumstances.

2 **Discuss management's information requirements.**

A management information system (MIS) is a means of providing managers with the information they need to perform their jobs as effectively as possible. The purpose of an MIS is to distribute timely and useful information from both internal and external sources to the decision makers who need it. The specific types of information managers need depend on their area of management and level within the firm. The size and complexity of an MIS must be tailored to the information needs of the organization it serves.

3 **Outline the five functions of an information system.**

The five functions performed by an MIS system are collecting data, storing data, updating data, processing data into information, and presenting information to users. Data can be collected from such internal sources as company records, reports, and minutes of meetings, as well as from the firm's managers. External sources include customers, suppliers, bankers, trade and financial publications, industry conferences, online computer services, and information-gathering organizations.

4 **Describe how the Internet helps employees to make decisions and communicate, assists a firm's sales force, and recruits and trains employees.**

Today, many employees use computers and the Internet to improve productivity. Three applications—decision-support systems, executive information systems, and expert systems—can help managers and employees to speed and improve the decision-making process. Another application in the workplace is electronic mail, or simply e-mail, which provides for communication within and outside the firm at any time, twenty-four hours a day, seven days a week. An extension of e-mail is groupware, which is software that facilitates the management of large projects among geographically dispersed employees as well as such group activities as problem solving and brainstorming. The Internet and a sales force automation software program can provide a database of information that can be used to assist a sales representative. The Internet also can be used to improve employee recruitment and training and recruitment while lowering costs. Business application software has been developed to satisfy almost every business need.

5 **Analyze how computers and technology change the way information is acquired, organized, and used.**

We live in an information society—one in which large groups of employees generate or depend on information to perform their jobs. To find needed information, many businesses and individuals use the Internet. The Internet is a worldwide network of computers linked through telecommunications. Firms also can use an intranet to distribute information within the firm. Both the Internet and intranets are examples of a computer network. A computer network is a group of two or more computers linked together to allow users to share data and information. Today, two basic types—local-area networks (LANs) and wide-area networks (WAN)—affect the way employees and the general public obtain data and information. Because of standardization, it is possible to use the Internet to access websites, search engines, and web pages to obtain a wealth of information with the click of a computer's mouse.

6 **Explain the meaning of e-business.**

e-Business, or electronic business, can be defined as the organized effort of individuals to produce and sell, for a profit, the products and services that satisfy society's needs *through the facilities available on the Internet.* The term *e-business* refers to all business activities and practices conducted on the Internet by an individual firm or the general concept of e-business. The human, material, information, and financial resources that any business requires are highly specialized for e-business. In an effort to reduce the cost of e-business resources, many firms have turned to outsourcing. Using e-business activities, it is possible to satisfy new customer needs created by the Internet as well as traditional ones in unique ways. Meeting customer needs is especially important when an e-business is trying to earn profits by increasing sales and reducing expenses. Each source of revenue flowing into the firm is referred to as a *revenue stream.*

7 **Describe the fundamental models of e-business.**

e-Business models focus attention on the identity of a firm's customers. Firms that use the Internet mainly to conduct business with other businesses generally are referred to as having a business-to-business, or B2B, model. Currently, the vast majority of e-business is B2B in nature. When examining B2B business firms, two clear types emerge. In the first type of B2B, the focus is simply on facilitating sales transactions between businesses. A second, more complex type of the B2B model involves a company and its suppliers. Firms such as Amazon and eBay clearly are focused on individual consumers and so are referred to as having a business-to-consumer, or B2C, model. In a B2C situation, understanding how consumers behave online is critical to the firm's success.

8 **Understand the factors that influence an e-business plan.**

For a new Internet business, a good e-business plan should provide detailed answers to basic questions about potential customers and their needs. Once the answers and initial research have been completed, it is time to choose a business model. Options include the B2B model, the B2C model, or one of the specialized models. A business that already has a physical location and a customer base generally looks at e-business as a way to expand sales to current customers and to add new customers who are beyond the reach of the firm's geographic location.

9 **Explore the growth trends, future opportunities, and challenges of e-business.**

Since the advent of commercial activity on the Internet, developments in e-business have been rapid and formidable. The long-term view held by the vast majority of analysts is that the Internet will continue to expand along with related technologies. Although the environmental forces at work are complex, it is useful to think of them as either internal or external forces that affect an e-business. Internal environmental forces are those that are closely associated with the actions and decisions taking place within a firm. In contrast, external environmental forces are those factors affecting an e-business originating outside an organization.

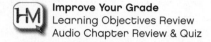

Improve Your Grade
Learning Objectives Review
Audio Chapter Review & Quiz

Review Questions

1. In your own words, describe how information and information rules reduces risk when you make a personal or work-related decision.
2. What is the difference between data and information? Give one example of accounting data and one example of accounting information.
3. How do the information requirements of managers differ by management area?
4. Why must a management information system (MIS) be tailored to the needs of the organization it serves?
5. List five functions of an MIS.
6. What are the differences among the mean, median, and mode of a set of data? How can a few extremely small or large numbers affect the mean?
7. What are the components of a typical business report?
8. Describe how the Internet and software can help a firm's employees make decisions and recruit and train employees.
9. How do e-businesses generate revenue streams?
10. What are the two fundamental e-business models?
11. How do internal and external forces change the way an e-business operates?

Discussion Questions

1. Do managers really need all the kinds of information discussed in this chapter? If not, which kinds can they do without?
2. How can confidential data and information (such as the wages of individual employees) be kept confidential and yet still be available to managers who need them?
3. Why are computers so well suited to management information systems (MISs)? What are some things computers *cannot* do in dealing with data and information?
4. Is outsourcing good for an e-business firm? the firm's employees? Explain your answer.
5. Do you think that the Internet will continue to grow as fast as it has in the past? Why?

CASE STUDY

Travelocity Takes e-Business a Long Way

One of the original online travel agency sites, Travelocity, has been bookmarked by millions of people seeking low prices on airline tickets, hotel rooms, cruises, and rental cars. The site books $5 billion worth of travel annually to destinations near and far. Customers can search for flights on six major carriers, read descriptions before reserving at one of 20,000 participating hotels, compare car-rental prices, and click to browse and buy specially priced travel packages.

Intense competition from Expedia and other online rivals has prompted Travelocity to find new ways of differentiating itself and keeping customers loyal. CEO Michelle Peluso says that the company is particularly interested in crating "an emotional connection with customers, one that builds more trust and bookings." Instead of focusing solely on low prices, Travelocity has invested $80 million in its "Roaming Gnome" multimedia ad campaign. The colourful garden gnome attracts attention in a crowded marketplace. It also brings personality and humour to the message that Travelocity stands for the whole travel experience, not just low prices.

In addition, the site has posted a Customer Bill of Rights guaranteeing customers that "everything about your booking will be right, or we'll work with our partners to make it right and right away." Although many e-businesses offer customer service by live chat, e-mail, and FAQ (frequently asked questions) pages, Travelocity encourages customers to call if something goes wrong with their travel arrangements so that company representatives can fix the problem. Peluso observes that customers whose problems are resolved satisfactorily have a 90 percent return rate, compared with an 80 percent rate for customers who have a good experience.

Not long ago, Travelocity had the opportunity to put the spotlight on its guarantee when it posted a superlow airfare for flights to Fiji. The rock-bottom price was supposed to apply to companion tickets only, but because the fare was posted in error, travelers were unsure initially whether Travelocity really would issue the tickets. The company decided to honour the fare, despite the mistake, to prove its commitment to taking care of customers. This brought a lot of positive media coverage, further enhancing Travelocity's reputation.

The company recently redesigned its website so that customers can find exactly what they want and have more tools for planning all aspects of a trip. For example, customers can buy tickets to city tours, price travel insurance, buy gift certificates, check flight status, read about different destinations, and read what travelers have to say about the hotels.

Travelocity operates a number of other travel sites, including holidayautos.com, lastminute.com, showtickets.com, and site59.com. The company has been branching out into corporate travel services and specialized travel sites for international markets. It also provides travel services for the members of AARP and other organizations. Where in the world will Travelocity's Roaming Gnome turn up next?[7]

For more information about this company, go to www.travelocity.com.

Questions:

1. Each year Travelocity helps millions of customers find low prices on airline tickets, hotel rooms, cruises, and rental cars by providing a website that is easy to use. What type of business model is Travelocity using? Support your answer.

2. Today, competition between Internet travel firms such as Travelocity, Expedia, and other online travel agencies has never been greater. What steps has Travelocity taken to retain its market share and increase revenues and profits?

3. Why would Travelocity publicize the availability of telephone customer service when higher call volume raises the company's costs?

BUILDING SKILLS FOR CAREER SUCCESS

1. Exploring the Internet

Computer technology is a fast-paced, highly competitive industry in which product life cycles sometimes are measured in months or even weeks. To keep up with changes and trends in hardware and software, MIS managers routinely must scan computer publications and websites that discuss new products.

A major topic of interest among MIS managers is groupware, software that facilitates the management of large projects among geographically dispersed employees, as well as group activities such as problem solving and brainstorming.

Assignment

1. Use a search engine and enter the keyword *groupware* to locate companies that provide this type of software. Try the demonstration edition of the groupware if it is available.

2. Based on your research of this business application, why do you think groupware is growing in popularity?

3. Describe the structure of one of the groupware programs you examined as well as your impressions of its value to users.

2. Building Team Skills

An interesting approach taken by Yahoo.com and several other websites is to provide viewers with the tools needed to create a personal web page or community. Yahoo's GeoCities site (http://geocities.yahoo.com) provides simple instructions for creating a site and posting your own content, such as articles and photographs.

Assignment

1. Working in a group, examine some of the GeoCities communities and personal web pages. Discuss which sites you think work well and which do not. Explain your reasoning.

2. Develop an idea for your own website. Draw a sketch of how you would like the site to appear on the Internet. You can use ideas that look good on other personal pages.

3. Who is your target audience, and why do you think they will want to visit the site?

3. Researching Different Careers

Firms today expect employees to be proficient in using computers and computer software. Typical business applications include e-mail, word processing, spreadsheets, and graphics. By improving your skills in these areas, you can increase your chances not only of being employed but also of being promoted once you are employed.

Assignment

1. Assess your computer skills by placing a check in the appropriate column in the following table:

Skill Level				
SOFTWARE	NONE	LOW	AVERAGE	HIGH
Word Processing				
Desktop Publishing				
Accounting				
Database management				
Graphics				
Spreadsheet				
Groupware				

2. Describe your self-assessment in a written report. Specify the software programs in which you need to become more proficient, and outline a plan for doing this.

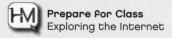
Prepare for Class
Exploring the Internet

CHAPTER 5

Choosing a Form of Business Ownership

Your Guide to Success in Business

Why this chapter matters
There's a good chance that during your lifetime you will work for a business or even start your own business.

LEARNING OBJECTIVES

1. Describe the advantages and disadvantages of sole proprietorships.

2. Explain the different types of partners and the importance of partnership agreements.

3. Describe the advantages and disadvantages of partnerships.

4. Summarize how a corporation is formed.

5. Describe the advantages and disadvantages of a corporation.

6. Examine special types of corporations, including government-owned corporations and not-for-profit corporations.

7. Discuss the purpose of a cooperative, joint venture, and syndicate.

8. Explain how growth from within and growth through mergers can enable a business to expand.

Canadian Tire Stores—
From Humble Beginnings

From coast to coast to coast, throughout Canada, the venerable Canadian Tire Corporation is a retailing institution. About 85 percent of Canadians live within a 15-minute drive of a store and more than 10,000 of them have their cars serviced there each and every day. Canadian Tire is visited by 40 percent of the adult population at least once a week making it the most visited non-grocery retailer in the country. Not surprising, Canadian Tire is the top national retailer in gardening, home appliances, home-improvement products and power tools, not to mention auto parts and accessories. Today, there are 430 associated dealer and corporate owned stores across Canada employing over 28,000 people.

But it wasn't always this way. Hard though it may be to image, in 1922 there were only about 200,000 automobiles in Ontario when brothers John W. and Alfred J. Billes bought the Hamilton Tire & Garage Ltd. in Toronto. Just at the time that Canadians began thinking about the automobile as a serious form of personal transportation, the Billes brothers provided parts, repair service, storage in the winter and fuel to keep local motorists on the move. As the popularity of automobile ownership soared, companies like Canadian Tire competed for the attention of customers who would need services for their automobile and farm vehicles. The Canadian Tire Corporation has grown tremendously and over the years has become an auto, sports, leisure, and home products retail centre.

The Canadian Tire catalogue, which was first introduced in 1928 to reach customers in rural and remote areas of the country, is so popular today that nine million copies are printed each year. Perhaps the only thing more appreciated by Canadians when they need to get something for their house than the convenience of their local Canadian Tire store or catalogue is finding a stack of Canadian Tire money in their glove compartment. First introduced in 1961 to reward cash paying customers and increase return visits, Canadian Tire money has proven to be an enormous customer-loyalty plan success.

continued on next page
● ● ●

DID YOU KNOW?

Canadian retailing giants like the T. Eaton Co. and Simpson's Co. have come and gone from the competitive landscape. Smart strategic responses to the changing retail market have ensured the success of Canadian Tire Corp.

K E Y   T E R M S

sole proprietorship (138)
unlimited liability (140)
partnership (141)
general partner (141)
general partnership (141)
limited partner (142)
limited partnership (142)
corporation (145)

stock (145)
stockholder (145)
private corporation (146)
public corporation (146)
corporate charter (147)
common stock (147)
preferred stock (147)
dividend (148)

proxy (148)
board of directors (148)
corporate officers (149)
limited liability (149)
government-owned corporation (152)
not-for-profit corporation (152)
cooperative (154)

joint venture (154)
syndicate (154)
merger (156)
hostile takeover (156)
tender offer (156)
proxy fight (156)
leveraged buyout (LBO) (159)

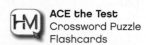

ACE the Test
Crossword Puzzle
Flashcards

Today, Canadian Tire Stores in major city centres and regional shopping malls bear little resemblance to the small retailer that seemed to show up in every small town across Canada selling provincial hunting and fishing licenses and sports gear. The pace of store renovations has been accelerated to attract more shoppers after early results pointed to quick acceptance by customers of the new look and product selections in stores. The introduction of financial services, such as bank savings accounts, guaranteed investment certificates, credit cards and mortgages, as well as the acquisition of Marks Work Warehouse casual clothing shops has further helped position the firm for future revenue growth. As customers continue to respond to new, larger store formats, Canadian Tire earnings and profits reach ever higher levels. In 2005, gross revenues rose to $7.8 billion, doubling in five years, and profits increased more than 13 % over the previous year to $330 million. From humble beginnings, the small Billes family enterprise has grown over the years to become the huge Canadian franchise corporation we recognize today.

Source: Based on information available on the Canadian Tire Corporation website accessed December 03, 2006, http://www2.canadiantire.ca/.

There are a variety of reasons business people choose to operate under one of several legally recognized forms of business and, from time-to-time, even decide to change to another. The type of legal structure and organization that is right for a particular business depends on a number of factors that will be discussed in this chapter. We begin this chapter by describing the three common forms of business ownership: sole proprietorships, partnerships, and corporations. We discuss how these types of businesses are formed and note the advantages and disadvantages of each. Next, we consider several types of business ownership usually chosen for special purposes, including government-owned corporations, not-for-profit corporations, and cooperatives. We conclude the chapter with a discussion of how businesses can grow through internal expansion or through mergers with other companies.

Sole Proprietorships

Learning Objective ❶

Describe the advantages and disadvantages of sole proprietorships.

sole proprietorship a business that is owned (and usually operated) by one person

A **sole proprietorship** is a business that is owned (and usually operated) by one person. Although a few sole proprietorships are large and have many employees, most are small. Sole proprietorship is the simplest form of business ownership and the easiest to start. In most instances, the owner (the *sole* proprietor) simply decides that he or she is in business and begins operations. Many retirees and executives seeking new employment readily identify themselves as consultants and typically set themselves up as sole proprietors.

Although it is difficult to know how many true sole proprietors there are in business, Statistics Canada estimates there were over 2.5 million Canadians actively self-employed in 2005, out of a total labour force of about 16.1 million, representing about 15 percent. This is a far cry from the 25 percent level of the 1930s when agriculture dominated the Canadian economy but a substantial increase from the 7 percent range of the 1970s.[1] Sole proprietorships are most common in retailing, service businesses like snow removal and landscaping, and fishing and agriculture.

Advantages of Sole Proprietorships

Most of the advantages of sole proprietorships arise from the two main characteristics of this form of ownership: simplicity and individual control.

Ease of Start-up and Closure Sole proprietorship is the simplest and cheapest way to start a business. Often, start-up requires no contracts, agreements, or other legal documents. Thus a sole proprietorship can be, and most often is, established without the services of an attorney. The legal requirements often are limited to registering the name of the business and obtaining any necessary licenses or permits.

If the enterprise does not succeed, the firm can be closed as easily as it was opened. Creditors must be paid, of course, but generally, the owner does not have to go through any legal procedure before hanging up an "Out of Business" sign.

Pride of Ownership A successful sole proprietor is often very proud of her or his accomplishments—and rightfully so. In almost every case the owner deserves a great deal of credit for assuming the risks and solving the day-to-day problems associated with operating sole proprietorships. Unfortunately, the reverse is also true. When the business fails, it is often the sole proprietor who is to blame.

Retention of All Profits Because all profits become the personal earnings of the owner, the owner has a strong incentive to succeed. This direct financial reward attracts many entrepreneurs to the sole proprietorship form of business and, if the business succeeds, is a source of great satisfaction.

Flexibility of Being Your Own Boss A sole proprietor is completely free to make decisions about the firm's operations. Without asking or waiting for anyone's approval, a sole proprietor can switch from retailing to wholesaling, move a shop's location, open a new store, or close an old one. Suppose that the sole proprietor of an appliance store finds that many customers now prefer to shop on Sunday afternoons. He or she can make an immediate change in business hours to take advantage of this information (provided that local laws allow such stores to open on Sunday). The manager of a store in a large corporate chain such as Best Buy Company may have to seek the approval of numerous managers and company officials before making such a change.

No Special Taxes Profits earned by a sole proprietorship are taxed as the personal income of the owner. As a result, sole proprietors must report certain financial information on their personal tax returns and make estimated quarterly tax payments to the federal and provincial governments. Thus a sole proprietorship does not pay any separate income taxes that corporations pay.

Disadvantages of Sole Proprietorships

The disadvantages of a sole proprietorship stem from the fact that these businesses are owned by one person. Some capable sole proprietors experience no problems. Individuals who start out with few management skills and little money are most at risk for failure.

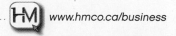

unlimited liability a legal concept that holds a business owner personally responsible for all the debts of the business

Unlimited Liability Unlimited liability is a legal concept that holds a business owner personally responsible for all the debts of the business. There is legally no difference between the debts of the business and the debts of the proprietor. If the business fails, or if the business is involved in a lawsuit and loses, the owner's personal property—including savings and other assets—can be seized (and sold if necessary) to pay creditors.

Unlimited liability is perhaps the major factor that tends to discourage would-be entrepreneurs with substantial personal wealth from using this form of business organization.

Lack of Continuity Legally, the sole proprietor *is* the business. If the owner retires, dies, or is declared legally incompetent, the business essentially ceases to exist. In many cases, however—especially when the business is a profitable enterprise—the owner's heirs take it over and either sell it or continue to operate it. The business also can suffer if the sole proprietor becomes ill and cannot work for an extended period of time. If the owner, for example, has a heart attack, there is often no one who can step in and manage the business. An illness can be devastating if the sole proprietor's personal skills are what determine if the business is a success or a failure.

Lack of Money Banks, suppliers, and other lenders usually are unwilling to lend large sums of money to sole proprietorships. Only one person—the sole proprietor—can be held responsible for repaying such loans, and the assets of most sole proprietors usually are limited. Moreover, these assets may have been used already as the basis for personal borrowing (a home mortgage or car loan) or for short-term credit from suppliers. Lenders also worry about the lack of continuity of sole proprietorships: Who will repay a loan if the sole proprietor dies? Finally, many lenders are concerned about the large number of sole proprietorships that fail—a topic discussed in Chapter 6.

The limited ability to borrow money can prevent a sole proprietorship from growing. It is the main reason that many business owners, when in need of relatively large amounts of capital, change from a sole proprietorship to a partnership or corporate form of ownership.

Limited Management Skills The sole proprietor is often the sole manager—in addition to being the only salesperson, buyer, accountant, and, on occasion, janitor. Even the most experienced business owner is unlikely to have expertise in all these areas. Consequently, unless he or she obtains the necessary expertise by hiring employees, assistants, or consultants, the business can suffer in the areas in which the owner is less knowledgeable. For the many sole proprietors

▲

Once a sole proprietor, now a corporation

Ayisha Bennett began her career as a fashion designer as a sole proprietorship. Now, after phenomenal success designing clothing that is not only trend setting but also comfortable, her company, Envi, is incorporated.

who cannot hire the help they need, there just are not enough hours in the day to do everything that needs to be done.

Difficulty in Hiring Employees The sole proprietor may find it hard to attract and keep competent help. Potential employees may feel that there is no room for advancement in a firm whose owner assumes all managerial responsibilities. And when those who *are* hired are ready to take on added responsibility, they may find that the only way to do so is to quit the sole proprietorship and go to work for a larger firm or start up their own businesses. The lure of higher salaries and increased benefits can also cause existing employees to change jobs.

Beyond the Sole Proprietorship

Like many others, you may decide that the major disadvantage of a sole proprietorship is the limited amount that one person can do in a workday. One way to reduce the effect of this disadvantage (and retain many of the advantages) is to have more than one owner.

Partnerships

Learning Objective

Explain the different types of partners and the importance of partnership agreements.

A person who would not think of starting and running a business alone may enthusiastically seize the opportunity to enter into a business partnership. A **partnership** is a voluntary association of two or more persons to act as co-owners of a business for profit. Although there is no legal maximum on the number of partners a partnership may have, most have only two. Large accounting, law, and advertising partnerships, however, are likely to have multiple partners. Regardless of the number of people involved, a partnership often represents a pooling of special managerial skills and talents; at other times, it is the result of a sole proprietor's taking on a partner for the purpose of obtaining more capital.

partnership a voluntary association of two or more persons to act as co-owners of a business for profit

Types of Partners

All partners are not necessarily equal. Some may be active in running the business, whereas others may have a limited role.

General Partners A **general partner** is a person who assumes full or shared responsibility for operating a business. General partners are active in day-to-day business operations, and each partner can enter into contracts on behalf of the other partners. He or she also assumes unlimited liability for all debts, including debts incurred by any other general partner without his or her knowledge or consent. A **general partnership** is a business co-owned by two or more general partners who are liable for everything the business does. To avoid future liability, a general partner who withdraws from the partnership must give notice to creditors, customers, and suppliers.

general partner a person who assumes full or shared responsibility for operating a business

general partnership a business co-owned by two or more general partners who are liable for everything the business does

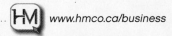

limited partner a person who contributes capital to a business but has no management responsibility or liability for losses beyond the amount he or she invested in the partnership

limited partnership a business co-owned by one or more general partners who manage the business and limited partners who invest money in it

Limited Partners A limited partner is a person who contributes capital to a business but who has no management responsibility or liability for losses beyond his or her investment in the partnership. A limited partnership is a business co-owned by one or more general partners who manage the business and limited partners who invest money in it.

The Partnership Agreement

Articles of partnership are an agreement listing and explaining the terms of the partnership. Although both oral and written partnership agreements are legal and can be enforced in the courts, a written agreement has an obvious advantage: It is not subject to lapses of memory.

Figure 5.1 shows a typical partnership agreement. The partnership agreement should state who will make the final decisions, what each partner's duties will be, and

Figure 5.1

Articles of Partnership

Articles of partnership is a written or oral agreement that lists and explains the terms of a partnership.

Source: Adapted from Goldman and Sigismond, *Business Law,* 5th edition. Boston: Houghton Mifflin, 2004. Copyright © 2004 by Houghton Mifflin Company. Reprinted with permission.

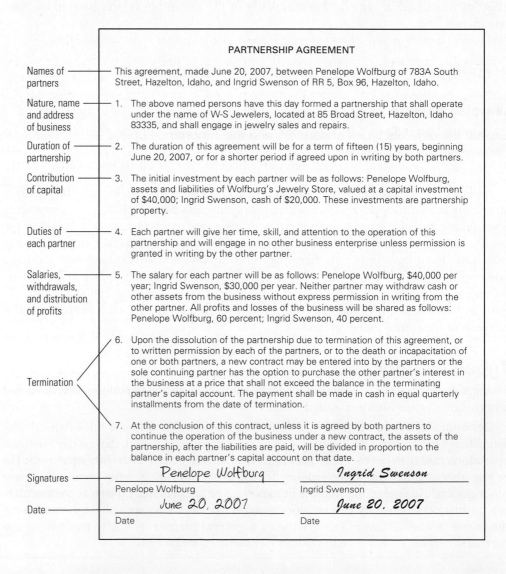

PARTNERSHIP AGREEMENT

Names of partners — This agreement, made June 20, 2007, between Penelope Wolfburg of 783A South Street, Hazelton, Idaho, and Ingrid Swenson of RR 5, Box 96, Hazelton, Idaho.

Nature, name and address of business — 1. The above named persons have this day formed a partnership that shall operate under the name of W-S Jewelers, located at 85 Broad Street, Hazelton, Idaho 83335, and shall engage in jewelry sales and repairs.

Duration of partnership — 2. The duration of this agreement will be for a term of fifteen (15) years, beginning June 20, 2007, or for a shorter period if agreed upon in writing by both partners.

Contribution of capital — 3. The initial investment by each partner will be as follows: Penelope Wolfburg, assets and liabilities of Wolfburg's Jewelry Store, valued at a capital investment of $40,000; Ingrid Swenson, cash of $20,000. These investments are partnership property.

Duties of each partner — 4. Each partner will give her time, skill, and attention to the operation of this partnership and will engage in no other business enterprise unless permission is granted in writing by the other partner.

Salaries, withdrawals, and distribution of profits — 5. The salary for each partner will be as follows: Penelope Wolfburg, $40,000 per year; Ingrid Swenson, $30,000 per year. Neither partner may withdraw cash or other assets from the business without express permission in writing from the other partner. All profits and losses of the business will be shared as follows: Penelope Wolfburg, 60 percent; Ingrid Swenson, 40 percent.

6. Upon the dissolution of the partnership due to termination of this agreement, or to written permission by each of the partners, or to the death or incapacitation of one or both partners, a new contract may be entered into by the partners or the sole continuing partner has the option to purchase the other partner's interest in the business at a price that shall not exceed the balance in the terminating partner's capital account. The payment shall be made in cash in equal quarterly installments from the date of termination.

Termination

7. At the conclusion of this contract, unless it is agreed by both partners to continue the operation of the business under a new contract, the assets of the partnership, after the liabilities are paid, will be divided in proportion to the balance in each partner's capital account on that date.

Signatures —

Penelope Wolfburg   *Ingrid Swenson*
Penelope Wolfburg   Ingrid Swenson

Date —

June 20, 2007   *June 20, 2007*
Date   Date

the investment each partner will make. The partnership agreement also should state how much profit or loss each partner receives or is responsible for. Finally, the partnership agreement should state what happens if a partner wants to dissolve the partnership or dies. Although the people involved in a partnership can draft their own agreement, most experts recommend consulting an attorney.

When entering into a partnership agreement, partners would be wise to let a neutral third party—a consultant, an accountant, a lawyer, or a mutual friend—assist with any disputes that might arise.

Advantages of Partnerships

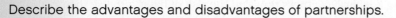

Learning Objective ❸

Describe the advantages and disadvantages of partnerships.

Partnerships have many advantages. The most important are described below.

Ease of Start-up Partnerships are relatively easy to form. As with a sole proprietorship, the legal requirements often are limited to registering the name of the business and obtaining any necessary licenses or permits. It may not even be necessary to prepare written articles of partnership, although doing so is generally a good idea.

Availability of Capital and Credit Because partners can pool their funds, a partnership usually has more capital available than a sole proprietorship does. This additional capital, coupled with the general partners' unlimited liability, can form the basis for a better credit rating. Banks and suppliers may be more willing to extend credit or grant larger loans to such a partnership than to a sole proprietor. This does not mean that partnerships can borrow all the money they need. Many partnerships have found it hard to get long-term financing simply because lenders worry about the possibility of management disagreements and lack of continuity.

Personal Interest General partners are very concerned with the operation of the firm—perhaps even more so than sole proprietors. After all, they are responsible for the actions of all other general partners, as well as for their own. The pride of ownership from solving the day-to-day problems of operating a business—with the help of another person(s)—is a strong motivating force and often makes all the people involved in the partnership work harder to become more successful.

Combined Business Skills and Knowledge Partners often have complementary skills. The weakness of one partner—in manufacturing, for example—may be offset by another partner's strength in that area. Moreover, the ability to discuss important decisions with another concerned individual often relieves some pressure and leads to more effective decision making.

Retention of Profits As in a sole proprietorship, all profits belong to the owners of the partnership. The partners share directly in the financial rewards and therefore are highly motivated to do their best to make the firm succeed. As noted, the partnership agreement should state how much profit or loss each partner receives or is responsible for.

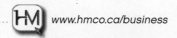

No Special Taxes Although a partnership pays no income tax, each partner is required to report his or her share of profit (or loss) from the partnership business on his or her individual tax return and is taxed on his or her share of the profit—in the same way a sole proprietor is taxed.

Disadvantages of Partnerships

Although partnerships have many advantages when compared with sole proprietorships and corporations, they also have some disadvantages, which anyone thinking of forming a partnership should consider.

Unlimited Liability As we have noted, each *general* partner has unlimited liability for all debts of the business. Each partner is legally and personally responsible for the debts and actions of any other partner, even if that partner did not incur those debts or do anything wrong. General partners thus run the risk of having to use their personal assets to pay creditors. *Limited* partners, however, risk only their original investment.

Management Disagreements What happens to a partnership if one of the partners brings a spouse or a relative into the business? What happens if a partner wants to withdraw more money from the business? Notice that each of the preceding situations—and for that matter, most of the other problems that can develop in a partnership—involves one partner doing something that disturbs the other partner(s). This human factor is especially important because business partners—with egos, ambitions, and money on the line—are especially susceptible to friction. When partners begin to disagree about decisions, policies, or ethics, distrust may build and get worse as time passes—often to the point where it is impossible to operate the business successfully.

Lack of Continuity Partnerships are terminated if any one of the general partners dies, withdraws, or is declared legally incompetent. However, the remaining partners can purchase that partner's ownership share. For example, the partnership agreement may permit surviving partners to continue the business after buying a deceased partner's interest from his or her estate. However, if the partnership loses an owner whose specific management or technical skills cannot be replaced, it is not likely to survive.

Frozen Investment It is easy to invest money in a partnership, but it is sometimes quite difficult to get it out. This is the case, for example, when remaining partners are unwilling to buy the share of the business that belongs to a partner who retires or wants to relocate to another city. To avoid such difficulties, the partnership agreement should include some procedure for buying out a partner.

In some cases, a partner must find someone outside the firm to buy his or her share. How easy or difficult it is to find an outsider depends on how successful the business is and how willing existing partners are to accept a new partner.

Beyond the Partnership

The main advantages of a partnership over a sole proprietorship are the added capital and management expertise of the partners. However, some of the basic disadvantages of the sole proprietorship also plague the general partnership. One disadvantage in particular—unlimited liability—can cause problems. A third form of business ownership, the corporation, overcomes this disadvantage.

Corporations

Learning Objective ❹
Summarize how a corporation is formed.

A **corporation** is an artificial person created by law, with most of the legal rights of a real person. These include the rights to start and operate a business, to buy or sell property, to borrow money, to sue or be sued, and to enter into binding contracts. Unlike a real person, however, a corporation exists only on paper.

The largest corporation in the world, ranked according to sales, is the giant U.S. owned retailer Wal-Mart Stores. For the 12 months ending in October 2006, Wal-Mart earned over $11,231 million net profit on over $315,654 million in sales ($13,500 million of that in Canada), while employing more than 1.8 million people worldwide.[2]

By comparison, Wal-Mart's sales are about 10 times those of Canada's top ranked corporations. Table 5.1 lists the ten largest Canadian corporations, ranked according to sales. Notice also that the although their revenues are large and relatively similar, profits vary more dramatically, as do the number of employees who operate these businesses.

Corporate Ownership

The shares of ownership of a corporation are called **stock.** The people who own a corporation's stock—and thus own part of the corporation—are called **stockholders** or sometimes *shareholders*. Once a corporation has been formed, it may sell its stock to

corporation an artificial person created by law with most of the legal rights of a real person, including the rights to start and operate a business, to buy or sell property, to borrow money, to sue or be sued, and to enter into binding contracts

stock the shares of ownership of a corporation

stockholder a person who owns a corporation's stock

RANK 2005	RANK 2004	COMPANY	REVENUES ($ MILLIONS)	PROFITS ($ MILLIONS)	EMPLOYEES
1	1	General Motors of Canada Ltd.	34,991	n.a.	20,000
2	4	Manulife Financial Corp.	32,047	3,291	20,100
3	3	George Weston Ltd.	31,363	698	150,000
4	6	Royal Bank of Canada	29,403	3,387	60,012
5	8	Imperial Oil Ltd.	27,797	2,600	6,100
6	5	Magna International Inc.	27,624	773	82,000
7	7	Power Corp. of Canada	26,613	1,053	21,800
8	2	Alcan Inc.	24,607	156	69,000
9	9	Sun Life Financial Inc.	21,918	1,876	14,300
10	12	DaimlerChrysler Canada Inc.	20,819	n.a.	11,000

Table 5.1

The Seven Largest Canadian Corporations, Ranked by Sales

Source: *Financial Post, Business Special Issue,* 42nd Edition, June 2006, p.64.

private corporation a corporation whose stock is owned by relatively few people and is not sold to the general public

public corporation a corporation whose stock can be bought and sold by any individual

individuals or other companies that want to invest in the corporation. It also may issue stock as a reward to key employees in return for certain services or as a return to investors (in place of cash payments).

A **private corporation** is a corporation whose stock is owned by relatively few people and is not sold to the general public. As an example, Mr. and Mrs. DeWitt Wallace owned virtually all the stock of Reader's Digest Association, making it one of the largest corporations of this kind. A person who wishes to sell the stock of a private corporation generally arranges to sell it *privately* to another stockholder or a close acquaintance.

Although founded in 1922 as a closed corporation, the Reader's Digest Association became an open corporation when it sold stock to investors for the first time in 1990. A **public corporation** is one whose stock can be bought and sold by any individual. Examples of open corporations include WestJet, Telus, General Motors, Microsoft, and Wal-Mart.

Forming a Corporation

Although you may think that incorporating a business guarantees success, it does not. There is no special magic about placing the word *Incorporated* or the abbreviation *Inc.* after the name of a business. Unfortunately, like sole proprietorships or partnerships, incorporated businesses can go broke. The decision to incorporate a business therefore should be made only after carefully considering whether the corporate form of ownership suits your needs better than the sole proprietorship or partnership forms.

If you decide that the corporate form is the best form of organization for you, most experts recommend that you begin the incorporation process by consulting a lawyer to be sure that all legal requirements are met. While it may be possible to incorporate a business without legal help, it is well to keep in mind the old saying, "A man who acts as his own attorney has a fool for a client." Table 5.2 lists some aspects of starting and running a business that may require legal help.

Where to Incorporate A business can incorporate federally under the *Canada Business Corporations Act* or according to one of the provincial acts. The rules governing corporate behaviour are different under each charter. Most importantly, a business that is likely to carry on activities in more than one province should incorporate federally. Otherwise, the business would be obliged to register and pay licensing fees in each province it operates in separately. Most small and medium-sized businesses

BIZ TECH

Where can you find out more about starting and managing a business? The Canadian government's Strategis website explores a number of business topics that are beneficial to new businesses as well as those currently in operation. The site answers typical questions such as which legal form is best and how to get financing and has an answer service where you can submit written questions about any specific concerns. Your gateway to Strategis website is at http://strategis.ic.gc.ca/.

1. Choosing either the sole proprietorship, partnership, or corporate form of ownership
2. Constructing a partnership agreement
3. Obtaining a corporate charter
4. Registering a corporation's stock
5. Obtaining a trademark, patent, or copyright
6. Filing for licenses or permits at the local, provincial, and federal levels
7. Purchasing an existing business or real estate
8. Creating valid contracts
9. Hiring employees and independent contractors
10. Extending credit and collecting debts

Table 5.2

Aspects of Business Requiring Legal Counsel

such as restaurants and other retail businesses that will only operate in their local trading area are incorporated in the province where their business is located. The founders of larger corporations, or of those that will do business nationwide will usually elect to incorporate federally.

The Corporate Charter Federal incorporators submit *articles of incorporation* to the Department of Consumer and Corporate Affairs in Ottawa. If the articles of incorporation are approved, they become the firm's corporate charter. A **corporate charter** is a contract between a corporation and the provincial or federal legislature, in which the legislature recognizes the formation of the artificial person that is the corporation. Usually the charter (and thus the articles of incorporation) includes the following information:

* The firm's name and address
* The incorporators' names and addresses
* The purpose of the corporation
* The maximum amount of stock and types of stock to be issued
* The rights and privileges of stockholders
* The length of time the corporation is to exist

Each of these key details is the result of decisions the incorporators must make as they organize the firm—before they submit the articles of incorporation. Let's look at two such areas: considering stockholders' rights and the final organizational meeting to select the board of directors.

Stockholders' Rights There are two basic types of stock. Owners of **common stock** may vote on corporate matters. Generally, an owner of common stock has one vote for each share owned. However, any claims of common-stock owners on profit and assets of the corporation are subordinate to the claims of others. The owners of **preferred stock** usually have no voting rights, but their claims on dividends are paid before those of common-stock owners. While large corporations may issue both common and preferred stock, generally small corporations issue only common stock.

corporate charter a contract between a corporation and the provincial or federal legislature, in which the legislature recognizes the formation of the artificial person that is the corporation

common stock stock owned by individuals or firms who may vote on corporate matters but whose claims on profit and assets are subordinate to the claims of others

preferred stock stock owned by individuals or firms who usually do not have voting rights but whose claims on dividends are paid before those of common-stock owners

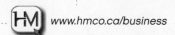 *www.hmco.ca/business*

dividend a distribution of earnings to the stockholders of a corporation

proxy a legal form listing issues to be decided at a stockholders' meeting and enabling stockholders to transfer their voting rights to some other individual or individuals

board of directors the top governing body of a corporation, the members of which are elected by the stockholders

Perhaps the most important right of owners of both common and preferred stock is to share in the profit earned by the corporation through the payment of dividends. A **dividend** is a distribution of earnings to the stockholders of a corporation. Other rights include receiving information about the corporation, voting on changes to the corporate charter, and attending the corporation's annual stockholders' meeting, where they may exercise their right to vote.

Because common stockholders usually live all over the country, very few actually may attend a corporation's annual meeting. Instead, they vote by proxy. A **proxy** is a legal form listing issues to be decided at a stockholders' meeting and enabling stockholders to transfer their voting rights to some other individual or individuals. The stockholder can register a vote and transfer voting rights simply by signing and returning the form. Today, most corporations also allow stockholders to exercise their right to vote by proxy by accessing the Internet or using a toll-free phone number.

Organizational Meeting As the last step in forming a corporation, the incorporators and original stockholders meet to adopt corporate by-laws and elect their first board of directors. (Later, directors will be elected or re-elected at the corporation's annual meetings.) The board members are directly responsible to the stockholders for the way they operate the firm.

Corporate Structure

The organizational structure of most corporations is more complicated than that of a sole proprietorship or partnership. This is especially true as the corporation begins to grow and expand. In a corporation, both the board of directors and the corporate officers are involved in management.

Board of Directors As an artificial person, a corporation can act only through its directors, who represent the corporation's stockholders. The **board of directors** is the top governing body of a corporation, and as we noted, directors are elected by the stockholders. Board members can be chosen from within the corporation or from outside it. *Note:* For a small corporation, only one director is required although you can choose to have more.

Directors who are elected from within the corporation are usually its top managers—the president and executive vice presidents, for example. Those elected from outside the corporation generally are experienced managers or entrepreneurs with proven leadership ability and/or specific talents the organization seems to need. In smaller corporations, majority stockholders usually serve as board members.

The major responsibilities of the board of directors are to set company goals and develop general

What's Bill Gates doing in Beijing?

While most people around the world recognize Bill Gates as the co-founder and chairman of Microsoft, Mr. Gates has been elevated to "rock star" status in many countries because of the corporation's products.

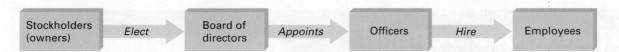

| Stockholders (owners) | *Elect* | Board of directors | *Appoints* | Officers | *Hire* | Employees |

plans (or strategies) for meeting those goals. The board also is responsible for the firm's overall operation.

Corporate Officers Corporate officers are appointed by the board of directors. The chairman of the board, president, executive vice presidents, corporate secretary, and treasurer are all corporate officers. They help the board to make plans, carry out strategies established by the board, hire employees, and manage day-to-day business activities. Periodically (usually each month), they report to the board of directors. And at the annual meeting, the directors report to the stockholders. In theory, then, the stockholders are able to control the activities of the entire corporation through its directors because they are the group that elects the board of directors (see Figure 5.2).

Advantages of Corporations

Learning Objective 5

Describe the advantages and disadvantages of a corporation.

Because a corporation is an artificial person or legal entity, it has some definite advantages when compared with other forms of ownership including limited liability, ease of raising capital, ease of transfer of ownership, perpetual life, and specialized management.

Limited Liability One of the most attractive features of corporate ownership is limited liability. With few exceptions, each owner's financial liability is limited to the amount of money he or she has paid for the corporation's stock. This feature arises from the fact that the corporation is itself a legal being, separate from its owners. If a corporation fails, creditors have a claim only on the corporation's assets, not on the owners' personal assets. Because it overcomes the problem of unlimited liability connected with sole proprietorships and general partnerships, limited liability is one of the chief reasons why entrepreneurs often choose the corporate form of organization.

Ease of Raising Capital The corporation is by far the most effective form of business ownership for raising capital. Like sole proprietorships and partnerships, corporations can borrow from lending institutions. However, they also can raise additional sums of money by selling stock. Individuals are more willing to invest in corporations than in other forms of business because their liability is limited, and they can sell their stock more easily—for a profit, they hope.

Ease of Transfer of Ownership Accessing a brokerage firm website or a telephone call to a stockbroker is all that is required to put stock up for sale. Willing buyers are available for most stocks at the market price. Ownership is transferred when the sale is made, and practically no restrictions apply to the sale and purchase of stock issued by public corporation.

Figure 5.2

Hierarchy of Corporate Structure

Stockholders exercise a great deal of influence through their right to elect the board of directors.

corporate officers the chairman of the board, president, executive vice presidents, corporate secretary, treasurer, and any other top executive appointed by the board of directors

limited liability a feature of corporate ownership that limits each owner's financial liability to the amount of money that he or she has paid for the corporation's stock

Perpetual Life Since it is essentially a legal "person," a corporation exists independently of its owners and survives them. The withdrawal, death, or incompetence of a key executive or owner does not cause the corporation to be terminated. Sears, Roebuck, which started as a partnership in 1887 and incorporated in 1893, is one of the U.S.'s largest retailing corporations, even though its original owners, Richard Sears and Alvah Roebuck, have been dead for decades.

Specialized Management Typically, corporations are able to recruit more skilled, knowledgeable, and talented managers than proprietorships and partnerships. This is because they tend to be able to pay bigger salaries, offer excellent fringe benefits, and are large enough to offer considerable opportunity for advancement. Within the corporate structure, administration, human resources, finance, marketing, and operations are placed in the charge of experts in these fields.

Disadvantages of Corporations

Like its advantages, many of a corporation's disadvantages stem from its legal definition as an artificial person or legal entity. Table 5.3 compares some of the advantages and disadvantages of a sole proprietorship, general partnership, and corporation.

Difficulty and Expense of Formation Forming a corporation can be a relatively complex and costly process. A lawyer usually has to complete the legal forms and apply for a charter. Charter fees, lawyer's fees, and registration costs associated with selling stock, and other organizational costs can amount to thousands of dollars for even a medium-sized corporation. The costs of incorporating, in both time and money, discourage many owners of smaller businesses from forming corporations.

	SOLE PROPRIETORSHIP	GENERAL PARTNERSHIP	REGULAR CORPORATION
Protecting against liability for debts	Difficult	Difficult	Easy
Raising money	Difficult	Difficult	Easy
Ownership transfer	Difficult	Difficult	Easy
Preserving continuity	Difficult	Difficult	Easy
Government regulations	Few	Few	Many
Formation	Easy	Easy	Difficult
Income taxation	Once	Once	Twice

Table 5.3

Some Advantages and Disadvantages of a Sole Proprietorship, Partnership, and Corporation

Government Regulation and Increased Paperwork A corporation must meet various government standards before it can sell its stock to the public. Then it must file many reports on its business operations and finances with local, provincial, and federal governments. In addition, the corporation must make periodic reports to its stockholders about various aspects of the business. To prepare all the necessary reports, even small corporations often need the regular help of an attorney, accountant, and other professionals. In addition, a corporation's activities are restricted by law to those spelled out in its charter.

Conflict Within the Corporation Because a large corporation might employ thousands of employees, some conflict is inevitable. For example, the pressure to increase sales revenue, reduce expenses, and increase profits, often leads to increased stress and tension for both managers and employees. This is especially true when a corporation operates in a competitive industry, attempts to develop and market new products, or must downsize its workforce to reduce employee salary expense.

Double Taxation Corporations must pay a tax on their profits. In addition, stockholders must pay personal income tax on profits received as dividends. Corporate profits thus are taxed twice—once as corporate income and a second time as the personal income of stockholders.

Lack of Secrecy Because open corporations are required to submit detailed reports to government agencies and to stockholders, they cannot keep their operations confidential. Competitors can study these corporate reports and then use the information to compete more effectively. In effect, every public corporation has to share some of its secrets with its competitors.

Special Types of Business Ownership

Learning Objective 6

Examine special types of corporations, including government-owned corporations and not-for-profit corporations.

In addition to the sole proprietorship, partnership, and the regular corporate form of organization, some entrepreneurs choose other forms of organization that meet their special needs. Additional organizational options include government-owned corporations and not-for-profit corporations.

Government-Owned Corporations

government-owned corporation a corporation owned and operated by a local, provincial, or federal government

A **government-owned corporation** is owned and operated by a local, provincial, or federal government. The Canadian Broadcasting Corporation, Canada Post, Atomic Energy of Canada, and the many provincial power utilities including Hydro-Quebec and Ontario's HydroOne are all government-owned corporations. City-owned corporations run most municipal transit lines such as the Toronto Transit Commission.

A government corporation usually provides a service the business sector is reluctant or unable to offer. Profit is secondary in such corporations. In fact, they may continually operate at a loss, particularly if they are involved in public transportation. Their main objective is to ensure that a particular service is available.

Not-for-Profit Corporations

not-for-profit corporation a corporation organized to provide a social, educational, religious, or other service rather than to earn a profit

A **not-for-profit corporation** (sometimes referred to as *nonprofit*) is a corporation organized to provide a social, educational, religious, or other service rather than to earn a profit. Various charities, museums, associations, private schools, and colleges are organized in this way, primarily to ensure limited liability. The Canadian Society for the Prevention of Cruelty to Animals better known as the C.S.P.C.A., or the Humane Society, and the Y.M.C.A. are examples of nonprofit organizations driven to serve their publics without a profit motive. Even though these corporations may receive more money than they spend, any surplus funds are "reinvested" in expanded activities. They are not-for-profit corporations because their primary purpose is to provide a social service. The laws governing the organization and operation of not-for-profit corporations are different from profit motivated corporations. These organizations do not issue stock certificates because no dividends are paid and no one is interested in buying or selling their stock. They are also exempt from paying income tax.

COMPANY	CATEGORY
General Motors of Canada Ltd.	most sales of any firm foreign owned vehicle and parts manufacturers
Royal Bank of Canada	financial institutions banks market capitalization
ManuLife Financial	insurance companies
Hydro-Quebec	utility government owned indebted ($31 billion)
George Weston Ltd.	employees (150,000)
Maple Leaf Foods Inc.	food and beverage manufacturers
Abitibi-Consolidated Inc.	forestry and paper companies
Gerdau Ameristeel Corp.	general manufacturers
Bombardier Inc.	hi-tech manufacturers
McKesson Canada	health care and biotech
CGI Group Inc.	information technology
Wal-Mart Canada Corp.	merchandisers
Alcan Inc.	mining
CanWest Global Communications Corp.	multimedia
Imperial Oil Ltd.	oil and gas
BCE Inc.	telecommunications
Mouvement des caisses Desjardins	credit unions
The Canada Trust Co.	trust companies
Deloitte & Touche LLP	accounting firms
Mercer Human Resources Consulting Ltd.	human resources consulting
Intrawest Corp.	real estate
Ontario Teachers' Pension Plan	pension funds
Gowling Lafleur Henderson LLP	law firms
World Vision Canada	charities
Fondation Lucie et Andre Chagnon	foundations

Table 5.4

Canada's Top-Ranked Corporations by Business Category

Source: *Financial Post, Business Special Issue,* 42nd Edition, June 2006.

Cooperatives, Joint Ventures, and Syndicates

Learning Objective 7

Discuss the purpose of a cooperative, joint venture, and syndicate.

Today, three additional types of business organizations—cooperatives, joint ventures, and syndicates—are used for special purposes. Each of these forms of organization is unique when compared with more traditional forms of business ownership.

Cooperatives

cooperative an association of individuals or firms whose purpose is to perform some business function for its members

A **cooperative** is an association of individuals or firms whose purpose is to perform some business function for its members. The cooperative can perform its function more effectively than any member could by acting alone. For example, cooperatives purchase goods in bulk and distribute them to members; thus the unit cost is lower than it would be if each member bought the goods in a much smaller quantity.

Although cooperatives are found in all segments of our economy, they are most prevalent in agriculture. Farmers use cooperatives to purchase supplies, to buy services such as trucking and storage, and to process and market their products. Ocean Spray Cranberries, Inc., for example, is a cooperative of some 650 cranberry growers and more than 100 citrus growers.

Joint Ventures

joint venture an agreement between two or more groups to form a business entity in order to achieve a specific goal or to operate for a specific period of time

A **joint venture** is an agreement between two or more groups to form a business entity in order to achieve a specific goal or to operate for a specific period of time. Both the scope of the joint venture and the liabilities of the people or businesses involved usually are limited to one project. Once the goal is reached, the period of time elapses, or the project is completed, the joint venture is dissolved.

Corporations, as well as individuals, can enter into joint ventures. Major oil producers often have formed a number of joint ventures to share the extremely high cost of exploring for offshore petroleum deposits. In the entertainment industry, Walt Disney formed a joint venture with Pixar Animation Studios to create movies. Finally, Japanese consumer electronics manufacturer Sony and Swedish telecom giant Ericsson have formed a joint venture to manufacture and market mobile communications equipment. Now, after more than four years, that joint venture is profitable and projects even larger sales revenues and profits in the immediate future.[3]

Syndicates

syndicate a temporary association of individuals or firms organized to perform a specific task that requires a large amount of capital

A **syndicate** is a temporary association of individuals or firms organized to perform a specific task that requires a large amount of capital. The syndicate is formed because no one person or firm is willing to put up the entire amount required for the

Caution Ahead for Automotive Joint Ventures?

Racing for higher revenues, car companies sometimes form joint ventures to enter or expand in overseas markets. However, joint ventures can have a dark side. Will carmakers put the brakes on joint ventures for fear that a partner might become a competitor?

In India. India's Tata Motors and Italy's Fiat have a joint venture to build cars for India's fast-growing middle class. Both partners are pleased with this venture. Tata, India's second-largest car manufacturer, benefits from Fiat's technology and supplier network; Fiat gains from Tata's experience and customer knowledge.

In China. General Motors and Volkswagen have separate joint ventures with the Shanghai Automotive Industry Corp. (SAIC) to produce cars in China. Yet SAIC recently created a new division, staffed by engineers who previously worked in the joint ventures, to make cars under a new brand. Publicly, VW and GM have said they value their ventures with SAIC and understand its desire to develop cars independently. What will happen to these ventures as SAIC's division increases competitive tension in an already pressured industry?

Sources: Based on information from Paulo Soares de Oliveira, "SAIC Plans European Launch 2007," *Automotive News Europe,* August 21, 2006, p. 12; "Tata Motors Ltd.: Truck Maker Joins with Fiat to Build, Sell Cars in India," *Wall Street Journal,* July 26, 2006, n.p.; Keith Bradsher, Micheline Mayner, "Chinese Partner of G.M. and VW to Offer Its Own Cars," *New York Times,* April 11, 2006, p. C6.

undertaking. Like a joint venture, a syndicate is dissolved as soon as its purpose has been accomplished.

Syndicates are used most commonly to underwrite large insurance policies, loans, and investments. Stock brokerage firms usually join together in the same way to market a new issue of stock. For example, Morgan Stanley, Credit Suisse First Boston, and other Wall Street firms formed a syndicate to sell shares of stock in Google. The initial public offering (IPO) was one of the largest in U.S. history—too large for Morgan Stanley and Credit Suisse First Boston to handle without help from other Wall Street firms. (An *initial public offering* is the term used to describe the first time a corporation sells stock to the general public.)

Corporate Growth

Learning Objective 8

Explain how growth from within and growth through mergers can enable a business to expand.

Growth seems to be a basic characteristic of business. One reason for seeking growth has to do with profit: A larger firm generally has greater sales revenue and

thus greater profit. Another reason is that in a growing economy, a business that does not grow is actually shrinking relative to the economy. A third reason is that business growth is a means by which some executives boost their power, prestige, and reputation.

Growth From Within

Most corporations grow by expanding their present operations. Some introduce and sell new but related products. Others expand the sale of present products to new geographic markets or to new groups of consumers in geographic markets already served. Currently, Wal-Mart has over 3,700 stores in the United States and over 1,600 stores in nine other countries and has long-range plans for expanding into additional international markets.[4]

Growth from within, especially when carefully planned and controlled, can have relatively little adverse effect on a firm. For the most part, the firm continues to do what it has been doing, but on a larger scale. For instance, Larry Ellison, founder and CEO of Oracle Corporation of Redwood City, California, built the firm's annual revenues up from a mere $282 million in 1988 to approximately $12 billion today.[5] Much of this growth has taken place since 1994 as Oracle capitalized on its global leadership in information management software.

Growth Through Mergers and Acquisitions

Another way a firm can grow is by purchasing another company. The purchase of one corporation by another is called a **merger.** An *acquisition* is essentially the same thing as a merger, but the term usually is used in reference to a large corporation's purchases of other corporations. Although most mergers and acquisitions are friendly, hostile takeovers also occur. A **hostile takeover** is a situation in which the management and board of directors of a firm targeted for acquisition disapprove of the merger.

When a merger or acquisition becomes hostile, a corporate raider—another company or a wealthy investor—may make a tender offer or start a proxy fight to gain control of the target company. A **tender offer** is an offer to purchase the stock of a firm targeted for acquisition at a price just high enough to tempt stockholders to sell their shares. Corporate raiders also may initiate a proxy fight. A **proxy fight** is a technique used to gather enough stockholder votes to control a targeted company.

If the corporate raider is successful and takes over the targeted company, existing management usually is replaced. Faced with this probability, existing management may take specific actions sometimes referred to as "poison pills," "shark repellents," or "porcupine provisions" to maintain control of the firm and avoid the hostile takeover. Whether mergers are friendly or hostile, they are generally classified as *horizontal*, *vertical*, or *conglomerate* (see Figure 5.3).

Horizontal Mergers A *horizontal merger* is a merger between firms that make and sell similar products or services in similar markets. The merger between SBC and AT&T is an example of a horizontal merger because both firms are in the telecommunications industry. This type of merger tends to reduce the number of firms in an industry—and thus may reduce competition. For this reason, each merger may be reviewed carefully by federal agencies before it is permitted.

merger the purchase of one corporation by another

hostile takeover a situation in which the management and board of directors of a firm targeted for acquisition disapprove of the merger

tender offer an offer to purchase the stock of a firm targeted for acquisition at a price just high enough to tempt stockholders to sell their shares

proxy fight a technique used to gather enough stockholder votes to control a targeted company

Vertical Mergers A *vertical merger* is a merger between firms that operate at different but related levels in the production and marketing of a product. Generally, one of the merging firms is either a supplier or a customer of the other. A vertical merger occurred when IBM acquired Candle Corporation—an IBM business partner since 1976. At the time of the merger, Candle Corporation, a privately held software and consulting company, was a leading provider of software solutions to help customers develop, deploy, and manage their enterprise infrastructure. At the same time, IBM needed this type of software to add to its own line of software products and remain competitive in the ever-changing software industry. Rather than develop its own software or purchase needed software from Candle Corporation, it simply purchased the company.[6]

Conglomerate Mergers A *conglomerate merger* takes place between firms in completely different industries. One of the largest conglomerate mergers in recent history occurred when Procter & Gamble merged with Gillette. While both companies were known for their consumer products, Procter & Gamble is the manufacturer and distributor for many household products, and Gillette is well known for personal-care products. According to Procter & Gamble, the addition of Gillette's products "will broaden the ways in which we can continue to provide the kinds of helpful solutions to assist our customers in taking care of their families, their homes—and themselves!"[7]

Canadian merger activity approached a near record $166-billion of corporate takeovers in 2005 and the pace of activity continued into 2006. For example, among the bigger deals, Brazilian mining company Companhia Vale do Rio Doce (CVRD) obtained control of Inco Limited, Advanced Micro Devices Inc. agreed to buy ATI Technologies Inc. of Toronto, and after Barrick Gold Corp. merged with NovaGold Resources Inc. and Pioneer Metals Corp., the Toronto-based mining giant became the biggest gold mining company in the world. [8]

Standoff or merger?

Canadians have not warmed to the idea of bank mergers, which would result in larger banks better positioned to compete internationally, but causing less competition in the Canadian market at the same time.

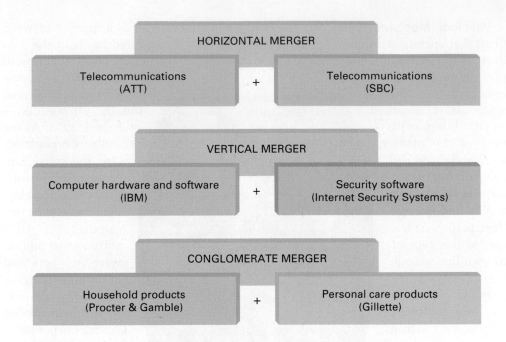

Current Merger Trends

Economists, financial analysts, corporate managers, and stockholders still hotly debate whether takeovers are good for the economy—or for individual companies—in the long run.

One thing is clear, however: There are two sides to the takeover question. Takeover advocates argue that for companies that have been taken over, the purchasers have been able to make the company more profitable and productive by installing a new top-management team and by forcing the company to concentrate on one main business.

Takeover opponents argue that takeovers do nothing to enhance corporate profitability or productivity. These critics argue that threats of takeovers have forced managers to devote valuable time to defending their companies from takeover, thus robbing time from new-product development and other vital business activities. This, they believe, is why North American companies may be less competitive with companies in such countries as Japan, Germany, and South Korea, where takeovers occur only rarely. Finally, the opposition argues that the only people who benefit from takeovers are investment bankers, brokerage firms, and takeover "artists," who receive financial rewards by manipulating corporations rather than by producing tangible products or services.

Most experts now predict that mergers and acquisitions during the first part of the twenty-first century will be the result of cash-rich companies looking to acquire businesses that will enhance their position in the marketplace. Analysts also anticipate more mergers that involve companies or investors from other countries. Regardless of the companies involved or where the companies are from, future mergers and acquisitions will be driven by solid business logic, the desire to compete in the international marketplace, and the explosion of information technology.

BUSINESS AROUND THE WORLD

International Mergers and Acquisitions Face Protectionism

Cross-border mergers and acquisitions are nothing new. One of the highest-profile acquisitions in the auto industry was the deal in which Germany's Daimler-Benz bought U.S.-based Chrysler to form DaimlerChrysler. However, in 2007 this deal came undone when Daimler sold its money-losing Chryster division to Cerberus Capital Corp. of NewYork.[9]

France

Just the rumour that the U.S. snack firm PepsiCo. might try to acquire Groupe Danone spurred government officials to say that they want Danone to remain under French ownership. In fact, France will protect ten industries (including casinos and defence firms) from cross-border takeovers. The minister for industry notes, however, that "our policy is not to oppose by principle every acquisition of a French company."

United States

China National Offshore Oil Company (CNOOC), owned by China, tried to buy California's Unocal. The U.S. Congress opposed the move, citing the need to protect the country's energy producers, and CNOOC withdrew its bid (leaving Chevron to buy Unocal). "It's a tremendous precedent setter for a government to interfere and declare that national security is at stake," comments an oil industry expert. What is this going to mean for American oil companies that want to invest in natural resources in different nations from Algeria to Zanzibar?

Finally, experts predict more leveraged buyouts in the future. A **leveraged buyout (LBO)** is a purchase arrangement that allows a firm's managers and employees or a group of investors to purchase the company. (LBO activity is sometimes referred to as *taking a firm private*.) To gain control of a company, LBOs usually rely on borrowed money to purchase stock from existing stockholders. The borrowed money is later repaid through the company's earnings, sale of assets, or money obtained from selling more stock. Perhaps Canada's best-known LBO strategist is Gerald Schwartz, founder of Onex Corporation. Onex has grown since its inception in 1983 to become one of Canada's largest companies, with $15 billion of assets, annual revenues of $19 billion, and 136,000 employees around the world. Firms under the Onex umbrella include Celestica Inc, ClientLogic, and the Cineplex chain of theatres.[10]

Whether they are sole proprietorships, partnerships, corporations, or some other form of business ownership, most North American businesses are small. In the next chapter we focus on these small businesses. We examine, among other things, the meaning of the word *small* as it applies to business and the place of small business in the Canadian economy.

leveraged buyout (LBO) a purchase arrangement that allows a firm's managers and employees or a group of investors to purchase the company

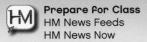

Prepare for Class
HM News Feeds
HM News Now

→ **RETURN TO INSIDE BUSINESS**

Canadian Tire Financial Services Limited is a wholly owned subsidiary of Canadian Tire Corporation, Limited. Canadian Tire Financial Services is primarily engaged in financing and managing the Canadian Tire Options MasterCard to over 4 million card members. The acquisition of Marks Work Warehouse (L'Équipeur stores in Quebec.) clothing store is another relatively recent addition to the family of financial and banking products that Canadian Tire stores are now offering customers as a means to increase revenues.

Questions

1. What other products do you think could be considered by Canadian Tire?

2. Why do you think these products would be successful with their current customer base?

CHAPTER REVIEW

1 Describe the advantages and disadvantages of sole proprietorships.

A successful sole proprietorship can be a great source of pride for the owner. It is the simplest form of business to enter, control, and leave. Sole proprietorships nevertheless have disadvantages, such as unlimited liability and limits on one person's ability to borrow or to be an expert in all fields.

2 Explain the different types of partners and the importance of partnership agreements.

Like sole proprietors, general partners are responsible for running the business and for all business debts. Limited partners receive a share of the profit in return for investing in the business. However, they are not responsible for business debts beyond the amount they have invested. Regardless of the type of partnership, it is always a good idea to have a written agreement (or articles of partnership) setting forth the terms of a partnership.

3 Describe the advantages and disadvantages of partnerships.

The major advantages of a partnership include ease of start-up, availability of capital and credit, personal interest, combined skills and knowledge, retention of profits, and possible tax advantages. The effects of management disagreements are one of the major disadvantages of a partnership. Other disadvantages include unlimited liability (in a general partnership), lack of continuity, and frozen investment.

4 Summarize how a corporation is formed.

A corporation is an artificial person created by law, with most of the legal rights of a real person, including the right to start and operate a business, to own property, to borrow money, to be sued or sue, and to enter into contracts. With the corporate form of ownership, stock can be sold to individuals to raise capital. Generally, corporations are classified as private corporations (few stockholders) or public corporations (many stockholders). The process of forming a corporation is called incorporation.

5   **Describe the advantages and disadvantages of a corporation.**

Perhaps the major advantage of the corporate form is limited liability—stockholders are not liable for the corporation's debts beyond the amount they paid for its stock. Other important advantages include ease of raising capital, ease of transfer of ownership, perpetual life, and specialized management. A major disadvantage of a large corporation is double taxation: all profits are taxed once as corporate income and again as personal income because stockholders must pay a personal income tax on the profits they receive as dividends. Other disadvantages include difficulty and expense of formation, government regulation, conflict within the corporation, and lack of secrecy.

 6   **Examine special types of corporations, including government-owned corporations and not-for profit corporations.**

Government-owned corporations provide particular services, such as public transportation, to citizens. Not-for-profit corporations are formed to provide social services rather than to earn profits.

 7   **Discuss the purpose of a cooperative, joint venture, and syndicate.**

A cooperative is an association of individuals or firms whose purpose is to perform some business function for its members. A joint venture is formed when two or more groups form a business entity in order to achieve a specific goal or to operate for a specific period of time. A syndicate is a temporary association of individuals or firms organized to perform a specific task that requires large amounts of capital.

 8   **Explain how growth from within and growth through mergers can enable a business to expand.**

A corporation may grow by expanding its present operations or through a merger or acquisition. Mergers generally are classified as horizontal, vertical, or conglomerate mergers.

 Improve Your Grade
Learning Objectives Review
Audio Chapter Review & Quiz

Review Questions

1. How does a partnership differ from a sole proprietorship? Which disadvantages of sole proprietorship does the partnership tend to eliminate or reduce?
2. What is the difference between a general partner and a limited partner?
3. What issues should be included in a partnership agreement? Why?
4. Explain the difference between a public corporation and a private corporation.
5. Outline the incorporation process, and describe the basic corporate structure.
6. What rights do stockholders have? What are the duties of a corporation's board of directors?
7. What are the major advantages and disadvantages associated with the corporate form of business ownership?
8. Why are cooperatives formed? Explain how they operate.
9. In what ways are joint ventures and syndicates alike? In what ways do they differ?
10. Describe the three types of mergers.

Discussion Questions

1. If you were to start a business, which ownership form would you choose? What factors might affect your choice?
2. Discuss the following statement: "Corporations are not really run by their owners."
3. Is growth a good thing for all firms? How does management know when a firm is ready to grow?
4. Are mergers and acquisitions good for the company, a firm's stockholders, or the economy?

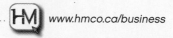

CASE STUDY

Stockholders Make Their Voices Heard at Disney

How much influence do stockholders wield over decisions made by and about the board of directors? Many stockholders of Walt Disney have been pushing for more say in key corporate governance issues such as how the board of directors is chosen and how corporate officers are supervised. Little by little, their voices have been heard. Disney has made a number of changes to the way directors are elected, reduced the size of its board, increased the number of independent members, and separated the role of chairman of the board from the role of chief executive officer.

Stockholders were looking forward to new leadership and new ideas when Michael Eisner was named CEO of Disney in the mid-1980s. The company's earnings were down, and its movies weren't drawing the huge audiences that management had hoped for. Eisner and his management team supercharged the theme park business, brought the company into the television industry by buying Cap Cities ABC, and put the magic back into Disney movies.

More than a decade into Eisner's revival of the Magic Kingdom's fortunes, however, some stockholders were grumbling. Disney had to write off millions that it had invested in its go.com Internet initiative as it changed its online strategy. Profits at the ABC Network were not up to par, and theme-park attendance was down following the terrorist attacks of 2001. Roy Disney, the last member of the Disney family to serve as a director, complained publicly about Eisner's management and the company's lagging share price. Eventually, he and another director resigned from the board and continued to push for management changes.

Eisner came under even more pressure when the cable company Comcast launched an unsolicited acquisition bid for Disney. As the company struggled against this unwanted takeover attempt—which it ultimately rebuffed—stockholders showed their displeasure with the CEO's performance. Eisner was running unopposed for re-election to the board, usually a routine event for a CEO who is also serving as chairman of the board. At this annual meeting, however, the CEO received a "withhold" vote from 45 percent of the shares.

Shareholders' voices were heard: The Disney board took the chairman's title away from Eisner that night, although he remained a director. No longer would the CEO be able to chair Disney's board of directors. Within months, Eisner announced he would soon retire. In preparation, the board scheduled a meeting with officials of major pension funds, which own sizable blocks of Disney stock, to hear their concerns about corporate governance and to discuss choosing Eisner's successor.

In the next few months, the board cut the total number of directors and added a new director considered to be independent of the company's management. It committed to rotating members among the board's committees to bring new viewpoints to such key areas of corporate governance as executive compensation. And most important, it changed the voting rules to require any director who receives a majority of "withhold" votes to submit a letter of resignation. George J. Mitchell, who replaced Eisner as chairman of the board, said in announcing the new voting rules: "Today's action is the latest in a series of steps we have taken to further strengthen Disney's corporate governance practices."

Questions:

1. Generally, stockholders of a large corporation such as Disney are fairly complacent with existing management. And yet, these same stockholders eventually changed the way that Disney was managed. In this case, what actions provoked stockholders to become so vocal?

2. Do you agree with the Disney board's decision to meet with the managers of large pension funds that own sizable blocks of Disney stock? Why or why not?

3. Why is it important for a board to have a certain number of directors who are not corporate officers and have no personal connection with corporate officers? What can board members who are outside the corporation contribute to the overall management of a large corporation?

BUILDING SKILLS FOR CAREER SUCCESS

1. Exploring the Internet

Arguments about mergers and acquisitions often come down to an evaluation of who benefits and by how much. Sometimes the benefits include access to new products, talented management, new customers, or new sources of capital. Often the debate is complicated by the involvement of firms based in different countries.

The Internet is a fertile environment for information and discussion about mergers. The firms involved will provide their view about who will benefit and why it is either a good thing or not. Journalists will report facts and offer commentary as to how they see the future result of any merger, and of course, chat rooms located on the websites of many journals promote discussion about the issues. Visit the text website for updates to this exercise.

Assignment

1. Using an Internet search engine such as Google or Yahoo!, locate two or three sites providing information about a recent merger (use a keyword such as *merger*).

2. After examining these sites and reading journal articles, report information about the merger, such as the dollar value, the reasons behind the merger, and so forth.

3. Based on your assessment of the information you have read, do you think the merger is a good idea or not for the firms involved, the employees, the investors, the industry, and society as a whole? Explain your reasoning.

2. Building Team Skills

Suppose that you have decided to quit your job as an insurance adjuster and open a bakery. Your business is now growing, and you have decided to add a full line of catering services. This means more work and responsibility. You will need someone to help you, but you are undecided about what to do. Should you hire an employee or find a partner? If you add a partner, what type of decisions should be made to create a partnership agreement?

Prepare for Class
Exploring the Internet

Assignment

1. In a group, discuss the following questions:
   a. What are the advantages and disadvantages of adding a partner versus hiring an employee?
   b. How would you go about finding a partner?

2. As a group, prepare an articles-of-partnership agreement. Be prepared to discuss the pros and cons of your group's agreement with other groups from your class, as well as to examine their agreements.

3. Summarize your group's answers to these questions, and present them to your class.

3. Researching Different Careers

Many people spend their entire lives working in jobs that they do not enjoy. Why is this so? Often it is because they have taken the first job they were offered without giving it much thought. How can you avoid having this happen to you? First, you should determine your "personal profile" by identifying and analyzing your own strengths, weaknesses, things you enjoy, and things you dislike. Second, you should identify the types of jobs that fit your profile. Third, you should identify and research the companies that offer those jobs.

Assignment

1. Take two sheets of paper and draw a line down the middle of each sheet, forming two columns on each page. Label column 1 "Things I Enjoy or Like to Do," column 2 "Things I Do Not Like Doing," column 3 "My Strengths," and column 4 "My Weaknesses."

2. Record data in each column over a period of at least one week. You may find it helpful to have a relative or friend give you input.

3. Summarize the data, and write a profile of yourself.

4. Research the companies that offer the types of jobs that fit your profile.

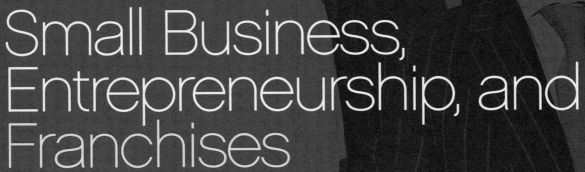

CHAPTER 6

Small Business, Entrepreneurship, and Franchises

Your Guide to Success in Business

Why this chapter matters
Small businesses drive the Canadian economy. Therefore, it is probable that you will work for a small business or start your own business.

LEARNING OBJECTIVES

1. Define what a small business is and recognize the fields in which small businesses are concentrated.

2. Identify the people who start small businesses and the reasons why some succeed and many fail.

3. Assess the contributions of small businesses to our economy.

4. Judge the advantages and disadvantages of operating a small business.

5. Explain how governments help small businesses.

6. Appraise the concept and types of franchising.

7. Analyze the growth of franchising and franchising's advantages and disadvantages.

Canadian Apparel Manufacturers in Transition

The Canadian apparel industry is the tenth largest manufacturing sector in Canada and, according to Statistics Canada, is comprised of some 2,150 mostly small business manufacturers, located primarily in Quebec, Ontario, Manitoba, and British Columbia. Quebec accounts for 55 percent of all industry activity, with more than 1,000 businesses located in Montreal—the historical capital of the industry. Over 33,500 people work in the apparel industry in Montreal, which has traditionally provided semi-skilled jobs, such as sewing, to locals and, especially, new immigrants to the city for more than a century. Only 5 percent of Montreal-based apparel businesses employ more that 100 people, 95 percent employ fewer than 100 people, 66 percent employ fewer than 10 employees, and the average is only 29 employees per establishment. Much of the reason for this lies in the ability to outsource various steps in the production process to other local firms that might specialize and have made investments in labour saving machinery.

Peerless, Main Knitting, Golden Brand, Samuelson, and Kovac are but a few corporate names well known to apparel industry insiders, but probably not familiar to most Canadians. Besides producing under their own brands, some of the larger firms, such as Peerless Clothing Inc., produce clothing under contract for popular brand names such as Chaps, Ralph Lauren, IZOD, Calvin Klein, and Anne Klein. Smaller producers, such as Kovac Manufacturing Inc., market their women's line of fashions throughout North America to large retailers such as Wal-Mart and smaller independent retailers under their own KovacTouché and 24 K brands.

In 2005, the Canadian industry employed about 70,000 workers and shipped over $5.5 billion worth of clothing, of which 39.5 percent was exported mainly to the U.S. market. Smaller Canadian producers can take advantage of their proximity to American customers, smaller production runs, and quick delivery times. However, the industry is facing increasing difficulties due to rising costs for labour, fabrics,

continued on next page

● ● ●

DID YOU KNOW?

The Canadian apparel industry accounts for 1.2% of manufacturing Gross Domestic Product, 1.2 percent of manufacturing investment, and 4.5 percent of manufacturing employment.

KEY TERMS

small business (166)
business plan (175)
Business Development Bank of Canada (BDC) (178)
venture capital (179)

franchise (180)
franchising (180)
franchisor (180)
franchisee (180)

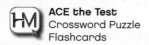

ACE the Test
Crossword Puzzle
Flashcards

marketing; and the rising exchange rate on the American dollar. The lower valued Canadian dollar, which acted as a subsidy for exporters in 2003 when it was US65 cents, is now presenting considerable challenge to Canadian manufacturers in the face of a U.S.dollar at par or near with the Canadian dollar and increasingly heavier competition from lower cost imports to North America from China and India.

Less than 20 years ago, about 70 percent of the textile and clothing products consumed in Canada were made in Canada. A major factor contributing to the decline in domestic manufacturing has been the dismantling of barriers to multilateral trade. As a result of the Uruguay Round of negotiations, World Trade Organization member countries agreed to remove all quotas in four stages between 1995 and 2005. With the end of quotas, protection from imports was virtually eliminated for domestic manufacturers. According to the Canadian Apparel Federation, the clothing manufacturing industry lost over 40,000 jobs from 2001 to 2006.

In response to these factors, Canadian manufacturers have increased investment in more efficient machinery and equipment, automated more of the production process, focused on fewer lines of products, increased marketing effort into new markets, and, over the past decade, outsourced more large-scale production runs to China and India where labour costs are significantly lower.

Sources: Allan Swift, "Stretching with the times," *Montreal Gazette*, November 20, 2006, p. B1-B2; Peter Diekmeyer, "On the flip side of a weak loonie," *National Post*, October 17, 2006, p. SR 1 and SR3.; Industry Canada, Strategis, Canadian Apparel, accessed December 18, 2006, http://strategis.ic.gc.ca/epic/internet/inapparel-vetements.nsf/en/ap03282e.html#industry; Ville de Montreal, "L'industrie du vêtement à Montréal," accessed December 18, 2006, http://ville.montreal.qc.ca/pls/portal/docs/page/MTL_STATISTIQUES_FR/media/documents/Profil_vetement_v2.pdf.

Most small businesses that survive usually stay small. They provide a solid foundation for our economy—as employers, suppliers, and purchasers of goods and services, and as taxpayers.

In this chapter we do not take small businesses for granted. Instead, we look closely at this important business sector—beginning with a definition of small business, a description of industries that often attract small businesses, and a profile of some of the people who start small businesses. Next, we consider the importance of small businesses to our economy. We also present the advantages and disadvantages of smallness in business. We then describe services provided by the various levels of government and their agencies formed to assist owners and managers of small businesses. We conclude the chapter with a discussion of the pros and cons of franchising, an approach to small-business ownership that has become very popular in the last thirty years.

Small Business: A Profile

Learning Objective 1

Define what a small business is and recognize the fields in which small businesses are concentrated.

small business one that is independently owned and operated for profit and is not dominant in its field

Although there are different guidelines used to describe small businesses, in Canada it is generally agreed that a **small business** is considered such if it is independently owned and operated for profit and not dominant in its field.

Various government agencies and banks use additional criteria when establishing whether a business can be considered small for a loan application or for the lower, small business tax rate. Usually the criteria include a limit on the number of employees and total sales revenue. For example, the definition offered by Statistics Canada sets revenues at no more than $2 million in annual sales and fewer than 50 employees for a service business.[1]

Annual sales in the millions of dollars may not seem very small. However, for many firms, profit is only a small percentage of total sales. Thus a firm might earn only $40,000 or $50,000 on yearly sales of $1 million—and that *is* small in comparison with the profits earned by most medium-sized and large firms.

The Small-Business Sector

A surprising number of Canadians take advantage of their freedom to start a business. According to Statistics Canada, the number of self-employed workers nearly doubled from 1976 to 2002. In 2002, a full 15 percent of all Canadian workers were self-employed—almost as many as were working in the public sector.[2]

Statistically, over 70 percent of new businesses can be expected to fail within their first five years.[3]

The primary reason for these failures is mismanagement resulting from a lack of business know-how. The makeup of the small-business sector thus is constantly changing. Despite the high failure rate, many small businesses succeed modestly. Some are extremely successful—to the point where they can no longer be considered small. Taken together, small businesses are also responsible for providing a high percentage of the jobs in Canada. According to some estimates, the figure is well over 50 percent.[4]

Industries That Attract Small Businesses

Some industries, such as auto manufacturing, require huge investments in machinery and equipment. Businesses in such industries are big from the day they are started—if an entrepreneur or group of entrepreneurs can gather the capital required to start one.

By contrast, a number of other industries require only a low initial investment and some special skills or knowledge. It is these industries that tend to attract new businesses. Growing industries, such as outpatient-care facilities, are attractive because of their profit potential. However, knowledgeable entrepreneurs choose areas with which they are familiar, and these are most often the more established industries.

Small enterprise spans the gamut from corner newspaper vending to the development of optical fibres. The owners of small businesses sell gasoline, flowers, and coffee to go. They publish magazines, haul freight, teach languages, and program computers. They make wines, movies, and high-fashion clothes. They build new homes and restore old ones. They fix appliances, recycle metals, and sell used cars. They drive cabs and fly planes. They make us well when we are ill, and they sell us the products of corporate giants. The various kinds of businesses generally fall into three broad categories of industry: distribution, service, and production.

Distribution Industries This category includes retailing, wholesaling, transportation, and communications—industries concerned with the movement of goods from producers to consumers. Clothing and jewellery stores, pet shops, bookstores, and grocery stores, for example, are all retail firms. Slightly less than one-quarter of the small distribution firms are wholesalers. Wholesalers purchase products in quantity from manufacturers and then resell them to retailers.

Service Industries This category accounts for close to three-quarters of all self-employed Canadian small businesses.[5] They provide non-financial services such as medical and dental care; watch, shoe, and TV repairs; haircutting and styling; restaurant meals; and dry cleaning and. financial services including accounting, insurance, real estate, and investment counselling. An increasing number of self-employed Canadians run service businesses from their homes.

Production Industries This last category includes the construction, mining, and manufacturing industries. Small firms that do venture into production generally make parts and subassemblies for larger manufacturing firms or supply special skills to larger construction firms.

The People in Small Businesses: The Entrepreneurs

Learning Objective 2

Identify the people who start small businesses and the reasons why some succeed and many fail.

Small businesses are typically managed by the people who started and own them. Most of these people have held jobs with other firms and could still be so employed if they wanted. Yet owners of small businesses would rather take the risk of starting and operating their own firms, even if the money they make is less than the salaries they might otherwise earn.

Researchers have suggested a variety of personal factors as reasons why individuals go into business. One that is often cited is the "entrepreneurial spirit"—the desire

Figure 6.1

How Old Is the Average Entrepreneur?

People in all age groups become entrepreneurs, but more than 70 percent are between 24 and 44 years of age.

Source: Data developed and provided by the National Federation of Independent Business Foundation and sponsored by the American Express Travel Related Services Company, Inc. Used by permission of NFIB.

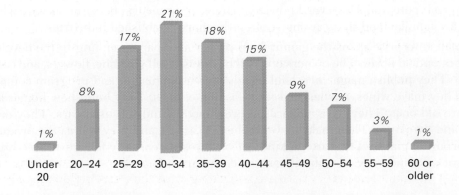

Under 20	20–24	25–29	30–34	35–39	40–44	45–49	50–54	55–59	60 or older
1%	8%	17%	21%	18%	15%	9%	7%	3%	1%

to create a new business. Other factors, such as independence, the desire to determine your own destiny, and the willingness to find and accept a challenge, certainly play a part. Background may exert an influence as well. In particular, researchers think that people whose families have been in business (successfully or not) are most apt to start and run their own businesses. Statistics Canada reports more than 800,000 women are now self-employed. These women make up only one-third of the total number of self-employed Canadians and men are still more likely to be running their own businesses across all age groups.[6] Those who start their own businesses also tend to cluster around certain ages—more than 70 percent are between 24 and 44 years of age[7] (see Figure 6.1).

In some people, the motivation to start a business develops slowly as they gain the knowledge and ability required for success as a business owner. Knowledge and ability—especially management ability—are probably the most important factors involved. A new firm is very much built around the entrepreneur. The owner must be able to manage the firm's finances, its personnel (if there are any employees), and its day-to-day operations. He or she must handle sales, advertising, purchasing, pricing, and a variety of other business functions. The knowledge and ability to do so are acquired most often through experience working for other firms in the same area of business.

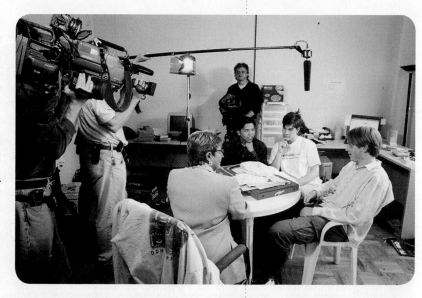

Teen entrepreneurs

In 1999 partners Albert Lai, 20, Michael Furdyk, 16, and Michael Hayman, 18, sold their Internet company for an estimated $1M. Albert Lai has gone on to create several web-based successes including the photo-sharing site Bubbleshare.com. The site allows users to easily upload photos and, if they care to, remix them and add comments or their own voice, turning the user's digital media quickly and easily into highly interactive presentations.

Why Small Businesses Fail

Small businesses are prone to failure. Capital, management, and planning are the key ingredients in the survival of a small business, as well as the most common reasons for failure. Businesses can experience a number of money-related problems. It can take several years before a business begins to show a profit. Entrepreneurs need to have not only the capital to open a business but also the money to operate it in its possibly lengthy start-up phase. One cash-flow obstacle often leads to others. And a series of cash-flow predicaments usually ends in a business failure. This scenario is played out all too often by small and not-so-small start-up Internet firms that fail to meet their financial backers' expectations and so are denied a second wave of investment dollars to continue their drive to establish a profitable online firm. For example, in one month alone, Digital Entertainment Network shut its video-streaming site, clothing distributor boo.com closed after spending more than $100 million in only six

BIZ TECH

Making a Small Business Look Big Through Technology

Technology isn't just a way to get things done more efficiently—it also can help a small business make a big impression. Here are three examples.

@ Using the Internet
Robert Singer of Richmond Hill, Ontario, has built an international business using his website (http://www.runsoft.ca) to sell what he calls the "easiest Point of Sale System to learn and administer." RunSoft's customer base includes restaurants and retailers that need multiple tasks, such as sales and inventory, controlled through their point of sale computer systems, which replaced conventional cash registers. By using the Internet and telephone, RunSoft is able to reduce marketing costs to serve clients who are particularly price sensitive.

Oriel Wines
Having a sophisticated website packed with useful information and equipped with powerful technology for customer service and marketing functions allows newcomer Oriel Wines to look like a major international wine importer. "We're a luxury brand, so customers have to think we're bigger than we really are," says Kelly Ford, Oriel's managing director.

Fog Creek Software
A company blog—a web log—can attract lots of attention on a tiny budget. Fog Creek's CEO wanted a blog because, he says, "I was trying to launch a new product and at the same time get some sort of audience on opening day to try it out." He asked the students developing the new product to write candidly about their experiences. Within weeks, their comments were drawing 15,000 regular readers. What's more, 700 of those readers agreed to pretest the software, which had the added benefit of building anticipation for the product's release.

months of business, and healthshop.com shut its doors completely after failing to meet its investors' expectations.[8]

Many entrepreneurs lack the management skills required to run a business. Money, time, personnel, and inventory all need to be managed effectively if a small business is to succeed. Starting a small business requires much more than optimism and a good idea.

Success and expansion sometimes lead to problems. Frequently, entrepreneurs with successful small businesses make the mistake of overexpansion. Fast growth often results in dramatic changes in a business. Thus the entrepreneur must plan carefully and adjust competently to new and potentially disruptive situations.

Every day, and in every part of the country, people open new businesses. According to Statistics Canada studies, about 125,000 businesses enter and exit the economy every year—with more entering than exiting in every year—regardless of economic conditions at the time.[9]

ENTREPRENEURIAL CHALLENGE

Buried in Paperwork

A Statistics Canada report suggests that smaller businesses face an unfair and disproportionate level of costs for mandatory compliance with government paperwork. The report estimated that regulatory compliance costs businesses over $33 billion a year, but for small businesses, with the cost of their compliance at $1.5 billion, it is a greater cause of difficulty than for larger businesses that can afford the bureaucratic structures and employees needed to meet-

ing reporting requirements. The report found that 41 percent of compliance spending went for filing tax forms, 17 percent for filing federal and provincial sales taxes, and 14 percent for employee remittances. Besides these filing obligations, businesses are sidetracked from their primary business activities by requirements associated with licence and permit applications and surveys of business activity for Statistics Canada.

Source: Eric Beauchesne, "Small firms buried by paperwork," *The Montreal Gazette,* December 13, 2006, p. B5.

Although many fail, others represent well-conceived ideas developed by entrepreneurs who have the expertise, resources, and determination to make their businesses succeed. As these well-prepared entrepreneurs pursue their individual goals, our society benefits in many ways from their work and creativity. Billion-dollar companies such as Canadian Tire Corporation and Bombardier Inc. are only two examples of small businesses that expanded into Canadian industry giants.

The Importance of Small Businesses in Our Economy

Learning Objective

Assess the contributions of small businesses to our economy.

Canadian economic history abounds with stories of ambitious men and women who turned their ideas into business dynasties. Joseph-Armand Bombardier's ideas for better vehicular mobility over snow started the giant transportation production company that bares his name around the world. And Tilley Endurables and Roots stores began with simple notions that helped them stand out in the retailing crowd.

Providing Technical Innovation

Invention and innovation are part of the foundations of our economy. The increases in productivity that have characterized our history are all rooted in one principal source: new ways to do a job with less effort for less money. Studies show that the incidence of innovation among small-business workers is significantly higher than among workers in large businesses. Small firms produce two and a half times as many innovations as large firms relative to the number of persons employed. In fact, small firms employ 41 percent of all high-tech workers such as scientists, engineers, and computer specialists. No wonder small firms produce thirteen to fourteen times more patents per employee than large patenting firms.[10]

According to the U.S. Office of Management and Budget, more than half the major technological advances of the twentieth century originated with individual inventors and small companies.

Perhaps even more remarkable—and important—is that many of these inventions sparked major new industries or contributed to an established industry by adding some valuable service.

Providing Employment

Small firms traditionally have added more than their proportional share of new jobs to the economy. According to Statistics Canada, small businesses have been responsible for creating 76 percent of all new jobs since the 1980s. Small businesses have thus contributed significantly to solving unemployment problems. For six years, in 1996 and 1997 and from 2000 to 2003, small businesses made the greatest contribution to net job creation. On the other hand, at the beginning of this period, in 1995, medium-sized businesses created the most jobs, while large businesses played the leading job-creation role in 1998, 1999, 2004, and 2005.[11]

Providing Competition

Small businesses challenge larger, established firms in many ways, causing them to become more efficient and more responsive to consumer needs. A small business cannot, of course, compete with a large firm in all respects. But a number of small firms, each competing in its own particular area and its own particular way, together have the desired competitive effect. Thus, several small clothing boutiques in the local mall together add up to reasonable competition for the larger department stores such as The Bay and Sears. In fact, many would argue that the smaller boutiques have contributed to the weakening of these once dominant department stores because of better customer response provided by the boutiques.

Filling the Needs of Society and Other Businesses

By their nature, large firms must operate on a large scale. Many may be unwilling or unable to meet the special needs of smaller groups of consumers. Such groups create almost perfect markets for small companies that can tailor their products to these groups and fill their needs profitably. A prime example is a firm that modifies automobile controls to accommodate handicapped drivers.

Small firms also provide a variety of goods and services to each other and to much larger firms. Sears, purchases merchandise from approximately 12,000 suppliers—and most of them are small businesses. General Motors relies on more than 32,000 companies for parts and supplies and depends on more than 11,000 independent deal-

ENTREPRENEURIAL CHALLENGE

When Should Entrepreneurs Use Outsourcing?

Small businesses are not necessarily sending jobs overseas when they choose outsourcing. For entrepreneurs and established companies alike, outsourcing can mean hiring local or national vendors to handle specialized functions such as payroll, manufacturing, information technology, and food services. Before outsourcing, an entrepreneur should ask:

- Is the function so strategically important or sensitive that it must be handled by my own staff only?

- Does my company have the people, expertise, and equipment to do the job more efficiently than an outsource vendor?

- Can my company weather the possible disruption if an outsource vendor experiences supply, labour, technical, or weather problems?

- How will the vendor handle any liability issues that might arise in managing the outsourced function?

- How long has the vendor been in business, and what do its customers say about its performance?

- Is the outsourcing contract too expensive, too restrictive, or too lengthy?

- What will my company need to do to manage the outsource vendor properly?

ers to sell its automobiles and trucks. Large firms generally buy parts and assemblies from smaller firms for one very good reason: it is less expensive than manufacturing the parts in their own factories. This lower cost eventually is reflected in the price that consumers pay for their products.

It is clear that small businesses are a vital part of our economy and that, as consumers and as members of the labour force, we all benefit enormously from their existence. Now let us look at the situation from the viewpoint of the owners of small businesses.

The Pros and Cons of Smallness

Learning Objective ❹

Judge the advantages and disadvantages of operating a small business.

Do most owners of small businesses dream that their firms will grow into giant corporations—managed by professionals—while they serve only on the board of directors? Or would they rather stay small, in a firm where they have the opportunity (and the responsibility) to do everything that needs to be done? The answers depend on the personal characteristics and motivations of the individual owners. For many, the advantages of remaining small far outweigh the disadvantages.

Advantages of Small Business

Small-business owners with limited resources often must struggle to enter competitive new markets. They also have to deal with increasing international competition. However, they enjoy several unique advantages.

Shoes with a personal touch

In 1994 Sandra Wilson designed a pair of shoes for her son, Robert. She hand stitched twenty pairs that she then sold at a gift fair in Vancouver. From there, her company, Robeez, grew, and grew, and grew.

Personal Relationships with Customers and Employees For those who like dealing with people, small business is the place to be. The owners of retail shops get to know many of their customers by name and deal with them on a personal basis. Through such relationships, small-business owners often become involved in the social, cultural, and political life of the community.

Relationships between owner-managers and employees also tend to be closer in smaller businesses. In many cases the owner is a friend and counsellor as well as the boss.

These personal relationships provide an important business advantage. The personal service small businesses offer to customers is a major competitive weapon—one that larger firms try to match but often cannot. In addition, close relationships with employees often help the small-business owner to keep effective workers who might earn more with a larger firm.

Ability to Adapt to Change Being his or her own boss, the owner-manager of a small business does not need anyone's permission to adapt to change. An owner can add or discontinue merchandise or services, change store hours, and experiment with various price strategies in response to changes in market conditions. And through personal relationships with customers, the owners of small businesses quickly become aware of changes in people's needs and interests, as well as in the activities of competing firms.

Simplified Record Keeping Many small firms need only a simple set of records. Record keeping might consist of a checkbook, a cash-receipts journal in which to record all sales, and a cash-disbursements journal in which to record all amounts paid out. Obviously, enough records must be kept to allow for producing and filing accurate tax returns.

Independence Small-business owners do not have to punch in and out, bid for vacation times, take orders from superiors, or worry about being fired or laid off. They are the masters of their own destinies—at least with regard to employment. For many people, this is the prime advantage of owning a small business.

Other Advantages Small-business owners also enjoy all the advantages of sole proprietorships, which were discussed in Chapter 5. These include being able to keep all profits, the ease and low cost of going into business and (if necessary) going out of business, and being able to keep business information secret.

Disadvantages of Small Business

Personal contacts with customers, closer relationships with employees, being one's own boss, less cumbersome record-keeping chores, and independence are the bright side of small business. In contrast, the dark side reflects problems unique to these firms.

Risk of Failure As we have noted, small businesses (especially new ones) run a heavy risk of going out of business—about two out of three close their doors within the first six years. Older, well-established small firms can be hit hard by a business recession mainly because they do not have the financial resources to weather an extended difficult period.

Limited Potential Small businesses that survive do so with varying degrees of success. Many are simply the means of making a living for the owner and his or her family. The owner may have some technical skill—as a hair stylist or electrician, for example—and may have started a business to put this skill to work. Such a business is unlikely to grow into big business. Also, employees' potential for advancement is limited.

Limited Ability to Raise Capital Small businesses typically have a limited ability to obtain capital. Figure 6.2 shows that most small-business financing comes out of the owner's pocket. Personal loans from lending institutions provide only about one-fourth of the capital required by small businesses. In fact, almost half of new firms begin with less than $10,000, usually provided by the owner or family members and friends.[12]

Although every person who considers starting a small business should be aware of the hazards and pitfalls we have noted, a well-conceived business plan can help the owner avoid the risk of failure. The Canadian and provincial governments are also dedicated to helping small businesses make it.

Developing a Business Plan

Lack of planning can be as deadly as lack of money to a new small business. Planning is important to any business, large or small, and never should be overlooked or taken lightly. A **business plan** is a carefully constructed guide for the person starting a business. Consider it as a tool with three basic purposes: communication, management,

business plan a carefully constructed guide for the person starting a business

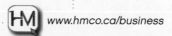

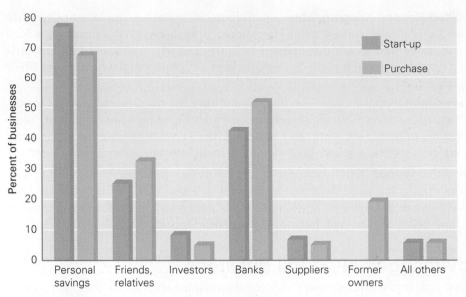

Figure 6.2

Sources of Capital for Entrepreneurs

Small businesses get financing from various sources; the most important is personal savings.

Source: Data developed and provided by the National Federation of Independent Business Foundation and sponsored by the American Express Travel Related Services Company, Inc. Used by permission of NFIB.

and planning. As a communication tool, a business plan serves as a concise document that potential investors can examine to see if they would like to invest or assist in financing a new venture. It shows whether a business has the potential to make a profit. As a management tool, the business plan helps to track, monitor, and evaluate the progress. The business plan is a living document; it is modified as the entrepreneur gains knowledge and experience. It also serves to establish timelines and milestones and allows comparison of growth projections against actual accomplishments. Finally, as a planning tool, the business plan guides a business person through the various phases of business. For example, the plan helps to identify obstacles to avoid and to establish alternatives.

Components of a Business Plan

Table 6.1 shows the twelve sections that a business plan should include. When constructing a business plan, the business person should strive to keep it easy to read, uncluttered, and complete. Like other busy executives, officials of financial institu-

BIZ TECH

According to a recent Ipso Reid-Royal Bank of Canada Small Business Survey, 74 percent rely on word-of-mouth for marketing and only 29 percent have a website. The survey found that 38 percent of small business owners used the Internet as their primary source of information for starting and running their business.

Source: Tom Barrett, "Lack of help doesn't dampen optimism," *The National Post*, October 17, 2006, p. SR 3.

1. *Introduction.* Basic information such as the name, address, and phone number of the business; the date the plan was issued; and a statement of confidentiality to keep important information away from potential competitors.

2. *Executive Summary.* A one- to two-page overview of the entire business plan, including a justification why the business will succeed.

3. *Benefits to the Community.* Information on how the business will have an impact on economic development, community development, and human development.

4. *Company and Industry.* The background of the company, choice of the legal business form, information on the products or services to be offered; and examination of the potential customers, current competitors, and the business's future.

5. *Management Team.* Discussion of skills, talents, and job descriptions of management team;managerial compensation;management training needs; and professional assistance requirements.

6. *Manufacturing and Operations Plan.* Discussion of facilities needed, space requirements, capital equipment, labour force, inventory control, and purchasing requirement.

7. *Labour Force.* Discussion of the quality of skilled workers available and the training, compensation, and motivation of workers.

8. *Marketing Plan.* Discussion of markets, market trends, competition, market share, pricing, promotion, distribution, and service policy.

9. *Financial Plan.* Summary of the investment needed, sales and cash-flow forecasts, break-even analysis, and sources of funding.

10. *Exit Strategy.* Discussion of a succession plan or going public. Who will take over the business?

11. *Critical Risks and Assumptions.* Evaluation of the weaknesses of the business and how the company plans to deal with these and any other business problems.

12. *Appendix.* Supplementary information crucial to the plan, such as résumés of owners and principal managers, advertising samples, organization chart, and any related information.

Table 6.1

Components of a Business Plan

Source: Adapted from Timothy S. Hatten, *Small Business Management: Entrepreneurship and Beyond,* 3d ed. (Boston: Houghton Mifflin, 2006), pp. 108-120.

tions do not have the time to wade through pages of extraneous data. The business plan should answer the four questions banking officials and investors are most interested in: (1) What exactly is the nature and mission of the new venture? (2) Why is this new enterprise a good idea? (3) What are the business person's goals? (4) How much will the new venture cost?

The great amount of time and consideration that should go into creating a business plan probably will end up saving time later. For example, Sharon Burch, who was running a computer software business while earning a degree in business administration, had to write a business plan as part of one of her courses. Burch has said, "I wish I'd taken the class before I started my business. I see a lot of things I could have done differently. But it has helped me since because I've been using the business plan as a guide for my business." Table 6.2 provides a business plan checklist.

Accuracy and realistic expectations are crucial to an effective business plan. It is unethical to deceive loan officers, and it is unwise to deceive yourself.

Table 6.2

Business Plan Checklist

Source: Kathleen R. Allen, *Launching New Ventures: An Entrepreneurial Approach,* 4th ed. (Boston: Houghton Mifflin, 2006), p. 197.

1. Does the executive summary grab the reader's attention and highlight the major points of the business plan?.

2. Does the business-concept section clearly describe the purpose of the business, the customers, the value proposition, and the distribution channel and convey a compelling story?

3. Do the industry and market analyses support acceptance and demand for the business concept in the marketplace and define a first customer in depth?

4. Does the management-team plan persuade the reader that the team could implement the business concept successfully? Does it assure the reader that an effective infrastructure is in place to facilitate the goals and operations of the company?

5. Does the product/service plan clearly provide details on the status of the product, the timeline for completion, and the intellectual property that will be acquired?

6. Does the operations plan prove that the product or service could be produced and distributed efficiently and effectively?

7. Does the marketing plan successfully demonstrate how the company will create customer awareness in the target market and deliver the benefit to the customer?.

8. Does the financial plan convince the reader that the business model is sustainable—that it will provide a superior return on investment for the investor and sufficient cash flow to repay loans to potential lenders?

9. Does the growth plan convince the reader that the company has long-term growth potential and spin-off products and services?

10. Does the contingency and exit-strategy plan convince the reader that the risk associated with this venture can be mediated? Is there an exit strategy in place for investors?

Small Business Assistance

Learning Objective 5

Explain how governments help small businesses.

Business Development Bank of Canada (BDC) a governmental agency that assists, counsels, and protects the interests of small businesses in the Canada

The **Business Development Bank of Canada (BDC),** created by an Act of Parliament in 1944, is a governmental agency that assists, counsels, and protects the interests of small businesses in Canada. It helps people get into business and stay in business. The agency provides assistance to owners and managers of prospective, new, and established small businesses. Through offices and resource centres throughout the nation, the BDC provides both long term financial assistance and management counselling. The BDC also provides training, technical assistance, and education to help small businesses prepare to enter foreign markets.

BDC Management Assistance

Statistics show that most failures in small business are related to poor management. For this reason, the BDC places special emphasis on improving the management

BIZ TECH

Using Productivity Tools

According to a recent Ipso Reid-Royal Bank of Canada Small Business Survey, 58 percent of small business people reported that simply writing a "to-do" list was a primary tool used to improve their productivity. This was the second highest ranked action, next to using online banking at 60 percent. Besides these two productivity tools, small business people also reported using accounting software (38 percent), telecommunications technologies (35 percent), delegating responsibilities to others (16 percent), outsourcing accounting responsibilities (12 percent), hiring better skilled employees (8 percent), using wireless tools like Blackberries (7 percent), and establishing clearly defined management processes for everyone to follow (6 percent) as the means by which they try to improve their productivity at work.

Source: Brian Morton, "It might be old school, but it still works," Canwest News Service, *The Montreal Gazette,* October 17, 2006, p. F13

ability of the owners and managers of small businesses. Individual counselling, courses, conferences, workshops, and a wide range of publications are available.

Management Courses and Workshops The management courses offered by the BDC cover all the functions, duties, and roles of managers. Instructors might be teachers from local colleges and universities or other professionals, such as management consultants, bankers, lawyers, and accountants. Fees for these courses are quite low. The most popular such course is a general survey of eight to ten different areas of business management. In follow-up studies, business people may concentrate in-depth on one or more of these areas depending on their particular strengths and weaknesses. The BDC occasionally offers one-day conferences. These conferences are aimed at keeping owner-managers up-to-date on new management developments, tax laws, and the like. A small-business owner who has a particular problem can request counselling from BDC. An assigned counsellor visits the owner in his or her establishment and, through careful observation, analyzes the business situation and the problem. If the problem is complex, the counsellor may call on other volunteer experts to assist. Finally, the counsellor offers a plan for solving the problem and helping the owner through the critical period.

Financial Assistance

Most small businesses borrow money directly from Canada's financial institutions, which actively support lending to this sector. The Small Business Loan program, which is administered under the Canada Business Loan Act, is typical of federal and provincial government assistance. If the bank that makes the loan is not paid by the small business, the government will guarantee payment for as much as 85 percent of the loan. Those small businesses that cannot borrow from traditional lending institutions because of the absence of a track record can be funded by the BDC or other organizations willing to help higher risk firms.

Venture capital is money that is invested in small (and sometimes struggling) firms that have the potential to become very successful. In many cases, only a lack of

venture capital money that is invested in small (and sometimes struggling) firms that have the potential to become very successful

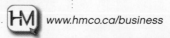

franchise a license to operate an individually owned business as though it were part of a chain of outlets or stores

franchising the actual granting of a franchise

franchisor an individual or organization granting a franchise

franchisee a person or organization purchasing a franchise

capital keeps these firms from rapid and solid growth. The people who invest in such firms expect that their investments will grow with the firms and become quite profitable. The popularity of these investments has increased over the past ten years, but most small firms still have difficulty obtaining venture capital. One drawback to dealing with venture capital groups is the common demand for a share in ownership and managerial involvement in running the business.

Venture capital loans in the $250,000 range are also available from government agencies including the BDC, BC Discovery Enterprises, Alberta Opportunities Company, Innovation Ontario, and the Société de développement industriel-Développement technologique.[13]

We have discussed the importance of the small-business segment of our economy. We have weighed the advantages and drawbacks of operating a small business compared to a large one. But is there a way to achieve the best of both worlds? Can a person preserve his or her independence as a business owner and still enjoy some of the benefits of "bigness"? Let's take a close look at franchising.

Franchising

> **Learning Objective 6**
>
> Appraise the concept and types of franchising.

A **franchise** is a license to operate an individually owned business as if it were part of a chain of outlets or stores. Often the business itself is also called a *franchise*. Among the most familiar franchises are Canadian-based Tim Horton's Donuts, Second Cup, and Van Houtte Coffee Shops as well as American-based McDonald's and Dairy Queen. Many other franchises carry familiar names; this method of doing business has become very popular in the last thirty years or so. It is an attractive means of starting and operating a small business.

What Is Franchising?

Franchising is the actual granting of a franchise. A **franchisor** is an individual or organization granting a franchise. A **franchisee** is a person or organization purchasing a franchise. The franchisor supplies a known and advertised business name, management skills, the required training and materials, and a method of doing business. The franchisee supplies labour and capital, operates the franchised business, and agrees to abide by the provisions of the franchise agreement. Table 6.3 lists some items that would be covered in a typical franchise agreement.

Types of Franchising

Franchising arrangements fall into three general categories. In the first approach, a manufacturer authorizes a number of retail stores to sell a certain brand-name item. This type of franchising arrangement, one of the oldest, is prevalent in sales of passenger cars and trucks, farm equipment, shoes, paint, earth-moving equipment, and

MCDONALD'S (FRANCHISOR) PROVIDES	INDIVIDUAL (FRANCHISEE) SUPPLIES
1. Nationally recognized trademarks and an established reputation for quality	1. Total investment of approximately $494,750 to $1,030,500, which includes initial franchise fee of $45,000
2. Designs and colour schemes for restaurants, signs, and equipment	2. Approximate cash requirement of 40 percent of total investment; a minimum of $200,000 of nonborrowed personal funds
3. Specifications for certain food products	3. A monthly base rent or rent based on a percentage of monthly sales
4. Proven methods of inventory and operations control	4. A minimum of 4 percent of gross sales annually for marketing and advertising
5. Bookkeeping, accounting, and policies manuals specially geared toward a franchised restaurant	5. Payment of a service fee of 4 percent of monthly gross sales to McDonald's
6. A franchise term of up to twenty years	6. Payment of a variable rent percent of monthly gross sales to McDonald's based on McDonald's investment and/or sales
7. Formal training program completed on a part-time basis in approximately eighteen to twenty-four months in a McDonald's restaurant	7. Kitchen equipment, seating, decor, lighting, and signs in conformity with McDonald's standards (included in total investment figure)
8. Five weeks of classroom training, including two weeks at Hamburger University	8. Taxes, insurance, and maintenance costs on the restaurant building and land
9. Ongoing regional support services and field service staff	9. Commitment to ensuring high-quality standards and upholding the McDonald's reputation
10. Research and development of labour-saving equipment and methods	
11. Monthly bulletins, periodicals, or meetings to inform franchisees about management and marketing techniques	
12. Site selection (purchase or lease) and development, including building	

Table 6.3

McDonald's Conventional Franchise Agreement

Source: "McDonald's Conventional Franchise Agreement as of November 2005," From *McDonald's Franchising*, McDonald's Corporation, Oak Brook, IL, www.mcdonalds.com/corp/franchise, accessed November 7, 2005. Used with permission from McDonald's Corporation.

petroleum. About 90 percent of all gasoline is sold through franchised, independent retail service stations, and franchised dealers handle virtually all sales of new cars and trucks. In the second type of franchising arrangement, a producer licenses distributors to sell a given product to retailers. This arrangement is common in the soft-drink industry. Most national manufacturers of soft-drink syrups—the Coca-Cola Company, Dr. Pepper/Seven-Up Companies, PepsiCo, Royal Crown Companies, Inc.—franchise independent bottlers who then serve retailers. In a third form of franchising, a franchisor supplies brand names, techniques, or other services instead of a complete product. Although the franchisor may provide certain production and distribution services, its primary role is the careful development and control of marketing strategies. This approach to franchising, which is the most typical today, is used by Holiday Inns, Howard Johnson Company, AAMCO Transmissions, McDonald's, Dairy Queen, Avis, Hertz Corporation, KFC (Kentucky Fried Chicken), and SUBWAY, to name but a few.

The Growth of Franchising

Learning Objective 7

Analyze the growth of franchising and franchising's advantages and disadvantages.

Franchising, which has been around for over a hundred years, was used originally by large firms, such as the Canadian Tire Corporation, to distribute their products. Franchising has been increasing steadily in popularity since the early 1900s, primarily for filling stations and car dealerships; however, this retailing strategy has experienced enormous growth since the mid-1970s. The franchise proliferation generally has paralleled the expansion of the fast-food industry. As Table 6.4 shows, five of *Entrepreneur* magazine's top-rated franchises for 2005 were in this category.

Of course, franchising is not limited to fast foods. Hair salons, tanning parlours, and dentists and lawyers are expected to participate in franchising arrangements in growing numbers. Franchised health clubs, pest exterminators, and campgrounds are already widespread, as are franchised tax preparers and travel agencies. The real estate industry also has experienced a rapid increase in franchising.

▲
Franchising: one way to begin

The Singer Sewing Company was one of the first large firms to distribute its sewing machines through franchising. In 2001, Singer celebrated the 150th anniversary of Isaac Singer's patent on the first practical sewing machine. In 1870, the Red "S" girl trademark made her debut and was destined to become one of the best-known emblems in the world.

Are Franchises Successful?

Franchising is designed to provide a tested formula for success, along with ongoing advice and training. The success rate for businesses owned and operated by franchisees is significantly higher than the success rate for other independently owned small businesses. In a recent U.S. Gallup poll of 944 franchise owners, 94 percent of franchisees indicated that they were very or somewhat successful, only 5 percent believed that they were very unsuccessful or somewhat unsuccessful, and 1 percent did not know. Despite

RANK	FRANCHISE	TOTAL INVESTMENT	FRANCHISE FEE	ROYALTY FEE	NET-WORTH REQUIREMENT	CASH REQUIREMENT	COMMENTS
1	SUBWAY	$70,000–$220,000	$12,500	8%	$30,000–$90,000	$30,000–$90,000	20-year renewable term
2	Curves for Women	$36,400–$42,900	$39,900	5%	$75,000	$50,000	5-year renewable term
3	Quizno's Franchise Co.	$208,400–$243,800	$25,000	7%	$125,000	$60,000	15-year renewable term; renewable fee $1,000
4	Jackson Hewitt Tax Service	$51,700–$85,500	$25,000	15%	$100,000–$200,000	$50,000	10-year renewable term
5	UPS Store	$138,700–$245,500	$29,950	5%	—	—	10-year renewable term; renewal fee: 25% of current fee
6	Sonic Drive In Restaurants	$710,000–$2,300,000	$30,000	1%–5%	$1,000,000	$500,000	20-year renewable term; renewal fee 10 years for $6,000
6	Taco Bell Corp.	$3,000,000	$45,000	5.5%	—	—	
7	Jani-King	$11,300–$34,100	$8,600–$16,300	10%	Varies	Varies	20-year renewable term
8	7-Eleven, Inc.	Varies	Varies	Varies	Varies	Varies	15-year renewable term
9	Dunkin Donuts	$255,700–$1,100,000	$40,000–$80,000	5.9%	$1,300,000	$750,000	—
10	RE/MAX Int'l	$20,000–$200,000	$10,000–$25,000	Varies	—	—	5-year renewable term; renewal fee varies

these impressive statistics, franchising is not a guarantee of success for either franchisees or franchisors. Too rapid expansion, inadequate capital or management skills, and a host of other problems can cause failure for both franchisee and franchisor.

Advantages of Franchising

Franchising plays a vital role in our economy and soon may become the dominant form of retailing. Why? Because franchising offers advantages to both the franchisor and the franchisee.

To the Franchisor The franchisor gains fast and well-controlled distribution of its products without incurring the high cost of constructing and operating its own outlets. The franchisor thus has more capital available to expand production and to use for advertising. At the same time, it can ensure, through the franchise agreement, that outlets are maintained and operated according to its own standards.

The franchisor also benefits from the fact that the franchisee—a sole proprietor in most cases—is likely to be very highly motivated to succeed. The success of the franchise means more sales, which translate into higher royalties for the franchisor.

Table 6.4

Entrepreneur's Top Ten Franchises in 2005

Source: Reprinted with permission from *Entrepreneur* Magazine, November 2005, www.entrepreneur.com.

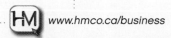

To the Franchisee The franchisee gets the opportunity to start a business with limited capital and to make use of the business experience of others. Moreover, an outlet with a nationally advertised name, such as Tim Hortons, McDonald's, or Century 21 Real Estate, has guaranteed customers as soon as it opens.

If business problems arise, the franchisor gives the franchisee guidance and advice. This counselling is primarily responsible for the very high degree of success enjoyed by franchises. In most cases, the franchisee does not pay for such help.

The franchisee also receives materials to use in local advertising and can take part in national promotional campaigns sponsored by the franchisor. McDonald's and its franchisees, for example, constitute one of the nation's top twenty purchasers of advertising. Finally, the franchisee may be able to minimize the cost of advertising, supplies, and various business necessities by purchasing them in cooperation with other franchisees.

Disadvantages of Franchising

The main disadvantage of franchising affects the franchisee, and it arises because the franchisor retains a great deal of control. The franchisor's contract can dictate every aspect of the business: decor, design of employee uniforms, types of signs, and all the details of business operations. All Burger King French fries taste the same because all Burger King franchisees have to make them the same way.

Contract disputes are the cause of many lawsuits. For example, Rekha Gabhawala, a Dunkin' Donuts franchisee in Milwaukee, alleged that the franchisor was forcing her out of business so that the company could profit by reselling the downtown franchise to someone else; the company, on the other hand, alleged that Gabhawala breached the contract by not running the business according to company standards. In another case, Dunkin' Donuts sued Chris Romanias, its franchisee in Pennsylvania, alleging that Romanias intentionally underreported gross sales to the company. Romanias, on the other hand, alleged that Dunkin' Donuts, Inc., breached the contract because it failed to provide assistance in operating the franchise. Other franchisees claim that contracts are unfairly tilted toward the franchisors. Yet others have charged that they lost their franchise and investment because their franchisor would not approve the sale of the business when they found a buyer.

Franchise holders pay for their security, usually with a one-time franchise fee and continuing royalty and advertising fees, collected as a percentage of sales. In some fields, franchise agreements are not uniform. One franchisee may pay more than another for the same services.

Even success can cause problems. Sometimes a franchise is so successful that the franchisor opens its own outlet nearby, in direct competition—although franchisees may fight back. For example, a court recently ruled that Burger King could not enter into direct competition with the franchisee because the contract was not specific on the issue. A spokesperson for one franchisor contends that the company "gives no geographical protection" to its franchise holders and thus is free to move in on them. Franchise operators work hard. They often put in ten- and twelve-hour days, six or seven days a week. The International Franchise Association advises prospective franchise purchasers to investigate before investing and to approach buying a franchise

BUSINESS AROUND THE WORLD

Dos and Don'ts of International Franchising

Small businesses that are thinking about transplanting a franchise from one country to another should think about these dos and don'ts:

DO	DON'T
• Find out what support the franchisor offers in each country.	• Assume that customers everywhere need or want what the franchise offers.
• Check trade laws before buying a franchise in another country.	• Expect hiring, training, and marketing practices to be identical in all countries.
• Thoroughly research the competitive situation.	• Underestimate the amount of money needed to fund international operations.
• Understand the laws and regulations governing franchising in each country.	• Forget that strong local management is needed to keep an international franchise going.

Doug Howard, CEO of Drama Kids International, the U.S. franchisor of an Australian-based drama program, stresses that franchisees can import a franchise successfully "as long as they are passionate about the basic concept, are prepared for a reasonable and necessary testing period, and realize that numerous changes—and sometimes dramatic challenges—are part of the process."

cautiously. Franchises vary widely in approach as well as in products. Some, such as Dunkin' Donuts and Baskin-Robbins, demand long hours, while others are more appropriate for those who do not want to spend many hours at their stores.

Global Perspectives in Small Business

For small Canadian businesses, the world is becoming smaller. National and international economies are growing more and more interdependent as political leadership and national economic directions change and trade barriers diminish or disappear. Globalization and instant worldwide communications are rapidly shrinking distances at the same time that they are expanding business opportunities. According to a recent study, the Internet is increasingly important to small-business strategic thinking, with more than 50 percent of those surveyed indicating that the Internet represented their most favoured strategy for growth. This was more than double the next-favoured choice, strategic alliances reflecting the opportunity to reach both global and domestic customers. The Internet and online payment systems enable even very small businesses to serve international customers. In fact, technology now gives small businesses the leverage and power to reach markets that were once limited solely to large corporations. No wonder the number of businesses exporting their goods and services continues to grow.

International trade will become more important to small-business owners as they face unique challenges in the new century. Small businesses, which are expected to remain the dominant form of organization in this country, must be prepared to adapt to significant demographic and economic changes in the world marketplace.

This chapter ends our discussion of Canadian business today. From here on we shall be looking closely at various aspects of business operations. We begin, in the next chapter, with a discussion of management—what management is, what managers do, and how they work to coordinate the basic economic resources within a business organization.

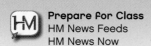
Prepare for Class
HM News Feeds
HM News Now

→ **RETURN TO INSIDE BUSINESS**

Small business entrepreneurs have always dominated the Canadian garment industry. Entrepreneurs would generally learn the business first by working for someone else and then set out on their own when they felt ready to take the plunge.

In general, barriers to entry, such as the required capital investment, have remained relatively low, in comparison to most other manufacturing industries and as anyone in the fashion business will tell you, "you're only as good as your last season." With every new season, the process starts all over again as manufacturers seek distinguishing styles, fabrics, and colours that will bring them sales, profits, and sustainability.

Questions

1. If you were working on a business plan for a small Canadian ski-wear manufacturer, how would you suggest that they deal with rising costs of production?

2. What are the arguments for and against importing more production from China and India?

CHAPTER REVIEW

1 Define what a small business is and recognize the fields in which small businesses are concentrated.

A small business is one that is independently owned and operated for profit and is not dominant in its field. Small businesses employ more than half the nation's workforce. More than half of all small businesses are in retailing and services.

2 Identify the people who start small businesses and the reasons why some succeed and many fail.

Such personal characteristics as independence, desire to create a new enterprise, and willingness to accept a challenge may encourage individuals to start small businesses. Various external circumstances, such as special expertise or even the loss of a job, also can supply the motivation to strike out on one's own. Poor planning and lack of capital and management experience are the major causes of small-business failures.

3 Assess the contributions of small businesses to our economy.

Small businesses have been responsible for a wide variety of inventions and innovations, some of which have given rise to new industries. Historically, small businesses have created the bulk of the nation's new jobs. Further, they have mounted effective competition to larger firms. They provide things that society needs, act as suppliers to larger firms, and serve as customers of other businesses, both large and small.

4 Judge the advantages and disadvantages of operating a small business.

The advantages of smallness in business include the opportunity to establish personal relationships with customers and employees, the ability to adapt to changes quickly, independence, and simplified record keeping. The major disadvantages are the high risk of failure, the limited potential for growth, and the limited ability to raise capital.

5 Explain how governments help small businesses.

The Business Development Bank of Canada (BDC) was created in 1944 to assist and counsel the nation's small-business owners. The BDC offers management courses and workshops; managerial help, including one-to-one counselling; various publications; and financial assistance through guaranteed loans.

6 Appraise the concept and types of franchising.

A franchise is a license to operate an individually owned business as though it were part of a chain. The franchisor provides a known business name, management skills, a method of doing business, and the training and required materials. The franchisee contributes labour and capital, operates the franchised business, and agrees to abide by the provisions of the franchise agreement. There are three major categories of franchise agreements.

7 Analyze the growth of franchising and franchising's advantages and disadvantages.

Franchising has grown tremendously since the mid-1970s. The franchisor's major advantage in franchising is fast and well-controlled distribution of products with minimal capital outlay. In return, the franchisee has the opportunity to open a business with limited capital, to make use of the business experience of others, and to sell to an existing clientele. For this, the franchisee usually must pay both an initial franchise fee and a continuing royalty based on sales. He or she also must follow the dictates of the franchise with regard to operation of the business. Worldwide business opportunities are expanding for small businesses. The next century will present unique challenges and opportunities for small-business owners.

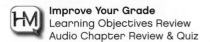

Improve Your Grade
Learning Objectives Review
Audio Chapter Review & Quiz

Review Questions

1. What information would you need to determine whether a particular business is small according to most guidelines?
2. Which two areas of business generally attract the most small businesses? Why are these areas attractive to small business?
3. Distinguish among service industries, distribution industries, and production industries.
4. What kinds of factors encourage certain people to start new businesses?
5. What are the major causes of small-business failure? Do these causes also apply to larger businesses?
6. Briefly describe four contributions of small business to the Canadian economy.
7. What are the major advantages and disadvantages of smallness in business?
8. What are the major components of a business plan? Why should an individual develop a business plan?
9. Identify the ways in which the BDC provides management assistance to small businesses.
10. Identify the ways in which the BDC provides financial assistance to small businesses.
11. Why does the BDC concentrate on providing management and financial assistance to small businesses?
12. What is venture capital? How does the BDC help small businesses to obtain it?
13. Explain the relationships among a franchise, the franchisor, and the franchisee.
14. What does the franchisor receive in a franchising agreement? What does the franchisee receive? What does each provide?
15. Cite one major benefit of franchising for the franchisor. Cite one major benefit of franchising for the franchisee.

Discussion Questions

1. Most people who start small businesses are aware of the high failure rate and the reasons for it. Why, then, do some take no steps to protect their firms from failure? What steps should they take?
2. Are the so-called advantages of small business really advantages? Wouldn't every small-business owner like his or her business to grow into a large firm?
3. Do average citizens benefit from the activities of the BDC, or is the BDC just another way to spend our tax money?
4. Would you rather own your own business independently or become a franchisee? Why?

CASE STUDY

No Funny Business at Newbury Comics

The success of Newbury Comics suggests that a single focus can be a great way to start a business, but diversification allows the firm to more easily adapt to new opportunities as they arise—including using the Internet as an important sales tool. The two university students who started Newbury Comics have become serious business owners. Mike Dreese and John Brusger started Newbury Comics in 1978 with $2,000 and a valuable comic book collection. Their first store was actually a tiny apartment on Boston's popular Newbury Street, which they rented for $260 per month. Three decades later, the company operates twenty-six stores in Massachusetts, Maine, New Hampshire, and Rhode Island. It still does business on Newbury Street—in a spacious storefront that rents for $23,000 per month.

How did Newbury Comics grow into a multimillion-dollar business? First, the owners identified a need that they could fill. They understood what kind of comic books collectors were interested in buying, and they enjoyed dealing with these customers.

Second, Reese and Brusger thought of their business as a business. As much as they liked comics, they recognized the profit potential of carrying other products. Over time, they started stocking music and added movies, novelty items, and clothing accessories.

Third, the entrepreneurs didn't do everything themselves—they knew when to delegate to others. As Newbury Comics expanded beyond comics and opened new stores, the owners hired professionals to negotiate leases, make buying decisions, and select the exact merchandise assortment for each store. They also hired technology experts to design systems for tracking what was in stock, what had been sold, how much the company was spending, and how much each store was contributing to total sales.

Fourth, Reese and Brusger have paid close attention to Newbury Comics' financial situation. They're careful to pay suppliers on time and, in exchange, they can get fast-selling products even when supplies are limited.

The company has formalized its store payroll budgets, assigned employees to check the quality of customer service at each store, and begun offering more products for sale online. Many competitors are far bigger, but no competitor knows its customers and its products better than the team at Newbury Comics.

Questions:

1. This chapter cites five advantages of small business. Which of these seem to apply to the owners' experience with Newbury Comics?

2. This chapter cites three disadvantages of small business. Based on what you know of Newbury Comics, which of these is likely to be the biggest problem in the coming years?

3. Newbury Comics was started without a formal business plan. If you were writing its plan today, what critical risks and assumptions would you examine—and why?

BUILDING SKILLS FOR CAREER SUCCESS

1. Exploring the Internet

Perhaps the most challenging difficulty for small businesses is operating with scarce resources, especially people and money. To provide information and point small-business operators in the right direction, many Internet sites offer helpful products and services. Although most are sponsored by advertising and may be free of charge, some charge a fee, and others are a combination of both. The BDC provides a wide array of free information and resources. You can find your way to the BDC through http://www.bdc.ca/en/home.htm. Visit the text website for updates to this exercise.

Assignment

1. Describe the various services provided by the BDC-SBA site.

2. What sources of funding are there?

3. What service would you like to see improved? How?

2. Building Team Skills

A business plan is a written statement that documents the nature of a business and how that business intends to achieve its goals. Although entrepreneurs should prepare a business plan before starting a business, the plan also serves as an effective guide later on. The plan should concisely describe the business's mission, the amount of capital it requires, its target market, competition, resources, production plan, marketing plan, organizational plan, assessment of risk, and financial plan.

Assignment

1. Working in a team of four students, identify a company in your community that would benefit from using a business plan, or create a scenario in which a hypothetical entrepreneur wants to start a business.

HM Prepare for Class
Exploring the Internet

2. Using the resources of the library or the Internet and/or interviews with business owners, write a business plan incorporating the information in Table 6.1

3. Present your business plan to the class.

3. Researching Different Careers

Many people dream of opening and operating their own businesses. Are you one of them? To be successful, entrepreneurs must have certain characteristics; their profiles generally differ from those of people who work for someone else. Do you know which personal characteristics make some entrepreneurs succeed and others fail? Do you fit the successful entrepreneur's profile? What is your potential for opening and operating a successful small business?

Assignment

1. Use the resources of the library or the Internet to establish what a successful entrepreneur's profile is and to determine whether your personal characteristics fit that profile. Internet addresses that can help you are www.smartbiz.com/sbs/arts/ieb1.html and www.sba.gov (see "Starting Your Business" and "FAQs"). These sites have quizzes online that can help you to assess your personal characteristics. The SBA also has helpful brochures.

2. Interview several small-business owners. Ask them to describe the characteristics they think are necessary for being a successful entrepreneur.

3. Using your findings, write a report that includes the following:

   a. A profile of a successful small-business owner

   b. A comparison of your personal characteristics with the profile of the successful entrepreneur

   c. A discussion of your potential as a successful small-business owner

RUNNING A BUSINESS PART II
Finagle A Bagel:
A Fast-Growing Small Business

Finagle A Bagel, a fast-growing small business co-owned by Alan Litchman and Laura Trust, is at the forefront of one of the freshest concepts in the food-service business: fresh food. Each of the twenty stores bakes a new batch of bagels every hour, and each receives new deliveries of cheeses, vegetables, fruits, and other ingredients every day. Rather than prepackage menu items, store employees make everything to order so that they can satisfy the specific needs of each guest (Finagle A Bagel's term for a customer). As a result, customers get fresh food prepared to their exact preferences—whether it's extra cheese on a bagel pizza or no onions in a salad—along with prompt, friendly service.

"Every sandwich, every salad is built to order, so there's a lot of communication between the customers and the cashiers, the customers and the sandwich makers, the customers and the managers," explains Trust. This allows Finagle A Bagel's store employees ample opportunity to build customer relationships and encourage repeat business. Many, like Mirna Hernandez of the Tremont Street store in downtown Boston, are so familiar with what certain customers order that they spring into action when regulars enter the store. "We know what they want, and we

just ring it in and take care of them," she says. Some employees even know their customers by name and make conversation as they create a sandwich or fill a coffee container.

Buying and Building the Business and Brand

The combination of a strong local following and favourable brand image is what attracted the entrepreneurs to Finagle A Bagel. Looking back, Litchman says that he and his wife recognized that building a small business would require more than good business sense. "It has a lot to do with having a great brand and having great food and reinforcing the brand every day," he remembers. "That's one of the key things that we bought."

To further reinforce the brand and reward customer loyalty, Finagle A Bagel created the Frequent Finagler card. Cardholders receive one point for every dollar spent in a Finagle A Bagel store and can redeem accumulated points for coffee, juice, sandwiches, or other rewards. To join, customers visit the company's website (www.finagleabagel.com) and complete a registration form asking for name, address, and other demographics. Once the account is set up, says Litchman, "It's a web-based program where customers

can log on, check their points, and receive free gifts by mail. The Frequent Finagler is our big push right now to use technology as a means of generating store traffic."

Bagels Online?

Soon Litchman plans to expand the website so that customers can order food and catering services directly online. Although some competitors already invite online orders, Finagle A Bagel has a more extensive menu, and its fresh-food concept is not as easily adapted to e-commerce. "In our stores, all the food is prepared fresh, and it is very customized," Litchman notes. "This entails a fair amount of interaction between employees and customers: 'What kind of croutons do you want? What kind of dressing? What kind of mustard?' When we're ready to go in that direction, it is going to be a fairly sizable technology venture for us to undertake."

Finagle A Bagel occasionally receives web or phone orders from customers hundreds or thousands of miles away. Still, the copresidents have no immediate plans to expand outside the Boston metropolitan area. Pointing to regional food-service firms that have profited by opening more stores in a wider geographic domain, Trust says, "We see that the most successful companies have really dominated their area first. Cheesecake Factory is an example of a company that's wildly successful right now, but they were a concept in California for decades before they moved beyond that area. In-and-Out Burger is an outstanding example of a food-service company in the west that's done what we're trying to do. They had seventeen stores at one time, and now they have hundreds of stores. They're very successful, but they never left their backyard. That's kind of why we're staying where we are."

Financing a Small Business

Some small businesses achieve rapid growth through franchising. The entrepreneurs running Finagle A Bagel resisted franchising for a long time. "When you franchise, you gain a large influx of capital," says Trust, "but you begin to lose control over the people, the place, and the product." Since the beginning, the owners and their senior managers routinely popped into different Finagle A Bagel stores every day to check quality and service. Now the company says that it will begin granting franchises in the near future and institute a stringent quality-control regimen to maintain the highest standards wherever the brand name appears.

As a corporation, Finagle a Bagel could, as some other small businesses do, raise money for growth through an initial public offering (IPO) of corporate stock. The co-presidents prefer not to transform their company into an open corporation at this time. "Going public is very tricky in the food-service business," Trust observes. "Some people have done it very successfully; others have not." The copresidents want to maintain total control over the pace and direction of growth rather than feeling pressured to meet the growth expectations of securities analysts and shareholders. Running a fast-growing small business is their major challenge for now.

Questions

1. Why would Finagle A Bagel maintain a business-to-customer (B2C) website even though it is not yet set up to process online orders from individuals?

2. Do you agree with Finagle A Bagel's plan to franchise its fresh-food concept and brand name? Support your answer.

3. Although opening new stores is costly, the copresidents have chosen not to raise money through an IPO. Do you agree with this decision? Discuss the advantages and disadvantages.

4. If you were writing the executive summary of Finagle A Bagel's business plan to show to lenders, what key points would you stress?

CHAPTER 7

Understanding the Management Process

Your Guide to Success in Business

Why this chapter matters
Most of the people who read this chapter will not spend much time at the bottom of organizations. They will advance upward and become managers. Thus an overview of the field of management is essential.

LEARNING OBJECTIVES

1. Define what management is.

2. Describe the four basic management functions: planning, organizing, leading and motivating, and controlling.

3. Distinguish among the various kinds of managers in terms of both level and area of management.

4. Identify key management skills and managerial roles.

5. Explain the different types of leadership.

6. Discuss the steps in the managerial decision-making process.

7. Describe how organizations benefit from total quality management.

8. Summarize what it takes to become a successful manager today.

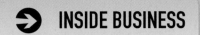

Managing a Hockey League . . .

Managing a hockey league is like trying to manufacture several products at the same time. There are obviously the workers—in this case the players who are represented by a union—The NHL Player's Association (NHLPA). There are also the owners of the teams and arenas, the marketing companies, the hockey memorabilia vendors, and let's not forget the various media interests, from radio and TV to the Internet.

At the helm of this sport sits Gary Bettman, a former lawyer for the National Basketball Association (NBA) who became the NHL Commissioner in 1993. While Bettman enjoyed considerable success assisting in managing the affairs of the NBA, his record at the NHL has been undermined to a degree by a strike and by the failure of the league to compete with other professional sports such as football, baseball, and basketball.

Since taking over from Gil Stein, Bettman's mandate has been clear—sell hockey in the United States where twenty-four of the thirty franchises are located. Compounding that problem is the fact that the league has lost its television contract with ESPN. The NBC has been airing a limited number of games on a revenue-sharing basis with the NHL, and cable broadcasts on OLN and satellite radio have been trying to fill the void, but without a national broadcast carrier, the game is unlikely to infiltrate the American marketplace.

In this chapter we will focus on what it takes to become a successful manager. Our discussions will focus on how we motivate people to perform to the best of their abilities. We will examine successful management theories and their impact on both employee and management functions.

For Mr. Bettman and his management team, the growth of the NHL "product" is measured by TV ratings, game revenue, and franchise values. And, as in selling any other product, the key is to develop brand loyalty. But whereas a product's life cycle is counted in months and years, the NHL's life cycle is measured in eighty-two game seasons.

continued on next page

DID YOU KNOW?

Founders of some successful companies don't have jobs for life.

KEY TERMS

management (196)
planning (198)
mission (198)
strategic planning (198)
goal (198)
objective (198)
plan (199)
strategic plan (200)
tactical plan (200)
operational plan (200)

contingency plan (200)
organizing (200)
leading (201)
motivating (201)
directing (201)
controlling (201)
top manager (203)
middle manager (203)
first-line manager (204)
financial manager (204)

production manager (204)
marketing manager (204)
human resources manager (205)
administrative manager (205)
technical skill (206)
conceptual skill (206)
interpersonal skill (207)
decisional role (207)
interpersonal role (207)
informational role (207)

leadership (208)
authoritarian leader (208)
laissez-faire leader (208)
democratic leader (208)
decision making (209)
problem (209)
total quality management (TQM) (212)

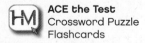

ACE the Test
Crossword Puzzle
Flashcards

Management innovations such as new product designs and improvements also take place in sport. The NHL's decision to allow a shootout to decide overtime tied games, decreasing the size of a goalie's padding, and increasing the size of the offensive zone in the hope of more goals were all been designed to garner fan interest.

But key to the success of the league will be management's continued attention to the development of human capital that stays in touch with the customer base and generates both interest and innovation in the game of hockey. All the management theories in the world will fail if Mr. Bettman and his team don't keep their eyes focused on finding ways to expand the customer base, particularly in the United States.

The leadership challenges faced by the management team at the NHL illustrate that management can be one of the most exciting and rewarding professions available today. Depending on its size, an organization employs a number of specialized managers who are responsible for particular areas of management, such as marketing, finance, and operations. That same organization also includes managers at several levels within the firm. In this chapter we define *management* and describe the four basic management functions of planning, organizing, leading and motivating, and controlling. Then we focus on the types of managers with respect to levels of responsibility and areas of expertise. Next, we focus on the skills of effective managers and the different roles managers must play. We examine several styles of leadership and explore the process by which managers make decisions. We also describe how total quality management can improve customer satisfaction. We conclude the chapter with a discussion of what it takes to be a successful manager today.

What Is Management?

Learning Objective ❶

Define what management is.

management the process of coordinating people and other resources to achieve the goals of an organization

Management is the process of coordinating people and other resources to achieve the goals of an organization. As we saw in Chapter 1, most organizations make use of four kinds of resources: material, human, financial, and informational (see Figure 7.1). *Material resources* are the tangible, physical resources an organization uses. For example, General Motors and Honda use steel, glass, and fibreglass to produce cars and trucks on complex machine-driven assembly lines. Seneca College and the University of Regina use books, classroom buildings, desks, and computers to educate students. And the Foothills Hospital in Calgary uses beds, operating room equipment, and diagnostic machines to provide healthcare.

Perhaps the most important resources of any organization are its *human resources*—people. In fact, some firms live by the philosophy that their employees are their most important assets. Evidence suggests that the way employees are developed and managed may have more impact on an organization than other vital components such as marketing, sound financial decisions about large expenditures, production, or use of technology.[1]

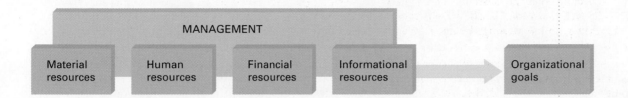

Figure 7.1

The Four Main Resources of Management

Managers coordinate an organization's resources to achieve the goals of the organization.

Financial resources are the funds an organization uses to meet its obligations to investors and creditors. A convenience store obtains money from customers at the check-out counters and uses a portion of that money to pay its suppliers. The Royal Bank of Canada, the largest Canadian bank, borrows and lends money. Your college or university obtains money in the form of tuition, income from its endowments, and provincial and federal government grants. It uses the money to pay utility bills, building maintenance, and professors' salaries.

Finally, many organizations increasingly find that they cannot afford to ignore *information*. External environmental conditions—including the economy, consumer markets, technology, politics, and cultural forces—are all changing so rapidly that a business that does not adapt probably will not survive. And to adapt to change, the business must know what is changing and how it is changing. Companies are finding it increasingly important to gather information about their competitors to increase their knowledge about changes in their industry and to learn from other companies' failures and successes.

It is important to realize that the four types of resources described earlier are only general categories of resources. Within each category are hundreds or thousands of more specific resources. It is this complex mix of specific resources—and not simply "some of each" of the four general categories—that managers must coordinate to produce goods and services.

Another interesting way to look at management is in terms of the different functions managers perform. These functions have been identified as planning, organizing, leading and motivating employees, and controlling. We look at each of these management functions in the next section.

Basic Management Functions

Learning Objective ❷

Describe the four basic management functions: planning, organizing, leading and motivating, and controlling.

A couple of years ago, AOL was struggling financially because it was losing significant market share to competitors such as Yahoo! and Google. At the time, AOL was primarily providing Internet service to dial-up customers. To turn the company around, top management had to make significant changes that included redesigning its format to offer a Yahoo!-like portal. In addition, this change forced AOL to provide

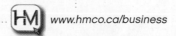

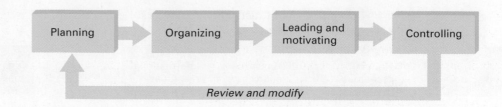

Review and modify

customers with its rich content for free. These major changes have resulted in a turnaround for AOL. Now AOL is a financially sound organization.[2]

Management decisions, such as those just described, do not occur according to some rigid, preset timetable. Managers do not plan in January, organize in February, lead and motivate in March, and control in April. At any given time, managers engage in a number of functions simultaneously. However, each function tends to lead naturally to others. Figure 7.2 provides a visual framework for a more detailed discussion of the four basic management functions. How well managers perform these key functions determines whether a business is successful.

Planning

planning establishing organizational goals and deciding how to accomplish them

Planning, in its simplest form, is establishing organizational goals and deciding how to accomplish them. It is often referred to as the "first" management function because all other management functions depend on planning. Organizations such as WestJet Airlines Ltd. and Tim Horton's begin the planning process by developing a mission statement.

mission a statement of the basic purpose that makes an organization different from others

An organization's **mission** is a statement of the basic purpose that makes that organization different from others. WestJet's mission statement is "to provide safe, friendly and affordable air travel."[3] Once an organization's mission has been described in a mission statement, the next step is to develop organizational goals and objectives, usually through strategic planning. **Strategic planning** is the process of establishing an organization's major goals and objectives and allocating the resources to achieve them.

strategic planning the process of establishing an organization's major goals and objectives and allocating the resources to achieve them

Establishing Goals and Objectives A **goal** is an end result that an organization is expected to achieve over a one- to ten-year period. An **objective** is a specific statement detailing what the organization intends to accomplish over a shorter period of time.

goal an end result that an organization is expected to achieve over a one- to ten-year period

Goals and objectives can deal with a variety of factors, such as sales, company growth, costs, customer satisfaction, and employee morale. Whereas a small manufacturer may focus primarily on sales objectives for the next six months, a large firm may be more interested in goals for several years ahead. A company's managers know that goals take time to achieve, and they are willing to invest to reach their goals. Finally, goals are set at every level of an organization. Every member of an organization—the president of the company, the head of a department, and an operating employee at the lowest level—has a set of goals that he or she hopes to achieve.

objective a specific statement detailing what an organization intends to accomplish over a shorter period of time

The goals developed for these levels must be consistent. However, it is likely that some conflict will arise. A production department, for example, may have a goal of minimizing costs. One way to do this is to produce only one type of product and offer "no frills." Marketing may have a goal of maximizing sales. One way to implement this goal is to offer customers a wide range of products and options. As part of goal setting, the manager who is responsible for *both* departments must achieve some sort of balance between conflicting goals. This balancing process is called *optimization*.

The optimization of conflicting goals requires insight and ability. Faced with the marketing-versus-production conflict just described, most managers probably would not adopt either viewpoint completely. Instead, they might decide on a reasonably diverse product line offering only the most widely sought-after options. Such a compromise would seem to be best for the whole organization.

Establishing Plans to Accomplish Goals and Objectives Once goals and objectives have been set for the organization, managers must develop plans for achieving them. A **plan** is an outline of the actions by which an organization intends to accomplish its goals and objectives. Just as it has different goals and objectives, the organization also develops several types of plans, as shown in Figure 7.3

The mission of WestJet.

WestJet is dedicated to serving the western region of Canada with the highest quality service, friendliness, pride, and company spirit.

plan an outline of the actions by which an organization intends to accomplish its goals and objectives

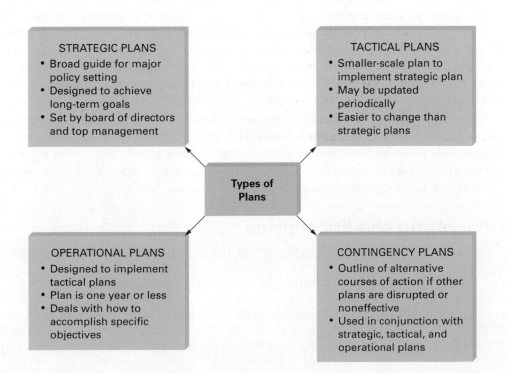

STRATEGIC PLANS
- Broad guide for major policy setting
- Designed to achieve long-term goals
- Set by board of directors and top management

TACTICAL PLANS
- Smaller-scale plan to implement strategic plan
- May be updated periodically
- Easier to change than strategic plans

Types of Plans

OPERATIONAL PLANS
- Designed to implement tactical plans
- Plan is one year or less
- Deals with how to accomplish specific objectives

CONTINGENCY PLANS
- Outline of alternative courses of action if other plans are disrupted or noneffective
- Used in conjunction with strategic, tactical, and operational plans

Figure 7.3

Types of Plans

Managers develop and rely on several types of plans.

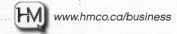
www.hmco.ca/business

strategic plan an organization's broadest plan, developed as a guide for major policy setting and decision making

tactical plan a smaller-scale plan developed to implement a strategy

operational plan a type of plan designed to implement tactical plans

contingency plan a plan that outlines alternative courses of action that may be taken if an organization's other plans are disrupted or become ineffective

organizing the grouping of resources and activities to accomplish some end result in an efficient and effective manner

Resulting from the strategic planning process, an organization's **strategic plan** is its broadest plan, developed as a guide for major policy setting and decision making. Strategic plans are set by the board of directors and top management and generally are designed to achieve the long-term goals of the organization. Thus a firm's strategic plan defines what business the company is in or wants to be in and the kind of company it is or wants to be. When medical researchers across Canada issued reports linking smoking and cancer, top management at cigarette manufacturers recognized that the industry's survival was being threatened. Executives needed to develop a strategic plan to diversify into non-tobacco products. The Internet has challenged traditional strategic thinking. For example, reluctant to move from a face-to-face sales approach to a less personal website approach, many companies have created an Internet presence to support its established sales force.

In addition to strategic plans, most organizations also employ several narrower kinds of plans. A **tactical plan** is a smaller-scale plan developed to implement a strategy. Most tactical plans cover a one- to three-year period. If a strategic plan will take five years to complete, the firm may develop five tactical plans, one covering each year. Tactical plans can be updated periodically as dictated by conditions and experience. Their more limited scope permits them to be changed more easily than strategies. Recognizing the public's growing aversion to smoking, Imasco developed tactical plans to eliminate tobacco-related products at Shoppers Drug Mart before governments legislated such changes.

An **operational plan** is a type of plan designed to implement tactical plans. Operational plans usually are established for one year or less and deal with how to accomplish the organization's specific objectives. Assume that after Imasco eliminated tobacco-related products, Shoppers Drug Mart managers adopted the objective of increasing overall sales by 5 percent the first year. A sales increase this large does not just happen, however. Management must develop an operational plan that describes certain activities the firm can undertake over the next year to increase sales. Specific components of the operational plan might include increasing the range of products and services offered, newspaper and television advertising, reduced prices, and coupon offers—all designed to increase sales.

Regardless of how hard managers try, sometimes business activities do not go as planned. Today, most corporations also develop contingency plans along with strategies, tactical plans, and operational plans. A **contingency plan** is a plan that outlines alternative courses of action that may be taken if an organization's other plans are disrupted or become ineffective.

Organizing the Enterprise

After goal setting and planning, the second major function of the manager is organization. **Organizing** is the grouping of resources and activities to accomplish some end result in an efficient and effective manner. Consider the case of an inventor who creates a new product and goes into business to sell it. At first, the inventor will do everything on his or her own—purchase raw materials, make the product, advertise it, sell it, and keep business records. Eventually, as business grows, the inventor will need help. To begin with, he or she might hire a professional sales representative and a part-time bookkeeper. Later, it also might be necessary to hire sales staff, people to assist with production, and an accountant. As the inventor hires new personnel, he or she must decide what each person will do, to whom each person will report, and how each person can best take part in the organization's activities. We discuss these and other facets of the organizing function in much more detail in Chapter 8.

Leading and Motivating

The leading and motivating function is concerned with the human resources within an organization. Specifically, **leading** is the process of influencing people to work toward a common goal. **Motivating** is the process of providing reasons for people to work in the best interests of an organization. Together, leading and motivating are often referred to as **directing.**

We have already noted the importance of an organization's human resources. Because of this importance, leading and motivating are critical activities. Obviously, different people do things for different reasons—that is, they have different *motivations*. Some are interested primarily in earning as much money as they can. Others may be spurred on by opportunities to get promoted. Part of a manager's job, then, is to determine what factors motivate workers and to try to provide those incentives to encourage effective performance. For example, Nissan's CEO, Carlos Ghosn, has been successful at motivating his employees to give their best efforts. His leadership style involves never punishing or giving orders to his employees. Through his leadership, Ghosn has helped Nissan to exceed its three-year Nissan Revival goals in just two years.[4] Owing to the success of his leadership, Ghosn has taken on an unprecedented challenge in the auto industry. He has assumed the duties of CEO of Renault SA in France, and he remains the head of Nissan in Japan. Ghosn is trying to leverage his leadership and motivation skills to run two auto manufacturers simultaneously in different parts of the world.[5]

A lot of research has been done on both motivation and leadership. As you will see in Chapter 11, research on motivation has yielded very useful information. Research on leadership has been less successful. Despite decades of study, no one has discovered a general set of personal traits or characteristics that makes a good leader. Later in this chapter we discuss leadership in more detail.

Controlling Ongoing Activities

Controlling is the process of evaluating and regulating ongoing activities to ensure that goals are achieved. To see how controlling works, consider a rocket launched by NASA to place a satellite in orbit. Do NASA personnel simply fire the rocket and then check back in a few days to find out whether the satellite is in place? Of course not. The rocket is monitored constantly, and its course is regulated and adjusted as needed to get the satellite to its destination.

The control function includes three steps (see Figure 7.4). The first is *setting standards* with which performance can be compared. The second is *measuring actual performance* and comparing it with the standard. And the third is *taking corrective action* as necessary. Notice that the control function is circular in nature. The steps in the

leading the process of influencing people to work toward a common goal

motivating the process of providing reasons for people to work in the best interests of an organization

directing the combined processes of leading and motivating

controlling the process of evaluating and regulating ongoing activities to ensure that goals are achieved

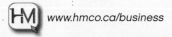

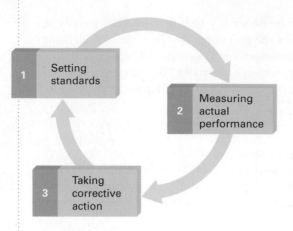

Figure 7.4

The Control Function

The control function includes three steps: setting standards, measuring actual performance, and taking corrective action.

control function must be repeated periodically until the goal is achieved. For example, suppose that WestJet Airlines establishes a goal of increasing its annual profit by 12 percent. To ensure that this goal is reached, WestJet's management might monitor its profit on a monthly basis. After three months, if profit has increased by 3 percent, management might be able to assume that plans are going according to schedule. Probably no action will be taken. However, if profit has increased by only 1 percent after three months, some corrective action would be needed to get the firm on track. The particular action that is required depends on the reason for the small increase in profit.

Examining ethics

What Makes an Ethical Leader?

Business leaders at all levels face ethical issues as they juggle responsibilities to customers, investors, colleagues, employees, competitors, regulators, and other groups. Do you have what it takes to be an ethical leader? Ask yourself:

1. Do I set a good example for others by acting ethically every day?

2. Do I tolerate questionable or unethical behaviour around me?

3. Do I act honestly and fairly, with my company's long-term priorities and interests in mind, rather than putting myself first?

4. If my company has an ethical code, do I understand and apply it every day?

5. If there is no ethical code, can I play a role in helping my company to develop and adopt one?

Ethical leaders can influence individual behaviour and, over time, shape a company's culture of ethics. A company's board of directors plays a major role in ensuring that top management is engaging in ethical business practices. And they have to be prepared to act immediately when questionable conduct surfaces, even when it means terminating the CEO.

Kinds of Managers

Learning Objective

Distinguish among the various kinds of managers in terms of both level and area of management.

Managers can be classified in two ways: according to their level within an organization and according to their area of management. In this section we use both perspectives to explore the various types of managers.

Levels of Management

For the moment, think of an organization as a three-storey structure (as illustrated in Figure 7.5). Each storey corresponds to one of the three general levels of management: top managers, middle managers, and first-line managers.

Top Managers A **top manager** is an upper-level executive who guides and controls the overall fortunes of an organization. Top managers constitute a small group. In terms of planning, they are generally responsible for developing the organization's mission. They also determine the firm's strategy. Michael Dell, founder of Dell Computers, determined the need for a direct-to-consumer computer company. Many analysts attribute Michael Dell's long-term success to the significant amount of time he spends with customers that helps him to make effective strategy and product decisions. Dell has continued to gain market share at a time when computer industry sales have decreased.[6] (It takes years of hard work, long hours, and perseverance, as well as talent and no small share of good luck, to reach the ranks of top management in large companies. Common job titles associated with top managers are president, vice president, chief executive officer (CEO), and chief operating officer (COO).

Middle Managers Middle management probably makes up the largest group of managers in most organizations. A **middle manager** is a manager who implements the strategy and major policies developed by top management. Middle managers develop tactical plans and operational plans, and they coordinate and supervise the activities of first-line managers. Titles at the middle-management level include division manager, department head, plant manager, and general manager.

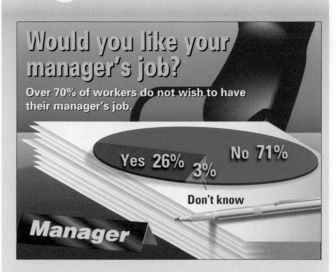

SP☉TLIGHT

Would you like your manager's job?

Over 70% of workers do not wish to have their manager's job.

Yes 26% 3% No 71%

Don't know

Manager

Source: Office Team Survey, www.officeteam.com/PressRoom?LOBName= OT&releaseid=1564.

Figure 7.5

Management Levels Found in Most Companies

The coordinated effort of all three levels of managers is required to implement the goals of any company.

Top management

Middle management

First-line management

top manager an upper-level executive who guides and controls the overall fortunes of an organization

middle manager a manager who implements the strategy and major policies developed by top management

first-line manager
a manager who coordinates and supervises the activities of operating employees

First-Line Managers A **first-line manager** is a manager who coordinates and supervises the activities of operating employees. First-line managers spend most of their time working with and motivating their employees, answering questions, and solving day-to-day problems. Most first-line managers are former operating employees who, owing to their hard work and potential, were promoted into management. Many of today's middle and top managers began their careers on this first management level. Common titles for first-line managers include office manager, supervisor, and foreman.

Areas of Management Specialization

Organizational structure also can be divided into areas of management specialization (see Figure 7.6). The most common areas are finance, production, marketing, human resources, and administration. Depending on its mission, goals, and objectives, an organization can include other areas—research and development (R&D), for example.

Figure 7.6

Areas of Management Specialization

Other areas may have to be added, depending on the nature of the firm and the industry.

| Finance | Production | Marketing | Human resources | Administration | Other (e.g., research and development) |

financial manager
a manager who is primarily responsible for an organization's financial resources

Financial Managers A **financial manager** is primarily responsible for an organization's financial resources. Accounting and investment are specialized areas within financial management. Because financing affects the operation of the entire firm, many of the CEOs and presidents of this country's largest companies are people who got their "basic training" as financial managers.

production manager a manager who manages the systems that convert resources into goods and services

Production Managers A **production manager** manages the systems that convert resources into goods and services. Traditionally, production management has been equated with manufacturing—the production of goods. However, in recent years, many of the techniques and procedures in production management have been applied to the production of services and to a variety of non-business activities. As with financial management, production management has produced a large percentage of today's company CEOs and presidents.

marketing manager a manager who is responsible for facilitating the exchange of products between an organization and its customers or clients

Marketing Managers A **marketing manager** is responsible for facilitating the exchange of products between an organization and its customers or clients. Specific areas within marketing are marketing research, product management, advertising, promotion, sales, and distribution. A sizable number of today's company presidents have risen from the ranks of marketing management.

Human Resources Managers A human resources manager is charged with managing an organization's human resources programs. He or she engages in human resources planning; designs systems for hiring, training, and evaluating the performance of employees; and ensures that the organization follows government regulations concerning employment practices. Some human resources managers are making effective use of technology. For example, over one million job openings are posted on Monster.com, which attracts about eighteen million visitors monthly.

Administrative Managers An administrative manager is not associated with any specific functional area but provides overall administrative guidance and leadership. A hospital administrator is an example of an administrative manager. He or she does not specialize in operations, finance, marketing, or human resources management but instead coordinates the activities of specialized managers in all these areas. In many respects, most top managers are really administrative managers.

Whatever their level in the organization and whatever area they specialize in, successful managers generally exhibit certain key skills and are able to play certain managerial roles. However, as we shall see, some skills are likely to be more critical at one level of management than at another.

human resources manager a person charged with managing an organization's human resources programs

administrative manager a manager who is not associated with any specific functional area but who provides overall administrative guidance and leadership

BUSINESS AROUND THE WORLD

Managing Globally, Managing Locally

How should a multinational corporation manage operations in different countries? No two companies handle this challenge in exactly the same way. Here's how two major computer firms manage globally while managing locally.

Lenovo

Lenovo, China's largest PC manufacturer, faced the challenge of managing across national borders after it bought IBM's worldwide PC business. After the merger, Lenovo moved its headquarters to New York and, to enhance its global perspective, added U.S. executives to the senior management team. Yet Yuanqing Yang, Lenovo's chairman, also relies heavily on local management to gauge demand and respond quickly because "we want to build a local company that is entrepreneurial in nature."

IBM

IBM once ran each country's operations as a mini-IBM, with regional executives coordinating all local operations. Now CEO Samuel Palmisano has eliminated the regional bureaucracies, allowing local managers to make speedier decisions. At the same time, he has reduced duplication by creating regional centres for research and development and other functions. The increased efficiency is helping IBM to free up resources to invest in fast-growing markets such as Brazil and India.

What Makes Effective Managers?

Learning Objective ④

Identify key management skills and managerial roles.

In general, effective managers are those who (1) possess certain important skills and (2) are able to use those skills in a number of managerial roles. Probably no manager is called on to use any particular skill *constantly* or to play a particular role *all the time*. However, these skills and abilities must be available when they are needed.

Key Management Skills

The skills that typify effective managers fall into three general categories: technical, conceptual, and interpersonal.

Dealing with people is part of a manager's job

Annette Vershuren, president of Home Depot Canada has been able to motivate her employees through her loyalty, vision, and compassion. ▼

technical skill a specific skill needed to accomplish a specialized activity

conceptual skill the ability to think in abstract terms

Technical Skills A techni- to accomplish a specialized skills engineers and ma- jobs are technical skills. to a lesser extent, mid- technical skills relevant manage. Although not perform the tech- they must be able to swer questions, and guidance and di- manager in the ac- of the Four Seasons ample, must be able erized accounting employees complete task. In general, top on technical skills as at other levels. Still, technical side of a effective management

Conceptual Skills ability to think in ab- skill allows a manager to understand how the vari- or idea can fit together. wide range of situations, includ-

cal skill is a specific skill needed activity. For example, the chinists need to do their First-line managers (and, dle managers) need the to the activities they these managers may nical tasks themselves, train subordinates, an- otherwise provide rection. A first-line counting department Hotel chain, for ex- to perform comput- transactions and help the same accounting managers do not rely heavily as managers understanding the business is an aid to at every level.

Conceptual skill is the stract terms. Conceptual see the "big picture" and ous parts of an organization These skills are useful in a ing the optimization of goals described earlier. They are usually more useful for top managers than for middle or first-line managers.

Interpersonal Skills An interpersonal skill is the ability to deal effectively with other people, both inside and outside an organization. Examples of interpersonal skills are the ability to relate to people, understand their needs and motives, and show genuine compassion. One reason Annette Verschuren, President of Home Depot Canada, has been so successful is her ability to motivate her employees and to inspire their loyalty to her vision for the firm. And although it is obvious that a CEO such as Verschuren must be able to work with employees throughout the organization, what is not so obvious is that middle and first-line managers also must possess interpersonal skills. For example, a first-line manager on an assembly line at Procter & Gamble must rely on employees to manufacture Tide detergent. The better the manager's interpersonal skills, the more likely the manager will be able to lead and motivate those employees. When all other things are equal, the manager able to exhibit these skills will be more successful than the arrogant and brash manager who does not care about others.

interpersonal skill the ability to deal effectively with other people

Managerial Roles

Research suggests that managers must, from time to time, act in ten different roles if they are to be successful.[7] (By *role*, we mean a set of expectations that he or she must fulfill.) These ten roles can be grouped into three broad categories: decisional, interpersonal, and informational.

Decisional Roles A decisional role involves various aspects of management decision making. The decisional role can be subdivided into the following four specific managerial roles: In the role of *entrepreneur*, the manager is the voluntary initiator of change. A second role is that of *disturbance handler*. A manager who settles a strike is handling a disturbance. Third, the manager also occasionally plays the role of *resource allocator*. In this role, the manager might have to decide which departmental budgets to cut and which expenditure requests to approve. The fourth role is that of *negotiator*. Being a negotiator might involve settling a dispute between a manager and a worker assigned to the manager's work group.

decisional role a role that involves various aspects of management decision making

Interpersonal Roles Dealing with people is an integral part of the manager's job. An interpersonal role is a role in which the manager deals with people. Like the decisional role, the interpersonal role can be broken down according to three managerial functions. The manager may be called on to serve as a *figurehead*, perhaps by attending a ribbon-cutting ceremony or taking an important client to dinner. The manager also may have to play the role of *liaison* by serving as a go-between for two different groups. As a liaison, a manager might represent his or her firm at meetings of an industry-wide trade organization. Finally, the manager often has to serve as a *leader*. Playing the role of leader includes being an example for others in the organization as well as developing the skills, abilities, and motivation of employees.

interpersonal role a role in which the manager deals with people

Informational Roles An informational role is one in which the manager either gathers or provides information. The informational role can be subdivided as follows: In the role of *monitor*, the manager actively seeks information that may be of value to the organization. For example, a manager who hears about a good business opportunity is engaging in the role of monitor. The second informational role is that of *disseminator*.

informational role a role in which the manager either gathers or provides information

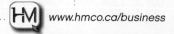

In this role, the manager transmits key information to those who can use it. As a disseminator, the manager who heard about a good business opportunity would tell the appropriate marketing manager about it. The third informational role is that of *spokesperson*. In this role, the manager provides information to people outside the organization, such as the press, television reporters, and the public.

Leadership

Learning Objective 5

Explain the different types of leadership.

leadership the ability to influence others

Leadership has been defined broadly as the ability to influence others. A leader has power and can use it to affect the behaviour of others. Leadership is different from management in that a leader strives for voluntary cooperation, whereas a manager may have to depend on coercion to change employee behaviour.

Formal and Informal Leadership

Some experts make distinctions between formal leadership and informal leadership. Formal leaders have legitimate power of position. They have *authority* within an organization to influence others to work for the organization's objectives. Informal leaders usually have no such authority and may or may not exert their influence in support of the organization. Both formal and informal leaders make use of several kinds of power, including the ability to grant rewards or impose punishments, the possession of expert knowledge, and personal attraction or charisma. Informal leaders who identify with the organization's goals are a valuable asset to any organization. However, a business can be brought to its knees by informal leaders who turn work groups against management.

authoritarian leader one who holds all authority and responsibility, with communication usually moving from top to bottom

laissez-faire leader one who gives authority to employees and allows subordinates to work as they choose with a minimum of interference; communication flows horizontally among group members

democratic leader one who holds final responsibility but also delegates authority to others, who help to determine work assignments; communication is active upward and downward

Styles of Leadership

For many years, leadership was viewed as a combination of personality traits, such as self-confidence, concern for people, intelligence, and dependability. Achieving a consensus on which traits were most important was difficult, however, and attention turned to styles of leadership behaviour. In the last few decades, several styles of leadership have been identified: authoritarian, laissez-faire, and democratic.[8] The **authoritarian leader** holds all authority and responsibility, with communication usually moving from top to bottom. This leader assigns workers to specific tasks and expects orderly, precise results. At the other extreme is the **laissez-faire leader,** who gives authority to employees. With the laissez-faire style, subordinates are allowed to work as they choose with a minimum of interference. Communication flows horizontally among group members. The **democratic leader** holds final responsibility but also delegates authority to others, who determine work assignments. In this leadership style, communication is active upward and downward. Employee commitment is high because of participation in the decision-making process.

Which Managerial Leadership Style Is Best?

Today, most management experts agree that no "best" managerial leadership style exists. Each of the styles described—authoritarian, laissez-faire, and democratic—has advantages and disadvantages. Democratic leadership can motivate employees to work effectively because they are implementing *their own* decisions. However, the decision-making process in democratic leadership takes time that subordinates could be devoting to the work itself.

Although hundreds of research studies have been conducted to prove which leadership style is best, there are no definite conclusions. The "best" leadership seems to occur when the leader's style matches the situation. Each of the leadership styles can be effective in the right situation. The *most* effective style depends on interaction among employees, characteristics of the work situation, and the manager's personality.

Managerial Decision Making

Learning Objective ⑥

Discuss the steps in the managerial decision-making process.

Decision making is the act of choosing one alternative from a set of alternatives.[9] In ordinary situations, decisions are made casually and informally. We encounter a problem, mull it over, settle on a solution, and go on. Managers, however, require a more systematic method for solving complex problems. As shown in Figure 7.7, managerial decision making involves four steps: (1) identifying the problem or opportunity, (2) generating alternatives, (3) selecting an alternative, and (4) implementing and evaluating the solution.

decision making the act of choosing one alternative from a set of alternatives

Identifying the Problem or Opportunity

A **problem** is the discrepancy between an actual condition and a desired condition—the difference between what is occurring and what one wishes would occur. For example, a marketing manager at Campbell Soup Company has a problem if sales revenues for Campbell's Hungry Man frozen dinners are declining (the actual condition). To solve this problem, the marketing manager must take steps to increase sales revenues (desired condition). Most people consider a problem to be "negative"; however, a problem also can be "positive." A positive problem should be viewed as an "opportunity."

Although accurate identification of a problem is essential before it can be solved or turned into an opportunity, this stage of decision making creates many difficulties for managers. Sometimes managers' preconceptions of the problem prevent them from seeing the actual situation. They produce an answer before the proper question has

Figure 7.7

Major Steps in the Managerial Decision-Making Process

Managers require a systematic method for solving problems in a variety of situations.

problem the discrepancy between an actual condition and a desired condition

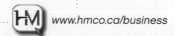

Your Career

The Heat Is On— and You're the Decision-Maker

Do you know how to make a decision when the pressure is on? Here are some tips for building your decision-making skills:

Stay calm. Getting panicky can distract you from key information and prompt hasty decisions. Calming your anxiety before attacking a problem will help you to make a better decision.

Look for a pattern. Is the current problem similar to one you solved in the past? If you can identify a similar pattern, you can apply the same decision guidelines you used previously or modify them for the current situation.

Simplify, simplify, simplify. Even if a problem seems complex, you usually can find a simple way to organize the symptoms and analyze possible alternatives and outcomes.

Use your intuition. You won't always have enough data or reliable data to make decisions. Keep an open mind, analyze the data at hand, and ask experts or experienced managers for input. Then let your intuition point you toward the best decision under the circumstances.

been asked. In other cases, managers overlook truly significant issues by focusing on unimportant matters. Also, managers may mistakenly analyze problems in terms of symptoms rather than underlying causes.

Effective managers learn to look ahead so that they are prepared when decisions must be made. They clarify situations and examine the causes of problems, asking whether the presence or absence of certain variables alters a situation. Finally, they consider how individual behaviours and values affect the way problems or opportunities are defined.

Generating Alternatives

After a problem has been defined, the next task is to generate alternatives. The more important the decision, the more attention is devoted to this stage. Managers should be open to fresh, innovative ideas as well as obvious answers.

Certain techniques can aid in the generation of creative alternatives. Brainstorming, commonly used in group discussions, encourages participants to produce many new ideas. Other group members are not permitted to criticize or ridicule. Another approach, developed by the U.S. Navy, is called "Blast! Then Refine." Group members tackle a recurring problem by erasing all previous solutions and procedures. The group then re-evaluates its original objectives, modifies them if necessary, and devises new solutions. Other techniques—including trial and error—are also useful in this stage of decision making.

Selecting an Alternative

Final decisions are influenced by a number of considerations, including financial constraints, human and informational resources, time limits, legal obstacles, and political factors. Managers must select the alternative that will be most effective and practical. At times, two or more alternatives or some combination of alternatives will be equally appropriate. After considering several alternatives to become more competitive, IBM management decided to outsource the manufacturing of more products such as disk drives and even low-end servers and to sell off its PC division to China's top PC maker, Lenovo.[10]

Managers can choose solutions to problems on several levels. The coined word "satisfice" describes solutions that are only adequate and not ideal. When lacking time or information, managers often make decisions that "satisfice." Whenever possible, managers should try to investigate alternatives carefully and select the ideal solution.

Implementing and Evaluating the Solution

Implementation of a decision requires time, planning, preparation of personnel, and evaluation of results. Managers usually deal with unforeseen consequences even when they carefully considered the alternatives.

The final step in managerial decision making entails evaluating the effectiveness of a decision. If the alternative that was chosen removes the difference between the actual condition and the desired condition, the decision is judged effective. If the problem still exists, managers can

* Decide to give the chosen alternative more time to work.
* Adopt a different alternative.
* Start the problem identification process all over again.

Failure to evaluate decisions adequately can result in negative consequences. Hewlett Packard's former CEO, Carly Fiorina, suffered negative consequences after the controversial merger with Compaq Computer did not help the company's earnings performance. Because Hewlett Packard's hardware units still were not highly competitive against the market leaders, Fiorina was replaced.[11]

Managing Total Quality

Learning Objective 7

Describe how organizations benefit from total quality management.

The management of quality is a high priority in some organizations today. Major reasons for a greater focus on quality include foreign competition, more demanding customers, and poor financial performance resulting from reduced market share and higher costs. Over the last few years, several Canadian firms have lost the dominant competitive positions they had held for decades.

total quality management (TQM) the coordination of efforts directed at improving customer satisfaction, increasing employee participation, strengthening supplier partnerships, and facilitating an organizational atmosphere of continuous quality improvement

Total quality management is a much broader concept than just controlling the quality of the product itself (which is discussed in Chapter 9). **Total quality management (TQM)** is the coordination of efforts directed at improving customer satisfaction, increasing employee participation, strengthening supplier partnerships, and facilitating an organizational atmosphere of continuous quality improvement. For TQM programs to be effective, management must address each of the following components:

* *Customer satisfaction.* Ways to improve include producing higher-quality products, providing better customer service, and showing customers that the company cares.

* *Employee participation.* This can be increased by allowing employees to contribute to decisions, develop self-managed work teams, and assume responsibility for improving the quality of their work.

* *Strengthening supplier partnerships.* Developing good working relationships with suppliers can ensure that the right supplies and materials will be delivered on time at lower costs.

* *Continuous quality improvement.* This should not be viewed as achievable through one single program that has a target objective. A program based on continuous improvement has proven to be the most effective long-term approach.

Although many factors influence the effectiveness of a TQM program, two issues are crucial. First, top management must make a strong commitment to a TQM program by treating quality improvement as a top priority and giving it frequent attention. Firms that establish a TQM program but then focus on other priorities will find that their quality-improvement initiatives will fail. Second, management must coordinate the specific elements of a TQM program so that they work in harmony with each other.

Although not all Canadian companies have TQM programs, these programs provide many benefits. Overall financial benefits include lower operating costs, higher return in sales and investments, and an improved ability to use premium rather than competitive pricing.

What It Takes to Become a Successful Manager Today

Learning Objective 8

Summarize what it takes to become a successful manager today.

Everyone hears stories about the corporate elite who make salaries in excess of $1 million a year, travel to and from work in chauffeur-driven limousines, and enjoy lucrative pension plans that provide a luxurious lifestyle after they retire. Although management obviously can be a rewarding career, what is not so obvious is the amount of time and hard work needed to achieve the impressive salaries and perks.

A Day in the Life of a Manager

Organizations pay managers for performance. As already pointed out, managers coordinate an organization's resources. They also perform the four basic management functions: planning, organizing, leading and motivating, and controlling. And managers make decisions and then implement and evaluate those decisions. This heavy workload requires that managers work long hours, and most do not get paid overtime. Typically, the number of hours increases as a manager advances.

Today's managers have demanding jobs. Managers spend a great deal of time talking with people on an individual basis. The purpose of these conversations is usually to obtain information or to resolve problems. In addition, a manager often spends time in meetings with other managers and employees. In most cases, the purpose of the meetings—some brief and some lengthy—is to resolve problems. And if the work is not completed by the end of the day, the manager usually packs his or her unfinished tasks in a briefcase.

Skills Required for Success

To be successful in today's competitive business environment, you must possess a number of skills. Some of these skills—technical, conceptual, and interpersonal skills—were discussed earlier in this chapter. However, you also need "personal" skills. Oral and written communication skills, computer skills, and critical-thinking skills may give you the edge in getting an entry-level management position.

* *Oral communication skills.* Because a large part of a manager's day is spent conversing with others, the ability to speak *and* listen is critical. Oral communication skills are used when a manager makes sales presentations, conducts interviews, and holds press conferences.

* *Written communication skills.* A manager's ability to prepare letters, e-mails, memos, sales reports, and other written documents can spell the difference between success and failure.

* *Computer skills.* Most employers do not expect you to be an expert computer programmer, but they do expect that you should know how to use a computer to prepare written and statistical reports and to communicate with other managers and employees.

* *Critical-thinking skills.* Employers expect managers to use the steps for effective managerial decision making. They also expect managers to use critical-thinking skills to identify problems correctly, generate reasonable alternatives, and select the "best" alternatives to solve problems.

The Importance of Education and Experience

Although most experts agree that management skills must be learned on the job, the concepts that you learn in business courses lay the foundation for a successful career. In addition, successful completion of college courses or obtaining a university degree can open doors to job interviews and career advancement.

Your Career

Making the Most of Your Résumé

There are methods you can use to "beef up" your résumé and to capitalize on your work experience. First, obtain summer jobs that provide opportunities to learn about the field that interests you. Chosen carefully, part-time jobs can provide work experience that other job applicants may not have. Some colleges and universities sponsor cooperative work/school programs that give students college credit for job experience. Even with solid academics and work experience, many would-be managers find it difficult to land the "right" job. Often they start in an entry-level position to gain more experience.

 Prepare for Class
HM News Feeds
HM News Now

 RETURN TO INSIDE BUSINESS

Gary Bettman deals with a number of people, from players to owners to television executives in his job as the NHL Commissioner. The need to adapt his management skills to meet the needs of these different groups is a management skill in itself. Keeping this in mind, and considering the management styles we have discussed in this chapter, what management style would you suggest would work best in the following situations:

a. Negotiating a new collective bargaining agreement with the NHL Player's Association?

b. Dealing with an on-ice disciplinary infraction involving a player and/or coach?

CHAPTER REVIEW

1 Define what management is.

Management is the process of coordinating people and other resources to achieve the goals of an organization. Managers are concerned with four types of resources—material, human, financial, and informational.

2 Describe the four basic management functions: planning, organizing, leading and motivating, and controlling.

Managers perform four basic functions. Management functions do not occur according to some rigid, preset timetable, though. At any time, managers may engage in a number of functions simultaneously. However, each function tends to lead naturally to others. First, managers engage in planning—determining where the firm should be going and how best to get there. Three types of plans, from the broadest to the most specific, are strategic plans, tactical plans, and operational plans. Managers also organize resources and activities to accomplish results in an efficient and effective manner, and they lead and motivate others to work in the best interests of the organization. In addition, managers control ongoing activities to keep the organization on course. There are three steps in the control function: setting standards, measuring actual performance, and taking corrective action.

3 Distinguish among the various kinds of managers in terms of both level and area of management.

Managers—or management positions—can be classified from two different perspectives. From the perspective of level within the organization, there are top managers, who control the fortunes of the organization; middle managers, who implement strategies and major policies; and first-line managers, who supervise the activities of operating employees. From the viewpoint of area of management, managers most often deal with the areas of finance, operations, marketing, human resources, and administration.

4 Identify key management skills and managerial roles.

Effective managers tend to possess a specific set of skills and to fill three basic managerial roles. Technical, conceptual, and interpersonal skills are all important, although the relative importance of each varies with the level of management within the organization. The primary managerial roles can be classified as decisional, interpersonal, or informational.

5 Explain the different types of leadership.

Managers' effectiveness often depends on their styles of leadership—that is, their ability to influence others, either formally or informally. Leadership styles include the authoritarian "do-it-my-way" style, the laissez-faire "do-it-your-way" style, and the democratic "let's-do-it-together" style.

6 Discuss the steps in the managerial decision-making process.

Decision making, an integral part of a manager's work, is the process of developing a set of possible alternative solutions to a problem and choosing one alternative from among the set. Managerial decision making involves four steps: managers must accurately identify problems, generate several possible solutions, choose the solution that will be most effective under the circumstances, and implement and evaluate the chosen course of action.

7 Describe how organizations benefit from total quality management.

Total quality management (TQM) is the coordination of efforts directed at improving customer satisfaction, increasing employee participation, strengthening supplier partnerships, and facilitating an organizational atmosphere of continuous quality improvement. To have an effective TQM program, top management must make a strong, sustained commitment to the effort and must be able to coordinate all the program's elements so that they work in harmony. Overall financial benefits of TQM include lower operating costs, higher return in sales and investment, and an improved ability to use premium pricing rather than competitive pricing.

8 **Summarize what it takes to become a successful manager today.**

Organizations pay managers for their performance. Managers coordinate resources. They also plan, organize, lead, motivate, and control. They make decisions that can spell the difference between an organization's success and failure. To complete their tasks, managers work long hours at a hectic pace. To be successful, they need personal skills (oral and written communication skills, computer skills, and critical-thinking skills), an academic background that provides a foundation for a management career, and practical work experience.

Improve Your Grade
Learning Objectives Review
Audio Chapter Review & Quiz

Review Questions

1. Define the term *manager* without using the word *management* in your definition.
2. What is the mission of a neighbourhood restaurant? Of the Salvation Army? What might be reasonable objectives for these organizations?
3. What does the term *optimization* mean?
4. How do a strategic plan, a tactical plan, and an operational plan differ? What do they all have in common?
5. What exactly does a manager organize, and for what reason?
6. Why are leadership and motivation necessary in a business in which people are paid for their work?
7. Explain the steps involved in the control function.
8. How are the two perspectives on kinds of managers—that is, level and area—different from each other?
9. In what ways are management skills related to the roles managers play? Provide a specific example to support your answer.
10. Compare and contrast the major styles of leadership.
11. Discuss what happens during each of the four steps of the managerial decision-making process.
12. What are the major benefits of a total quality management program?
13. What personal skills should a manager possess in order to be successful?

Discussion Questions

1. Does a healthy firm (one that is doing well) have to worry about effective management? Explain.
2. Which of the management functions, skills, and roles do not apply to the owner-operator of a sole proprietorship?
3. Which leadership style might be best suited to each of the three general levels of management within an organization?
4. According to this chapter, the leadership style that is *most* effective depends on the interaction among the employees, the characteristics of the work situation, and the manager's personality. Do you agree or disagree? Explain your answer.
5. Do you think that people are really as important to an organization as this chapter seems to indicate?
6. As you learned in this chapter, managers often work long hours at a hectic pace. Would this type of career appeal to you? Explain your answer.

New Leadership, New Opportunities for Hewlett Packard

Hewlett Packard (HP) was born in somebody's garage. Over six decades later, the company founded by Bill Hewlett and Dave Packard annually sells $82 billion worth of computers, printers, data storage systems, and digital cameras. Yet, in all these years, only six CEOs have led the company—and only two CEOs have been outsiders.

The first was Carly Fiorina, brought in from Lucent Technologies to become CEO in 1999. Fiorina's bold strategy included the acquisition of Compaq in 2002 to create an integrated technology superpower. Within three years, however, HP's financial performance was not hitting the expected heights. And although HP was the world's largest printer maker, competitor Dell had surged ahead to become top PC company in the United States. The board of directors forced Fiorina out as HP continued losing PC market share and replaced her with another outsider: Mark Hurd, the CEO of business technology firm NCR.

Hurd knew that planning would be vitally important to putting HP back on track. He began digging into the company's current strategy, learning about its various businesses, and meeting with employees and managers at all levels. He quickly realized that HP would be better positioned for future opportunities if he and his management team looked closely at organizing, leading and motivating, and controlling.

One of Hurd's early decisions was to step back from Fiorina's integration strategy and refocus the company on individual products. To do this, he organized PCs into one division and printer products into another. Because many large companies prefer to buy complete systems, however, HP continued its integrated sales approach for these customers, sending a team of product experts to assess needs and recommend solutions.

Starting at the top, the CEO tackled the function of leading and motivating. "When you look at the ability to build a great company and great management teams, management is really a team sport," he said after joining HP. "On a personal-style basis, I believe in very engaged management." He added, "I like to move through multiple levels of the company, and I like my management to do that. Great companies have boards, CEOs, and management that all have one script."

Hurd discovered strong motivation throughout the workforce: "If there's anything that struck me in coming to HP, it's the desire on the part of employees to see this company succeed." This was important because "when a company has the kind of passion that HP-ers have, it shows up not only inside the company in a positive way but it bleeds into how we support and treat our customers," he said. And this made Hurd enthusiastic about his job: "The CEO actually gets motivated by the employees, sometimes. Everyone thinks the CEO doesn't have emotion around all this stuff, but I get motivated by it, too."

Hurd made controlling a high priority to adjust HP's day-to-day activities for top performance. However, he didn't want employees confused or distracted by having to check too many standards and measure too many activities. Therefore, he established a specific set of standards for assessing performance based on efficiency, revenue, profitability, and other key measures.

In his first year as CEO, Hurd improved HP's financial results and continued to make changes designed to position the company for future growth. Still, high-tech businesses operate within a notoriously uncertain environment, so Hurd will have to apply all his management expertise to continue HP's good performance.

For more information about this company, go to www.hp.com.

Questions:

1. Do you think that Mark Hurd was emphasizing decisional roles, interpersonal roles, or informational roles when he became HP's CEO—and why?

2. How can Hurd apply the management function of controlling to improve HP's decision-making process?

3. From a management perspective, what are the benefits and limitations of appointing an outsider as CEO?

BUILDING SKILLS FOR CAREER SUCCESS

1. Exploring the Internet

Most large companies call on a management consulting firm for a variety of services, including employee training, help in the selection of an expensive purchase such as a computer system, recruitment of employees, and direction in reorganization and strategic planning.

Large consulting firms generally operate globally and provide information to companies considering entry into foreign countries or business alliances with foreign firms. They use their websites, along with magazine-style articles, to celebrate achievements and present their credentials to clients. Business students can acquire an enormous amount of up-to-date information in the field of management by perusing these sites.

Assignment

1. Explore each of the following websites:

   www.deloitte.com

   www.kpmg.com

   www.mckinsey.com

Visit the text website for updates to this exercise.

2. Judging from the articles and notices posted, what are the current areas of activities of one of these firms?

3. Explore one of these areas in more detail by comparing postings from each firm's site. For instance, if "global business opportunities" appears to be a popular area of management consulting, how has each firm distinguished itself in this area? Who would you call first for advice?

4. Given that consulting firms are always trying to fill positions for their clients and to meet their own recruitment needs, it is little wonder that employment postings are a popular area on their sites. Examine these in detail. Based on your examination of the site and the registration format, what sort of recruit are they interested in?

Prepare for Class
Exploring the Internet

2. Developing Critical Thinking Skills

As defined in the chapter, an organization's mission is a statement of the basic purpose that makes the organization different from others. Clearly, a mission statement, by indicating the purpose of a business, directly affects the company's employees, customers, and stockholders.

Assignment

1. Find the mission statements of three large corporations in different industries. The Internet is one source of mission statements.

2. Compare the mission statements on the basis of what each reflects about the philosophy of the company and its concern for employees, customers, and stockholders.

3. Which company would you like to work for and why?

4. Prepare a report on your findings.

3. Building Team Skills

Over the past few years, an increasing number of employees, stockholders, and customers have been demanding to know what their companies are about. As a result, more companies have been taking the time to analyze their operations and to prepare mission statements that focus on the purpose of the company. The mission statement is becoming a critical planning tool for successful companies. To make effective decisions, employees must understand the purpose of their company.

Assignment

1. Divide into teams and write a mission statement for one of the following types of businesses:

   Food service, restaurant

   Banking

   Airline

   Auto repair

   Cabinet manufacturing

2. Discuss your mission statement with other teams. How did the other teams interpret the

purpose of your company? What is the mission statement saying about the company?

3. Write a one-page report on what you learned about developing mission statements.

4. Researching Different Careers

A successful career requires planning. Without a plan, or roadmap, you will find it very difficult, if not impossible, to reach your desired career destination. The first step in planning is to establish what your career goal is. You then must set objectives and develop plans for accomplishing those objectives. This kind of planning takes time, but it will pay off later.

Assignment

Complete the following statements:

1. My career goal is to _____.

This statement should encapsulate what you want to accomplish over the long run. It can include the type of job you want and the type of business or industry you want to work in. Examples include

- My career goal is to work as a top manager in the food industry.
- My career goal is to supervise aircraft mechanics.
- My career goal is to win the top achievement award in the advertising industry.

2. My career objectives are to _____.

Objectives are benchmarks along the route to a career destination. They are more specific than a career goal. A statement about a career objective should specify what you want to accomplish, when you will complete it, and any other details that will serve as criteria against which you can measure your progress. Examples include

- My objective is to be promoted to supervisor by January 1, 20xx.

- My objective is to enroll in a management course at college/university in the spring semester 20xx.
- My objective is to earn an A in the management course at college/university in the spring semester 20xx.
- My objective is to prepare a status report by September 30 covering the last quarter's activities by asking Charlie in Quality Control to teach me the procedures.

3. Exchange your goal and objectives statements with another class member. Can your partner interpret your objectives correctly? Are the objectives concise and complete? Do they include criteria against which you can measure your progress? If not, discuss the problem and rewrite the objective.

5. Improving Communication Skills

Being a successful employee today requires personal and managerial skills. Without proficiency in these skills, promotions and other rewards are unlikely to be forthcoming. To be competitive, employees must assess their skill levels periodically and, when necessary, work to improve them. How do your personal and managerial skills measure up?

Assignment

1. Rate yourself and have at least two other people rate you on the skills listed in the following table.

2. Prepare a plan for improving your weak areas. The plan should specify exactly how, where, and when you will accomplish your goal. It also should include criteria for measuring your level of improvement.

Skill Assessment

	BELOW AVERAGE	AVERAGE	ABOVE AVERAGE	SPECIFIC EXAMPLES
Personal skills				
Oral communication skills				
Written communication skills				
Computer skills				
Critical-thinking skills				
Managerial skills				
Conceptual skills				
Technical skills				
Interpersonal skills				
Decision-making skills				

CHAPTER 8

Creating a Flexible Organization

Your Guide to Success in Business

Why this chapter matters

To operate a business at an acceptable level of profitability, those in charge must create an organization that is able to attract resources and develop long-term customer relationships.

LEARNING OBJECTIVES

1. Understand what an organization is and identify its characteristics.

2. Explain why job specialization is important.

3. Identify the various bases for departmentalization.

4. Explain how decentralization follows from delegation.

5. Understand how the span of management describes an organization.

6. Understand how the chain of command is established by using line and staff management.

7. Describe the four basic forms of organizational structure: bureaucratic, matrix, cluster, and network.

8. Summarize the use of corporate culture, intrapreneurship, committees, coordination techniques, informal groups, and the grapevine.

Four Seasons Hotels and Resorts

Isadore Sharp had a vision—one that he hoped to translate into a luxury hotel operation around the world. It would be different with an unprecedented focus on the customer. Personal service would be "personal" and the prospect of return customers meant that that service would change as the customer changed. Mr. Sharp recognized that life cycles do not just happen to products, but to people as well. And as people grew older, their tastes and needs changed along with their age.

But to advance his vision he first had to identify what was important to his customers and then put in place an organization that could deliver what the customer wanted.

Since opening the first Four Seasons Motor Hotel in Toronto, in 1961, Mr. Sharp has expanded his operations to include approximately seventy hotels in over thirty countries. His success has been due to his obsession with giving people what they want in a luxury hotel. Privacy, security, discretion, and exclusivity have all become part of the Four Seasons' experience. First class services and amenities are available at each of the hotels. In more recent years, Four Seasons has expanded its operations to include resort properties in some of the most exclusive destinations.

But the real success in Mr. Sharp's vision lies in the training and skills of Four Seasons staff and management. The organization is constantly improving the services that it offers and continually training staff on how to provide premier personalized service. Knowing both what customers like and then how to deliver those services is what distinguishes Four Seasons from most of its competitors.

Achieving consistency in its operations and delivering its services to the highest standards has become a Four Seasons' tradition. Everything from the design of the hotel to the training of staff has had this objective. And while it does cost more for customers, they appear not to mind as the hotels enjoy high occupancy rates.

continued on next page

• • •

DID YOU KNOW?

Being a smaller company like Four Seasons Hotels has some major advantages when competing against bigger organizations.

K E Y   T E R M S

organization (225)
organization chart (226)
chain of command (226)
job specialization (227)
job rotation (228)
departmentalization (228)
departmentalization by function (228)
departmentalization by product (228)
departmentalization by location (229)

departmentalization by customer (229)
delegation (230)
responsibility (230)
authority (230)
accountability (230)
decentralized organization (231)
centralized organization (231)
span of management (or span of control) (232)

organizational height (232)
line management position (233)
staff management position (233)
bureaucratic structure (236)
matrix structure (236)
cross-functional team (237)
cluster structure (238)
network structure (238)
corporate culture (239)

intrapreneur (241)
ad hoc committee (241)
standing committee (241)
task force (241)
managerial hierarchy (241)
informal organization (242)
informal group (242)
grapevine (243)

ACE the Test
Crossword Puzzle
Flashcards

A successful business like Four Seasons does not just happen by chance. It requires a dedicated and disciplined approach from management throughout the entire organization. It evolves through the recruitment of qualified staff, the development of training programs designed to maximize their potential, and compensation packages aligned with meeting and exceeding company targets. It requires leadership and—as Mr. Sharp has demonstrated throughout his career—leadership starts at the top.

To survive and to grow, companies such as Four Seasons must constantly look for ways to improve their methods of doing business. Managers at Four Seasons, like those at many other organizations, deliberately reorganize the company to achieve its goals and objectives and to create satisfying products that foster long-term customer relationships.

When firms are organized, or reorganized, the focus is sometimes on achieving low operating costs. Other firms, such as Nike, emphasize providing high-quality products to ensure customer satisfaction. A firm's organization influences its performance. Thus the issue of organization is important.

We begin this chapter by examining the business organization—what it is and how it functions in today's business environment. Next, we focus one by one on five characteristics that shape an organization's structure. We discuss job specialization within a company, the grouping of jobs into manageable units or departments, the delegation of power from management to workers, the span of management, and establishment of a chain of command. Then we step back for an overall view of four approaches to organizational structure: the bureaucratic structure, the matrix structure, the cluster structure, and the network structure. Finally, we look at the network of social interactions—the informal organization—that operates within the formal business structure.

Figure 8.1

A Typical Corporate Organization Chart

A company's organization chart represents the positions and relationships within the organization and shows the managerial chains of command.

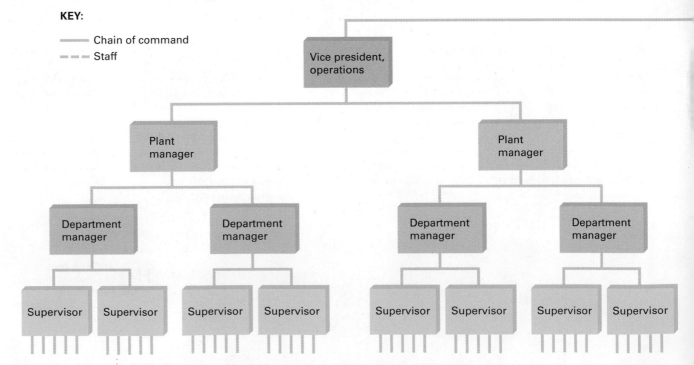

KEY:

———— Chain of command

– – – Staff

What Is an Organization?

Learning Objective ❶

Understand what an organization is and identify its characteristics.

We used the term *organization* throughout Chapter 7 without really defining it mainly because its everyday meaning is close to its business meaning. Here, however, let us agree that an **organization** is a group of two or more people working together to achieve a common set of goals. A neighbourhood dry cleaner owned and operated by a husband-and-wife team is an organization. Bombardier and Magna, which employ thousands of workers worldwide, are also organizations in the same sense. Although each corporation's organizational structure is more complex than the dry-cleaning establishment, all must be organized to achieve their goals.

An inventor who goes into business to produce and market a new invention hires people, decides what each will do, determines who will report to whom, and so on.

organization a group of two or more people working together to achieve a common set of goals

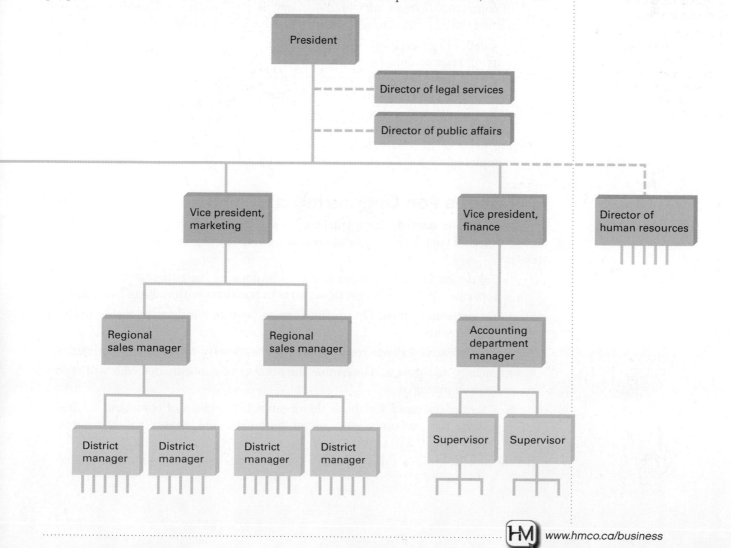

These activities are the essence of organizing, or creating, the organization. One way to create this "picture" is to create an organization chart.

Developing Organization Charts

organization chart a diagram that represents the positions and relationships within an organization

An **organization chart** is a diagram that represents the positions and relationships within an organization. An example of an organization chart is shown in Figure 8.1. Each rectangle represents a particular position or person in the organization. At the top is the president; at the next level are the vice presidents. The solid vertical lines connecting the vice presidents to the president indicate that the vice presidents are in the chain of command. The **chain of command** is the line of authority that extends from the highest to the lowest levels of the organization. Moreover, each vice president reports directly to the president. Similarly, the plant managers, regional sales managers, and accounting department manager report to the vice presidents. The chain of command can be short or long.

chain of command the line of authority that extends from the highest to the lowest levels of an organization

In the chart, the connections to the directors of legal services, public affairs, and human resources are shown as broken lines; these people are not part of the direct chain of command. Instead, they hold *advisory*, or *staff*, positions. This difference will be examined later in this chapter when we discuss line and staff positions.

Most smaller organizations find organization charts useful. They clarify positions and reporting relationships for everyone in the organization, and they help managers to track growth and change in the organizational structure. For two reasons, however, many large organizations do not maintain complete, detailed charts. First, it is difficult to chart even a few dozen positions accurately, much less the thousands that characterize larger firms. And second, larger organizations are almost always changing parts of their structure. An organization chart would be outdated before being completed.

Five Steps for Organizing a Business

When a firm is started, management must decide how to organize the firm. These decisions are all part of five major steps that sum up the organizing process. The five steps are

1. *Job design.* Divide the work that is to be done by the entire organization into separate parts, and assign those parts to positions within the organization.
2. *Departmentalization.* Group the various positions into manageable units or departments.
3. *Delegation.* Distribute responsibility and authority within the organization.
4. *Span of management.* Determine the number of subordinates who will report to each manager.
5. *Chain of command.* Establish the organization's chain of command by designating the positions with direct authority and those that are support positions.

In the next several sections we discuss major issues associated with these steps.

Job Design

Explain why job specialization is important.

In Chapter 1 we defined *specialization* as the separation of a manufacturing process into distinct tasks and the assignment of different tasks to different people. Here we are extending that concept to *all* the activities performed within an organization.

Job Specialization

Job specialization is the separation of all organizational activities into distinct tasks and the assignment of different tasks to different people. Adam Smith, the eighteenth-century economist whose theories gave rise to capitalism, was the first to emphasize the power of specialization in his book *The Wealth of Nations*. According to Smith, the various tasks in a particular pin factory were arranged so that one worker drew the wire for the pins, another straightened the wire, a third cut it, a fourth ground the point, and a fifth attached the head. Smith claimed that ten men were able to produce 48,000 pins per day. Before specialization, they could produce only 200 pins per day because each worker had to perform all five tasks!

job specialization the separation of all organizational activities into distinct tasks and the assignment of different tasks to different people

The Rationale for Specialization

For a number of reasons, some job specialization is necessary in every organization because the "job" of most organizations is too large for one person to handle. In a firm such as Honda Canada, located in Alliston, Ontario, thousands of people are needed to manufacture automobiles. Others are needed to sell the cars to dealerships, control the firm's finances, and so on.

Second, when a worker has to learn one specific, highly specialized task, that individual should be able to learn it very efficiently. Third, a worker repeating the same job does not lose time changing from operations, as the pin workers did when producing complete pins. Fourth, the more specialized the job, the easier it is to design specialized equipment. And finally, the more specialized the job, the easier is the job training.

Alternatives to Job Specialization

Unfortunately, specialization can have negative consequences as well. The most significant drawback is the boredom and dissatisfaction employees may feel when repeating

Job Specialization

At this production facility in Calgary, workers build office furniture. These workers' jobs are the result of job specialization, which increases the productivity of this factory.

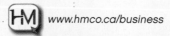

the same job. Bored employees may be absent from work frequently, may not put much effort into their work, and may even sabotage the company's efforts to produce quality products.

To combat these problems, managers often turn to job rotation. **Job rotation** is the systematic shifting of employees from one job to another. For example, a worker may be assigned a different job every week for a four-week period and then return to the first job in the fifth week. Job rotation provides a variety of tasks so that workers are less likely to become bored and dissatisfied.

Two other approaches—job enlargement and job enrichment—also can provide solutions to the problems caused by job specialization. These topics, along with other methods used to motivate employees, are discussed in Chapter 11.

job rotation the systematic shifting of employees from one job to another

Departmentalization

 Learning Objective 3

Identify the various bases for departmentalization.

After jobs are designed, they must be grouped together into "working units," or departments. This process is called *departmentalization*. More specifically, **departmentalization** is the process of grouping jobs into manageable units. Several departmentalization bases are used commonly. In fact, most firms use more than one. Today, the most common bases for organizing a business into effective departments are by function, by product, by location, and by customer.

departmentalization the process of grouping jobs into manageable units

By Function

Departmentalization by function groups jobs that relate to the same organizational activity. Under this scheme, all marketing personnel are grouped together in the marketing department, all production personnel in the production department, and so on.

Most smaller and newer organizations departmentalize by function. Supervision is simplified because everyone is involved in the same activities, and coordination is easy. The disadvantages of this method of grouping jobs are that it can lead to slow decision making and that it tends to emphasize the department over the whole organization.

departmentalization by function grouping jobs that relate to the same organizational activity

By Product

Departmentalization by product groups activities related to a particular good or service. This approach is used often by older and larger firms that produce and sell a variety of products. Each department handles its own marketing, production, financial management, and human resources activities.

Departmentalization by product makes decision making easier and provides for the integration of all activities associated with each product. However, it causes some duplication of specialized activities—such as finance—from department to department. And the emphasis is placed on the product rather than on the whole organization.

departmentalization by product grouping activities related to a particular product or service

By Location

Departmentalization by location groups activities according to the defined geographic area in which they are performed. Departmental areas may range from whole countries (for international firms) to regions within countries (for national firms) to areas of several city blocks (for police departments organized into precincts). Departmentalization by location allows the organization to respond readily to the unique demands or requirements of different locations. Nevertheless, a large administrative staff and an elaborate control system may be needed to coordinate operations in many locations.

departmentalization by location grouping activities according to the defined geographic area in which they are performed

By Customer

Departmentalization by customer groups activities according to the needs of various customer populations. A local General Motors dealership, for example, may have one sales staff to deal with individual consumers and a different sales staff to work with corporate fleet buyers. The obvious advantage of this approach is that it allows the firm to deal efficiently with unique customers or customer groups. The biggest drawback is that a larger-than-usual administrative staff is needed.

departmentalization by customer grouping activities according to the needs of various customer populations

Combinations of Bases

Many organizations use more than one of these departmentalization bases.

Take a moment to examine Figure 8.2. Notice that departmentalization by customer is used to organize New-Wave Fashions, Inc., into three major divisions: men's, women's, and children's clothing. Then functional departmentalization is used to distinguish the firm's production and marketing activities. Finally, location is used to organize the firm's marketing efforts.

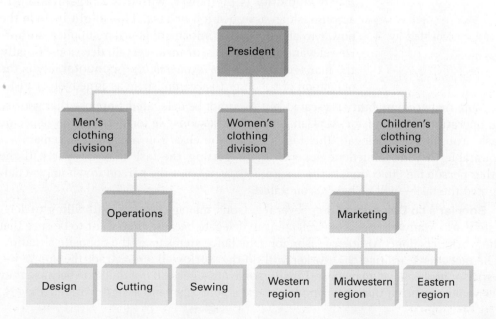

Figure 8.2

Multibase Departmentalization for New-Wave Fashions, Inc.

Most firms use more than one basis for departmentalization to improve efficiency and to avoid overlapping positions.

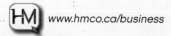

Delegation, Decentralization, and Centralization

Learning Objective ④

Explain how decentralization follows from delegation.

delegation assigning part of a manager's work and power to other workers

The third major step in the organizing process is to distribute power in the organization. **Delegation** assigns part of a manager's work and power to other workers. The degree of centralization or decentralization of authority is determined by the overall pattern of delegation within the organization.

Delegation of Authority

Because no manager can do everything, delegation is vital to completion of a manager's work. Delegation is also important in developing the skills and abilities of subordinates. It allows those who are being groomed for higher-level positions to play increasingly important roles in decision making.

Steps in Delegation The delegation process generally involves three steps (see Figure 8.3). First, the manager must *assign responsibility*. **Responsibility** is the duty to do a job or perform a task. In most job settings, a manager simply gives the worker a job to do. Typical job assignments might range from having a worker prepare a report on the status of a new quality control program to placing the person in charge of a task force. Second, the manager must *grant authority*. **Authority** is the power, within the organization, to accomplish an assigned job or task. This might include the power to obtain specific information, order supplies, authorize relevant expenditures, or make certain decisions. Finally, the manager must *create accountability*. **Accountability** is the obligation of a worker to accomplish an assigned job or task.

THE DELEGATION PROCESS

Figure 8.3

Steps in the Delegation Process

To be successful, a manager must learn how to delegate. No one can do everything alone.

responsibility the duty to do a job or perform a task

authority the power, within an organization, to accomplish an assigned job or task

accountability the obligation of a worker to accomplish an assigned job or task

Note that accountability is created, but it cannot be delegated. Suppose that you are an operations manager for Air Canada and are responsible for performing a specific task. You, in turn, delegate this task to someone else. You nonetheless remain accountable to your immediate supervisor for getting the task done properly. If the other person fails to complete the assignment, you—not the person to whom you delegated the task—will be held accountable.

Barriers to Delegation For several reasons, managers may be unwilling to delegate work. Many managers are reluctant to delegate because they want to be sure that the work gets done. Another reason for reluctance stems from the opposite situation. The manager fears that the worker will do the work well and attract the approving notice of higher-level managers. Finally, some managers do not delegate because they are so disorganized that they simply are not able to plan and assign work effectively.

ENTREPRENEURIAL CHALLENGE

Five Ways to Improve Delegation

Accustomed to doing everything alone, entrepreneurs may have difficulty delegating. By learning to delegate, entrepreneurs benefit from the skills and knowledge of others—and create more time to build the business. Experts suggest these five ways to improve delegation:

1. *Identify tasks that can be delegated.* Which tasks are so important that only the owner can deal with them? Which can be delegated to capable employees?

2. *Explain the purpose of each task.* Articulate not only what must be done, but why. Understanding how the business will benefit gives employees context.

3. *Provide the appropriate tools.* Be sure that employees have the information, equipment, contacts, and training to complete their tasks.

4. *Focus on the outcome.* Instead of dictating every action, focus on coaching toward the desired outcome. This allows employees to apply their creativity and hone their skills.

5. *Invest the time.* Although delegating can be time-consuming at first, investing the time upfront will save lots of time later.

decentralized organization an organization in which management consciously attempts to spread authority widely in the lower levels of the organization

centralized organization an organization that systematically works to concentrate authority at the upper levels of the organization

Decentralization of Authority

The pattern of delegation throughout an organization determines the extent to which that organization is decentralized or centralized. In a **decentralized organization,** management consciously attempts to spread authority widely across various organization levels. A **centralized organization,** on the other hand, systematically works to concentrate authority at the upper levels. For example, many publishers of university and college-level textbooks are centralized organizations, with authority concentrated at the top. Large organizations may have characteristics of both decentralized and centralized organizations. Wal-Mart centralizes its operations in Bentonville, Arkansas, but usually permits tremendous independence in stocking the stores with items local customers want. The top-management team in Bentonville focuses primarily on only the least successful of its stores and tends to leave the rest alone.[1]

A number of factors can influence the extent to which a firm is decentralized. One is the external environment in which the firm operates. The more complex and unpredictable this environment, the

Delegation

Wal-Mart has both a centralized and decentralized management structure, depending on the size of the store.

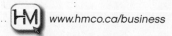

more likely it is that top management will let lower-level managers make important decisions. After all, lower-level managers are closer to the problems. Another factor is the nature of the decision itself. The riskier or more important the decision, the greater is the tendency to centralize decision making. A third factor is the abilities of lower-level managers. If these managers do not have strong decision-making skills, top managers will be reluctant to decentralize. And, in contrast, strong lower-level decision-making skills encourage decentralization. Finally, a firm that traditionally has practised centralization or decentralization is likely to maintain that posture in the future.

The Span of Management

Learning Objective 5

Understand how the span of management describes an organization.

span of management (or span of control) the number of workers who report directly to one manager

The fourth major step in organizing a business is establishing the **span of management** (or **span of control**), which is the number of workers who report directly to one manager. For hundreds of years, theorists have searched for an ideal span of management. When it became apparent that there is no perfect number of subordinates for a manager to supervise, they turned their attention to the general issue of whether the span should be wide or narrow. This issue is complicated because the span of management can change by department within the same organization. For example, the span of management at FedEx varies within the company. Departments in which workers do the same tasks on a regular basis—customer service agents, handlers and sorters, couriers—usually have a span of management of fifteen to twenty employees per manager. Groups performing multiple and different tasks are more likely to have smaller spans of management consisting of five or six employees.[2] Thus FedEx uses a wide span of control in some departments and a narrower one in others.

Wide and Narrow Spans of Control

A *wide* span of management exists when a manager has a larger number of subordinates. A *narrow* span exists when the manager has only a few subordinates. Several factors determine the span that is better for a particular manager (see Figure 8.4). Generally, the span of control may be wide when (1) the manager and the subordinates are very competent, (2) the organization has a well-established set of standard operating procedures, and (3) few new problems are expected to arise. The span should be narrow when (1) workers are physically located far from one another, (2) the manager has much work to do in addition to supervising workers, (3) a great deal of interaction is required between supervisor and workers, and (4) new problems arise frequently.

Organizational Height

organizational height the number of layers, or levels, of management in a firm

The span of management has an obvious impact on relations between managers and workers. It has a more subtle but equally important impact on the height of the organization. **Organizational height** is the number of layers, or levels, of management

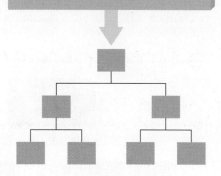

WIDE SPAN	NARROW SPAN
• High level of competence in managers and workers • Standard operating procedures • Few new problems	• Physical dispersion of subordinates • Manager has additional tasks • High level of interaction required between manager and workers • High frequency of new problems

Flat organization

Figure 8.4

The Span of Management

Several criteria determine whether a firm uses a wide span of management, in which a number of workers report to one manager, or a narrow span, in which a manager supervises only a few workers.

in a firm. The span of management plays a direct role in determining the height of the organization, as shown in Figure 8.4. If spans of management are wider, fewer levels are needed, and the organization is *flat*. If spans of management generally are narrow, more levels are needed, and the resulting organization is *tall*.

In a taller organization, administrative costs are higher because more managers are needed. And communication among levels may become distorted because information has to pass up and down through more people. When companies are cutting costs, one option is to decrease organizational height in order to reduce related administrative expenses. Although flat organizations avoid these problems, their managers may perform more administrative duties simply because there are fewer managers. Wide spans of management also may require managers to spend considerably more time supervising and working with subordinates.

Chain of Command: Line and Staff Management

Learning Objective ⑥

Understand how the chain of command is established by using line and staff management.

Establishing the chain of command is another step in organizing a business. It reaches from the highest to the lowest levels of management. A **line management position** is part of the chain of command; it is a position in which a person makes decisions and gives orders to subordinates to achieve the goals of the organization. A **staff management position**, by contrast, is a position created to provide support, advice,

line management position a position that is part of the chain of command and that includes direct responsibility for achieving the goals of the organization

staff management position a position created to provide support, advice, and expertise within an organization

 www.hmco.ca/business

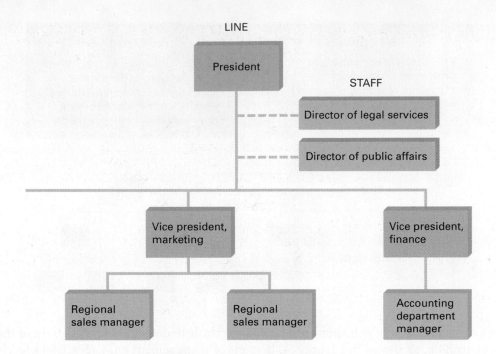

Figure 8.5

Line and Staff Management

A line manager has direct responsibility for achieving the company's goals and is in the direct chain of command. A staff manager supports and advises the line managers.

and expertise to someone in the chain of command. Staff managers are not part of the chain of command but do have authority over their assistants (see Figure 8.5).

Line and Staff Positions Compared

Both line and staff managers are needed for effective management, but the two positions differ in important ways. The basic difference is in terms of authority. Line managers have *line authority*, which means that they can make decisions and issue directives relating to the organization's goals.

Staff managers seldom have this kind of authority. Instead, they usually have either advisory authority or functional authority. *Advisory authority* is the expectation that line managers will consult the appropriate staff manager when making decisions. Functional authority is stronger. *Functional authority* is the authority of staff managers to make decisions and issue directives about their areas of expertise. For example, a legal adviser for Loblaw's can decide whether to retain a particular clause in a contract (their area of expertise) but does not engage in product pricing, The legal advisor therefore, occupies a staff position

Line-Staff Conflict

For a variety of reasons, conflict between line managers and staff managers is fairly common in businesses. Staff managers often have more formal education and sometimes are younger (and perhaps more ambitious) than line managers. Line managers may perceive staff managers as a threat to their own authority and thus may resent them. For their part, staff managers may become annoyed or angry if their expert recommendations—in public relations or human resources management, for example—are not adopted by line management.

DIMENSION	PURPOSE
Job design	To divide the work performed by an organization into parts and assign each part a position within the organization.
Departmentalization	To group various positions in an organization into manageable units. Departmentalization may be based on function, product, location, customer, or a combination of these bases.
Delegation	To distribute part of a manager's work and power to other workers. A deliberate concentration of authority at the upper levels of the organization creates a centralized structure. A wide distribution of authority into the lower levels of the organization creates a decentralized structure.
Span of management	To set the number of workers who report directly to one manager. A narrow span has only a few workers reporting to one manager. A wide span has a large number of workers reporting to one manager.
Line and staff management	To distinguish between those positions that are part of the chain of command and those that provide support, advice, or expertise to those in the chain of command.

Table 8.1

Five Characteristics of Organizational Structure

Fortunately, there are several ways to minimize the likelihood of such conflict. One way is to integrate line and staff managers into one team. Another is to ensure that the areas of responsibility of line and staff managers are clearly defined. Finally, line and staff managers both can be held accountable for the results of their activities.

Before studying the next topic—forms of organizational structure—you may want to review the five organization-shaping characteristics that we have just discussed. See Table 8.1 for a summary.

Forms of Organizational Structure

Learning Objective ❼

Describe the four basic forms of organizational structure: bureaucratic, matrix, cluster, and network.

Up to this point we have focused our attention on the major characteristics of organizational structure. In many ways this is like discussing the parts of a jigsaw puzzle one by one. It is time to put the puzzle together. In particular, we discuss four basic forms of organizational structure: bureaucratic, matrix, cluster, and network.

The Bureaucratic Structure

The term *bureaucracy* is used often in an unfavourable context to suggest rigidity and red tape. This image may be negative, but it does capture some of the essence of the bureaucratic structure.

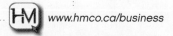 www.hmco.ca/business

bureaucratic structure a management system based on a formal framework of authority that is outlined carefully and followed precisely

A **bureaucratic structure** is a management system based on a formal framework of authority that is outlined carefully and followed precisely. A bureaucracy is likely to have the following characteristics:

1. A high level of job specialization
2. Departmentalization by function
3. Formal patterns of delegation
4. A high degree of centralization
5. Narrow spans of management, resulting in a tall organization
6. Clearly defined line and staff positions with formal relationships between the two

Perhaps the best examples of contemporary bureaucracies are government agencies and colleges and universities. Consider the very rigid university entrance and registration procedures. The reason for such procedures is to ensure that the organization is able to deal with large numbers of people in an equitable and fair manner. We may not enjoy them, but regulations and standard operating procedures guarantee uniform treatment.

Another example of a bureaucratic structure is Canada Post Corporation. Like colleges and universities, Canada Post relies on procedures and rules to accomplish the organization's goals. However, Canada Post has streamlined some of its procedures and initiated new services in order to compete with FedEx, United Parcel Service, and other delivery services. As a result, customer satisfaction has begun to improve.

The biggest drawback to the bureaucratic structure is lack of flexibility. A bureaucracy has trouble adjusting to change and coping with the unexpected. Because today's business environment is dynamic and complex, many firms have found that the bureaucratic structure is not an appropriate organizational structure.

▲
Working together to achieve a common task

The Campbell's soup company employs cross-functional teams to combat stiff competition with its soup division.

matrix structure an organizational structure that combines vertical and horizontal lines of authority, usually by superimposing product departmentalization on a functionally departmentalized organization

The Matrix Structure

When the matrix structure is used, individuals report to more than one superior at the same time. The **matrix structure** combines vertical and horizontal lines of authority. The matrix structure occurs when product departmentalization is superimposed on a functionally departmentalized organization. In a matrix organization, authority flows both down and across.

To understand the structure of a matrix organization, consider the usual functional arrangement, with people working in departments such as engineering, finance, and marketing. Now suppose that we assign people from these departments to a special

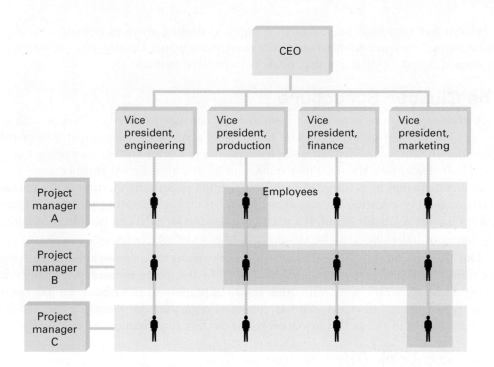

Figure 8.6

A Matrix Structure

A matrix is usually the result of combining product departmental-ization with function departmentalization. It is a complex structure in which employees have more than one supervisor.

Source: Ricky W. Griffin, *Management*, 8th ed. (Boston: Houghton Mifflin, 2005) Copyright © 2005 by Houghton Mifflin Company. Adapted with permission.

group that is working on a new project as a team. This team is called a **cross-functional team.** Frequently, cross-functional teams are charged with the responsibility of developing new products. The manager in charge of a team is usually called a *project manager*. Any individual who is working with the team reports to *both* the project manager and the individual's superior in the functional department (see Figure 8.6).

Cross-functional team projects may be temporary, in which case the team is disbanded once the mission is accomplished, or they may be permanent. These teams often are empowered to make major decisions. Campbell Soup Company recently broadened its innovation group into a permanent cross-functional work team to develop innovative new products and marketing techniques. Campbell's has encountered stiff competition in the soup industry and hopes that this team will create ways to increase the per capita soup consumption in its North American markets.[3] When a cross-functional team is employed, prospective team members might receive special training because effective teamwork can require different skills. For cross-functional teams to be successful, team members must be given specific information on the job each performs. The team also must develop a sense of cohesiveness and maintain good communications among its members.

Matrix structures offer advantages over other organizational forms. Added flexibility is probably the most obvious advantage. The matrix structure also can increase productivity, raise morale, and nurture creativity and innovation. In addition, employees experience personal development through doing a variety of jobs.

The matrix structure also has disadvantages. Having employees report to more than one supervisor can cause confusion about who is in charge. Like committees, teams may take longer to resolve problems and issues than individuals working alone. Other difficulties include personality clashes, poor communication, undefined individual

cross-functional team a group of employees from different departments who work together on a specific project

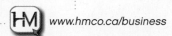

roles, unclear responsibilities, and challenges to finding ways to reward individual and team performance simultaneously. Because more managers and support staff may be needed, a matrix structure may be more expensive to maintain.

The Cluster Structure

cluster structure an organization that consists primarily of teams with no or very few underlying departments

A **cluster structure** is a type of business that consists primarily of teams with no or very few underlying departments. This type of structure is also called *team* or *collaborative.* In this type of organization, team members work together on a project until it is finished, and then the team may remain intact and be assigned another project, or team members may be reassigned to different teams, depending on their skills and the needs of the organization. In a cluster organization, the operating unit is the team, and it remains relatively small. If a team becomes too large, it can be split into multiple teams, or individuals can be assigned to other existing teams.

The cluster organizational structure has both strengths and weaknesses. Keeping the teams small provides the organization with the flexibility necessary to change directions quickly, to try new techniques, and to explore new ideas. Some employees in these types of organizations express concerns regarding job security and the increased amount of stress that arises owing to the fact that changes occur rapidly.[4]

The Network Structure

network structure an organization in which administration is the primary function, and most other functions are contracted out to other firms

In a **network structure** (sometimes called a *virtual organization*), administration is the primary function performed, and other functions such as engineering, production, marketing, and finance are contracted out to other organizations. Frequently, a network organization does not manufacture the products it sells. This type of organization has a few permanent employees consisting of top management and hourly clerical workers. Leased facilities and equipment, as well as temporary workers, are increased or decreased as the needs of the organization change. Thus there is rather limited formal structure associated with a network organization.

An obvious strength of a network structure is flexibility that allows the organization to adjust quickly to changes. Some of the challenges faced by managers in network-structured organizations include controlling the quality of work performed by other organizations, low morale and high turnover among hourly workers, and the vulnerability associated with relying on outside contractors.

Additional Factors That Influence an Organization

Learning Objective **8**

Summarize the use of corporate culture, intrapreneurship, committees, coordination techniques, informal groups, and the grapevine.

As you might expect, other factors in addition to those already covered in this chapter affect the way a large corporation operates on a day-to-day basis. To get a "true picture" of the organizational structure of a huge corporation such as Bell Canada Enterprises (BCE) for example, you need to consider the topics discussed in this section.

Corporate Culture

Most managers function within a corporate culture. A **corporate culture** is generally defined as the inner rites, rituals, heroes, and values of a firm. An organization's culture has a powerful influence on how employees think and act. It also can determine public perception of the organization.

Corporate culture generally is thought to have a very strong influence on a firm's performance over time. Hence it is useful to be able to assess a firm's corporate culture. Common indicators include the physical setting (building, office layouts), what the company says about its corporate culture (in advertising and news releases), how the company greets guests (does it have formal or informal reception areas?), and how employees spend their time (working alone in an office or working with others).

Goffee and Jones have identified four distinct types of corporate cultures (see Figure 8.7). One is called the *networked culture*, characterized by a base of trust and friendship among employees, a strong commitment to the

SPOTLIGHT

Should coworkers date?

About half say *yes*, and about half say *no*.

Yes 45%

5% Don't know

No 50%

Source: Maritz poll.

corporate culture the inner rites, rituals, heroes, and values of a firm

BIZ TECH

Meet the Avatars

How can you go to a meeting without leaving your desk? As the pace of business gets faster and travel becomes more expensive, a growing number of companies are calling meetings on the Internet. Sites such as Second Life (www.secondlife.com) offer affordable online meeting "spaces" and cutting-edge digital tools to make communication fast, easy, and out-of-the-ordinary.

Second Life is a virtual world inhabited by computer-generated, three-dimensional images called avatars, each customized to represent a particular person. To attend a meeting in Second Life, employees log on from anywhere and navigate their personal avatars to the meeting space—which can even be a virtual replica of the firm's actual conference room. Attendees sit in their real-world offices and converse by instant messaging text or, in some cases, Internet phone calls supplemented by web-cam video. Companies also gain from the hands-on experience with cutting-edge technologies. "To explore the new world, you have to live in it," observes an executive at the advertising agency Leo Burnett Worldwide, which holds Second Life meetings with employees worldwide.

Sources: Based on information from Emily Steel, "Avatars at the Office," *Wall Street Journal*, November 13, 2006, p. B1; Andrew Adam Newman, "The Reporter Is Real, but the World He Covers Isn't," *New York Times*, October 16, 2006, p. C6; www.secondlife.com; Richard Siklos, "A Virtual World but Real Money," *New York Times*, October 19, 2006, p. C1.

High

Networked Culture
- Extrovert energized by relationships
- Tolerant of ambiguities and have low needs for structure
- Can spot politics and act to stop "negative" politics
- Consider yourself easygoing, affable, and loyal to others

Communal Culture
- You consider yourself passionate
- Strong need to identify with something bigger than yourself
- You enjoy being in teams
- Prepared to make sacrifices for the greater good

Sociability

Fragmented Culture
- Are a reflective and self-contained introvert
- Have a high autonomy drive and strong desire to work independently
- Have a strong sense of self
- Consider yourself analytical rather than intuitive

Mercenary Culture
- Goal-oriented and have an obsessive desire to complete tasks
- Thrive on competitive energy
- Keep "relationships" out of work—develop them only to achieve your goals
- Keep things clear-cut and see the world in black and white

Low

Low   High

Solidarity

Figure 8.7

Types of Corporate Cultures

Which corporate culture would you choose?

Source: "Types of Corporate Culture," in Rob Goffee and Gareth Jones, *The Character of a Corporation* (New York: HarperCollins, 1998). Copyright © 1998 by Rob Goffee and Gareth Jones. Reprinted by permission of HarperCollins Publishers, Inc.

organization, and an informal environment. The *mercenary culture* embodies the feelings of passion, energy, sense of purpose, and excitement for one's work. The term *mercenary* does not imply that employees are motivated to work only for the money, but this is part of it. In this culture, employees are very intense, focused, and determined to win. In the *fragmented culture*, employees do not become friends, and they work "at" the organization, not "for" it. Employees have a high degree of autonomy, flexibility, and equality. The *communal culture* combines the positive traits of the networked culture and the mercenary culture—those of friendship, commitment, high focus on performance, and high energy. People's lives revolve around the product in this culture, and success by anyone in the organization is celebrated by all.[5]

Some experts believe that cultural change is needed when a company's environment changes, when the industry becomes more competitive, the company's performance is mediocre, and when the company is growing or is about to become a truly large organization. For example, the PC industry has become highly competitive as PC sales stagnated. Fast growth used to be Dell's top concern, but now Michael Dell and other executives are focusing on developing the company's culture. "The Soul of Dell" is the computer giant's guide to corporate culture and ethics, and management hopes that a strong culture will increase employee loyalty and the success of the company.[6]

In the future organizations will look quite different. Experts predict that tomorrow's businesses will be comprised of small, task-oriented work groups, each with control over its own activities. These small groups will be coordinated through an elaborate computer network and held together by a strong corporate culture. Businesses operating in fast-changing industries will require leadership that supports trust and risk taking. Creating a culture of trust in an organization can lead to increases in growth, profit, productivity, and job satisfaction. A culture of trust can retain the best people, inspire customer loyalty, develop new markets, and increase creativity.

Another area where corporate culture plays a vital role is the integration of two or more companies. Business leaders often cite the role of corporate cultures in the integration process as one of the primary factors affecting the success of a merger or acquisition. Experts note that corporate culture is a way of conducting business both within the company and externally. If two merging companies do not address differences in corporate culture, they are setting themselves up for missed expectations and possibly failure.[7]

Intrapreneurship

Since innovations and new-product development are important to companies, and since entrepreneurs are innovative people, it seems almost natural that an entrepreneurial character would surface prominently in many of today's larger organizations. An **intrapreneur** is an employee who takes responsibility for pushing an innovative idea, product, or process through an organization.[8] An intrapreneur possesses the confidence and drive of an entrepreneur but is allowed to use organizational resources for idea development. For example, Art Fry, inventor of the colourful Post-it-Notes that people can't live without, is a devoted advocate of intrapreneurship. Nurturing his notepad idea at Minnesota Mining and Manufacturing (3M) for years, Fry speaks highly of the intrapreneurial commitment at 3M. Fry indicates that an *intrapreneur* is an individual who does not have all the skills to get the job done and thus has to work within an organization, making use of its skills and attributes.

intrapreneur an employee who pushes an innovative idea, product, or process through an organization

Committees

Today, business firms use several types of committees that affect organizational structure. An **ad hoc committee** is created for a specific short-term purpose, such as reviewing the firm's employee benefits plan. Once its work is finished, the ad hoc committee disbands. A **standing committee** is a relatively permanent committee charged with performing a recurring task. A firm might establish a budget review committee, for example, to review departmental budget requests on an ongoing basis. Finally, a **task force** is a committee established to investigate a major problem or pending decision. A firm contemplating a merger with another company might form a task force or special committee to assess the pros and cons of the merger. Governments also use task forces to deal with special problems and issues.

Committees offer some advantages over individual action. Their several members are able to bring information and knowledge to the task at hand. Furthermore, committees tend to make more accurate decisions and to transmit their results through the organization more effectively. However, committee deliberations take longer than individual actions. In addition, unnecessary compromise can take place within the committee. Or the opposite can occur, as one person dominates (and thus negates) the committee process.

ad hoc committee a committee created for a specific short-term purpose

standing committee a relatively permanent committee charged with performing some recurring task

task force a committee established to investigate a major problem or pending decision

Coordination Techniques

A large organization is forced to coordinate organizational resources to minimize duplication and to maximize effectiveness. One technique is simply to make use of the **managerial hierarchy,** which is the arrangement that provides increasing authority

managerial hierarchy the arrangement that provides increasing authority at higher levels of management

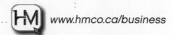

at higher levels of management. One manager is placed in charge of all the resources being coordinated. That person is able to coordinate them by virtue of the authority accompanying his or her position.

Resources also can be coordinated through rules and procedures. For example, a rule can govern how a firm's travel budget is allocated. This particular resource, then, would be coordinated in terms of that rule.

In complex situations, more sophisticated coordination techniques may be called for. One approach is to establish a liaison. A *liaison* is a go-between—a person who coordinates the activities of two groups. Suppose that General Motors is negotiating a complicated contract with a supplier of steering wheels. The supplier might appoint a liaison whose primary responsibility is to coordinate the contract negotiations. Finally, for *very* complex coordination needs, a committee could be established. Suppose that Research in Motion is in the process of purchasing a rolling-ball supplier. In this case, a committee might be appointed to integrate the new firm into RIM's' larger organizational structure.

The Informal Organization

So far we have discussed the organization as a formal structure consisting of interrelated positions. This is the organization that is shown on an organization chart. There is another kind of organization, however, that does not show up on any chart. We define this **informal organization** as the pattern of behaviour and interaction that stems from personal rather than official relationships. Firmly embedded within every informal organization are informal groups and the notorious grapevine.

Informal Groups An **informal group** is created by the group members themselves to accomplish goals that may or may not be relevant to the organization. Workers might create an informal group to go bowling, form a union, get a particular manager fired or transferred, or go for lunch. The group might last for several years or a few hours.

Informal groups can be powerful forces in organizations. They can restrict output, or they can help managers through tight spots. They can cause disagreement and conflict or they can help to boost morale and job satisfaction. They can show new people how to contribute to the organization or they can help people get away with substandard performance. Clearly, managers should be aware of these informal groups.

informal organization the pattern of behaviour and interaction that stems from personal rather than official relationships

informal group a group created by the members themselves to accomplish goals that may or may not be relevant to an organization

▲
Informal groups

Informal groups, such as the Cinga employee softball league, can be a source of information and camaraderie for participants. Although informal groups can sometimes create problems for the organization, they can also provide significant benefits.

Those who make the mistake of fighting the informal organization have a major obstacle to overcome.

The Grapevine The grapevine is the informal communications network within an organization. It is completely separate from—and sometimes much faster than—the organization's formal channels of communication. Formal communications usually follow a path that parallels the organizational chain of command. Information can be transmitted through the grapevine in any direction—up, down, diagonally, or horizontally across the organizational structure. Subordinates may pass information to their bosses, an executive may relay something to a maintenance worker, or there may be an exchange of information between people who work in totally unrelated departments. Grapevine information can cover topics ranging from the latest management decisions to gossip.

grapevine the informal communications network within an organization

How should managers treat the grapevine? Certainly it would be a mistake to try to eliminate it. People working together, day in and day out, are going to communicate. A more rational approach is to recognize its existence. For example, managers should respond promptly and aggressively to inaccurate grapevine information to minimize the damage that such misinformation might do. Moreover, the grapevine can come in handy when managers are on the receiving end of important communications from the informal organization.

In the next chapter we apply these and other management concepts to an extremely important business function: the production of goods and services.

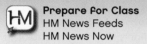

Prepare for Class
HM News Feeds
HM News Now

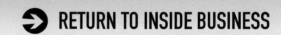

→ **RETURN TO INSIDE BUSINESS**

After starting with one motor hotel in Toronto, Four Seasons has expanded its operations around the world. Some projects include apartment-style hotels and resorts. In each location, the organizational structure is determined to a large extent by the types of operations and services the site offers its customers.

Questions

1. Consider the typical managerial jobs that you would find at a Four Seasons Hotel. Which ones would be classified as line positions and which would be considered staff positions?

2. Which type of organizational structure would work best at a Four Seasons Hotel?

CHAPTER REVIEW

1 Understand what an organization is and identify its characteristics.

An organization is a group of two or more people working together to achieve a common set of goals. The relationships among positions within an organization can be illustrated by means of an organization chart. Five specific characteristics—job design, departmentalization, delegation, span of management, and chain of command—help to determine what an organization chart and the organization itself look like.

2 Explain why job specialization is important.

Job specialization is the separation of all the activities within an organization into smaller components and the assignment of those different components to different people. Several factors combine to make specialization a useful technique for designing jobs, but high levels of specialization may cause employee dissatisfaction and boredom. One technique for overcoming these problems is job rotation.

3 Identify the various bases for departmentalization.

Departmentalization is the grouping of jobs into manageable units. Typical bases for departmentalization are by function, product, location, or customer. Because each of these bases provides particular advantages, most firms—especially larger ones—use a combination of different bases in different organizational situations.

4 Explain how decentralization follows from delegation.

Delegation is the assigning of part of a manager's work to other workers. It involves the following three steps: (a) assigning responsibility, (b) granting authority, and (c) creating accountability. A decentralized firm is one that delegates as much power as possible to people in the lower management levels. In a centralized firm, on the other hand, power is systematically retained at the upper levels.

5 Understand how the span of management describes an organization.

The span of management is the number of workers who report directly to a manager. Spans generally are characterized as wide (many workers per manager) or narrow (few workers per manager). Wide spans generally result in flat organizations (few layers of management); narrow spans generally result in tall organizations (many layers of management).

6 Understand how the chain of command is established by using line and staff management.

A line position is one that is in the organization's chain of command or line of authority. A manager in a line position makes decisions and gives orders to workers to achieve the goals of the organization. On the other hand, a manager in a staff position provides support, advice, and expertise to someone in the chain of command. Staff positions may carry some authority, but it usually applies only within staff areas of expertise.

7 Describe the four basic forms of organizational structure: bureaucratic, matrix, cluster, and network.

There are four basic forms of organizational structure. The bureaucratic structure is characterized by formality and rigidity. With the bureaucratic structure, rules and procedures are used to ensure uniformity. The matrix structure may be visualized as product departmentalization superimposed on functional departmentalization. With the matrix structure, an employee on a cross-functional team reports to both the project manager and the individual's supervisor in a functional department. A cluster structure is an organization that consists primarily of teams with very few underlying functional departments. In an organization with a network structure, the primary function performed internally is administration, and other functions are contracted out to other firms.

Summarize the use of corporate culture, intrapreneurship, committees, coordination techniques, informal groups, and the grapevine.

Corporate culture—the inner rites, rituals, heroes, and values of a firm—is thought to have a very strong influence on a firm's performance over time. An intrapreneur is an employee in an organizational environment who takes responsibility for pushing an innovative idea, product, or process through the organization. Additional elements that influence an organization include the use of commit-

tees and the development of techniques for achieving coordination among various groups within the organization. Finally, both informal groups created by group members and an informal communication network called the grapevine may affect an organization and its performance.

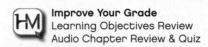 **Improve Your Grade**
Learning Objectives Review
Audio Chapter Review & Quiz

Review Questions

1. In what way do organization charts create a picture of an organization?
2. What is the chain of command in an organization?
3. What determines the degree of specialization within an organization?
4. Describe how job rotation can be used to combat the problems caused by job specialization.
5. What are the major differences among the four departmentalization bases?
6. Why do most firms employ a combination of departmentalization bases?
7. What three steps are involved in delegation? Explain each.
8. How does a firm's top management influence its degree of centralization?
9. How is organizational height related to the span of management?
10. What are the key differences between line and staff positions?
11. Contrast the bureaucratic and matrix forms of organizational structure.
12. What are the differences between the cluster structure and the network structure?
13. What is corporate culture? Describe the major types.
14. Which form of organizational structure probably would lead to the strongest informal organization? Why?
15. How might managerial hierarchy be used to coordinate the organization's resources?

Discussion Questions

1. Explain how the five steps of the organizing process determine the characteristics of the resulting organization. Which steps are most important?
2. Which kinds of firms probably would operate most effectively as centralized firms? As decentralized firms?
3. How do decisions concerning span of management, the use of committees, and coordination techniques affect organizational structure?
4. How might a manager go about formalizing the informal organization?

CASE STUDY

Saturn: Still a Different Kind of Company?

S aturn was only an idea in 1983—General Motors' new idea about how to organize a car company. The idea was to give the company and its employees a lot more autonomy instead of imposing the rigid rules and conventions under which auto factories normally operated. Yet, since 1990, when the Saturn plant opened in Spring Hill, Tennessee, GM has changed the organization little by little. Is today's Saturn still a different kind of car company?

The Saturn project went into high gear after GM and the United Auto Workers came to agreement about having plant employees take a more active role. Instead of operating under an inflexible system of narrow job specialization, the plan was for Saturn's employees to work in teams and handle a variety of tasks as needed. The new company was to be managed as a separate entity and therefore hired its own engineers, developed its own vehicles, and purchased its own supplies and raw materials. GM also built Saturn a new state-of-the-art plant at a cost of $3.5 billion. And to reinforce Saturn's independence from the GM hierarchy, its top manager was designated its CEO.

By the time the first sedans started rolling off the assembly line, Saturn had established itself as a different kind of car company. Customers welcomed the "no haggle, no hassle" pricing policy as a change from the back-and-forth price negotiation they usually had to endure when buying a car. Just as important, Saturn's dealers put extra emphasis on service and satisfaction, making customers feel especially appreciated.

Such a mystique surrounded Saturn that happy customers began dropping by the factory to thank the employees. Saturn soon channelled their enthusiasm into a "homecoming" festival at Spring Hill that drew more than 40,000 customers from all over the United States. The CEO even gave the bride away when the employees of two competing Saturn dealers decided to hold their wedding at Spring Hill. Sales soared and the plant strained to keep up with demand. For a time, Saturn was more than just a car company—it was a national phenomenon.

By end of the 1990s, however, Saturn had lost its novelty. While GM's officials debated whether to invest in new models, tastes were changing. Competitors' sport-utility vehicles (SUVs)

and light pickup trucks had captured the public's imagination and gained market share at Saturn's expense. Eventually, Saturn did introduce the Vue SUV, but it was unable to generate the same kind of magic as the company's original sedan.

Meanwhile, GM was under great pressure to improve its financial performance, and top management was determined to cut costs worldwide. In the past, the president of each region (North America, Europe, Latin America, and Asia-Pacific) was responsible for that region's product development and other key functions. As a result, corporate officials could request but not order changes that would lower costs, such as following one set of engineering standards. By centralizing engineering, purchasing, and product development, the corporate office gained the direct control necessary to squeeze out redundancies.

This move toward centralization touched Saturn as well. Although the Spring Hill plant was highly efficient, maintaining a separate engineering staff for Saturn was costly. Thus GM moved Saturn's engineers to Michigan, where they joined the corporate design staff. In addition, GM eliminated the CEO title at Saturn and began managing the brand in the same way as Chevrolet and all other brands in the corporate lineup. In the future, the Spring Hill factory may very well manufacture Chevrolets, whereas Saturns may be produced in Ohio or Mexico. Already the Saturn minivan is being made in Georgia. With all these changes, is Saturn still a new kind of car company?

For more information about this company, go to www.saturn.com and www.gm.com.

Questions:

1. In a factory such as Saturn's, where certain tasks must be completed in exactly the same way to produce each car, why would the company not push for job specialization?

2. Does GM appear to be organized by function, product, location, customer, or more than one of these departmentalization bases?

3. How does eliminating the CEO position at Saturn affect the chain of command at GM?

BUILDING SKILLS FOR CAREER SUCCESS

1. Exploring the Internet

After studying the various organizational structures described in this chapter and the reasons for employing them, you may be interested in learning about the organizational structures in place at large firms. As noted in the chapter, departmentalization typically is based on function, product, location, and customer. Many large firms use a combination of these organizational strategies successfully. You can gain a good sense of which organizational theme prevails in an industry by looking at several corporate sites.

Assignment

1. Explore the website of any large firm that you believe is representative of its industry, and find its organization chart or a description of its organization. Create a brief organization chart from the information you have found. (You may choose one of the consulting firms listed in the Internet exercise for Chapter 7.)

2. Describe the bases on which this firm is departmentalized.

2. Developing Critical-Thinking Skills

A firm's culture is a reflection of its most basic beliefs, values, customs, and rituals. Because it can have a powerful influence on how employees think and act, this culture also can have a powerful influence on a firm's performance. The influence may be for the better, of course or it may be for the worse, as in the case of a bureaucratic organization whose employees feel hopelessly tied up in red tape. When a company is concerned about mediocre performance and declining sales figures, its managers would do well to examine the cultural environment to see what might be in need of change.

Assignment

1. Analyze the cultural environment in which you work. (If you have no job, consider your school as your workplace and your instructor as your supervisor.) Ask yourself and your coworkers (or classmates) the following questions and record the answers:

   a. Do you feel that your supervisors welcome your ideas and respect them even when they may disagree with them? Do you take pride in your work? Do you feel that your work is appreciated? Do you think that the amount of work assigned to you is reasonable? Are you compensated adequately for your work?

   b. Are you proud to be associated with the company? Do you believe what the company says about itself in its advertisements? Are there any company policies or rules, written or unwritten, that you feel are unfair? Do you think that there is an opportunity for you to advance in this environment?

   c. How much independence do you have in carrying out your assignments? Are you ever allowed to act on your own, or do you feel that you have to consult with your supervisor on every detail?

   d. Do you enjoy the atmosphere in which you work? Is the physical setting pleasant? How often do you laugh in an average workday? How well do you get along with your supervisor and coworkers?

   e. Do you feel that the company cares about you? Will your supervisor give you time off when you have some pressing personal need? If the company had to downsize, how do you think you would be treated?

2. Using the responses to these questions, write a two-page paper describing how the culture of your workplace affects your performance and the overall performance of the firm. Point out the cultural factors that have the most beneficial and negative effects. Include your thoughts on how negative effects could be reversed.

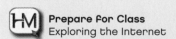
Prepare for Class
Exploring the Internet

3. Building Team Skills

An organization chart is a diagram showing how employees and tasks are grouped and how the lines of communication and authority flow within an organization. These charts can look very different depending on a number of factors, including the nature and size of the business, the way it is departmentalized, its patterns of delegating authority, and its span of management.

Assignment

1. Working in a team, use the following information to draw an organization chart: The ABC Design Centre works closely with two home-construction companies, Canex and Midpoint. ABC's role is to help customers select materials for their new homes and to ensure that their selections are communicated accurately to the builders. The company is also a retailer of wallpaper, blinds, and drapery. The retail department, the Canex accounts, and the Midpoint accounts make up ABC's three departments. The company has the following positions:

    President

    Executive vice president

    Managers, 2

    Appointment coordinators, 2

    Canex coordinators, 2

    Midpoint coordinators, 2

    Consultants/designers for the Canex and Midpoint accounts, 15

    Retail positions, 4

    Payroll and billing personnel, 1

2. After your team has drawn the organization chart, discuss the following:

    a. What type of organizational structure does your chart depict? Is it a bureaucratic, matrix, cluster, or network structure? Why?

    b. How does ABC use departmentalization?

    c. To what extent is authority in the company centralized or decentralized?

    d. What is the span of management within ABC?

    e. Which positions are line positions and which are staff? Why?

3. Prepare a three-page report summarizing what the chart revealed about relationships and tasks at the ABC Design Centre and what your team learned about the value of organization charts. Include your chart in your report.

4. Researching Different Careers

In the past, company loyalty and ability to assume increasing job responsibility usually ensured advancement within an organization. While the reasons for seeking advancement (the desire for a better-paying position, more prestige, and job satisfaction) have not changed, the qualifications for career advancement have. In today's business environment, climbing the corporate ladder requires packaging and marketing yourself. To be promoted within your company or to be considered for employment with another company, it is wise to improve your skills continually. By taking workshops and seminars or enrolling in community college courses, you can keep up with the changing technology in your industry. Networking with people in your business or community can help you to find a new job. Most jobs are filled through personal contacts. Who you know can be important.

A list of your accomplishments on the job can reveal your strengths and weaknesses. Setting goals for improvement helps to increase your self-confidence.

Be sure to recognize the signs of job dissatisfaction. It may be time to move to another position or company.

Assignment

Are you prepared to climb the corporate ladder? Do a self-assessment by analyzing the following areas, and summarize the results in a two-page report.

1. Skills

-   What are your most valuable skills?
-   What skills do you lack?
-   Describe your plan for acquiring new skills and improving your skills.

2. Networking
- How effectively are you at using a mentor?
- Are you a member of a professional organization?
- In which community, civic, or church groups are you participating?
- Whom have you added to your contact list in the last six weeks?

3. Accomplishments
- What achievements have you reached in your job?

- What would you like to accomplish? What will it take for you to reach your goal?

4. Promotion or new job
- What is your likelihood for getting a promotion?
- Are you ready for a change? What are you doing or willing to do to find another job?

CHAPTER 9

Producing Quality Goods and Services

Your Guide to Success in Business

Why this chapter matters
Think for a moment about the products and services you bought in the past week. If it weren't for the activities in this chapter, those products and services would not be available.

1. Explain the nature of production.

2. Outline how the conversion process transforms raw materials, labour, and other resources into finished products or services.

3. Describe how research and development lead to new products and services.

4. Discuss the components involved in planning the production process.

5. Explain how purchasing, inventory control, scheduling, and quality control affect production.

6. Summarize how productivity and technology are related.

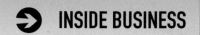

Honda Canada Inc.—Location, location, location . . .

We normally speak of the importance of location in determining the success of retail and service outlets, particularly fast food chains. But location is also critically important in choosing the location of manufacturing facilities.

In 1986, Honda Canada Inc., through their subsidiary, Honda of Canada Mfg., began production of the Accord in Alliston, Ontario, a small farming community located north of Toronto. Considering that most of the automobile manufacturing in Canada was centred in the Windsor-Detroit corridor, Oakville (Ford), and Oshawa (General Motors), it seemed an odd choice of location for what was planned to be a major footprint for the Japanese company.

But Honda executives knew what they were doing. The original plant with production capacity of approximately 40,000 vehicles per year has grown tenfold, and now employs over 4,000 Honda "associates." It produces vehicles to support both the Honda and Acura brands including the Odyssey minivan and the Acura MDX SUV.

In choosing a location to establish a manufacturing facility in Canada, Honda considered several factors. One was the availability and cost of land. Expansion of the plant was always a consideration, so the location had to have room to grow. The farming community in and around Alliston was contracting and large tracts of land were available. The proximity of both Toronto and Barrie assisted in two other major considerations—access to sales markets and workers. Access to major transportation routes was also important. The 400 series of highways was right next door and rail lines could be connected directly to the plant.

Honda used a "just in time" inventory management system, whereby suppliers provided their parts when needed, shipping daily to accommodate the production schedule. To ensure delivery, many of the

continued on next page

● ● ●

> **DID YOU KNOW?**
>
> Since it began in 1986, the Honda plant in Alliston has produced more than 3 million vehicles for the North American market. The location of the plant is one of the primary elements of its success.

KEY TERMS

operations management (252)
mass production (254)
analytical process (254)
synthetic process (254)
utility (255)
form utility (255)
service economy (256)
research and development (R&D) (258)
design planning (260)
product line (260)
product design (261)

capacity (261)
labour-intensive technology (261)
capital-intensive technology (261)
plant layout (263)
planning horizon (264)
purchasing (265)
inventory control (266)
materials requirements planning (MRP) (266)
just-in-time inventory system (267)
scheduling (267)
Gantt chart (268)

PERT (Program Evaluation and Review Technique) (268)
critical path (269)
International Organization for Standardization (269)
quality control (270)
statistical process control (SPC) (270)
statistical quality control (SQC) (271)
inspection (271)
Six Sigma (271)
quality circle (271)
productivity (272)

automation (273)
robotics (273)
computer-aided design (CAD) (273)
computer-aided manufacturing (CAM) (273)
computer-integrated manufacturing (CIM) (273)
continuous process (274)
flexible manufacturing system (FMS) (274)
intermittent process (274)

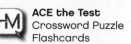
ACE the Test
Crossword Puzzle
Flashcards

suppliers needed warehouse space located close to the plant—Alliston could accommodate their needs as well.

Finally, the municipal and provincial governments had to support the project—modified land use restrictions and financial incentives such as tax concessions helped Alliston compete with other sites that Honda was considering.

Alliston won the day and more than 3 million vehicles have since been produced there, fuelling a local economic boom that has been boosted by continual investment in the Honda manufacturing facility.

As Honda continues to grow its manufacturing operation in Alliston, Ontario, they must constantly look for ways to improve its methods of doing business to improve not only quality but also manufacturing productivity. The fact is that no industry illustrates this chapter's content—the production of quality goods and services—better than the automobile industry. Auto manufacturers, such as Honda, take all kinds of raw materials—steel, aluminum, rubber, plastic, vinyl, and leather—and transform them into finely tuned cars that are sold to demanding customers around the globe. Today people expect more when purchasing an automobile, and now Honda is working to produce a product that people want.

We begin this chapter with an overview of operations management—the activities required to produce products and services that meet the needs of customers. In this section we also discuss competition in the global marketplace and careers in operations management. Next, we describe the conversion process that makes production possible and also note the growing role of services in our economy. Then we examine more closely three important aspects of operations management: developing ideas for new products, planning for production, and effectively controlling operations after production has begun. We close the chapter with a look at productivity trends and ways that productivity can be improved through the use of technology.

What Is Production?

 Learning Objective 1

Explain the nature of production.

Have you ever wondered where a new pair of Parassuco jeans comes from? Or a new Mitsubishi big-screen colour television, Tommy Hilfiger pullover sweater, or Michelin tires? Even factory service on a IBM notebook computer or a Maytag clothes dryer would be impossible if it weren't for the activities described in this chapter. In fact, these products and services and millions of others like them would not exist if it weren't for production activities.

Let's begin this chapter by reviewing what an operating manager does. In Chapter 7 we described an *operations manager* as a person who manages the systems that convert resources into goods and services. This area of management is usually referred to as **operations management**, which consists of all the activities managers engage in to produce goods and services.

To produce a product or service successfully, a business must perform a number of specific activities. For example, suppose that an organization such as Toyota has an idea for a new Toyota Highlander Hybrid sport-utility vehicle (SUV) that will cost in

operations management all activities managers engage in to produce goods and services

excess of $3,000 and features a new gas/electric engine. Marketing research must determine not only if customers are willing to pay the price for this product but also what special features they want. Then Toyota's operations managers must turn the concept into reality.

Toyota's managers cannot just push the "start" button and immediately begin producing the new automobile. Production must be planned. As you will see, planning takes place both *before* anything is produced and *during* the production process.

Managers also must concern themselves with the control of operations to ensure that the organization's goals are achieved. For a product such as Toyota's Highlander Hybrid SUV, control of operations involves a number of important issues, including product quality, performance standards, the amount of inventory of both raw materials and finished products, and production costs.

We discuss each of the major activities of operations management later in this chapter. First, however, let's take a closer look at Canadian and U.S. manufacturers and how they compete in the global marketplace.

Competition in the Global Marketplace

After World War II, the United States became the most productive country in the world. As its largest and closest trading partner, Canada has tracked almost simultaneously the changes in production and manufacturing that U.S. firms have experienced. For almost thirty years, until the late 1970s, the United States' leadership was never threatened. By then, however, manufacturers in Japan, Germany, Great Britain, Italy, Korea, Sweden, and other industrialized nations were offering U.S. firms increasing competition. And now the Chinese are manufacturing everything from sophisticated electronic equipment and automobiles to less expensive everyday items—often for lower cost than the same goods can be manufactured in other countries. As a result, the goods North Americans purchase may have been manufactured in the United States, Canada *or* in other countries around the globe and shipped to North America.

Competition has never been fiercer, and in some ways the world has never been smaller.

In an attempt to regain a competitive edge on foreign manufacturers, Canadian firms have taken another look at the importance of improving quality and meeting the needs of their customers. The most successful Canadian firms also have focused on the following:

1. Motivating employees to cooperate with management and improve productivity

2. Reducing production costs by selecting suppliers that offer higher-quality raw materials and components at reasonable prices

3. Replacing outdated equipment with state-of-the-art manufacturing equipment

4. Using computer-aided and flexible manufacturing systems that allow a higher degree of customization

5. Improving control procedures to help ensure lower manufacturing costs

6. Building new manufacturing facilities in foreign countries where labour costs are lower

Although competing in the global economy is a major challenge, it is a worthwhile pursuit. For most firms, competing in the global marketplace is not only profitable, but it is also an essential activity that requires the cooperation of everyone within the organization.

Careers in Operations Management

mass production a manufacturing process that lowers the cost required to produce a large number of identical or similar products over a long period of time

analytical process a process in operations management in which raw materials are broken into different component parts

synthetic process a process in operations management in which raw materials or components are combined to create a finished product

Although it is hard to provide information about specific career opportunities in operations management, some generalizations do apply to this management area. First, you must appreciate the manufacturing process and the steps required to produce a product or service. A basic understanding of mass production and the difference between an analytical process and a synthetic process is essential. **Mass production** is a manufacturing process that lowers the cost required to produce a large number of identical or similar products over a long period of time. An **analytical process** breaks raw materials into different component parts. For example, a barrel of crude oil refined by PetroCanada—an Alberta-based oil refiner—can be broken down into gasoline, oil and lubricants, and many other petroleum by-products. A **synthetic process** is just the opposite of the analytical one; it combines raw materials or components to create a finished product. Research In Motion uses a synthetic process when it combines plastic, steel, rechargeable batteries, and other components to produce its successful BlackBerry device.

Once you understand that operations managers are responsible for producing tangible products or services that customers want, you must determine how you fit into the production process. Today's successful operations managers must

1. be able to motivate and lead people.
2. understand how technology can make a manufacturer more productive and efficient.
3. appreciate the control processes that help lower production costs and improve product quality.
4. understand the relationship between the customer, the marketing of a product, and the production of a product.

If operations management seems like an area you might be interested in, why not do more career exploration? You could take an operations management course if your college or university offers one, or you could obtain a part-time job during the school year or a summer job in a manufacturing company.

A synthetic process

Oil from Petro-Canada's refineries produces a range of products including gasoline, oil, lubricants, plastics, paints, and fertilizers.

The Conversion Process

Learning Objective ❷

Outline how the conversion process transforms raw materials, labour, and other resources into finished products or services.

To have something to sell, a business must convert resources into goods and services. The resources are materials, finances, people, and information—the same resources discussed in Chapters 1 and 7. The goods and services are varied, ranging from consumer products to heavy manufacturing equipment to fast food. The purpose of this conversion of resources into goods and services is to provide utility to customers. **Utility** is the ability of a good or service to satisfy a human need. Although there are four types of utility—form, place, time, and possession—operations management focuses primarily on form utility. **Form utility** is created by converting raw materials, people, finances, and information into finished products. The other types of utility—place, time, and possession—are discussed in Chapter 13.

But how does the conversion take place? How does Kellogg convert wheat, corn, sugar, salt, and other ingredients; money from previous sales and stockholders' investments; production workers and managers; and economic and marketing forecasts into cereal products? How does Sun Life Assurance Company of Canada convert office buildings, insurance premiums, actuaries, and mortality tables into life insurance policies? They do so through the use of a conversion process like the one illustrated in Figure 9.1. As indicated by our Sun Life Assurance example, the conversion process is not limited to manufacturing products. The conversion process also can be used to produce services.

Manufacturing Using a Conversion Process

The conversion of resources into products and services can be described in several ways. We limit our discussion here to three: the focus or major resource used in the conversion process, its magnitude of change, and the number of production processes employed.

Focus By the *focus* of a conversion process we mean the resource or resources that make up the major or most important *input*. For a bank such as the Royal Bank of Canada, financial resources are the major resource. An energy company such as PetroCanada concentrates on material and natural resources. A college or university is concerned primarily with information. And a temporary employment service focuses on the use of human resources.

Magnitude of Change The *magnitude* of a conversion process is the degree to which the resources are physically changed.

utility the ability of a good or service to satisfy a human need

form utility utility created by converting raw materials, people, finances, and information into finished products

INPUTS
- Concept for a new good or service
- Financial, material, human, and information resources

CONVERSION
- Develop specifications to convert an idea to a good or service
- Planning for production
- Actual production

OUTPUTS
- Completed good or service

Figure 9.1

The Conversion Process

The conversion process converts resources such as materials, finances, people, and information into useful goods, services, and ideas. The ability to produce products, services, and ideas is a crucial step in the economic development of any nation.

At one extreme lie such processes where the original resources are totally unrecognizable in the finished product, such as in the manufacture of plastic food wraps. At the other extreme, Air Canada produces *no* physical change in its original resources. The airline simply provides a service and transports people from one place to another.

Number of Production Processes A single firm may employ one production process or many. In general, larger firms that make a variety of products use multiple production processes. For example, General Electric manufactures some of its own products, buys other merchandise from suppliers, and operates a credit division, an insurance company, an entertainment division, and a medical equipment division. Smaller firms, by contrast, may operate in one fairly narrow market in which few production processes are required.

The Increasing Importance of Services

The application of the basic principles of operations management to the production of services has coincided with a dramatic growth in the number and diversity of service businesses. Statistics Canada figures for the years 2002 through 2006 indicated that fully two-thirds of the total number of employment opportunities in Canada are derived from the service sector. In fact, the Canadian economy is now characterized as a **service economy** (see Table 9.1). A service economy is one in which more effort is devoted to the production of services than to the production of goods. Although it is often more difficult to measure customer satisfaction, today's successful service firms work hard at providing the services customers want. Compared with manufacturers, service firms often listen more carefully to customers and respond more quickly to the market's changing needs.

Today, the managers of restaurants, laundries, real estate agencies, banks, movie theatres, airlines, travel bureaus, and other service firms have realized that they can benefit from the experience of manufacturers. And yet the production of services is very different from the production of manufactured goods in the following four ways:

1. Services are consumed immediately and, unlike manufactured goods, cannot be stored. For example, a hair stylist cannot store completed haircuts.

2. Services are provided when and where the customer desires the service. In many cases customers will not travel far to obtain a service.

3. Services are usually labour-intensive because the human resource is often the most important resource used in the production of services.

4. Services are intangible, and it is therefore more difficult to evaluate customer satisfaction.[1]

Now that we understand something about the production process that is used to transform resources into goods and services, we can consider three major activities involved in operations management. These are new product development, planning for production, and operations control.

service economy an economy in which more effort is devoted to the production of services than to the production of goods

	2002	2003	2004	2005	2006
			THOUSANDS		
All industries	**15,310.4**	**15,672.3**	**15,947.0**	**16,169.7**	**16,484.3**
Goods-producing sector	3,878.6	3,925.7	3,989.8	4,002.4	3,985.9
Agriculture	325.4	332.4	326.0	343.7	346.4
Forestry, fishing, mining, oil and gas	270.3	281.6	286.6	306.4	330.1
Utilities	131.9	130.5	133.3	125.3	122.0
Construction	865.2	906.0	951.7	1,019.5	1,069.7
Manufacturing	2,285.9	2,275.2	2,292.1	2,207.4	2,117.7
Services-producing sector	11,431.8	11,746.6	11,957.2	12,167.3	12,498.4
Trade	2,409.3	2,467.8	2,507.1	2,574.6	2,633.5
Transportation and warehousing	760.7	790.9	799.4	793.6	802.2
Finance, insurance, real estate and leasing	895.1	917.0	960.6	987.8	1,040.5
Professional, scientific and technical services	987.1	1,003.6	1,018.3	1,050.0	1,089.9
Business, building and other support services[a]	579.6	608.7	630.2	654.4	690.0
Educational services	1,007.4	1,027.1	1,035.7	1,106.1	1,158.4
Health care and social assistance	1,617.3	1,679.2	1,733.4	1,734.6	1,785.5
Information, culture and recreation	715.1	714.6	738.0	735.1	745.0
Accommodation and food services	985.1	1,005.5	1,012.4	1,004.5	1,015.0
Other services	686.2	713.1	696.6	693.4	701.0
Public administration	788.9	819.0	825.5	833.1	837.4

[a]Formerly Management of companies, administrative and other support services.

Table 9.1

Employment by Industry

Source: Statistics Canada, CANSIM, table (for fee) 282-0008 and Catalogue no. 71F0004XCB. Last modified: 2007-01-04. Statistics Canada information is used with the permission of Statistics Canada. Users are forbidden to copy this material and/or redisseminate the data, in an original or modified form, for commercial purposes, without the expressed permission of Statistics Canada.

Where Do New Products and Services Come From?

Learning Objective ③

Describe how research and development lead to new products and services.

No firm can produce a product or service until it has an idea. In other words, someone first must come up with a new way to satisfy a need—a new product or an improvement in an existing product. Starbucks' milkshake-like coffee drink and Apple's iPod, began as an idea. While no one can predict with 100 percent accuracy what types of products will be available in the next five years, it is safe to say that companies will continue to introduce new products that will change the way we take care of ourselves, interact with others, and find the information and services we need.

Research and Development

How did we get personal computers and DVD players? We got them the same way we got light bulbs and automobile tires—from people working with new ideas. Alexander Graham Bell invented the telephone in a small laboratory in a Boston boarding house, and Frederick Banting discovered insulin in his University of Toronto laboratory. In the same way, scientists and researchers working in businesses and universities have produced many of the newer products we already take for granted.

These activities generally are referred to as *research and development*. For our purposes, **research and development (R&D)** are a set of activities intended to identify new ideas that have the potential to result in new goods and services.

Today, business firms use three general types of R&D activities. *Basic research* consists of activities aimed at uncovering new knowledge. The goal of basic research is scientific advancement, without regard for its potential use in the development of goods and services. *Applied research*, in contrast, consists of activities geared toward discovering new knowledge with some potential use. *Development and implementation* are research activities undertaken specifically to put new or existing knowledge to use in producing goods and services. The 3M Company has always been known for its development and implementation research activities. At the end of the twentieth century, the company had developed more than 55,000 products, including Post-It Notes, designed to make people's lives easier. Does a company like 3M quit innovating because it has developed successful products? No, not at all! Just recently the 3M company used development and implementation when it created a new line of Nexcare braces and supports for sport-related injuries, arthritic joints, and pain caused by repetitive-motion injuries. For people with knee, ankle, elbow, wrist, or back injuries, the new products are reducing both immediate pain and the time required for healing. There is even a line of Nexcare youth braces and supports for smaller customers— kids who twist their joints in sports activities or just playing around.[2]

research and development (R&D) a set of activities intended to identify new ideas that have the potential to result in new goods and services

Product Extension and Refinement

When a brand-new product is first marketed, its sales are zero and slowly increase from that point. If the product is successful, annual sales increase more and more rapidly until they reach some peak. Then, as time passes, annual sales begin to decline, and they continue to decline until it is no longer profitable to manufacture the product. (This rise-and-decline pattern, called the *product life cycle*, is discussed in more detail in Chapter 14.)

If a firm sells only one product, when that product reaches the end of its life cycle, the firm will die too. To stay in business, the firm must, at the very least, find ways to refine or extend the want-satisfying capability of its product. Consider television sets. Since they were introduced in the late 1930s, television sets have been constantly *refined* so that they now provide clearer, sharper pictures with less dial adjusting. During the same time, television sets also were *extended.* There are colour sets, television-only sets, and others that include VCR and DVD players. There are even television sets that allow their owners to access the Internet. And the latest development—high-definition (HD) television—is already available. Although initial prices were high, prices now have dropped and are more affordable.

Each refinement or extension results in an essentially "new" product whose sales make up for the declining sales of a product that was introduced earlier. When consumers discovered that the original five varieties of Campbell's Soup were of the highest quality, as well as inexpensive, the soups were an instant success. Although one of the most successful companies at the beginning of the 1900s, Campbell's had to continue to innovate, refine, and extend its product line. For example, many consumers in Canada live in what is called an on-the-go society. To meet this need, Campbell's Soup has developed ready-to-serve products that can be popped into a microwave at work or school. In other countries, customer feedback is also used to adapt products to meet the needs of local customers. For example, Liebig Pur, a thick vegetable soup, is sold in cartons with a long shelf life in France.[3] For most firms, extension and refinement are expected results of their development and implementation effort. Most often they result from the application of new knowledge to existing products. For instance, improved technology affects the content companies can distribute on the Internet. The Disney Corporation currently has a clear advantage over competitors because much of its content is animation. Animation is the easiest content to transfer to the Internet.

Product extension

Research and development at 3M has resulted in over 55,000 products, including Post-It notes.

How Do Managers Plan for Production?

Learning Objective **4**

Discuss the components involved in planning the production process.

Only a few of the many ideas for new products, refinements, and extensions ever reach the production stage. For those ideas that do, however, the next step is planning for production.

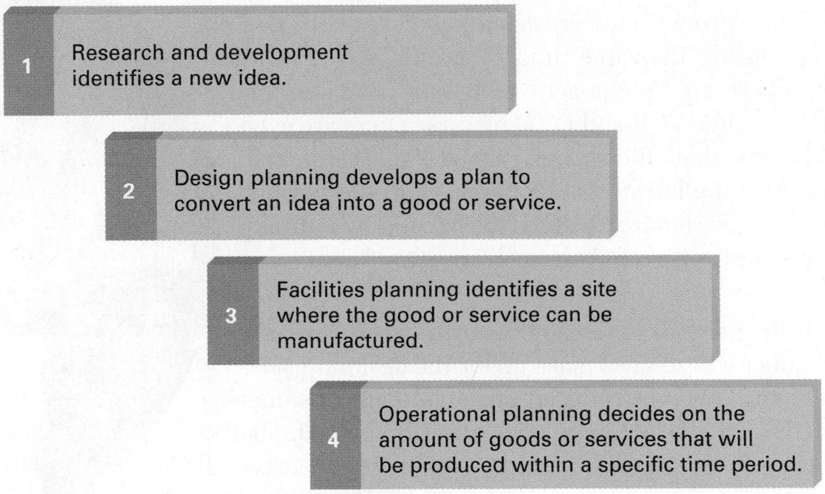

Figure 9.2

Planning for Production

Once research and development have identified an idea that meets customer needs, manufacturers use three phases to convert the idea to an actual product or service.

1. Research and development identifies a new idea.

2. Design planning develops a plan to convert an idea into a good or service.

3. Facilities planning identifies a site where the good or service can be manufactured.

4. Operational planning decides on the amount of goods or services that will be produced within a specific time period.

Design Planning

When the R&D staff at Research In Motion recommended to top management that the firm produce and market an affordable BlackBerry with special options geared to the broader consumer market, the company could not simply swing into production the next day. Instead, a great deal of time and energy had to be invested in determining what the new BlackBerry would look like, where and how it would be produced, and what options would be included. These decisions are a part of design planning and the result was the BlackBerry Pearl. **Design planning** is the development of a plan for converting a product idea into an actual product or service. The major decisions involved in design planning deal with product line, required capacity, and use of technology.

design planning the development of a plan for converting a product idea into an actual product or service

product line a group of similar products that differ only in relatively minor characteristics

Product Line A **product line** is a group of similar products that differ only in relatively minor characteristics. During the design-planning stage, a manufacturer such as Research In Motion needs to determine how many different models to produce and what major options to offer. A restaurant chain such as The Keg must decide how many menu items to offer.

An important issue in deciding on the product line is to balance customer preferences and production requirements. For this reason, marketing managers play an important role in making product-line decisions. Typically, marketing personnel want a "long" product line that offers customers many options. Because a long product line with more options gives customers choice, it is easier to sell products that meet the needs of individual customers. On the other hand, production personnel generally want a "short" product line because fewer products are easier to produce. With a short product line, the production process is less complex because there are fewer options, and most products are produced using the same basic steps. In many cases the actual choice between a long and short product line involves balancing customer preferences with the cost and problems associated with a more complex production process.

Once the product line has been determined, each distinct product within the product line must be designed. **Product design** is the process of creating a set of specifications from which a product can be produced. When designing a new product, specifications are extremely important. For example, product engineers for Whirlpool Corporation must make sure that a new frost-free refrigerator keeps food frozen in the freezer compartment. At the same time, they must make sure that lettuce and tomatoes do not freeze in the crisper section of the refrigerator. The need for a complete product design is fairly obvious; products that work cannot be manufactured without it. But services should be designed carefully as well—and *for the same reason.*

Required Production Capacity **Capacity** is the amount of products or services that an organization can produce in a given period of time. Operations managers—again working with the firm's marketing managers—must determine the required capacity. This, in turn, determines the size of the production facility. Capacity means about the same thing to service businesses. For example, the capacity of a restaurant such as The Keg, is the number of customers it can serve at one time.

Use of Technology During the design-planning stage, management must determine the degree to which *automation* will be used to produce a product or service. Here, there is a tradeoff between high initial costs and low operating costs (for automation) and low initial costs and high operating costs (for human labour). Ultimately, management must choose between a labour-intensive technology and a capital-intensive technology. A **labour-intensive technology** is a process in which people must do most of the work. Housecleaning services and the Toronto Blue Jays baseball team, for example, are labour-intensive. A **capital-intensive technology** is a process in which machines and equipment do most of the work. A Bombardier automated assembly plant is capital-intensive.

Facilities Planning and Site Selection

Once initial decisions have been made about a new product line, required capacity, and the use of technology, it is time to determine where the products or services are going to be produced. Generally, a business will choose to produce a new product in an existing factory as long as (1) the existing factory has enough capacity to handle customer demand for both the new product and established products and (2) the cost of refurbishing an existing factory is less than the cost of building a new one.

After exploring the capacity of existing factories, management might decide to build a new production facility. Once again, a number of decisions must be made. Should all the organization's production capacity be placed in one or two large facilities? Or should it be divided among several smaller facilities? In general, firms that

product design the process of creating a set of specifications from which a product can be produced

capacity the amount of products or services that an organization can produce in a given time

labour-intensive technology a process in which people must do most of the work

capital-intensive technology a process in which machines and equipment do most of the work

market a wide variety of products find it more economical to have a number of smaller facilities. Firms that produce only a small number of products tend to have fewer but larger facilities.

In determining where to locate production facilities, management must consider a number of variables, including the following:

* Locations of major customers and transportation costs to deliver finished products
* Geographic locations of suppliers of parts and raw materials
* Availability and cost of skilled and unskilled labour
* Quality of life for employees and management in the proposed location
* The cost of both land and construction required to build a new production facility
* Local, provincial, and federal taxes; environmental regulations; and zoning laws
* The amount of financial support, if any, offered by local, provincial, and federal governments
* Special requirements, such as great amounts of energy or water used in the production process

This is exactly the process that Honda undertook before deciding to build their manufacturing plant in Alliston, Ontario. The location, approximately an hour north of Toronto, was close to their market and suppliers. Both highway and rail transportation routes were well developed in the area and the local and provincial governments provided inducements such as tax concessions and land development. There was an available pool of skilled and unskilled labour both to the south (Greater Toronto Area) and north (Barrie), as well as hospitals and schools to support the plant personnel and their families.

It may, of course, be impossible to find the perfect location for a production facility. In fact, the choice of a location often involves balancing the most important variables for each production facility. Before making a final decision about where a proposed plant will be located and how it will be organized, two other factors—human resources and plant layout—should be examined.

Human Resources Several issues involved in facilities planning and site selection fall within the province of the human resources manager. Thus, at this stage, human resources and operations managers work closely together. For example, suppose that a Canadian

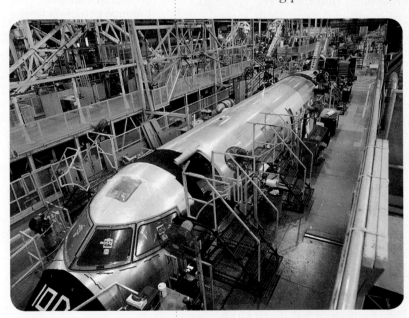

▲

Can anyone put all the pieces back together?

For a product like a C-class jetliner, there are literally thousands of parts that must be assembled to build just one plane. At the Bombardier plant in Montreal, a fixed position layout is used because the product is too large and difficult to move during the assembly process.

firm such as Magna wants to lower labour costs by constructing a sophisticated production plant in Mexico. The human resources manager will have to recruit managers and employees with the appropriate skills who are willing to relocate to a foreign country or develop training programs for local Mexican workers or both.

Plant Layout Plant layout is the arrangement of machinery, equipment, and personnel within a production facility. Three general types of plant layout are used (see Figure 9.3).

The *process layout* is used when different operations are required for creating small batches of different products or working on different parts of a product. The plant is arranged so that each operation is performed in its own particular area. An auto repair facility at a local automobile dealership provides an example of a process layout. The various operations may be engine repair, body work, wheel alignment, and safety inspection. Each operation is performed in a different area. If you take your Honda Accord for a wheel alignment, your car "visits" only the area where alignments are performed.

plant layout the arrangement of machinery, equipment, and personnel within a production facility

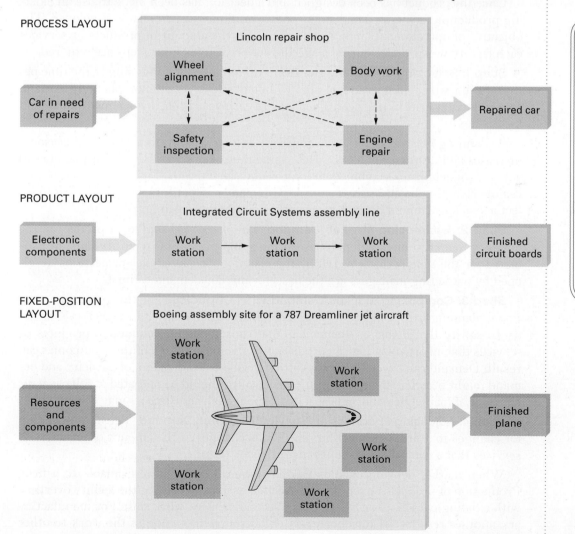

PROCESS LAYOUT

PRODUCT LAYOUT

FIXED-POSITION LAYOUT

Figure 9.3

Facilities Planning

The process layout is used when small batches of different products are created or when working on different parts of a product. The product layout (assembly line) is used when all products undergo the same operations in the same sequence. The fixed-position layout is used in producing a product too large to move.

A *product layout* (sometimes referred to as an *assembly line*) is used when all products undergo the same operations in the same sequence. Workstations are arranged to match the sequence of operations, and work flows from station to station. An assembly line is the best example of a product layout. For example, Honda uses a product layout to manufacture their automobiles and SUVs in their Alliston, Ontario plant.

A *fixed-position layout* is used when a very large product is produced. Aircraft manufacturers and shipbuilders apply this method because of the difficulty of moving a large product such as an airliner or ship. The product remains stationary, and people and machines are moved as needed to assemble the product. Bombardier, for example, uses the fixed-position layout to build aircraft at its Quebec-based Canadair Division manufacturing facility.

Operational Planning

Once the product has been designed and a decision has been made to use an existing production facility or build a new one, operational plans must be developed. The objective of operational planning is to decide on the amount of products or services each facility will produce during a specific period of time. Four steps are required.

Step 1: Selecting a Planning Horizon   A planning horizon is simply the time period during which an operational plan will be in effect. A common planning horizon for production plans is one year. Then, before each year is up, management must plan for the next.

A planning horizon of one year generally is long enough to average out seasonal increases and decreases in sales. At the same time, it is short enough for planners to adjust production to accommodate long-range sales trends. Firms that operate in a rapidly changing business environment with many competitors may find it best to select a shorter planning horizon to keep their production planning current.

Step 2: Estimating Market Demand   The *market demand* for a product is the quantity that customers will purchase at the going price. This quantity must be estimated for the time period covered by the planning horizon. Sales projections developed by marketing managers are the basis for market-demand estimates.

Step 3: Comparing Market Demand with Capacity   The third step in operational planning is to compare the estimated market demand with the facility's capacity to satisfy that demand. (Remember that capacity is the amount of products or services that an organization can produce in a given time.) One of three outcomes can result: Demand can exceed capacity, capacity can exceed demand, or capacity and demand might be equal. If they are equal, the facility should be operated at full capacity. However, if market demand and capacity are not equal, adjustments may be necessary.

Step 4: Adjusting Products or Services to Meet Demand   The biggest reason for changes to a firm's production schedule is changes in the amount of products or services that a company sells to its customers.

When market demand exceeds capacity, several options are available to a firm. Production of products or services can be increased by operating the facility overtime with existing personnel or by starting a second or third work shift. For manufacturers, another response is to subcontract or outsource a portion of the work to other

planning horizon the period during which an operational plan will be in effect

producers. If the excess demand is likely to be permanent, the firm might expand the current facility or build another facility.

What happens when capacity exceeds market demand? Again, there are several options. To reduce output temporarily, workers might be laid off and part of the facility shut down. Or the facility might be operated on a shorter-than-normal work week for as long as the excess capacity persists. To adjust to a permanently decreased demand, management might shift the excess capacity of a manufacturing facility to the production of other goods or services. The most radical adjustment is to eliminate the excess capacity by selling unused facilities.

Operations Control

Learning Objective 5

Explain how purchasing, inventory control, scheduling, and quality control affect production.

We have discussed the development of an idea for a product or service and the planning that translates that idea into the reality. Now we are ready to push the "start" button to begin the production process and examine four important areas of operations control: purchasing, inventory control, scheduling, and quality control (see Figure 9.4).

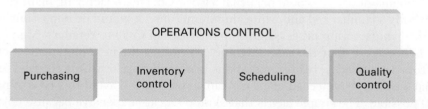

Purchasing

Purchasing consists of all the activities involved in obtaining required materials, supplies, components (or subassemblies), and parts from other firms. Levi Strauss must purchase denim cloth, thread, and zippers before it can produce a single pair of jeans. Similarly, Nike, Inc., must purchase leather, rubber, cloth for linings, and laces before manufacturing a pair of athletic shoes. For all firms, the purchasing function is far from routine, and its importance should not be underestimated. Purchased materials make up more than 50 percent of the wholesale costs of some products. The objective of purchasing is to ensure that required materials are available when they are needed, in the proper amounts, and at minimum cost. Generally, the company with purchasing needs and suppliers must develop a working relationship built on trust. In addition to a working relationship built on trust, many companies believe that purchasing is one area where they can promote diversity.

Purchasing personnel should be on the lookout constantly for new or backup suppliers, even when their needs are being met by their present suppliers, because problems

Figure 9.4

Four Aspects of Operations Control

Implementing the operations control system in any business requires the effective use of purchasing, inventory control, scheduling, and quality control.

purchasing all the activities involved in obtaining required materials, supplies, components, and parts from other firms

such as strikes and equipment breakdowns can cut off the flow of purchased materials from a primary supplier at any time.

The choice of suppliers should result from careful analysis of a number of factors. The following are especially critical:

* *Price.* Comparing prices offered by different suppliers is always an essential part of selecting a supplier. Even tiny differences in price add up to enormous sums when large quantities are purchased.

* *Quality.* Purchasing specialists always try to buy materials at a level of quality in keeping with the type of product being manufactured. The minimum acceptable quality is usually specified by product designers.

* *Reliability.* An agreement to purchase high-quality materials at a low price is the purchaser's dream. But such an agreement becomes a nightmare if the supplier does not deliver.

* *Credit terms.* Purchasing specialists should determine if the supplier demands immediate payment or will extend credit. Also, does the supplier offer a cash discount or reduction in price for prompt payment?

* *Shipping Costs.* One of the most overlooked factors in purchasing is the geographic location of the supplier. Low prices and favourable credit terms offered by a distant supplier can be wiped out when the buyer must pay the shipping costs. Above all, the question of who pays the shipping costs should be answered before any supplier is chosen.

Inventory Control

Can you imagine what would happen if a Coca-Cola manufacturing plant ran out of the company's familiar red and white aluminum cans? It would be impossible to complete the manufacturing process and ship the cases of Coke to retailers. Management would be forced to shut the assembly line down until the next shipment of cans arrived from a supplier. In reality, operations managers for Coca-Cola realize the disasters that a shortage of needed materials can cause and will avoid this type of problem if at all possible. The simple fact is that shutdowns are expensive because costs such as rent, wages, and insurance still must be paid.

Operations managers are concerned with three types of inventories. A *raw-materials inventory* consists of materials that will become part of the product during the production process. The *work-in-process inventory* consists of partially completed products. The *finished-goods inventory* consists of completed goods.

Associated with each type of inventory are a *holding cost*, or storage cost, and a *stock-out cost*, the cost of running out of inventory. **Inventory control** is the process of managing inventories in such a way as to minimize inventory costs, including both holding costs and potential stock-out costs. Today, computer systems are used to keep track of inventories, provide periodic inventory reports, and alert managers to impending stock-outs.

One of the most sophisticated methods of inventory control used today is materials requirements planning. **Materials requirements planning (MRP)** is a computerized system that integrates production planning and inventory control. One of the great advantages of an MRP system is its ability to juggle delivery schedules and lead times effectively. It is virtually impossible for individual managers to oversee the hundreds

inventory control the process of managing inventories in such a way as to minimize inventory costs, including both holding costs and potential stock-out costs

materials requirements planning (MRP) a computerized system that integrates production planning and inventory control of parts that go into the finished product of one as complex as an automobile or airplane. However, a manager using an MRP system can arrange both order and delivery schedules so that materials, parts, and supplies arrive when they are needed.

Two extensions of MRP are used by manufacturing firms today. The first is known as *manufacturing resource planning*, or simply *MRP II*. The primary difference between the two systems is that MRP involves just production and inventory personnel, whereas MRP II involves the entire organization. Thus MRP II provides a single common set of facts that can be used by all the organization's managers to make effective decisions. The second extension of MRP is known as *enterprise resource planning (ERP)*. The primary difference between ERP and the preceding methods is that ERP software is more sophisticated and can monitor not only inventory and production processes but also quality, sales, and even such variables as inventory at a supplier's location.

Because large firms can incur huge inventory costs, much attention has been devoted to inventory control. The just-in-time system used by some businesses is one result of all this attention. A **just-in-time inventory system** is designed to ensure that materials or supplies arrive at a facility just when they are needed so that storage and holding costs are minimized. The customer must specify what will be needed, when, and in what amounts. The supplier must be sure that the right supplies arrive at the agreed-on time and location. For example, managers using a just-in-time inventory system at a Honda assembly plant determine the number of automobiles that will be assembled in a specified time period. Then Honda purchasing personnel order *just* the parts needed to produce those automobiles. In turn, suppliers deliver the parts *in time* or when they are needed on the assembly line.

Without proper inventory control, it is impossible for operations managers to schedule the work required to produce goods that can be sold to customers.

Scheduling

Scheduling is the process of ensuring that materials and other resources are at the right place at the right time. The materials and resources may be moved from a warehouse to the workstations, they may move from station to station along an assembly line, or they may arrive at workstations "just in time" to be made part of the work in process there.

As our definition implies, both place and time are important to scheduling. (This is no different from, say, the scheduling of classes. You cannot attend your classes unless you know *both* where and when they are held.) The *routing* of materials is the sequence of workstations that the materials will follow. Assume that Shermag, a Sherbrooke, Quebec, furniture manufacturer—is scheduling production of an oval coffee table made from cherry wood. Operations managers would route the needed materials (wood, screws, packaging materials, and so on) through a series of individual workstations along an assembly line. At each workstation, a specific task would be performed, and then the partially finished coffee table would move to the next workstation. When routing materials, operations managers are especially concerned with the sequence of each step of the production process. For the coffee table, the top and legs must be cut to specifications before the wood is finished. (If the wood were finished before being cut, the finish would be ruined, and the coffee table would have to be stained again.)

just-in-time inventory system a system designed to ensure that materials or supplies arrive at a facility just when they are needed so that storage and holding costs are minimized

scheduling the process of ensuring that materials and other resources are at the right place at the right time

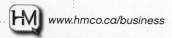

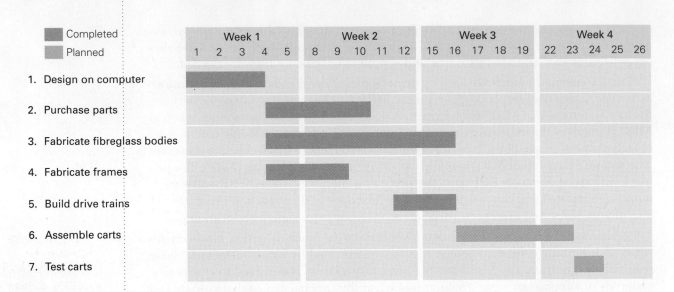

Completed
Planned

	Week 1	Week 2	Week 3	Week 4
	1 2 3 4 5	8 9 10 11 12	15 16 17 18 19	22 23 24 25 26

1. Design on computer
2. Purchase parts
3. Fabricate fibreglass bodies
4. Fabricate frames
5. Build drive trains
6. Assemble carts
7. Test carts

Figure 9.5

A Gantt Chart

This chart details the job of building three dozen electric golf carts.

Source: Robert Kreitner, *Management*, 9th ed. Copyright © 2004 by Houghton Mifflin Company. Reprinted with permission.

Gantt chart a graphic scheduling device that displays the tasks to be performed on the vertical axis and the time required for each task on the horizontal axis

PERT (Program Evaluation and Review Technique) a scheduling technique that identifies the major activities necessary to complete a project and sequences them based on the time required to perform each one

When scheduling production, managers also are concerned with timing. The *timing* function specifies when the materials will arrive at each station and how long they will remain there. It might take workers thirty minutes to cut the table top and legs and another thirty minutes to drill the holes and assemble the cherry coffee table. Before packaging the coffee table for shipment, it must be finished with cherry stain and allowed to dry. This last step may take as long as three days depending on weather conditions and humidity.

Whether or not the finished product requires a simple or complex production process, operations managers are responsible for monitoring schedules—called *follow-up*—to ensure that the work flows according to a timetable. For complex products, many operations managers prefer to use Gantt charts or the PERT technique.

Scheduling Through Gantt Charts Developed by Henry L. Gantt, a **Gantt chart** is a graphic scheduling device that displays the tasks to be performed on the vertical axis and the time required for each task on the horizontal axis. Gantt charts

* allow you to determine how long a project should take.

* lay out the order in which tasks need to be completed.

* determine the resources needed.

* monitor progress of different activities required to complete the project.

A Gantt chart that describes the activities required to build three dozen golf carts is illustrated in Figure 9.5. Gantt charts usually are not suitable for scheduling extremely complex situations. Nevertheless, using them forces a manager to plan the steps required to get a job done and to specify time requirements for each part of the job.

Scheduling via PERT Another technique for scheduling a complex process or project and maintaining control of the schedule is **PERT (Program Evaluation and Review Technique)**. To use PERT, we begin by identifying all the major *activities* involved in the project. For example, the activities involved in producing your textbook are illustrated in Figure 9.6.

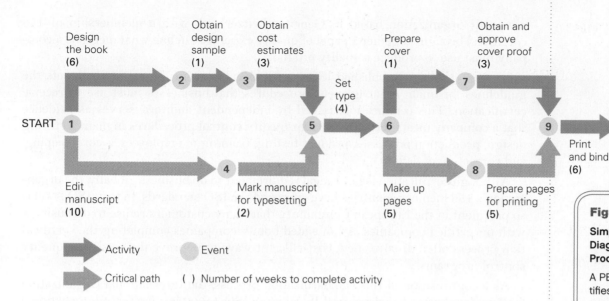

Figure 9.6

Simplified PERT Diagram for Producing This Book

A PERT diagram identifies the activities necessary to complete a given project and arranges the activities based on the total time required for each to become an event. The activities on the critical path determine the minimum time required.

All events are arranged in a sequence. In doing so, we must be sure that an event that must occur before another event in the actual process also occurs before that event on the PERT chart. For example, the manuscript must be edited before the type is set. Therefore, in our sequence, the event "edit manuscript" must precede the event "set type."

Next, we use arrows to connect events that must occur in sequence. We then estimate the time required for each activity and mark it near the corresponding arrow. The sequence of production activities that take the longest time from start to finish is called the **critical path.** The activities on this path determine the minimum time in which the process can be completed. These activities are the ones that must be scheduled and controlled carefully. A delay in any one of them will cause a delay in completion of the project as a whole. The critical path runs from event 1 to event 4 to event 5. It then runs through events 6, 8, and 9 to the finished book at event 10. Note that even a six-week delay in preparing the cover will not delay the production process. However, *any* delay in an activity on the critical path will hold up publication. Thus, if necessary, resources could be diverted from cover preparation to, say, making up of pages or preparing pages for printing.

critical path the sequence of production activities that takes the longest time from start to finish

Quality Control

As mentioned earlier in this chapter, Canadian business firms that compete in the very competitive global marketplace have taken another look at the importance of improving quality.

World Quality Standards: ISO 9000 and ISO 14000 Different companies have different perceptions of quality. Without a common standard of quality, however, customers would be at the mercy of manufacturers and vendors. As the number of companies competing in the world marketplace has increased, so has the seriousness of this problem. To deal with it, the **International Organization for Standardization** (a

International Organization for Standardization a nonprofit organization based in Geneva, Switzerland, with a membership of 156 countries, that develops standards for products to facilitate trade across national borders

nonprofit organization based in Geneva, Switzerland, with a membership of 156 countries) brought together a panel of quality experts to define what methods a company must use to produce a quality product.

In 1987, the panel published ISO 9000 (*iso* is Greek for "equal"), which sets the guidelines for quality management procedures that businesses must use to receive certification. This certification, issued by independent auditors, serves as evidence that a company meets the standards for quality control procedures in manufacturing design, production processes, product testing, training of employees, record keeping, and correction of defects.

Although certification is not a legal requirement to do business globally, the organization's 156 member countries have approved the ISO standards. In fact, ISO 9000 is so prevalent in the European Community that many customers refuse to do business with uncertified companies. As an added bonus, companies completing the certification process often discover new, cost-efficient ways to improve their existing quality control programs.

As a continuation of this standardization process, the International Organization for Standardization has developed ISO 14000. ISO 14000 is a family of international standards for incorporating environmental concerns into operations and product standards. As with ISO 9000 certification, ISO 14000 requires that a company's procedures be documented by independent auditors. It also requires that a company develop an environmental management system that will help it to achieve environmental goals, objectives, and targets. Both the ISO 9000 and ISO 14000 family of standards are updated periodically. For example, ISO 9001:2000 reflects new standards for quality when compared with the original ISO standards.

Many companies find that conforming to the ISO standards results in

* better employee relations,
* higher productivity,
* greater customer satisfaction,
* increased market share, and
* improved profitability.

While meeting the ISO standards can mean prestige and recognition, the companies all have one factor in common: They use quality control to improve their firm's products or services.

Quality control is the process of ensuring that goods and services are produced in accordance with design specifications. The major objective of quality control is to see that the organization lives up to the standards it has set for itself on quality. Some firms, such as Research In Motion and The Bay, have built their reputations on quality. Customers pay more for their products in return for assurances of high quality. Other firms adopt a strategy of emphasizing lower prices along with reasonable (but not particularly high) quality.

Many U.S firms use two systems to gather statistical information about the quality of their products and study the way they operate. **Statistical process control (SPC)** is a system that uses sampling to obtain data that are plotted on control charts and

quality control the process of ensuring that goods and services are produced in accordance with design specifications

statistical process control (SPC) a system that uses sampling to obtain data that are plotted on control charts and graphs to see if the production process is operating as it should and to pinpoint problem areas

graphs to see if the production process is operating as it should and to pinpoint problem areas. **Statistical quality control (SQC),** a similar technique, is a set of specific statistical techniques used to monitor all aspects of the production process to ensure that both work in progress and finished products meet the firm's quality standards. A firm can use the information provided by both these to correct problems in the production process and to improve the quality of its products.

Increased effort is also being devoted to **inspection,** which is the examination of the quality of work in process. Inspections are performed at various times during production. Purchased materials might be inspected when they arrive at the production facility. Subassemblies and manufactured parts might be inspected before they become part of a finished product. And finished goods might be inspected before they are shipped to customers. Items that are within design specifications continue on their way. Those that are not within design specifications are removed from production.

Improving Quality Through Employee Participation   Historically, efforts to ensure quality increased the costs associated with making that good or service. For this reason, quality and productivity were viewed as conflicting: One was increased at the other's expense. Over the years, more and more managers have realized that quality is an essential "ingredient" of the good or service being provided. This view of quality provides several benefits. The number of defects decreases, which causes profits to increase. Making products right the first time reduces many of the rejects and much of the rework. And making employees responsible for quality often eliminates the need for inspection. An employee is indoctrinated to accept full responsibility for the quality of his or her work.

Because of increased global competition, many Canadian manufacturers have adopted a goal that calls for better quality in their products. As noted in Chapter 7, a *total quality management* (TQM) program coordinates the efforts directed at improving customer satisfaction, increasing employee participation, strengthening supplier partnerships, and facilitating an organizational atmosphere of continuous quality improvement. Firms such as Dofasco Inc. (steel) and Suncor Energy Inc. (integrated oil and gas) have used TQM to improve product quality and, ultimately, customer satisfaction. Another technique that businesses use to improve not only quality but also overall performance is Six Sigma. **Six Sigma** is a disciplined approach that relies on statistical data and improved methods to eliminate defects in a firm's products and services. While many experts agree that Six Sigma is similar to TQM, Six Sigma often has more top-level support, more training for employees, much more teamwork, and a new corporate attitude or culture.[4] For more information about Six Sigma go to www.isixsigma.com.

The use of a **quality circle,** a team of employees who meet on company time to solve problems of product quality, is another way manufacturers are achieving better quality at the operations level. Quality circles have been used successfully in such companies as Honda and Toyota.

statistical quality control (SQC) a set of specific statistical techniques used to monitor all aspects of the production process to ensure that both work in progress and finished products meet the firm's quality standards

inspection the examination of the quality of work in process

Six Sigma a disciplined approach that relies on statistical data and improved methods to eliminate defects for a firm's products and services

quality circle a team of employees who meet on company time to solve problems of product quality

Management of Productivity and Technology

Learning Objective 6
Summarize how productivity and technology are related.

No coverage of production and operations management would be complete without a discussion of productivity. Productivity concerns all managers, but it is especially important to operations managers, the people who must oversee the creation of a firm's goods or services. We define **productivity** as the average level of output per worker per hour. Hence, if each worker at plant A produces seventy-five units per day and each worker at plant B produces only seventy units per day, the workers at plant A are more productive. If one bank teller serves twenty-five customers per hour and another serves twenty-eight per hour, the second teller is more productive.

productivity the average level of output per worker per hour

Productivity Trends

Productivity growth rates in Canada have been stagnant for the past several years. An important factor that has hurt the Canadian productivity growth rate is the tremendous growth of the service sector in Canada. While this sector grew in the number of employees and economic importance, its productivity levels did not grow. Today, many economic experts agree that improving service-sector productivity is the next major hurdle facing Canadian business.

Improving Productivity Growth Rates

Several techniques and strategies have been suggested to improve current productivity growth rates. For example, various government policies that may be hindering productivity could be eliminated or at least modified.

In addition, increased cooperation between management and labour could improve productivity. When unions and management work together, quite often the result is improved productivity. In a related area, many managers believe that increased employee motivation and participation can enhance productivity.

Still another potential solution to productivity problems is to change work incentives. Many firms sim-

▲ **Does this product meet design specifications?**

Erik Blake poses next to a drilling assembly design at his office in Whitehorse, Yukon. Blake's drill will be used on a future mission to Mars assuming it meets all the NASA design specifications.

ply pay employees for their time, regardless of how much or how little they produce. By changing the reward system so that people are paid for what they contribute rather than for the time they put in, it may be possible to motivate employees to produce at higher levels.

Finally, business must invest more money in facilities, equipment, and employee training. There is hard evidence that investments in technological innovations are linked to job growth, higher employee wages, new products, *and* increased productivity.

The Impact of Computers and Robotics on Production

Automation, a development that has been revolutionizing the workplace, is the total or near-total use of machines to do work. The rapid increase in automated procedures has been made possible by the microprocessor, a silicon chip that led to the production of desktop computers for businesses, homes, and schools. In factories, microprocessors are used in robotics and in computerized manufacturing systems.

Robotics Robotics is the use of programmable machines to perform a variety of tasks by manipulating materials and tools. Robots work quickly, accurately, and steadily.

Robots are especially effective in tedious, repetitive assembly-line jobs as well as in handling hazardous materials. They are also useful as artificial "eyes" that can check the quality of products as they are being processed on the assembly lines. To date, the automotive industry has made the most extensive use of robotics, but robots also have been used to mine coal, inspect the inner surfaces of pipes, assemble computer components, provide certain kinds of patient care in hospitals, and clean and guard buildings at night.

Computer Manufacturing Systems People are quick to point out how computers have changed their everyday lives, but most people do not realize the impact computers have had on manufacturing. In simple terms, the factory of the future has already arrived. For most manufacturers, the changeover began with the use of computer-aided design and computer-aided manufacturing. **Computer-aided design (CAD)** is the use of computers to aid in the development of products. Using CAD, Ford speeds up car design and Canon designs new cameras and photocopiers.

Computer-aided manufacturing (CAM) is the use of computers to plan and control manufacturing processes. A well-designed CAM system allows manufacturers to become much more productive. Not only are a greater number of products produced, but speed and quality also increase.

If you are thinking that the next logical step is to combine the CAD and CAM computer systems, you are right. Today, the most successful manufacturers use CAD and CAM together to form a computer-integrated manufacturing system. Specifically, **computer-integrated manufacturing (CIM)** is a computer system that not only helps to design products but also controls the machinery needed to produce the finished product. Other advantages of using CIM include improved flexibility, more efficient scheduling, and higher product quality—all factors that make a production facility more competitive in today's global economy. Furthermore, specialized management software from firms such as Maxager.com enables managers to optimize plant operations by providing information about manufacturing costs. Instead of simply guessing

automation the total or near-total use of machines to do work

robotics the use of programmable machines to perform a variety of tasks by manipulating materials and tools

computer-aided design (CAD) the use of computers to aid in the development of products

computer-aided manufacturing (CAM) the use of computers to plan and control manufacturing processes

computer-integrated manufacturing (CIM) a computer system that not only helps to design products but also controls the machinery needed to produce the finished product

 www.hmco.ca/business

which product lines are most profitable, the software uses machinery performance data to analyze profits, including the opportunity costs of the machinery used to produce the products. As a result, client firms such as Motorola believe that paybacks in improved production schedules and the product-selection process are well worth the investment.[5]

Flexible Manufacturing Systems Manufacturers have known for a number of years that the old-style, traditional assembly lines used to manufacture products present a number of problems. For example, although traditional assembly lines turn out extremely large numbers of identical products economically, the system requires expensive, time-consuming retooling of equipment whenever a new product is to be manufactured. This type of manufacturing is often referred to as a continuous process. **Continuous process** is a manufacturing process in which a firm produces the same product(s) over a long period of time. Now it is possible to use flexible manufacturing systems to solve such problems. A **flexible manufacturing system (FMS)** combines robotics and computer-integrated manufacturing in a single production system. Instead of having to spend vast amounts of time and effort to retool the traditional mechanical equipment on an assembly line for each new product, an FMS is rearranged simply by reprogramming electronic machines. Because FMSs require less time and expense to reprogram, manufacturers can produce smaller batches of a variety of products without raising the production cost. Flexible manufacturing is sometimes referred to as an intermittent process. An **intermittent process** is a manufacturing process in which a firm's manufacturing machines and equipment are changed to produce different products. When compared with the continuous process (longer production runs), an intermittent process has a shorter production run.

For most manufacturers, the driving force behind flexible manufacturing systems is the customer. In fact, the term *customer-driven production* is often used by operations managers to describe a manufacturing system that is driven by customer needs and what customers want to buy. For example, advanced software and a flexible manufacturing system have enabled Dell Computer to change to a more customer-driven manufacturing process. The process starts when a customer phones a sales representative on a toll-free line or accesses Dell's website. Then the representative or the customer enters the specifications for the new product directly into a computer. The order then is sent to a nearby plant. Once the order is received, a team of employees with the help of a reprogrammable assembly line can build the product just the way the customer wants it. Products include desktop computers, notebook computers, and other Dell equipment.[6] Although the costs of designing and installing an FMS such as this are high, the electronic equipment is used more frequently and efficiently than the machinery on a traditional assembly line.

Technological Displacement Automation has increased productivity by cutting manufacturing time, reducing error, and simplifying retooling procedures. Many of the robots being developed for use in manufacturing will not replace human employees. Rather, these robots will work with employees in making their jobs easier and helping to prevent accidents. No one knows, however, what the effect will be on the workforce. Some experts estimate that automation will bring new changes to more than half of all jobs within the next ten years. Total unemployment may not increase, but many workers will be faced with the choice of retraining for new jobs or seeking

continuous process a manufacturing process in which a firm produces the same product(s) over a long period of time

flexible manufacturing system (FMS) a single production system that combines robotics and computer-integrated manufacturing

intermittent process a manufacturing process in which a firm's manufacturing machines and equipment are changed to produce different products

jobs in other sectors of the economy. Government, business, and education will have to cooperate to prepare workers for new roles in an automated workplace.

The next chapter discusses many of the issues caused by technological displacement. In addition, a number of major components of human resources management are described, and we see how managers use various reward systems to boost motivation, productivity, and morale.

 Prepare for Class
HM News Feeds
HM News Now

→ **RETURN TO INSIDE BUSINESS**

Having chosen to build their manufacturing plant in Alliston, Ontario, Honda still had to convince suppliers that they could still meet their just-in-time inventory management requirements. But many of the same reasons why Honda chose Alliston also worked for their suppliers. Access to transportation, the availability of land, workers, and government incentives all contributed to suppliers' decisions to bid on the Honda supplier contracts.

Questions

1. What is the advantage to Honda's suppliers of building warehouse facilities near the Honda manufacturing plant?
2. What risks do parts suppliers face when working with Honda?

CHAPTER REVIEW

1 Explain the nature of production.

Operations management consists of all the activities that managers engage in to create goods and services. Operations are as relevant to service organizations as to manufacturing firms. Generally, three major activities are involved in producing goods or services: product development, planning for production, and operations control. Today, Canadian manufacturers are forced to compete in an ever-smaller world to meet the needs of more demanding customers. In an attempt to regain a competitive edge, they have taken another look at the importance of improving quality and meeting the needs of their customers. They also have used new techniques to motivate employees, reduced production costs, replaced outdated equipment, used computer-aided and flexible manufacturing systems, improved control procedures, and built new manufacturing facilities in foreign countries where labour costs are lower. Competing in the global economy is

not only profitable, but it is also an essential activity that requires the cooperation of everyone within an organization.

2 Outline how the conversion process transforms raw materials, labour, and other resources into finished products or services.

A business transforms resources into goods and services in order to provide utility to customers. Utility is the ability of a good or service to satisfy a human need. Form utility is created by converting raw materials, people, finances, and information into finished products. Conversion processes vary in terms of the major resources used to produce goods and services (focus), the degree to which resources are changed (magnitude), and the number of production processes that a business uses. The application of the basic principles of operations management to the production of services has coincided with the growth and importance of service businesses in Canada.

3 Describe how research and development lead to new products and services.

Operations management often begins with product research and development (R&D). R&D can result in entirely new products or extensions and refinements of existing products. R&D activities are classified as basic research (aimed at uncovering new knowledge), applied research (discovering new knowledge with some potential use), and development and implementation (using new or existing knowledge to produce goods and services). If a firm sells only one product, when that product reaches the end of its life cycle, the firm will die, too. To stay in business, the firm must, at the very least, find ways to refine or extend the want-satisfying capability of its product.

4 Discuss the components involved in planning the production process.

Planning for production involves three major phases: design planning, facilities planning and site selection, and operational planning. First, design planning is undertaken to address questions related to the product line, required production capacity, and the use of technology. Then production facilities, site selection, human resources, and plant layout must be considered. Operational planning focuses on the use of production facilities and resources. The steps for operational planning include (a) selecting a planning horizon, (b) estimating market demand, (c) comparing market demand with capacity, and (d) adjusting production of products or services to meet demand.

5 Explain how purchasing, inventory control, scheduling, and quality control affect production.

The major areas of operations control are purchasing, inventory control, scheduling, and quality control. Purchasing involves selecting suppliers. The choice of suppliers should result from careful analysis of a number of factors, including price, quality, reliability, credit terms, and shipping costs. Inventory control is the management of stocks of raw materials, work in process, and finished goods to minimize the total inventory cost. Today, most firms use a computerized system to maintain inventory records. In addition, many firms use a just-in-time inventory system, in which materials or supplies arrive at a facility just when they are needed

so that storage and holding costs are minimized. Scheduling ensures that materials and other resources are at the right place at the right time—for use within the facility or for shipment to customers. Both Gantt charts and PERT can be used to improve a firm's ability to schedule the production of products. Quality control guarantees that products meet the design specifications for those products. The major objective of quality control is to see that the organization lives up to the standards it has set for itself on quality. Some firms, such as Research In Motion and Bombardier, have built their reputations on quality. Customers pay more for their products in return for assurances of high quality. Other firms adopt a strategy of emphasizing lower prices along with reasonable (but not particularly high) quality.

6 Summarize how productivity and technology are related.

The productivity growth rate in Canada has fallen behind the pace of growth in some of the other industrialized nations in recent years. Several factors have been cited as possible causes for this disturbing trend, and managers have begun to explore solutions for overcoming them. Possible solutions include less government regulation, increased cooperation between management and labour, increased employee motivation and participation, new incentives for work, and additional investment by business to fund new or renovated facilities, equipment, employee training, and the use of technology. Automation, the total or near-total use of machines to do work, has for some years been changing the way work is done in Canadian factories. A growing number of industries are using programmable machines called robots to perform tasks that are tedious or hazardous to human beings. Computer-aided design, computer-aided manufacturing, and computer-integrated manufacturing use computers to help design and manufacture products. The flexible manufacturing system combines robotics and computer-integrated manufacturing to produce smaller batches of products more efficiently than on the traditional assembly line. Instead of having to spend vast amounts of time and effort to retool the traditional mechanical equipment on an assembly line for each new product, an FMS is rearranged simply by reprogramming electronic machines. Because FMSs require less time and expense to reprogram, manufacturers can produce smaller batches of a variety of products without raising the production cost.

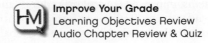

Improve Your Grade
Learning Objectives Review
Audio Chapter Review & Quiz

Review Questions

1. List all the activities involved in operations management.
2. What is the difference between an analytical and a synthetic manufacturing process? Give an example of each type of process.
3. Characterize the production processes used by a local pizza parlour, a dry-cleaning establishment, and an auto repair shop in terms of focus, magnitude, and number.
4. Describe how research and development lead to new products.
5. Explain why product extension and refinement are important.
6. What are the major elements of design planning?
7. What factors should be considered when selecting a site for a new manufacturing facility?
8. What is the objective of operational planning? What four steps are used to accomplish this objective?
9. If you were an operations manager, what would you do if market demand exceeded the production capacity of your manufacturing facility? What action would you take if the production capacity of your manufacturing facility exceeded market demand?
10. Why is selecting a supplier so important?
11. What costs must be balanced and minimized through inventory control?
12. How can materials requirements planning (MRP), manufacturing resource planning (MRP II), and enterprise resource planning (ERP) help to control inventory and a company's production processes?
13. How does the just-in-time-inventory system help to reduce inventory costs?
14. Explain in what sense scheduling is a *control* function of operations managers.
15. How can management and employees use statistical process control, statistical quality control, inspection, and quality circles to improve a firm's products?
16. How might productivity be measured in a restaurant? In a department store? In a public school system?
17. How can CIM and FMS help a manufacturer to produce products?

Discussion Questions

1. Why would Bombardier—a successful Canadian company—need to expand and sell its products to customers in foreign countries?
2. Do certain kinds of firms need to stress particular areas of operations management? Explain.
3. Is it really necessary for service firms to engage in research and development? In planning for production and operations control?
4. How are the four areas of operations control interrelated?
5. In what ways can employees help to improve the quality of a firm's products?
6. Is operations management relevant to non-business organizations such as colleges and hospitals? Why or why not?

CASE STUDY

Cutting-Edge Production at Remington

Remington—long known for its shavers—has been associated with a number of manufacturing "firsts." It produced the first commercial typewriter in 1873, the first electric dry shaver in 1937, and the first cordless shaver in 1960. Despite several changes in ownership, management, and focus, once the company began making shavers, it never stopped. In 2003, Remington was acquired by Spectrum Brands, which also owns Rayovac batteries, Vigoro lawn-care products, and many other name-brand products.

Today, Remington offers a wide variety of electric shavers, hair trimmers, hair dryers, curling irons, and other small appliances for personal grooming. Its products are available in North and South America, Europe, Asia, Australia, and New Zealand where the company's products are sold through drug, department, and discount stores, as well as through online retailers.

Remington uses marketing research to gain an in-depth understanding of its customers' needs so as to develop new technology and product designs to meet those needs. Its products have changed dramatically over the years, but not men's beards. Yet what men and women are looking for in shavers has evolved over time. For example, knowing that some women prefer to shave in the shower or bath and others prefer to shave before or after bathing, Remington has introduced a line of wet/dry shavers. For maximum convenience and flexibility, some of these shavers operate on household batteries, whereas others are recharged using an electric adapter. Other trends affecting Remington's product lineup are changing lifestyles and an aging population.

New products, new technology, and new production methods are all helping Remington meet the needs of customers all over the world. In fact, new technology is just as important as product styling. Not long ago Remington won a favourable ruling from the European Court of Justice in a battle over three-headed rotary razors. Philips trademarked the three-headed design in the 1960s. Decades later, it sued Remington for introducing a three-headed razor of its own, saying that three heads were part of the Philips brand. Remington won by arguing that a trademark cannot cover improved technical performance. In other words, although the hourglass Coca-Cola bottle does not improve the beverage's taste, the three-headed design does improve a razor's shaving ability.

Once Remington has completed a new design, the product is manufactured and assembled overseas. Some products may have up to a hundred components, which adds complexity to the production process. Using specialized machinery, production workers punch blades out of steel and make cutters out of miles of aluminum coil. One shaver may require as many as seventy-five blades and three cutters, carefully manufactured, ground for sharpness, and tested before assembly.

To meet global demand for Remington shavers, the plant must turn out one million blades per day. Therefore, plant managers must plan in advance to buy and store supplies and materials, have everything in place when and where needed, and inspect the finished blades to ensure quality. Then the blades go to the foreign factories, where they are incorporated into shavers and trimmers. After production is complete, the finished products are transported to an international network of independent distributors for delivery to retail outlets in dozens of countries.

Under Spectrum Brands, Remington has moved its blade production from Connecticut to Wisconsin. The parent company employs 10,000 people worldwide and rings up nearly $3 billion in annual sales. Remington continues to be a strong competitor to Braun, Philips, Panasonic, and other makers of electric shaving products. However, now that Braun has the financial and marketing power of Procter & Gamble behind it, Remington will face even greater competitive challenges in the coming years. To keep sales and profits growing, the company must keep introducing innovative products to meet customer needs and continue to fine-tune its production methods for ever-higher productivity and quality.

Questions:

1. Which plant layout would you suggest that Remington use when making blades in its U.S. factory? Why?

2. Why would Remington choose to produce only blades in the United States rather than assembling entire shavers as well?

3. What is the focus of the conversion process in Remington's U.S. factory?

BUILDING SKILLS FOR CAREER SUCCESS

1. Exploring the Internet

Improvements in the quality of products and services is an ever-popular theme in business management. Besides the obvious increase to profitability to be gained by such improvements, a company's demonstration of its continuous search for ways to improve operations can be a powerful statement to customers, suppliers, and investors. Two of the larger schools of thought in this field are Six Sigma and the European-based International Organization for Standardization. Visit the text website for updates to this exercise.

Assignment

1. Use Internet search engines to find more information about each of these topics.

2. From the information on the Internet, can you tell whether there is any real difference between these two approaches?

3. Describe one success story of a firm that realized improvement by adopting either approach.

3. Building Team Skills

Suppose that you are planning to build a house in the country. It will be a brick, one-storey structure of approximately 186 square metres, centrally heated and cooled. It will have three bedrooms, two bathrooms, a family room, a dining room, a kitchen with a breakfast nook, a study, a utility room, an entry foyer, a two-car garage, a covered patio, and a fireplace. Appliances will operate on electricity and propane fuel. You have received approval and can be connected to the cooperative water system at any time. Public sewerage services are not available; therefore, you must rely on a septic system. You want to know how long it will take to build the house.

Assignment

1. Identify the major activities involved in the project, and sequence them in the proper order.

2. Estimate the time required for each activity, and establish the critical path.

3. Working in a group, prepare a PERT diagram to show the steps involved in building your house.

4. Present your PERT diagram to the class, and ask for comments and suggestions.

5. Improving Communication Skills

Total quality management (TQM) is a much broader concept than just controlling the quality of a single product. It is a philosophy that places quality at the centre of everything a company does. In particular, TQM is aimed at improving customer satisfaction, increasing employee participation, strengthening supplier partnerships, and facilitating an organizational atmosphere of continuous quality improvement. For TQM to work successfully, it must start with a company's mission statement, be ingrained in the company's goals and objectives, and be implemented through the strategies that ultimately satisfy customer needs. Today, many companies use TQM.

Assignment

1. Read articles or use the Internet to find out how at least two different companies implement TQM.

2. Prepare a three-page report on your findings. The report should include answers to the following questions:

   a. Exactly how does each company focus on quality?

   b. How are the TQM programs of these two companies alike? How do they differ?

   c. How will TQM influence their operations in the twenty-first century?

   d. Using quality as a criterion, which company would you rather work for? Why?

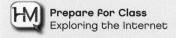

Prepare for Class
Exploring the Internet

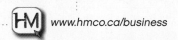

RUNNING A BUSINESS PART III
Finagle A Bagel's Management, Organization, and Production Finesse

We don't have a traditional corporate organizational chart," states Heather Robertson, Finagle A Bagel's director of marketing, human resources, and research and development. When she hires new employees, Robertson draws the usual type of organization chart showing the co-presidents on the top and the store employees on the bottom. Then she turns it upside down, explaining: "The most important people in our stores are the crew members, and the store manager's role is to support those crew members. Middle management's role is to support the store managers. And the co-presidents' responsibility is to support us," referring to herself and her middle-management colleagues.

In short, the co-presidents and all the people in corporate headquarters work as a team to help the general managers (who run the stores) and their crew members. Every store strives to achieve preset sales goals within budget guidelines. Higher-level managers are available to help any general manager whose store's performance falls outside the expected ranges. Moreover, each general manager is empowered to make decisions that will boost sales and make the most of opportunities to build positive relationships with local businesses and community organizations. "We want our general managers to view the store as their business," copresident Laura Trust emphasizes. "If a general manager wants to do something that will alleviate a store problem or increase sales, we give him [or her] the leeway to do it."

Many Bagels, One Factory

Although the co-presidents decentralized authority for many store-level decisions, they achieved more efficiency by centralizing the authority and responsibility for food procurement and preparation. For example, headquarters handles payroll, invoices, and many other time-consuming activities on behalf of all the stores. This reduces the paperwork burden on general managers and frees them to concentrate on managing store-level food service to satisfy customers.

Finagle A Bagel also decided to centralize production and supply functions in its recently opened Newton headquarters, where the factory has enough capacity to supply up to 100 stores. "We outgrew our old facility, and we wanted to find some place we could expand our operations," copresident Laura Trust explains. Production employees prepare and shape dough for 100,000 bagels and mix over 900 kilos of flavoured cream cheese spreads every day. In addition, they slice 680 kilos of fruit every week.

Then they gather whatever each store needs—raw dough, salad fixings, packages of condiments, or plastic bowls—and load it on the truck for daily delivery.

Baking Bagels and More

Once the raw dough reaches a store, crew members follow the traditional New York-style method of boiling and baking bagels in various varieties, ranging from year-round favourites such as sesame to seasonal offerings such as pumpkin raisin. In line with Finagle A Bagel's fresh-food concept, the stores bake bagels every hour and tumble them into a line of bins near the front counter. Each store has a unique piece of equipment, dubbed the "bagel buzz saw," to slice and move bagels to the sandwich counter after customers have placed their orders. This equipment not only helps to prevent employee accidents and speeds food preparation, but it also entertains customers as they wait for their sandwiches.

Finagle A Bagel is constantly introducing new menu items to bring customers back throughout the day. One item the company has perfected is the bagel pizza. Earlier bagel pizzas turned out soggy, but the newest breakfast pizzas are both crunchy and tasty. The central production facility starts by mixing egg bagel dough, forms it into individual flat breads, grills the rounds, and ships them to the stores. There, a crew member tops each round with the customer's choice of ingredients, heats it, and serves it toasty fresh.

Managing a Bagel Restaurant

Finagle A Bagel's general managers stay busy from the early morning, when they open the store and help crew members to get ready for customers, to the time they close the store at night after one last look to see whether everything is in order for the next day. General managers such as Paulo Pereira, who runs the Harvard Square Finagle A Bagel in Cambridge, must have the technical skills required to run a fast-paced food-service operation.

General managers also need good conceptual skills so that they can look beyond each individual employee and task to see how everything should fit together. One way Pereira does this is by putting himself in the customer's shoes. He is constantly evaluating how customers would judge the in-store experience, from courteous, attentive counter service to the availability of fresh foods, clean tables, and well-stocked condiment containers.

Just as important, Pereira—like other Finagle A Bagel general managers—must have excellent interpersonal skills to work effectively with customers, crew members, colleagues, and higher-level managers. Pereira knows that he can't be successful without being able to work well with other people, especially those he supervises. "You need to have a good crew behind you to help you every single hour of the day," he says. "Every employee needs to feel special and appreciated. I try to treat employees as fairly as possible, and I try to accommodate their needs."

Questions

1. What does Finagle A Bagel's upside-down organization chart suggest about the delegation of authority and coordination techniques within the company?

2. Is Finagle A Bagel a tall or flat organization? How do you know?

3. What values seem to permeate Finagle A Bagel's corporate culture?

4. Why would Finagle A Bagel build a dough factory that has more capacity than the company needs to supply its stores and its wholesale customers?

Sources: Based on information from Donna Hood Crecca, "Higher Calling," *Chain Leader*, December 2002, p. 14; "While Finagle Flaunts a Breakfast Bagel Pizza," *Restaurant Business Menu Strategies*, November 12, 2002, www .restaurantbusiness.com; Finagle A Bagel website: www.finagleabagel .com; interview with Laura B. Trust and Alan Litchman, February 25, 2003.

CHAPTER 10

Attracting and Retaining the Best Employees

Your Guide to Success in Business

Why this chapter matters
Being able to understand how to attract and keep the right people is crucial. Also, you can better understand about your own interactions with your coworkers.

LEARNING OBJECTIVES

1. Describe the major components of human resources management.

2. Identify the steps in human resources planning.

3. Describe cultural diversity and understand some of the challenges and opportunities associated with it.

4. Explain the objectives and uses of job analysis.

5. Describe the processes of recruiting, employee selection, and orientation.

6. Discuss the primary elements of employee compensation and benefits.

7. Explain the purposes and techniques of employee training, development, and performance appraisal.

8. Outline the major legislation affecting human resources management.

McDonald's Canada Chosen Top Employer

The *Globe and Mail* selected McDonald's Canada as one of the country's 50 best employers in 2006. McDonald's Canada has received the award five other times and continues to set an example for other Canadian employers.

Management has the challenge of attracting, retaining and rewarding employees to not only keep them happy with their work, but also help minimize the cost and disruption of employee turnover.

McDonald's starts with the makeup of its workforce—from burger builders to board members. Mirroring the communities in which it operates, McDonald's hires people of every background and ethnicity, as well as people with disabilities. Women are well represented at all levels—nearly half of McDonald's middle managers are women—and seniors often work alongside teenagers.

"We have a tremendous diversity," confirms Don Thompson, executive vice president and chief operations officer for McDonald's. As a result, the company has "an even stronger ability to tap into and respond to the diversity that our customers represent." In fact, the company's policy of inclusion extends beyond the workforce. No other fast-food company has as many minority and women franchisees. What's more, the company buys $3 billion worth of goods and services every year from suppliers owned by women and minorities.

McDonald's launched its diversity strategy thirty years ago with a series of seminars to educate employees about ongoing changes in the workforce. This diversity training has been offered, with updates and revisions, ever since.

McDonald's human resources policies build on their commitment to the community. Respect and recognition are the cornerstones to their management practices. Ongoing training, educational opportunities, including scholarships for college and university studies, ensure a loyal and appreciative workforce.

continued on next page

DID YOU KNOW?

Companies such as McDonald's go to considerable efforts to support their workforces.

KEY TERMS

human resources management (HRM) (284)
human resources planning (286)
replacement chart (287)
skills inventory (287)
cultural (workplace) diversity (288)
job analysis (291)
job description (291)

job specification (292)
recruiting (292)
external recruiting (292)
internal recruiting (293)
selection (293)
orientation (295)
compensation (295)
compensation system (295)

wage survey (296)
job evaluation (296)
comparable worth (297)
hourly wage (297)
salary (297)
commission (298)
incentive payment (298)
lump-sum salary increase (298)

profit sharing (298)
employee benefit (298)
flexible benefit plan (299)
employee training (300)
management development (300)
performance appraisal (302)

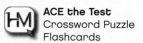

ACE the Test
Crossword Puzzle
Flashcards

Pay for performance and employee recognition awards, reward employees for their efforts and further support McDonald's mission to be one of the top employers in Canada.

For more information about this company, go to www.mcdonalds.ca.

Source: McDonald's Corporation website, www.mcdonalds.ca. Based on information from Sakina P. Spruell, "The 30 Best Companies for Diversity," *Black Enterprise*, July 2005, pp. 112+; "Diversity at McDonald's: A Way of Life," *Nation's Restaurant News*, April 11, 2005, pp. S92+; "Human Resources: A Challenge Best Addressed One Unit at a Time," *Nation's Restaurant News*, April 11, 2005, p. S100; Sarah E. Lockyer, "McD Boosts Morale, Ante at Managers' Vegas Confab," *Nation's Restaurant News*, July 4, 2005, pp. 1, 45; www.mcdonalds.com.

McDonald's encourages the hiring and training of employees from diverse ethnic backgrounds. Hiring a diverse mix of employees helps the company to serve a diverse customer base. Many companies consider these as important factors when attracting, motivating, and retaining the appropriate mix of human resources.

We begin our study of human resources management (HRM) with an overview of how businesses acquire, maintain, and develop their human resources. After listing the steps by which firms match their human resource needs with the supply available, we explore several dimensions of cultural diversity. Then we examine the concept of job analysis. Next, we focus on a firm's recruiting, selection, and orientation procedures as the means of acquiring employees. We also describe forms of employee compensation that motivate employees to remain with a firm and to work effectively. Then we discuss methods of employee training, management development, and performance appraisal. Finally, we consider legislation that affects HRM practices.

Human Resources Management: An Overview

(Learning Objective ❶

Describe the major components of human resources management.

The human resource is not only unique and valuable, but it is also an organization's most important resource. It seems logical that an organization would expend a great deal of effort to acquire and make full use of such a resource. This effort is known as *human resources management* (HRM). It also has been called *staffing* and *personnel management*.

human resources management (HRM) all the activities involved in acquiring, maintaining, and developing an organization's human resources

Human resources management (HRM) consists of all the activities involved in acquiring, maintaining, and developing an organization's human resources. As the definition implies, HRM begins with acquisition—getting people to work for the organization. The acquisition process can be quite competitive for certain types of qualified employees. For example, brokerage houses such as RBC Dominion Securities, BMO Nesbitt Burns Inc., and Genuity Capital Markets often recruit experienced traders from other brokerage firms. Next, steps must be taken to keep these valuable resources. (After all, they are the only business resources that can leave an organization.) Finally, the human resources should be developed to their full capacity.

HRM Activities

Each of the three phases of HRM—acquiring, maintaining, and developing human resources—consists of a number of related activities. Acquisition, for example, includes planning and the various activities that lead to hiring new personnel. Altogether this phase of HRM consists of five separate activities. They are

* *Human resources planning*—determining the firm's future human resources needs
* *Job analysis*—determining the exact nature of the positions
* *Recruiting*—attracting people to apply for positions
* *Selection*—choosing and hiring the most qualified applicants
* *Orientation*—acquainting new employees with the firm

Maintaining human resources consists primarily of encouraging employees to remain with the firm and to work effectively by using a variety of HRM programs, including

* *Employee relations*—increasing employee job satisfaction through satisfaction surveys, employee communication programs, exit interviews, and fair treatment
* *Compensation*—rewarding employee effort through monetary payments
* *Benefits*—providing rewards to ensure employee well-being

The development phase of HRM is concerned with improving employees' skills and expanding their capabilities. The two important activities within this phase are

* *Training and development*—teaching employees new skills, new jobs, and more effective ways of doing their present jobs
* *Performance appraisal*—assessing employees' current and potential performance levels

These activities will be discussed in more detail shortly, when we have completed this overview of HRM.

Responsibility for HRM

In general, HRM is a responsibility shared by line managers and staff HRM specialists. In very small organizations, the owner handles all or most HRM activities. As a firm grows, a human resources manager is hired to take over staff responsibilities. In firms as large as Bell Canada Enterprises Inc. (BCE), HRM activities tend to be very highly specialized. There are separate groups to deal with compensation, benefits, training and development, and other staff activities.

Specific HRM activities are assigned to those who are in the best position to perform them. Human resources planning and job analysis usually are done by staff specialists, with input from line managers. Similarly, recruiting and selection are handled by staff experts, although line managers are involved in hiring decisions. Orientation programs are devised by staff specialists and carried out by both staff specialists and line managers. Compensation systems (including benefits) most often are developed

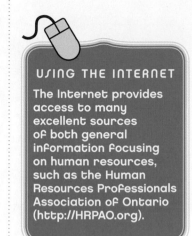

USING THE INTERNET

The Internet provides access to many excellent sources of both general information focusing on human resources, such as the Human Resources Professionals Association of Ontario (http://HRPAO.org).

and administered by the HRM staff. However, line managers recommend pay increases and promotions. Training and development activities are the joint responsibility of staff and line managers. Performance appraisal is the job of the line manager although, in many organizations, HRM personnel design the firm's appraisal system.

Human Resources Planning

Learning Objective

Identify the steps in human resources planning.

human resources planning the development of strategies to meet a firm's future human resources needs

Human resources planning is the development of strategies to meet a firm's future human resources needs. The starting point is the organization's overall strategic plan. From this, human resources planners can forecast future demand for human resources. Next, the planners must determine whether the needed human resources will be available. Finally, they have to take steps to match supply with demand.

Forecasting Human Resources Demand

Planners should base forecasts of the demand for human resources on as much relevant information as is available. The firm's overall strategic plan will provide information about future business ventures, new products, and projected expansions or contractions of specific product lines. Information on past staffing levels, evolving technologies, industry staffing practices, and projected economic trends can also be helpful.

HRM staff use this information to determine both the number of employees required and their qualifications. Planners use a wide range of methods to forecast specific personnel needs. For example, in one simple method, personnel requirements are projected to increase or decrease in the same proportion as sales revenue. Thus, if a 30 percent increase in sales volume is projected over the next two years, then up to a 30 percent increase in personnel requirements may be expected for the same period. (This method can be applied to specific positions as well as to the workforce in general. It is not, however, a very precise forecasting method.) At the other extreme are elaborate, computer-based personnel planning models used by some large firms.

Forecasting Human Resources Supply

Forecasting the supply of human resources must take into account both the present workforce and any changes that might occur within it. For example, suppose that planners project that in five years a firm that currently employs 100 engineers will need to employ a total of 200 engineers. Planners simply cannot assume that they will have to hire 100 engineers; during that period, some of the firm's present engineers are likely to be promoted, leave the firm, or move to other jobs within the firm. Thus planners may project the supply of engineers in five years at 87, which means that the firm will have to hire a total of 113 new engineers. When forecasting supply, planners should analyze the organization's existing employees to determine who can be retrained to perform the required tasks.

Two useful techniques for forecasting human resources supply are the replacement chart and the skills inventory. A **replacement chart** is a list of key personnel and their possible replacements within a firm. The chart is maintained to ensure that top-management positions can be filled fairly quickly in the event of an unexpected death, resignation, or retirement. Some firms also provide additional training for employees who might eventually replace top managers.

A **skills inventory** is a computerized data bank containing information on the skills and experience of all present employees. It is used to search for candidates to fill available positions. For example, for a special project, a manager might seek a current employee with specific information technology skills, at least six years of experience, and fluency in French. The skills inventory can quickly identify employees who possess such qualifications.

Matching Supply with Demand

Once they have forecast the supply and demand for personnel, planners can devise a course of action for matching the two. When demand is predicted to be greater than supply, plans must be made to recruit new employees. The timing of these actions depends on the types of positions to be filled. Suppose that a firm expects to open another plant in five years. Along with other employees, the firm will need a plant manager and twenty-five maintenance workers. It probably can wait quite a while before beginning to recruit maintenance personnel. However, because the job of plant manager is so critical, the firm might start searching for the right person for that position immediately.

When supply is predicted to be greater than demand, the firm must take steps to reduce the size of its workforce. When the oversupply is expected to be temporary, some employees may be *laid off*—dismissed from the workforce until they are needed again.

Perhaps the most humane method for making personnel cutbacks is through attrition. *Attrition* is the normal reduction in the workforce that occurs when employees leave a firm. If these employees are not replaced, the workforce eventually shrinks to the point where supply matches demand. Of course, attrition can be a very slow process—often too slow to help the firm. For example, Ford Motor Company, facing declining market share and reduced profits, announced that they would achieve the desired cost savings needed through a combination of job cuts and employee attrition.

Early retirement is another option. Under early retirement, people who are within a few years of retirement are permitted to retire early with full benefits. Depending on the age makeup of the workforce, this may or may not reduce the staff enough.

As a last resort, unneeded employees are sometimes simply *fired* or let go. However, because of its negative impact, this method generally is used only when absolutely necessary, and it is not without cost, as these layoffs generally attract some form of compensation such as severance pay.

replacement chart a list of key personnel and their possible replacements within a firm

skills inventory a computerized data bank containing information on the skills and experience of all present employees

Cultural Diversity in Human Resources

Learning Objective ③

Describe cultural diversity and understand some of the challenges and opportunities associated with it.

The value of cultural diversity

Diversity brings together different backgrounds, viewpoints and skill sets and reflects Canada's multicultural population.

cultural (workplace) diversity differences among people in a workforce owing to race, ethnicity, and gender

SPOTLIGHT

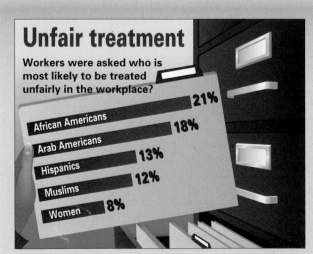

Unfair treatment

Workers were asked who is most likely to be treated unfairly in the workplace?

African Americans   21%
Arab Americans   18%
Hispanics   13%
Muslims   12%
Women   8%

Source: *USA Today*, April 10, 2002, p. B1.

Today's workforce is made up of people from many backgrounds. Firms can no longer assume that every employee has similar beliefs or expectations. Whereas North American white males may believe in challenging authority, Asians tend to respect and defer to it. In Hispanic cultures, people often bring music, food, and family members to work, a custom that Canadian businesses traditionally have not allowed. A job applicant who will not make eye contact during an interview may be rejected for being unapproachable, when, according to his or her culture, he or she was just being polite.

Since a larger number of women, minorities, and immigrants have entered the Canadian workforce, the workplace is more diverse. For example, it is estimated that women make up about approximately 47 percent of the Canadian workforce. **Cultural** (or **workplace**) **diversity** refers to the differences among people in a workforce owing to race, ethnicity, and gender. Increasing cultural diversity is forcing managers to learn to supervise and motivate people with a broader range of value systems. The flood of women into the workforce, combined with a new emphasis on participative parenting by men, has brought many family-related issues to the workplace. Today's more educated employees also want greater independence and flexibility. In return for their efforts, they want both compensation and a better quality of life.

Although cultural diversity presents a challenge, managers should view it as an opportunity rather than a limitation. When managed properly, cultural diversity can provide competitive advantages for an organization. Table 10.1 shows

Cost	As organizations become more diverse, the cost of a poor job in integrating workers will increase. Companies that handle this well thus can create cost advantages over those that do a poor job. In addition, companies also experience cost savings by hiring people with knowledge of various cultures as opposed to having to train Canadians, for example, about how Chinese people do business.
Resource acquisition	Companies develop reputations as being favourable or unfavourable prospective employers for women and ethnic minorities. Those with the best reputations for managing diversity will win the competition for the best personnel.
Marketing edge	For multinational organizations, the insight and cultural sensitivity that members with roots in other countries bring to marketing efforts should improve these efforts in important ways. The same rationale applies when marketing to diverse local groups.
Flexibility	Culturally diverse employees often are open to a wider array of positions within a company and are more likely to move up the corporate ladder more rapidly, given excellent performance.
Creativity	Diversity of perspectives and less emphasis on conformity to norms of the past should improve the level of creativity.
Problem solving	Differences within decision-making and problem-solving groups potentially produce better decisions through a wider range of perspectives and more thorough critical analysis of issues.
Language skills	Cultural diversity in the workplace brings with it language skills and cultural sensitivity that are advantageous in the ever-growing global marketplace. Employees with knowledge about how other cultures work can not only speak to clients in their language but also prevent their company from making embarrassing moves owing to a lack of cultural sophistication. These companies should seek job applicants with a background in the cultures with which the company does business.

Table 10.1

Competitive Advantages of Cultural Diversity

Sources: Taylor H. Cox and Stacy Blake, "Managing Cultural Diversity: Implications for Organizational Competitiveness," *Academy of Management Executive* 5(3):46, 1991; Graciela Kenig, "Yo Soy Ingeniero: The Advantages of Being Bilingual in Technical Professions," *Diversity Monthly*, February 28, 1999, p. 13; and "Dialogue Skills in the Multicultural Workplace," *North American Post*, March 19, 1999, p. 2.

several benefits that creative management of cultural diversity can offer. A firm that manages diversity properly can develop cost advantages over other firms. Moreover, organizations that manage diversity creatively are in a much better position to attract the best personnel. A culturally diverse organization can gain a marketing edge because it understands different cultural groups. Proper guidance and management of diversity in an organization also can improve the level of creativity. Culturally diverse people frequently are more flexible in the types of positions they will accept. Employees skilled in more than one language bring numerous benefits to an organization.

Because cultural diversity creates challenges along with advantages, it is important for an organization's employees to understand it. To accomplish this goal, numerous Canadian firms have trained their managers to respect and manage diversity. Diversity training programs might include recruiting minorities, training minorities to be managers, training managers to view diversity positively, teaching English as a second language, and facilitating support groups for immigrants. Many organizations are realizing the importance of diversity training. Universities and colleges have increased their efforts to promote diversity in their faculty. These institutions have realized that a valid education includes cultural diversity. Many companies have realized

Here's How to Negotiate Higher Compensation

Consider making a case for higher compensation if you've taken on more responsibilities, completed a challenging assignment, or achieved exceptionally high performance. Some negotiating tips:

Do your homework. Research typical salaries for your job by checking classified ads, websites, and other sources. This is a starting point for your negotiation.

List your accomplishments. Document how you've contributed to your firm's success or completed tasks beyond those in your job description. Susan Hackley, head of the Harvard Law School's Program on Negotiation, advises: "This is the one chance you've got to convey to your boss that you deserve everything you're asking for."

Approach your boss. Make an appointment with your boss and go in prepared. Be positive but not pushy, and be patient. Your manager may need higher-level approval to grant a raise. Finally, be flexible. Incentive pay may be a possibility, if a raise is not.

that diversity training goes beyond racial issues to include age, religious practices, weight, sexual orientation, and even hobbies should be considered part of diversity.[1] Owing to the high quality of its program, the Royal Bank of Canada has received several awards for being one of the best places in Canada for minorities to work. RBC's cultural diversity program involves training and education, employee diversity groups, and corporate policies that support advancement of minorities. Hundreds of managers, supervisors, and employees from all parts of the company have attended diversity training programs that taught them to value the cultural differences in RBC.[2]

A diversity program will be successful only if it is systematic and ongoing and has a strong, sustained commitment from top leadership. Cultural diversity is here to stay. Its impact on organizations is widespread and will continue to grow within corporations. Management must learn to overcome the obstacles and capitalize on the advantages associated with culturally diverse human resources.

Job Analysis

Learning Objective 4

Explain the objectives and uses of job analysis.

There is no sense in hiring people unless the firm knows what it is hiring them to do. In other words, the firm needs to know the nature of a job before finding the right person to do it.

Job analysis is a systematic procedure for studying jobs to determine their various elements and requirements. Consider the position of clerk, for example. In a large corporation, there may be fifty kinds of clerk positions. They all may be called "clerk," but each position differs from the others in the activities to be performed, the level of proficiency required for each activity, and the particular set of qualifications that the position demands. These distinctions are the focus of job analysis.

The job analysis for a particular position typically consists of two parts—a job description and a job specification. A **job description** is a list of the elements that make up a particular job. It includes the duties to be performed, the working conditions, responsibilities, and the tools and equipment that must be used on the job (see Figure 10.1).

job analysis a systematic procedure for studying jobs to determine their various elements and requirements

job description a list of the elements that make up a particular job

---

TITLE: Sales Coordinator   **DATE:** 25/3/08
DEPARTMENT: Sales
REPORTS TO: Regional Manager

BRIEF SUMMARY:
Supervise one other Alberta-based sales representative to gain supervisory experience. Captain the four members of the outside sales rep team assigned to the universities and colleges in Western Canada. Oversee, coordinate, advise, and make decisions regarding Alberta sales activities. Based upon broad contact with customers across the region, the person will make recommendations regarding issues specific to the needs of higher education including distance learning, institution-wide adoptions, and faculty support and in-service.

PRINCIPAL ACCOUNTABILITIES:

1. Supervises/manages/trains one other Alberta-based sales rep.
2. Advises two other sales reps regarding the institutions in their territories.
3. Increases overall sales in the region.
4. Assists regional manager.
5. Initiates a dialogue with faculty members in the areas of distance learning and course development.

DIMENSIONS:
This position will have one direct report in addition to the leadership role played within the region. Revenue most directly impacted will be within the individually assigned territory, the supervised territory, and the overall sales for the region.

KNOWLEDGE AND SKILLS:
Must have displayed a history of consistently outstanding sales in personal territory. Must demonstrate clear teamwork and leadership skills and be willing to extend beyond the individual territory goals. Should have a clear understanding of the company's systems and product offerings in order to train and lead other sales representatives. Must have the communication skills and presence to communicate articulately with faculty and faculty administrators and to serve as a bridge between the company and higher education in the region.

Figure 10.1

Job Description and Job Specification

This job description explains the job of sales coordinator and lists the responsibilities of the position. The job specification is contained in the last paragraph.

Source: Used with permission of Houghton Mifflin Company.

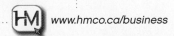

job specification a list of the qualifications required to perform a particular job

A **job specification** is a list of the qualifications required to perform a particular job. Included are the skills, abilities, education, and experience the jobholder must have. When attempting to hire an investment analyst, the Royal Bank of Canada used the following job requirements: " 2 to 3 years of relevant work experience (VC/PE, investment banking, consulting) excellent academic credentials; willingness to be part of a small team and handle a wide range of responsibilities."[3]

The job analysis is not only the basis for recruiting and selecting new employees; it is also used in other areas of HRM, including evaluation and the determination of equitable compensation levels.

Recruiting, Selection, and Orientation

Learning Objective ⑤

Describe the processes of recruiting, employee selection, and orientation.

In an organization with jobs waiting to be filled, HRM personnel need to (1) find candidates for those jobs and (2) match the right candidate with each job. Three activities are involved: recruiting, selection, and (for new employees) orientation.

Recruiting

recruiting the process of attracting qualified job applicants

Recruiting is the process of attracting qualified job applicants. Because it is a vital link in a costly process (the cost of hiring an employee can be several thousand dollars), recruiting needs to be a systematic process. One goal of recruiters is to attract the "right number" of applicants. The right number is enough to allow a good match between applicants and open positions but not so many that matching them requires too much time and effort. For example, if there are five open positions and five applicants, the firm essentially has no choice. It must hire those five applicants (qualified or not), or the positions will remain open. At the other extreme, if several hundred job seekers apply for the five positions, HRM personnel will have to spend weeks processing their applications.

Recruiters can seek applicants outside the firm, within the firm, or both. The source used depends on the nature of the position, the situation within the firm, and, sometimes, the firm's established or traditional recruitment policies.

external recruiting the attempt to attract job applicants from outside an organization

External Recruiting **External recruiting** is the attempt to attract job applicants from outside an organization. External recruiting might include newspaper advertising, employment agencies, recruiting on college and university campuses, soliciting recommendations from present employees, conducting "open houses," and recruiting online. The biggest of online job-search sites is Monster.com, which has as clients about 490 of the *Fortune 500* companies.[4] In Canada, Workopolis is the leading online job-search site. In addition, many people simply apply at a firm's employment office.

Clearly, it is best to match the recruiting means with the kind of applicant being sought. For example, private employment agencies most often handle executive and professional personnel, while public employment agencies often handle a broader range of personnel needs, from civil service positions to student internships.

The primary advantage of external recruiting is that it brings in people with new perspectives and varied business backgrounds. A disadvantage of external recruiting is that it is often expensive, especially if private employment agencies must be used. External recruiting also may provoke resentment among present employees.

Internal Recruiting Internal recruiting means considering present employees as applicants for available positions. Generally, current employees are considered for *promotion* to higher-level positions. However, employees may be considered for *transfer* from one position to another at the same level.

Promoting from within provides strong motivation for current employees and helps the firm to retain quality personnel. The practice of *job posting*, or informing current employees of upcoming openings, may be a company policy or required by union contract. The primary disadvantage of internal recruiting is that promoting a current employee leaves another position to be filled. Not only does the firm still incur recruiting and selection costs, but it must also train two employees instead of one.

In many situations it is impossible to recruit internally. For example, a new position may be such that no current employee is qualified. Or the firm may be growing so rapidly that there is no time to reassign positions that promotion or transfer requires.

> **internal recruiting** considering present employees as applicants for available positions

Selection

Selection is the process of gathering information about applicants for a position and using that information to choose the most appropriate applicant. Note the use of the word *appropriate*. In selection, the idea is not to hire the person with the *most* qualifications but rather the applicant who is *most appropriate*. The selection of an applicant is made by line managers responsible for the position. However, HRM personnel usually help by developing a pool of applicants and by expediting the assessment of these applicants. Common means of obtaining information about applicants' qualifications are employment applications, interviews, references, and assessment centres.

> **selection** the process of gathering information about applicants for a position and using that information to choose the most appropriate applicant

Employment Applications An employment application is useful in collecting factual information on a candidate's education, work experience, and personal history. The data obtained from applications usually are used for two purposes: to identify applicants who are worthy of further scrutiny and to familiarize interviewers with their backgrounds.

Many job candidates submit résumés, with a covering letter of application, and some firms require them. A *résumé* is a one- or two-page summary of the candidate's background and qualifications. It may include a description of the type of job the applicant is seeking. A résumé might be sent to a firm to request consideration for available jobs, or it can be submitted along with an employment application. The letter of application can tell the firm a lot about the candidate, such as the ability to express thoughts clearly, grammatically, and in an organized way.

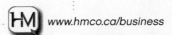

To improve the usefulness of information, HRM specialists ask current employees about factors in their backgrounds most related to their current jobs. Then these factors are included on the applications and may be weighted more heavily when evaluating new applicants' qualifications.

Employment Tests Tests administered to job candidates usually focus on aptitudes, skills, abilities, or knowledge relevant to the job. Such tests (basic computer skills tests, for example) indicate how well the applicant will do the job. Occasionally, companies use general intelligence or personality tests, but these are seldom helpful in predicting specific job performance. However, many large companies, as well as an increasing number of medium and small companies, are using predictive-behaviour personality tests as the cost of administering them decreases. Darden Restaurants, parent company of The Olive Garden and Red Lobster, uses a work-style inventory in its hiring process for all positions, whereas firms such as Disney use similar tests for management positions.[5]

At one time, a number of companies were criticized for using tests that were biased against certain minority groups. The test results were, to a great extent, unrelated to job performance. Today, a firm must be able to prove that a test is not discriminatory by demonstrating that it accurately measures one's ability to perform.

Interviews The interview is perhaps the most widely used selection technique. Job candidates are interviewed by at least one member of the HRM staff and by the person for whom they will be working. Candidates for higher-level jobs might meet with a department head or vice president over several interviews.

Interviews provide an opportunity for applicants and the firm to learn more about each other. Interviewers can pose problems to test the candidate's abilities, probe employment history, and learn something about the candidate's attitudes and motivation. The candidate has a chance to find out more about the job and potential coworkers.

Unfortunately, interviewing can be the stage at which discrimination begins. For example, suppose that a female applicant mentions that she is the mother of small children. Her interviewer might assume that she would not be available for job-related travel. In addition, interviewers can be unduly influenced by such factors as appearance. Or they may ask different questions of different applicants so that it becomes impossible to compare candidates' qualifications.

Some of these problems can be solved through interviewer training and use of structured interviews. In a *structured interview*, the interviewer asks only a prepared set of job-related questions. The firm also may consider using several different interviewers for each applicant, but this is likely to be costly.

▲
Recruiting

The modern day interview will include reference checks, skills assessments and a personal meeting with the company's human resources department.

References A job candidate generally is asked to furnish the names of references—people who can verify background information and provide personal evaluations. Naturally, applicants tend to list only references who are likely to say good things. Thus personal evaluations obtained from references may not be of much value. However, references are often contacted to verify such information as previous job responsibilities and the reason an applicant left a former job.

Assessment Centres An assessment centre is used primarily to select current employees for promotion to higher-level positions. Typically, a group of employees is sent to the centre for a few days. While there, they participate in activities designed to simulate the management environment and to predict managerial effectiveness. Trained observers make recommendations regarding promotion possibilities. Although this technique is gaining popularity, the expense involved limits its use.

Orientation

Once all information about job candidates has been collected and analyzed, a job offer is extended. If it is accepted, the candidate becomes an employee.

Soon after a candidate joins a firm, he or she goes through the firm's orientation program. **Orientation** is the process of acquainting new employees with an organization. Orientation topics range from the location of the company cafeteria to career paths within the firm. The orientation itself may consist of a half-hour informal presentation by a human resources manager. Or it may be an elaborate program involving dozens of people and lasting several days or weeks.

orientation the process of acquainting new employees with an organization

Compensation and Benefits

Learning Objective 6

Discuss the primary elements of employee compensation and benefits.

An effective employee reward system must (1) enable employees to satisfy basic needs, (2) provide rewards comparable with those offered by other firms, (3) be distributed fairly within the organization, and (4) recognize that different people have different needs.

A firm's compensation system can be structured to meet the first three of these requirements. The fourth is more difficult because it must account for many variables. Most firms offer a number of benefits that, taken together, generally help to provide for employees' varying needs.

Compensation Decisions

Compensation is the payment employees receive in return for their labour. Its importance to employees is obvious. And because compensation can account for up to 80 percent of a firm's operating costs, it is equally important to management. The firm's **compensation system,** the policies and strategies that determine employee compensation, therefore must be designed carefully to provide for employee needs while keeping

compensation the payment employees receive in return for their labour

compensation system the policies and strategies that determine employee compensation

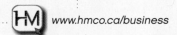

labour costs within reasonable limits. For most firms, designing an effective compensation system requires three separate management decisions—wage level, wage structure, and individual wages.

Wage Level   Management first must position the firm's general pay level relative to pay levels of comparable firms. Most firms choose a pay level near the industry average. A firm that is not in good financial shape might pay less than average and large, prosperous organizations might pay more than average.

To determine what the average is, the firm may use wage surveys. A **wage survey** is a collection of data on prevailing wage rates within an industry or a geographic area. Such surveys are compiled by industry associations, local governments, personnel associations, and (occasionally) individual firms.

Wage Structure   Next, management must decide on relative pay levels for all the positions within the firm. Will managers be paid more than secretaries? Will secretaries be paid more than custodians? The result of this set of decisions is often called the firm's *wage structure*.

The wage structure almost always is developed on the basis of a job evaluation. **Job evaluation** is the process of determining the relative worth of the various jobs within a firm. Most observers probably would agree that a secretary should make more money than a custodian, but how much more? Job evaluation should provide the answer to this question.

A number of techniques may be used to evaluate jobs. The simplest is to rank all the jobs within the firm according to value. A more frequently used method is based on the job analysis. Points are allocated to each job for each of its elements and requirements. For example, "university degree required" might be worth fifty points, whereas the need for a high school education might count for only twenty-five points. The more points a job is allocated, the more important it is presumed to be (and the higher its level in the firm's wage structure).

Individual Wages   Finally, the specific payments individual employees will receive must be determined. Consider the case of two secretaries working side by side. Job evaluation has been used to determine the relative level of secretarial pay within the firm's wage structure. However, suppose that one secretary has fifteen years of experience and can type eighty words per minute accurately. The other has two years of experience and can type only fifty-five words per minute. In most firms these two people would not receive the same pay. Instead, a wage range would be established for the secretarial position. In this case, the range might be $12.00 to $15.00 per hour. The more experienced and proficient secretary then would be paid an amount near the top of the range (say, $14.50 per hour); the less experienced secretary would receive an amount that is lower but still within the range (say, $12.25 per hour).

Two wage decisions come into play here. First, the employee's initial rate must be established. It is based on experience, other qualifications, and expected performance. Later, the employee may be given pay increases based on seniority and performance.

Comparable Worth

One reason women in the workforce are paid less may be that a proportion of women occupy female-dominated jobs—nurses, secretaries, and medical records analysts, for

---

wage survey a collection of data on prevailing wage rates within an industry or a geographic area

job evaluation the process of determining the relative worth of the various jobs within a firm

---

—EXAMINING ETHICS—
CEO Compensation: How Much Is Too Much?

Are CEOs overpaid? Although the CEO of Yahoo! earned $230 million in total compensation during one recent year, not all CEOs enjoy such a hefty pay package. Still, CEO compensation has increased dramatically in the past decade, raising a number of questions:

Should CEO compensation be based on performance? Ideally, yes—in practice, not always. If the company's profits are flat or the stock price barely budges, should the CEO receive a big raise?

What does compensation include? CEOs often receive club memberships and other extras. Should shareholders know about these extras?

Should the CEO's salary be hundreds of times greater than an average worker's salary? The organic grocery chain Whole Foods is against such a huge pay disparity. Its CEO's total compensation cannot be more than fourteen times that of the average employee, and for the year 2007, CEO John Mackey's annual salary will be just $1.00 (*The Wall Street Journal*—July 23, 2007). Will more companies follow its lead in capping CEO pay?

---

example—that require education, skills, and training equal to higher-paid positions but are undervalued. **Comparable worth** is a concept that seeks equal compensation for jobs that require about the same level of education, training, and skills. Most provinces have enacted laws requiring equal pay for comparable work.

Critics of comparable worth argue that the market has determined the worth of jobs and laws should not tamper with the pricing mechanism of the market. Critics also argue that artificially inflating salaries for female-dominated occupations encourages women to keep these jobs rather than seek out higher-paying jobs.

comparable worth a concept that seeks equal compensation for jobs requiring about the same level of education, training, and skills

Types of Compensation

Compensation can be paid in a variety of forms. Most forms of compensation fall into the following categories: hourly wage, weekly or monthly salary, commissions, incentive payments, lump-sum salary increases, and profit sharing.

Hourly Wage An **hourly wage** is a specific amount of money paid for each hour of work. People who earn wages are paid their hourly wage for the first forty hours worked in any week. They are then paid one and one-half times their hourly wage for time worked in excess of forty hours. (That is, they are paid "time and a half" for overtime.) Workers in retailing and fast-food chains, on assembly lines, and in clerical positions usually are paid an hourly wage.

hourly wage a specific amount of money paid for each hour of work

Weekly or Monthly Salary A **salary** is a specific amount of money paid for an employee's work during a set calendar period, regardless of the actual number of hours worked. Salaried employees receive no overtime pay, but they do not lose pay when they are absent from work. Most professional and managerial positions are salaried.

salary a specific amount of money paid for an employee's work during a set calendar period, regardless of the actual number of hours worked

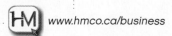 www.hmco.ca/business

commission a payment that is a percentage of sales revenue

incentive payment a payment in addition to wages, salary, or commissions

lump-sum salary increase an entire pay raise taken in one lump sum

profit sharing the distribution of a percentage of a firm's profit among its employees

employee benefit a reward in addition to regular compensation that is provided indirectly to employees

Commissions A **commission** is a payment that is a percentage of sales revenue. Sales representatives and sales managers often are paid entirely through commissions or through a combination of commissions and salary.

Incentive Payments An **incentive payment** is a payment in addition to wages, salary, or commissions. Incentive payments are really extra rewards for outstanding job performance. They might be distributed to all employees or only to certain employees. Some firms distribute incentive payments to all employees annually. The size of the payment depends on the firm's earnings and, at times, on the particular employee's length of service with the firm. Firms sometimes offer incentives to employees who exceed specific sales or production goals, a practice called *gain sharing*.

To avoid yearly across-the-board salary increases, some organizations reward outstanding workers individually through *merit pay*. This pay-for-performance approach allows management to control labour costs while encouraging employees to work more efficiently. An employee's merit pay depends on his or her achievements relative to those of others.

Lump-Sum Salary Increases In traditional reward systems, an employee who receives an annual pay increase is given part of the increase in each pay period. For example, suppose an employee on a monthly salary gets a 10 percent annual pay hike. He or she actually receives 10 percent of the former monthly salary added to each month's paycheque for a year. Companies that offer a **lump-sum salary increase** give the employee the option of taking the entire pay raise in one lump sum. The employee then draws his or her "regular" pay for the rest of the year. The lump-sum payment typically is treated as an interest-free loan that must be repaid if the employee leaves the firm during the year.

Profit Sharing **Profit sharing** is the distribution of a percentage of a firm's profit among its employees. The idea is to motivate employees to work effectively by giving them a stake in the company's financial success. Some firms—including Sears, Roebuck—have linked their profit-sharing plans to employee retirement programs; that is, employees receive their profit-sharing distributions, with interest, when they retire.

Employee Benefits

An **employee benefit** is a reward in addition to regular compensation that is provided indirectly to employees. Employee benefits consist mainly of services (such as insurance) that

Sharing profits

Profit sharing grants employees a portion of the company's profits and serves as an incentive and motivator for employees.

are paid for partially or totally by employers and employee expenses (such as tuition for continuing education) that are reimbursed by employers.

Types of Benefits Employee benefits take a variety of forms. *Pay for time not worked* covers such absences as vacation time, holidays, and sick leave. *Insurance packages* may include extra health coverage, such as dental and vision care, and life and long-term care insurance for employees and their families. Some firms pay the entire cost of the insurance package, and others share the cost with the employee. The costs of *pension and retirement programs* also may be borne entirely by the firm or shared with the employee.

Some benefits are required by law. For example, employers must maintain *workers' compensation insurance*, which pays medical bills for injuries that occur on the job and provides income for employees who are disabled by job-related injuries. Employers also must contribute to *employment insurance* and the Canada Pension Plan. Vacation pay, at a minimum of 4 percent, is also mandated by law.

Other benefits provided by employers might include tuition-reimbursement plans, credit unions, child care, company cafeterias, exercise rooms, and broad stock purchase plans available to all employees.

Flexible Benefit Plans Through a flexible benefit plan, an employee receives a predetermined amount of benefit dollars and can allocate those dollars to various categories of benefits in the mix that best fits his or her needs. Some flexible benefit plans offer a broad array of benefit options, including extra health care, dental care, life insurance, accidental death, and dismemberment coverage for both the worker and dependents, long-term disability coverage, extra vacation benefits, retirement savings, and dependent-care benefits. Other firms offer limited options, primarily in health and life insurance and retirement plans.

Although the cost of administering flexible plans is high, a number of organizations, including Coca-Cola, have implemented this option for several reasons. Because employees' needs are so diverse, flexible plans help firms to offer benefit packages that more specifically meet their employees' needs. Flexible plans can, in the long run, help a company to contain costs because a specified amount is allocated to cover the benefits of each employee. Furthermore, organizations that offer flexible plans with many choices might be perceived as employee-friendly. Thus they are in a better position to attract and retain qualified employees.

flexible benefit plan compensation plan whereby an employee receives a predetermined amount of benefit dollars to spend on a package of benefits he or she has selected to meet individual needs

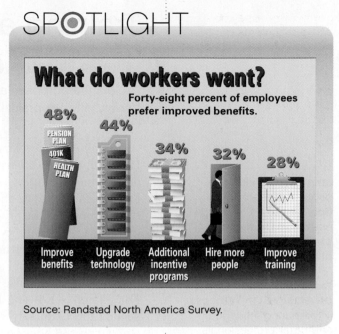

SP🔘TLIGHT

What do workers want?

Forty-eight percent of employees prefer improved benefits.

48% — Improve benefits
44% — Upgrade technology
34% — Additional incentive programs
32% — Hire more people
28% — Improve training

Source: Randstad North America Survey.

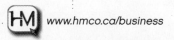

Training and Development

Learning Objective 7

Explain the purposes and techniques of employee training, development, and performance appraisal.

employee training the process of teaching operations and technical employees how to do their present jobs more effectively and efficiently

management development the process of preparing managers and other professionals to assume increased responsibility in both present and future positions

Training and development are both aimed at improving employees' skills and abilities. However, the two are usually differentiated as either employee training or management development. **Employee training** is the process of teaching operations and technical employees how to do their present jobs more effectively and efficiently. **Management development** is the process of preparing managers and other professionals to assume increased responsibility in both present and future positions. Thus training and development differ in who is being taught and the purpose of the teaching. Both are necessary for personal and organizational growth. Companies that hope to stay competitive typically make huge commitments to employee training and development. For example, Edward Jones, the stockbroker with nearly 500 branches in Canada, spends approximately 3.8 percent of its payroll on training. These expenditures average out to 146 hours per year for each employee, with new hires receiving about four times this amount of training. This dedication to its employees has helped Edward Jones to be named one of the "50 Best Employers in Canada" in the *Globe and Mail*'s annual listing in *Report on Business* magazine for the fifth consecutive year (2007).[6] Internet-based e-learning is growing. Driven by cost, travel, and time savings, online learning alone, and in conjunction with face-to-face situations, is a strong alternative strategy. Development of a training program usually has three components: analysis of needs, determination of training and development methods, and creation of an evaluation system to assess the program's effectiveness.

Analysis of Training Needs

When thinking about developing a training program, managers first must determine if training is needed and, if so, what types of training needs exist. At times, what at first appears to be a need for training is actually, on assessment, a need for motivation. Training needs can vary considerably. For example, some employees may need training to improve their technical skills, or they may need training about organizational procedures. Training also can focus on business ethics, product information, or customer service. Because training is expensive, it is critical that the correct training needs are identified.

Training and Development Methods

A number of methods are available for employee training and management development. Some of these methods may be more suitable for one or the other, but most can be applied to both.

* *On-the-job methods.* The trainee learns by doing the work under the supervision of an experienced employee.

* *Simulations.* The work situation is simulated in a separate area so that learning takes place away from the day-to-day pressures of work.

* *Classroom teaching and lectures.* You probably already know these methods quite well.

* *Conferences and seminars.* Experts and learners meet to discuss problems and exchange ideas.

* *Role playing.* Participants act out the roles of others in the organization for better understanding of those roles (primarily a management development tool).

Evaluation of Training and Development

Training and development are very expensive. The training itself costs quite a bit, and employees are usually not working—or are working at a reduced load and pace—during training sessions. To ensure that training and development are cost-effective, the managers responsible should evaluate the company's efforts periodically.

The starting point for this evaluation is a set of verifiable objectives that are developed *before* the training is undertaken. Suppose that a training program is expected to improve the skills of machinists. The objective of the program might be stated as follows: "At the end of the training period, each machinist should be able to process thirty parts per hour with no more than one defective part per ninety parts completed." This objective clearly specifies what is expected and how training results may be measured or verified. Evaluation then consists of measuring machinists' output and the ratio of defective parts produced after the training.

The results of training evaluations should be made known to all those involved in the program—including trainees and upper management. For trainees, the results of

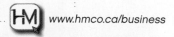

evaluations can enhance motivation and learning. For upper management, the results may be the basis for making decisions about the training program itself.

Performance Appraisal

performance appraisal
the evaluation of employees' current and potential levels of performance to allow managers to make objective human resources decisions

Performance appraisal is the evaluation of employees' current and potential levels of performance to allow managers to make objective human resources decisions. The process has three main objectives. First, managers use performance appraisals to let workers know how well they are doing and how they can do better in the future. Second, a performance appraisal provides an effective basis for distributing rewards, such as pay raises and promotions. Third, performance appraisal helps the organization monitor its employee selection, training, and development activities. If large numbers of employees continually perform below expectations, the firm may need to revise its selection process or strengthen its training and development activities.

Common Evaluation Techniques

The various techniques and methods for appraising employee performance are either objective or judgmental in nature.

Objective Methods Objective appraisal methods use some measurable quantity as the basis for assessing performance. Units of output, dollar volume of sales, number of defective products, and number of insurance claims processed are all objective, measurable quantities. Thus an employee who processes an average of twenty-six insurance claims per week is given a higher evaluation than one whose average is nineteen claims per week.

Such objective measures may require some adjustment for the work environment. Suppose that the first of our insurance-claims processors works in Montreal, Quebec, and the second works in rural Saskatchewan. Both must visit each client because they are processing homeowners' insurance claims. The difference in their average weekly output may be due entirely to the distance the employee must travel to visit clients. In this case, the two workers may very well be equally competent and motivated. Thus a manager must take into account circumstances that may be hidden by a purely statistical measurement.

Judgmental Methods Judgmental appraisal methods are used much more frequently than objective methods. They require that the manager judge or estimate the employee's performance level. However, judgmental methods are not capricious. These methods are based on employee ranking or rating scales. When ranking is used, the manager ranks subordinates from best to worst. This approach has a number of drawbacks, including the lack of any absolute standard. Rating scales are the most popular judgmental appraisal technique. A *rating scale* consists of a number of statements; each employee is rated on the degree to which the statement applies. For example, one statement might be, "This employee always does high-quality work." The supervisor would give the employee a rating, from 5 down to 1, corresponding to gradations ranging from "strongly agree" to "strongly disagree." The ratings on all the statements are added to obtain the employee's total evaluation.

Avoiding Appraisal Errors Managers must be cautious if they are to avoid making mistakes when appraising employees. It is common to overuse one portion of an evaluation instrument (such as a performance evaluation form) thus overemphasizing some issues and underemphasizing others. A manager must guard against allowing an employee's poor performance on one activity to influence his or her judgment of that subordinate's work on other activities. Similarly, putting too much weight on recent performance distorts an employee's evaluation. For example, if the employee is being rated on performance over the last year, a manager should not permit last month's disappointing performance to overshadow the quality of the work done in the first eleven months of the year. Finally, a manager must guard against discrimination on the basis of race, age, gender, religion, national origin, or sexual orientation.

Performance Feedback

No matter which appraisal technique is used, the results should be discussed with the employee soon after the evaluation is completed. The manager should explain the basis for present rewards and should let the employee know what he or she can do to be recognized as a better performer in the future. The information provided to an employee in such discussions is called a *performance feedback*, and the process is known as a *performance feedback interview*.

There are three major approaches to performance feedback interviews: tell and sell, tell and listen, and problem solving. In a *tell-and-sell* feedback interview, the superior tells the employee how good or bad the employee's performance has been and then attempts to persuade the employee to accept this evaluation. Since the employee has no input into the evaluation, the tell-and-sell interview can lead to defensiveness, resentment, and frustration on the part of the subordinate. The employee may not accept the results of the interview and may not be committed to achieving the goals that are set.

With the *tell-and-listen* approach, the supervisor tells the employee what has been right and wrong with the employee's performance and then gives the employee a chance to respond. The subordinate simply may be given an opportunity to react to the supervisor's statements or may be permitted to offer a full self-appraisal, challenging the supervisor's assessment.

In the *problem-solving* approach, employees evaluate their own performance and set their own goals for future performance. The supervisor is more a colleague than a judge and offers comments and advice in a noncritical manner. An active and open dialogue ensues in which goals for improvement are established mutually. The problem-solving interview is more likely to result in the employee's commitment to the established goals.

To avoid some of the problems associated with the tell-and-sell interview, a mixed approach sometimes is used. The mixed interview uses the tell-and-sell approach to communicate administrative decisions and the problem-solving approach to discuss employee-development issues and future performance goals.[7]

An appraisal approach that has become popular is called a *360-degree evaluation*. A 360-degree evaluation collects anonymous reviews about an employee from his or her peers, subordinates, and supervisors and then compiles these reviews into a feedback report that is given to the employee. Companies that invest significant resources in employee-development efforts are especially likely to use 360-degree evaluations. An

employee should not be given a feedback report without first having a one-on-one meeting with his or her supervisor. The most appropriate way to introduce a 360-degree evaluation system in a company is to begin with upper-level management. Then managers should be trained on how to interpret feedback reports so that they can coach their employees on how to use the feedback to achieve higher-level job-related skills and behaviours.[8]

Finally, we should note that many managers find it difficult to discuss the negative aspects of an appraisal. Unfortunately, they may ignore performance feedback altogether or provide it in a very weak and ineffectual manner. In truth, though, most employees have strengths that can be emphasized to soften the discussion of their weaknesses. An employee may not even be aware of weaknesses and their consequences. If such weaknesses are not pointed out through performance feedback, they cannot possibly be eliminated. Only through tactful, honest communication can the results of an appraisal be fully utilized.

The Legal Environment of HRM

Learning Objective 8

Outline the major legislation affecting human resources management.

Legislation regarding HRM practices has been passed at both the federal and provincial levels primarily to protect the rights of employees, promote job safety, and stop discrimination in the workplace. The Canadian Charter of Rights and Freedoms, which supersedes any other legislation in Canada, is the primary source of protection against workplace discrimination on the basis of gender, age, skin colour, marital status, and so forth. In addition to the Charter of Rights and Freedoms, managers need to be cognizant of any provincial rights legislation that may apply only in that one province, and specific bodies of law such as the Unemployment Insurance Act, Worker's Compensation, and pay equity legislation that may pertain to particular work issues or industries.

Needless to say, legislation in HR is fluid and management constantly needs to be aware of changes that can affect them.[9] Changes over the last thirty years to the way Canadian society and the courts now regard issues such as hiring and interviewing practices, employment application form questions, unfair termination of employees, sexual harassment, and privacy clearly indicate just how much HR legislation and application of the laws have changed.

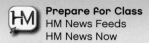

Prepare for Class
HM News Feeds
HM News Now

→ **RETURN TO INSIDE BUSINESS**

In addition to the extensive recruiting efforts and employee satisfaction initiatives employed by McDonald's, the company is also very active in communities across Canada. The creation of Ronald McDonald Houses that provide assistance to

families suffering serious illness and the support the company provides to other local charities shows a financial commitment to the communities where they do business. This is an example of corporate social responsibility and some would argue that this is also just good business.

Questions

1. Is corporate social responsibility good for business? How?
2. Do supportive efforts in the community assist in attracting and retaining employees?

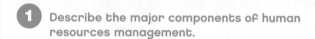

CHAPTER REVIEW

1 **Describe the major components of human resources management.**

Human resources management (HRM) is the set of activities involved in acquiring, maintaining, and developing an organization's human resources. Responsibility for HRM is shared by specialized staff and line managers. HRM activities include human resources planning, job analysis, recruiting, selection, orientation, compensation, benefits, training and development, and performance appraisal.

2 **Identify the steps in human resources planning.**

Human resources planning consists of forecasting the human resources that a firm will need and those that it will have available and then planning a course of action to match supply with demand. Layoffs, attrition, early retirement, and (as a last resort) firing are ways to reduce the size of the workforce. Supply is increased through hiring.

3 **Describe cultural diversity and understand some of the challenges and opportunities associated with it.**

Cultural diversity refers to the differences among people in a workforce owing to race, ethnicity, and gender. With an increasing number of women, minorities, and immigrants entering the Canadian workforce, management is faced with both challenges and competitive advantages. Some organizations are implementing diversity-related training programs and working to make the most of cultural diversity. With the proper guidance and management, a culturally diverse organization can prove beneficial to all involved.

4 **Explain the objectives and uses of job analysis.**

Job analysis provides a job description and a job specification for each position within a firm. A job description is a list of the elements that make up a particular job. A job specification is a list of qualifications required to perform a particular job. Job analysis is used in evaluation and in determining compensation levels and serves as the basis for recruiting and selecting new employees.

5 Describe the processes of recruiting, employee selection, and orientation.

Recruiting is the process of attracting qualified job applicants. Candidates for open positions may be recruited from within or outside a firm. In the selection process, information about candidates is obtained from applications, résumés, tests, interviews, references, or assessment centres. This information then is used to select the most appropriate candidate for the job. Newly hired employees then will go through a formal or informal orientation program to acquaint them with the firm.

6 Discuss the primary elements of employee compensation and benefits.

Compensation is the payment employees receive in return for their labour. In developing a system for paying employees, management must decide on the firm's general wage level (relative to other firms), the wage structure within the firm, and individual wages. Wage surveys and job analyses are useful in making these decisions. Employees may be paid hourly wages, salaries, or commissions. They also may receive incentive payments, lump-sum salary increases, and profit-sharing payments.

7 Explain the purposes and techniques of employee training, development, and performance appraisal.

Employee training and management-development programs enhance the ability of employees to contribute to a firm. When developing a training program, training needs should be analyzed. Then training methods should be selected. Because training is expensive, an organization periodically should evaluate the effectiveness of its training programs.

Performance appraisal, or evaluation, is used to provide employees with performance feedback, to serve as a basis for distributing rewards, and to monitor selection and training activities. Both objective and judgmental appraisal techniques are used. Their results are communicated to employees through three performance feedback approaches: tell and sell, tell and listen, and problem solving.

8 Outline the major legislation affecting human resources management.

A number of laws have been passed that affect HRM practices and that protect the rights and safety of employees. At the federal level, the Charter of Rights and Freedoms is the primary piece of legislation that protects workers against various forms of discrimination. At the provincial level, all provinces have an Employment Standards Act and Human Rights Code, as well as further legislation dealing with such issues as occupational health and safety, labour relations, workplace safety, and pay equity.

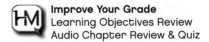

Improve Your Grade
Learning Objectives Review
Audio Chapter Review & Quiz

Review Questions

1. List the three main HRM activities and their objectives.
2. In general, on what basis is responsibility for HRM divided between line and staff managers?
3. How is a forecast of human resources demand related to a firm's organizational planning?
4. How do human resources managers go about matching a firm's supply of workers with its demand for workers?
5. What are the major challenges and benefits associated with a culturally diverse workforce?
6. How are a job analysis, job description, and job specification related?
7. What are the advantages and disadvantages of external recruiting? Of internal recruiting?
8. In your opinion, what are the two best techniques for gathering information about job candidates?
9. Why is orientation an important HRM activity?
10. Explain how the three wage-related decisions result in a compensation system.
11. How is a job analysis used in the process of job evaluation?
12. Suppose that you have just opened a new Ford sales showroom and repair shop. Which of your employees would be paid wages, which would receive salaries, and which would receive commissions?
13. What is the difference between the objective of employee training and the objective of management development?
14. Why is it so important to provide feedback after a performance appraisal?

Discussion Questions

1. How accurately can managers plan for future human resources needs?
2. How might an organization's recruiting and selection practices be affected by the general level of employment?
3. Are employee benefits really necessary? Why?
4. As a manager, what actions would you take if an operations employee with six years of experience on the job refused ongoing training and ignored performance feedback?
5. Why are there so many laws relating to HRM practices? Which are the most important laws, in your opinion?

CASE STUDY

People Make the Difference at the New England Aquarium

From porpoises and penguins to seals and sea turtles, the nonprofit New England Aquarium houses an incredibly diverse array of the world's sea life. The aquarium's official mission statement is "to present, promote, and protect the world of water." It also wants to appeal to the broadest possible audience and build a workforce of paid and unpaid staff that reflects the diversity of the Boston community.

Volunteers are a major resource for the New England Aquarium. Its staff of 1,000 volunteers—one of the nonprofit world's largest—contributes 100,000 hours of service yearly. Many high school and college students volunteer to try out possible career choices. Adults with and without specialized college degrees (in fields such as marine biology and environmental affairs) volunteer their time as well. And the New England Aquarium's internships offer college students and recent graduates hands-on experience in veterinary services, communications, and other key areas.

Maureen C. Hentz, director of volunteer programs, is a champion for workplace diversity. Most organizations "are good at putting diversity in their mission statements and talking about it, but not actually accomplishing it," she observes. In contrast, she and her New England Aquarium colleagues aggressively reach out to recruit volunteers, interns, and employees of different races, ethnicities, socioeconomic levels, physical abilities, and ages. In addition, they welcome people of diverse educational backgrounds, personalities, and viewpoints because of the new ideas these differences can bring to the organization's opportunities and challenges.

The New England Aquarium must plan for employees, volunteers, or interns to handle certain tasks whenever the facility is open. For example, it needs cashiers to collect admission fees during daytime, evening, and weekend hours. Volunteers are often available to work during weekend hours, but filling daytime positions can be difficult. This is another reason why Hentz and her staff attend community meetings and find other ways to encourage volunteerism.

It is much the same operation at the Vancouver Aquarium in Canada. Volunteers as young as fourteen years of age can become involved in just about every aspect of the aquarium's operations. Their volunteer program includes opportunities for completing school sponsored community service requirements and training for possible careers in marine conservation.

At the Toronto Zoo, volunteers must complete a twelve-week course and agree to a two-year commitment to work as tour guides and ambassadors for the zoo in various outreach programs designed to teach groups more about the zoo's activities.

Both the Vancouver Aquarium and the Toronto Zoo benefit from this win-win scenario—they get trained volunteer assistance, and volunteers gain valuable experience and the enjoyment of working with organizations in which they are truly interested.

Candidates for internships must send a letter expressing interest in working as an intern and include a résumé plus two academic or professional references. As an option, candidates can send a letter of reference and a college transcript to support the application letter. The New England Aquarium's internship coordinators interview the most promising candidates and make the final selections. Interns, like volunteers, gain valuable experience and can list their New England Aquarium positions on their résumés when looking for future employment.

Paid employees receive a full package of valuable benefits, including paid holidays and sick days, insurance, and tuition reimbursement. Just as important, employees gain an opportunity to make a difference. When hired, they become part of an organization that protects the underwater environment, educates the public, and saves the lives of whales and other marine life.

For more information about these organizations, go to www.neaq.org, www.vanaqua.org/home/, and www.torontozoo.com.

Questions:

1. Why would the New England Aquarium require people to apply in writing for unpaid volunteer and internship positions?

2. In addition to using the web and attending community meetings, what other external recruiting techniques would you suggest that Hentz use? Why?

3. Do you think that the New England Aquarium should evaluate the performance of its volunteers periodically? Support your answer.

BUILDING SKILLS FOR CAREER SUCCESS

1. Exploring the Internet

Although you may believe that your formal learning will end when you graduate and enter the working world, it won't. Companies both large and small spend billions of dollars annually in training employees and updating their knowledge and skills. Besides supporting employees who attend accredited continuing-education programs, companies also may provide more specialized in-house course work on new technologies, products, and markets for strategic planning. The Internet is an excellent search tool to find out about course work offered by private training organizations, as well as by traditional academic institutions. Learning online over the Internet is a fast-growing alternative, especially for busy employees requiring updates to skills in the information technology (IT) field, where software knowledge must be refreshed continuously. Visit the text website for updates to this exercise.

Assignment

1. Visit the websites of several academic institutions and examine their course work offerings. Also examine the offerings of some of the following private consulting firms:

   Learning Tree International: www .learningtree.com

   Accenture: www.accenture.com

   KPMG: www.kpmg.com

   Ernst & Young: www.ey.com/global

2. What professional continuing-education training and services are provided by one of the academic institutions whose site you visited?

3. What sort of training is offered by one of the preceding consulting firms?

4. From the company's point of view, what is the total real cost of a day's worth of employee training? What is the money value of one day of study for a full-time college student? Can you explain why firms are willing to pay higher

HM **Prepare for Class**
Exploring the Internet

starting salaries for employees with higher levels of education?

2. Developing Critical-Thinking Skills

Suppose that you are the manager of the six supervisors described in the following list. They have all just completed two years of service with you and are eligible for an annual raise. How will you determine who will receive a raise and how much each will receive?

- Joe Garcia has impressed you by his above-average performance on several difficult projects. Some of his subordinates, however, do not like the way he assigns jobs. You are aware that several family crises have left him short of cash.

- Sandy Vance meets her goals, but you feel that she could do better. She is single, likes to socialize, and at times arrives late for work. Several of her subordinates have low skill levels, but Sandy feels that she has explained their duties to them adequately. You believe that Sandy may care more about her friends than about coaching her subordinates. Her workers never complain and appear to be satisfied with their jobs.

- Paul Steiberg is not a good performer, and his work group does not feel that he is an effective leader. You also know that his group is the toughest one to manage. The work is hard and dirty. You realize that it would be very difficult to replace him, and you therefore do not want to lose him.

- Anna Chen runs a tight ship. Her subordinates like her and feel that she is an excellent leader. She listens to them and supports them. Recently, her group won the TOP (The Outstanding Performance) Award. Anna's husband is CEO of a consulting firm, and as far as you know, she is not in financial need.

- Jill Foster has completed every assignment successfully. You are impressed by this, particularly since she has a very difficult job. You recently learned that she spends several hours every week taking classes on her own time to improve her skills. Jill seems to be motivated more by recognition than by money.

- Fred Hammer is a jolly person who gets along with everyone. His subordinates like him, but you do not think that he is getting the job done to your expectations. Twice he has missed a critical delivery date and this cost the firm over $5,000 each time. He recently divorced his wife and is having an extremely difficult time meeting his financial obligations.

Assignment

1. You have $25,000 available for raises. As you think about how you will allot the money, consider the following:
   a. What criteria will you use in making a fair distribution?
   b. Will you distribute the entire $25,000? If not, what will you do with the remainder?
2. Prepare a four-column table in the following manner:
   a. In column 1, write the name of the employee.
   b. In column 2, write the amount of the raise.
   c. In column 3, write the percentage of the $25,000 the employee will receive.
   d. In column 4, list the reasons for your decision.

3. Building Team Skills

The New Therapy Company is soliciting a contract to provide five nursing homes with physical, occupational, speech, and respiratory therapy. The therapists will float among the five nursing homes. The therapists have not yet been hired, but the nursing homes expect them to be fully trained and ready to go to work in three months. The previous therapy company lost its contract because of high staff turnover owing to "burnout" (a common problem in this type of work), high cost, and low quality care. The nursing homes want a plan specifying how the New Therapy Company will meet staffing needs, keep costs low, and provide high quality care.

Assignment

1. Working in a group, discuss how the New Therapy Company can meet the three-month deadline and still ensure that the care its therapists provide is of high quality. Also discuss the following:
   a. How many of each type of therapist will the company need?
   b. How will it prevent therapists from "burning out"?
   c. How can it retain experienced staff and still limit costs?
   d. Are promotions available for any of the staff? What is the career ladder?
   e. How will the company manage therapists at five different locations? How will it keep in touch with them (computer, voice mail, monthly meetings)? Would it make more sense to have therapists work permanently at each location rather than rotate among them?
   f. How will the company justify the travel costs? What other expenses might it expect?
2. Prepare a plan for the New Therapy Company to present to the nursing homes.

4. Researching Different Careers

A résumé provides a summary of your skills, abilities, and achievements. It can also include a description of the type of job you want. A well-prepared résumé indicates that you know what your career objectives are, shows that you have given serious thought to your career, and tells a potential employer what you are qualified to do. The way a résumé is prepared can make a difference in whether you are considered for a job.

Assignment

1. Prepare a résumé for a job that you want.
   a. First, determine what your skills are and decide which skills are needed to do this particular job.

b. Decide which type of format—chronological or functional—would be most effective in presenting your skills and experience.

c. Keep the résumé to one page, if possible (definitely no more than two pages). (Note that portfolio items, such as artwork, may need to be attached for certain types of jobs.)

2. Have several people review the résumé for accuracy.

3. Ask your instructor to comment on your résumé.

CHAPTER *11*

Motivating and Satisfying Employees and Teams

Your Guide to Success in Business

Why this chapter matters
As you move up into management positions or operate your own business, you will need to understand what motivates others in an organization.

LEARNING OBJECTIVES

1 Explain what motivation is.

2 Understand some major historical perspectives on motivation.

3 Describe three contemporary views of motivation: equity theory, expectancy theory, and goal-setting theory.

4 Explain several techniques for increasing employee motivation.

5 Understand the types, development, and uses of teams.

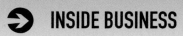
The Best Places to Work in Canada

In 2007, Rocky Mountaineer Vacations was ranked by the *Globe and Mail* as one of the top fifty employers in Canada. At number 23 on the list, the ranking highlighted its commitment to its employees, and the employees' commitment to the company. "At its core, the . . . study measures how engaged employees are or how passionate, motivated and excited they are to come to work. This is an award that recognizes how well we work together and how much we enjoy working with one another," says Paul Dyck, Vice President, Human Resources & Corporate Administration at Rocky Mountaineer Vacations. "We have long recognized that our employees are the foundation of our team, and as such we strive to be an employer of choice by attracting, training, supporting and retaining the very best people."*

Is that, in fact, what the ranking really means? Certainly, there have been various attempts to rank the best companies to work for in Canada, and the criteria, methods, and results are perhaps rarely the same. The *Globe and Mail*, *Financial Post*, and *Canadian Business* magazine all publish something along these lines and it is interesting to see what companies make each of their lists.

What they each strive to recognize, however, is the principle reflected in Dyke's comment about what the ranking meant to his company: what motivates employees is most often not financial remuneration or hard cash, but rather the "softer" benefits that come from a better work-life balance and a collegial atmosphere at work. In fact, fair compensation based on performance is what people expect. After that, respectful interactions between staff and management, transparent decision-making practices, and a feeling that their work matters are what employees say motivates them.

But perks still are important. Back in Motion Rehab, a small rehab company in Surrey, B.C., provides funding and paid time off so that employees can further their professional training and qualifications. At Environics Communications in Toronto, employees are given an extra week of holidays and a

continued on next page

● ● ●

> **DID YOU KNOW?**
>
> All of the most highly ranked businesses in Canada offer more than just competitive wages, including travel subsidies, child support, and professional development programs.

K E Y   T E R M S

motivation (314)
morale (314)
scientific management (315)
piece-rate system (316)
need (317)
Maslow's hierarchy of needs (317)
physiological needs (317)
safety needs (317)
social needs (317)
esteem needs (318)

self-actualization needs (318)
motivation-hygiene theory (319)
motivation factors (319)
hygiene factors (319)
Theory X (320)
Theory Y (320)
Theory Z (321)
reinforcement theory (322)
equity theory (323)
expectancy theory (324)

goal-setting theory (325)
management by objectives (MBO) (325)
job enrichment (326)
job enlargement (327)
job redesign (327)
behaviour modification (328)
flextime (329)
part-time work (329)
job sharing (329)

telecommuting (330)
empowerment (330)
employee ownership (331)
team (332)
problem-solving team (332)
virtuoso team (332)
self-managed teams (332)
cross-functional team (333)
virtual team (333)

ACE the Test
Crossword Puzzle
Flashcards

$5,000 travel subsidy when they reach their fifth year anniversary with the company. Saskcentral, a credit union in Regina, covers the tuition so that employees can study for a MBA. Monster Canada, the online recruiting firm based in Montreal, gives away free trips to outstanding performers, as judged by their peers. And S.C. Johnson and Son of Brantford, has several cottages in Muskoka, Ontario, that employees can rent during the summer. Rocky Mountain Vacations motivates employees through travel incentives.

Motivation theories abound but attention to fairness and the odd perk can go a long way to ensuring that you attract and retain the top employees, which results in great companies.

* http://www.rockymountaineer.com/media/media_kit/press_releases/2007/01-08.aspx accessed December 20, 2007.

Sources: *Canadian Business* magazine, "The Best Workplaces in Canada," April 23, 2007.

To achieve its goals, any organization—whether it's Ernst & Young LLP, Four Seasons Hotels, Saskcentral, or your local convenience store—must be sure that its employees have more than the right raw materials, adequate facilities, and equipment that works. The organization also must ensure that its employees are *motivated*. A high level of employee motivation derives, to a certain extent, from effective management practices.

In this chapter, after first explaining what motivation is, we present several views of motivation that have influenced management practices over the years: Taylor's ideas of scientific management, Mayo's Hawthorne Studies, Maslow's hierarchy of needs, Herzberg's motivation-hygiene theory, McGregor's Theory X and Theory Y, Ouchi's Theory Z, and reinforcement theory. Then, turning our attention to contemporary ideas, we examine equity theory, expectancy theory, and goal-setting theory. Finally, we discuss specific techniques managers can use to foster employee motivation and satisfaction.

What Is Motivation?

Learning Objective ①

Explain what motivation is.

motivation the individual internal process that energizes, directs, and sustains behaviour; the personal "force" that causes you or me to behave in a particular way

A *motive* is something that causes a person to act. A successful athlete is said to be "highly motivated." A student who avoids work is said to be "unmotivated." We define **motivation** as the individual internal process that energizes, directs, and sustains behaviour. It is the personal "force" that causes you or me to act in a particular way. For example, job rotation might increase your job satisfaction and your enthusiasm for your work so that you devote more energy to it but, perhaps, job rotation would not have the same impact on me.

morale an employee's feelings about his or her job and superiors and about the firm itself

Morale is an employee's attitude or feelings about the job, about superiors, and about the firm itself. To achieve organizational goals effectively, employees need more than the right raw materials, adequate facilities, and equipment that works. High morale results mainly from the satisfaction of needs on the job or as a result of the job.

One need that might be satisfied on the job is the need *to be recognized* as an important contributor to the organization. A need satisfied as a result of the job is the need for *financial security*. High morale, in turn, leads to dedication and loyalty, as well as to the desire to do the job well. Low morale can lead to shoddy work, absenteeism, and high turnover rates as employees leave to seek more satisfying jobs with other firms. Sometimes creative solutions are needed to motivate people and boost morale. This is especially true where barriers to change are deeply rooted in cultural stereotypes of the job and in the industry.

Motivation, morale, and the satisfaction of employees' needs are thus intertwined. Along with productivity, they have been the subject of much study since the end of the nineteenth century. We continue our discussion of motivation by outlining some landmarks of that early research.

Historical Perspectives on Motivation

Learning Objective ②

Understand some major historical perspectives on motivation.

Researchers often begin a study with a fairly narrow goal in mind. After they develop an understanding of their subject, however, they realize that both their goal and their research should be broadened. This is exactly what happened when early research into productivity blossomed into the more modern study of employee motivation.

Scientific Management

Toward the end of the nineteenth century, Frederick W. Taylor became interested in improving the efficiency of individual workers. This interest stemmed from his own experiences in manufacturing plants. It eventually led to **scientific management,** the application of scientific principles to management of work and workers.

One of Taylor's first jobs was with the Midvale Steel Company in Philadelphia, where he developed a strong distaste for waste and inefficiency. He also observed a practice he called "soldiering." Workers "soldiered," or worked slowly, because they feared that if they worked faster, they would run out of work and lose their jobs. Taylor realized that managers were not aware of this practice because they had no idea what the workers' productivity levels *should* be.

Taylor later left Midvale and spent several years at Bethlehem Steel. It was there that he made his most significant contribution. In particular, he suggested that each job should be broken down into separate tasks. Then, management should determine (1) the best way to perform these tasks and (2) the job output to expect when the tasks were performed properly. Next, management should carefully choose the best person for each job and train that person to do the job properly. Finally, management should cooperate with workers to ensure that jobs were performed as planned.

scientific management
the application of scientific principles to management of work and workers

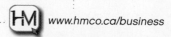

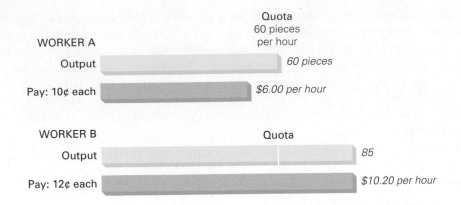

Figure 11.1

Taylor's Piece-Rate System

Workers who exceeded their quota were rewarded by being paid at a higher rate per piece for all the pieces they produced.

piece-rate system a compensation system under which employees are paid a certain amount for each unit of output they produce

Taylor also developed the idea that most people work only to earn money. He therefore reasoned that pay should be tied directly to output. The more a person produced, the more he or she should be paid. This gave rise to the **piece-rate system**, under which employees are paid a certain amount for each unit of output they produce. Under Taylor's piece-rate system, each employee was assigned an output quota. Those exceeding the quota were paid a higher per-unit rate for *all* units they produced (see Figure 11.1). Today, the piece-rate system is still used by some manufacturers and by farmers who grow crops that are harvested by farm labourers.

When Taylor's system was put into practice at Bethlehem Steel, the results were dramatic. Average earnings per day for steel handlers rose from $1.15 to $1.88. (Don't let the low wages that prevailed at the time obscure the fact that this was an increase of more than 60 percent!) The average amount of steel handled per day increased from sixteen to fifty-seven Imperial tons.

Taylor's revolutionary ideas had a profound impact on management practices. However, his view of motivation soon was recognized as overly simplistic and narrow. It is true that most people expect to be paid for their work, but it is also true that people work for a variety of reasons other than pay. Simply increasing a person's pay may not increase that person's motivation or productivity.

The Hawthorne Studies

Between 1927 and 1932, Elton Mayo conducted two experiments at the Hawthorne plant of the Western Electric Company in Chicago. The original objective of these studies, now referred to as the *Hawthorne Studies*, was to determine the effects of the work environment on employee productivity.

In the first set of experiments, lighting in the workplace was varied for one group of workers but not for a second group. Then the productivity of both groups was measured to determine the effect of the light. To the amazement of the researchers, productivity increased for *both* groups. And

SPOTLIGHT

Why not switch jobs?

Here are the most common reasons employees stay in their jobs.

- 41% Interesting responsibilities
- 31% Long-term potential
- 18% Loyalty to the company
- 6% Compensation
- 4% Loyalty to a manager

Source: Fortune Personnel Consultants survey.

for the group whose lighting was varied, productivity remained high until the light was reduced to the level of moonlight!

The second set of experiments focused on the effectiveness of the piece-rate system in increasing the output of *groups* of workers. Researchers expected that output would increase because faster workers would put pressure on slower workers to produce more. Again, the results were not as expected. Output remained constant no matter what "standard" rates management set.

The researchers came to the conclusion that *human factors* were responsible for the results of the two experiments. In the lighting experiments, researchers had given both groups of workers a *sense of involvement* in their jobs merely by asking them to participate in the research. These workers—perhaps for the first time—felt as though they were an important part of the organization. In the piece-rate experiments, each group of workers informally set the acceptable rate of output for the group. To gain or retain the *social acceptance* of the group, each worker had to produce at that rate. Slower or faster workers were pressured to maintain the group's pace.

The Hawthorne Studies showed that such human factors are at least as important to motivation as pay rates. From these and other studies, the *human relations movement* was born. Its premise was simple: employees who are happy and satisfied with their work are motivated to perform better. Hence management would do best to provide a work environment that maximizes employee satisfaction.

Maslow's Hierarchy of Needs

Abraham Maslow, an American psychologist whose best-known works were published in the 1960s and 1970s, developed a theory of motivation based on a hierarchy of needs. A **need** is a personal requirement. Maslow assumed that humans are "wanting" beings who seek to fulfill a variety of needs. He observed that these needs can be arranged according to their importance in a sequence now known as **Maslow's hierarchy of needs** (see Figure 11.2).

At the most basic level are **physiological needs**, the things we require to survive. They include food and water, clothing, shelter, and sleep. In the employment context, these needs usually are satisfied through adequate wages.

At the next level are **safety needs**, the things we require for physical and emotional security. Safety needs may be satisfied through job security, supplemental health insurance, pension plans, and safe working conditions. During a time of falling corporate profits, many companies are forced to limit bonus payouts or forgo some company functions, such as year-end parties or sales conferences.

Next are the **social needs**, the human requirements for love and affection and a sense of belonging. To an extent, these needs can be satisfied through relationships in the work environment and

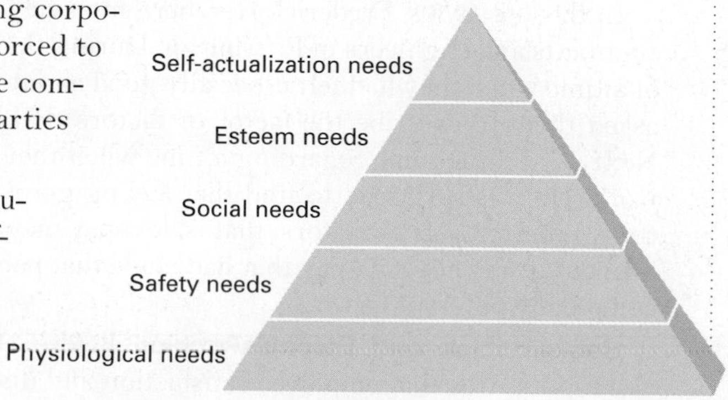

need a personal requirement

Maslow's hierarchy of needs a sequence of human needs in the order of their importance

physiological needs the things we require for survival

safety needs the things we require for physical and emotional security

social needs the human requirements for love and affection and a sense of belonging

Self-actualization needs

Esteem needs

Social needs

Safety needs

Physiological needs

Figure 11.2

Maslow's Hierarchy of Needs

Maslow believed that people act to fulfill five categories of needs.

▲

Esteem needs

Employee recognition helps to satisfy esteem needs. Recognition of this type shows respect for an individual and his or her accomplishments.

esteem needs our need for respect, recognition, and a sense of our own accomplishment and worth

self-actualization needs the need to grow and develop and to become all that we are capable of being

the informal organization. However, social networks beyond the workplace—with family and friends, for example—are usually necessary.

At the level of **esteem needs** we require respect and recognition from others and a sense of our own accomplishment and worth (self-esteem). These needs can be satisfied through personal accomplishment, promotion to more responsible jobs, various honors and awards, and other forms of recognition.

At the top of the hierarchy are our **self-actualization needs,** the need to grow and develop and to become all that we are capable of being. These are the most difficult needs to satisfy, and the means of satisfying them tend to vary with the individual. For some people, learning a new skill, starting a new career after retirement, or becoming "the best there is" at some endeavour might be the way to self-actualization.

Maslow suggested that people work to satisfy their physiological needs first, then their safety needs, and so on up the "needs ladder." In general, they are motivated by the needs at the lowest level that remain unsatisfied. However, needs at one level do not have to be satisfied completely before needs at the next-higher level come into play. If the majority of a person's physiological and safety needs are satisfied, that person will be motivated primarily by social needs. But any physiological and safety needs that remain unsatisfied also will be important.

Maslow's hierarchy of needs provides a useful way of viewing employee motivation, as well as a guide for management. By and large, Canadian businesses have satisfied workers' basic needs, but the higher-order needs present more of a challenge. These needs are not satisfied in a simple manner, and the means of satisfaction vary from one employee to another.

Herzberg's Motivation-Hygiene Theory

In the late 1950s, Frederick Herzberg interviewed approximately two hundred accountants and engineers in Pittsburgh. During the interviews, he asked them to think of a time when they had felt especially good about their jobs and their work. Then he asked them to describe the factor or factors that had caused them to feel that way. Next, he did the same regarding a time when they had felt especially bad about their work. He was surprised to find that feeling good and feeling bad resulted from entirely different sets of factors; that is, low pay may have made a particular person feel bad, but it was not high pay that had made that person feel good. Instead, it was some completely different factor.

Satisfaction and Dissatisfaction Before Herzberg's interviews, the general assumption was that employee satisfaction and dissatisfaction lay at opposite ends of

Figure 11.3

Herzberg's Motivation-Hygiene Theory

Herzberg's theory takes into account that there are different dimensions to job satisfaction and dissatisfaction and that these factors do not overlap.

the same scale. People felt satisfied, dissatisfied, or somewhere in between. But Herzberg's interviews convinced him that satisfaction and dissatisfaction may be different dimensions altogether. One dimension might range from satisfaction to no satisfaction, and the other might range from dissatisfaction to no dissatisfaction. In other words, the opposite of satisfaction is not dissatisfaction. The idea that satisfaction and dissatisfaction are separate and distinct dimensions is referred to as the **motivation-hygiene theory** (see Figure 11.3).

The job factors that Herzberg found most frequently associated with satisfaction are achievement, recognition, responsibility, advancement, growth, and the work itself. These factors are generally referred to as **motivation factors** because their presence increases motivation. However, their absence does not necessarily result in feelings of dissatisfaction. When motivation factors are present, they act as *satisfiers*.

Job factors cited as causing dissatisfaction are supervision, working conditions, interpersonal relationships, pay, job security, and company policies and administration. These factors, called **hygiene factors,** reduce dissatisfaction when they are present to an acceptable degree. However, they do not necessarily result in high levels of motivation. When hygiene factors are absent, they act as *dissatisfiers*.

Using Herzberg's Motivation-Hygiene Theory Herzberg provides explicit guidelines for using the motivation-hygiene theory of employee motivation. He suggests that the hygiene factors must be present to ensure that a worker can function comfortably. He warns, however, that a state of *no dissatisfaction* never exists. In any situation, people always will be dissatisfied with something.

According to Herzberg, managers should make hygiene as positive as possible but should expect only short-term improvement in motivation. Managers must focus instead on providing those motivation factors that presumably *will* enhance motivation and long-term effort.

We should note that employee pay has more effect than Herzberg's theory indicates. He suggests that pay provides only short-term change and not true motivation. Yet, in many organizations, pay constitutes a form of recognition and reward for achievement—and recognition and achievement are both motivation factors. The effect of pay may depend on how it is distributed. If a pay increase does not depend on performance (as in across-the-board or cost-of-living raises), it may not motivate people. However, if pay is increased as a form of recognition (as in bonuses or incentives), it can play a powerful role in motivating employees to higher performance.

motivation-hygiene theory the idea that satisfaction and dissatisfaction are separate and distinct dimensions

motivation factors job factors that increase motivation but whose absence does not necessarily result in dissatisfaction

hygiene factors job factors that reduce dissatisfaction when present to an acceptable degree but that do not necessarily result in high levels of motivation

Theory X and Theory Y

The concepts of Theory X and Theory Y were advanced by Douglas McGregor in his book *The Human Side of Enterprise*[1] They are, in essence, sets of assumptions that underlie management's attitudes and beliefs regarding worker behaviour.

Theory X is a concept of employee motivation generally consistent with Taylor's scientific management. Theory X assumes that employees dislike work and will function effectively only in a highly controlled work environment. According to Theory X,

1. People dislike work and try to avoid it.
2. Because people dislike work, managers must coerce, control, and, frequently, threaten employees to achieve organizational goals.
3. People generally must be led because they have little ambition and will not seek responsibility; they are concerned mainly with security.

The logical outcome of such assumptions will be a highly controlled work environment—one in which managers make all the decisions and employees take all the orders.

On the other hand, **Theory Y** is a concept of employee motivation generally consistent with the ideas of the human relations movement. Theory Y assumes that employees accept responsibility and work toward organizational goals if by so doing they also achieve personal rewards. According to Theory Y,

1. People do not naturally dislike work; in fact, work is an important part of their lives.
2. People will work toward goals to which they are committed.
3. People become committed to goals when it is clear that accomplishing the goals will bring personal rewards.
4. People often seek out and willingly accept responsibility.
5. Employees have the potential to help accomplish organizational goals.
6. Organizations generally do not make full use of their human resources.

Obviously, this view is quite different from—and much more positive than—that of Theory X. McGregor argued that most managers behave in accordance with Theory X. But he maintained that Theory Y is more appropriate and effective as a guide for managerial action (see Table 11.1).

Theory X a concept of employee motivation generally consistent with Taylor's scientific management; assumes that employees dislike work and will function only in a highly controlled work environment

Theory Y a concept of employee motivation generally consistent with the ideas of the human relations movement; assumes that employees accept responsibility and work toward organizational goals if by so doing they also achieve personal rewards

Table 11.1

Theory X and Theory Y Contrasted

AREA	THEORY X	THEORY Y
Attitude toward work	Dislike	Involvement
Control systems	External	Internal
Supervision	Direct	Indirect
Level of commitment	Low	High
Employee potential	Ignored	Identified
Use of human resources	Limited	Not limited

The human relations movement and Theories X and Y increased managers' awareness of the importance of social factors in the workplace. However, human motivation is a complex and dynamic process to which there is no simple key. Neither money nor social factors alone can provide the answer. Rather, a number of factors must be considered in any attempt to increase motivation.

Theory Z

William Ouchi, a management professor at UCLA, studied business practices in American and Japanese firms. He concluded that different types of management systems dominate in these two countries.[2] In Japan, Ouchi found what he calls *type J* firms. They are characterized by lifetime employment for employees, collective (or group) decision making, collective responsibility for the outcomes of decisions, slow evaluation and promotion, implied control mechanisms, non-specialized career paths, and a holistic concern for employees as people.

American industry is dominated by what Ouchi calls *type A* firms that follow a different pattern. They emphasize short-term employment, individual decision making, individual responsibility for the outcomes of decisions, rapid evaluation and promotion, explicit control mechanisms, specialized career paths, and a segmented concern for employees only as employees.

A few very successful American firms represent a blend of the type J and type A patterns. These firms, called *type Z* organizations, emphasize long-term employment, collective decision making, individual responsibility for the outcomes of decisions, slow evaluation and promotion, informal control along with some formalized measures, moderately specialized career paths, and a holistic concern for employees.

Ouchi's **Theory Z** is the belief that some middle ground between his type A and type J practices is best for American business (see Figure 11.4). A major part of Theory Z is the emphasis on participative decision making. The focus is on "we" rather than on "us versus them." Theory Z employees and managers view the organization as a family. This participative spirit fosters cooperation and the dissemination of information and organizational values.

Theory Z the belief that some middle ground between Ouchi's type A and type J practices is best for American business

Figure 11.4

The Features of Theory Z

The best aspects of Japanese and American management theories combine to form the nucleus of Theory Z.

TYPE J FIRMS (Japanese)
- Lifetime employment
- Collective decision making
- Collective responsibility
- Slow promotion
- Implied control mechanisms
- Nonspecialized career paths
- Holistic concern for employees

TYPE Z FIRMS (Best choice for American firms)
- Long-term employment
- Collective decision making
- Individual responsibility
- Slow promotion
- Informal control
- Moderately specialized career paths
- Holistic concern for employees

TYPE A FIRMS (American)
- Short-term employment
- Individual decision making
- Individual responsibility
- Rapid promotion
- Explicit control mechanisms
- Specialized career paths
- Segmented concern for employees

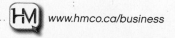

Reinforcement Theory

Reinforcement theory is based on the premise that behaviour that is rewarded is likely to be repeated, whereas behaviour that is punished is less likely to recur. A *reinforcement* is an action that follows directly from a particular behaviour. It might be a pay raise following a particularly large sale to a new customer or a reprimand for coming to work late.

Reinforcements can take a variety of forms and can be used in a number of ways. A *positive reinforcement* is one that strengthens desired behaviour by providing a reward. For example, many employees respond well to praise; recognition from their supervisors for a job well done increases (strengthens) their willingness to perform well in the future. A *negative reinforcement* strengthens desired behaviour by eliminating an undesirable task or situation. Suppose that a machine shop must be cleaned thoroughly every month—a dirty, miserable task. During one particular month when the workers do a less-than-satisfactory job at their normal work assignments, the boss requires the workers to clean the factory rather than bringing in the usual private maintenance service. The employees will be motivated to work harder the next month to avoid the unpleasant cleaning duty again.

Punishment is an undesired consequence of undesirable behaviour. Common forms of punishment used in organizations include reprimands, reduced pay, disciplinary layoffs, and termination (firing). Punishment often does more harm than good. It tends to create an unpleasant environment, fosters hostility and resentment, and suppresses undesirable behaviour only until the supervisor's back is turned.

Managers who rely on *extinction* hope to eliminate undesirable behaviour by not responding to it. The idea is that the behaviour eventually will become "extinct." Suppose, for example, that an employee has the habit of writing memo after memo to his or her manager about insignificant events. If the manager does not respond to any of these memos, the employee probably will stop writing them, and the behaviour will have been squelched.

The effectiveness of reinforcement depends on which type is used and how it is timed. One approach may work best under certain conditions, but some situations lend themselves to the use of more than one approach. Generally, positive reinforcement is considered the most effective, and it is recommended when the manager has a choice.

Continual reinforcement can become tedious for both managers and employees, especially when the same behaviour is being reinforced over and over in the same way. At the start, it may be necessary to reinforce a desired behaviour every time it occurs. However, once a desired behaviour has become more or less established, occasional reinforcement seems to be most effective.

Contemporary Views on Motivation

Learning Objective ③

Describe three contemporary views of motivation: equity theory, expectancy theory, and goal-setting theory.

Maslow's hierarchy of needs and Herzberg's motivation-hygiene theory are popular and widely known theories of motivation. Each is also a significant step up from the relatively narrow views of scientific management and Theories X and Y. But they do have one weakness: each attempts to specify *what* motivates people, but neither explains *why* or *how* motivation develops or is sustained over time. In recent years, managers have begun to explore three other models that take a more dynamic view of motivation. These are equity theory, expectancy theory, and goal-setting theory.

Equity Theory

The **equity theory** of motivation is based on the premise that people are motivated to obtain and preserve equitable treatment for themselves. As used here, *equity* is the distribution of rewards in direct proportion to the contribution of each employee to the organization. Everyone need not receive the *same* rewards, but the rewards should be in accordance with individual contributions.

According to this theory, we tend to implement the idea of equity in the following way: First, we develop our own input-to-outcome ratio. *Inputs* are the time, effort, skills, education, experience, and so on that we contribute to the organization. *Outcomes* are the rewards we get from the organization, such as pay, benefits, recognition, and promotions. Next, we compare this ratio with what we perceive as the input-to-outcome ratio for some other person. It might be a coworker, a friend who works for another firm, or even an average of all the people in our organization. This person is called the *comparison other*. Note that our perception of this person's input-to-outcome ratio may be absolutely correct or completely wrong. However, we believe that it is correct.

If the two ratios are roughly the same, we feel that the organization is treating us equitably. In this case we are motivated to leave things as they are. However, if our ratio is the higher of the two, we feel under-rewarded and are motivated to make changes. We may (1) decrease our own inputs by not working so hard, (2) try to increase our total outcome by asking for a raise in pay, (3) try to get the comparison other to increase some inputs or receive decreased outcomes, (4) leave the work situation, or (5) do a new comparison with a different comparison other.

Equity theory is most relevant to pay as an outcome. Because pay is a very real measure of a person's worth to an organization, comparisons involving pay are a natural part of organizational life. Managers can try to avoid problems arising from inequity by making sure that rewards are distributed on the basis of performance and that everyone clearly understands the basis for his or her own pay.

equity theory a theory of motivation based on the premise that people are motivated to obtain and preserve equitable treatment for themselves

Expectancy Theory

expectancy theory a model of motivation based on the assumption that motivation depends on how much we want something and on how likely we think we are to get it

Expectancy theory, developed by Victor Vroom, is a very complex model of motivation based on a deceptively simple assumption. According to expectancy theory, motivation depends on how much we want something and on how likely we think we are to get it (see Figure 11.5). Consider, for example, the case of three sales representatives who are candidates for promotion to one sales manager's job. Bill has had a very good sales year and always gets good performance evaluations. However, he isn't sure that he wants the job because it involves a great deal of travel, long working hours, and much stress and pressure. Paul wants the job badly but doesn't think he has much chance of getting it. He has had a terrible sales year and gets only mediocre performance evaluations from his present boss. Susan wants the job as much as Paul, and she thinks that she has a pretty good shot at it. Her sales have improved significantly this past year, and her evaluations are the best in the company.

Expectancy theory would predict that Bill and Paul are not very motivated to seek the promotion. Bill doesn't really want it, and Paul doesn't think that he has much of a chance of getting it. Susan, however, is very motivated to seek the promotion because she wants it *and* thinks that she can get it.

Expectancy theory is complex because each action we take is likely to lead to several outcomes; some we may want and others we may not want. For example, a person who works hard and puts in many extra hours may get a pay raise, be promoted, and gain valuable new job skills. However, that person also may be forced to spend less time with his or her family and be forced to cut back on his or her social life.

For one person, the promotion may be paramount, the pay raise and new skills fairly important, and the loss of family and social life of negligible importance. For someone else, the family and social life may be most important, the pay raise of moderate importance, the new skills unimportant, and the promotion undesirable because of the additional hours it would require. The first person would be motivated to work hard and put in the extra hours, whereas the second person would not be at all motivated to do so. In other words, it is the entire bundle of outcomes—and the individual's evaluation of the importance of each outcome—that determines motivation.

Expectancy theory is difficult to apply, but it does provide several useful guidelines for managers. It suggests that managers must recognize that (1) employees work for a variety of reasons, (2) these reasons, or expected outcomes, change over time, and (3) it is necessary to clearly show employees how they can attain the outcomes they desire.

Figure 11.5

Expectancy Theory

Vroom's theory is based on the idea that motivation depends on how much people want something and on how likely they think they are to get it.

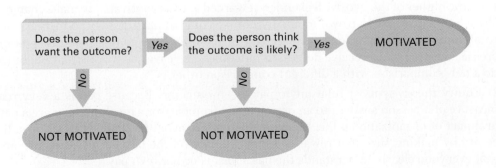

Goal-Setting Theory

Goal-setting theory suggests that employees are motivated to achieve goals that they and their managers establish together. The goal should be very specific, moderately difficult, and one the employee will be committed to achieve.[3] Rewards should be tied directly to goal achievement. Using goal-setting theory, a manager can design rewards that fit employee needs, clarify expectations, maintain equity, and provide reinforcement. A major benefit of this theory is that it provides a good understanding of the goal the employee is to achieve and the rewards that will accrue to the employee if the goal is accomplished.

goal-setting theory a theory of motivation suggesting that employees are motivated to achieve goals that they and their managers establish together

Key Motivation Techniques

Learning Objective 4

Explain several techniques for increasing employee motivation.

Today, it takes more than a generous salary to motivate employees. Increasingly, companies try to motivate employees by satisfying their less tangible needs. In this section we discuss several specific—and somewhat more orthodox—techniques that help managers to boost employee motivation and job satisfaction.

Management by Objectives

Management by objectives (MBO) is a motivation technique in which managers and employees collaborate in setting goals. The primary purpose of MBO is to clarify the roles employees are expected to play in reaching the organization's goals. By allowing individuals to participate in goal setting and performance evaluation, MBO increases their motivation. Most MBO programs consist of a series of five steps.

management by objectives (MBO) a motivation technique in which managers and employees collaborate in setting goals

The first step in setting up an MBO program is to secure the acceptance of top management. It is essential that top managers endorse and participate in the program if others in the firm are to accept it. The commitment of top management also provides a natural starting point for educating employees about the purposes and mechanics of MBO.

Next, preliminary goals must be established. Top management also plays a major role in this activity because the preliminary goals reflect the firm's mission and strategy. The intent of an MBO program is to have these goals filter down through the organization.

The third step, which actually consists of several smaller steps, is the heart of MBO:

1. The manager explains to each employee that he or she has accepted certain goals for the group (the manager as well as the employees) and asks the individual to think about how he or she can help to achieve these goals.

2. The manager later meets with each employee individually. Together they establish goals for the employee. Whenever possible, the goals should be measurable and should specify the time frame for completion (usually one year).

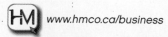

Make Your Job Application Stand Out

You want your job application, résumé, and cover letter to stand out—so does every other applicant. So how do you catch the eye of a prospective employer?

Add a little personality. Alison Hager sent her résumé to twenty advertising agencies but got no response until she wrote in one cover letter, "It would be a dream for me" to work at a small agency. She was called for an interview—and landed the job.

Show what you can do. Show that you understand the challenges the company is facing, and suggest how you might help. Lisa Jacobson, who owns a tutoring company, received dozens of applications for a recent job opening but interviewed (and hired) the one candidate who explained "what she was going to do to make my company better."

Be creative but don't go overboard. Depending on the position you want, an outlandish attention-getting technique can hurt your chances. However, consider an imaginative approach when the job requires creativity. One applicant impressed the head of human resources by submitting a home video about marketing the company's product with his résumé—and he marketed himself into a marketing job.

3. The manager and the employee decide what resources the employee will need to accomplish his or her goals.

As the fourth step, the manager and each employee meet periodically to review the employee's progress. They might agree to modify certain goals during these meetings if circumstances have changed. For example, a sales representative may have set a goal of increasing sales by 20 percent. However, an aggressive competitor may have entered the marketplace, making this goal unattainable. In light of this circumstance, the goal may be revised downward to 10 or 15 percent.

The fifth step is evaluation. At the end of the designated time period, the manager and each employee meet again to determine which of the individual's goals were met, which were not met, and why. The employee's reward (in the form of a pay raise, praise, or promotion) is based primarily on the degree of goal attainment.

As with every other management method, MBO has advantages and disadvantages. MBO can motivate employees by involving them actively in the life of the firm. The collaboration on goal setting and performance appraisal improves communication and makes employees feel that they are an important part of the organization. Periodic review of progress also enhances control within an organization. A major problem with MBO is that it does not work unless the process begins at the top of an organization. In some cases MBO results in excessive paperwork. Also, a manager may not like sitting down and working out goals with subordinates and may instead just assign them goals. Finally, MBO programs prove difficult to implement unless goals are quantifiable.

Job Enrichment

job enrichment a motivation technique that provides employees with more variety and responsibility in their jobs

Job enrichment is a method of motivating employees by providing them with variety in their tasks while giving them some responsibility for, and control over, their jobs. At the same time, employees gain new skills and acquire a broader perspective about how their individual work contributes to the goals of the organization. Earlier in this chapter we noted that Herzberg's motivation-hygiene theory is one rationale for the use of job enrichment; that is, the added responsibility and control that job enrichment confers on employees increases their satisfaction and motivation. Employees at 3M get to spend 15 percent of their time at work on whatever projects they choose regardless of the relationship of these "pet projects" to the employees' regular duties. This type of enrichment can motivate employees and create a variety of benefits for the company.[4] The program produced an unexpected hit product—Post-It Notes.

At times, **job enlargement,** expanding a worker's assignments to include additional but similar tasks, can lead to job enrichment. Job enlargement might mean that a worker on an assembly line who used to connect three wires to components moving down the line now connects five wires. Unfortunately, the added tasks often are just as routine as those the worker performed before the change. In such cases, enlargement may not be effective.

job enlargement
expanding a worker's assignments to include additional but similar tasks

Whereas job enlargement does not really change the routine and monotonous nature of jobs, job enrichment does. Job enrichment requires that added tasks give an employee more responsibility for what he or she does. It provides workers with both more tasks to do and more control over how they perform them. In particular, job enrichment removes many controls from jobs, gives workers more authority, and assigns work in complete, natural units. Moreover, employees frequently are given fresh and challenging job assignments. By blending more planning and decision making into jobs, job enrichment gives work more depth and complexity.

Job redesign is a type of job enrichment in which work is restructured in ways that cultivate the worker-job match. Job redesign can be achieved by combining tasks, forming work groups, or establishing closer customer relationships. Employees often are more motivated when jobs are combined because the increased variety of tasks presents more challenge and therefore more reward. Work groups motivate employees by showing them how their jobs fit within the organization as a whole and how they contribute to its success. Establishing client relationships allows employees to interact directly with customers. Not only does this type of redesign add a personal dimension to employment, but it also provides workers with immediate and relevant feedback about how they are doing their jobs.

job redesign a type of job enrichment in which work is restructured to cultivate the worker-job match

Job enrichment works best when employees seek more challenging work. Of course, not all workers respond positively to job-enrichment programs. Employees must desire personal growth and have the skills and knowledge to perform enriched jobs. Lack of self-confidence, fear of failure, or distrust of management's intentions are likely to lead to ineffective performance on enriched jobs. In addition, some workers do not view their jobs as routine and boring, and others even prefer routine jobs because they find them satisfying. Companies that use job

Job enrichment

Employees at this New Balance plant are enrolled in a job enrichment program. Each person on this work team has been cross-trained to do other team members' jobs.

enrichment as an alternative to specialization also face extra expenses, such as the cost of retraining. Another motivation for job redesign is to reduce employees' stress at work. A job redesign that carefully matches worker to job can prevent stress-related injuries, which constitute about 60 to 80 percent of all work-related injuries. The reduced stress also creates greater motivation.[5]

Behaviour Modification

Behaviour modification is a systematic program of reinforcement to encourage desirable behaviour. Behaviour modification involves both rewards to encourage desirable actions and punishments to discourage undesirable actions. However, studies have shown that rewards, such as compliments and expressions of appreciation, are much more effective behaviour modifiers than punishments, such as reprimands and scorn.

When applied to management, behaviour modification strives to encourage desirable organizational behaviour. Use of this technique begins with identification of a *target behaviour*—the behaviour that is to be changed. (It might be low production levels or a high rate of absenteeism, for example.) Existing levels of this behaviour then are measured. Next, managers provide positive reinforcement in the form of a reward when employees exhibit the *desired behaviour* (such as increased production or less absenteeism). The reward might be praise or a more tangible form of recognition, such as a gift, meal, or trip. Finally, the levels of the target behaviour are measured again to determine whether the desired changes have been achieved. If they have, the reinforcement is maintained. However, if the target behaviour has not changed significantly in the desired direction, the reward system must be changed to one that is likely to be more effective. John Kotter, a renowned Harvard Business School professor, states that this is difficult because the kind of emotional persuasion needed for these changes is not taught in business schools and is not often properly considered in many business settings.[6] The key is to devise effective rewards that not only will modify employees' behaviour in desired ways but also will motivate them. To this end, experts suggest that management should reward quality, loyalty, and productivity.

Flextime

To most people, a work schedule means the standard nine-to-five, forty-hour work week. In reality, though, many people have work schedules that are quite different from this. Police officers, firefighters, restaurant personnel, airline employees, and medical personnel usually have work schedules that are far from standard. Some manufacturers also rotate personnel from shift to shift. And many professional people—such as managers, artists, and lawyers—need more than forty hours each week to get their work done.

The needs and lifestyles of today's workforce are changing. Dual-income families make up a much larger share of the workforce than ever before, and women are one of its fastest-growing sectors. Many employees are responsible for the care of elderly relatives. Recognizing that these changes increase the demand for family time, many employers offer flexible work schedules that not only help employees to manage their time better but also increase employee motivation and job satisfaction.

Flextime is a system in which employees set their own work hours within certain limits determined by employers. Typically, the firm establishes two bands of time: the *core time*, when all employees must be at work, and the *flexible time*, when employees may choose whether to be at work. The only condition is that every employee must work a total of eight hours each day. For example, the hours between 9 and 11 a.m. and 1 and 3 p.m. might be core time, and the hours between 6 and 9 a.m., between 11 a.m. and 1 p.m., and between 3 and 6 p.m. might be flexible time. This would give employees the option of coming in early and getting off early, coming in later and leaving later, or taking an extra long lunch break. But flextime also ensures that everyone is present at certain times, when, for example, conferences with supervisors and department meetings can be scheduled. Another type of flextime allows employees to work a forty-hour work week in four days instead of five. Workers who put in ten hours a day instead of eight get an extra day off each week. Sometimes, smaller firms use flextime to attract and retain employees, especially when they cannot match the salary and benefits package provided by larger companies. By offering a customized work schedule and part-time positions with full-time benefits, firms are able to remain competitive with larger companies.[7]

The sense of independence and autonomy employees gain from having a say in what hours they work can be a motivating factor. In addition, employees who have enough time to deal with non-work issues often work more productively and with greater satisfaction when they are on the job. Two common problems associated with using flextime are (1) supervisors sometimes find their jobs complicated by having employees who come and go at different times and (2) employees without flextime sometimes resent coworkers who have it.

flextime a system in which employees set their own work hours within employer-determined limits

part-time work permanent employment in which individuals work less than a standard work week

job sharing an arrangement whereby two people share one full-time position

Part-Time Work and Job Sharing

Part-time work is permanent employment in which individuals work less than a standard work week. The specific number of hours worked varies, but part-time jobs are structured so that all responsibilities can be completed in the number of hours an employee works. Part-time work is of special interest to parents who want more time with their children and people who simply desire more leisure time. One disadvantage of part-time work is that it often does not provide the benefits that come with a full-time position. This is not, however, the case at Starbucks, where approximately 80 percent of its employees work part time. Starbucks does not treat its part-time employees any differently from its full-time employees; all receive the same access to numerous benefits, which even includes a free pound of coffee every week.[8]

Job sharing (sometimes referred to as *work sharing*) is an arrangement whereby two people share one full-time position. One job sharer might work from 8 a.m. to noon, and the other, from 1 to 5 p.m., one might work from Monday at 8 a.m. to 1 p.m. on Wednesday and the other from noon on Wednesday to

Part-time work

At Starbucks, part-time employees receive the same level of benefits as full-time employees.

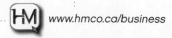

5 p.m. on Friday, or they might alternate work days. Job sharing combines the security of a full-time position with the flexibility of a part-time job.

Job sharing provides a unique opportunity for firms to attract highly skilled employees who might not be available on a full-time basis. In addition, companies can save on expenses by reducing the cost of benefits and avoiding the disruptions of employee turnover. Employees who opt for the flexibility of job sharing may be giving up some of the benefits received for full-time work. In addition, job sharing is difficult if tasks are not easily divisible or if two people do not work or communicate well with one another.

Telecommuting

A growing number of companies allow **telecommuting,** working at home all the time or for a portion of the work week. Personal computers, modems, fax machines, voice mail, cellular phones, and overnight couriers all facilitate the work-at-home trend. Working at home means that individuals can set their own hours and have more time with their families.

Employees equipped with the right technology can work for companies around the corner or around the world. Companies generally require telecommuters to participate in regular teleconference or videoconference meetings, file weekly e-mail reports, and stay in close touch by phone or instant messaging as needed.

Companies that allow telecommuting experience several benefits, including increased productivity, lower real estate and travel costs, reduced employee absenteeism and turnover, increased work-life balance and improved morale, and access to additional labour pools. Pitney Bowes reports that an additional benefit gained when employees work from home is the company's image as a good corporate citizen because the program helps to decrease pollution and traffic congestion.[9] Among the disadvantages to telecommuting are feelings of isolation, putting in longer hours, and being distracted by family or household responsibilities. In addition, some supervisors have difficulty monitoring productivity. Although most bosses say that they trust their staff to work from home, many think that home workers are work-shy and less productive than office-based staff. A survey conducted in the United Kingdom found that up to 38 percent of managers surveyed believe that home workers are less productive and 22 percent think that working from home is an excuse for time off. In addition, some supervisors have difficulty monitoring productivity.[10]

Employee Empowerment

Many companies increase employee motivation and satisfaction through the use of empowerment. **Empowerment** means making employees more involved in their jobs and in the operations of the organization by increasing their participation in decision making. With empowerment, control no longer flows exclusively from the top levels of the organization downward. Empowered employees have a voice in what they do and how and when they do it. In some organizations, employees' input is restricted to individual choices, such as when to take breaks. In other companies, their responsibilities may encompass more far-reaching issues, including ensuring customer satisfaction through the granting of minor concessions or perks.

For empowerment to work effectively, management must be involved. Managers should set expectations, communicate standards, institute periodic evaluations, and guarantee follow-up. Effectively implemented, empowerment can lead to increased job satisfaction, improved job performance, higher-self esteem, and increased organizational commitment. Obstacles to empowerment include resistance on the part of management, distrust of management on the part of workers, insufficient training, and poor communication between management and employees.

Employee Ownership

Some organizations are discovering that a highly effective technique for motivating employees is **employee ownership**, that is, employees own the company they work for because they are stockholders. Employee-owned businesses directly reward employees for success. When the company enjoys increased sales or lower costs, employees benefit directly. As a means to motivate top executives and, frequently, middle-ranking managers who are working long days for what are generally considered poor salaries, some firms provide stock options as part of the employee compensation package. The option is simply the right to buy shares of the firm within a prescribed time at a set price. If the firm does well and its stock price rises past the set price (presumably because of all the work being done by the employee), the employee can exercise the option and immediately sell the stock and cash in on the company's success.

employee ownership a situation in which employees own the company they work for because they are stockholders

There has been some controversy surrounding stock options in recent years, primarily involving backdating. Options are supposed to be recorded at the price of the stock on the grant date, however, some companies have used earlier dates, when the stock was at a lower price, thus creating a situation where the options are already "in the money." Most Canadian firms are looking at alternatives such as Deferred Share Units (DSU) and Restricted Share Units (RSU), which are similar to actual shares. The intention is to line senior management and employees up with shareholders so they benefit equally when the share price appreciates. This presumably provides an incentive to management to avoid gaming, a process whereby the share price is artificially inflated through increased trades and other actions, to create value in the options.

Teams and Teamwork

Learning Objective 5
Understand the types, development, and uses of teams.

The concepts of teams and teamwork may be most commonly associated with sports, but they also are integral parts of business organizations. This organizational structure is popular because it encourages employees to participate more fully in business decisions.

The growing number of companies organizing their workforces into teams reflects an effort to increase employee productivity and creativity because team members work on specific goals and are given greater autonomy. This leads to greater job satisfaction as employees feel more involved in the management process.[11]

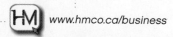

What Is a Team?

In a business organization, a **team** is a group of workers functioning together as a unit to complete a common goal or purpose. A team may be assigned any number of tasks or goals, from development of a new product to selling that product.[12] Although teamwork might seem like a simple concept learned on soccer or football fields, since teams function as a microcosm of the larger organization, it is important to understand the types, development, and general nature of teams.

Types of Teams

There are several types of teams within businesses that function in specific ways to achieve different purposes including problem-solving teams, self-managed teams, cross-functional teams, and virtual teams.

Problem-Solving Teams The most common type of team in business organizations is the **problem-solving team.** It is generally used temporarily in order to bring knowledgeable employees together to tackle a specific problem. Once the problem is solved, the team typically is disbanded. For example, when General Motors (GM) announced its plans to close an assembly plant in Wilmington, Delaware, employees formed problem-solving teams with managers to improve quality control and reduce costs. The teams' suggested changes were so effective that within two years, the factory became the lowest-cost producer of all General Motors' factories. This prompted GM to keep the plant open, and the employees' jobs were saved.[13]

In extraordinary cases, an expert team may be needed to generate groundbreaking ideas. A **virtuoso team** consists of exceptionally highly skilled and talented individuals brought together to produce significant change. As with other kinds of problem-solving teams, virtuoso teams usually are assembled on a temporary basis. Instead of being task-oriented, they focus on producing ideas and provoking change that could have an impact on the company and its industry. Because of the high skill level of their members, virtuoso teams can be difficult to manage. And unlike traditional teams, virtuoso teams place an emphasis on individuality over teamwork, which can cause further conflict. However, their conflicts usually are viewed as competitive and therefore productive in generating the most substantial ideas.[14]

Self-Managed Work Teams **Self-managed teams** are groups of employees with the authority and skills to manage themselves. Experts

team a group of workers functioning together as a unit to complete a common goal or purpose

problem-solving team a team of knowledgeable employees brought together to tackle a specific problem

virtuoso team a team of exceptionally highly skilled and talented individuals brought together to produce significant change

self-managed teams groups of employees with the authority and skills to manage themselves

▲
What type of team is this?

At New Balance, team members discuss ideas for improving efficiency during a bi-weekly meeting of workers and supervisors. Ideas from factory workers have led to improved performance and, in turn, have helped the employees keep their jobs from going overseas.

ADVANTAGES	DISADVANTAGES
• Boosts employee morale	• Additional training costs
• Increases productivity	• Teams may be disorganized
• Aids innovation	• Conflicts may arise
• Reduces employee boredom	• Leadership role may be unclear

Figure 11.6

Advantages and Disadvantages of Self-Managed Teams

While self-managed teams provide benefits, managers must recognize their limitations.

suggest that workers on self-managed teams are more motivated and satisfied because they have more task variety and job control. On many work teams, members rotate through all the jobs for which the team is responsible. Some organizations cross-train the entire team so that everyone can perform everyone else's job. In a traditional business structure, management is responsible for hiring and firing employees, establishing budgets, purchasing supplies, conducting performance reviews, and taking corrective action. Self-managed teams can take over some or all of these management functions. Xerox, Procter & Gamble, and Ferrari have used self-managed teams successfully. At the Ferrari factory, work teams perform a variety of tasks for about an hour and a half before a vehicle moves on to the next team. Employees learn more job skills, are more interested in their work, and develop a greater sense of pride in and loyalty to Ferrari.[15] The major advantages and disadvantages of self managed teams are mentioned in Figure 11.6.

Cross-Functional Teams Traditionally, businesses have organized employees into departments based on a common function or specialty. However, increasingly, business organizations are faced with projects that require a diversity of skills not available within a single department. A **cross-functional team** consists of individuals with varying specialties, expertise, and skills who are brought together to achieve a common task. For example, a purchasing agent might create a cross-functional team with representatives from various departments to gain insight into useful purchases for the company. This structure avoids departmental separation and allows greater efficiency when there is a single goal. Although cross-functional teams aren't necessarily self-managed, most self-managed teams are cross-functional. They can also be cross-divisional, such as at Mercedes Benz, which has begun assembling cross-functional teams to improve quality and cut costs in research and development. Instead of a single team per model, cross-functional teams will develop standard parts to be used in different Mercedes vehicles.[16] Cross-functional teams also can include a variety of people from outside the company, such as the cross-functional team of ergonomists, users, and university scientists that developed the new natural ergonomic keyboard for Microsoft. Owing to their speed, flexibility, and increased employee satisfaction, it is likely that the use of cross-functional teams will increase.

cross-functional team a team of individuals with varying specialties, expertise, and skills that are brought together to achieve a common task

Virtual Teams With the advent of sophisticated communications technology, it is no longer necessary for teams to be geographically close. A **virtual team** consists of members who are geographically dispersed but communicate electronically. In fact, team members may never meet in person but rely solely on e-mail, teleconferences, faxes, voice mail, and other technological interactions. In today's global environment, virtual teams connect employees on a common task across continents, oceans, time zones, and organizations. In some cases, the physical distances between participants and the lack of face-to-face interaction can be difficult when deadlines approach or communication is not clear.

virtual team a team consisting of members who are geographically dispersed but communicate electronically

Developing and Using Effective Teams

When a team is first developed, it takes time for the members to establish roles, relationships, delegation of duties, and other attributes of an effective team. As a team matures, it passes through five stages of development, shown in Figure 11.7.

Forming In the first stage, *forming*, team members are introduced to one another and begin to develop a social dynamic. The members of the team are still unsure how to relate to one another, what behaviours are considered acceptable, and what the ground rules for the team are. Through group member interaction over time, team members become more comfortable, and a group dynamic begins to emerge.

Storming During the *storming* stage, the interaction may be volatile, and the team may lack unity. Because the team is still relatively new, this is the stage at which goals and objectives begin to develop. Team members will brainstorm to develop ideas and plans and establish a broad-ranging agenda. It is important at this stage for team members to grow more comfortable around the others so that they can contribute openly. At this time, the leadership role likely will be formally undefined. A team member might emerge as the informal leader. The success or failure of the ideas in storming determines how long until the team reaches the next stage.

Norming After storming and the first large burst of activity, the team begins to stabilize during the *norming* stage. During this process, each person's role within the group starts to become apparent, and members begin to recognize the roles of others. A sense of unity will become stronger. If it hasn't already occurred, an identified leader will emerge. The group still may be somewhat volatile at this point and may regress back to the second stage if any conflict, especially over the leadership role, occurs.

Performing The fourth stage, *performing*, is when the team achieves its full potential. It is usually slow to develop and occurs when the team begins to focus strongly on the assigned task and away from team-development issues. The members of the team work in harmony under the established roles to accomplish the necessary goals.

Adjourning In the final stage, *adjourning*, the team is disbanded because the project has been completed. Team members may be reassigned to other teams or tasks. This stage does not always occur if the team is placed together for a task with no specific date for completion. For example, a marketing team for Best Buy might continue to develop promotional efforts for a store even after a specific promotional task has been accomplished. This stage is especially common in problem-solving teams that are dismantled after the assigned problem has been resolved.

Figure 11.7

Stages of Team Development

When attempting to develop teams, managers must understand that multiple stages are generally required.

FORMING
The team is new. Members get to know each other.

STORMING
The team may be volatile. Goals and objectives are developed.

NORMING
The team stabilizes. Roles and duties are accepted and recognized.

PERFORMING
The team is dynamic. Everyone makes a focused effort to accomplish goals.

ADJOURNING
The team is finished. The goals have been accomplished and the team is disbanded.

Roles Within a Team

Within any team, each member has a role to play in helping the team attain its objectives. Each of these roles adds important dimensions to team member interactions. The group member who pushes forward toward goals and places the objective first is playing the *task-specialist role* by concentrating fully on the assigned task. In a cross-functional team this might be the person with the most expertise relating to the current task. The *socio-emotional role* is played by the individual who supports and encourages the emotional needs of the other members. This person places the team members' personal needs over the task of the team. While this might sound unimportant, the socio-emotional member's dedication to team cohesiveness will lead to greater unity and higher productivity. The leader of the team and, possibly, others, will play a *dual role*. This dual role is a combination of both the socio-emotional and task-specialist roles because this individual focuses on both the task and the team. The team leader might not always play a dual role, but the team is likely to be most successful when he or she does. Sometimes an individual assumes the *non-participant role*. This role behaviour is characterized by a person who does not contribute to accomplishing the task and does not provide favourable input with respect to team members' socio-emotional needs.

Team Cohesiveness

Developing a unit from a diverse group of personalities, specialties, backgrounds, and work styles can be challenging and complicated. In a cohesive team, the members get along and are able to accomplish their tasks effectively. There are factors that affect cohesiveness within a team. Teams generally are ideal when they contain five to twelve people. Fewer than five people is too few to accomplish tasks and generate a variety of ideas. More than twelve is too large because members do not develop relationships, might feel too intimidated to speak, or might disconnect. It also may be beneficial to have team members introduce themselves and describe their past work experiences. This activity will foster familiarity and shared experiences. One of the most reliable ways to build cohesiveness within a team is through competition with other teams. When two teams are competing for a single prize or recognition, they are forced to put aside conflict and accomplish their goal. By adding an incentive to finishing the task, the team automatically becomes more goal-oriented. Also, a favourable appraisal from an outsider can strengthen team cohesiveness. Since the team is being praised as a group, team members recognize their contribution as a unit. Teams are also more successful when goals have become agreed on. A team that is clear about its objective will focus more on accomplishing it. Frequent interaction also builds cohesiveness as relationships strengthen and familiarity increases.

Team Conflict and How to Resolve It

Conflict occurs when a disagreement arises between two or more team members. Conflict traditionally has been viewed as negative but, if handled properly, conflict can improve a team. For example, if two team members disagree about a certain decision, both might analyze the situation more closely to determine the best choice. As long as conflict is handled in a respectful and professional manner, it can improve the quality

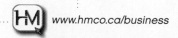 www.hmco.ca/business

of work produced. If conflict turns hostile and affects the work environment, steps must be taken to arrive at a suitable compromise. Compromises can be difficult in a business organization because neither party ends up getting everything he or she wants. The best solution is a middle-ground alternative in which each party is satisfied to some degree. It is best to avoid attempting to minimize or ignore conflicts within a group because this can cause the conflict to grow as members concentrate on the problem instead of the task. However the conflict is resolved, it is important to remember that conflict must be acknowledged if it is to be either resolved or serve a constructive purpose.

Benefits and Limitations of Teams

Teamwork within a company has been credited as a key to reducing turnover and costs and increasing production, quality, and customer service. There is also evidence that working in teams leads to higher levels of job satisfaction among employees and a harmonious work environment. Thus an increasingly large number of companies are considering teams as a viable organizational structure. However, the process of reorganizing into teams can be stressful and time-consuming with no guarantee that the team will develop effectively. If a team lacks cohesiveness and is unable to resolve conflict, the company may experience lower productivity.

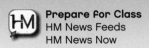
Prepare for Class
HM News Feeds
HM News Now

→ **RETURN TO INSIDE BUSINESS**

While different theories can explain employees' behaviour and provide an insight into why some employees succeed more than others, it is still important to develop an atmosphere where employees feel important—that their work matters. And, of course, it does—we would not have the goods and services that we enjoy if not for the talents and expertise of the many people who provide for our needs and requirements each day.

When asked, employees note that it is the softer side of management—the human resource functions that can make or break their job satisfaction. And part of that relates to compensation or rewards for a job well done. At issue in many companies that espouse unique and intriguing benefits (use of cottages, sabbaticals, advanced education) is that they usually apply to all employees equally, regardless of performance. How do we recognize exemplary service to the company without triggering a system that has been set up to be "performance neutral"?

Questions
1. Propose a compensation plan that rewards only the top performers in your company.
2. What are the risks of such a plan?
3. Consider what motivates you—what benefits or perks would you accept in place of a cash bonus?

CHAPTER REVIEW

1 **Explain what motivation is.**

Motivation is the individual internal process that energizes, directs, and sustains behaviour. Motivation is affected by employee morale—that is, the employee's feelings about the job, superiors, and the firm itself. Motivation, morale, and job satisfaction are closely related.

2 **Understand some major historical perspectives on motivation.**

One of the first approaches to employee motivation was Frederick Taylor's scientific management, the application of scientific principles to the management of work and workers. Taylor believed that employees worked only for money and that they must be closely supervised and managed. This thinking led to the piece-rate system, under which employees were paid a certain amount for each unit they produced. The Hawthorne Studies attempted to determine the effects of the work environment on productivity. Results of these studies indicated that human factors affect productivity more than do physical aspects of the workplace. Maslow's hierarchy of needs suggests that people are motivated by five sets of needs. In ascending order of importance, these motivators are physiological, safety, social, esteem, and self-actualization needs. People are motivated by the lowest set of needs that remains unfulfilled. As needs at one level are satisfied, people try to satisfy needs at the next level. Frederick Herzberg found that job satisfaction and dissatisfaction are influenced by two distinct sets of factors. Motivation factors, including recognition and responsibility, affect an employee's degree of satisfaction, but their absence does not necessarily cause dissatisfaction. Hygiene factors, including pay and working conditions, affect an employee's degree of dissatisfaction but do not affect satisfaction.

Theory X is a concept of motivation that assumes that employees dislike work and will function effectively only in a highly controlled work environment. Thus, to achieve an organization's goals, managers must coerce, control, and threaten employees. This theory generally is consistent with Taylor's scientific management. Theory Y is more in keeping with the results of the Hawthorne Studies and the human relations movement. It suggests that employees can be motivated to behave as responsible members of the organization. Theory Z emphasizes long-term employment, collective decision making, individual responsibility for the outcomes of decisions, informal control, and a holistic concern for employees. Reinforcement theory is based on the idea that people will repeat behaviour that is rewarded and will avoid behaviour that is punished.

3 **Describe three contemporary views of motivation: equity theory, expectancy theory, and goal-setting theory.**

Equity theory maintains that people are motivated to obtain and preserve equitable treatment for themselves. Expectancy theory suggests that our motivation depends on how much we want something and how likely we think we are to get it. Goal-setting theory suggests that employees are motivated to achieve a goal that they and their managers establish together.

4 **Explain several techniques for increasing employee motivation.**

Management by objectives (MBO) is a motivation technique in which managers and employees collaborate in setting goals. MBO motivates employees by getting them more involved in their jobs and in the organization as a whole. Job enrichment seeks to motivate employees by varying their tasks and giving them more responsibility for and control over their jobs. Job enlargement, expanding a worker's assignments to include additional tasks, is one aspect of job enrichment. Job redesign is a type of job enrichment in which work is restructured to improve the worker-job match. Behaviour modification uses reinforcement to encourage desirable behaviour. Rewards for productivity, quality, and loyalty change employees' behaviour in desired ways and also increase motivation.

Allowing employees to work more flexible hours is another way to build motivation and job satisfaction. Flextime is a system of work scheduling that allows workers to set their own hours as long as they fall within limits established by employers. Part-time work is permanent employment in which individuals work less than a standard work week. Job sharing is an arrangement whereby two people share one full-time position. Telecommuting allows employees to work at home all or part of the work week. All these types of work arrangements give employees more time outside the workplace to deal with family responsibilities or to enjoy free time. Employee empowerment, self-managed work teams, and employee ownership are all techniques that boost employee motivation. Empowerment increases employees' involvement in their jobs by increasing their decision-making authority. Self-managed work teams are groups of employees with the authority and skills to manage themselves. When employees participate in ownership programs, such as employee stock ownership plans (ESOPs), they have more incentive to make the company succeed and therefore work more effectively.

5 Understand the types, development, and uses of teams.

A large number of companies use teams to increase their employees' productivity. In a business organization, a team is a group of workers functioning together as a unit to complete a common goal or purpose. There are several types of teams within businesses that function in specific ways to achieve different purposes. A problem-solving team is a team of knowledgeable employees brought to-

gether to tackle a specific problem. A virtuoso team is a team of highly skilled and talented individuals brought together to produce significant change A virtual team is a team consisting of members who are geographically dispersed but communicate electronically. A cross-functional team is a team of individuals with varying specialties, expertise, and skills.

The five stages of team development are forming, storming, norming, performing, and adjourning. As a team develops, it should become more productive and unified. The four roles within teams are task specialist, socio-emotional, dual, and non-participative. Each of these roles plays a specific part in the team's interaction. For a team to be successful, members must learn how to resolve and manage conflict so that the team can work cohesively to accomplish goals.

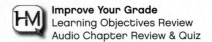

Improve Your Grade
Learning Objectives Review
Audio Chapter Review & Quiz

Review Questions

1. How do scientific management and Theory X differ from the human relations movement and Theory Y?
2. How did the results of the Hawthorne Studies influence researchers' thinking about employee motivation?
3. What are the five sets of needs in Maslow's hierarchy? How are a person's needs related to motivation?
4. What are the two dimensions in Herzberg's theory? What kinds of elements affect each dimension?
5. What is the fundamental premise of reinforcement theory?
6. According to equity theory, how does an employee determine whether he or she is being treated equitably?
7. According to expectancy theory, what two variables determine motivation?
8. Identify and describe the major techniques for motivating employees.
9. Describe the steps involved in the MBO process.
10. What are the objectives of MBO? What do you think might be its disadvantages?
11. How does employee participation increase motivation?
12. Describe the steps in the process of behaviour modification.
13. Identify and describe the major types of teams.
14. What are the major benefits and limitations associated with the use of self-managed teams?
15. Explain the major stages of team development.

Discussion Questions

1. How might managers make use of Maslow's hierarchy of needs in motivating employees? What problems would they encounter?
2. Do the various theories of motivation contradict each other or complement each other? Explain.
3. What combination of motivational techniques do you think would result in the best overall motivation and reward system?
4. Reinforcement theory and behaviour modification have been called demeaning because they tend to treat people "like mice in a maze." Do you agree?
5. In what ways are team cohesiveness and team conflict related?

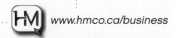

CASE STUDY

American Flatbread Fires up Employees

George Schenk's passion is making work meaningful, sustainable, and personal. He learned about wood-fired cooking from his grandmother in Vermont and, years later, rekindled his love of cooking with fire when he founded the American Flatbread Company. His company produces frozen wood-fired flatbread pizzas from all-natural, locally grown ingredients, hand-made by 100 employees in Waitsfield and Middlebury, Vermont.

On Mondays, Tuesdays, Wednesdays, and Thursdays, two shifts of employees stoke the bakeries' wood-fired ovens to a temperature of 800°F [427°C] and prepare the flatbreads. After the products are baked, frozen, and wrapped, they are shipped to grocery and specialty stores, such as Whole Foods supermarkets. Both bakeries are transformed into casual pizza restaurants on Friday and Saturday nights, where diners sit in view of the gigantic ovens to enjoy salads and flatbreads. Schenk also has licensed American Flatbread's brand and wood-fired cooking methods to bakeries and restaurants in New England and in Los Alamos, California. One-third of American Flatbread's annual revenue comes from the licensing deals and restaurant receipts, whereas the wholesale frozen pizza operation contributes the remaining two-thirds.

Schenk's enthusiasm for wood-fired cooking is matched by his enthusiasm for building a business in which the work has long-term significance to the employees and the community. Among American Flatbread's goals are to "create a pleasant, fulfilling, sustainable, and secure workplace" and "to trust one another and practice respectful relationships with everyone involved in this work."

Another goal mentioned in the mission statement is to be grateful, respectful, and forgiving—and to encourage the same in others. In line with this goal, Schenk has worked hard to avoid what he calls "founder's syndrome," the notion that the founder can do nothing wrong. His managers and employees know they can speak up about their mistakes and not lose the opportunity to try new things.

Jennifer Moffroid, the company's director of marketing, stresses that the founder has created an environment in which employees can do work that is in keeping with what they want for their lives.

Making the workday fun is one of Schenk's priorities, as is making the workplace an inviting place to be. Moffroid also notes that Schenk not only delegates, but he also "empowers employees and celebrates their work." The company's seven senior managers are involved in decision making, and every suggestion is evaluated on its merit, not on its source. "We're all in this together," Schenk says.

Since the beginning, American Flatbread has supported local food producers and given back to the community in a variety of ways. For example, the restaurants hold "benefit bakes" to raise money for causes such as public health clinics and habitat preservation. In turn, the community has come to the company's aid on more than one occasion. When flood waters inundated American Flatbread's bakery, people came from miles around to clean and rebuild the facility. Thanks to this outpouring of support, the bakery was able to reopen in only seven days.

Today, the Vermont bakeries turn out 10,000 flatbreads every week; the California bakery produces another 4,000 for distribution in western states. Schenk keeps the company's values in the spotlight by writing a dedication for each week's menu. These dedications focus employees on what's important and provide "food for thought" for restaurant customers. Sharing values, being "a good neighbour," and building trusting, respectful relationships with stakeholders have enabled American Flatbread to keep employees happy and productive, minimize turnover, and strengthen financial performance.

For more information about this company, go to www.americanflatbread.com.

Questions:

1. Does George Schenk manage American Flatbread as a type A or a type Z firm? Support your answer.

2. Would you recommend that American Flatbread offer bakery and restaurant employees flextime arrangements? Explain.

3. How has George Schenk paved the way for empowerment at his company?

BUILDING SKILLS FOR CAREER SUCCESS

1. Developing Critical-Thinking Skills

This chapter has described several theories managers can use as guidelines in motivating employees to do the best job possible for the company. Among these theories are Maslow's hierarchy of needs, equity theory, expectancy theory, and goal-setting theory. How effective would each of these theories be in motivating you to be a more productive employee?

Assignment

1. Identify five job needs that are important to you.
2. Determine which of the theories mentioned above would work best to satisfy your job needs.
3. Prepare a two-page report explaining how you reached these conclusions.

2. Building Team Skills

By increasing employees' participation in decision making, empowerment makes workers feel more involved in their jobs and the operations of the organization. While empowerment may seem like a commonsense idea, it is a concept not found universally in the workplace. If you had empowerment in your job, how would you describe it?

Assignment

1. Use brainstorming to explore the concept of empowerment.
   a. Write each letter of the word *empowerment* in a vertical column on a sheet of paper or on the classroom chalkboard.
   b. Think of several words that begin with each letter.
   c. Write the words next to the appropriate letter.
2. Formulate a statement by choosing one word from each letter that best describes what empowerment means to you.

3. Analyze the statement.
   a. How relevant is the statement for you in terms of empowerment? Or empowerment in your workplace?
   b. What changes must occur in your workplace for you to have empowerment?
   c. How would you describe yourself as an empowered employee?
   d. What opportunities would empowerment give to you in your workplace?
4. Prepare a report of your findings.

3. Improving Communication Skills

Suppose that you and a friend went into the auto repair business some years ago. You had the technical expertise, and he had the business knowledge. Although funds were tight for the first three years, your customer base grew, and you were able to hire extra help and expand business hours. Your business is now six years old and very successful. You have five people working under you. Henry, your most productive employee, wants to be promoted to a supervisory position. However, two other employees, Jack and Fred, have seniority over Henry, and you anticipate much dissension and poor morale if you go ahead and promote Henry. Henry clearly deserves the supervisory position because of his hard work and superior skills, but you stand to lose the other two employees if you promote him.

Assignment

1. Analyze the scenario, and answer these questions:
   a. Will you promote Henry? If so, why?
   b. How can you motivate Jack and Fred to stay with you if you promote Henry?
2. Refer to specific motivational techniques or theories to explain your reasoning in resolving the situation with Henry, Jack, and Fred.
3. Prepare a three-page report outlining and justifying your decision.

HM **Prepare for Class**
Exploring the Internet

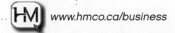

RUNNING A BUSINESS PART IV
Inside the People Business at Finagle A Bagel

People are a vital ingredient in Finagle A Bagel's recipe for success. As a quick-serve business, the company strives for high turnover in food, not employees. In fact, careful attention to human resources management has enabled Finagle A Bagel to continue expanding its market share without spending money on advertising. Low workforce turnover means less money and time spent on recruiting and training—an important financial consideration for a fast-growing business. It also means that Finagle A Bagel has the human resources strength to combine super service with fresh food for a distinctive competitive advantage in a crowded marketplace.

The Right People in the Right Place

"We depend on our crew at the store level—who are interacting with our guests every day—to know their jobs, to understand the company mission, and to communicate with the guests," says Heather Robertson, who directs the company's marketing, human resources, and research and development. "And once we get them on board, people don't leave our company. They just stay. They realize that it can be a career for them."

A sizable number of Finagle A Bagel's managers and employees (including Robertson) were hired years ago and became so excited about the product, the company, and the customers that they simply stayed. Many remain with Finagle A Bagel because they prefer the more personal atmosphere of a 320-employee business over the relatively faceless anonymity of a gigantic corporation. "It's really unusual to have one-on-one interaction on a daily basis with the president of the company or any senior executive member of the company," Robertson states. "Our cashiers, our café attendants, our bakers, and our managers know they can pick up the phone at any point and call anybody here and say, 'Here's my problem. How do I fix it?' or 'I need your help.' The size of our company allows us to do that, and the culture of the company encourages that."

Because bagels are an integral part of every menu item, employees who join Finagle A Bagel must "love" bagels, regardless of any other skills or experiences they bring to their jobs. When Robertson advertises to fill an open position in Finagle A Bagel's headquarters, for example, she always mentions this requirement. As résumés come in, she sorts them according to whether the candidates indicate a fondness for bagels. Those who fail to mention it are automatically disqualified from consideration.

Different Kinds of Managers for Different Locations

Alan Litchman, Finagle A Bagel's copresident, says that selecting a candidate to manage one of the Boston stores is easier than selecting one for a suburban store. Given the inner-city location of the company's support centre, he or another executive can get to the Boston stores more quickly if a problem arises. Moreover, the city stores compete by providing speedy, accurate service to busy customers who have little time to waste waiting in line. Paulo Pereira, general manager of the Harvard Square store in Cambridge, has become an expert at squeezing inefficiencies from the city stores so that customers are in and out more quickly. By increasing the number of customers served each day and slashing the number of bagels left over at closing, Pereira boosts both sales revenues and profits.

When selecting a manager for a suburban store, Litchman looks for people with an "owner-operator mentality" who have the drive, initiative, and know-how to build business locally. His message to a potential general manager is: "If you want to be a franchisee but don't have the capital, or if you want to own your own business, we're going to put you in business. You don't have to give us any money to do that. And if your store achieves more than a certain level of sales or profits, we'll start splitting the bottom line with you in a bonus program." Consider Nick Cochran, who worked his way up from assistant manager to general manager of the store in Wayland, an affluent Boston suburb. Cochran's enthusiasm for quality and service has drawn a highly loyal customer following and contributed to the Wayland store's success.

Hiring and Motivating Store Personnel

General managers such as Cochran and Pereira are responsible for recruiting, interviewing, hiring, training, motivating, and evaluating store-level personnel. They assign job responsibilities according to the skills and strengths of each manager and employee, but they also expect everyone to work as a team during extremely busy periods. In addition to motivating general managers by offering bonuses based on meeting revenue and profit goals, Finagle A Bagel encourages crew members to take advantage of extra training and internal promotions.

"In a company our size," stresses copresident Laura Trust, "there is always opportunity. You just have to find the right fit for the individual." In fact, says her husband, "The best supervisors, coordinators, assistant managers, or managers in any unit—by far—are the ones who have started with us at a lower level and worked their way up."

Diverse Workforce, Family Business

Finagle A Bagel has an extremely diverse workforce made up of people originally from Latin America, Europe, western Africa, and many other areas. Despite diversity's many advantages—including creativity, flexibility, and the ability to relate to a broader customer base—it also can create communications challenges when English is not an employee's native language. To avoid confusion, Litchman and Trust insist that employees speak only in English when addressing customers.

As a small, family-run business, Finagle A Bagel sees its workforce as a group of unique individuals, not interchangeable cogs in an impersonal corporate machine. Trust feels strongly that "there's a responsibility that you have to your employees and to your colleagues. These people work for you—they work hard to try and move your company forward—and their efforts need to be recognized." Because the business is still small, she adds, "the people who have become a part of the management team are very much like family to Alan and me. If you run your company that way, then you'll be successful because everybody believes that you care about not only the work they do but everything they do, and every part of their lives affects their job."

Questions

1. What effect has diversity had on Finagle A Bagel?

2. If you were the general manager of a downtown Finagle A Bagel store, what job description and job specification would you prepare for a cashier? Based on these, what kinds of questions would you ask when interviewing candidates for this position?

3. Which of Herzberg's motivation factors are Trust and Litchman emphasizing for general managers?

4. Would it be feasible for Finagle A Bagel to apply the concept of flextime to store employees? To senior managers at the headquarters facility? Explain.

CHAPTER 12

Building Customer Relationships Through Effective Marketing

Your Guide to Success in Business

Why this chapter matters
To develop competitive product offerings, businesses must be able to identify target customer groups and understand customer behaviour.

LEARNING OBJECTIVES

1. Understand *marketing* and management of customer relationships.

2. Explain how marketing adds value by creating utility.

3. Trace the development of the marketing concept.

4. Understand what markets are and how they are classified.

5. Identify the four elements of the marketing mix and be aware of their importance in developing a marketing strategy.

6. Explain how the marketing environment affects strategic market planning.

7. Understand the major components of a marketing plan.

8. Describe market measurement and sales forecasting.

9. Distinguish between a marketing information system and marketing research.

10. Identify the major steps in the consumer buying decision process and the sets of factors that can influence this process.

Trend Watching—Following Consumer Behaviour Trends

According to Industry Canada, the average Canadian household spending of $60,000 is dominated first by personal taxes (20 percent), shelter (18 percent), transportation (14 percent), and food (11 percent). The balance ranges from choices for recreation (5 percent) to reading material of various sorts (0.5 percent). Marketers can learn about the way consumers intend to spend their dollars by looking at trends. For example, the trend toward leasing rather than purchasing a personal vehicle has continued to grow since 1986 and is now over 11 percent in comparison to only 2 percent then. Similarly, Canadians are flying more than ever before, increasing spending by 4 percent per year since 1982 and currently averaging over $1,715 per household. More than 75 percent of the $6,684 we spend on food (compared to $4,131 in 1982) is bought from stores. And today's Canadian households only spend 15 to 30 minutes (versus 45 minutes 10 years ago) preparing an average meal resulting in an increase in the purchase and consumption of more processed foods. According to research by Health Canada, "the single most frequently mentioned obstacle to healthy eating was lack of time." And, interestingly, food choices are increasingly positioned as a wellness product by the industry—a trend that may have originated in response to baby boomers seeking to delay the aging process. For example, to help prevent certain health conditions, an increasing number of consumers are turning to what may be called "nutraceutical/functional foods," such as fish containing high levels of omega-3 oils. Furthermore, the growing health-conscious market, made up mostly of younger, college educated Canadians are identified as driving the organic food market.

Based on information from Industry Canada, Strategis website, *The Consumer Trends Report*, Chapter 9, Consumer Spending, accessed January 7, 2007, http://consumer.ic.gc.ca/epic/site/oca-bc.nsf/en/ca02117e.html#a95.

DID YOU KNOW?

Teens determine "what's cool," and they influence people slightly younger and slightly older than they are thereby helping to create trends in the marketplace.

KEY TERMS

marketing (346)
relationship marketing (347)
customer relationship management (CRM) (348)
customer lifetime value (348)
form utility (348)
utility (349)

place utility (349)
time utility (349)
possession utility (349)
marketing concept (350)
market (352)
marketing strategy (353)
marketing mix (353)

target market (353)
undifferentiated approach (354)
market segment (354)
market segmentation (354)
marketing plan (359)
sales forecast (361)
marketing information system (362)

marketing research (362)
buying behaviour (364)
consumer buying behaviour (364)
business buying behaviour (364)
personal income (366)
disposable income (366)
discretionary income (366)

ACE the Test
Crossword Puzzle
Flashcards

In today, out tomorrow—the quest for cool drives much of the buying done by teenagers and young adults. Companies that offer products based on the newest trend or latest pop culture development know that they have to move quickly, before a sales frenzy becomes a fizzle. This is why many companies hire trend consultants or specialized researchers to help them spot the new, new thing before it becomes the old, old thing.

How do marketers deal with shorter time frames between the emergence of a new product and the quickly changing "cool" must-have product, such as the latest iPhone or X-Box? Often what teenagers think is cool is heavily influenced by media. "Each season, teens get more fashionable," says Erin Conroy of Brown Shoe, a fashion shoe company. "They are tuned in to MTV and Hollywood and follow celebrities and other trend setters rather than setting the trends." Yet media coverage contributes to the speedy death of trends as well as to their birth. As soon as a celebrity wears a new style, word spreads through the Internet, television, magazines, and newspapers. Teens want what's cool right now, not what was cool yesterday. Trend analyst Irma Zandl stresses the importance of timing: Being the first to introduce a product in the hope of making it trendy is just as risky as being the last to market.

Moreover, teen tastes influence what preteens and young adults will buy. As other groups start to buy what teens in the vanguard are buying, trendy products become mainstream and much less appealing to the superhip. This is the signal for companies to put once-cool items on sale and gear up for the next trend.

Keeping up with cool also means keeping advertising up to date. Andrew Keller, creative director at ad agency CP+B, says that "advertising is disposable," and yet, he adds, "the faster we react to fads, the faster they'll go away." The bottom line for businesses is that the quest for cool never ends. Now more than ever, companies need to know their customers and look carefully for clues to the next cool thing.[1]

Marketing efforts are directed toward providing customer satisfaction. Understanding customers' needs, such as "what's cool," is crucial to providing customer satisfaction. Although marketing encompasses a diverse set of decisions and activities performed by individuals and by both business and non-business organizations, marketing always begins and ends with the customer. The American Marketing Association defines **marketing** as "an organizational function and a set of processes for creating, communicating, and delivering value to customers [and] for managing customer relationships in ways that benefit the organization and its stakeholders."[2] The marketing process involves eight major functions and numerous related activities (see Table 12.1). All these functions are essential if the marketing process is to be effective.

In this chapter we examine marketing activities that add value to products. We trace the evolution of the marketing concept and describe how organizations practise it. Next, our focus shifts to market classifications and marketing strategy. We analyze the four elements of a marketing mix and also discuss uncontrollable factors in the marketing environment. Then we examine the major components of a marketing plan. We consider tools for strategic market planning, including market measurement, sales forecasts, marketing information systems, and marketing research. Last, we look at the forces that influence consumer and organizational buying behaviour.

marketing an organizational function and a set of processes for creating, communicating, and delivering value to customers and for managing customer relationships in ways that benefit the organization and its stakeholders

Exchange functions: All companies—manufacturers, wholesalers, and retailers—buy and sell to market their merchandise.

1. **Buying** includes obtaining raw materials to make products, knowing how much merchandise to keep on hand, and selecting suppliers.

2. **Selling** creates possession utility by transferring the title of a product from seller to customer.

Physical distribution functions: These functions involve the flow of goods from producers to customers. Transportation and storage provide time and place utility and require careful management of inventory.

3. **Transporting** involves selecting a mode of transport that provides an acceptable delivery schedule at an acceptable price.

4. **Storing goods** is often necessary to sell them at the best selling time.

Facilitating functions: These functions help the other functions take place.

5. **Financing** helps at all stages of marketing. To buy raw materials, manufacturers often borrow from banks or receive credit from suppliers. Wholesalers may be financed by manufacturers, and retailers may receive financing from the wholesaler or manufacturer. Finally, retailers often provide financing to customers.

6. **Standardizing** sets uniform specifications for products or services. Grading classifies products by size and quality, usually through a sorting process. Together, standardization and grading facilitate production, transportation, storage, and selling.

7. **Risk taking**—even though competent management and insurance can minimize risks—is a constant reality of marketing because of such losses as bad-debt expense, obsolescence of products, theft by employees, and product-liability lawsuits.

8. **Gathering market information** is necessary for making all marketing decisions.

> **Table 12.1**
> **Major Marketing Functions**

Managing Customer Relationships

Learning Objective

Understand *marketing* and management of customer relationships.

Marketing relationships with customers are the lifeblood of all businesses. Maintaining positive relationships with customers is an important goal for marketers. The term **relationship marketing** refers to establishing "long-term, mutually beneficial arrangements in which both the buyer and seller focus on value enhancement through the creation of more satisfying exchanges."[3] Relationship marketing continually deepens the buyer's trust in the company, which, as the customer's loyalty grows, increases a company's understanding of the customer's needs and desires. Successful marketers respond to customer needs and strive to continually increase value to buyers over time. Eventually, this interaction becomes a solid relationship that allows for

relationship marketing establishing long-term, mutually satisfying buyer-seller relationships

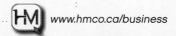
www.hmco.ca/business

cooperation and mutual dependency. For example, customers depend on the Coca-Cola Company to provide a standardized, reliable, satisfying soft drink or beverage anyplace in the world. Owing to its efforts to expand distribution to every possible location, Coca-Cola sells 33 percent of its volume in Europe and the Middle East, 31 percent in North America, 22 percent in the Asian/Pacific region, 10 percent in Latin America, and 5 percent in Africa.[4] The company continues to introduce new products, expand distribution, and maintain high-quality products. Coca-Cola is also a good "corporate citizen," donating millions of dollars to education, health and human services, and disaster-plagued regions each year.

customer relationship management (CRM) using information about customers to create marketing strategies that develop and sustain desirable customer relationships

To build long-term customer relationships, marketers increasingly are turning to marketing research and information technology. **Customer relationship management (CRM)** focuses on using information about customers to create marketing strategies that develop and sustain desirable customer relationships. By increasing customer value over time, organizations try to retain and increase long-term profitability through customer loyalty.[5]

Managing customer relationships requires identifying patterns of buying behaviour and using that information to focus on the most promising and profitable customers.[6] Companies must be sensitive to customers' requirements and desires, and establish communication to build customers' trust and loyalty. In some instances it may be more profitable for a company to focus on satisfying a valuable existing customer than to attempt to attract a new one who may never develop the same level of loyalty. This involves determining how much the customer will spend over his or her lifetime. The **customer lifetime value** is a combination of purchase frequency, average value of purchases, and brand-switching patterns over the entire span of a customer's relationship with a company.[7] There are intangible benefits to retaining lifetime-value customers, such as their ability to provide feedback to a company and refer new customers of similar value. The amount of money a company is willing to spend to retain such customers is also a factor. In general, when marketers focus on customers chosen for their lifetime value, they earn higher profits in the future than when they focus on customers selected for other reasons.[8] Because the loss of a potential lifetime customer can result in lower profits, managing customer relationships has become a major focus of marketers.

customer lifetime value a combination of purchase frequency, average value of purchases, and brand-switching patterns over the entire span of a customer's relationship with a company

Utility: The Value Added by Marketing

Learning Objective ❷

Explain how marketing adds value by creating utility.

form utility utility created by converting production inputs into finished products

Form utility is created by converting production inputs into finished products. Marketing efforts may influence form utility indirectly because the data gathered as part of marketing research frequently are used to determine the size, shape, and features of a product.

As defined in Chapter 9, **utility** is the ability of a good or service to satisfy a human need. A lunch at a Pizza Hut, an overnight stay at a Holiday Inn, and a Mercedes S500L all satisfy human needs. Thus each possesses utility. There are four kinds of utility.

The three kinds of utility that are created directly by marketing are place, time, and possession utility. **Place utility** is created by making a product available at a location where customers wish to purchase it. A pair of shoes is given place utility when it is shipped from a factory to a department store. **Time utility** is created by making a product available when customers wish to purchase it. For example, Halloween costumes might be manufactured in April but not displayed until late September, when consumers start buying them. By storing the costumes until they are wanted, the manufacturer or retailer provides time utility. **Possession utility** is created by transferring title (or ownership) of a product to a buyer. For a product as simple as a pair of shoes, ownership usually is transferred by means of a sales slip or receipt. For products such as automobiles and homes, the transfer of title is a more complex process. Along with the title to its products, the seller transfers the right to use that product to satisfy a need (see Figure 12.1).

utility the ability of a good or service to satisfy a human need

place utility utility created by making a product available at a location where customers wish to purchase it

time utility utility created by making a product available when customers wish to purchase it

possession utility utility created by transferring title (or ownership) of a product to a buyer

Wanted:
One pair of size 8 shoes in Duluth, immediately. Will pay $50.

	CAN SATISFY THE NEED WITH:	BUT CANNOT SATISFY THE NEED WITH:
Form utility	Size 8 shoes	Size 10 shoes
Place utility	Size 8 shoes in Duluth	Size 8 shoes in Los Angeles
Time utility	Size 8 shoes in Duluth available now	Size 8 shoes in Duluth available next month
Possession utility	Size 8 shoes in Duluth available now for $50	Size 8 shoes in Duluth available now for $80

Figure 12.1

Types of Utility

Form utility is created by the production process, but marketing creates place, time, and possession utility.

Place, time, and possession utility have real value in terms of both money and convenience. This value is created and added to goods and services through a wide variety of marketing activities—from research indicating what customers want to product warranties ensuring that customers get what they pay for. Overall, these marketing activities account for about half of every dollar spent by consumers. When they are part of an integrated marketing program that delivers maximum utility to the customer, many would agree that they are worth the cost.

Place, time, and possession utility are only the most fundamental applications of marketing activities. In recent years, marketing activities have been influenced by a broad business philosophy known as the *marketing concept.*

The Marketing Concept

Learning Objective

Trace the development of the marketing concept.

marketing concept a business philosophy that a firm should provide goods and services that satisfy customers' needs through a coordinated set of activities that allows the firm to achieve its objectives

The **marketing concept** is a business philosophy that a firm should provide goods and services that satisfy customers' needs through a coordinated set of activities that allows the firm to achieve its objectives. Thus, initially, the firm must communicate with potential customers to assess their product needs. Then the firm must develop a good or service to satisfy those needs. Finally, the firm must continue to seek ways to provide customer satisfaction. This process is an application of the marketing concept, or marketing orientation. Ben & Jerry's, for example, constantly assesses customer demand for ice cream and sorbet. On its website, it maintains a "flavour graveyard" listing combinations that were tried and ultimately failed. It also notes its top ten flavours each month. Thus the marketing concept emphasizes that marketing begins and ends with customers.

Evolution of the Marketing Concept

From the start of the Industrial Revolution until the early twentieth century, business efforts were directed mainly toward the production of goods. Consumer demand for manufactured products was so great that manufacturers could bank on selling everything they produced. Business had a strong *production orientation*, in which emphasis was placed on increased output and production efficiency. Marketing was limited to taking orders and distributing finished goods.

In the 1920s, production caught up with and began to exceed demand. Now producers had to direct their efforts toward selling goods rather than just producing goods that consumers readily bought. This new *sales orientation* was characterized by increased advertising, enlarged sales forces, and, occasionally, high-pressure selling techniques. Manufacturers produced the goods they expected consumers to want, and marketing consisted primarily of promoting products through personal selling and advertising, taking orders, and delivering goods.

During the 1950s, however, business people started to realize that even enormous advertising expenditures and the most thoroughly proven sales techniques were not enough. Something else was needed if products were to sell as well as expected. It was then that business managers recognized that they were not primarily producers or sellers but rather were in the business of satisfying customers' needs. Marketers realized that the best approach was to adopt a customer orientation—in other words, the organization had to first determine what customers need and then develop goods and services to fill those particular needs (see Table 13.2).

All functional areas—research and development (R&D), production, finance, human resources, and, of course, marketing—are viewed as playing a role in providing customer satisfaction.

Business managers recognized that they were not primarily producers or sellers but rather were in the business of satisfying customers' wants.

PRODUCTION ORIENTATION	SALES ORIENTATION	CUSTOMER ORIENTATION
Take orders	Increase advertising	Determine customer needs
Distribute goods	Enlarge sales force	Develop products to fill these needs
	Intensify sales techniques	Achieve the organization's goals

Table 12.2

Evolution of Customer Orientation

Implementing the Marketing Concept

The marketing concept has been adopted by many of the most successful business firms. Some firms, such as Ford Motor Company and Apple Computer, have gone through minor or major reorganizations in the process. Because the marketing concept is essentially a business philosophy, anyone can say, "I believe in it." To make it work, however, management must fully adopt and then implement it.

To implement the marketing concept, a firm first must obtain information about its present and potential customers. The firm must determine not only what customers' needs are but also how well those needs are being satisfied by products currently on the market—both its own products and those of competitors. It must ascertain how its products might be improved and what opinions customers have about the firm and its marketing efforts.

The firm then must use this information to pinpoint the specific needs and potential customers toward whom it will direct its marketing activities and resources. (Obviously, no firm can expect to satisfy all needs. And not every individual or firm can be considered a potential customer for every product manufactured or sold by a firm.) Next, the firm must mobilize its marketing resources to (1) provide a product that will satisfy its customers, (2) price the product at a level that is acceptable to buyers and that will yield an acceptable profit, (3) promote the product so that potential customers will be aware of its existence and its ability to satisfy their needs, and (4) ensure that the product is distributed so that it is available to customers where and when needed.

Finally, the firm again must obtain marketing information—this time regarding the effectiveness of its efforts. Can the product be improved? Is it being promoted properly? Is it being distributed efficiently? Is the price too high or too low? The firm must be ready to modify any or all of its marketing activities based on information about its customers and competitors. Toyota, for example, has taken the lead in the automotive industry through its promise of high quality yet sensible cars. But Toyota isn't satisfied

SPOTLIGHT

E-business races for parts suppliers

Major auto industry parts suppliers say e-business with their own suppliers will rise dramatically the next 2 years. How it will grow:

Today | In 2 years

Computer communication: 41% — 85%
Send orders and releases: 33% — 81%
Check parts availability: 0% — 66%
Procurement of parts: request for bids and proposals: 25% — 76%

Source: *USA Today*, October 18, 2001, p. B1.

with producing practical cars and is launching a new campaign to make consumers passionate about its product. Toyota is revamping its relationship with customers by forgoing traditional advertising and bringing its cars straight to the consumer. The Toyota Camry, the number-one selling car in North America, is being redesigned to integrate a flashier grill and a sportier body to add fun to its proven quality. When the hybrid version of the new Camry debuts, Toyota will team up with medical doctors to promote the vehicle as friendly to those with asthma. Toyota will test out its new FJ Cruiser sport-utility vehicle (SUV) at off-road and trail events instead of using more traditional television advertising. To market its truck line, Toyota will focus on fishing and hunting events.[9]

Markets and Their Classification

Learning Objective ❹

Understand what markets are and how they are classified.

market a group of individuals or organizations, or both, that need products in a given category and that have the ability, willingness, and authority to purchase such products

A **market** is a group of individuals or organizations, or both, that need products in a given category and that have the ability, willingness, and authority to purchase such products. The people or organizations must want the product. They must be able to purchase the product by exchanging money, goods, or services for it. They must be willing to use their buying power. Finally, they must be socially and legally authorized to purchase the product.

Markets are broadly classified as consumer or business-to-business markets. These classifications are based on the characteristics of the individuals and organizations within each market. Because marketing efforts vary depending on the intended market, marketers should understand the general characteristics of these two groups.

Consumer markets consist of purchasers and/or household members who intend to consume or benefit from the purchased products and who do not buy products to make profits. *Business-to-business markets*, also called *industrial markets*, are grouped broadly into producer, reseller, governmental, and institutional categories. These markets purchase specific kinds of products for use in making other products for resale or for day-to-day operations. *Producer markets* consist of individuals and business organizations that buy certain products to use in the manufacture of other products. *Reseller markets*

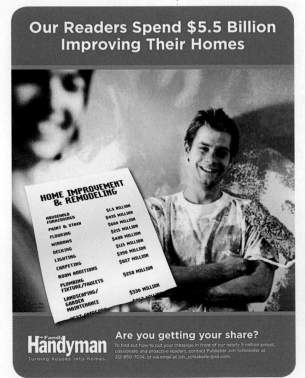

Reaching a target market

A company's marketing efforts for a brand or product group are aimed at a specific target market. This advertisement for *Family Handyman* magazine indicates that the magazine can help a company reach a target market of customers who do their own home improvement projects.

consist of intermediaries such as wholesalers and retailers that buy finished products and sell them for a profit. *Governmental markets* consist of federal, provincial, county, and municipal governments. They buy goods and services to maintain internal operations and to provide citizens with such products as highways, education, water, energy, and defence. Governmental purchases total billions of dollars each year. *Institutional markets* include religious organizations, private schools, hospitals, civic clubs, fraternities and sororities, charitable organizations, and foundations. Their goals are different from such typical business goals as profit, market share, or return on investment.

Developing Marketing Strategies

A **marketing strategy** is a plan that will enable an organization to make the best use of its resources and advantages to meet its objectives. A marketing strategy consists of (1) the selection and analysis of a target market and (2) the creation and maintenance of an appropriate **marketing mix,** a combination of product, price, distribution, and promotion developed to satisfy a particular target market.

Target Market Selection and Evaluation

A **target market** is a group of individuals or organizations, or both, for which a firm develops and maintains a marketing mix suitable for the specific needs and preferences of that group. In selecting a target market, marketing managers examine potential markets for their possible effects on the firm's sales, costs, and profits. The managers attempt to determine whether the organization has the resources to produce

marketing strategy a plan that will enable an organization to make the best use of its resources and advantages to meet its objectives

marketing mix a combination of product, price, distribution, and promotion developed to satisfy a particular target market

target market a group of individuals or organizations, or both, for which a firm develops and maintains a marketing mix suitable for the specific needs and preferences of that group

---

BUSINESS AROUND THE WORLD

OXO Comes to Grips with Global Markets

OXO's best-known products are the Good Grips line of kitchen tools, designed to fit the hand and please the eye. Targeting seniors whose grip strength or manual dexterity has declined, OXO's Good Grips are popular in the U.S. market but flopped when they were first introduced in Japan. After months of meticulous marketing research, however, OXO was able to improve its target marketing and create products especially for Japanese consumers.

It turns out that U.S. and Japanese consumers use kitchen tools differently. "Most Westerners hold a spatula like a tennis racket when they stir, flip, or cook," says OXO's CEO. "But the Japanese women we observed cooking all held it like a pen." After OXO redesigned the tools and made them smaller for compact Japanese kitchens, sales soared. In an unexpected twist, a smaller salad spinner that became OXO's top seller in Japan has caught on with those U.S. consumers who prefer space-saving devices.

Sources: Based on information in Helen Walters, "OXO: Remade in Japan," *BusinessWeek Online,* December 8, 2006, www.businessweek.com; Dalia Fahmy, "Making Necessities Stylish and Getting a Higher Price," *New York Times,* March 9, 2006, p. C7.

a marketing mix that meets the needs of a particular target market and whether satisfying those needs is consistent with the firm's overall objectives. They also analyze the strengths and numbers of competitors already marketing to people in this target market. Marketing managers may define a target market as a vast number of people or a relatively small group. Rolls-Royce, for example, targets its automobiles toward a small, very exclusive market: wealthy people who want the ultimate in a prestige automobile. Other companies target multiple markets with different products, prices, distribution systems, and promotion for each one. Nike uses this strategy, marketing different types of shoes to meet specific needs of cross-trainers, rock climbers, basketball players, aerobics enthusiasts, and other athletic-shoe buyers. When selecting a target market, marketing managers generally take either the undifferentiated approach or the market-segmentation approach.

Undifferentiated Approach A company that designs a single marketing mix and directs it at the entire market for a particular product is using an **undifferentiated approach** (see Figure 12.2). This approach assumes that individual customers in the target market for a specific kind of product have similar needs and that the organization therefore can satisfy most customers with a single marketing mix. This single marketing mix consists of one type of product with little or no variation, one price, one promotional program aimed at everyone, and one distribution system to reach all customers in the total market. Products that can be marketed successfully with the undifferentiated approach include staple food items, such as sugar and salt, and certain kinds of farm produce. An undifferentiated approach is useful in only a limited number of situations because for most product categories, buyers have different needs. When customers' needs vary, a company should use the market-segmentation approach.

Market-Segmentation Approach A firm that is marketing fifteen-metre yachts would not direct its marketing effort toward every person in the total boat market. Some might want a sailboat or a canoe. Others might want a speedboat or an outboard-powered fishing boat. Still others might be looking for something resembling a small ocean liner. Marketing efforts directed toward such boat buyers would be wasted.

Instead, the firm would direct its attention toward a particular portion, or *segment*, of the total market for boats. A **market segment** is a group of individuals or organizations within a market that shares one or more common characteristics. The process of dividing a market into segments is called **market segmentation.** As shown in Figure 12.2, there are two types of market-segmentation approaches: concentrated and differentiated. When an organization uses *concentrated* market segmentation, a single marketing mix is directed at a single market segment. If *differentiated* market segmentation is employed, multiple marketing mixes are focused on multiple market segments.

In our boat example, one common characteristic, or *basis*, for segmentation might be "end use of a boat." The firm would be interested primarily in that market segment whose uses for a boat could lead to the purchase of a forty-foot yacht. Another basis for segmentation might be income; still another might be geographic location. Each of these variables can affect the type of boat an individual might purchase. When choosing a basis for segmentation, it is important to select a characteristic that relates to differences in people's needs for a product. The yacht producer, for example, would not use religion to segment the boat market because people's needs for boats do not vary based on religion.

undifferentiated approach directing a single marketing mix at the entire market for a particular product

market segment a group of individuals or organizations within a market that shares one or more common characteristics

market segmentation the process of dividing a market into segments and directing a marketing mix at a particular segment or segments rather than at the total market

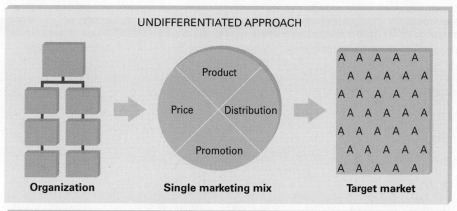

UNDIFFERENTIATED APPROACH

Organization   Single marketing mix   Target market

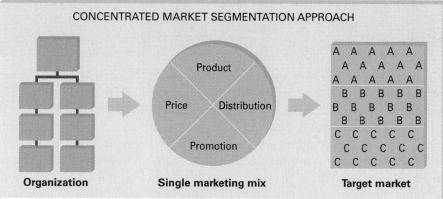

CONCENTRATED MARKET SEGMENTATION APPROACH

Organization   Single marketing mix   Target market

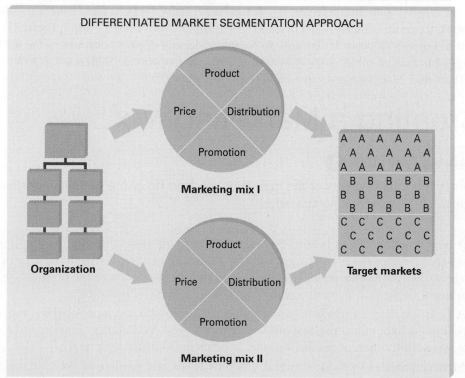

DIFFERENTIATED MARKET SEGMENTATION APPROACH

Marketing mix I

Organization   Target markets

Marketing mix II

Figure 12.2

General Approaches for Selecting Target Markets

The undifferentiated approach assumes that individual customers have similar needs and that most customers can be satisfied with a single marketing mix. When customers' needs vary, the market-segmentation approach—either concentrated or differentiated—should be used.

Source: William M. Pride and O. C. Ferrell, *Marketing: Concepts and Strategies* (Boston: Houghton Mifflin, 2006). Copyright © 2006 by Houghton Mifflin Company. Adapted with permission.

NOTE: The letters in each target market represent potential customers. Customers that have the same letters have similar characteristics and similar product needs.

 www.hmco.ca/business

Table 12.3

Common Bases of Market Segmentation

Source: William M. Pride and O. C. Ferrell, *Marketing: Concepts and Strategies* (Boston: Houghton Mifflin, 2006). Copyright © 2006 by Houghton Mifflin Company. Adapted with permission.

DEMOGRAPHIC	PSYCHOGRAPHIC	GEOGRAPHIC	BEHAVIOURISTIC
Age	Personality attributes	Region	Volume usage
Gender	Motives	Urban, suburban, rural	End use
Ethnicity	Lifestyles	Market density	Benefit expectations
Income		Climate	Brand loyalty
Education		Terrain	Price sensitivity
Occupation		City size	
Family size		County size	
Family life cycle		Province size	
Religion			
Social class			

Marketers use a wide variety of segmentation bases. Those bases most commonly applied to consumer markets are shown in Table 12.3. Each may be used as a single basis for market segmentation or in combination with other bases. For example, Vertu, a part of mobile phone maker Nokia, has segmented the market for cellular phones and is using a concentrated targeting strategy. The segment Vertu is after is very wealthy customers who want luxurious, social-status possessions. The company's mobile phones are made from precious materials, including gold, platinum, and sapphire crystal. The phones include a button that connects the owner to a personal assistant twenty-four hours a day. To reach its wealthy target market, Vertu sells its phones in private suites in select cities (for example, New York, London, Paris, Tokyo, and, of course, Beverly Hills) and at Nieman Marcus department stores for a price ranging from just under $5,000 to almost $20,000 per phone. Such stars as Gwyneth Paltrow and Madonna are some of Vertu's customers.[10]

Creating a Marketing Mix

Learning Objective 5

Identify the four elements of the marketing mix and be aware of their importance in developing a marketing strategy.

A business firm controls four important elements of marketing that it combines in a way that reaches the firm's target market. These are the *product* itself, the *price* of the product, the means chosen for its *distribution*, and the *promotion* of the product. When combined, these four elements form a marketing mix (see Figure 12.3).

A firm can vary its marketing mix by changing any one or more of these ingredients. Thus a firm might use one marketing mix to reach one target market and a second, somewhat different marketing mix to reach another target market.

Most automakers produce several different types and models of vehicles and aim them at different market segments based on age, income, and other factors. For exam-

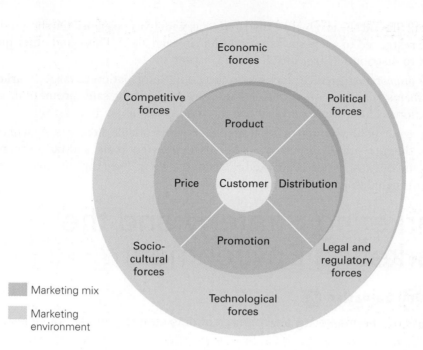

Figure 12.3

The Marketing Mix and the Marketing Environment

The marketing mix consists of elements that the firm controls—product, price, distribution, and promotion. The firm generally has no control over forces in the marketing environment.

Source: William M. Pride and O. C. Ferrell, *Marketing: Concepts and Strategies* (Boston: Houghton Mifflin, 2006). Copyright © 2006 by Houghton Mifflin Company. Adapted with permission.

ple, Toyota's marketing research about Generation Y drivers found that they practically live in their cars, and many even keep a change of clothes in their vehicles. As a result of this research, Toyota designed its Scion as a "home on wheels," with a 15-volt outlet for plugging in a computer, reclining front seats for napping, and a powerful audio system for listening to MP3 music files, all for a $12,500 price tag.[11]

The *product* ingredient of the marketing mix includes decisions about the product's design, brand name, packaging, warranties, and the like. When McDonald's decides on brand names, package designs, sizes of orders, flavours of sauces, and recipes, these choices are all part of the product ingredient.

The *pricing* ingredient is concerned with both base prices and discounts of various kinds. Pricing decisions are intended to achieve particular goals, such as to maximize profit or even to make room for new models. The rebates offered by automobile manufacturers are a pricing strategy developed to boost low auto sales. Product and pricing are discussed in detail in Chapter 13.

The *distribution* ingredient involves not only transportation and storage but also the selection of intermediaries. How many levels of intermediaries should be used in the distribution of a particular

Is this ad aimed at all women?

The maker of RoC Retinol Correxion is not aiming its product at all women, but is using market segmentation. This product is targeted to women aged forty and older.

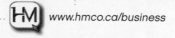

product? Should the product be distributed as widely as possible? Or should distribution be restricted to a few specialized outlets in each area? These and other questions related to distribution are considered in Chapter 14.

The *promotion* ingredient focuses on providing information to target markets. The major forms of promotion are advertising, personal selling, sales promotion, and public relations. These four forms are also discussed in Chapter 14.

These ingredients of the marketing mix are controllable elements. A firm can vary each of them to suit its organizational goals, marketing goals, and target markets. As we extend our discussion of marketing strategy, we will see that the marketing environment includes a number of *uncontrollable* elements.

Marketing Strategy and the Marketing Environment

Learning Objective 6

Explain how the marketing environment affects strategic market planning.

The marketing mix consists of elements that a firm controls and uses to reach its target market. In addition, the firm has control over such organizational resources as finances and information. These resources, too, can be used to accomplish marketing goals. However, the firm's marketing activities are also affected by a number of external—and generally uncontrollable—forces. As Figure 12.3 illustrates, the forces that make up the external *marketing environment* are

* *Economic forces*—the effects of economic conditions on customers' ability and willingness to buy

* *Sociocultural forces*—influences in a society and its culture that result in changes in attitudes, beliefs, norms, customs, and lifestyles

* *Political forces*—influences that arise through the actions of elected and appointed officials

* *Competitive forces*—the actions of competitors, who are in the process of implementing their own marketing plans

* *Legal and regulatory forces*—laws that protect consumers and competition and government regulations that affect marketing

* *Technological forces*—technological changes that, on the one hand, can create new marketing opportunities or, on the other, can cause products to become obsolete almost overnight

These forces influence decisions about marketing-mix ingredients. Changes in the environment can have a major impact on existing marketing strategies. In addition, changes in environmental forces can lead to abrupt shifts in customers' needs. Technological forces, for example, are having a major impact at Intel, the world's largest producer of computer microchips. With competition from iPods, BlackBerrys, cell phones, and other handheld devices, the PC industry is slowing, and Intel is re-

BIZ TECH

Leaping from Virtual to Reality

When some people saw the Internet as the end of the greeting card business, Hallmark took it as a new beginning. The company has integrated its online and off-line marketing efforts to build customer relationships, launch new products, and keep profits growing.

"If you get customers to interact with you both online and in the stores, they're better customers," states Hallmark's marketing manager. This is the idea behind Hallmark's free e-cards, electronic greeting cards that customers can personalize and e-mail to friends and relatives. Customers who come to the Hallmark site to send e-cards also see other Hallmark products.

What's more, e-cards are a good way to test new product ideas. Hallmark's talking cartoon dogs, Hoops and YoYo, became so popular on e-cards that Hallmark put them on nonvirtual products like T-shirts, dolls, wallets, wristwatches, and even a CD—sold online and in Hallmark stores.

Sources: Information based on Chris Batchik, "Integration: Bridging the Online/Offline Gap," *B to B*, March 13, 2006, p. 12; Bob Tedeschi, "The Resurgence of E-Cards," *New York Times*, January 30, 2006, p. C6; "Online Marketing: Trust and the Blogging Stranger," *Marketing Week*, November 23, 2006, p. 38.

vamping its focus and its brand in an effort to remain relevant. Intel is launching more new products than at any time in the company's history. The Viiv will be a new chip designed to replace your TiVo, stereo, and potentially, cable or satellite box. It can download first-run movies, music, and games. In addition to its expanding product range, Intel is hiring software developers, sociologists, ethnographers, and even doctors for product development.[12]

Developing a Marketing Plan

> ## Learning Objective 7
> Understand the major components of a marketing plan.

A **marketing plan** is a written document that specifies an organization's resources, objectives, marketing strategy, and implementation and control efforts to be used in marketing a specific product or product group. The marketing plan describes the firm's current position or situation, establishes marketing objectives for the product, and specifies how the organization will attempt to achieve these objectives. Marketing plans vary with respect to the time period involved. Short-range plans are for one year or less, medium-range plans cover from over one year up to five years, and long-range plans cover periods of more than five years.

Although time-consuming, developing a clear, well-written marketing plan is important. The plan will be used for communication among the firm's employees. It covers the assignment of responsibilities, tasks, and schedules for implementation. It specifies

marketing plan a written document that specifies an organization's resources, objectives, strategy, and implementation and control efforts to be used in marketing a specific product or product group

Table 12.4

Components of the Marketing Plan

Source: William M. Pride and O. C. Ferrell, *Marketing: Concepts and Strategies* (Boston: Houghton Mifflin, 2006). Copyright © 2006 by Houghton Mifflin Company. Reprinted with permission.

PLAN COMPONENT	COMPONENT SUMMARY	HIGHLIGHTS
Executive summary	One- to two-page synopsis of the entire marketing plan	Usually written after all the other steps.
Environmental analysis	Information about the company's current situation with respect to the marketing environment	1. Assessment of marketing environment factors 2. Assessment of target market(s) 3. Assessment of current marketing objectives and performance
SWOT analysis	Assessment of the organization's strengths, weaknesses, opportunities, and threats	1. Strengths 2. Weaknesses 3. Opportunities 4. Threats
Marketing objectives	Specification of the firm's marketing objectives	Qualitative measures of what is to be accomplished
Marketing strategies	Outline of how the firm will achieve its objectives	1. Target market(s) 2. Marketing mix
Marketing implementation	Outline of how the firm will implement its marketing strategies	1. Marketing organization 2. Activities and responsibilities 3. Implementation timetable
Evaluation and control	Explanation of how the firm will measure and evaluate the results of the implemented plan	1. Performance standards 2. Financial controls 3. Monitoring procedures (audits)

how resources are to be allocated to achieve marketing objectives. It helps marketing managers monitor and evaluate the performance of the marketing strategy. Because the forces of the marketing environment are subject to change, marketing plans have to be updated frequently. Disney, for example, recently made changes to its marketing plans by combining all activities and licensing associated with the Power Rangers, Winnie the Pooh, and Disney Princess into one marketing plan with a $500 million budget. The primary goal is to send consistent messages about branding to customers. As the new marketing plan is implemented, Disney will have to respond quickly to customers' reactions and make adjustments to the plan.[13] The major components of a marketing plan are shown in Table 12.4.

Market Measurement and Sales Forecasting

Learning Objective 8

Describe market measurement and sales forecasting.

Measuring the sales potential of specific types of market segments helps an organization to make some important decisions. It can evaluate the feasibility of entering new segments. The organization also can decide how best to allocate its marketing resources and activities among market segments in which it is already active. All such estimates should identify the relevant time frame. As with marketing plans, these estimates can be short range, covering periods of less than one year; medium range, covering one to five years; or long range, covering more than five years. The estimates also should define the geographic boundaries of the forecast. For example, sales potential can be estimated for a city, county, province, or group of nations. Finally, analysts should indicate whether their estimates are for a specific product item, a product line, or an entire product category.

A **sales forecast** is an estimate of the amount of a product that an organization expects to sell during a certain period of time based on a specified level of marketing effort. Managers in different divisions of an organization rely on sales forecasts when they purchase raw materials, schedule production, secure financial resources, consider plant or equipment purchases, hire personnel, and plan inventory levels. Because the accuracy of a sales forecast is so important, organizations often use several forecasting methods, including executive judgments, surveys of buyers or sales personnel, time-series analyses, correlation analyses, and market tests. The specific methods used depend on the costs involved, type of product, characteristics of the market, time span of the forecast, purposes for which the forecast is used, stability of historical sales data, availability of the required information, and expertise and experience of forecasters.

sales forecast an estimate of the amount of a product that an organization expects to sell during a certain period of time based on a specified level of marketing effort

Marketing Information

Learning Objective 9

Distinguish between a marketing information system and marketing research.

The availability and use of accurate and timely information are critical to making effective marketing decisions. A wealth of marketing information is obtainable. There are two general ways to obtain it: through a marketing information system and through marketing research.

Marketing Information Systems

marketing information system a system for managing marketing information that is gathered continually from internal and external sources

A **marketing information system** is a system for managing marketing information that is gathered continually from internal and external sources. Most such systems are computer-based because of the amount of data the system must accept, store, sort, and retrieve. *Continual* collection of data is essential if the system is to incorporate the most up-to-date information.

In concept, the operation of a marketing information system is not complex. Data from a variety of sources are fed into the system. Data from *internal* sources include sales figures, product and marketing costs, inventory levels, and activities of the sales force. Data from *external* sources relate to the organization's suppliers, intermediaries, and customers; competitors' marketing activities; and economic conditions. All these data are stored and processed within the marketing information system. Its output is a flow of information in the form that is most useful for making marketing decisions. This information might include daily sales reports by territory and product, forecasts of sales or buying trends, and reports on changes in market share for the major brands in a specific industry. Both the information outputs and their form depend on the requirements of the personnel in the organization.

Marketing Research

marketing research the process of systematically gathering, recording, and analyzing data concerning a particular marketing problem

Marketing research is the process of systematically gathering, recording, and analyzing data concerning a particular marketing problem. Thus marketing research is used in specific situations to obtain information not otherwise available to decision makers. It is an intermittent, rather than a continual, source of marketing information. In the United States, with the help of a new software company, Dunkin' Donuts is using marketing research to remain competitive against Tim Hortons, Krispy Kreme, and Starbucks, as well as McDonald's, which recently entered the espresso-drink market. A survey of Dunkin' Donuts customers revealed that they welcomed menu changes such as iced beverages, espresso drinks, and scrambled eggs and cheese on a bagel. The firm's research also suggested that it should continue its strategy of targeting workday on-the-go customers and not taking on Starbucks directly.[14]

Table 12.5 outlines a six-step procedure for conducting marketing research. This procedure is particularly well suited to testing new products, determining various characteristics of consumer markets, and evaluating promotional activities. Food-processing companies, such as Kraft Foods and Kellogg's, use a variety of marketing research methods to avoid costly mistakes in introducing the wrong products or products in the wrong way or at the wrong time. Virtually all food companies are either eliminating or reducing the use of unhealthy trans-fats. Understanding of the food preferences, loyalties, and purchase motivators of consumer groups enables these companies to serve them better.

Using Technology to Gather and Analyze Marketing Information

Technology is making information for marketing decisions increasingly accessible. The ability of firms to track the purchase behaviours of customers electronically and to better determine what they want is changing the nature of marketing. The integra-

1. Define the problem	In this step, the problem is stated clearly and accurately to determine what issues are involved in the research, what questions to ask, and what types of solutions are needed. This is a crucial step that should not be rushed.	**Table 12.5** **The Six Steps of Marketing Research**
2. Make a preliminary investigation	The objective of preliminary investigation is to develop both a sharper definition of the problem and a set of tentative answers. The tentative answers are developed by examining internal information and published data, and by talking with persons who have some experience with the problem. These answers will be tested by further research.	
3. Plan the research	At this stage, researchers know what facts are needed to resolve the identified problem and what facts are available. They make plans on how to gather needed but missing data.	
4. Gather factual information	Once the basic research plan has been completed, the needed information can be collected by mail, telephone, or personal interviews; by observation; or from commercial or government data sources. The choice depends on the plan and the available sources of information.	
5. Interpret the information	Facts by themselves do not always provide a sound solution to a marketing problem. They must be interpreted and analyzed to determine the choices available to management.	
6. Reach a conclusion	Sometimes the conclusion or recommendation becomes obvious when the facts are interpreted. However, in other cases, reaching a conclusion may not be so easy because of gaps in the information or intangible factors that are difficult to evaluate. If and when the evidence is less than complete, it is important to say so.	

tion of telecommunications with computing technology provides marketers with access to accurate information not only about customers and competitors but also about industry forecasts and business trends. Among the communication tools that are radically changing the way marketers obtain and use information are databases, online information services, and the Internet.

A *database* is a collection of information arranged for easy access and retrieval. Using databases, marketers tap into internal sales reports, newspaper articles, company news releases, government economic reports, bibliographies, and more. Many marketers use commercial databases, such as LEXIS-NEXIS, to obtain useful information for marketing decisions. Many of these commercial databases are available in printed form (for a fee), online (for a fee), or on purchasable CD-ROMs. Other marketers develop their own databases in-house. Some firms sell their databases to other organizations. *Reader's Digest*, for example, markets a database that provides information on 100 million households. Dun & Bradstreet markets a database that includes information on the addresses, phone numbers, and contacts of businesses located in specific areas.

Information provided by a single firm on household demographics, purchases, television viewing behaviour, and responses to promotions such as coupons and free samples is called *single-source data*. For example, Behavior Scan, offered by Information Resources, Inc., screens about 60,000 households in twenty-six U.S. markets. This single-source information service monitors household televisions and records the programs and commercials viewed. When buyers from these households shop in stores equipped with scanning registers, they present Hotline cards (similar to credit cards) to cashiers. This enables each customer's identification to be coded electronically so that the firm can track each product purchased and store the information in a database.

Online information services offer subscribers access to e-mail, websites, files for downloading (and reading via Acrobat Reader), news, databases, and research materials. By subscribing to mailing lists, marketers can receive electronic newsletters and participate in online discussions with other network users. This ability to communicate online with customers, suppliers, and employees improves the capability of a firm's marketing information system and helps the company track its customers' changing desires and buying habits.

The *Internet* has evolved as a powerful communication medium, linking customers and companies around the world via computer networks with e-mail, forums, web pages, and more. Growth in Internet use has given rise to an entire industry that makes marketing information easily accessible to both companies and customers. Among the many web pages useful for marketing research are the home pages of Nielsen marketing research and *Advertising Age*. While most web pages are open to all Internet users, many companies also maintain internal web pages, called *intranets*, that allow employees to access internal data and facilitate communication among departments.

Table 12.6 lists a number of websites where you might find valuable information for marketing research.

Types of Buying Behaviour

Buying behaviour may be defined as the decisions and actions of people involved in buying and using products.[15] **Consumer buying behaviour** refers to the purchasing of products for personal or household use, not for business purposes. **Business buying behaviour** is the purchasing of products by producers, resellers, governmental

buying behaviour the decisions and actions of people involved in buying and using products

consumer buying behaviour the purchasing of products for personal or household use, not for business purposes

business buying behaviour the purchasing of products by producers, resellers, governmental units, and institutions

Table 12.6

Internet Sources of Marketing Information

Source: William M. Pride and O. C. Ferrell, *Marketing: Concepts and Strategies* (Boston: Houghton Mifflin, 2006). Copyright © 2006 by Houghton Mifflin Company. Reprinted with permission.

Government sources	Periodicals and books
Canadian Census www12.Statcan.ca/english/census01/home	adage.com
Strategis, Industry Canada www.strategis.ic.gc.ca	salesandmarketing.com
Statistics Canada www.statcan.ca	Fortune.com
U.S. Census www.census.gov	inc.com
	businessweek.com
	bloomberg.com

Commercial sources	
acnielsen.com	arbitron.com
Infores.com	chamber-of-commerce.com
gallup.com	

units, and institutions. Since a firm's success depends greatly on buyers' reactions to a particular marketing strategy, it is important to understand buying behaviour. Marketing managers are better able to predict customer responses to marketing strategies and to develop a satisfying marketing mix if they are aware of the factors that affect buying behaviour.

Consumer Buying Behaviour

Learning Objective 10

Identify the major steps in the consumer buying decision process and the sets of factors that may influence this process.

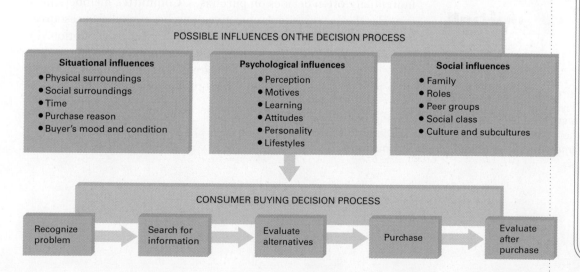

SP⊙TLIGHT

Buying a home via the Net

Over 40% of first time home buyers used the Internet to search for house listings.

41% Search listings

18% Research values

8% Research location

6% Research schools and city/county

Source: Real Estate.com survey.

Consumers' buying behaviours differ when they buy different types of products. For frequently purchased low-cost items, a consumer employs routine response behaviour involving very little search or decision-making effort. The buyer uses limited decision making for purchases made occasionally or when more information is needed about an unknown product in a well-known product category. When buying an unfamiliar, expensive item or one that is seldom purchased, the consumer engages in extensive decision making.

A person deciding on a purchase goes through some or all of the steps shown in Figure 12.4. First, the consumer acknowledges that a problem exists. A problem is usually the lack of a product or service that is desired or needed. Then the buyer looks for information that can include brand names, product characteristics, warranties, and

POSSIBLE INFLUENCES ON THE DECISION PROCESS

Situational influences	Psychological influences	Social influences
• Physical surroundings • Social surroundings • Time • Purchase reason • Buyer's mood and condition	• Perception • Motives • Learning • Attitudes • Personality • Lifestyles	• Family • Roles • Peer groups • Social class • Culture and subcultures

CONSUMER BUYING DECISION PROCESS

Recognize problem → Search for information → Evaluate alternatives → Purchase → Evaluate after purchase

Figure 12.4

Consumer Buying Decision Process and Possible Influences on the Process

A buyer goes through some or all of these steps when making a purchase.

Source: William M. Pride and O. C. Ferrell, *Marketing: Concepts and Strategies* (Boston: Houghton Mifflin, 2006). Copyright © 2006 by Houghton Mifflin Company. Adapted with permission.

personal income the income an individual receives from all sources

disposable income personal income *less* all personal taxes

discretionary income disposable income *less* savings and expenditures on food, clothing, and housing

other features. Next, the buyer weighs the various alternatives he or she has discovered, and then finally makes a choice and acquires the item. In the after-purchase stage, the consumer evaluates the suitability of the product. This judgment will affect future purchases. As Figure 12.4 shows, the buying process is influenced by situational factors (physical surroundings, social surroundings, time, purchase reason, and buyer's mood and condition), psychological factors (perception, motives, learning, attitudes, personality, and lifestyle), and social factors (family, roles, peer groups, social class, culture, and subculture).

Consumer buying behaviour is also affected by ability to buy or buying power, which is largely determined by income. As every taxpayer knows, not all income is available for spending. For this reason, marketers consider income in three different ways. **Personal income** is the income an individual receives from all sources. **Disposable income** is personal income *less* all personal taxes. These taxes include income, goods and services, capital gains, and property taxes levied by local, provincial, and federal governments. **Discretionary income** is disposable income *less* savings and expenditures on food, clothing, and housing. Discretionary income is of particular interest to marketers because consumers have the most choice in spending it. Consumers use their discretionary income to purchase items ranging from automobiles and vacations to movies and pet food.

Business Buying Behaviour

Business buyers consider a product's quality, its price, and the service provided by suppliers. Marketers at GraniteRock Company understand the value of customer service and thus concentrate their efforts on on-time delivery to distinguish GraniteRock from its competitors.[16] Business buyers usually are better informed than consumers about products and generally buy in larger quantities. In a business, a committee or group of people, rather than single individuals, often decides on purchases. Committee members must consider the organization's objectives, purchasing policies, resources, and personnel. Business buying occurs through description, inspection, sampling, or negotiation. A number of organizations buy a variety of products online.

▲

Recognizing a problem

Some advertisements, such as this one for Uni-Ball pens, are aimed at a particular stage of the consumer's buying-decision process. This Uni-Ball pen ad is meant to stimulate the problem-recognition stage of the buying-decision process.

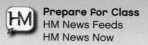

Prepare for Class
HM News Feeds
HM News Now

→ **RETURN TO INSIDE BUSINESS**

From colas to cars, jeans to jerseys, music to mobile phones, cool makes a difference in many product categories—especially when young adults are the target market. Firms that cater to trendy teens cannot afford the luxury of waiting months for

items to be manufactured and shipped from the Far East or other distant places because the window of opportunity closes much sooner these days. When teens want a cool product, they want it now. Price is a secondary consideration.

Many companies use the Internet to keep their brands cool. Coca-Cola, for example, sponsors an interactive website called MyCoke.com. Millions of teens have registered to create music mixes, record songs, play games, download screensavers, and more. The head of Coke's online agency explains that companies are particularly keen to keeping teens interested because "if you can be cool, then you're going to be talked about, and that's going to produce results."

Questions

1. MyCoke.com members are asked to list their birth date and e-mail address (but not their names) when they register. How might this information be valuable to Coca-Cola's marketers?

2. How does the concept of time utility apply to trendy products?

CHAPTER REVIEW

1 **Understand** *marketing* **and management of customer relationships.**

Marketing is an organizational function and a set of processes for creating, communicating, and delivering value to customers and for managing customer relationships in ways that benefit the organization and its stakeholders. Maintaining positive relationships with customers is crucial. Relationship marketing is establishing long-term, mutually satisfying buyer-seller relationships. Customer relationship management uses information about a customer to create marketing strategies that develop and sustain desirable customer relationships. Managing customer relationships requires identifying patterns of buying behaviour and focusing on the most profitable customers. Customer lifetime value is a combination of purchase frequency, average value of purchases, and brand-switching patterns over the entire span of a customer's relationship with the company.

2 **Explain how marketing adds value by creating utility.**

Marketing adds value in the form of utility or the power of a product or service to satisfy a need. It creates place utility by making products available where customers want them, time utility by making products available when customers want them, and possession utility by transferring the ownership of products to buyers.

3 **Trace the development of the marketing concept.**

From the Industrial Revolution until the early twentieth century, business people focused on the production of goods; from the 1920s to the 1950s, the emphasis moved to the selling of goods. During the 1950s, however, business people recognized that their enterprises involved not only producing and selling products but also satisfying customers' needs. They began to implement

the marketing concept, a business philosophy that involves the entire organization in the dual processes of meeting the customers' needs and achieving the organization's goals. Implementation of the marketing concept begins and ends with customers—first to determine what customers' needs are and later to evaluate how well the firm is meeting those needs.

4 Understand what markets are and how they are classified.

A market consists of people with needs, the ability to buy, and the desire and authority to purchase. Markets are classified as consumer and industrial (producer, reseller, governmental, and institutional) markets.

5 Identify the four elements of the marketing mix and be aware of their importance in developing a marketing strategy.

A marketing strategy is a plan for the best use of an organization's resources to meet its objectives. Developing a marketing strategy involves selecting and analyzing a target market and creating and maintaining a marketing mix that will satisfy that target market. A target market is chosen through either the undifferentiated approach or the market-segmentation approach. A market segment is a group of individuals or organizations within a market that has similar characteristics and needs. Businesses that use an undifferentiated approach design a single marketing mix and direct it at the entire market for a particular product. The market-segmentation approach directs a marketing mix at a segment of a market. The four elements of a firm's marketing mix are product, price, distribution, and promotion. The product ingredient includes decisions about the product's design, brand name, packaging, and warranties. The pricing ingredient is concerned with both base prices and various types of discounts. Distribution involves not only transportation and storage but also the selection of intermediaries. Promotion focuses on providing information to target markets. The elements of the marketing mix can be varied to suit broad organizational goals, marketing objectives, and target markets.

6 Explain how the marketing environment affects strategic market planning.

To achieve a firm's marketing objectives, marketing-mix strategies must begin with an assessment of the marketing environment, which, in turn, will influence decisions about marketing-mix ingredients. Marketing activities are affected by a number of external forces that make up the marketing environment. These forces include economic forces, sociocultural forces, political forces, competitive forces, legal and regulatory forces, and technological forces. Economic forces affect customers' ability and willingness to buy. Sociocultural forces are societal and cultural factors, such as attitudes, beliefs, and lifestyles, that affect customers' buying choices. Political forces and legal and regulatory forces influence marketing planning through laws that protect consumers and regulate competition. Competitive forces are the actions of competitors who are implementing their own marketing plans. Technological forces can create new marketing opportunities or quickly cause a product to become obsolete.

7 Understand the major components of a marketing plan.

A marketing plan is a written document that specifies an organization's resources, objectives, strategy, and implementation and control efforts to be used in marketing a specific product or product group. The marketing plan describes a firm's current position, establishes marketing objectives, and specifies the methods the organization will use to achieve these objectives. Marketing plans can be short range, covering one year or less; medium range, covering two to five years; or long range, covering periods of more than five years.

8 Describe market measurement and sales forecasting.

Market measurement and sales forecasting are used to estimate sales potential and predict product sales in specific market segments.

9 Distinguish between a marketing information system and marketing research.

Strategies are monitored and evaluated through marketing research and the marketing information system that stores and processes internal and external data in a form that aids marketing decision making. A marketing information system is a system for managing marketing information that is gathered continually from internal and external sources. Marketing research is the process of systematically gathering, recording, and analyzing data concerning a particular marketing problem. It is an intermittent rather than a continual source of marketing information. Technology is making information for marketing decisions more accessible. Electronic communication tools can be very useful for accumulating accurate information with minimal customer interaction. Information technologies that are changing the way marketers obtain and use information are databases, online information services, and the Internet.

10 Identify the major steps in the consumer buying decision process and the sets of factors that may influence this process.

Buying behaviour consists of the decisions and actions of people involved in buying and using products. Consumer

buying behaviour refers to the purchase of products for personal or household use. Organizational buying behaviour is the purchase of products by producers, resellers, governments, and institutions. Understanding buying behaviour helps marketers to predict how buyers will respond to marketing strategies. The consumer buying decision process consists of five steps, including recognizing the problem, searching for information, evaluating alternatives, purchasing, and evaluating after purchase. Factors affecting the consumer buying decision process fall into three categories: situational influences, psychological influences, and social influences.

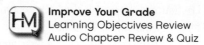

Improve Your Grade
Learning Objectives Review
Audio Chapter Review & Quiz

Review Questions

1. How, specifically, does marketing create place, time, and possession utility?
2. What is relationship marketing?
3. How is a marketing-oriented firm different from a production-oriented firm or a sales-oriented firm?
4. What are the major requirements for a group of individuals and organizations to be a market? How does a consumer market differ from a business-to-business market?
5. What are the major components of a marketing strategy?
6. What is the purpose of market segmentation? What is the relationship between market segmentation and the selection of target markets?
7. What are the four elements of the marketing mix? In what sense are they "controllable"?
8. Describe the forces in the marketing environment that affect an organization's marketing decisions.
9. What is a marketing plan, and what are its major components?
10. What major issues should be specified before conducting a sales forecast?
11. What is the difference between a marketing information system and a marketing research project? How might the two be related?

12. What new information technologies are changing the ways that marketers keep track of business trends and customers?
13. Why do marketers need to understand buying behaviour?
14. How are personal income, disposable income, and discretionary income related? Which is the best indicator of consumer purchasing power?

Discussion Questions

1. Are there any problems for a company that focuses mainly on the most profitable customers?
2. In what way is each of the following a marketing activity?
   a. The provision of sufficient parking space for customers at a suburban shopping mall
   b. The purchase by a clothing store of seven dozen sweaters in assorted sizes and colours
   c. The inclusion of a longer and more comprehensive warranty on an automobile
3. How might adoption of the marketing concept benefit a firm? How might it benefit the firm's customers?
4. Is marketing information as important to small firms as it is to larger firms? Explain.
5. How does the marketing environment affect a firm's marketing strategy?

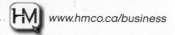

CASE STUDY

IKEA Targets Do-It-Yourselfers

Every day, more than 1 million customers visit IKEA stores worldwide to buy everything from beds and baskets to bookcases and bathmats. The Swedish-based retailer has grown to more than 225 stores worldwide with annual sales of $18 billion by offering 7,000 home furnishings that are well designed, functional, and affordably priced. Its customers like the contemporary look of IKEA's products—and they don't mind assembling their purchases to save money.

IKEA is always driving costs down in manufacturing, marketing, warehousing, and raw materials so that it can pass the savings along to customers. Year after year, the retailer lowers its prices by an average of 2 to 3 percent by buying in bulk, searching for the most efficient suppliers, and sticking to simple, contemporary styles. For a company that buys from 1,700 suppliers, including some that are thousands of miles from company headquarters, even small efficiencies quickly add up to significant savings.

Although IKEA's customers are frugal, they want fashionable furniture that fits their personalities and lifestyles. In fact, the store's appeal cuts across demographic lines. Some customers who can well afford to shop at posh emporiums come to IKEA because they like the combination of chic design, down-to-earth functionality, and speedy assembly. Any item that must be assembled at home is accompanied by clear step-by-step instructions and illustrations, reassuring to even the most inexperienced do-it-yourselfer.

Customers in many countries have responded enthusiastically to IKEA's formula. After expanding beyond Sweden to Norway and Denmark, the company opened stores in Europe, Australia, and North America. More recently, IKEA has come to Russia, Israel, Japan, and China. By 2010, more than sixty IKEA stores will dot North America from coast to coast.

Product names such as Billy bookcases and Klippan sofas are standard throughout the world and reflect the company's Swedish origins. However, IKEA's designers are careful to modify products for local tastes. "North Americans want more comfortable sofas, higher-quality textiles, bigger glasses, more spacious entertainment units," says the head of IKEA North America. Designers and researchers visit customers' homes to observe how they use furniture. As a result, when IKEA makes bedroom furniture for the North American market, it adds deeper drawers because "Americans prefer to store most of their clothes folded," notes the product manager. In Europe, product measurements are provided in centimetres, whereas in the United States, measurements are provided in inches.

IKEA translates its catalogues into thirty-six languages and distributes 160 million copies every year. Here again, IKEA looks for ways to minimize expenses. It has all products photographed at a large European studio and transmits the images electronically to printing plants in the regions where catalogues will be distributed, saving on shipping and mailing costs. Every detail, from paper quality to type size, is scrutinized to identify new cost efficiencies.

IKEA's formula of fashionable, affordable, and functional furniture has won it a loyal following. Customers have been known to line up a week ahead of opening day for a chance to win prizes and fifteen minutes of local fame as the first to see the new store. If customers get hungry while they shop, they can drop into the informal store restaurant for a quick snack or a light meal of Scandinavian delicacies. The most popular dish is Swedish meatballs: Customers devour 150 million of these tiny meatballs every year.

As popular as IKEA has become, CEO Anders Dahlvig sees plenty of room for growth because "awareness of our brand is much bigger than the size of our company." Still, no matter how large and fast IKEA grows, its focus will remain on keeping costs low to satisfy the target market's need for reasonably priced, well-designed assemble-it-yourself home furnishings.

For more information about this company, go to www.ikea.com.

Questions:

1. Is IKEA's targeting strategy concentrated or undifferentiated? Explain your answer.

2. Which of the variables for segmenting consumer markets is IKEA using, and why are these variables appropriate?

3. What combination of techniques might IKEA apply when preparing sales forecasts for North America?

BUILDING SKILLS FOR CAREER SUCCESS

1. Exploring the Internet

Consumer products companies with a variety of famous brand names known around the world are making their presence known on the Internet through websites and online banner advertising. The giants in consumer products include U.S.-based Procter & Gamble (www.pg .com/), Swiss-based Nestlé (www.nestle.com/), and British-based Unilever (www.unilever.com/).

According to a spokesperson for the Unilever Interactive Brand Center in New York, the firm is committed to making the Internet part of its marketing strategy. The centre carries out research and development (R&D) and serves as a model for others now in operation in the Netherlands and Singapore. Information is shared with interactive marketers assigned to specific business units. Eventually, centres will be established globally, reflecting the fact that most of Unilever's $52 billion in sales takes place in about 100 countries.

Unilever's view that online consumer product sales are the way of the future was indicated by online alliances established with Microsoft Network, America Online, and NetGrocer.com. Creating an online dialogue with consumers on a global scale is no simple task. Cultural differences often are subtle and difficult to explain but nonetheless are perceived by the viewers interacting with a site. Unilever's website, which is its connection to customers all over the world, has a global feel to it. The question is whether or not it is satisfactory to each target audience. Visit the text website for updates to this exercise.

Assignment

1. Examine the Unilever, Procter & Gamble, and Nestlé sites and describe the features that you think would be most interesting to consumers.
2. Describe those features you do not like and explain why.
3. Do you think that the sites can contribute to better consumer buyer behaviour? Explain your thinking.

HM Prepare for Class
Exploring the Internet

2. Building Team Skills

Review the text definitions of *market* and *target market*. Markets can be classified as consumer or industrial. Buyer behaviour consists of the decisions and actions of those involved in buying and using products or services. By examining aspects of a company's products, you usually can determine the company's target market and the characteristics important to members of that target market.

Assignment

1. Working in teams of three to five, identify a company and its major products.
2. List and discuss characteristics that customers may find important. These factors include price, quality, brand name, variety of services, salespeople, customer service, special offers, promotional campaign, packaging, convenience of use, convenience of purchase, location, guarantees, store/office decor, and payment terms.
3. Write a description of the company's primary customer (target market).

3. Researching Different Careers

Before interviewing for a job, you should learn all you can about the company. With this information, you will be prepared to ask meaningful questions about the firm during the interview, and the interviewer no doubt will be impressed with your knowledge of the business and your interest in it. To find out about a company, you can conduct some market research.

Assignment

1. Choose at least two local companies for which you might like to work.
2. Contact your local Chamber of Commerce. (The Chamber of Commerce collects information about local businesses and most of its services are free.) Ask for information about the companies.

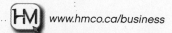

CHAPTER 13

Creating and Pricing Products That Satisfy Customers

Your Guide to Success in Business

Why this chapter matters
To be successful, a business person must understand how to develop a mix of appropriately priced products and to recognize that products will have to be changed with changing customer needs.

LEARNING OBJECTIVES

1. Explain what a product is and how products are classified.

2. Discuss the product life cycle and how it leads to new product development.

3. Define *product line* and *product mix* and distinguish between the two.

4. Identify the methods available for changing a product mix.

5. Explain the uses and importance of branding, packaging, and labelling.

6. Describe the economic basis of pricing and the means by which sellers can control prices and buyers' perceptions of prices.

7. Identify the major pricing objectives used by businesses.

8. Examine the three major pricing methods that firms employ.

9. Explain the strategies available to companies for setting prices.

10. Describe three major types of pricing associated with business products.

The Apple of My iPod

The Apple brand is shinier than ever, thanks to a never-ending stream of high-tech products with the human touch. A pioneer in the computer industry in the 1980s, Apple has long concentrated on developing cutting-edge products that are good looking and user-friendly. Its easy-to-use Macintosh computers have a loyal customer following. Still, they account for only a small share of the personal computer market, dominated by computers that run on Microsoft Windows systems.

However, the company's iPod portable digital media players have really polished Apple's reputation for breaking new ground. When the iPod was introduced, it faced considerable competition from established products—yet its stylish design and innovative features immediately captured the public imagination. The original iPod was designed specifically for music; the next-generation model accommodated photos, followed by models that also allowed viewing of videos. Today, the iPod product line holds a commanding lead in digital media players, with an estimated 75 percent share of the North American market.

A key part of Apple's product mix is its popular web-based iTunes Music Store. Here, songs sell for 99 cents each, and episodes of television programs such as *Desperate Housewives* sell for $1.99 each. Customers also can choose from thousands of music videos and short movies. Each downloaded song nets Apple just 10 cents in profits, but it helps sell iPods.

Both iPod and iTunes face an ever-more-crowded field of competitors. For example, Wal-Mart's website sells music downloads for just 88 cents each. As another example, Rogers has teamed up with Fido to offer hundreds of thousands of songs and video clips that can be downloaded from Rogers MusicStore directly to Fido cellphones or PCs. Can Apple remain at the top of the tree?

Not to be outdone, in early 2007 Apple announced the introduction of the iPhone, a cellphone/iPod hybrid and Apple TV, a wireless device that connects computers and other devices holding iTunes music,

continued on next page

● ● ●

DID YOU KNOW?

The iPod's stylish design is one reason why this product is so successful.

KEY TERMS

product (374)
consumer product (375)
business product (375)
convenience product (375)
shopping product (375)
specialty product (376)
raw material (376)
major equipment (376)
accessory equipment (376)
component part (376)
process material (376)
supply (376)
business service (376)
product life cycle (377)
product line (379)
product mix (380)
product modification (381)

line extension (381)
product deletion (382)
brand (385)
brand name (385)
brand mark (385)
trademark (385)
trade name (385)
manufacturer (or producer) brand (386)
store (or private) brand (386)
generic product (or brand) (386)
brand loyalty (387)
brand equity (387)
individual branding (389)
family branding (389)
brand extension (389)
packaging (389)

labelling (391)
express warranty (391)
price (392)
supply (392)
demand (393)
price competition (393)
non-price competition (393)
product differentiation (394)
markup (396)
break-even quantity (397)
total revenue (397)
fixed cost (397)
variable cost (397)
total cost (397)
price skimming (400)
penetration pricing (400)
negotiated pricing (400)

secondary-market pricing (400)
periodic discounting (401)
random discounting (401)
odd-number pricing (401)
multiple-unit pricing (401)
reference pricing (401)
bundle pricing (401)
everyday low prices (EDLPs) (402)
customary pricing (402)
captive pricing (402)
premium pricing (402)
price lining (403)
price leaders (403)
special-event pricing (403)
comparison discounting (403)
transfer pricing (404)
discount (404)

ACE the Test
Crossword Puzzle
Flashcards

photos, podcasts, films, and television content to their television screens. Using Apple TV's interface, anyone can quickly browse and view their entire collection of digital media. Not coincidently, these announcements came from CEO Steven Jobs on the same day it was also announced that henceforth, Apple Computer would simply be named Apple, reflecting the new focus on consumer electronic devices and services.

As a result of these technological developments, production and distribution of content can economically meet the needs of smaller markets. For example, Canadian artists are readily available at the iTunes store and are accessible to the online global market as well. "The demand across Canada for the iTunes Music Store has been overwhelming," said Eddy Cue, Apple's vice president of Applications. "We are excited to be able to offer music fans in Canada their own customized iTunes Music Store featuring many top Canadian artist exclusives."

The iTunes Music Store in Canada features over 700,000 songs and dozens of exclusive tracks from a wide variety of leading worldwide artists, including songs from Alanis Morissette, The Tragically Hip, Sarah McLachlan, Auf der Maur, Delerium, Black Eyed Peas, Chingy, Toby Keith, Diana Krall, and 3 Doors Down.

Based on www.apple.com/ca; and press release, "Apple Launches iTunes Music Store in Canada," December 2, 2004, http://www.apple.com/ca/press/2004/12/itunes_canada.html; and information from Phil Patton, "Style Meets Function, and Technology Gets a Human Touch," *New York Times*, November 2, 2005, p. G5; Eric A. Taub, "The Small Screen, Redefined," *New York Times*, November 10, 2005, p. C11; Peter Grant and Dionne Searcey, "How to Watch TV," *Wall Street Journal*, November 9, 2005, p. D1; "IPod's Cool Factor May Be Fading," *InformationWeek*, November 7, 2005, www.informationweek.com; www.rogers.com, accessed December 16, 2007.

product everything one receives in an exchange, including all tangible and intangible attributes and expected benefits; it can be a good, service, or idea

A **product** is everything one receives in an exchange, including all tangible and intangible attributes and expected benefits. An Apple iPod purchase, for example, includes not only the iPod itself but also earphones, instructions, and a warranty. A car includes a warranty, an owner's manual, and perhaps free emergency road service for a year. Some of the intangibles that come with an automobile include the status associated with ownership and the memories generated from past rides. Developing and managing products effectively are crucial to an organization's ability to maintain successful marketing mixes.

A product can be a good, a service, or an idea. A *good* is a real, physical thing that we can touch, such as a Classic Sport football. A *service* is the result of applying human or mechanical effort to a person or thing—a change we pay others to make for us. A real estate agent's services result in a change in the ownership of real property. A barber's services result in a change in your appearance. An *idea* can take the form of philosophies, lessons, concepts, or advice. Often ideas are included with a good or service. Thus we might buy a book (a good) that provides ideas on how to lose weight. Or we might join Weight Watchers for ideas on how to lose weight and for help (services) in doing so.

In this chapter we look first at products. We examine product classifications and describe the four stages, or life cycle, through which every product moves. Next, we illustrate how firms manage products effectively by modifying or deleting existing products and by developing new ones. We also discuss branding, packaging, and labelling of products. Then our focus shifts to pricing. We explain competitive factors that influence sellers' pricing decisions and also explore buyers' perceptions of prices.

After considering organizational objectives that can be accomplished through pricing, we outline several methods for setting prices. Finally, we describe pricing strategies by which sellers can reach target markets successfully.

Classification of Products

Learning Objective ❶

Explain what a product is and how products are classified.

Different classes of products are directed at particular target markets. A product's classification largely determines what kinds of distribution, promotion, and pricing are appropriate in marketing the product.

Products can be grouped into two general categories: consumer and business (also called *business-to-business* or *industrial products*). A product purchased to satisfy personal and family needs is a **consumer product.** A product bought for resale, for making other products, or for use in a firm's operations is a **business product.** The buyer's use of the product determines the classification of an item. Note that a single item can be both a consumer and a business product. A broom is a consumer product if you use it in your home. However, the same broom is a business product if you use it in the maintenance of your business. After a product is classified as a consumer or business product, it can be categorized further as a particular type of consumer or business product.

Consumer Product Classifications

The traditional and most widely accepted system of classifying consumer products consists of three categories: convenience, shopping, and specialty products. These groupings are based primarily on characteristics of buyers' purchasing behaviour.

A **convenience product** is a relatively inexpensive, frequently purchased item for which buyers want to exert only minimal effort. Examples include bread, gasoline, newspapers, soft drinks, and chewing gum. The buyer spends little time in planning the purchase of a convenience item or in comparing available brands or sellers.

A **shopping product** is an item for which buyers are willing to expend considerable effort on planning and making the purchase. Buyers allocate ample time for comparing stores and brands with

consumer product
a product purchased to satisfy personal and family needs

business product
a product bought for resale, for making other products, or for use in a firm's operations

convenience product
a relatively inexpensive, frequently purchased item for which buyers want to exert only minimal effort

shopping product an item for which buyers are willing to expend considerable effort on planning and making the purchase

Shopping products

Most brands of watches are shopping products. However, very expensive watches that are sold in few outlets are classified as specialty products.

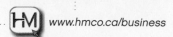

specialty product an item that possesses one or more unique characteristics for which a significant group of buyers is willing to expend considerable purchasing effort

raw material a basic material that actually becomes part of a physical product; usually comes from mines, forests, oceans, or recycled solid wastes

major equipment large tools and machines used for production purposes

accessory equipment standardized equipment used in a firm's production or office activities

component part an item that becomes part of a physical product and is either a finished item ready for assembly or a product that needs little processing before assembly

process material a material that is used directly in the production of another product but is not readily identifiable in the finished product

supply an item that facilitates production and operations but does not become part of a finished product

business service an intangible product that an organization uses in its operations

respect to prices, product features, qualities, services, and, perhaps, warranties. Appliances, upholstered furniture, men's suits, bicycles, and cellular phones are examples of shopping products. These products are expected to last for a fairly long time and thus are purchased less frequently than convenience items.

A **specialty product** possesses one or more unique characteristics for which a group of buyers is willing to expend considerable purchasing effort. Buyers actually plan the purchase of a specialty product; they know exactly what they want and will not accept a substitute. In searching for specialty products, purchasers do not compare alternatives. Examples include unique sports cars, a specific type of antique dining table, a rare imported beer, or, perhaps, specially handcrafted stereo speakers.

One problem with this approach to classification is that buyers behave differently when purchasing a specific type of product. Thus a single product can fit into more than one category. To minimize this problem, marketers think in terms of how buyers are most likely to behave when purchasing a specific item.

Business Product Classifications

Based on their characteristics and intended uses, business products can be classified into the following categories: raw materials, major equipment, accessory equipment, component parts, process materials, supplies, and services.

A **raw material** is a basic material that actually becomes part of a physical product. It usually comes from mines, forests, oceans, or recycled solid wastes. Raw materials usually are bought and sold according to grades and specifications.

Major equipment includes large tools and machines used for production purposes. Examples of major equipment are lathes, cranes, and stamping machines. Some major equipment is custom-made for a particular organization, but other items are standardized products that perform one or several tasks for many types of organizations.

Accessory equipment is standardized equipment used in a firm's production or office activities. Examples include hand tools, fax machines, fractional-horsepower motors, and calculators. Compared with major equipment, accessory items are usually much less expensive and are purchased routinely with less negotiation.

A **component part** becomes part of a physical product and is either a finished item ready for assembly or a product that needs little processing before assembly. Although it becomes part of a larger product, a component part often can be identified easily. Clocks, tires, computer chips, and switches are examples of component parts.

A **process material** is used directly in the production of another product. Unlike a component part, however, a process material is not readily identifiable in the finished product. Like component parts, process materials are purchased according to industry standards or to the specifications of the individual purchaser. Examples include industrial glue and food preservatives.

A **supply** facilitates production and operations but does not become part of a finished product. Paper, pencils, oils, and cleaning agents are examples. A **business service** is an intangible product that an organization uses in its operations. Examples include financial, legal, online, janitorial, and marketing research services. Purchasers must decide whether to provide their own services internally or to hire them from outside the organization.

The Product Life Cycle

Learning Objective

Discuss the product life cycle and how it leads to new product development.

In a way, products are like people. They are born, they live, and they die. Every product progresses through a **product life cycle,** a series of stages in which a product's sales revenue and profit increase, reach a peak, and then decline. A firm must be able to launch, modify, and delete products from its offering of products in response to changes in product life cycles. Otherwise, the firm's profits will disappear, and the firm will fail. Depending on the product, life-cycle stages will vary in length. In this section we discuss the stages of the life cycle and how marketers can use this information.

product life cycle a series of stages in which a product's sales revenue and profit increase, reach a peak, and then decline

Stages of the Product Life Cycle

Generally, the product life cycle is assumed to be composed of four stages—introduction, growth, maturity, and decline—as shown in Figure 13.1. Some products progress through these stages rapidly, in a few weeks or months. Others can take years to go through each stage. The original Rubik's Cube (now experiencing a revival) had a relatively short life cycle. Parker Brothers' Monopoly game, which was introduced over seventy years ago, is still going strong.

Introduction In the *introduction stage*, customer awareness and acceptance of the product are low. Sales rise gradually as a result of promotion and distribution activities, but initially, high development and marketing costs result in low profit or even in a loss. There are relatively few competitors. The price is sometimes high, and purchasers are primarily people who want to be "the first" to own the new product. The marketing challenge at this stage is to make potential customers aware of the product's existence and its features, benefits, and uses.

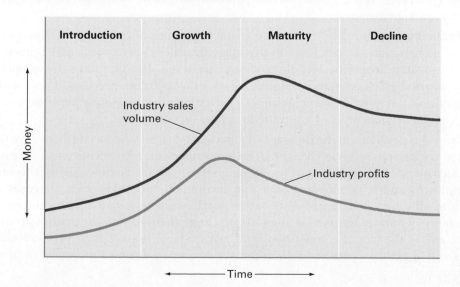

Figure 13.1

Product Life Cycle

The graph shows sales volume and profits during the life cycle of a product.

Source: William M. Pride and O. C. Ferrell, *Marketing: Concepts and Strategies* (Boston: Houghton Mifflin, 2006). Copyright © 2006 by Houghton Mifflin Company. Adapted with permission.

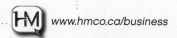

A new product is seldom an immediate success. Marketers must watch early buying patterns carefully and be prepared to modify the new product promptly if necessary. The product should be priced to attract the particular market segment that has the greatest desire and ability to buy the product. Plans for distribution and promotion should suit the targeted market segment. As with the product itself, the initial price, distribution channels, and promotional efforts may need to be adjusted quickly to maintain sales growth during the introduction stage.

Growth In the *growth stage*, sales increase rapidly as the product becomes well known. Other firms probably have begun to market competing products. The competition and lower unit costs (owing to mass production) result in a lower price, which reduces the profit per unit. Note that industry profits reach a peak and begin to decline during this stage. To meet the needs of the growing market, the originating firm offers modified versions of its product and expands its distribution. The 3M Company, the maker of Post-it Notes, has developed a variety of sizes, colours, and designs.

Management's goal in the growth stage is to stabilize and strengthen the product's position by encouraging brand loyalty. To beat the competition, the company may further improve the product or expand the product line to appeal to additional market segments. Apple, for example, has introduced several variations on its wildly popular iPod MP3 player. The iPod Mini is a smaller, more colourful device, and the iPod Shuffle, is a more affordable version. The iPod Nano is a pencil-thin device that weighs 49.2 grams. The Video iPod can store and play movies, television shows, and music videos. Apple has expanded its iTunes Music Store to include downloadable versions of popular shows such as *Saturday Night Live*, *Desperate Housewives*, and *Lost*, as well as exclusive music videos from artists such as U2. Continuous product innovation and service expansion have helped to expand Apple's market penetration in the competitive MP3 player industry.[1] Management can also compete by lowering prices if increased production efficiency has resulted in savings for the company. As the product becomes more widely accepted, marketers may be able to broaden the network of distributors. Marketers also can emphasize customer service and prompt credit for defective products. During this period, promotional efforts attempt to build brand loyalty among customers.

Maturity Sales are still increasing at the beginning of the *maturity stage*, but the rate of increase has slowed. Later in this stage the sales curve peaks and begins to decline. Industry profits decline throughout this stage. Product lines are simplified, markets are segmented more carefully, and price competition increases. The increased competition forces weaker competitors to leave the industry. Refinements and extensions of the original product continue to appear on the market.

During a product's maturity stage, its market share may be strengthened by redesigned packaging or style changes. Also, consumers may be encouraged to use the product more often or in new ways. Pricing strategies are flexible during this stage. Markdowns and price incentives are not uncommon, although price increases may work to offset production and distribution costs. Marketers may offer incentives and assistance of various kinds to dealers to encourage them to support mature products, especially in the face of competition from private-label brands. New promotional efforts and aggressive personal selling may be necessary during this period of intense competition.

Decline During the *decline stage*, sales volume decreases sharply. Profits continue to fall. The number of competing firms declines, and the only survivors in the marketplace are firms that specialize in marketing the product. Production and marketing costs become the most important determinant of profit.

When a product adds to the success of the overall product line, the company might retain it; otherwise, management must determine when to eliminate the product. A product usually declines because of technological advances, environmental factors, or because consumers have switched to competing brands. Therefore, few changes are made in the product itself during this stage. Instead, management might raise the price to cover costs, re-price it to maintain market share, or lower the price to reduce inventory. Similarly, management will narrow distribution of the declining product to the most profitable existing markets. During this period, the company probably will not spend heavily on promotion, although it may use some advertising and sales incentives to slow the product's decline. The company may choose to eliminate less profitable versions of the product from the product line or may decide to drop the product entirely.

Using the Product Life Cycle

Marketers should be aware of the life-cycle stage of each product for which they are responsible. And they should try to estimate how long the product is expected to remain in that stage. Both must be taken into account in making decisions about the marketing strategy for a product. If a product is expected to remain in the maturity stage for a long time, a replacement product might be introduced later in the stage. If the maturity stage is expected to be short, however, a new product should be introduced much earlier. For example, Logitech, a leading manufacturer of computer mice, finds that its technology-driven accessories face a short product life cycle. In an industry with powerful competitors such as Microsoft, Logitech must introduce new products frequently particularly due to the current trend toward everything wireless. Logitech also has introduced its Laser Mouse, engineered specifically for use in gaming. The company has made strides against the competition with significant growth in sales in recent years.[2] In some cases a firm may be willing to take the chance of speeding up the decline of existing products. In other situations a company will attempt to extend a product's life cycle. For example, General Mills has extended the life of Bisquick baking mix (launched in the mid-1930s) by improving the product's formulation significantly and creating and promoting a variety of uses.

Product Line and Product Mix

Define *product line* and *product mix* and distinguish between the two.

A **product line** is a group of similar products that differ only in relatively minor characteristics. Generally, the products within a product line are related to each other in the way they are produced, marketed, or used. Procter & Gamble, for example,

product line a group of similar products that differ only in relatively minor characteristics

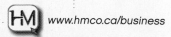

manufactures and markets several shampoos, including Prell, Head & Shoulders, Pert Plus, and Ivory.

Many organizations tend to introduce new products within existing product lines. This permits them to apply the experience and knowledge they have acquired to the production and marketing of new products. Other firms develop entirely new product lines.

product mix all the products a firm offers for sale

An organization's **product mix** consists of all the products the firm offers for sale. For example, Procter & Gamble, which recently acquired Gillette, has over 300 brands that fall into one of twenty-two product lines ranging from deodorants to paper products.[3] Two "dimensions" are often applied to a firm's product mix. The *width* of the mix is the number of product lines it contains. The *depth* of the mix is the average number of individual products within each line. These are general measures; we speak of a *broad* or a *narrow* mix rather than a mix of exactly three or five product lines. Some organizations provide broad product mixes to be competitive. For example, in the U.S., GE Financial Network (GEFN), a comprehensive Internet-based, consumer-friendly, financial services resource, provides an extensive product mix of financial services, including home mortgages, mutual funds, stock price quotes, annuities, life insurance, auto insurance, long-term care insurance, credit cards, and auto warranty plans.[4]

Managing the Product Mix

Learning Objective 4

Identify the methods available for changing a product mix.

To provide products that satisfy people in a firm's target market or markets and that also achieve the organization's objectives, a marketer must develop, adjust, and maintain an effective product mix. Seldom can the same product mix be effective for long. Because customers' product preferences and attitudes change, their desire for a product can diminish or grow. In some cases a firm needs to alter its product mix to adapt to competition. A marketer may have to eliminate a product from the mix because one or more competitors dominate that product's specific market segment. Similarly, an organization may have to introduce a new product or modify an existing one to compete more effectively. A marketer may expand the firm's product mix to take advantage of excess marketing and production capacity. For example, both Coca-Cola and Pepsi have expanded their lines by adding the bottled-water brands Dasani and Aquafina. More recently, they have launched berry- and citrus-flavoured waters. The bottled-water category leader, Nestlé, has released its own four-flavour line of water called Pure Life Splash in the United States in direct response to Coca-Cola and Pepsi's latest line extensions.[5] For whatever reason a product mix is altered, the product mix must be managed to bring about improvements in the mix. There are three major ways to improve a product mix: change an existing product, delete a product, or develop a new product.

Managing Existing Products

A product mix can be changed by deriving additional products from existing ones. This can be accomplished through product modifications and by line extensions.

Product Modifications Product modification refers to changing one or more of a product's characteristics. For this approach to be effective, several conditions must be met. First, the product must be modifiable. Second, existing customers must be able to perceive that a modification has been made, assuming that the modified item is still directed at the same target market. Third, the modification should make the product more consistent with customers' desires so that it provides greater satisfaction. For example, Ford modified its popular F-150 pickup by adding more interior room, better safety features, and an optional built-in DVD player. The company designed these modifications for the 80 percent of its F-150 customers who use the truck as family transportation.[6]

Existing products can be altered in three primary ways: in quality, function, and aesthetics. *Quality modifications* are changes that relate to a product's dependability and durability and usually are achieved by alterations in the materials or production process. *Functional modifications* affect a product's versatility, effectiveness, convenience, or safety; they usually require redesign of the product. Typical product categories that have undergone extensive functional modifications include home appliances, office and farm equipment, and consumer electronics. *Aesthetic modifications* are directed at changing the sensory appeal of a product by altering its taste, texture, sound, smell, or visual characteristics. Because a buyer's purchasing decision is affected by how a product looks, smells, tastes, feels, or sounds, an aesthetic modification can have a definite impact on purchases. Through aesthetic modifications, a firm can differentiate its product from competing brands and perhaps gain a sizable market share if customers find the modified product more appealing.

Line Extensions A line extension is the development of a product closely related to one or more products in the existing product line but designed specifically to meet somewhat different customer needs. For example, Nabisco extended its cookie line to include Reduced Fat Oreos and Double Stuf Oreos.

Many of the so-called new products introduced each year are in fact line extensions. Line extensions are more common than new products because they are a less expensive, lower-risk alternative for increasing sales. A line extension can focus on a different market segment or be an attempt to increase sales within the same market segment by more precisely satisfying the needs of people in that segment. Line extensions are also used to take market share from competitors.

product modification the process of changing one or more of a product's characteristics

line extension development of a new product that is closely related to one or more products in the existing product line but designed specifically to meet somewhat different customer needs

Line extensions

Gatorade Endurance Formula products are line extensions. These products are available in three ready-to-drink flavours and instant mixes.

Deleting Products

To maintain an effective product mix, an organization often has to eliminate some products. This is

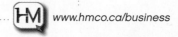

product deletion the elimination of one or more products from a product line

called **product deletion.** A weak product costs a firm time, money, and resources that could be used to modify other products or develop new ones. Also, when a weak product generates an unfavourable image among customers, the negative image may rub off on other products sold by the firm.

Most organizations find it difficult to delete a product. Some firms drop weak products only after they have become severe financial burdens. A better approach is some form of systematic review of the product's impact on the overall effectiveness of a firm's product mix. Such a review should analyze a product's contribution to a company's sales for a given period. It should include estimates of future sales, costs, and profits associated with the product and a consideration of whether changes in the marketing strategy could improve the product's performance.

A product-deletion program definitely can improve a firm's performance. Long-time rivals Coke and Pepsi went head to head when they both introduced their own midcalorie soft drinks: C2 and Pepsi Edge. Both were meant to appeal to regular soda drinkers who wanted fewer calories without diet taste. While neither product was successful, Pepsi was quick to cut its losses and deleted Edge, whereas Coke continued producing C2.[7]

Developing New Products

Developing and introducing new products is frequently time-consuming, expensive, and risky. Thousands of new products are introduced annually. Depending on how we define it, the failure rate for new products ranges between 60 and 75 percent. Although developing new products is risky, failing to introduce new products can be just as hazardous. New products generally are grouped into three categories on the basis of their degree of similarity to existing products. *Imitations* are products designed to be similar to—and to compete with—existing products of other firms. Examples are the various brands of whitening toothpastes that were developed to compete with Rembrandt. *Adaptations* are variations of existing products that are intended for an established market. For example, with increasing concerns nationwide about health issues such as diabetes and obesity, Hershey decided to introduce product adaptations with the launching of its sugar-free versions of twenty-four of its major chocolate brands in conjunction with a partnership with the American Diabetes Association. Instead of sugar, these candy bars contain Splenda.[8] Product refinements and extensions are the adaptations considered most often, although imitative products also may include some refinement and extension. *Innovations* are entirely new products. They may give rise to a new industry or revolutionize an existing one. The introduction of CDs, for example, has brought major changes to the recording industry. Innovative products take considerable time, effort, and money to develop. They are therefore less common than adaptations and imitations. As shown in Figure 13.2, the process of developing a new product consists of seven phases.

Idea Generation Idea generation involves looking for product ideas that will help a firm to achieve its objectives. Although some organizations get their ideas almost by chance, firms trying to maximize product-mix effectiveness usually develop systematic approaches for generating new product ideas. Ideas may come from managers, researchers, engineers, competitors, advertising agencies, management consultants, private research organizations, customers, salespersons, or top executives.

Screening During screening, ideas that do not match organizational resources and objectives are rejected. In this phase, a firm's managers consider whether the organization has personnel with the expertise to develop and market the proposed product. Management may reject a good idea because the company lacks the necessary skills and abilities. The largest number of product ideas are rejected during the screening phase.

Concept Testing Concept testing is a phase in which a product idea is presented to a small sample of potential buyers through a written or oral description (and perhaps a few drawings) to determine their attitudes and initial buying intentions regarding the product. For a single product idea, an organization can test one or several concepts of the same product. Concept testing is a low-cost means for an organization to determine consumers' initial reactions to a product idea before investing considerable resources in product research and development (R&D). Product development personnel can use the results of concept testing to improve product attributes and product benefits that are most important to potential customers. The types of questions asked vary considerably depending on the type of product idea being tested. The following are typical questions:

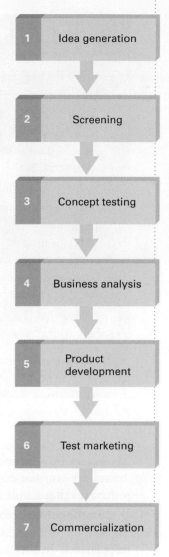

Figure 13.2

Phases of New Product Development

Generally, marketers follow these seven steps when developing a new product.

Source: William M. Pride and O. C. Ferrell, *Marketing: Concepts and Strategies* (Boston: Houghton Mifflin, 2006). Copyright © 2006 by Houghton Mifflin Company. Adapted with permission.

* Which benefits of the proposed product are especially attractive to you?

* Which features are of little or no interest to you?

* What are the primary advantages of the proposed product over the one you currently use?

* If this product were available at an appropriate price, how often would you buy it?

* How could this proposed product be improved?

Business Analysis Business analysis provides tentative ideas about a potential product's financial performance, including its probable profitability. During this stage, the firm considers how the new product, if it were introduced, would affect the firm's sales, costs, and profits. Marketing personnel usually work up preliminary sales and cost projections at this point, with the help of R&D and production managers.

Product Development In the product development phase, the company must find out first if it is technically feasible to produce the product and then if the product can be made at a cost low enough to justify a reasonable price. If a product idea makes it to this point, it is transformed into a working model, or *prototype*.

Test Marketing Test marketing is the limited introduction of a product in several towns or cities chosen to be representative of the intended target market. Its aim is to determine buyers' probable reactions. The product is left in the test markets long

BUSINESS AROUND THE WORLD

Carl Zeiss Makes New Products Pay Off

Just a decade ago, Carl Zeiss, the German maker of precision optical products such as microscopes and camera lenses, was in serious financial trouble. Today, however, it's a profitable $2.8 billion company, with two-thirds of its sales from products introduced within the past five years. Based on close attention to customers' needs and changing market conditions, Zeiss makes its rigorous new-product development pay off. Here's how:

1. Hold an annual innovation conference where hundreds of employees present their new product ideas.
2. Select the most promising 20 to 30 ideas for evaluation by a special "ideas board."
3. Allow six months to analyze the challenges and opportunities of the best ideas.
4. Based on this analysis, assign teams to create prototypes for the top 2 or 3 product ideas.
5. Test the prototypes and put the winner into production.

"Innovation is about more than invention," says CEO Dieter Kurz. "It is about creating something that gives the company an advantage."

Sources: Based on information in Jens Meyer, "Priming the R&D Machine," *Business 2.0,* September 2006, p. 60; "Zeiss Microscopy Unit Undergoes Change," *R & D,* March 2006, p. 13.

enough to give buyers a chance to repurchase the product if they are so inclined. Marketers can experiment with advertising, pricing, and packaging in different test areas and can measure the extent of brand awareness, brand switching, and repeat purchases that result from alterations in the marketing mix.

Commercialization During commercialization, plans for full-scale manufacturing and marketing must be refined and completed, and budgets for the project must be prepared. In the early part of the commercialization phase, marketing management analyzes the results of test marketing to find out what changes in the marketing mix are needed before the product is introduced. The results of test marketing may tell the marketers, for example, to change one or more of the product's physical attributes, to modify the distribution plans to include more retail outlets, to alter promotional efforts, or to change the product's price. Products usually are not introduced nationwide overnight. Most new products are marketed in stages, beginning in selected geographic areas and expanding into adjacent areas over a period of time.

Why Do Products Fail? Despite this rigorous process for developing product ideas, most new products end up as failures. In fact, many well-known companies have produced market failures (see Table 13.1).

Why does a new product fail? Mainly because the product and its marketing program are not planned and tested as completely as they should be. For example, to save on development costs, a firm may market-test its product but not its entire marketing mix. Or a firm may market a new product before all the "bugs" have been worked out.

COMPANY	PRODUCT
Orajel	Toddler training toothpaste
3M	Floptical storage disk
IncrEdibles Breakaway Foods	Push n' Eat
General Mills	Betty Crocker MicroRave Singles
Adams (Pfizer)	Body Smarts nutritional bars
General Motors Corp.	Cadillac Allante luxury sedan
Anheuser-Busch Companies	Bud Dry and Michelob Dry beer
Coca-Cola	Surge Citrus drink
Heinz	Ketchup Salsa
Noxema	Noxema Skin Fitness

Table 13.1

Examples of Product Failures

Sources: www .newproductworks.com; accessed January 23, 2006; Robert M. McMath, "Copycat Cupcakes Don't Cut It," *American Demographics*, January 1997, p. 60; Eric Berggren and Thomas Nacher, "Why Good Ideas Go Bust," *Management Review*, February 2000, pp. 32–36.

Or, when problems show up in the testing stage, a firm may try to recover its product development costs by pushing ahead with full-scale marketing anyway. Finally, some firms try to market new products with inadequate financing.

Branding, Packaging, and Labelling

Learning Objective 5

Explain the uses and importance of branding, packaging, and labelling.

Three important features of a product (particularly a consumer product) are its brand, package, and label. These features might be used to associate a product with a successful product line or to distinguish it from existing products. They could be designed to attract customers at the point of sale or to provide information to potential purchasers. Because the brand, package, and label are very real parts of the product, they deserve careful attention during product planning.

What Is a Brand?

A **brand** is a name, term, symbol, design, or any combination of these that identifies a seller's products as distinct from those of other sellers.[9] A **brand name** is the part of a brand that can be spoken. It may include letters, words, numbers, or pronounceable symbols, such as the ampersand in *Procter & Gamble*. A **brand mark**, on the other hand, is the part of a brand that is a symbol or distinctive design, such as the Nike "swoosh." A **trademark** is a brand name or brand mark that is registered with the Canadian Trademark Office and thus is legally protected from use by anyone except its owner. A **trade name** is the complete and legal name of an organization, such as Pizza Hut Incorporated, or Houghton Mifflin Harcourt Company (the publisher of this text).

brand a name, term, symbol, design, or any combination of these that identifies a seller's products as distinct from those of other sellers

brand name the part of a brand that can be spoken

brand mark the part of a brand that is a symbol or distinctive design

trademark a brand name or brand mark that is registered with the Canadian Trademark Office (part of the Canadian Intellectual Property Office of Industry Canada) and thus is legally protected from use by anyone except its owner

trade name the complete and legal name of an organization

SPOTLIGHT

Consumers often choose the store brand

Percentage of total product sales derived from store brand products:

57.8%   50.9%   51.7%   53.4%   45.4%

Sugar   Powdered milk   Dry beans/ vegetables   Marshmallows   Coffee creamer

Source: *PLMA's 2003 Private Label Yearbook: A Statistical Guide to Today's Store Brands*, p. 63.

manufacturer (or **producer**) **brand** a brand that is owned by a manufacturer

store (or **private**) **brand** a brand that is owned by an individual wholesaler or retailer

generic product (or **brand**) a product with no brand at all

Types of Brands

Brands often are classified according to who owns them: manufacturers or stores. A **manufacturer** (or **producer**) **brand,** as the name implies, is a brand that is owned by a manufacturer. Many foods (Frosted Flakes), major appliances (Whirlpool), gasolines (Exxon), automobiles (Honda), and clothing (Levis) are sold as manufacturers' brands. Some consumers prefer manufacturer brands because they usually are nationally known, offer consistent quality, and are widely available.

A **store** (or **private**) **brand** is a brand that is owned by an individual wholesaler or retailer. Among the better-known store brands are Kenmore and Craftsman, both owned by Sears, Roebuck. Owners of store brands claim that they can offer lower prices, earn greater profits, and improve customer loyalty with their own brands. Some companies that manufacture private brands also produce their own manufacturer brands. They often find such operations profitable because they can use excess capacity and at the same time avoid most marketing costs. Many private-branded grocery products are produced by companies that specialize in making private-label products. About 20 percent of products sold in supermarkets are private-branded items.[10]

Consumer confidence is the most important element in the success of a branded product, whether the brand is owned by a producer or by a retailer. Because branding identifies each product completely, customers can easily repurchase products that provide satisfaction, performance, and quality. And they can just as easily avoid or ignore products that do not. In supermarkets, the products most likely to keep their shelf space are the brands with large market shares and strong customer loyalty.

A **generic product** (sometimes called a **generic brand**) is a product with no brand at all. Its plain package carries only the name of the product—applesauce, peanut butter, potato chips, or whatever. Generic products, available in supermarkets since 1977, sometimes are made by the major producers that manufacture name brands. Even though generic brands may have accounted for as much as 10 percent of all grocery sales several years ago, they currently represent less than one-half of 1 percent.

Benefits of Branding

Both buyers and sellers benefit from branding. Because brands are easily recognizable, they reduce the amount of time buyers must spend shopping; buyers can quickly identify the brands they prefer. Choosing particular brands, such as Tommy Hilfiger, Polo, Nautica, and Nike, can be a way of expressing oneself. When buyers are unable to evaluate a product's characteristics, brands can help them to judge the quality of the product. For example, most buyers are not able to judge the quality of stereo components but may be guided by a well-respected brand name. Brands can symbolize a certain quality level to a customer, allowing that perception of quality to represent the actual quality of the item. Brands thus help to reduce a buyer's perceived risk of purchase. Finally, customers may receive a psychological reward that comes from owning a brand that symbolizes status. The Lexus brand is an example.

Because buyers are already familiar with a firm's existing brands, branding helps a firm to introduce a new product that carries the same brand name. For example, Unilever, the company that produces the Dove brand as well as many others, has continued to expand its Dove product line. Originally, Dove made bar soap and then extended the line to include deodorant, facial cleansing products, and body soap. The latest additions are Dove shampoos and conditioners. Unilever hopes to gain market share quickly because of customers' favourable perceptions of Dove products.[11] Branding aids sellers in their promotional efforts because promotion of each branded product indirectly promotes other products of the same brand. H.G. Heinz, for example, markets many products with the Heinz brand name, such as ketchup, vinegar, vegetarian beans, gravies, barbecue sauce, and steak sauce. Promotion of one Heinz product indirectly promotes the others.

One chief benefit of branding is the creation of **brand loyalty,** the extent to which a customer favours buying a specific brand. The stronger the brand loyalty, the greater is the likelihood that buyers will consistently choose the brand. There are three levels of brand loyalty: recognition, preference, and insistence. *Brand recognition* is the level of loyalty at which customers are aware that the brand exists and will purchase it if their preferred brands are unavailable or if they are unfamiliar with available brands. This is the weakest form of brand loyalty. *Brand preference* is the level of brand loyalty at which a customer prefers one brand over competing brands. However, if the preferred brand is unavailable, the customer is willing to substitute another brand. *Brand insistence* is the strongest level of brand loyalty. Brand-insistent customers strongly prefer a specific brand and will not buy substitutes. Brand insistence is the least common type of brand loyalty. Partly owing to marketers' increased dependence on discounted prices, coupons, and other short-term promotions, and partly because of the enormous array of new products with similar characteristics, brand loyalty in general seems to be declining.

Brand equity is the marketing and financial value associated with a brand's strength in a market. Although difficult to measure, brand equity represents the value of a brand to an organization. Some of the world's most valuable brands include Coca-Cola, Microsoft, IBM, General Electric, and Intel.[12] The four major factors that contribute to brand equity are brand awareness, brand associations, perceived brand quality, and brand loyalty. Brand awareness leads to brand familiarity, and buyers are more likely to select a familiar brand than an unfamiliar one. The associations linked to a brand can connect a personality type or lifestyle with a particular brand. For example, consumers may associate De Beers diamonds with loving, long-lasting relationships. When consumers are unable to judge for themselves the quality of a product, they may rely on their perception of the quality of the product's brand. Finally, brand loyalty is a valued element of brand equity because it reduces both a brand's vulnerability to competitors and the need to spend tremendous resources to attract new customers; it also provides brand visibility and encourages retailers to carry the brand. New companies, for example, have much work to do in establishing new brands to compete with well-known brands. For example, China's Beijing Li Ning Sports Goods

brand loyalty extent to which a customer favours buying a specific brand

brand equity marketing and financial value associated with a brand's strength in a market

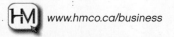

Company, started by the gymnastic gold medalist Li Ning, is establishing itself as a rival brand to Nike in shoes and sporting goods. Building brand equity will take both time and large investments of capital. Currently, Li Ning Company spends 11 percent of its revenue on marketing efforts to increase brand recognition and loyalty. The company is expanding internationally, and its "L" logo that resembles a wavy check mark is set up to rival the Nike swoosh in China and beyond.[13]

Marketing on the Internet sometimes is best done in collaboration with a better-known web brand. For instance, Weight Watchers, Tire Rack, wine.com, Office Depot, Toys "Я" Us, and Shutterfly all rely on partnerships with Internet retail giant Amazon to increase their sales. Amazon provides special sections on its website to promote its partners and their products. As with its own products, Amazon gives users the ability to post online reviews of its partners' products or to add them to an Amazon "wish list" that can be saved or e-mailed to friends. Amazon even labels its partners as "Amazon Trusted" when customers browse their sites, giving even these well-known real-world companies credibility in the online marketplace.[14]

Choosing and Protecting a Brand

A number of issues should be considered when selecting a brand name. The name should be easy for customers to say, spell, and recall. Short, one-syllable names such as *Tide* often satisfy this requirement. The brand name should suggest, in a positive way, the product's uses, special characteristics, and major benefits and should be distinctive enough to set it apart from competing brands. Choosing the right brand name has become a challenge because many obvious product names already have been used.

It is important that a firm select a brand that can be protected through registration, reserving it for exclusive use by that firm. Some brands, because of their designs, are infringed more easily upon than others. Although registration protects trademarks domestically for ten years and can be renewed indefinitely, a firm should develop a system for ensuring that its trademarks will be renewed as needed. To protect its exclusive right to the brand, the company must ensure that the selected brand will not be considered an infringement on any existing brand already registered with the Canadian Trademark Office. This task can be complicated by the fact that infringement is determined by the courts, which base their decisions on whether a brand causes consumers to be confused, mistaken, or deceived about the source of the product. Starbucks, the Seattle-based coffee company, recently took legal action against companies using similar brand names, including Sambuck's Coffeehouse, Black Bear's Charbucks Blend, and A&D Cafe's Warbucks coffee.[15]

▲
Building brand equity

The Toronto Raptors' mascot is a trade character. Companies employ trade characters to elicit positive brand associations in consumers' minds.

A firm must guard against a brand name's becoming a generic term that refers to a general product category. Generic terms cannot be legally protected as exclusive brand names. For example, names such as *yo-yo, aspirin, escalator,* and *thermos*—all exclusively brand names at one time—eventually were declared generic terms that refer to product categories. As such, they could no longer be protected. To ensure that a brand name does not become a generic term, the firm should spell the name with a capital letter and use it as an adjective to modify the name of the general product class, as in Jell-O Brand Gelatin. An organization can deal directly with this problem by advertising that its brand is a trademark and should not be used generically. Firms also can use the registered trademark symbol ® to indicate that the brand is trademarked.

Branding Strategies

The basic branding decision for any firm is whether to brand its products. A producer may market its products under its own brands, private brands, or both. A retail store may carry only producer brands, its own brands, or both. Once either type of firm decides to brand, it chooses one of two branding strategies: individual branding or family branding.

Individual branding is the strategy in which a firm uses a different brand for each of its products. For example, Procter & Gamble uses individual branding for its line of bar soaps, which includes Ivory, Camay, Zest, Safeguard, Coast, and Oil of Olay. Individual branding offers two major advantages. A problem with one product will not affect the good name of the firm's other products, and the different brands can be directed toward different market segments. For example, Marriotts' Fairfield Inns are directed toward budget-minded travellers and Marriott Hotels toward upscale customers.

individual branding the strategy in which a firm uses a different brand for each of its products

Family branding is the strategy in which a firm uses the same brand for all or most of its products. Sony, Dell, IBM, and Xerox use family branding for their entire product mixes. A major advantage of family branding is that the promotion of any one item that carries the family brand tends to help all other products with the same brand name. In addition, a new product has a head start when its brand name is already known and accepted by customers.

family branding the strategy in which a firm uses the same brand for all or most of its products

Brand Extensions A **brand extension** occurs when an organization uses one of its existing brands to brand a new product in a different product category. For example, Procter & Gamble employed a brand extension when it named a new product Ivory Body Wash. A brand extension should not be confused with a line extension. A *line extension* refers to using an existing brand on a new product in the same product category, such as a new flavour or new sizes. For example, when the makers of Tylenol introduced Extra Strength Tylenol PM, the new product was a line extension because it was in the same product category. One thing marketers must be careful of, however, is extending a brand too many times or extending too far outside the original product category, which can weaken the brand.

brand extension using an existing brand to brand a new product in a different product category

Packaging

Packaging consists of all the activities involved in developing and providing a container with graphics for a product. The package is a vital part of the product. It

packaging all the activities involved in developing and providing a container with graphics for a product

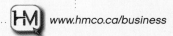

can make the product more versatile, safer, or easier to use. Through its shape, appearance, and printed message, a package can influence purchasing decisions.

Packaging Functions Effective packaging means more than simply putting products in containers and covering them with wrappers. The basic function of packaging materials is to protect the product and maintain its functional form. Fluids such as milk, orange juice, and hair spray need packages that preserve and protect them; the packaging should prevent damage that could affect the product's usefulness and increase costs. Since product tampering has become a problem for marketers of many types of goods, several packaging techniques have been developed to counter this danger. Some packages are also designed to foil shoplifting.

Another function of packaging is to offer consumer convenience. For example, small, aseptic packages—individual-serving boxes or plastic bags that contain liquids and do not require refrigeration—appeal strongly to children and to young adults with active lifestyles. The size or shape of a package may relate to the product's storage, convenience of use, or replacement rate. Small, single-serving cans of vegetables, for instance, might prevent waste and make storage easier. A third function of packaging is to promote a product by communicating its features, uses, benefits, and image. Sometimes a firm develops a reusable package to make its product more desirable. For example, the Cool Whip package doubles as a food-storage container.

Package Design Considerations Many factors must be weighed when developing packages. Obviously, one major consideration is cost. Although a number of packaging materials, processes, and designs are available, some are rather expensive. While Canadian buyers have shown a willingness to pay more for improved packaging, there are limits.

Marketers also must decide whether to package the product in single or multiple units. Multiple-unit packaging can increase demand by increasing the amount of the product available at the point of consumption (in the home, for example). However, multiple-unit packaging does not work for infrequently used products because buyers do not like to tie up their dollars in an excess supply or to store those products for a long time. However, multiple-unit packaging can make storage and handling easier (as in the case of six-packs used for soft drinks); it also can facilitate special price offers, such as two-for-one sales. In addition, multiple-unit packaging can increase consumer acceptance of a product by encouraging the buyer to try it several times. On the other hand, customers may hesitate to try the product at all if they do not have the option to buy just one.

Marketers should consider how much consistency is desirable among an organization's package designs. To promote an overall company image, a firm may decide that all packages must be similar or include one major element of the design. This approach, called *family packaging*, is sometimes used only for lines of products, as with Campbell's soups, Weight Watchers entrees, and Planters nuts. The best policy is sometimes no consistency, especially if a firm's products are unrelated or aimed at vastly different target markets.

Packages also play an important promotional role. Through verbal and nonverbal symbols, the package can inform potential buyers about the product's content, uses, features, advantages, and hazards. Firms can create desirable images and associations by choosing particular colours, designs, shapes, and textures. Many cosmetics manufacturers, for example, design their packages to create impressions of richness, luxury, and exclusiveness. The package performs another promotional function when it is designed to be safer or more convenient to use if such features help to stimulate demand.

Packaging also must meet the needs of intermediaries. Wholesalers and retailers consider whether a package facilitates transportation, handling, and storage. Resellers may refuse to carry certain products if their packages are cumbersome.

Finally, firms must consider the issue of environmental responsibility when developing packages. Companies must balance consumers' desires for convenience against the need to preserve the environment. About one-half of all garbage consists of discarded plastic packaging, such as plastic soft drink bottles and carryout bags. Plastic packaging material is not biodegradable, and paper necessitates destruction of valuable forest lands. Consequently, many companies are exploring packaging alternatives and recycling more materials.

Labelling

Labelling is the presentation of information on a product or its package. The *label* is the part that contains the information. This information can include the brand name and mark, the registered trademark symbol ®, the package size and contents, product claims, directions for use and safety precautions, a list of ingredients, the name and address of the manufacturer, and the Universal Product Code (UPC) symbol, which is used for automated checkout and inventory control.

A number of federal regulations specify information that *must* be included in the labelling for certain products. For example,

* Garments must be labelled with the name of the manufacturer, country of manufacture, fabric content, and cleaning instructions.

* Food labels must contain the most common term for ingredients.

* Any food product for which a nutritional claim is made must have nutrition labelling that follows a standard format.

* Food product labels must state the number of servings per container, the serving size, the number of calories per serving, the number of calories derived from fat, and amounts of specific nutrients.

* Nonedible items such as shampoos and detergents must carry safety precautions as well as instructions for their use.

Such regulations are aimed at protecting customers from both misleading product claims and the improper (and thus unsafe) use of products.

Labels also may carry the details of written or express warranties. An **express warranty** is a written explanation of the responsibilities of the producer in the event that a

labelling the presentation of information on a product or its package

express warranty a written explanation of the responsibilities of the producer in the event that a product is found to be defective or otherwise unsatisfactory

SPOTLIGHT

How much would you pay for a textbook?

Depending on a person's evaluation of price, he or she may be willing to spend across a broad range of prices for the same textbook.

Used book purchased from another student	$52.00
Used book from bookstore	$74.00
New book purchased online	$87.00
New book purchased from bookstore	$105.00

Source: *USA Today*, January 13, 2003, p. A1.

product is found to be defective or otherwise unsatisfactory. As a result of consumer discontent (along with some federal legislation), firms have begun to simplify the wording of warranties and to extend their duration.

Pricing Products

Learning Objective

Describe the economic basis of pricing and the means by which sellers can control prices and buyers' perceptions of prices.

A product is a set of attributes and benefits that has been carefully designed to satisfy its market while earning a profit for its seller. No matter how well a product is designed, however, it cannot help an organization to achieve its goals if it is priced incorrectly. Few people will purchase a product with too high a price, and a product with too low a price will earn little or no profit. Somewhere between too high and too low there is a "proper," effective price for each product. Let's take a closer look at how businesses go about determining a product's right price.

The Meaning and Use of Price

price the amount of money a seller is willing to accept in exchange for a product at a given time and under given circumstances

The **price** of a product is the amount of money a seller is willing to accept in exchange for the product at a given time and under given circumstances. At times, the price results from negotiations between buyer and seller. In many business situations, however, the price is fixed by the seller. Suppose that a seller sets a price of $10 for a particular product. In essence, the seller is saying, "Anyone who wants this product can have it here and now in exchange for $10."

Each interested buyer then makes a personal judgment regarding the utility of the product, often in terms of some dollar value. A particular person who feels that he or she will get at least $10 worth of want satisfaction (or value) from the product is likely to buy it. If that person can get more want satisfaction by spending $10 in some other way, however, he or she will not buy the product.

Price thus serves the function of *allocator.* First, it allocates goods and services among those who are willing and able to buy them. (As we noted in Chapter 1, the answer to the economic question "For whom to produce?" depends primarily on prices.) Second, price allocates financial resources (sales revenue) among producers according to how well they satisfy customers' needs. And third, price helps customers to allocate their own financial resources among various want-satisfying products.

Supply and Demand Affects Prices

supply the quantity of a product that producers are willing to sell at each of various prices

In Chapter 1 we defined the **supply** of a product as the quantity of the product that producers are willing to sell at each of various prices. We can draw a graph of the supply relationship for a particular product, say, jeans (see the left graph in Figure 13.3). Note that the quantity supplied by producers *increases* as the price increases along this *supply curve.*

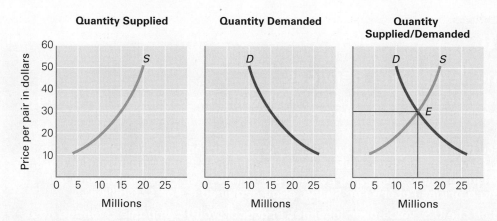

Figure 13.3

Supply and Demand Curves

Supply curve (*left*): The upward slope means that producers will supply more jeans at higher prices.
Demand curve (*center*): The downward slope (*to the right*) means that buyers will purchase fewer jeans at higher prices.
Supply and demand curves together (*right*): Point E indicates equilibrium in quantity and price for both sellers and buyers.

As defined in Chapter 1, the **demand** for a product is the quantity that buyers are willing to purchase at each of various prices. We also can draw a graph of the demand relationship (see the centre graph in Figure 13.3). Note that the quantity demanded by purchasers *increases* as the price decreases along the *demand curve*. The buyers and sellers of a product interact in the marketplace. We can show this interaction by superimposing the supply curve onto the demand curve for our product, as shown in the right graph in Figure 13.3. The two curves intersect at point *E*, which represents a quantity of fifteen million pairs of jeans and a price of $30 per pair. Point *E* is on the *supply curve*; thus producers are willing to supply fifteen million pairs at $30 each. Point *E* is also on the demand curve; thus buyers are willing to purchase fifteen million pairs at $30 each. Point *E* represents *equilibrium*. If fifteen million pairs are produced and priced at $30, they all will be sold. And everyone who is willing to pay $30 will be able to buy a pair of jeans.

demand the quantity of a product that buyers are willing to purchase at each of various prices

Price and Non-price Competition

Before the price of a product can be set, an organization must decide on the basis on which it will compete—on the basis of price alone or some combination of factors. The choice influences pricing decisions as well as other marketing-mix variables.

Price competition occurs when a seller emphasizes the low price of a product and sets a price that equals or beats competitors' prices. To use this approach most effectively, a seller must have the flexibility to change prices often and must do so rapidly and aggressively whenever competitors change their prices. Price competition allows a marketer to set prices based on demand for the product or in response to changes in the firm's finances. Competitors can do likewise, however, which is a major drawback of price competition. They, too, can quickly match or outdo an organization's price cuts. In addition, if circumstances force a seller to raise prices, competing firms may be able to maintain their lower prices.

price competition an emphasis on setting a price equal to or lower than competitors' prices to gain sales or market share

The Internet makes price comparison relatively easy for users. This ease of price comparison helps to drive competition. Examples of websites where customers can compare prices include mysimon.com, pricescan.com, bizrate.com, pricegrabber.com, pricecomparison.com, shopping.yahoo.com, nextag.com, and froogle.google.com.

Non-price competition is competition based on factors other than price. It is used most effectively when a seller can make its product stand out from the competition by

non-price competition competition based on factors other than price

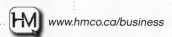

BIZ TECH

Talk Is Cheap: Online Telephone Services

Internet technology is making talk so cheap that traditional phone companies are reeling from the price competition. Some major players in this telephone service revolution include

Skype. More than fifty million people worldwide talk for free using Skype's software for PC-to-PC phone calls. Because calls are routed over the Internet, "we don't have any cost per user," says a Skype cofounder. Customers pay pennies per minute for PC-to-telephone or telephone-to-PC calls. Seeing a bright future for Skype, eBay acquired it for $2.6 billion.

Vonage. One of the largest of the U.S. voice-over-Internet Protocol (VoIP) companies, Vonage has one million subscribers who pay a flat monthly fee for telephone-to-telephone calls anywhere in the United States, Canada, and Puerto Rico. Rates on international calls run less than 10 cents per minute.

Time Warner and *Cablevision.* These giant cable companies have jumped on the VoIP bandwagon by bundling low-price phone service with television and pay-per-view subscription packages.

All this competition puts pricing pressure on traditional phone companies. Bell Canada, for instance, is vulnerable because voice calls account for more than half its revenue. What will ever-lower prices do to the telephone industry?

---

product differentiation
the process of developing and promoting differences between one's product and all similar products

distinctive product quality, customer service, promotion, packaging, or other features. Buyers must be able to perceive these distinguishing characteristics and consider them desirable. Once customers have chosen a brand for non-price reasons, they may not be attracted as easily to competing firms and brands. In this way, a seller can build customer loyalty to its brand. A method of non-price competition is **product differentiation** which is the process of developing and promoting differences between one's product and all similar products.

Buyers' Perceptions of Price

In setting prices, managers should consider the price sensitivity of people in the target market. How important is price to them? Is it always "very important"? Members of one market segment may be more influenced by price than members of another. For a particular product, the price may be a bigger factor to some buyers than to others. For example, buyers may be more sensitive to price when purchasing gasoline than when purchasing running shoes.

Buyers will accept different ranges of prices for different products; that is, they will tolerate a narrow range for certain items and a wider range for others. Consider the wide range of prices that consumers pay for soft drinks—from 15 cents per ounce at the movies down to 1.5 cents per ounce on sale at the grocery store. Management should be aware of these limits of acceptability and the products to which they apply. The firm also should take note of buyers' perceptions of a given product in relation to competing products. A premium price may be appropriate if a product is considered superior to others in its category or if the product has inspired strong brand loyalty.

Non-price competition

Tums competes with Prilosec on the basis of product attributes. There is no mention of price in this advertisement.

IN CASE OF HEARTBURN
BREAK GLASS

FOR RELIEF
NOW

FOR FULL EFFECT
IN 1-4 DAYS

When the alarm sounds for heartburn, think fast. Prilosec OTC® is not intended for immediate relief. It can take 1 to 4 days for full effect. But Tums neutralizes acid on contact. There's nothing faster. And Tums has calcium.

On the other hand, if buyers have even a hint of a negative view of a product, a lower price may be necessary.

Sometimes buyers relate price to quality. They may consider a higher price to be an indicator of higher quality. Managers involved in pricing decisions should determine whether this outlook is widespread in the target market. If it is, a higher price might improve the image of a product and, in turn, make the product more desirable. For example, German automobile manufacturer Porsche has always worked to keep its quality and image as a luxury sports car maker. In addition to its traditional 911 model and more recently the Boxster model, Porsche recently added a new model called the Cayenne. Porsche hopes this SUV-like vehicle will be very desirable to customers, equally for those who are willing to pay its $88,900 price.[16]

Pricing Objectives

Identify the major pricing objectives used by businesses.

Before setting prices for a firm's products, management must decide what it expects to accomplish through pricing. That is, management must set pricing objectives that are in line with both organizational and marketing objectives. Of course, one objective of pricing is to make a profit, but this may not be a firm's primary objective. One or more of the following factors may be just as important.

Survival

A firm may have to price its products to survive—either as an organization or as a player in a particular market. This usually means that the firm will cut its price to attract customers, even if it then must operate at a loss. Obviously, such a goal hardly can be pursued on a long-term basis, for consistent losses would cause the business to fail.

Profit Maximization

Many firms may state that their goal is to maximize profit, but this goal is impossible to define (and thus impossible to achieve). What, exactly, is the *maximum* profit? How does a firm know when it has been reached? Firms that wish to set profit goals

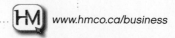

should express them as either specific dollar amounts or percentage increases over previous profits.

Target Return on Investment

The *return on investment* (ROI) is the amount earned as a result of that investment. Some firms set an annual percentage ROI as their pricing goal—such as a target after-tax ROI of 20 percent.

Market-Share Goals

A firm's *market share* is its proportion of total industry sales. Some firms attempt, through pricing, to maintain or increase their share of the market. To gain market share, Netzero priced unlimited hours of service for $6.95.[17]

Status-Quo Pricing

In pricing their products, some firms are guided by a desire to avoid "making waves," or to maintain the status quo. This is especially true in industries that depend on price stability. If such a firm can maintain its profit or market share simply by meeting the competition—charging about the same price as competitors for similar products—then it will do so.

Pricing Methods

Learning Objective 8

Examine the three major pricing methods that firms employ.

Once a firm has developed its pricing objectives, it must select a pricing method to reach that goal. Two factors are important to every firm engaged in setting prices. The first is recognition that the market, and not the firm's costs, ultimately determines the price at which a product will sell. The second is awareness that costs and expected sales can be used only to establish some sort of *price floor*, the minimum price at which the firm can sell its product without incurring a loss. In this section we look at three kinds of pricing methods: cost-based, demand-based, and competition-based pricing.

Cost-Based Pricing

markup the amount a seller adds to the cost of a product to determine its basic selling price

Using the simplest method of pricing, *cost-based pricing*, the seller first determines the total cost of producing (or purchasing) one unit of the product. The seller then adds an amount to cover additional costs (such as insurance or interest) and profit. The amount that is added is called the **markup.** The total of the cost plus the markup is the selling price of the product.

A firm's management can calculate markup as a percentage of its total costs. Suppose, for example, that the total cost of manufacturing and marketing 1,000 DVD players is $100,000, or $100 per unit. If the manufacturer wants a markup that is 20 percent above its costs, the selling price will be $100 plus 20 percent of $100, or $120 per unit.

Markup pricing is easy to apply, and it is used by many businesses (mostly retailers and wholesalers). However, it has two major flaws. The first is the difficulty of determining an effective markup percentage. If this percentage is too high, the product will be overpriced for its market; then too few units may be sold to return the total cost of producing and marketing the product. In contrast, if the markup percentage is too low, the seller is "giving away" profit it could have earned simply by assigning a higher price. In other words, the markup percentage needs to be set to account for the workings of the market, and that is very difficult to do.

The second problem with markup pricing is that it separates pricing from other business functions. The product is priced *after* production quantities are determined, *after* costs are incurred, and almost without regard for the market or the marketing mix. To be most effective, the various business functions should be integrated. *Each* should have an impact on *all* marketing decisions.

Cost-based pricing also can be facilitated through the use of break-even analysis. For any product, the **break-even quantity** is the number of units that must be sold for the total revenue (from all units sold) to equal the total cost (of all units sold). **Total revenue** is the total amount received from the sales of a product. We can estimate projected total revenue as the selling price multiplied by the number of units sold.

The costs involved in operating a business can be broadly classified as either fixed or variable costs. A **fixed cost** is a cost incurred no matter how many units of a product are produced or sold. Rent, for example, is a fixed cost; it remains the same whether 1 or 1,000 units are produced. A **variable cost** is a cost that depends on the number of units produced. The cost of fabricating parts for a stereo receiver is a variable cost. The more units produced, the higher is the cost of parts. The **total cost** of producing a certain number of units is the sum of the fixed costs and the variable costs attributed to those units.

If we assume a particular selling price, we can find the break-even quantity either graphically or by using a formula. Figure 13.4 graphs the total revenue earned and the

break-even quantity the number of units that must be sold for the total revenue (from all units sold) to equal the total cost (of all units sold)

total revenue the total amount received from sales of a product

fixed cost a cost incurred no matter how many units of a product are produced or sold

variable cost a cost that depends on the number of units produced

total cost the sum of the fixed costs and the variable costs attributed to a product

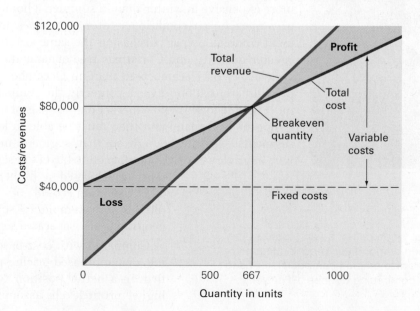

Figure 13.4

Break-even Analysis

Break-even analysis answers the question: what is the lowest level of production and sales at which a company can break even on a particular product?

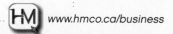

total cost incurred by the sale of various quantities of a hypothetical product. With fixed costs of $40,000, variable costs of $60 per unit, and a selling price of $120, the break-even quantity is 667 units. To find the break-even quantity, first deduct the variable cost from the selling price to determine how much money the sale of one unit contributes to offsetting fixed costs. Then divide that contribution into the total fixed costs to arrive at the break-even quantity. (The break-even quantity in Figure 13.4 is the quantity represented by the intersection of the total revenue and total cost axes.) If the firm sells more than 667 units at $120 each, it will earn a profit. If it sells fewer units, it will suffer a loss.

Demand-Based Pricing

Rather than basing the price of a product on its cost, companies sometimes use a pricing method based on the level of demand for the product: *demand-based pricing*. This method results in a high price when product demand is strong and a low price when demand is weak. Some long-distance telephone companies use demand-based pricing. Buyers of new cars that are in high demand, such as Hummer H3, Pontiac Solstice, Dodge Charger, Ford Mustang GT, and Toyota Prius, pay sticker prices plus a premium. To use this method, a marketer estimates the amount of a product that customers will demand at different prices and then chooses the price that generates the highest total revenue. Obviously, the effectiveness of this method depends on the firm's ability to estimate demand accurately.

A firm may favour a demand-based pricing method called *price differentiation* if it wants to use more than one price in the marketing of a specific product. Price differentiation can be based on such considerations as time of the purchase, type of customer, or type of distribution channel. For example, Florida hotel accommodations are more expensive in winter than in summer, a home owner pays more for air-conditioner filters than does an apartment complex owner purchasing the same size filters in greater quantity, and Christmas tree ornaments usually are cheaper on December 26 than on December 16. For price differentiation to work correctly, the company first must be able to segment a market on the basis of different strengths of demand and then must be able to keep the segments separate enough so that segment members who buy at lower prices cannot sell to buyers in segments that are charged a higher price. This isolation could be accomplished, for example, by selling to geographically separated segments.

Compared with cost-based pricing, demand-based pricing places a firm in a better position to attain higher profit levels, assuming that

Demand-based pricing

Airlines employ demand-based pricing. When demand for a particular flight is high, prices are elevated. When demand for a particular price is low, airfare is less expensive. Airlines also employ competition-based pricing, especially on routes on which competing airlines offer very low fares.

buyers value the product at levels sufficiently above the product's cost. To use demand-based pricing, however, management must be able to estimate demand at different price levels, which can be difficult to do accurately.

Competition-Based Pricing

In using *competition-based pricing*, an organization considers costs and revenue secondary to competitors' prices. The importance of this method increases if competing products are quite similar and the organization is serving markets in which price is the crucial variable of the marketing strategy. A firm that uses competition-based pricing may choose a price below competitors' prices, slightly above competitors' prices, or at the same level. The price that your bookstore paid to the publishing company of this text was determined using competition-based pricing. Competition-based pricing can help to attain a pricing objective to increase sales or market share. Competition-based pricing may be combined with other cost approaches to arrive at profitable levels. For example, Monster Gym, a Montreal-area facility recently established a fixed annual membership fee—for life—for membership renewals as a promotional means to keep their clients from leaving to join competing gyms.

Pricing Strategies

Learning Objective 9

Explain the strategies available to companies for setting prices.

A *pricing strategy* is a course of action designed to achieve pricing objectives. Generally, pricing strategies help marketers to solve the practical problems of setting prices. The extent to which a business uses any of the following strategies depends on its pricing and marketing objectives, the markets for its products, the degree of product differentiation, the life-cycle stage of the product, and other factors. Figure 13.5 contains a list of the major types of pricing strategies. We discuss these strategies in the remainder of this section.

Figure 13.5

Types of Pricing Strategies

Companies can choose from a variety of pricing strategies.

PRICING STRATEGIES

New-Product Pricing	Differential Pricing	Psychological Pricing	Product-Line Pricing	Promotional Pricing
• Price skimming • Penetration pricing	• Negotiated pricing • Secondary-market pricing • Periodic discounting • Random discounting	• Odd-number pricing • Multiple-unit pricing • Reference pricing • Bundle pricing • Everyday low prices • Customary pricing	• Captive pricing • Premium pricing • Price lining	• Price leaders • Special-event pricing • Comparison discounting

New Product Strategies

The two primary types of new product pricing strategies are price skimming and penetration pricing. An organization can use either one or even both over a period of time.

Price Skimming Some consumers are willing to pay a high price for an innovative product either because of its novelty or because of the prestige or status that ownership confers. **Price skimming** is the strategy of charging the highest possible price for a product during the introduction stage of its life cycle. The seller essentially "skims the cream" off the market, which helps to recover the high costs of R&D more quickly. Also, a skimming policy can hold down demand for the product, which is helpful if the firm's production capacity is limited during the introduction stage. The greatest disadvantage is that a skimming price may make the product appear lucrative to potential competitors, who then may attempt to enter that market.

Penetration Pricing At the opposite extreme, **penetration pricing** is the strategy of setting a low price for a new product. The main purpose of setting a low price is to build market share for the product quickly. The seller hopes that the building of a large market share quickly will discourage competitors from entering the market. If the low price stimulates sales, the firm also may be able to order longer production runs, which result in lower production costs per unit. A disadvantage of penetration pricing is that it places a firm in a less flexible position. It is more difficult to raise prices significantly than it is to lower them.

Differential Pricing

An important issue in pricing decisions is whether to use a single price or different prices for the same product. A single price is easily understood by both employees and customers, and since many salespeople and customers do not like having to negotiate a price, it reduces the chance of a marketer developing an adversarial relationship with a customer.

Differential pricing means charging different prices to different buyers for the same quality and quantity of product. For differential pricing to be effective, the market must consist of multiple segments with different price sensitivities. When this method is employed, caution should be used to avoid confusing or antagonizing customers. Differential pricing can occur in several ways, including negotiated pricing, secondary-market pricing, periodic discounting, and random discounting.

Negotiated Pricing **Negotiated pricing** occurs when the final price is established through bargaining between the seller and the customer. Negotiated pricing occurs in a number of industries and at all levels of distribution. Even when there is a predetermined stated price or a price list, manufacturers, wholesalers, and retailers still may negotiate to establish the final sales price. Consumers commonly negotiate prices for houses, cars, and used equipment.

Secondary-Market Pricing **Secondary-market pricing** means setting one price for the primary target market and a different price for another market. Often the price charged in the secondary market is lower. However, when the costs of serving a secondary market are higher than normal, secondary-market customers may have to pay a higher price. Examples of secondary markets include a geographically isolated domestic market, a market in a foreign country, and a segment willing to purchase a product during off-peak times (such as "early bird" diners at restaurants and off-peak users of cellular phones).

Periodic Discounting Periodic discounting is the temporary reduction of prices on a patterned or systematic basis. For example, many retailers have annual holiday sales, and some women's apparel stores have two seasonal sales each year—a winter sale in the last two weeks of January and a summer sale in the first two weeks of July. From the marketer's point of view, a major problem with periodic discounting is that customers can predict when the reductions will occur and may delay their purchases until they can take advantage of the lower prices.

periodic discounting temporary reduction of prices on a patterned or systematic basis

Random Discounting To alleviate the problem of customers' knowing when discounting will occur, some organizations employ **random discounting.** That is, they reduce their prices temporarily on a nonsystematic basis. When price reductions of a product occur randomly, current users of that brand are not likely to be able to predict when the reductions will occur and so will not delay their purchases in anticipation of buying the product at a lower price. Marketers also use random discounting to attract new customers.

random discounting temporary reduction of prices on an unsystematic basis

Psychological Pricing Strategies

Psychological pricing strategies encourage purchases based on emotional responses rather than on economically rational responses. These strategies are used primarily for consumer products rather than business products.

Odd-Number Pricing Many retailers believe that consumers respond more positively to odd-number prices such as $4.99 than to whole-dollar prices such as $5. Odd-number pricing is the strategy of setting prices using odd numbers that are slightly below whole-dollar amounts. Nine and five are the most popular ending figures for odd-number prices.

odd-number pricing the strategy of setting prices using odd numbers that are slightly below whole-dollar amounts

Sellers who use this strategy believe that odd-number prices increase sales. The strategy is not limited to low-priced items. Auto manufacturers may set the price of a car at $11,999 rather than $12,000. Odd-number pricing has been the subject of various psychological studies, but the results have been inconclusive.

Multiple-Unit Pricing Many retailers (especially supermarkets) practise **multiple-unit pricing,** setting a single price for two or more units, such as two cans for 99 cents rather than 50 cents per can. Especially for frequently purchased products, this strategy can increase sales. Customers who see the single price and who expect eventually to use more than one unit of the product regularly purchase multiple units to save money.

multiple-unit pricing the strategy of setting a single price for two or more units

Reference Pricing Reference pricing means pricing a product at a moderate level and positioning it next to a more expensive model or brand in the hope that the customer will use the higher price as a reference price (that is, a comparison price). Because of the comparison, the customer is expected to view the moderate price favourably. When you go to Sears to buy a DVD recorder, a moderately priced DVD recorder may appear especially attractive because it offers most of the important attributes of the more expensive alternatives on display and at a lower price.

reference pricing pricing a product at a moderate level and positioning it next to a more expensive model or brand

Bundle Pricing Bundle pricing is the packaging together of two or more products, usually of a complementary nature, to be sold for a single price. To be attractive

bundle pricing packaging together two or more complementary products and selling them for a single price

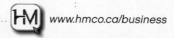

to customers, the single price usually is considerably less than the sum of the prices of the individual products. Being able to buy the bundled combination of products in a single transaction may be of value to the customer as well. Bundle pricing is used commonly for banking and travel services, computers, and automobiles with option packages. Bundle pricing can help to increase customer satisfaction. Bundling slow-moving products with ones with a higher turnover, an organization can stimulate sales and increase its revenues. The new term *all-distance* has emerged, but the bundling of services goes beyond just combined pricing for local and long-distance services. Companies like Bell Canada now offer packages that can include unlimited local, long-distance, wireless, DSL, and satellite television access.

Everyday Low Prices (EDLPs) To reduce or eliminate the use of frequent short-term price reductions, some organizations use an approach referred to as **everyday low prices (EDLPs)**. When EDLPs are used, a marketer sets a consistent, low price for its products rather than setting higher prices and frequently discounting them. EDLPs, though not deeply discounted, are set far enough below competitors' prices to make customers feel confident that they are receiving a fair price. EDLPs are employed by retailers such as Wal-Mart and by manufacturers such as Procter & Gamble. A company that uses EDLPs benefits from reduced promotional costs, reduced losses from frequent markdowns, and more stability in its sales. A major problem with this approach is that customers have mixed responses to it. In some instances, customers simply do not believe that EDLPs are what they say they are but are instead a marketing gimmick.

Customary Pricing In **customary pricing**, certain goods are priced primarily on the basis of tradition. Examples of customary, or traditional, prices would be those set for candy bars and chewing gum.

Product-Line Pricing

Rather than considering products on an item-by-item basis when determining pricing strategies, some marketers employ product-line pricing. *Product-line pricing* means establishing and adjusting the prices of multiple products within a product line. Product-line pricing can provide marketers with flexibility in price setting. For example, marketers can set prices so that one product is quite profitable, whereas another increases market share by virtue of having a lower price than competing products.

When marketers employ product-line pricing, they have several strategies from which to choose. These include captive pricing, premium pricing, and price lining.

Captive Pricing When **captive pricing** is used, the basic product in a product line is priced low, but the price on the items required to operate or enhance it are set at a higher level. For example, the manufacturer of the Polaroid Instant cameras and film priced its cameras at a low level to attract customers, but priced the film at a relatively high level because customers had to continue to purchase its special film in order to use their cameras.

Premium Pricing **Premium pricing** occurs when the highest-quality product or the most-versatile version of similar products in a product line is given the highest price. Other products in the line are priced to appeal to price-sensitive shoppers or to

---

everyday low prices (EDLPs) setting a low price for products on a consistent basis

customary pricing pricing on the basis of tradition

captive pricing pricing the basic product in a product line low, but pricing related items at a higher level

premium pricing pricing the highest-quality or most-versatile products higher than other models in the product line

those who seek product-specific features. Marketers that use premium pricing often realize a significant portion of their profits from premium-priced products. Examples of product categories in which premium pricing is common are small kitchen appliances, beer, ice cream, and television cable service.

Price Lining Price lining is the strategy of selling goods only at certain predetermined prices that reflect definite price breaks. For example, a shop may sell men's ties only at $22 and $37. This strategy is used widely in clothing and accessory stores. It eliminates minor price differences from the buying decision—both for customers and for managers who buy merchandise to sell in these stores.

price lining the strategy of selling goods only at certain predetermined prices that reflect definite price breaks

Promotional Pricing

Price, as an ingredient in the marketing mix, often is coordinated with promotion. The two variables sometimes are so interrelated that the pricing policy is promotion-oriented. Examples of promotional pricing include price leaders, special-event pricing, and comparison discounting.

Price Leaders Sometimes a firm prices a few products below the usual markup, near cost, or below cost, which results in prices known as price leaders. This type of pricing is used most often in supermarkets and restaurants to attract customers by giving them especially low prices on a few items. Management hopes that sales of regularly priced products will more than offset the reduced revenues from the price leaders.

price leaders products priced below the usual markup, near cost, or below cost

Special-Event Pricing To increase sales volume, many organizations coordinate price with advertising or sales promotions for seasonal or special situations. Special-event pricing involves advertised sales or price cutting linked to a holiday, season, or event. If the pricing objective is survival, then special sales events may be designed to generate the necessary operating capital.

special-event pricing advertised sales or price cutting linked to a holiday, season, or event

Comparison Discounting Comparison discounting sets the price of a product at a specific level and simultaneously compares it with a higher price. The higher price may be the product's previous price, the price of a competing brand, the product's price at another retail outlet, or a manufacturer's suggested retail price. Customers may find comparative discounting informative, and it can have a significant impact on them. However, because this pricing strategy on occasion has led to deceptive pricing practices, governments have established guidelines for comparison discounting. If the higher price against which the comparison is made is the price formerly charged for the product, sellers must have made the previous price available to customers for a reasonable period of time. If sellers present the higher price as the one charged by other retailers in the same trade area, they must be able to demonstrate that this claim is true. When they present the higher price as the manufacturer's suggested retail price, then the higher price must be similar to the price at which a reasonable proportion of the product was sold. Some manufacturers' suggested retail prices are so high that very few products actually are sold at those prices. In such cases, it would be deceptive to use comparison discounting.

comparison discounting setting a price at a specific level and comparing it with a higher price

Pricing Business Products

Learning Objective 10

Describe three major types of pricing associated with business products.

Many of the pricing issues discussed thus far in this chapter deal with pricing in general. Setting prices for business products can be different from setting prices for consumer products owing to several factors such as size of purchases, transportation considerations, and geographic issues. We examine three types of pricing associated with business products, including geographic pricing, transfer pricing, and discounting.

Geographic Pricing

Geographic pricing strategies deal with delivery costs. The pricing strategy that requires the buyer to pay the delivery costs is called *FOB origin pricing*. It stands for "free on board at the point of origin," which means that the price does not include freight charges, and thus the buyer must pay the transportation costs from the seller's warehouse to the buyer's place of business. *FOB destination* indicates that the price does include freight charges, and thus the seller pays these charges.

Transfer Pricing

transfer pricing prices charged in sales between an organization's units

When one unit in an organization sells a product to another unit, **transfer pricing** occurs. The price is determined by calculating the cost of the product. A transfer price can vary depending on the types of costs included in the calculations. The choice of the costs to include when calculating the transfer price depends on the company's management strategy and the nature of the units' interaction. An organization also must ensure that transfer pricing is fair to all units involved in the purchases.

Discounting

discount a deduction from the price of an item

A **discount** is a deduction from the price of an item. Producers and sellers offer a wide variety of discounts to their customers, including the following:

* *Trade discounts* are discounts from the list prices that are offered to marketing intermediaries, or middlemen. A furniture retailer, for example, may receive a 40 percent discount from the manufacturer. The retailer then would pay $60 for a lamp carrying a list price of $100. Intermediaries, discussed in Chapter 14, perform various marketing activities in return for trade discounts.

* *Quantity discounts* are discounts given to customers who buy in large quantities. The seller's per-unit selling cost is lower for larger purchases. The quantity discount is a way of passing part of these savings on to the buyer.

* *Cash discounts* are discounts offered for prompt payment. A seller may offer a discount of "2/10, net 30," meaning that the buyer may take a 2 percent discount if the bill is paid within ten days and that the bill must be paid in full within thirty days.

* A *seasonal discount* is a price reduction to buyers who purchase out of season. This discount lets the seller maintain steadier production during the year. For example, automobile rental agencies offer seasonal discounts in winter and early spring to encourage firms to use automobiles during the slow months of the automobile rental business.

* An *allowance* is a reduction in price to achieve a desired goal. Trade-in allowances, for example, are price reductions granted for turning in used equipment when purchasing new equipment. This type of discount is popular in the aircraft industry. Another example is a promotional allowance, which is a price reduction granted to dealers for participating in advertising and sales-support programs intended to increase sales of a particular item.

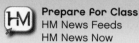
Prepare for Class
HM News Feeds
HM News Now

→ **RETURN TO INSIDE BUSINESS**

The Apple brand has become so desirable that noncompeting firms are lining up to link their products and brands with the Apple image. JBL and Bose are just two of many companies that make speaker systems specifically for docking with iPod models. BMW and Volvo are among the growing list of automakers that offer iPod connections as options on new vehicles.

Although iTunes downloads are inexpensive, new iPod models are premium-priced to reinforce their trendy, up-to-the-minute positioning and attract buyers who must have the latest "cool" product. At the same time, Apple has slowly lowered prices on older iPod models to maintain overall sales momentum by appealing to more cost-conscious buyers. Look for more innovations ahead as Apple continues to polish its brand through innovative new products.

Questions

1. Why would Apple use family branding rather than individual branding for the iPod and the Macintosh?

2. Do you think Apple is using cost-based pricing, demand-based pricing, or competition-based pricing for iPod products? Explain your answer.

CHAPTER REVIEW

1 **Explain what a product is and how products are classified.**

Products are classified according to their ultimate use. Classification affects a product's distribution, promotion, and pricing. Business products are purchased for resale, for making other products, or for use in a firm's operations. Business products can be classified as raw materials, major

equipment, accessory equipment, component parts, process materials, supplies, and services.

2 **Discuss the product life cycle and how it leads to new product development.**

Every product moves through a series of four stages—introduction, growth, maturity, and decline—which together

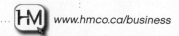

form the product life cycle. As the product progresses through these stages, its sales and profitability increase, peak, and then decline.

3 Define *product line* and *product mix* and distinguish between the two.

A product line is a group of similar products marketed by a firm. A product mix includes all the products it offers for sale. The width of a mix is the number of product lines it contains. The depth of the mix is the average number of individual products within each line.

4 Identify the methods available for changing a product mix.

Marketers may improve a product mix by changing existing products, deleting products, and developing new products. Most product failures result from inadequate product planning and development.

5 Explain the uses and importance of branding, packaging, and labelling.

A brand is a name, term, symbol, design, or any combination of these that identifies a seller's products as distinct from those of other sellers. Packaging protects goods, offers consumer convenience, and enhances marketing efforts by communicating product features, uses, benefits, and image. Labelling provides customers with product information, some of which is required by law.

6 Describe the economic basis of pricing and the means by which sellers can control prices and buyers' perceptions of prices.

Prices are determined through supply and demand. Firms must consider the relative importance of price to buyers in the target market before setting prices. Buyers' perceptions of prices are affected by the importance of the product to them, the range of prices they consider acceptable, their perceptions of competing products, and their association of quality with price.

7 Identify the major pricing objectives used by businesses.

Objectives of pricing include survival, profit maximization, target return on investment, achieving market goals, and maintaining the status quo. The firm sets an annual percentage ROI as the pricing goal.

8 Examine the three major pricing methods that firms employ.

The three major pricing methods are cost-based pricing, demand-based pricing, and competition-based pricing. When cost-based pricing is employed, a proportion of the cost is added to the total cost to determine the selling price. When demand-based pricing is used, the price will be higher when demand is higher, and the price will be lower when demand is lower. A firm that uses competition-based pricing may choose to price below competitors' prices, at the same level as competitors' prices, or slightly above competitors' prices.

9 Explain the strategies available to companies for setting prices.

Pricing strategies fall into five categories: new product pricing, differential pricing, psychological pricing, product-line pricing, and promotional pricing. Price skimming and penetration pricing are two strategies used for pricing new products. Differential pricing can be accomplished through negotiated pricing, secondary-market pricing, periodic discounting, and random discounting. Psychological pricing strategies are odd-number pricing, multiple-unit pricing, reference pricing, bundle pricing, everyday low prices, and customary pricing. Product-line pricing can be achieved through captive pricing, premium pricing, and price lining. The major types of promotional pricing are price-leader pricing, special-event pricing, and comparison discounting.

10 Describe three major types of pricing associated with business products.

Setting prices for business products can be different from setting prices for consumer products as a result of several factors, such as size of purchases, transportation considerations, and geographic issues. The three types of pricing associated with the pricing of business products are geographic pricing, transfer pricing, and discounting.

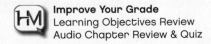
Improve Your Grade
Learning Objectives Review
Audio Chapter Review & Quiz

Review Questions

1. What does the purchaser of a product obtain besides the good, service, or idea itself?
2. What are the products of (a) a bank, (b) an insurance company, and (c) a university?
3. What major factor determines whether a product is a consumer or a business product?
4. Describe each of the classifications of business products.
5. What are the four stages of the product life cycle? How can a firm determine which stage a particular product is in?
6. What is the difference between a product line and a product mix? Give an example of each.
7. Under what conditions does product modification work best?
8. Why do products have to be deleted from a product mix?
9. Why must firms introduce new products?
10. Briefly describe the seven new product development stages.
11. What is the difference between manufacturer brands and store brands? Between family branding and individual branding?
12. What is the difference between a line extension and a brand extension?
13. How can packaging be used to enhance marketing activities?
14. For what purposes is labelling used?
15. What is the primary function of prices in our economy?
16. Compare and contrast the characteristics of price and non-price competition.
17. How might buyers' perceptions of price influence pricing decisions?
18. List and briefly describe the five major pricing objectives.
19. What are the differences among markup pricing, pricing by break-even analysis, and competition-based pricing?
20. In what way is demand-based pricing more realistic than markup pricing?
21. Why would a firm use competition-based pricing?
22. What are the five major categories of pricing strategies? Give at least two examples of specific strategies that fall into each category.
23. Identify and describe the main types of discounts that are used in the pricing of business products.

Discussion Questions

1. Why is it important to understand how products are classified?
2. What factors might determine how long a product remains in each stage of the product life cycle? What can a firm do to prolong each stage?
3. Some firms do not delete products until they become financially threatening. What problems may result from relying on this practice?
4. Which steps in the evolution of new products are most important? Which are least important? Defend your choices.
5. Do branding, packaging, and labelling really benefit consumers? Explain.
6. To what extent can a firm control its prices in our market economy? What factors limit such control?
7. Under what conditions would a firm be most likely to use non-price competition?
8. Can a firm have more than one pricing objective? Can it use more than one of the pricing methods discussed in this chapter? Explain.
9. What are the major disadvantages of price skimming?
10. What is an "effective" price?
11. Under what conditions would a business most likely decide to employ one of the differential pricing strategies?
12. For what types of products are psychological pricing strategies most likely to be used?

CASE STUDY

XM: 4 U 24/7/365

Satellite radio is gaining customers more quickly than any other new consumer technology in history—and XM Satellite Radio is leading the way. The company started on the road to static-free radio in 1997, when it paid more than $80 million for a federal licence to broadcast digital radio. Until then, AM and FM radio stations had been free to all listeners mainly because of commercial sponsorship. However, XM believed that commuters—and anyone travelling by car for long periods—would pay for perfect 24-hour radio reception and dozens of channel choices anywhere in North America. After all, millions of viewers were paying for cable television service, even though in many geographic areas they could watch broadcast television for free.

Turning the concept of digital radio into reality cost XM more than $1 billion. First, the company had to design and launch two satellites into orbit over North America. It set up satellite dishes to beam radio signals to the satellites and erected antennas on 800 buildings in major cities to reach local listeners across the continent. In addition, XM created a vast library of digital recordings and built two performance studios to broadcast and record live musical performances.

Meanwhile, XM was conducting marketing research to determine the target market's listening tastes. Based on this research, the company decided to devote most of its radio stations to specific types of music, such as country, rap, jazz, blues, rock and roll, classic rock, international pop, instrumental classical music, and movie soundtracks. For more variety, it planned news-only, sports-only, talk-only, comedy-only, and children's stations, among other special-interest stations. XM also has become the exclusive satellite radio home of Major League Baseball, the National Hockey League, and celebrities such as Ellen DeGeneres.

Pricing involved a delicate balancing act. On the one hand, XM wanted to build a sizable base of subscribers, so its pricing had to be within customers' reach. On the other hand, the company was planning for long-term profitability and wanted to recoup some of its high start-up costs. Initially, XM set a monthly subscription fee of $9.95 and priced its first radios at $300 or less. Within a year, the company launched smaller, less expensive radios for the home

and for listening on the go. "We are an entertainment company, but we also recognized that if we were going to be successful, we had to rapidly drive down the cost of the equipment people needed to get our service," recalls an XM marketing analyst.

XM's new product introduction has been successful. Even though XM has raised its monthly subscription fee to $12.95, more than six million subscribers already have signed up. Its only competitor, Sirius Satellite Radio, also charges a monthly subscription fee of $12.95 and has signed three million subscribers. Sirius channels are entirely commercial-free, whereas some XM channels broadcast commercials as well as music. To draw listeners with exclusive programming, Sirius has signed radio personality Howard Stern, lifestyle guru Martha Stewart, and other well-known names. Chrysler, BMW, and Ford all offer Sirius radio receivers as new-car options.

Today, XM customers must have its radio equipment to receive XM channels, just as Sirius customers must have its equipment to receive Sirius channels. This will change when new radios capable of receiving either company's channels become available. Still, XM's CEO expects to continue his company's market dominance by putting the emphasis on program content. "The technology is only the facilitator," he says. "Music connects so personally to people. We're putting the passion back into radio."

For more information about this company, go to www .xmradio.com/.

Questions:

1. At what stage of the product life cycle is satellite radio? What factors are likely to affect satellite radio's movement into the next stage?

2. Evaluate the brand names of XM Satellite Radio and Sirius Satellite Radio. What are the strengths and weaknesses of each brand? Which do you think is the better brand name—and why?

3. Why is XM Satellite Radio relying on non-price competition rather than price competition? Do you agree with this choice? Explain.

BUILDING SKILLS FOR CAREER SUCCESS

1. Exploring the Internet

The Internet has quickly taken comparison shopping to a new level. Several websites such as bizrate.com, pricescan.com, and mysimon.com have emerged boasting that they can find the consumer the best deal on any product. From computers to watches, these sites offer unbiased price and product information to compare virtually any product. Users can read reviews about products as well as provide their own input from personal experience. Some of these sites also offer special promotions and incentives in exchange for user information. Visit the text website for updates to this exercise.

Assignment

1. Search all three of the websites listed above for the same product.

2. Did you notice any significant differences between the sites and the information they provide?

3. What percentage of searches do you think lead to purchases as opposed to browsing? Explain your answer.

4. Which site are you most likely to use on a regular basis? Why?

5. In what ways do these websites contribute to price competition?

2. Building Team Skills

In his book, *The Post-Industrial Society,* Peter Drucker wrote:

> Society, community, and family are all conserving institutions. They try to maintain stability and to prevent, or at least slow down, change. But the organization of the post-capitalist society of organizations is a destabilizer. Because its function is to put knowledge to work—on tools, processes, and products; on work; on knowledge itself—it must be organized for constant change. It must be organized for innovation.

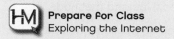

Prepare for Class
Exploring the Internet

New product development is important in this process of systematically abandoning the past and building a future. Current customers can be sources of ideas for new products and services and ways of improving existing ones.

Assignment

1. Working in teams of five to seven, brainstorm ideas for new products or services for your college or university.

2. Construct questions to ask currently enrolled students (your customers). Sample questions might include

   a. Why did you choose this college or university?

   b. How can this college or university be improved?

   c. What products or services do you wish were available?

3. Conduct the survey and review the results.

3. Researching Different Careers

Standard & Poor's Industry Surveys, designed for investors, provides insight into various industries and the companies that compete within those industries. The "Basic Analysis" section gives overviews of industry trends and issues. The other sections define some basic industry terms, report the latest revenues and earnings of more than 1,000 companies, and occasionally list major reference books and trade associations.

Assignment

1. Identify an industry in which you might like to work.

2. Find the industry in *Standard & Poor's.*

3. Identify the following:

   a. Trends and issues in the industry

   b. Opportunities and/or problems that might arise in the industry in the next five years

   c. Major competitors within the industry

4. Prepare a report of your findings.

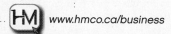

CHAPTER 14

Distributing and Promoting Products

Your Guide to Success in Business

Why this chapter matters
Not only is it important to create and maintain a mix of products that satisfies customers, but also to make these products available at the right place and time and to communicate with customers effectively.

1. Identify the various channels of distribution.

2. Understand how supply-chain management facilitates partnering among channel members.

3. Understand the types of wholesalers and the services they provide.

4. Distinguish the major types of retailers.

5. Explain the five most important physical distribution activities.

6. Describe integrated marketing communications.

7. Explain the purposes of the three types of advertising.

8. Recognize the various kinds of salespersons, the steps in the personal-selling process, and the major sales management tasks.

9. Describe sales promotion objectives and methods.

10. Understand the types and uses of public relations.

Fruits & Passion Sales Grow with Store Openings

Fruits & Passion, the Montreal-based beauty, body, and lifestyle products retailer is a remarkable success story in a very competitive global marketplace. The firm creates unique fragrances for oils, candles, and other personal care products using ingredients gathered from around the world and then wraps them in unusually attractive packaging.

Fruits & Passion was started in 1991 by Jean Hurteau, his wife France Menard, and brother Guy Hurteau at home. The trio believed that the "lifestyle market" for personal luxuries that enhanced a customer's quality of life in small ways was beginning to explode. Stores like The Body Shop were leading the way in the personal care market and the partners sensed that people's desire for personal lifestyle quality would transform into demand for other products for their homes. For instance, small decorative products like candles could enhance a room's quality if the design and fragrance were just right. Little things could make a big difference in their kitchens, bathrooms, and bedrooms.

Before long, the firm was selling their creative selections through twelve Canadian retail stores, which they still own and operate today. However, in order for potential sales to truly become realized, a large retail distribution network would be needed to provide products to customers in more markets.

Currently, the firm sells its products through 150 Fruits & Passion retailers—93 of which are in Canada—and over 2,000 independent retailers around the world. Fruits & Passion franchise retailers can be found in Taiwan, China, Morocco, Mexico, France, the United States, and Canada. But the big push to open more than 1,000 franchise dealers is now in the works after the purchase of 30 percent of the firm's shares by SGF, the Quebec-based venture capital firm. The new funds were used to finance franchise-based expansion into the United Kingdom, Spain, Italy, and Germany in 2007.

Source: Based on information available on the Fruits & Passion corporate website accessed February 11, 2007, www .fruits-passion.com.

DID YOU KNOW?

Fruits & Passion boutiques and retail distributors sell to over 30,000 customers around the world each week.

K E Y   T E R M S

channel of distribution (or marketing channel) (412)

middleman (or marketing intermediary) (412)

merchant middleman (412)

functional middleman (412)

retailer (413)

wholesaler (413)

intensive distribution (414)

selective distribution (414)

exclusive distribution (414)

supply-chain management (415)

merchant wholesaler (416)

full-service wholesaler (417)

general-merchandise wholesaler (417)

limited-line wholesaler (417)

specialty-line wholesaler (417)

limited-service wholesaler (417)

agent (417)

broker (417)

independent retailer (418)

chain retailer (418)

department store (418)

discount store (418)

warehouse showroom (420)

convenience store (420)

supermarket (420)

superstore (420)

warehouse club (420)

traditional specialty store (420)

off-price retailer (421)

category killer (421)

non-store retailing (421)

direct selling (421)

direct marketing (422)

catalogue marketing (423)

direct-response marketing (423)

telemarketing (423)

television home shopping (424)

online retailing (424)

automatic vending (424)

lifestyle shopping centre (425)

neighbourhood shopping centre (425)

community shopping centre (426)

regional shopping centre (426)

physical distribution (426)

inventory management (427)

order processing (427)

warehousing (428)

materials handling (428)

transportation (428)

carrier (429)

integrated marketing communications (430)

promotion (431)

promotion mix (431)

advertising (431)

personal selling (431)

sales promotion (432)

public relations (432)

primary-demand advertising (433)

selective-demand (or brand) advertising (433)

institutional advertising (433)

advertising agency (436)

order getter (437)

creative selling (437)

order taker (437)

sales support personnel (437)

missionary salesperson (437)

trade salesperson (438)

technical salesperson (438)

consumer sales promotion method (440)

trade sales promotion method (440)

rebate (441)

coupon (441)

sample (441)

premium (441)

frequent-user incentive (441)

point-of-purchase display (441)

trade show (441)

buying allowance (442)

cooperative advertising (442)

publicity (443)

news release (443)

feature article (443)

captioned photograph (443)

press conference (443)

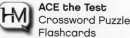

ACE the Test
Crossword Puzzle
Flashcards

Store chains such as Fruits & Passion, Starbucks, and Wal-Mart operate retail outlets where consumers make purchases. Some retailers, such as Avon Products and Amway, send their salespeople to the homes of customers. Other retailers, such as Lands' End and L. L. Bean, sell through catalogues or through both catalogues and online. Still others, such as Amazon, sell only online to customers.

In addition, there are more than half a million wholesalers in North America that sell merchandise to other firms. Most consumers know little about these firms, which work "behind the scenes" and rarely sell directly to consumers. These and other intermediaries are concerned with the transfer of both products and ownership. They thus help to create the time, place, and possession utilities that are critical to marketing. As we will see, they also perform a number of services for their suppliers and their customers.

In this chapter we initially examine various channels of distribution that products follow as they move from producer to ultimate user. Then we discuss wholesalers and retailers within these channels. Next, we examine the types of shopping centres. Then, we explore the physical distribution functions.

Next, we introduce four promotional methods and describe how they are used in an organization's marketing plans. First, we examine the role of advertising in the promotion mix. We discuss different types of advertising, the process of developing an advertising campaign, and social and legal concerns in advertising. Next, we consider several categories of personal selling, noting the importance of effective sales management. We also look at sales promotion—why firms use it and which sales promotion techniques are most effective. Then we explain how public relations can be used to promote an organization and its products.

Channels of Distribution

Learning Objective 1

Identify the various channels of distribution.

A **channel of distribution,** or **marketing channel,** is a sequence of marketing organizations that directs a product from the producer to the ultimate user. Every marketing channel begins with the producer and ends with either the consumer or the business user.

A marketing organization that links a producer and user within a marketing channel is called a **middleman,** or **marketing intermediary.** For the most part, middlemen are concerned with the transfer of *ownership* of products. A **merchant middleman** (or, more simply, a *merchant*) is a middleman who actually takes title to products by buying them. A **functional middleman,** on the other hand, helps in the transfer of ownership of products but does not take title to the products. Generally different channels of distribution are used to move consumer and business products. The six most commonly used channels are illustrated in Figure 14.1.

Producer to Consumer This channel, often called the *direct channel,* includes no marketing intermediaries. Practically all services and a few consumer goods are distributed through a direct channel. Examples of marketers that sell goods directly to

---

channel of distribution (or **marketing channel**) a sequence of marketing organizations that directs a product from the producer to the ultimate user

middleman (or **marketing intermediary**) a marketing organization that links a producer and user within a marketing channel

merchant middleman a middleman who actually takes title to products by buying them

functional middleman a middleman who helps in the transfer of ownership of products but does not take title to the products

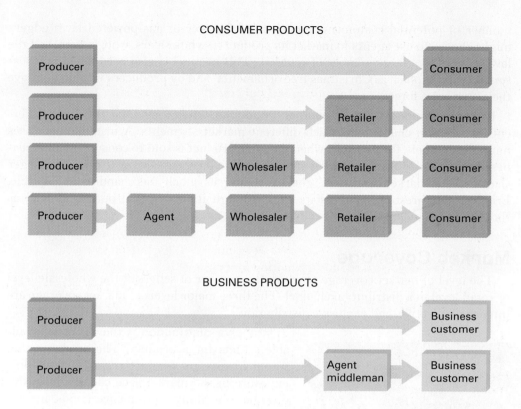

CONSUMER PRODUCTS

BUSINESS PRODUCTS

Figure 14.1

Distribution Channels

Producers use various channels to distribute their products.

consumers include Dell Computer, Mary Kay Cosmetics, and Avon Products. Producers sell directly to consumers for several reasons. They can better control the quality and price of their products. They do not have to pay (through discounts) for the services of intermediaries. And they can maintain closer ties with customers.

Producer to Retailer to Consumer A retailer is a middleman who buys from producers or other middlemen and sells to consumers. Producers sell directly to retailers when retailers (such as Wal-Mart) can buy in large quantities. This channel is used most often for products that are bulky, such as furniture and automobiles, for which additional handling would increase selling costs. It is also the usual channel for perishable products, such as fruits and vegetables, and for high-fashion products that must reach the consumer in the shortest possible time.

Producer to Wholesaler to Retailer to Consumer This channel is known as the *traditional channel* because many consumer goods (especially convenience goods) pass through wholesalers to retailers. A wholesaler is a middleman who sells products to other firms. These firms can be retailers, industrial users, or other wholesalers. A producer uses wholesalers when its products are carried by so many retailers that the producer cannot deal with all of them. For example, the maker of Wrigley's gum uses this type of channel.

Producer to Agent to Wholesaler to Retailer to Consumer Producers may use agents to reach wholesalers. Agents are functional middlemen who do not take title to products and are compensated by commissions paid by producers. Often these products are inexpensive, frequently purchased items. For example, to reach a large

retailer a middleman who buys from producers or other middlemen and sells to consumers

wholesaler a middleman who sells products to other firms

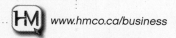

number of potential customers, a small manufacturer of gas-powered lawn edgers might choose to use agents to market its product to wholesalers, who, in turn, sell the lawn edgers to a large number of retailers. This channel is also used for highly seasonal products (such as Christmas tree ornaments) and by producers who do not have their own sales forces.

Multiple Channels for Consumer Products Often a manufacturer uses different distribution channels to reach different market segments. A manufacturer uses multiple channels, for example, when the same product is sold to consumers and business customers. Multiple channels are also used to increase sales or to capture a larger share of the market. With the goal of selling as much merchandise as possible, Bridgestone/Firestone markets its tires through its own retail outlets as well as through independent dealers.

Market Coverage

The level of market coverage refers to the number of sellers at the wholesale level or retail level in a distribution channel. The three major levels of market coverage are intensive, selective, and exclusive distribution.

intensive distribution the use of all available outlets for a product

selective distribution the use of only a portion of the available outlets for a product in each geographic area

exclusive distribution the use of only a single retail outlet for a product in a large geographic area

Intensive distribution is the use of all available outlets for a product. The producer that wants to give its product the widest possible exposure in the marketplace chooses intensive distribution. Many convenience goods, including candy, gum, and soft drinks, are distributed intensively.

Selective distribution is the use of only a portion of the available outlets for a product in each geographic area. Manufacturers of goods such as furniture, major home appliances, and clothing typically prefer selective distribution. **Exclusive distribution** is the use of only a single retail outlet for a product in a large geographic area. Exclusive distribution usually is limited to very prestigious products. It is appropriate, for instance, for specialty goods such as upscale pianos, fine china, and expensive jewellery. The producer usually places many requirements (such as inventory levels, sales training, service quality, and warranty procedures) on exclusive dealers.

▲
Selective distribution

Home appliances, such as those manufactured by Whirlpool, are usually distributed through selective distribution.

Partnering Through Supply-Chain Management

Learning Objective 2

Understand how supply-chain management facilitates partnering among channel members.

Supply-chain management is a long-term partnership among channel members working together to create a distribution system that reduces inefficiencies, costs, and redundancies while creating a competitive advantage and satisfying customers. Supply-chain management requires cooperation throughout the entire marketing channel, including research, manufacturing, sales, advertising, and shipping. Supply chains focus not only on producers, wholesalers, retailers, and customers but also on component-parts suppliers, shipping companies, communication companies, and other organizations that participate in product distribution. Suppliers have an increasing impact on determining what items retail stores carry. This phenomenon, called *category management*, is becoming common for mass merchandisers, supermarkets, and convenience stores. Through category management, the retailer asks a supplier in a particular category how to stock the shelves. For example, U.S. book retailer Borders asked publisher HarperCollins what books it should sell, which includes both HarperCollins' books and competitors' books. Many retailers and suppliers claim this process delivers maximum efficiency.[1]

Traditionally, buyers and sellers negotiating purchases have been adversaries. Supply-chain management, however, encourages cooperation in reducing the costs of inventory, transportation, administration, and handling; in speeding order-cycle times; and in increasing profits for all channel members. When buyers, sellers, marketing intermediaries, and facilitating agencies work together, customers' needs regarding delivery, scheduling, packaging, and other requirements are better met. Home Depot, North America's largest home-improvement retailer, is working to help its suppliers improve productivity and thereby supply Home Depot with better-quality products at lower costs. The company has even suggested a cooperative partnership with its competitors so that regional trucking companies making deliveries to all these organizations can provide faster, more efficient delivery.

supply-chain management long-term partnership among channel members working together to create a distribution system that reduces inefficiencies, costs, and redundancies while creating a competitive advantage and satisfying customers

Marketing Intermediaries: Wholesalers

Learning Objective

Understand the types of wholesalers and the services they provide.

The press, consumers, public officials, and other marketers often charge wholesalers, at least in principle, with inefficiency and parasitism. Consumers in particular feel strongly that the distribution channel should be made as short as possible. They assume that the fewer the intermediaries in a distribution channel, the lower the price of the product will be.

Wholesalers may be the most misunderstood of marketing intermediaries. Producers sometimes try to eliminate them from distribution channels by dealing directly with retailers or consumers. Yet wholesalers provide a variety of essential marketing services. Although wholesalers can be eliminated, their functions cannot; these functions *must* be performed by other channel members or by the consumer or ultimate user. Eliminating a wholesaler may or may not cut distribution costs.

Wholesalers Provide Services to Retailers and Manufacturers

Wholesalers help retailers by buying in large quantities and then selling to retailers in smaller quantities and by delivering goods to retailers. They also stock—in one place—the variety of goods that retailers otherwise would have to buy from many producers. And wholesalers provide assistance in three other vital areas: promotion, market information, and financial aid.

Some of the services that wholesalers perform for manufacturers are similar to those they provide to retailers. In addition, wholesalers can help manufacturers by providing a sales force, reducing inventory costs, assuming credit risks, and furnishing market information.

Types of Wholesalers

Wholesalers generally fall into three categories: merchant wholesalers; commission merchants, agents, and brokers; and manufacturers' sales branches and sales offices. Of these, merchant wholesalers constitute the largest portion. They account for about four-fifths of all wholesale establishments and employees.

Merchant Wholesalers A **merchant wholesaler** is a middleman who purchases goods in large quantities and then sells them to other wholesalers or retailers and to institutional, farm, government, professional, or industrial users. Merchant wholesalers usually operate one or more warehouses at which they receive, take title to, and store goods. These wholesalers are sometimes called *distributors* or *jobbers*.

merchant wholesaler a middleman who purchases goods in large quantities and then sells them to other wholesalers or retailers and to institutional, farm, government, professional, or industrial users

Most merchant wholesalers are businesses composed of salespeople, order takers, receiving and shipping clerks, inventory managers, and office personnel. The successful merchant wholesaler must analyze available products and market needs. It must be able to adapt the type, variety, and quality of its products to changing market conditions.

Merchant wholesalers can be classified as full-service or limited-service wholesalers depending on the number of services they provide. A **full-service wholesaler** performs the entire range of wholesaler functions described earlier in this section. These functions include delivering goods, supplying warehousing, arranging for credit, supporting promotional activities, and providing general customer assistance.

Under this broad heading are the general-merchandise wholesaler, limited-line wholesaler, and specialty-line wholesaler. A **general-merchandise wholesaler** deals in a wide variety of products, such as drugs, hardware, nonperishable foods, cosmetics, detergents, and tobacco. A **limited-line wholesaler** stocks only a few product lines but carries numerous product items within each line. A **specialty-line wholesaler** carries a select group of products within a single line. Food delicacies such as shellfish represent the kind of product handled by this type of wholesaler.

In contrast to a full-service wholesaler, a **limited-service wholesaler** assumes responsibility for a few wholesale services only. Other marketing tasks are left to other channel members or consumers. This category includes cash-and-carry wholesalers, truck wholesalers, drop shippers, and mail-order wholesalers.

Agents and Brokers Agents and brokers are functional middlemen. Functional middlemen do not take title to products. They perform a small number of marketing activities and are paid a commission that is a percentage of the sales price.

An **agent** is a middleman who expedites exchanges, represents a buyer or a seller, and often is hired permanently on a commission basis. When agents represent producers, they are known as *sales agents* or *manufacturer's agents.* As long as the products represented do not compete, a sales agent might represent one or several manufacturers on a commission basis. The agent solicits orders for the manufacturers within a specific territory. As a rule, the manufacturers ship the merchandise and bill the customers directly. The manufacturers also set the prices and other conditions of the sales. What do the manufacturers gain by using a sales agent? The sales agent provides immediate entry into a territory, regular calls on customers, selling experience, and a known, predetermined selling expense (a commission that is a percentage of sales revenue).

A **broker** is a middleman who specializes in a particular commodity, represents either a buyer or a seller, and is likely to be hired on a temporary basis. However, food brokers, who sell grocery products to resellers, generally have long-term relationships with their clients. Brokers may perform only the selling function, or both buying and selling, using established contacts or special knowledge of their fields.

full-service wholesaler a middleman who performs the entire range of wholesaler functions

general-merchandise wholesaler a middleman who deals in a wide variety of products

limited-line wholesaler a middleman who stocks only a few product lines but carries numerous product items within each line

specialty-line wholesaler a middleman who carries a select group of products within a single line

limited-service wholesaler a middleman who assumes responsibility only for a few wholesale services

agent a middleman who expedites exchanges, represents a buyer or a seller, and often is hired permanently on a commission basis

broker a middleman who specializes in a particular commodity, represents either a buyer or a seller, and is likely to be hired on a temporary basis

Marketing Intermediaries: Retailers

Learning Objective ❹

Distinguish the major types of retailers.

Retailers are the final link between producers and consumers. Retailers may buy from either wholesalers or producers. They sell not only goods but also such services as auto repairs, haircuts, and dry cleaning. Some retailers sell both. Sears Canada sells consumer goods, financial services, and repair services for home appliances bought at Sears.

Canadian retail chain stores account for just over two-fifths (43 percent) of total retail operating revenues or approximately $160 billion. Independent retailers continued to account for the largest share of the retail industry, with about 57 percent of total operating revenues.[2] Table 15.1 lists the ten largest Canadian and twenty largest American retail organizations and their approximate sales revenues and yearly profits.

Types of In-Store Retailers

One way to classify retailers is by the number of stores owned and operated by the firm. An **independent retailer** is a firm that operates only one retail outlet. Approximately three-fourths of retailers are independent. One-store operators, like all small businesses, generally provide personal service and a convenient location.

A **chain retailer** is a company that operates more than one retail outlet. By adding outlets, chain retailers attempt to reach new geographic markets. As sales increase, chains usually buy merchandise in larger quantities and thus take advantage of quantity discounts. They also wield more power in their dealings with suppliers. About one-fourth of retail organizations operate chains.

Another way to classify in-store retailers is by store size and the kind and number of products carried. Let's take a closer look at store types based on these dimensions.

Department Stores These large retail establishments consist of several sections, or departments, that sell a wide assortment of products. According to the U.S. Bureau of the Census, a **department store** is a retail store that (1) employs twenty-five or more persons and (2) sells at least home furnishings, appliances, family apparel, and household linens and dry goods, each in a different part of the store. Macy's in New York, Harrods in London, and Au Printemps in Paris are examples of large department stores. The Bay, Sears Canada, Sears, Roebuck, and JC Penney are also department stores. Traditionally, department stores have been service-oriented. Along with the goods they sell, these retailers provide credit, delivery, personal assistance, liberal return policies, and a pleasant shopping atmosphere.

Discount Stores A **discount store** is a self-service general-merchandise outlet that sells products at lower-than-usual prices. These stores can offer lower prices by operating on smaller markups, by locating large retail showrooms in low-rent areas,

independent retailer a firm that operates only one retail outlet

chain retailer a company that operates more than one retail outlet

department store a retail store that (1) employs twenty-five or more persons and (2) sells at least home furnishings, appliances, family apparel, and household linens and dry goods, each in a different part of the store

discount store a self-service general-merchandise outlet that sells products at lower-than-usual prices

RANK	COMPANY	ANNUAL SALES (MILLIONS)	ANNUAL PROFITS (MILLIONS)
1	Wal-Mart Canada	$13,500	n.a.
2	Costco	8,107	n.a.
3	Canadian Tire Corp.	7,774	330
4	Hudson's Bay Co.	6,946	(174)
5	Sears Canada Inc.	6,237	770
6	Home Depot Canada	5,500	n.a.
7	Home Hardware Stores	4,200	n.a.
8	Best Buy Canada	3,584	(2)
9	Liquor Control Board of Ontario	3,532	1,146
10	Direct Energy Marketing	3,380	n.a.

Table 14.1

The Ten Largest Retail Firms in Canada

Source: *Financial Post, Special Issue,* "Canada's Largest Corporations, Merchandisers, June 2006, p. 144.

RANK	COMPANY	ANNUAL SALES (MILLIONS)	ANNUAL PROFITS (MILLIONS)	NUMBER OF STORES
1	Wal-Mart Inc.	$285,222	$10,267	5,200
2	The Home Depot	73,094	5,001	2,000
3	Kroger	56,434	−100	2,532
4	Costco	47,146	882	400
5	Target	45,682	3,198	1,249
6	Albertson's	39,897	444	2,500
7	Walgreen's	37,508	1,350	5,240
8	Lowe's	36,464	2,176	2,300
9	Safeway	35,823	560	1,700
10	Sears	35,718	−507	2,400
11	CVS	30,594	919	4,122
12	Best Buy	27,433	984	750
13	Kmart	19,701	1,106	1,479
14	Publix	18,554	819	875
15	JC Penney	18,424	524	1,017
16	RiteAid	16,816	302	3,300
17	Gap	16,267	1,150	3,000
18	Federated Dept. Stores	15,630	689	459
19	TJX Cos. Inc.	14,913	664	1,900
20	May Inc.	14,441	524	1,229

The Twenty Largest Retail Firms in the United States

Source: 2006 Global Powers of Retailing, www.deloitte.com; accessed January 20, 2006.

and by offering minimal customer services. To keep prices low, discount stores operate on the basic principle of high turnover of such items as appliances, toys, clothing, automotive products, and sports equipment. To attract customers, many discount stores also offer some food and household items at low prices. Popular discount stores include Kmart, Wal-Mart, Dollar General, and Target.

A **warehouse showroom** is a retail facility with five basic characteristics: (1) a large, low-cost building, (2) warehouse materials-handling technology, (3) vertical merchandise displays, (4) a large on-premises inventory, and (5) minimal service. Some of the best-known showrooms are operated by big furniture retailers. These operations employ few personnel and offer few services. Most customers carry away purchases in the manufacturer's carton, although some warehouse showrooms will deliver for a fee.

Convenience Stores A **convenience store** is a small food store that sells a limited variety of products but remains open well beyond normal business hours. Their limited product mixes and higher prices keep convenience stores from becoming a major threat to other grocery retailers.

Supermarkets A **supermarket** is a large self-service store that sells primarily food and household products. It stocks canned, fresh, frozen, and processed foods; paper products; and cleaning supplies. Supermarkets also may sell such items as housewares, toiletries, toys and games, drugs, stationery, books and magazines, plants and flowers, and a few clothing items. Supermarkets are large-scale operations that emphasize low prices and one-stop shopping for household needs. A supermarket has annual sales of at least $2 million. Current top-ranking supermarkets include Loblaws and Sobey's.

Superstores A **superstore** is a large retail store that carries not only food and nonfood products ordinarily found in supermarkets but also additional product lines—housewares, hardware, small appliances, clothing, personal-care products, garden products, and automotive merchandise. Superstores also provide a number of services to entice customers. Typically, these include automotive repair, snack bars and restaurants, film developing, and banking.

Warehouse Clubs The **warehouse club** is a large-scale members-only establishment that combines features of cash-and-carry wholesaling with discount retailing. For a nominal annual fee (about $25), small retailers may purchase products at wholesale prices for business use or for resale. Warehouse clubs also sell to ultimate consumers. Instead of paying a membership fee, individual consumers pay about 5 percent more on each item than do small-business owners. Individual purchasers usually can choose to pay yearly dues for membership cards that allow them to avoid the 5 percent additional charge.

Warehouse clubs offer the same types of products offered by discount stores but in a limited range of sizes and styles. Because their product lines are shallow and sales volumes are high, warehouse clubs can offer a broad range of merchandise, including perishable and nonperishable foods, beverages, books, appliances, housewares, automotive parts, hardware, furniture, and sundries.

Traditional Specialty Stores A **traditional specialty store** carries a narrow product mix with deep product lines. Traditional specialty stores are sometimes called *limited-line retailers*. If they carry depth in one particular product category, they may

---

warehouse showroom a retail facility in a large, low-cost building with a large on-premises inventory and minimal service

convenience store a small food store that sells a limited variety of products but remains open well beyond normal business hours

supermarket a large self-service store that sells primarily food and household products

superstore a large retail store that carries not only food and nonfood products ordinarily found in supermarkets but also additional product lines

warehouse club a large-scale members-only establishment that combines features of cash-and-carry wholesaling with discount retailing

traditional specialty store a store that carries a narrow product mix with deep product lines

be called *single-line retailers*. Specialty stores usually sell such products as clothing, jewellery, sporting goods, fabrics, computers, flowers, baked goods, books, and pet supplies. Examples of specialty stores include the Gap, The Source, and Foot Locker.

Off-Price Retailers An **off-price retailer** is a store that buys manufacturers' seconds, overruns, returns, and off-season merchandise at below-wholesale prices and sells them to consumers at deep discounts. Off-price retailers sell limited lines of national-brand and designer merchandise, usually clothing, shoes, or housewares. Examples of off-price retailers include the 145 Canadian Winners stores and the U.S.-based T.J. Maxx, Burlington Coat Factory, and Marshalls. Off-price stores charge up to 50 percent less than department stores do for comparable merchandise but offer few customer services. They often include community dressing rooms and central checkout counters, and some off-price retailers have a no-returns, no-exchanges policy.

Traditional specialty stores

This Roots store is an example of a traditional specialty store.

Category Killers A **category killer** is a very large specialty store that concentrates on a single product line and competes by offering low prices and an enormous number of products. These stores are called *category killers* because they take business away from smaller, high-cost retail stores. Examples of category killers include Home Depot (building materials), Office Depot (office supplies and equipment), and Best Buy (electronics), all of which are leaders in their niche. Toys "R" Us, one of the original category killers, has a bleak future; the inability to maintain high sales year round with a market that focuses on the holidays has had its effect on the toy retailer. Some experts are predicting a decrease in the number of large-scale category killers in the not so distant future owing to other stores focusing on even smaller niches.[3]

Kinds of Non-store Retailing

Non-store retailing is selling that does not take place in conventional store facilities; consumers purchase products without visiting a store. This form of retailing accounts for an increasing percentage of total retail sales. Non-store retailers use direct selling, direct marketing, and vending machines.

Direct Selling **Direct selling** is the marketing of products to customers through face-to-face sales presentations at home or in the workplace. Traditionally called *door-to-door selling*, direct selling in North America began with peddlers more than a century ago and has since grown into a sizable industry that generates about $30 billion in sales annually.[4] Instead of the door-to-door approach, many companies today—such as Mary Kay, Kirby, Amway, and Avon—use other approaches. They identify customers by mail, telephone, the Internet, or at shopping malls and then set up appointments. Direct selling sometimes involves the "party plan," which can occur in

off-price retailer a store that buys manufacturers' seconds, overruns, returns, and off-season merchandise for resale to consumers at deep discounts

category killer a very large specialty store that concentrates on a single product line and competes on the basis of low prices and product availability

non-store retailing a type of retailing whereby consumers purchase products without visiting a store

direct selling the marketing of products to customers through face-to-face sales presentations at home or in the workplace

Apple's iTunes Becomes a Major Entertainment Success

Apple's online iTunes Store has revolutionized entertainment retailing by selling down-loadable music, television shows, feature films, games, audio books, and more. Launched in 2003 to support sales of Apple's iPod media player, iTunes has captured a whopping 72 percent of the online-music market and is now the fourth largest re-tailer of music in any form, anywhere. In addition, iTunes has done well with download-able movies. Walt Disney, the first studio to retail its movies through iTunes, sold 125,000 downloads worth $1 million in revenue during the first week alone.

However, iTunes faces increasingly aggressive competition from deep-pocketed rivals. Amazon .com, an online retailing pioneer, began selling movie downloads one week before iTunes got into the business, and both Wal-Mart and Blockbuster are moving into movie downloads. Microsoft is heavily promoting its own digital media players and online entertainment store, Zune Marketplace. Can iTunes stay on top?

Sources: Based on information in Jennifer Netherby, "Paid Downloads Slow to Catch On," *Video Business*, January 1, 2007, p. 1; "Wal-Mart Adds Net Offer," *Los Angeles Times*, November 29, 2006, p. C3; "Disney Posts $1 Million in Movie Sales on iTunes," *Los Angeles Times*, September 20, 2006, p. C9; Ethan Smith, "Can Anybody Catch iTunes?" *Wall Street Journal*, November 27, 2006. p. R.1.

---

the customer's home or workplace. One customer will act as a host and invite friends and coworkers to view merchandise in a group setting where the salesperson demonstrates the products. Direct selling through the party plan requires effective salespeople who can identify potential hosts and provide encouragement and incentives for them to organize a gathering of friends and associates. Companies that commonly use the party plan are Tupperware, Stanley Home Products, Pampered Chef, and Sarah Coventry. Mary Kay also uses the party plan by holding group pyjama parties, makeovers, and girls' nights out.

Direct selling has both benefits and limitations. It gives the marketer an opportunity to demonstrate the product in an environment—usually customers' homes—where it most likely would be used. Some companies, such as Kirby Vacuums, will even clean the carpet in your home while they demonstrate their product. The direct seller can give the customer personal attention, and the product can be presented to the customer at a convenient time and location. Personal attention to the customer is the foundation on which some direct sellers have built their businesses. For example, your Mary Kay salesperson can recommend beauty and skin products tailored to your special needs. Because commissions are so high, ranging from 30 to 50 percent of the sales price, and great effort is required to isolate promising prospects, overall costs of direct selling make it a very expensive form of retailing. Furthermore, some customers view direct selling negatively because of unscrupulous and fraudulent practices used by some direct sellers in the past. Some communities even have local ordinances that control or, in some cases, prohibit door-to-door selling.

Direct Marketing Direct marketing is the use of the telephone, Internet, and nonpersonal media to communicate product and organizational information to cus-

direct marketing the use of the telephone, Internet, and nonpersonal media to introduce products to customers, who then can purchase them via mail, telephone, or the Internet

tomers, who then can purchase products via mail, telephone, or the Internet. Direct marketing is one type of non-store retailing. Direct marketing can occur through catalogue marketing, direct-response marketing, telemarketing, television home shopping, and online marketing.

In **catalogue marketing,** an organization provides a catalogue from which customers make selections and place orders by mail, by telephone, or on the Internet. Catalogue marketing began in the 1800s, when the companies in Canada like T. Eaton Company and Montgomery Ward and Sears, Roebuck in the United States sent catalogues to rural families. Today, there are more than 7,000 catalogue marketing companies in North America, as well as a number of retail stores, such as Canadian Tire Stores, that engage in catalogue marketing. Some organizations offer a broad array of products spread over multiple product lines. Catalogue companies such as Lands' End, Pottery Barn, and J. Crew offer considerable depth in one major line of products. Still other catalogue companies specialize in only a few products within a single line. The advantages of catalogue marketing include efficiency and convenience for customers. The retailer benefits by being able to locate in remote, low-cost areas, save on expensive store fixtures, and reduce both personal selling and store operating expenses. On the other hand, catalogue marketing is inflexible, provides limited service, and is most effective for only a selected set of products.

Even though the cost of mailing catalogues continues to rise, catalogue sales are growing at double the rate of in-store retailing. Williams-Sonoma, for example, sells kitchenware and home and garden products through five catalogues, including Pottery Barn and Gardeners' Eden. Catalogue sales have been increasing owing to the convenience of catalogue shopping. Product quality is often high, and because consumers can call toll-free, 24 hours a day or order online, charge purchases to a credit card, and have the merchandise delivered to their door in one to two days, such shopping is much easier than going to a store.

Direct-response marketing occurs when a retailer advertises a product and makes it available through mail, telephone, or online orders. Examples of direct-response marketing include a television commercial offering a recording artist's musical collection, a newspaper or magazine advertisement for a series of children's books, and even a billboard promoting floral services available by calling 1-800-Flowers. Direct-response marketing is also conducted by sending letters, samples, brochures, or booklets to prospects on a mailing list and asking that they order the advertised products by mail, telephone, or online.

Telemarketing is the performance of marketing-related activities by telephone. Some organizations use a prescreened list of prospective clients. Telemarketing can help generate sales leads, improve customer service, speed up payments on past-due accounts, raise funds for nonprofit organizations, and gather marketing data.

Currently, the laws and regulations regarding telemarketing, while in a state of flux, are becoming more restrictive. Several American states have established do-not-call lists of customers who do not want to receive telemarketing calls from companies. On October 1, 2003, the U.S. Congress implemented the national do-not-call registry for consumers who do not want to receive telemarketing calls. After two years, the do-not-call registry listed over 100 million phone numbers. Regulations associated with the national do-not-call registry are enforced by the Federal Trade Commission

catalogue marketing a type of marketing in which an organization provides a catalogue from which customers make selections and place orders by mail, telephone, or the Internet

direct-response marketing a type of marketing in which a retailer advertises a product and makes it available through mail, telephone, or online orders

telemarketing the performance of marketing-related activities by telephone

(FTC). Companies are subject to fines of up to $12,000 for each call made to consumers listed on the national do-not-call registry.[5] For example, DirecTV recently was ordered to pay $5.3 million in fines by the FTC for violating the do-not-call list.[6] Certain exceptions apply to no-call lists. A company still can use telemarketing to communicate with existing customers. In addition, charitable, political, and telephone survey organizations are not restricted by the U.S. registry. Similar legislation was passed in Canada in 2005.

television home shopping a form of selling in which products are presented to television viewers, who can buy them by calling a toll-free number and paying with a credit card

Television home shopping, presents products to television viewers, encouraging them to order through toll-free numbers and pay with credit cards. Home Shopping Network (HSN) originated and popularized this format. The most popular products sold through television home shopping are jewellery (40 percent of total sales), clothing, housewares, and electronics. Home shopping channels have grown so rapidly in recent years that more than 60 percent of U.S. and most Canadian households have access to home shopping programs. HSN and QVC are two of the largest home shopping networks in the U.S., while the Shopping Channel serves the Canadian market. With the growing popularity of this medium, new channels are being added, even ones that specialize on one specific product category, such as Jewelry Television. Approximately 60 percent of home shopping sales revenues come from repeat purchasers.

The television home shopping format offers several benefits. Products can be demonstrated easily, and an adequate amount of time can be spent showing the product so as to make viewers well informed. The length of time a product is shown depends not only on the time required for doing the demonstration but also on whether the product is selling. Once the calls peak and begin to decline, a new product is shown. Another benefit is that customers can shop at their convenience from the comfort of their homes. HSN has made this even easier by teaming up with GoldPocket Interactive to equip television remotes with buying power. Users with a special set-top box and an HSN account will be able to charge the items being displayed to their accounts by pressing a button on their remote instead of calling by phone.[7]

online retailing retailing that makes products available to buyers through computer connections

Online retailing makes products available to buyers through computer connections. Most bricks-and-mortar retailers have websites to sell products, provide information about their company, or distribute coupons. Consumers also can bid on anything from concert tickets, automobiles, or even a piece of cheese shaped like Elvis on eBay. Zip.ca and Netflix have changed the video rental industry by offering online movie rental services completely online. Customers pay a monthly fee for unlimited rentals and browse the website to compose a list of videos they want to rent. Selections are mailed to their home, and customers are free to keep the rental as long as they want without the late fees typically charged by traditional stores.[8] Brokerage firms have established websites to give their customers direct access to manage their accounts and enable them to trade online. With advances in computer technology continuing and consumers ever more pressed for time, online retailing will continue to escalate. Although online retailing represents a major retailing venue, security remains an issue. In a recent survey conducted by the Business Software Alliance, some Internet users still expressed concerns about shopping online. The major issues are identity theft and credit card theft.

automatic vending the use of machines to dispense products

Automatic Vending **Automatic vending** is the use of machines to dispense products. It accounts for less than 2 percent of all retail sales. Video game machines provide an entertainment service, and many banks offer automated teller machines (ATMs) that dispense cash and perform other services.

Automatic vending is one of the most impersonal forms of retailing. Small, standardized, routinely purchased products (for example, chewing gum, candy, newspapers, cigarettes, soft drinks, and coffee) can be sold in machines because consumers usually buy them at the nearest available location. Machines in areas of heavy traffic provide efficient and continuous service to consumers. Such high-volume areas may have more diverse product availability—for example, hot and cold sandwiches, DVD rentals, or even iPods (yes, $200 iPods are available in machines with coin slots). San Francisco-based company Zoom Systems has expanded its vending machine offerings from snacks to digital cameras. But their number one seller is the iPod vending machine that offers Apple's popular MP3 players as well as accessories such as headphones, speakers, and battery chargers.[9]

Since vending machines need only a small amount of space and no sales personnel, this retailing method has some advantages over stores. These advantages are partly offset, however, by the high cost of equipment and the need for frequent servicing and repairs.

Planned Shopping Centres

The planned shopping centre is a self-contained retail facility constructed by independent owners and consisting of various stores. Shopping centres are designed and promoted to serve diverse groups of customers with widely differing needs. The management of a shopping centre strives for a coordinated mix of stores, a comfortable atmosphere, adequate parking, pleasant landscaping, and special events to attract customers. The convenience of shopping for most family and household needs in a single location is an important part of shopping-centre appeal.

A planned shopping centre is one of four types: lifestyle, neighbourhood, community, or regional. Although shopping centres vary, each offers a complementary mix of stores for the purpose of generating consumer traffic.

Lifestyle Shopping Centres

A **lifestyle shopping centre** is a shopping centre that has an open-air configuration and is occupied by upscale national chain specialty stores. The lifestyle centre is more convenient than a traditional enclosed mall but offers the same quality of upscale retail, department stores, movie theatres, and dining. A strong emphasis is placed on the architecture of the centre and creating a pleasant and "hip" shopping environment. Most lifestyle centres are found in affluent neighbourhoods.[10]

lifestyle shopping centre an open-air-environment shopping centre with upscale chain specialty stores

Neighbourhood Shopping Centres

A **neighbourhood shopping centre** typically consists of several small convenience and specialty stores. Businesses in neighbourhood shopping centres might include small grocery stores, drugstores, gas stations, and fast-food restaurants. These retailers serve consumers who live less than ten minutes away, usually within a three-to-four kilometre radius of the stores. Because most purchases in the neighbourhood

neighbourhood shopping centre a planned shopping centre consisting of several small convenience and specialty stores

◄
Community shopping centres

This mall in Ottawa is typical of the shopping centres that serve the needs of local shoppers in Canada.

shopping centre are based on convenience or personal contact, these retailers generally make only limited efforts to coordinate promotional activities among stores in the shopping centre.

Community Shopping Centres

community shopping centre a planned shopping centre that includes one or two department stores and some specialty stores, along with convenience stores

A **community shopping centre** includes one or two department stores and some specialty stores, along with convenience stores. It attracts consumers from a wider geographic area who will drive longer distances to find products and specialty items unavailable in neighbourhood shopping centres. Community shopping centres, which are carefully planned and coordinated, generate traffic with special events such as art exhibits, automobile shows, and sidewalk sales. The management of a community shopping centre maintains a balance of tenants so that the centre can offer wide product mixes and deep product lines.

Regional Shopping Centres

regional shopping centre a planned shopping centre containing large department stores, numerous specialty stores, restaurants, movie theatres, and sometimes even hotels

A **regional shopping centre** usually has large department stores, numerous specialty stores, restaurants, movie theatres, and sometimes even hotels. It carries most of the merchandise offered by a downtown shopping district. Downtown merchants, in fact, often have renovated their stores and enlarged their parking facilities to meet the competition of successful regional shopping centres. Urban expressways and improved public transportation also have helped many downtown shopping areas to remain vigorous.

Regional shopping centres carefully coordinate management and marketing activities to reach the 150,000 or more customers in their target market. These large centres usually advertise, hold special events, and provide transportation to certain groups of customers. They also maintain a suitable mix of stores. National chain stores can gain leases in regional shopping centres more easily than small independent stores because they are better able to meet the centres' financial requirements.

Physical Distribution

physical distribution all those activities concerned with the efficient movement of products from the producer to the ultimate user

Learning Objective 5

Explain the five most important physical distribution activities.

Physical distribution is all those activities concerned with the efficient movement of products from the producer to the ultimate user. Physical distribution therefore is the movement of the products themselves—both goods and services—through their channels of distribution. It is a combination of several interrelated business functions. The most important of these are inventory management, order processing, warehousing, materials handling, and transportation. These functions and their costs are highly interrelated. For example, using expensive air freight may reduce warehousing and inventory costs. Because of such interrelationships, marketers view physical distribution as an integrated effort that supports other important marketing activities such as getting the right product to the right place at the right time and at minimal total costs.

Inventory Management

In Chapter 9 we discussed inventory management from the standpoint of operations. We defined **inventory management** as the process of managing inventories in such a way as to minimize inventory costs, including both holding costs and potential stock-out costs. Both the definition and the objective of inventory control apply here as well.

Holding costs are the costs of storing products until they are purchased or shipped to customers. *Stock-out costs* are the costs of sales lost when items are not in inventory. Of course, holding costs can be reduced by minimizing inventories, but then stock-out costs could be financially threatening to the organization. And stock-out costs can be minimized by carrying very large inventories, but then holding costs would be enormous.

Inventory management therefore is a sort of balancing act between stock-out costs and holding costs. The latter include the cost of money invested in inventory, the cost of storage space, insurance costs, and inventory taxes. Often even a relatively small reduction in inventory investment can provide a relatively large increase in working capital. And sometimes this reduction can best be accomplished through a willingness to incur a reasonable level of stock-out costs. Companies frequently rely on technology and software to help manage inventory.

Order Processing

Order processing consists of activities involved in receiving and filling customers' purchase orders. It can include not only the means by which customers order products but also procedures for billing and for granting credit.

Fast, efficient order processing is an important marketing service—one that can provide a dramatic competitive edge. The people who purchase goods for intermediaries are especially concerned with their suppliers' promptness and reliability in order processing. To them, promptness and reliability mean minimal inventory costs as well as the ability to order goods when they are needed rather than weeks in advance. The Internet is providing new opportunities for improving services associated with order processing.

inventory management
the process of managing inventories in such a way as to minimize inventory costs, including both holding costs and potential stock-out costs

order processing
activities involved in receiving and filling customers' purchase orders

Inventory management technology

This handheld inventory management device allows employees to have an instant overview of every item—and its price—in the warehouse at any given time.

Warehousing

Warehousing is the set of activities involved in receiving and storing goods and preparing them for reshipment. Goods are stored to create time utility; that is, they are held until they are needed for use or sale. Warehousing includes:

* *Receiving goods*—The warehouse accepts delivered goods and assumes responsibility for them.
* *Identifying goods*—Records are made of the quantity of each item received. Items may be marked, coded, or tagged for identification.
* *Sorting goods*—Delivered goods may have to be sorted before being stored.
* *Dispatching goods to storage*—Items must be moved to specific storage areas, where they can be found later.
* *Holding goods*—The goods are kept in storage under proper protection until needed.
* *Recalling, picking, and assembling goods*—Items that are to leave the warehouse must be selected from storage and assembled efficiently.
* *Dispatching shipments*—Each shipment is packaged suitably and directed to the proper transport vehicle. Shipping and accounting documents are prepared.

A firm may use its own warehouses or rent space in public warehouses. A *private warehouse*, owned and operated by a particular firm, can be designed to serve the firm's specific needs. However, the organization must take on the task of financing the facility, determining the best location for it, and ensuring that it is used fully. Generally, only companies that deal in large quantities of goods can justify private warehouses.

Public warehouses offer their services to all individuals and firms. Most are huge one-story structures on the outskirts of cities, where rail and truck transportation are easily available. They provide storage facilities, areas for sorting and assembling shipments, and office and display spaces for wholesalers and retailers. Public warehouses also will hold—and issue receipts for—goods used as collateral for borrowed funds. Many organizations design and locate their warehouses to not only to be cost-efficient but also provide excellent customer service.

Materials Handling

Materials handling is the actual physical handling of goods—in warehouses as well as during transportation. Proper materials-handling procedures and techniques can increase the usable capacity of a warehouse or that of any means of transportation. Proper handling can reduce breakage and spoilage as well.

Modern materials handling attempts to reduce the number of times a product is handled. One method is called *unit loading*. Several smaller cartons, barrels, or boxes are combined into a single standard-size load that can be handled efficiently by forklift, conveyer, or truck.

Transportation

As a part of physical distribution, **transportation** is simply the shipment of products to customers. The greater the distance between seller and purchaser, the more important is the choice of the means of transportation and the particular carrier.

A firm that offers transportation services is called a **carrier**. A *common carrier* is a transportation firm whose services are available to all shippers. Railways, airlines, and most long-distance trucking firms are common carriers. A *contract carrier* is available for hire by one or several shippers. Contract carriers do not serve the general public. Moreover, the number of firms they can handle at any one time is limited by law. A *private carrier* is owned and operated by the shipper.

In addition, a shipper can hire agents called *freight forwarders* to handle its transportation. Freight forwarders pick up shipments from the shipper, ensure that the goods are loaded on selected carriers, and assume responsibility for safe delivery of the shipments to their destinations. Freight forwarders often group a number of small shipments into one large load (which is carried at a lower rate). This, of course, saves money for shippers.

The six major criteria used for selecting transportation modes are compared in Table 14.2. Obviously, the *cost* of a transportation mode is important to marketers. At times, marketers choose higher-cost modes of transportation because of the benefits they provide. *Speed* is measured by the total time that a carrier possesses the products, including time required for pickup and delivery, handling, and movement between point of origin and destination. Usually there is a direct relationship between cost and speed; that is, faster modes of transportation are more expensive. A transportation mode's *dependability* is determined by the consistency of service provided by that mode. *Load flexibility* is the degree to which a transportation mode can provide appropriate equipment and conditions for moving specific kinds of products and can be adapted for moving other kinds of products. For example, certain types of products may need controlled temperatures or humidity levels. *Accessibility* refers to a transportation mode's ability to move goods over a specific route or network. *Frequency* refers to how often a marketer can ship products by a specific transportation mode. Whereas pipelines provide continuous shipments, railways and waterways follow specific schedules for moving products from one location to another. In Table 14.2, each transportation mode is rated on a relative basis for these six selection criteria and the percentage of use (tonne-kilometres) for each mode.

Railways Railways are North America's most important mode of transportation in terms of total freight carried. They are also the least expensive for many products. Almost all railways are common carriers. Many commodities carried by railways could not be transported easily by any other means.

Trucks The trucking industry consists of common, contract, and private carriers. Trucks can move goods to suburban and rural areas not served by railways. They can

carrier a firm that offers transportation services

MODE	COST	SPEED	DEPENDABILITY	LOAD FLEXIBILITY	ACCESSIBILITY	FREQUENCY
Railways	Moderate	Average	Average	High	High	Low
Trucks	High	Fast	High	Average	Very high	High
Airplanes	Very high	Very fast	High	Low	Average	Average
Waterways	Very low	Very slow	Average	Very high	Limited	Very low
Pipelines	Low	Slow	High	Very low	Very limited	Very high

Table 14.2

Relative Ratings of Transportation Modes by Selection Criteria

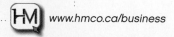

Waterways

The Welland Canal is one of the most important transportation routes in Canada. Waterway transportation is used to move heavy, non-perishable products, such as large equipment, grain, motor vehicles, and chemicals.

handle freight quickly and economically, and they carry a wide range of shipments. Many shippers favour this mode of transportation because it offers door-to-door service, less stringent packaging requirements than ships and airplanes, and flexible delivery schedules. Rail and truck carriers have teamed up to provide a form of transportation called *piggyback*. Truck trailers are carried from city to city on specially equipped flatcars. Within each city, the trailers are then pulled in the usual way by truck tractors.

Airplanes Air transport is the fastest but most expensive means of transportation. All certified airlines are common carriers. Supplemental or charter lines are contract carriers. Because of the high cost, lack of airport facilities in many areas, and reliance on weather conditions, airlines carry less than 1 percent of all intercity freight. Only high-value or perishable items, such as flowers, aircraft parts, and pharmaceuticals or goods that are needed immediately, usually are shipped by air.

Waterways Cargo ships and barges offer the least expensive but slowest form of transportation. They are used mainly for bulky nonperishable goods such as iron ore, bulk wheat, motor vehicles, and agricultural implements. Of course, shipment by water is limited to cities located on navigable waterways.

Pipelines Pipelines are a highly specialized mode of transportation. They are used primarily to carry petroleum and natural gas. Pipelines have become more important as North America's need for petroleum products has increased. Such products as semiliquid coal and wood chips also can be shipped through pipelines continuously, reliably, and with minimal handling.

What Is Integrated Marketing Communications?

> ## Learning Objective 6
>
> Describe integrated marketing communications.

integrated marketing communications
coordination of promotion efforts to ensure maximal informational and persuasive impact on customers

Integrated marketing communications is the coordination of promotion efforts to ensure maximal informational and persuasive impact on customers. A major goal of integrated marketing communications is to send a consistent message to customers. Integrated marketing communications provides an organization with a way to coordinate and manage its promotional efforts to ensure that customers do receive consistent messages. This approach fosters not only long-term customer relationships but also the efficient use of promotional resources.

The concept of integrated marketing communications has been increasingly accepted for several reasons. Mass-media advertising, a very popular promotional method in the past, is used less today because of its high costs and less predictable audience sizes. Marketers now can take advantage of more precisely targeted promotional tools, such as cable TV, direct mail, DVDs, the Internet, special-interest magazines, and podcasts. Database marketing also allows marketers to be more precise in targeting individual customers. Until recently, suppliers of marketing communications were specialists. Advertising agencies provided advertising campaigns, sales promotion companies provided sales promotion activities and materials, and public-relations organizations engaged in public-relations efforts. Today, a number of promotion-related companies provide one-stop shopping to the client seeking advertising, sales promotion, and public relations, thus reducing coordination problems for the sponsoring company. Because the overall costs of marketing communications are significant, management demands systematic evaluations of communications efforts to ensure that promotional resources are being used efficiently. Although the fundamental role of promotion has not changed, the specific communication vehicles employed and the precision with which they are used are changing.

The Promotion Mix: An Overview

Promotion is communication about an organization and its products that is intended to inform, persuade, or remind target-market members. The promotion with which we are most familiar—advertising—is intended to inform, persuade, or remind us to buy particular products. But there is more to promotion than advertising, and it is used for other purposes as well. Charities use promotion to inform us of their need for donations, to persuade us to give, and to remind us to do so in case we have forgotten. Even the Canada Revenue Agency uses promotion (in the form of publicity) to remind us of its April 30 deadline for filing tax returns.

A **promotion mix** (sometimes called a *marketing-communications mix*) is the particular combination of promotional methods a firm uses to reach a target market. The makeup of a mix depends on many factors, including the firm's promotional resources and objectives, the nature of the target market, the product characteristics, and the feasibility of various promotional methods.

Advertising, personal selling, sales promotion, and public relations are the four major elements in an organization's promotion mix (see Figure 14.2). While it is possible that one ingredient may be used, it is likely that two, three, or four of these ingredients will be used in a promotion mix depending on the type of product and target market involved.

Advertising is a paid nonpersonal message communicated to a select audience through a mass medium. Advertising is flexible enough that it can reach a very large target group or a small, carefully chosen one. **Personal selling** is personal communication aimed at

promotion communication about an organization and its products that is intended to inform, persuade, or remind target-market members

promotion mix the particular combination of promotion methods a firm uses to reach a target market

advertising a paid nonpersonal message communicated to a select audience through a mass medium

personal selling personal communication aimed at informing customers and persuading them to buy a firm's products

Figure 14.2

Possible Ingredients of a Promotion Mix

Depending on the type of product and target market involved, one or more of these ingredients are used in a promotion mix.

Source: William M. Pride and O. C. Ferrell, *Marketing: Concepts and Strategies* (Boston: Houghton Mifflin, 2006). Copyright © 2006 by Houghton Mifflin Company. Adapted with permission.

[Pie chart with four segments: Advertising, Personal selling, Sales promotion, Public relations]

―EXAMINING ETHICS―
Who's Behind the Blog Buzz?

I s it ethical to have a product mentioned in a blog (an online journal) without clearly identifying that a company is behind the attempt to build buzz? Here are two recent examples that caused controversy.

- *Wal-Mart*. The "Wal-Marting Across America" blog seemed to be written by two ordinary people who drove their RV to Wal-Mart parking lots and chatted with happy employees and customers. The blog included a banner from Working Families for Wal-Mart but never mentioned that funding came from Wal-Mart—a fact first revealed by *BusinessWeek* magazine.

- *Nokia*. When David Ponce of the OhGizmo.com blog reviewed a $600 multi-function Nokia cell phone, he wrote that although "some features lack a little polish . . . the phone is worth its weight in gold." Only careful readers of OhGizmo would notice a statement that reviewers accept free samples of products for review. Yet Ponce told *Smart Money* magazine that the Nokia was a great music player but not a very good phone.

So should bloggers and companies be required to disclose any connections they may have?

Sources: Based on information in Anne Kadet, "Romancing the Bloggers," *SmartMoney*, November 2006, pp. 92+; Pallavi Gogoi, "Wal-Mart vs. the Blogosphere," *BusinessWeek*, October 17, 2006, www.businessweek.com; Pallavi Gogoi, "Wal-Mart's Jim and Laura: The Real Story," *BusinessWeek*, October 8, 2006, www.businessweek.com; Howard Kurtz, "Post Photographer Repays Group for Trip Expenses," *Washington Post*, October 12, 2006, p. C2.

---

sales promotion the use of activities or materials as direct inducements to customers or salespersons

public relations communication activities used to create and maintain favourable relations between an organization and various public groups, both internal and external

informing customers and persuading them to buy a firm's products. It is more expensive to reach a consumer through personal selling than through advertising, but this method provides immediate feedback and often is more persuasive than advertising. **Sales promotion** is the use of activities or materials as direct inducements to customers or salespersons. It adds extra value to the product or increases the customer's incentive to buy the product. **Public relations** is a broad set of communication activities used to create and maintain favourable relationships between an organization and various public groups, both internal and external. Public-relations activities are numerous and varied and can be a very effective form of promotion.

Advertising

Learning Objective 7

Explain the purposes of three types of advertisings.

According to Statistics Canada there are more than 5,000 agencies among the 11,900 firms involved in advertising and related services. Agencies account for about 45 percent of revenues with most generated in Ontario (57 percent) and Quebec

(26 percent).[11] In 2004, organizations spent over $12 billion on advertising through the various media.[12]

Types of Advertising by Purpose

Depending on its purpose and message, advertising can be classified into one of three groups: primary demand, selective demand, or institutional.

Primary-Demand Advertising Primary-demand advertising is advertising aimed at increasing the demand for *all* brands of a product within a specific industry. Trade and industry associations, such as the Dairy Farmer's of Canada that promotes sales of all sorts of dairy products for its 16,000 members, are the major users of primary-demand advertising. Their advertisements promote broad product categories, such as beef, milk, pork, potatoes, and prunes, without mentioning specific brands.

Selective-Demand Advertising Selective-demand (or brand) advertising is advertising that is used to sell a particular brand of product. It is by far the most common type of advertising, and it accounts for the lion's share of advertising expenditures. Producers use brand-oriented advertising to convince us to buy everything from Blackberries to Buicks.

Selective advertising that aims at persuading consumers to make purchases within a short time is called *immediate-response advertising*. Most local advertising is of this type. Often local advertisers promote products with immediate appeal. Selective advertising aimed at keeping a firm's name or product before the public is called *reminder advertising*.

Comparative advertising compares the sponsored brand with one or more identified, competing brands. Of course, the comparison shows the sponsored brand to be as good as or better than the other identified competing brands.

Institutional Advertising Institutional advertising is advertising designed to enhance a firm's image or reputation. Many public utilities and larger firms, such as Telus, and the major oil companies, use part of their advertising dollars to build goodwill rather than to stimulate sales directly. A positive public image helps an organization to attract not only customers but also employees and investors.

Major Steps in Developing an Advertising Campaign

An advertising campaign is developed in several stages. These stages can vary in number and the order in which they are implemented depending on the company's resources, products, and audiences. The development of a campaign in any organization, however, will include the following steps in some form:

1. Identify and Analyze the Target Audience The target audience is the group of people toward which a firm's advertisements are directed. To pinpoint the organization's target audience and develop an effective campaign, marketers must analyze such information as the geographic distribution of potential customers; their age, sex, ethnicity, income, and education; and their attitudes toward both the advertiser's product and competing products. How marketers use this information will be influenced by the features of the product to be advertised and the nature of the competition.

primary-demand advertising advertising whose purpose is to increase the demand for *all* brands of a product within a specific industry

selective-demand (or brand) advertising advertising that is used to sell a particular brand of product

institutional advertising advertising designed to enhance a firm's image or reputation

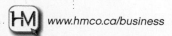

Precise identification of the target audience is crucial to the proper development of subsequent stages and, ultimately, to the success of the campaign itself.

2. Define the Advertising Objectives The goals of an advertising campaign should be stated precisely and in measurable terms. The objectives should include the current position of the firm, indicate how far and in what direction from that original reference point the company wishes to move, and specify a definite period of time for the achievement of the goals. Advertising objectives that focus on sales will stress increasing sales by a certain percentage or dollar amount or expanding the firm's market share. Communication objectives will emphasize increasing product or brand awareness, improving consumer attitudes, or conveying product information.

3. Create the Advertising Platform An advertising platform includes the important selling points or features that an advertiser wishes to incorporate into the advertising campaign. These features should be important to customers in their selection and use of a product and, if possible, they should be features that competing products lack. Although research into what consumers view as important issues is expensive, it is the most productive way to determine which issues to include in an advertising platform.

4. Determine the Advertising Appropriation The advertising appropriation is the total amount of money designated for advertising in a given period. This stage is critical to the success of the campaign because advertising efforts based on an inadequate budget will understimulate customer demand, and a budget too large will waste a company's resources. Advertising appropriations might be based on last year's (or next year's forecasted) sales, on what competitors spend on advertising, or on executive judgment.

5. Develop the Media Plan A media plan specifies exactly which media will be used in the campaign and when advertisements will appear. Although cost-effectiveness is not easy to measure, the primary concern of the media planner is to reach the largest number of persons in the target audience for each dollar spent. In addition to cost, media planners must consider the location and demographics of the advertising target audience, the content of the message, and the characteristics of the audiences reached by various media. The media planner begins with general media decisions, selects subclasses within each medium, and finally chooses particular media vehicles for the campaign. The advantages and disadvantages (and the proportion of ad spending) of the major media classes are shown in Table 14.3.

6. Create the Advertising Message The content and form of a message are influenced by the product's features, the characteristics of people in the target audience, the objectives of the campaign, and the choice of medium. An advertiser must consider these factors to choose words and illustrations that will be meaningful and appealing to persons in the target audience. The copy, or words, of an advertisement will vary depending on the media choice but should attempt to move the audience through attention, interest, desire, and action. Artwork and visuals should complement copy by attracting the audience's attention and communicating an idea quickly. Creating a cohesive advertising message is especially difficult for a company such as eBay that offers such a broad mix of products. eBay developed a "whatever it is" campaign that features a variety of consumers of every age using a variety of products (a car, a television, a dress, and a laptop) all shaped like the letters "it." The tagline,

MEDIUM	PERCENTAGE OF TOTAL*	ADVANTAGES	DISADVANTAGES
Television	25.1 percent	Reaches large audiences, high frequency available, dual impact of audio and video, highly visible, high prestige, geographic and demographic selectivity, difficult to ignore	Very expensive, highly perishable message, size of audience not guaranteed, amount of prime time limited, lack of selectivity in target market
Direct mail	20.4 percent	Little wasted circulation, highly selective, circulation controlled by advertiser, few distractions, personal, stimulates actions, use of novelty, relatively easy to measure performance, hidden from competitors	Very expensive, lacks editorial content to attract readers, often thrown away unread as junk mail, criticized as invasion of privacy, consumers must choose to read the ad
Newspapers	17.4 percent	Reaches large audience, purchased to be read, geographic flexibility, short lead time, frequent publication, favourable for cooperative advertising, merchandising services	Not selective for socioeconomic groups or target market, short life, limited reproduction capabilities, large advertising volume limits exposure to any one advertisement
Radio	7.2 percent	Reaches 95 percent of consumers, highly mobile and flexible, very low relative costs, ad can be changed quickly, high level of geographic and demographic selectivity, encourages use of imagination	Lacks visual imagery, short life of message, listeners' attention limited because of other activities, market fragmentation, difficult buying procedures, limited media and audience research
Yellow Pages	5.2 percent	Wide availability, action and product category oriented, low relative costs, ad frequency and longevity, nonintrusive	Market fragmentation, extremely localized, slow updating, lack of creativity, long lead times, requires large space to be noticed
Magazines	4.7 percent	Demographic selectivity, good reproduction, long life, prestige, geographic selectivity when regional issues are available, read in leisurely manner	High costs, 30–90 day average lead time, high level of competition, limited reach, communicates less frequently
Internet	2.9 percent	Immediate response, potential to reach a precisely targeted audience, ability to track customers and build databases, highly interactive medium	Costs of precise targeting are high, inappropriate ad placement, effects difficult to measure, concerns about security and privacy
Outdoor	2.3 percent	Allows for frequent repetition, low cost, message can be placed close to point of sale, geographic selectivity, operable 24 hours a day, high creativity and effectiveness	Message must be short and simple, no demographic selectivity, seldom attracts readers' full attention, criticized as traffic hazard and blight on countryside, much wasted coverage, limited capabilities

*Spending on miscellaneous advertising accounts for 13.2 percent of total expenditures.

Table 14.3

Percentage Use and Advantages and Disadvantages of Major Media Classes

Sources: William F. Arens, *Contemporary Advertising* (Burr Ridge, IL: Irwin/McGraw-Hill, 2004); George E. Belch and Michael Belch, *Advertising and Promotion* (Burr Ridge, IL: Irwin/McGraw-Hill, 2004). Advertising Age, Ad Spending Totals by Media, June 26, 2006, p. S-8.

"Whatever *it* is, you can get it on eBay," emphasizes the massive range of products available from the site and effectively showcases the service that the company provides.

7. Execute the Campaign Execution of an advertising campaign requires extensive planning, scheduling, and coordinating because many tasks must be completed on time. The efforts of many people and firms are involved. Production companies, research organizations, media firms, printers, photoengravers, and commercial artists are just a few of the people and firms that can contribute to a campaign. Advertising managers constantly must assess the quality of the work and take corrective action when necessary. In some instances, advertisers make changes during the campaign to meet objectives more effectively.

8. Evaluate Advertising Effectiveness A campaign's success should be measured in terms of its original objectives before, during, and/or after the campaign. An advertiser should at least be able to estimate whether sales or market share went up because of the campaign or whether any change occurred in customer attitudes or brand awareness. Data from past and current sales and responses to coupon offers and customer surveys administered by research organizations are some of the ways in which advertising effectiveness can be evaluated.

Advertising Agencies

advertising agency an independent firm that plans, produces, and places advertising for its clients

Advertisers can plan and produce their own advertising with help from media personnel, or they can hire advertising agencies. An **advertising agency** is an independent firm that plans, produces, and places advertising for its clients. Many large ad agencies offer help with sales promotion and public relations as well. The media usually pay a commission of 15 percent to advertising agencies. Thus the cost to the agency's client can be quite moderate. The client may be asked to pay for selected services that the agency performs. Other methods for compensating agencies are also used.

Firms that do a lot of advertising might use both an in-house advertising department and an independent agency. This approach gives the firm the advantage of being able to call on the agency's expertise in particular areas of advertising. An agency also can bring a fresh viewpoint to a firm's products and advertising plans.

Social and Legal Considerations in Advertising

Critics of advertising have two main complaints—that it is wasteful and that it can be deceptive. Although advertising (like any other activity) can be performed inefficiently, it is far from wasteful. Let's look at the evidence:

* Advertising is the most effective and least expensive means of communicating product information to a large number of individuals and organizations.

* Advertising encourages competition and is, in fact, a means of competition. It thus leads to the development of new and improved products, wider product choices, and lower prices.

* Advertising revenues support our mass-communications media—newspapers, magazines, radio, and television. This means that advertising pays for much of our news coverage and entertainment programming.

* Advertising provides job opportunities in fields ranging from sales to film production.

Personal Selling

Learning Objective 8

Recognize the various kinds of salespersons, the steps in the personal-selling process, and the major sales management tasks.

Personal selling is the most adaptable of all promotional methods because the person who is presenting the message can modify it to suit the individual buyer. However, personal selling is also the most expensive method of promotion.

Most successful salespeople are able to communicate with others on a one-to-one basis and are strongly motivated. They strive to have a thorough knowledge of the products they offer for sale. And they are willing and able to deal with the details involved in handling and processing orders. Sales managers tend to emphasize these qualities when recruiting and hiring.

Many selling situations demand the face-to-face contact and adaptability of personal selling. This is especially true of industrial sales, in which a single purchase can amount to millions of dollars. Obviously, sales of that size must be based on carefully planned sales presentations, personal contact with customers, and thorough negotiations.

Kinds of Salespersons

Because most businesses employ different salespersons to perform different functions, marketing managers must select the kinds of sales personnel who will be most effective in selling the firm's products. Salespersons might be identified as order getters, order takers, and support personnel. A single individual can, and often does, perform all three functions.

Order Getters An **order getter** is responsible for what is sometimes called **creative selling**—selling a firm's products to new customers and increasing sales to current customers. An order getter must perceive buyers' needs, supply customers with information about the firm's product, and persuade them to buy the product. Some order-getters focus on current customers while others focus on new customers.

Order Takers An **order taker** handles repeat sales in ways that maintain positive relationships with customers. An order taker sees that customers have products when and where they are needed and in the proper amounts. *Inside order takers* receive incoming mail and telephone orders in some businesses; salespersons in retail stores are also inside order takers. *Outside* (or *field*) *order takers* travel to customers. Often the buyer and the field salesperson develop a mutually beneficial relationship of placing, receiving, and delivering orders. Both inside and outside order takers are active salespersons and often produce most of their companies' sales.

Support Personnel Sales support personnel aid in selling but are more involved in locating *prospects* (likely first-time customers), educating customers, building goodwill for the firm, and providing follow-up service.

The most common categories of support personnel are missionary, trade, and technical salespersons. A **missionary salesperson,** who usually works for a manufacturer,

order getter a salesperson who is responsible for selling a firm's products to new customers and increasing sales to present customers

creative selling selling products to new customers and increasing sales to present customers

order taker a salesperson who handles repeat sales in ways that maintain positive relationships with customers

sales support personnel employees who aid in selling but are more involved in locating prospects, educating customers, building goodwill for the firm, and providing follow-up service

missionary salesperson a salesperson—generally employed by a manufacturer—who visits retailers to persuade them to buy the manufacturer's products

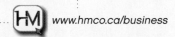

trade salesperson a salesperson—generally employed by a food producer or processor—who assists customers in promoting products, especially in retail stores

technical salesperson a salesperson who assists a company's current customers in technical matters

visits retailers to persuade them to buy the manufacturer's products. If the retailers agree, they buy the products from wholesalers, who are the manufacturer's actual customers. A **trade salesperson**, who generally works for a food producer or processor, assists customers in promoting products, especially in retail stores. A trade salesperson might obtain additional shelf space for the products, restock shelves, set up displays, and distribute samples. Because trade salespersons usually are order takers as well, they are not strictly support personnel. A **technical salesperson** assists a company's current customers in technical matters. He or she may explain how to use a product, how it is made, how to install it, or how a system is designed. A technical salesperson should be formally educated in science or engineering.

Marketers usually need sales personnel from several of these categories. Factors that affect hiring and other personnel decisions include the number of customers and their characteristics; the product's attributes, complexity, and price; the distribution channels used by the company; and the company's approach to advertising.

The Personal-Selling Process

No two selling situations are exactly alike, and no two salespeople perform their jobs in exactly the same way. Most salespeople, however, follow the six-step procedure illustrated in Figure 14.3.

Prospecting The first step in personal selling is to research potential buyers and choose the most likely customers, or prospects. Sources of prospects include business associates and customers, public records, telephone and trade-association directories, and company files. The salesperson concentrates on those prospects who have the financial resources, willingness, and authority to buy the product.

Approaching the Prospect First impressions are often lasting impressions. Thus the salesperson's first contact with the prospect is crucial to successful selling. The best approach is one based on knowledge of the product, the prospect's needs, and how the product can meet those needs. Salespeople who understand each customer's particular situation are likely to make a good first impression—and to make a sale.

Making the Presentation The next step is actual delivery of the sales presentation. In many cases this includes demonstrating the product. The salesperson points out the product's features, its benefits, and how it is superior to competitors' merchandise. If the product has been used successfully by other firms, the salesperson may mention this as part of the presentation.

During a demonstration, the salesperson may suggest that the prospect try out the product personally. The demonstration and product trial should underscore specific points made during the presentation.

Answering Objections The prospect is likely to raise objections or ask questions at any time. This gives the salesperson a chance to eliminate objections that might

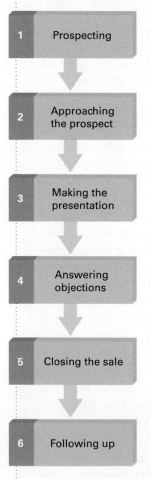

Figure 14.3

The Six Steps of the Personal-Selling Process

Personal selling is not only the most adaptable of all promotional methods but also the most expensive.

Source: William M. Pride and O. C. Ferrell, *Marketing: Concepts and Strategies* (Boston: Houghton Mifflin, 2006). Copyright © 2006 by Houghton Mifflin Company. Adapted with permission.

1 Prospecting

2 Approaching the prospect

3 Making the presentation

4 Answering objections

5 Closing the sale

6 Following up

prevent a sale, to point out additional features, or to mention special services the company offers.

Closing the Sale To close the sale, the salesperson asks the prospect to buy the product. This is considered the critical point in the selling process. Many experienced salespeople make use of a *trial closing*, in which they ask questions based on the assumption that the customer is going to buy the product. The questions "When would you want delivery?" and "Do you want the standard model or the one with the special options package?" are typical of trial closings. They allow the reluctant prospect to make a purchase without having to say, "I'll take it."

Following Up The salesperson must follow up after the sale to ensure that the product is delivered on time, in the right quantity, and in proper operating condition. During follow-up, the salesperson also makes it clear that he or she is available in case problems develop. Follow-up leaves a good impression and eases the way toward future sales. Hence it is essential to the selling process. The salesperson's job does not end with a sale. It continues as long as the seller and the customer maintain a working relationship.

Managing Personal Selling

A firm's success often hinges on the competent management of its sales force. Although some companies operate efficiently without a sales force, most firms rely on a strong sales force—and the sales revenue it brings in—for their success.

Sales managers have responsibilities in a number of areas. They must set sales objectives in concrete, quantifiable terms and specify a certain period of time and a certain geographic area. They must adjust the size of the sales force to meet changes in the firm's marketing plan and the marketing environment. Sales managers must attract and hire effective salespersons. For example, Guitar centre, the largest musical instrument chain in the United States, has only one requirement for members of its sales force—that they be able to play a musical instrument. The company believes that a rocking sales force will care more deeply about the product and sell it more effectively to customers.[13] Sales managers must develop a training program and decide where, when, how, and for whom to conduct the training. They must formulate a fair and adequate compensation plan to keep qualified employees. They must motivate salespersons to boost their productivity. They must define sales territories and determine scheduling and routing of the sales force. Finally, sales managers must evaluate the operation as a whole through sales reports, communications with customers, and invoices.

Sales Promotion

Describe sales promotion objectives and methods.

Sales promotion consists of activities or materials that are direct inducements to customers or salespersons. Are you a member of an airline frequent-flyer program? Did you recently receive a free sample in the mail or at a supermarket? Have you recently

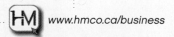

received a rebate from a manufacturer? Do you use coupons? All these are examples of sales promotion efforts. Sales promotion techniques often are used to enhance and supplement other promotional methods. They can have a significant impact on sales.

The dramatic increase in spending for sales promotion shows that marketers have recognized the potential of this promotional method. Many firms now include numerous sales promotion efforts as part of their overall promotion mix.

Sales Promotion Objectives

Sales promotion activities can be used singly or in combination, both offensively and defensively, to achieve one goal or a set of goals. Marketers use sales promotion activities and materials for a number of purposes, including

1. To attract new customers
2. To encourage trial of a new product
3. To invigorate the sales of a mature brand
4. To boost sales to current customers
5. To reinforce advertising
6. To increase traffic in retail stores
7. To steady irregular sales patterns
8. To build up reseller inventories
9. To neutralize competitive promotional efforts
10. To improve shelf space and displays[14]

Any sales promotion objectives should be consistent with the organization's general goals and with its marketing and promotional objectives.

Sales Promotion Methods

Most sales promotion methods can be classified as promotional techniques for either consumer sales or trade sales. A **consumer sales promotion method** attracts consumers to particular retail stores and motivates them to purchase certain new or established products. A **trade sales promotion method** encourages wholesalers and retailers to stock and actively promote a manufacturer's product. Incentives such as money, merchandise, marketing assistance, and gifts are commonly awarded to resellers who buy products or respond positively in other ways. Of the combined dollars spent on sales promotion and advertising *last year*, about one-half was spent on trade promotions, one-fourth on consumer promotions, and one-fourth on advertising.

A number of factors enter into marketing decisions about which and how many sales promotion methods to use. Of greatest importance are the objectives of the promotional effort. Product characteristics—size, weight, cost, durability, uses, features, and hazards—and target market profiles—age, gender, income, location, density, usage rate, and buying patterns—likewise must be considered. Distribution channels and availability of appropriate resellers also influence the choice of sales promotion methods, as do the competitive and regulatory forces in the environment. Let's now discuss a few important sales promotion methods.

consumer sales promotion method a sales promotion method designed to attract consumers to particular retail stores and to motivate them to purchase certain new or established products

trade sales promotion method a sales promotion method designed to encourage wholesalers and retailers to stock and actively promote a manufacturer's product

Rebates A **rebate** is a return of part of the purchase price of a product. Usually the refund is offered by the producer to consumers who send in a coupon along with a specific proof of purchase. Rebating is a relatively low-cost promotional method. One problem with rebates is that many people perceive the redemption process as too complicated. Only about half of individuals who purchase rebated products actually apply for the rebates.

Coupons A **coupon** reduces the retail price of a particular item by a stated amount at the time of purchase. Coupons can be worth anywhere from a few cents to a few dollars. They are made available to customers through newspapers, magazines, direct mail, online, and shelf dispensers in stores. Some coupons are precisely targeted at customers. For Example, All Online Coupons is an Internet site that provides visitors with links to all online coupons currently being offered. Customers can find coupons by category or store name. Other companies, such as Old Navy and The Gap, offer coupons on their websites that can be used online or in stores. Billions of coupons are distributed annually. Of these, just under 2 percent are redeemed by consumers.

Samples A **sample** is a free product given to customers to encourage trial and purchase. Marketers use free samples to stimulate trial of a product, increase sales volume in the early stages of a product's life cycle, and obtain desirable distribution. Samples may be offered via online coupons, direct mail, or in stores. Many customers prefer to receive their samples by mail. It is the most expensive sales promotion technique, and although it is used often to promote new products, it can be used to promote established brands, too, such as cosmetics companies that use samples to attract customers. In designing a free sample, organizations must consider such factors as seasonal demand for the product, market characteristics, and prior advertising.

Premiums A **premium** is a gift that a producer offers a customer in return for buying its product. They are used to attract competitors' customers, introduce different sizes of established products, add variety to other promotional efforts, and stimulate consumer loyalty. Creativity is essential when using premiums; to stand out and achieve a significant number of redemptions, the premium must match both the target audience and the brand's image. Premiums also must be easily recognizable and desirable. Premiums are placed on or inside packages and also can be distributed through retailers or through the mail.

Frequent-User Incentives A **frequent-user incentive** is a program developed to reward customers who engage in repeat (frequent) purchases. Such programs are used commonly by service businesses such as airlines, hotels, and auto rental agencies. Frequent-user incentives foster customer loyalty to a specific company or group of cooperating companies because the customer is given an additional reason to continue patronizing the business.

Point-of-Purchase Displays A **point-of-purchase display** is promotional material placed within a retail store. The display is usually located near the product being promoted. It actually can hold merchandise (as do L'eggs hosiery displays) or inform customers about what the product offers and encourage them to buy it. Most point-of-purchase displays are prepared and set up by manufacturers and wholesalers.

Trade Shows A **trade show** is an industry-wide exhibit at which many sellers display their products. Some trade shows are organized exclusively for dealers—to

rebate a return of part of the purchase price of a product

coupon reduces the retail price of a particular item by a stated amount at the time of purchase

sample a free product given to customers to encourage trial and purchase

premium a gift that a producer offers a customer in return for buying its product

frequent-user incentive a program developed to reward customers who engage in repeat (frequent) purchases

point-of-purchase display promotional material placed within a retail store

trade show an industry-wide exhibit at which many sellers display their products

permit manufacturers and wholesalers to show their latest lines to retailers. Others are promotions designed to stimulate consumer awareness and interest. Among the latter are the boat, home, and flower shows put on each year in large cities.

Buying Allowances A buying allowance is a temporary price reduction to resellers for purchasing specified quantities of a product. For example, a laundry detergent manufacturer might give retailers $1 for each case of detergent purchased. A buying allowance may serve as an incentive to resellers to handle new products and may stimulate purchase of items in large quantities. While the buying allowance is simple, straightforward, and easily administered, competitors can respond quickly by offering a better buying allowance.

Cooperative Advertising Cooperative advertising is an arrangement whereby a manufacturer agrees to pay a certain amount of a retailer's media cost for advertising the manufacturer's products. To be reimbursed, a retailer must show proof that the advertisements actually did appear. A large percentage of all cooperative advertising dollars are spent on newspaper advertisements. Not all retailers take advantage of available cooperative advertising offers because they cannot afford to advertise or do not choose to do so.

buying allowance
a temporary price reduction to resellers for purchasing specified quantities of a product

cooperative advertising
an arrangement whereby a manufacturer agrees to pay a certain amount of a retailer's media cost for advertising the manufacturer's product

Public Relations

Learning Objective 10

Understand the types and uses of public relations.

As noted earlier, public relations is a broad set of communication activities used to create and maintain favourable relationships between an organization and various public groups, both internal and external. These groups can include customers, employees, stockholders, suppliers, educators, the media, government officials, and society in general.

Types of Public-Relations Tools

Organizations use a variety of public-relations tools to convey messages and create images. Public-relations professionals prepare written materials, such as brochures, newsletters, company magazines, annual reports, and news releases. They also create corporate-identity materials, such as logos, business cards, signs, and stationery. Speeches are another public-relations tool. Speeches can affect an organization's image and therefore must convey the desired message clearly.

Another public-relations tool is event sponsorship, in which a company pays for all or part of a special event, such as a concert, sports competition, festival, or play. Sponsoring special events is an effective way for organizations to increase brand recognition and receive media coverage with comparatively little investment. For example, pharmaceutical company Bristol-Myers Squibb sponsored the Tour of Hope, a nine-day bike trek from San Diego, California, to Washington, D.C., to raise money for cancer research. Bristol-Myers spokesman, seven-time Tour de France winner and cancer survivor Lance Armstrong, led twenty-four other cyclists on the tour.[15]

Some public-relations tools traditionally have been associated specifically with publicity, which is a part of public relations. **Publicity** is communication in news-story form about an organization, its products, or both. Publicity is transmitted through a mass medium, such as newspapers or radio, at no charge. Organizations use publicity to provide information about products; to announce new product launches, expansions, or research; and to strengthen the company's image. Public-relations personnel sometimes organize events, such as grand openings with prizes and celebrities, to create news stories about a company.

The most widely used type of publicity is the **news release.** It is generally one typed page of about 300 words provided by an organization to the media as a form of publicity. The release includes the firm's name, address, phone number, and contact person. There are also several other kinds of publicity-based public-relations tools. A **feature article,** which can be as long as 3,000 words, is usually written for inclusion in a particular publication. For example, a software firm might send an article about its new product to a computer magazine. A **captioned photograph,** a picture accompanied by a brief explanation, is an effective way to illustrate a new or improved product. A **press conference** allows invited media personnel to hear important news announcements and to receive supplementary text and photographs. Finally, letters to the editor, special newspaper or magazine editorials, films, and tapes may be prepared and distributed to appropriate media for possible use.

Uses of Public Relations

Public relations can be used to promote people, places, activities, ideas, and even countries. Public relations focuses on enhancing the reputation of the total organization by making people aware of a company's products, brands, or activities and by creating specific company images such as that of innovativeness or dependability. For example, ice-cream maker Ben and Jerry's uses news stories and other public-relations efforts to reinforce its reputation as a socially responsible company. By getting the media to report on a firm's accomplishments, public relations helps a company to maintain positive public visibility. Effective management of public-relations efforts also can reduce the unfavourable effects of negative events.

publicity communication in news-story form about an organization, its products, or both

news release a typed page of about 300 words provided by an organization to the media as a form of publicity

feature article a piece (of up to 3,000 words) prepared by an organization for inclusion in a particular publication

captioned photograph a picture accompanied by a brief explanation

press conference a meeting at which invited media personnel hear important news announcements and receive supplementary textand photographs

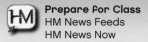

Prepare for Class
HM News Feeds
HM News Now

→ **RETURN TO INSIDE BUSINESS**

To reach even more customers Fruits & Passion operates a retail website at www.fruits-passion.com. Websites fill the retail gaps between physical store locations and serve those customers that are already familiar with the firm's brand and

product characteristics. Websites allow customers to re-order favourite products or perhaps purchase gifts to send to others 24/7. As other retailers have discovered, the Internet is an excellent retail distribution service that can help a firm increase sales in more markets around the world.

Questions:

1. How can the firm's website assist developing retail stores around the world?

2. How important is physical contact with Fruits & Passion products in order to make a purchase decision? Explain your answer.

CHAPTER REVIEW

1 **Identify the various channels of distribution.**

A marketing channel is a sequence of marketing organizations that directs a product from producer to ultimate user. The marketing channel for a particular product is concerned with the transfer of ownership of that product. Merchant middlemen (merchants) actually take title to products, whereas functional middlemen simply aid in the transfer of title. The channels used for consumer products include the direct channel from producer to consumer; the channel from producer to retailer to consumer; the channel from producer to wholesaler to retailer to consumer; and the channel from producer to agent to wholesaler to retailer to consumer. Channels and intermediaries are chosen to implement a given level of market coverage. Intensive distribution is the use of all available outlets for a product, providing the widest market coverage. Selective distribution uses only a portion of the available outlets in an area. Exclusive distribution uses only a single retail outlet for a product in a large geographic area.

2 **Understand how supply-chain management facilitates partnering among channel members.**

Supply-chain management is a long-term partnership among channel members working together to create a distribution system that reduces inefficiencies, costs, and redundancies while creating a competitive advantage and satisfying customers. Cooperation is required among all channel members, including manufacturing, research, sales, advertising, and shipping. When all channel partners work together, delivery, scheduling, packaging, and other customer requirements are better met. Technology, such as bar coding and electronic data exchange (EDI), makes supply-chain management easier to implement.

3 Understand the types of wholesalers and the services they provide.

Wholesalers are intermediaries who purchase from producers or other intermediaries and sell to industrial users, retailers, or other wholesalers. Wholesalers perform many functions in a distribution channel. If they are eliminated, other channel members—such as the producer or retailers—must perform these functions. Wholesalers provide retailers with help in promoting products, collecting information, and financing. They provide manufacturers with sales help, reduce their inventory costs, furnish market information, and extend credit to retailers. Merchant wholesalers buy and then sell products. Agents do not take title to the goods they distribute.

4 Distinguish the major types of retailers.

Retailers are intermediaries who buy from producers or wholesalers and sell to consumers. In-store retailers include department stores, discount stores, warehouse showrooms, convenience stores, supermarkets, superstores, warehouse clubs, traditional specialty stores, off-price retailers, and category killers. Non-store retailers do not sell in conventional store facilities. Instead, they use direct selling, direct marketing, and automatic vending. Types of direct marketing include catalogue marketing, direct-response marketing, telemarketing, television home shopping, and online retailing. There are three major types of shopping centres: neighbourhood, community, and regional. A centre fits one of these categories based on its mix of stores and the size of the geographic area it serves.

5 Explain the five most important physical distribution activities.

Physical distribution consists of activities designed to move products from producers to ultimate users. Its five major functions are inventory management, order processing, warehousing, materials handling, and transportation. These interrelated functions are integrated into the marketing effort.

6 Describe integrated marketing communications.

Integrated marketing communications is the coordination of promotion efforts to achieve maximum informational and persuasive impact on customers.

7 Explain the purposes of the three types of advertising.

Advertising is a paid non-personal message communicated to a specific audience through a mass medium. Primary-demand advertising promotes the products of an entire industry rather than just a single brand. Selective-demand advertising promotes a particular brand of product. Institutional advertising is image-building advertising for a firm. An advertising campaign is developed in several stages. A firm's first task is to identify and analyze its advertising target. The goals of the campaign also must be clearly defined. Then the firm must develop the advertising platform, or statement of important selling points, and determine the size of the advertising budget. The next steps are to develop a media plan, create the advertising message, and execute the campaign. Finally, promotion managers must evaluate the effectiveness of the advertising efforts before, during, and/or after the campaign.

8 Recognize the various kinds of salespersons, the steps in the personal-selling process, and the major sales management tasks.

Personal selling is personal communication aimed at informing customers and persuading them to buy a firm's products. It is the most adaptable promotional method because the salesperson can modify the message to fit each buyer. Three major kinds of salespersons are order getters, order takers, and support personnel. The six steps in the personal-selling process are prospecting, approaching the prospect, making the presentation, answering objections, closing the sale, and following up. Sales managers are involved directly in setting sales force objectives; recruiting, selecting, and training salespersons; compensating and motivating sales personnel; creating sales territories; and evaluating sales performance.

Describe sales promotion objectives and methods.

Sales promotion is the use of activities and materials as direct inducements to customers and salespersons. The primary objective of sales promotion methods is to enhance and supplement other promotional methods. Methods of sales promotion include rebates, coupons, samples, premiums, frequent-user incentives, point-of-purchase displays, trade shows, buying allowances, and cooperative advertising.

 Understand the types and uses of public relations.

Public relations is a broad set of communication activities used to create and maintain favourable relationships between an organization and various public groups, both internal and external. Organizations use a variety of public-relations tools to convey messages and create images. Brochures, newsletters, company magazines, and annual reports are written public-relations tools. Speeches, event sponsorship, and publicity are other public-relations tools. Publicity is communication in news-story form about an organization, its products, or both. Types of publicity include news releases, feature articles, captioned photographs, and press conferences. Public relations can be used to promote people, places, activities, ideas, and even countries. It can be used to enhance the reputation of an organization and also to reduce the unfavourable effects of negative events.

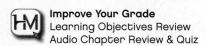

Improve Your Grade
Learning Objectives Review
Audio Chapter Review & Quiz

Review Questions

1. What are the most common marketing channels for consumer products?
2. List the services performed by wholesalers. For whom is each service performed?
3. What is the basic difference between a merchant wholesaler and an agent?
4. Identify three kinds of full-service wholesalers. What factors are used to classify wholesalers into one of these categories?
5. What is the basic difference between wholesalers and retailers?
6. How do (a) convenience stores, (b) traditional specialty stores, and (c) category killers compete with other retail outlets?
7. What can non-store retailers offer their customers that in-store retailers cannot?
8. What is physical distribution? Which major functions does it include?
9. What activities besides storage are included in warehousing?
10. What is integrated marketing communications, and why is it becoming increasingly accepted?
11. Identify and describe the major ingredients of a promotion mix.
12. How are selective-demand, institutional, and primary-demand advertising different from one another? Give an example of each.
13. List the three major print media, and give an advantage and a disadvantage of each.
14. Outline the main steps involved in developing an advertising campaign.
15. Explain how each step in the personal selling process leads to the next step.
16. What is cooperative advertising? What sorts of firms use it?
17. What is the difference between publicity and public relations? What is the purpose of each?

Discussion Questions

1. Many producers sell to consumers both directly and through middlemen. How can such a producer justify competing with its own middlemen?
2. If a middleman is eliminated from a marketing channel, under what conditions will costs decrease? Under what conditions will costs increase? Will the middleman's functions be eliminated? Explain.
3. Which types of retail outlets are best suited to intensive distribution? To selective distribution? To exclusive distribution? Explain your answer in each case.
4. A number of companies have shifted a portion of their promotion dollars from advertising to trade sales promotion methods? Why?
5. Why would a producer offer rebates or coupons rather than simply lowering the price of its products?
6. How can public-relations efforts aimed at the general public help an organization?
7. Why do firms use event sponsorship?

CASE STUDY

Harry Potter and the Wizards of Public Relations

Public-relations magic has catapulted every Harry Potter book to the top of the best-seller lists and transformed every Harry Potter movie into a box-office hit. Worldwide, more than 300 million copies of J. K. Rowling's Harry Potter books and $3.5 billion worth of tickets to Harry Potter movies have been sold. The enormous popularity of the series has made reading "an event with the glitz of a movie premiere," in the words of one children's literature expert. It also has made the author an instant celebrity—and now a billionaire. The seventh and last book in the series, *Harry Potter and the Deathly Hallows,* was released in July 2007. Publishers announced a record-breaking 12 million copies for the first print run in the U.S. alone.

The magic started with the U.K. release of *Harry Potter and the Philosopher's Stone* (published by Raincoast in Canada and published by Scholastic in the United States as *Harry Potter and the Sorcerer's Stone*). Sales picked up quickly, fueled by publicity about Hogwarts and wizardry, the author's background, and even the hefty length of the book. As the buzz carried across the Atlantic, the publishers started by printing more than 50,000 copies for the North American market. However, they were unprepared for the unprecedented demand and had to reprint this debut book again and again. Readers remained enchanted with the young wizard's adventures, boosting sales of each successive book in the series.

To build anticipation and excitement for the sixth book, *Harry Potter and the Half-Blood Prince* and seventh, *Harry Potter and the Deathly Hallows,* none of the millions of copies printed for the North American market were sold before midnight on their official launch dates. Advertising and sales promotion not only boosted sales, but they also provoked considerable media coverage as well. Bookstores invited readers to preorder the new book and show up at 12:01 A.M.—dressed up as Harry, Hermione, or another character from the series—to pick up their purchases.

Raincoast Books set up a special website for Canadian Harry Potter fans at http://www.raincoast.com/harrypotter/index.html. Barnes & Noble, the largest American book retailer, offered the book at a 40 percent discount and sold 1.3 million copies in the first forty-eight hours. Libraries and schools kept enthusiasm high with Harry Potter parties, parades, and trivia contests.

In addition, all kinds of people connected with the book made public appearances, including author Rowling and Jim Dale, the Shakespearean actor who narrated the audiobook. Reporters sought out children and parents, educators, librarians, literacy professionals, and child psychologists to discuss the "Harry Potter phenomenon." Media coverage continued for weeks as a prelude to the holiday-season release of the fourth movie, *Harry Potter and the Goblet of Fire,* just a few months after the sixth book was released.

As the premiere date approached, Warner Bros. briefed reporters on every detail of the production. The studio also posted movie previews, games, newsletters, and more on its Harry Potter website (www.harrypotter.com). The film's teenage stars made news everywhere as they met fans, reporters, and television personalities. The public-relations barrage paid off: *Harry Potter and the Goblet of Fire* smashed box-office records, with $400 million worth of movie tickets sold worldwide in the first ten days.

Then, months before the release of the fifth film, *Harry Potter and the Order of the Phoenix,* Warner Bros. put public relations to work again. Fans were treated to special online previews and photos; interviews with the director and stars filled the media. By the time the movie opened at the height of the busy summer movie season, the magic of Potter-mania had caught the public's imagination—showing, once again, that Harry Potter's marketers are wizards of public relations.

Questions:

1. What would you suggest that Scholastic do to increase sales of earlier Harry Potter books through public relations?

2. How might Warner Bros. use event sponsorship to promote sales of Harry Potter movies on DVD?

3. From the retailer's perspective, what are the advantages and disadvantages of running ads that trumpet sizable discounts on a new Harry Potter book or DVD?

BUILDING SKILLS FOR CAREER SUCCESS

1. Exploring the Internet

One reason the Internet has generated so much excitement and interest among both buyers and distributors of products is that it is a highly effective method of direct marketing. Already a multibillion dollar industry, e-commerce is growing as more businesses recognize the power of the Internet to reach customers twenty-four hours a day anywhere in the world. In addition to using the Internet to provide product information to potential customers, businesses can use it to process orders and accept payment from customers. Quick delivery from warehouses or stores by couriers such as UPS and FedEx adds to the convenience of Internet shopping.

Businesses whose products traditionally have sold well through catalogues are clear leaders in the electronic marketplace. Books, CDs, clothing, and other frequently purchased, relatively low-cost items sell well through both the Internet and catalogues. As a result, many successful catalogue companies are including the Internet as a means of communicating about products. And many of their customers are finding that they prefer the more dynamic online versions of the catalogues.

Assignment

1. Explore the websites listed below, or just enter "shopping" on one of the web search engines—then stand back! Also visit the text website for updates to this exercise.

   www.llbean.com

   www.jcpenney.com

   www.sears.com

   www.landsend.com

   www.barnesandnoble.com

   www.amazon.com

2. Which website does the best job of marketing merchandise? Explain your answer.

3. Find a product that you would be willing to buy over the Internet and explain why you would buy it. Name the website and describe the product.

4. Find a product that you would be unwilling to buy over the Internet and, again, explain your reasoning. Name the website and describe the product.

2. Building Team Skills

Surveys are a commonly used tool in marketing research. The information they provide can reduce business risk and facilitate decision making. Retail outlets often survey their customers' wants and needs by distributing comment cards or questionnaires. The customer survey (on p. 450) is an example of a survey that a local photography shop might distribute to its customers.

Assignment

1. Working in teams of three to five, choose a local retailer.

2. Classify the retailer according to the major types of retailers.

3. Design a survey to help the retailer to improve customer service. (You may find it beneficial to work with the retailer and actually administer the survey to the retailer's customers. Prepare a report of the survey results for the retailer.)

4. Present your findings to the class.

3. Researching Different Careers

Most public libraries maintain relatively up-to-date collections of occupational or career materials. Begin your library search by looking at the computer listings under "vocations" or "careers" and then under specific fields. Check the library's periodicals section, where you will find trade and professional magazines and journals about specific occupations and industries. (*Business Periodicals Index*, published by H. W. Wilson, is an index to articles in major business publications. Arranged alphabetically, it is easy to use.) Familiarize yourself with the concerns and activities of potential employers by skimming their annual reports and other information they distribute to the public. You can also find occupational information on videocassettes, in kits, and through computerized information systems.

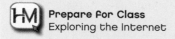
Prepare For Class
Exploring the Internet

Assignment

1. Choose a specific occupation.
2. Conduct a library search of the occupation.
3. Prepare an annotated bibliography for the occupation.

Customer Survey

To help us to serve you better, please take a few minutes while your photographs are being developed to answer the following questions. Your opinions are important to us.

1. Do you live/work in the area? (Circle one or both if they apply.)
2. Why did you choose us? (Circle all that apply.)
   Close to home
   Close to work
   Convenience
   Good service
   Quality
   Full-service photography shop
   Other
3. How did you learn about us? (Circle one.)
   Newspaper
   Flyer/coupon
   Passing by
   Recommended by someone
   Other

4. How frequently do you print pictures from your cell phone or digital camera?
   _____ Times per month
   _____ Times per year
5. Which aspects of our photography shop do you think need improvement?
6. Our operating hours are from 8:00 A.M. to 7:00 P.M. weekdays and Saturdays from 9:30 A.M. to 6:00 P.M. We are closed on Sundays and legal holidays. If changes in our operating hours would serve you better, please specify how you would like them changed.
7. Age (Circle one.)
   Under 25
   26-39
   40-59
   Over 60

Comments:

RUNNING A BUSINESS PART V
Finagle A Bagel's Approach to Marketing

Round, flat, seeded, plain, crowned with cheese, or cut into croutons, bagels form the basis of every menu item at Finagle A Bagel. "So many other shops will just grab onto whatever is hot, whatever is trendy, in a 'me-too' strategy," observes Heather Robertson, the director of marketing, human resources, and research and development. In contrast, she says, "We do bagels—that's what we do best. And any menu item in our stores really needs to reaffirm that as our core concept." That's the first of Finagle A Bagel's marketing rules.

In addition to its retailing activities, the company wholesales its bagels in bulk to hospitals, schools, and other organizations. It also wholesales a line of Finagle A Bagel–branded bagels for resale in Shaw's Market stores. Whether selling wholesale or retail, the company is always hunting for new product ideas involving bagels.

Product Development: Mix, Bake, Bite, and Try Again

To identify a new product idea, Robertson and her colleagues conduct informal research by talking with both customers and employees. They also browse food magazines and cookbooks for ideas about out-of-the-ordinary flavours, taste combinations, and preparation methods. When developing a new bagel variety, for example, Robertson says

that she looks for ideas that are uncommon and innovative yet appealing: "If someone else has a sun-dried tomato bagel, that's all the more reason for me not to do it. People look at Finagle A Bagel as kind of the trendsetter."

Once the marketing staff comes up with a promising idea, the next step is to write up a formula or recipe, walk downstairs to the dough factory, and mix up a test batch. Through trial and error, they refine the idea until they like the way the bagel or sandwich looks and tastes. Occasionally, Finagle A Bagel has to put an idea on hold until it can find just the right ingredients.

For example, when Robertson was working on a new bagel with jalapeno peppers and cheddar cheese, she had difficulty finding a cheese that would melt during baking but not dissolve and disappear into the batter. Ultimately, she found a supplier willing to cook up cheese formulas especially for Finagle A Bagel. The supplier would send a batch of cheese overnight for Robertson to incorporate into the next day's test batch of bagels. After baking, Robertson would send some of the bagels overnight to the supplier so that the two of them could discuss the flavour, consistency, and other details.

The cheeses and bagels flew back and forth for eight months until Finagle A Bagel hit on a recipe that worked well. "When we finally got

it done," Robertson says, "we shipped test batches to our stores, three stores at a time. And we just gave the product away. We'd make several batches during the week, and guess who would come back wanting to buy dozens of these bagels?" That's when she knew the new product was going to be a hit. Not every new flavour becomes popular, however. Dark chocolate bagels with white chocolate chips sold poorly, as did pineapple-mango-coconut bagels. Today, plain bagels remain the best-selling flavour, followed by sesame.

Samples and Coupons Spark Word-of-Mouth Communication

The story of the jalapeno-and-cheese bagel illustrates another of Finagle A Bagel's marketing rules: Spend nothing on advertising. Many quick-serve food companies use television and radio commercials, newspaper advertisements, and other mass-media messages to build brand awareness, promote products, and attract customers. However, Robertson and her colleagues believe that the best way to build the Finagle A Bagel brand and whet customers' appetites for a new menu item is to give them a free taste.

Consider what happened when Finagle A Bagel used samples and coupons to build lunchtime sales by promoting bagel sandwiches in one of the suburban stores. Instead of placing an ad in the local newspaper, Robertson and her staff went to the store and prepared 100 bagel sandwiches. They cut each in half and wrapped the halves individually. Then they set up 200 Finagle A Bagel bags, put a half-sandwich into each, and added a coupon for a free bagel sandwich without any risk. They piled all the bags into a big basket, attached a sign reading, "Free Bagel Sandwiches," and headed to a large intersection just a block from the store.

"Every time the light turned red, we would run out into the middle of the street and throw a bag through someone's car window," Robertson recalls. "We got a lot of strange looks. A few people would roll up their car windows . . . but a lot of people just thought it was hysterically funny. They would be motioning, waving us over, saying, 'What have you got?' And then they'd go back to their office and tell their coworkers, 'Hey, you know what happened to me today? Some crazy lady threw a bagel through my car window, and it was great. You should check it out.'" The entire effort cost $100—and convinced a large number of customers to look around the store, try a sandwich risk-free, and talk up the experience to colleagues, friends, and family.

The popular Finagle A Bagel headquarters tour has become an effective public-relations tool. Community groups, students, and bagel lovers of all ages can visit the "World Headquarters" building and walk through exhibits representing the company's successes and mistakes. In the factory area, visitors watch through a huge window as hundreds of pounds of dough are mixed, cut, and shaped into bagels. The window is set low so even the youngest visitors can get a great view of the process.

Buy a Branded Bagel—Again and Again

Although some restaurant companies want each unit to look distinctly different, Finagle A Bagel uses consistency to reinforce the brand image—another of its marketing rules. "We believe the stores should have a very similar look and feel so that you can walk into any Finagle A Bagel and know what to expect," says co-president Alan Litchman. For example, every Finagle A Bagel store sports an eye-catching burgundy-and-yellow sign featuring an oversized bagel with a few bites taken out. This bagel icon is repeated on posters highlighting menu items as well as on other store decorations.

Still, the suburban stores are not exactly like the downtown stores. Many of the suburban stores have children's furniture and cushiony chairs so that families can sit and relax. Free weekly concerts by the "Music Man"—a local musician— make these stores decidedly family friendly. The city stores have no children's furniture because they cater to busy working people who want to be in and out in a hurry. The Harvard Square store is unique: It has a liquor licence and attracts a large student crowd, which means it is busier on weekends than on weekdays.

One of the most effective sales promotion techniques the company uses is the Frequent Finagler loyalty card, which rewards customers for making repeat purchases. For every dollar customers spend on bagels or other menu items, they receive Frequent Finagler points that can be redeemed for free coffee, free sandwiches, and so on. Customers are pleased because they receive extra value for the money they spend—and Finagle A Bagel is pleased because its average sale to loyal customers is higher.

Pricing a Bagel

Pricing is an important consideration in the competitive world of quick-serve food. This is where another of Finagle A Bagel's marketing rules comes in. Regardless of cost, the company will not compromise quality. Therefore, the first step in pricing a new product is to find the best possible ingredients and then examine the costs and calculate an approximate retail price. After thinking about what a customer might expect to pay for such a menu item, shopping the competition, and talking with some customers, the company settles on a price that represents "a great product for a fair value," says Robertson.

Although Finagle A Bagel's rental costs vary, the co-presidents price menu items the same in higher-rent stores as in lower-rent stores. "We have considered adjusting prices based upon the location of the store, but we haven't done it because it can backfire in a very significant way," co-president Laura Trust explains. "People expect to be treated fairly, regardless of where they live."

Questions

1. Does Finagle A Bagel apply all seven phases of the new product development process when working on a new menu item such as the jalapeno-and-cheese bagel? Explain.

2. Do you agree with Laura Trust's assessment that adjusting prices based on store location can backfire? What arguments can you offer for and against Finagle A Bagel raising prices in higher-rent stores?

3. Finagle A Bagel is both a wholesaler and a retailer. Which of these two marketing intermediary roles do you think the company should develop more

aggressively in the next few years? Why?

4. Should Finagle A Bagel continue to spend nothing on media advertising and rely instead primarily on sales promotion techniques such as samples and coupons?

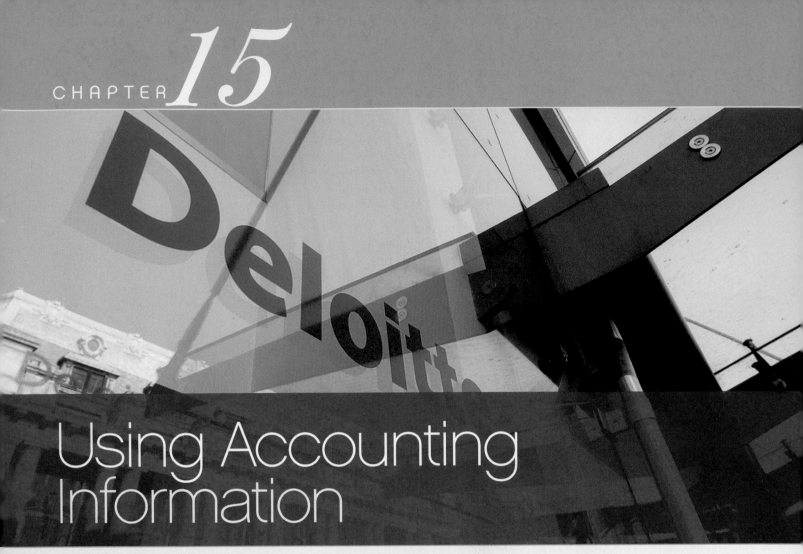

CHAPTER *15*

Using Accounting Information

Your Guide to Success in Business

Why this chapter matters
It is impossible to manage a business without accurate and up-to-date information supplied by the firm's accountants.

LEARNING OBJECTIVES

1. Explain why accurate accounting information and audited financial statements are important.

2. Identify the people who use accounting information and possible careers in the accounting industry.

3. Discuss the accounting process.

4. Read and interpret a balance sheet.

5. Read and interpret an income statement.

6. Describe business activities that affect a firm's cash flow.

7. Summarize how managers evaluate the financial health of a business.

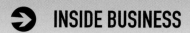

Counting on the Big Four

Most of Canada's largest corporations count on one of the "Big Four" accounting firms to double-check internal accounting procedures, review financial records, and sign off on annual reports. The Big Four consist of Deloitte, Ernst & Young, PricewaterhouseCoopers, and KPMG, each employing tens of thousands of accounting and tax experts around the world.

The number of big accounting firms has dropped in the past two decades as firms merged to gain economies of scale and diversify their services. High-profile legal problems have brought even more dramatic changes to the industry. Arthur Andersen, for example, was convicted of obstructing justice in the U.S. government investigation of client Enron's sudden (and massive) bankruptcy. This effectively put Andersen out of business, even though the Supreme Court eventually overturned the conviction. Then, months after Enron's collapse, WorldCom filed for bankruptcy following the disclosure of accounting frauds involving billions of dollars.

In the wake of these and other big-money scandals in both Canada and the U.S., accounting and financial reporting rules have been modified to improve compliance and transparency. As a result, corporations have put in place more stringent controls to ensure that the accounting process runs smoothly and that their financial records are both accurate and complete. Now the biggest accounting firms are busier than ever, conducting in-depth audits for clients and complying with government's tougher documentation requirements.

All this extra work is generating extra revenue but also putting extra pressure on the employees of major accounting firms. As well, changes in conflict-of-interest rules make it difficult for accounting firms to offer other services—such as consulting and tax and pension advice—to their audit clients. And who's auditing these busy auditors? An independent board has been established to investigate how well the big accounting firms handle their reviews of corporate clients' accounting practices and financial statements.

continued on next page

DID YOU KNOW?

Most of Canada's largest corporations count on one of the "Big Four" accounting firms to double-check internal accounting procedures, review financial records, and sign off on annual reports.

K E Y   T E R M S

accounting (456)
audit (459)
generally accepted accounting principles (GAAPs) (459)
managerial accounting (462)
financial accounting (462)
chartered accountant (CA) (463)
certified management accountant (CMA) (464)
assets (464)

liabilities (464)
owners' equity (464)
accounting equation (464)
double-entry bookkeeping system (465)
trial balance (465)
annual report (465)
balance sheet (or statement of financial position) (466)
liquidity (469)
current assets (469)

fixed assets (469)
depreciation (469)
intangible assets (469)
current liabilities (470)
long-term liabilities (470)
retained earnings (470)
income statement (471)
revenues (473)
gross sales (473)

net sales (473)
cost of goods sold (473)
gross profit (473)
operating expenses (473)
net income (474)
net loss (474)
statement of cash flows (474)
financial ratio (477)

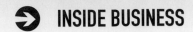

For more information about these companies, go to www.deloitte.com, www.ey.com, www.pwcglobal.com, and www.kpmg.com.

Sources: "Annual Reports Could Use Some Life," *PR Week (US)*, October 9, 2006, p. 10; "Sears' Lampert Shows Value of Annual Report as Comms Tool," *PR Week (US)*, April 10, 2006, p. 9; Charles Keenan, "If It's Spring, It Must Be Annual Report Season," *Community Banker*, May 2006, pp. 64+.

For investors, corporate executives and employees, lenders, and government regulators, the financial reporting problems at Enron and WorldCom were a wake-up call for more exacting accounting standards. After these financial horror stories, the U.S. Congress tightened key accounting and financial reporting rules through legislation called the Sarbanes-Oxley Act. Because of the large number of corporations doing business in both Canada and the U.S., these rules also apply to many Canadian operations— subsidiaries of U.S. parent companies. And Canadian authorities, including the federal and provincial governments, securities commissions, stock exchanges, and accounting standards' professional bodies are enacting changes that mirror many of the provisions of the Sarbanes-Oxley legislation. As a result, corporations have implemented more stringent controls to ensure that the accounting process runs smoothly and that their financial records are both accurate and complete. And the Big Four accounting firms—responsible for auditing a corporation's accounting records and signing off on annual reports—are busier than ever. The message now is clear: accounting and financial information is too important and the penalties too severe to "doctor" the books and report inflated revenues and phony earnings.

We begin this chapter by looking at why accounting information is important, the recent problems in the accounting industry, and attempts to improve financial reporting. Then we look at how managers, employees, individuals, and groups outside a firm use accounting information. We also identify different types of accountants and career opportunities in the accounting industry. Next, we focus on the accounting process and the basics of an accounting system. We also examine the three most important financial statements: the balance sheet, the income statement, and the statement of cash flows. Finally, we show how ratios are used to measure specific aspects of a firm's financial health.

Why Accounting Information Is Important

Learning Objective ❶

Explain why accurate accounting information and audited financial statements are important.

accounting the process of systematically collecting, analyzing, and reporting financial information

Accounting is the process of systematically collecting, analyzing, and reporting financial information. Today it is impossible to manage a business without accurate and up-to-date information supplied by the firm's accountants. Just for a moment, think about the following three questions:

1. How much profit did a business earn last year?
2. How much tax does a business owe Revenue Canada?
3. How much cash does a business have on hand?

The firm's accountants and its accounting system provide the answers to these questions and many others. And, while accounting information can be used to answer questions about what has happened in the past, it also can be used to help make decisions about the future. For these reasons, accounting is one of the most important areas within a business organization.

Because the information provided by a firm's accountants and its accounting system is so important, managers and other groups interested in a business firm's financial records must be able to "trust the numbers." Unfortunately, the recent number of accounting scandals have caused people to doubt not only the numbers but also the accounting industry.

Recent Accounting Problems for Corporations and Their Auditors

Today, much of the pressure on corporate executives to "cook" the books is driven by the desire to look good to analysts and investors. Every three months companies report their revenues, expenses, profits, and projections for the future. If a company meets or exceeds "the street's" expectations, everything is usually fine. However, if a company reports financial numbers that are lower than expected, the company's stock value can drop dramatically. An earnings report that is lower by even a few pennies per share than expected can cause a company's stock value to drop immediately by as much as 30 to 40 percent or more. Greed—especially when salary and bonuses are tied to a company's stock value—is another factor that can lead some corporate executives to use questionable accounting methods to inflate a firm's financial performance. Lower-level managers may go along with dubious accounting schemes because they stand to profit from cooperating, because they fear retaliation from senior executives, or because they worry about losing their jobs—especially when new employment opportunities are scarce.

In a perfect world, the accountants who inspect the corporate books would catch mistakes and disclose questionable accounting practices. Unfortunately, we do not live in a perfect world. Consider the part that auditors for the accounting firm Arthur Andersen played in the Enron meltdown in the United States. When the Securities and Exchange Commission (SEC) launched its inquiry into Enron's financial affairs, Andersen employees shredded the documents related to the audit. As a result, both the SEC and the Department of Justice began to investigate Andersen's role in the failure of Enron. Eventually, Andersen was convicted of obstruction of justice and was forced to cease auditing public companies. Simply put, Andersen—the once-proud accounting firm—was found guilty.[1] Less than a month after admitting accounting errors that inflated earnings by almost $600 million since 1994, Enron filed for bankruptcy.[2] Other high-profile companies, including Adelphia, Quest Communications, and Tyco International, have been hauled into court to explain their accounting practices.

In Canada, Nortel Networks and Hollinger Inc. have been investigated over allegations of improper record keeping and management malfeasance. And more accounting firms—including KPMG and PricewaterhouseCoopers—have been targeted by trial lawyers and government regulators for providing questionable audit work for major corporate clients.[3] Make no mistake; the penalties for what some critics call "executive crime" are real. Consider the following:

* Bernard Ebbers, WorldCom CEO, was sentenced to twenty-five years in prison for his part in defrauding investors, employees, pension holders, and other groups that lost money on WorldCom stock.[4]

* Former Tyco CEO Dennis Kozlowski was found guilty of looting more than $600 million from the company and sentenced to 20 years in jail.[5]

* Enron executives Ken Lay and Jeff Skilling were convicted of conspiracy to commit securities and wire fraud in May 2006.[6]

Ken Lay passed away before an appeal of his conviction could be heard, and although Jeff Skilling will have another day in court, the cases show that corporate executives can't escape responsibility for reporting inaccurate or misleading accounting information. Unfortunately, the ones hurt most often are not the high-paid corporate executives; in many cases, it's the employees who lose their jobs and often the money they invested in the company's retirement program, and it's the investors, lenders, and suppliers who relied on fraudulent accounting information when deciding to invest in or lend money to the company.

In Canada, we have not experienced, to the same degree, the accounting scandals that have rocked their business world, but is this because of weaker regulations and enforcement? It would be naïve to suggest that these types of activities occur only in the United States, and only time will tell if Canadian courts find themselves dealing with increased cases of white collar crime.

In an indirect way, the recent accounting scandals underscore how important accurate accounting information is for a corporation. To see how the auditing process can improve accounting information, read the next section.

Why Audited Financial Statements Are Important

Assume that you are a bank officer responsible for evaluating loan applications. How do you make a decision to approve or reject a loan request? In this situation, most bank officers rely on the information contained in the firm's balance sheet, income statement, and statement of cash flows, along with other information provided by the prospective borrower. In fact, most lenders insist that these financial statements be audited by a chartered accountant (CA).

BUSINESS AROUND THE WORLD

China's Answer to GAAP: CASS

Accounting changes are sweeping through China. Why? "To become an economic superpower, China needs capital to fund growth," observes the CEO of the Hong Kong Institute of Certified Public Accountants, "and it will help if its companies speak the same business language as the rest of the world." So the country has been changing the accounting standards for the 1,100 public companies traded on the Shanghai and Shenzhen stock exchanges.

The goal is to make the China Accounting Standards System (CASS) consistent with the generally accepted accounting practices (GAAPs) that apply in Western countries. This will give investors a clearer picture of each company's financial performance. More than 150 Chinese companies listed on foreign stock exchanges already use international accounting standards. Huaneng Power International, for instance, is listed on the Shanghai and Hong Kong exchanges and must therefore prepare two sets of financial statements. The switch to CASS goes well beyond numbers: it's also creating thousands of new jobs for accounting professionals.

Sources: Based on information in James T. Areddy, "Adding Up Chinese Data," *Wall Street Journal,* February 27, 2006, p. C10; Nisha Gopalan, "Mainland-Listed Chinese Firms to Follow Global Accounting Rules," *Wall Street Journal,* July 19, 2006, n.p.

An **audit** is an examination of a company's financial statements and the accounting practices that produced them. The purpose of an audit is to make sure that a firm's financial statements have been prepared in accordance with generally accepted accounting principles. Today, **generally accepted accounting principles (GAAPs)** have been developed to provide an accepted set of guidelines and practices for companies reporting financial information and the accounting profession.

If an accountant determines that a firm's financial statements present financial information fairly and conform to GAAPs, then he or she will issue the following statement:

In our opinion, the financial statements . . . present fairly, in all material respects . . . in conformity with generally accepted accounting principles.

While an audit and the resulting report do not *guarantee* that a company has not "cooked" the books, it does imply that, on the whole, the company has followed GAAPs. Bankers, creditors, investors, and government agencies are willing to rely on an auditor's opinion because of the historically ethical reputation and independence of auditors and accounting firms. Even with the recent scandals involving corporations and their accountants that falsified or misled the general public, most accountants still abide by the rules. And, although it is easy to indict an entire profession because of the actions of a few, there are many more accountants who adhere to the rules and are

audit an examination of a company's financial statements and the accounting practices that produced them

generally accepted accounting principles (GAAPs) an accepted set of guidelines and practices for companies reporting financial information and for the accounting profession

honest, hard-working professionals. Finally, it should be noted that without the audit function and GAAPs, there would be very little oversight or supervision. The validity of a firm's financial statements and its accounting records would drop quickly, and firms would find it difficult to obtain debt financing, acquire goods and services from suppliers, find investor financing, or prepare documents requested by government agencies.

Reform: The Sarbanes-Oxley Act of 2002

To help ensure that corporate financial information is accurate and in response to the many accounting scandals that surfaced in the last part of the 1990s and the first part of the twenty-first century, the United States Congress enacted the Sarbanes-Oxley Act. Key components include the following:

* The SEC is required to establish a full-time five-member federal oversight board that will police the accounting industry.

* Chief executive and financial officers are required to certify periodic financial reports and are subject to criminal penalties for violations of securities reporting requirements.

* Accounting firms are prohibited from providing many types of non-audit and consulting services to the companies they audit.

* Auditors must maintain financial documents and audit work papers for five years.

* Auditors, accountants, and employees can be imprisoned for up to twenty years for destroying financial documents and willful violations of the securities laws.

* A public corporation must change its lead auditing firm every five years.

* There is added protection for whistle-blowers who report violations of the Sarbanes-Oxley Act.

While most people welcome the Sarbanes-Oxley Act, complex rules make compliance more expensive and time-consuming for corporate management and more difficult for accounting firms. And yet, most people agree that the cost of compliance is justified. As you read the next section, you will see just how important accurate accounting information is.

In Canada, many of the provisions enacted through the Sarbanes-Oxley Act are being incorporated through changes to accounting standards, legislation enacted by provincial securities commissions, and stock exchange regulations. The absence of a national securities regulator makes this a much more cumbersome process than that employed in the United States.

Who Uses Accounting Information

Learning Objective 2

Identify the people who use accounting information and possible careers in the accounting industry.

Managers and employees, lenders, suppliers, stockholders, and government agencies all rely on the information contained in three financial statements, each no more than one page in length. These three reports—the balance sheet, the income statement, and the statement of cash flows—are concise summaries of a firm's activities during a specific time period. Together they represent the results of perhaps tens of thousands of transactions that have occurred during the accounting period. Moreover, the form of the financial statements is pretty much the same for all businesses, from a neighbourhood video store or small dry cleaner to giant conglomerates such as Home Depot, Magna, and the Bank of Montreal. This information has a variety of uses both within the firm and outside it. However, first and foremost, accounting information is management information.

The People Who Use Accounting Information

The primary users of accounting information are *managers* and *employees*. The firm's accounting system provides information that can be compiled for the entire firm and for each product; sales territory, store, or salesperson; for each division or department; and generally in any way that will help those who manage the organization. Much of this accounting information is *proprietary*; it is not divulged to anyone outside the firm. This type of information is used by a firm's managers and employees to plan and set goals, organize, lead, motivate, and control—all the management functions that were described in Chapter 7. To see how important accounting is, just think about what happens when a manager plans to purchase a new piece of equipment. Immediately, everyone involved in the decision begins discussing how much it will cost and what effect it will have on the firm's profits, sales, and expenses. It is the firm's accounting system that provides the answers to these important questions.

How did he get so rich?

Although there are many reasons why Warren Buffett, chairman on the board of Berkshire Hathaway, has become one of the wealthiest people on the continent, his ability to understand accounting information has enabled him to identify investments that are extremely profitable. This same appreciation for numbers is one reason why Berkshire Hathaway subsidiary companies are known to have lower operating costs and larger bottom-line profits than their competitors.

Table 15.1

Users of Accounting Information

The primary users of accounting information are a company's managers and employees, but individuals and organizations outside the company also require information on its finances.

MANAGEMENT	LENDERS AND SUPPLIERS	STOCKHOLDERS AND POTENTIAL INVESTORS	GOVERNMENT AGENCIES
Plan and set goals, organize, lead and motivate, and control—all management functions described in Chapter 7.	Evaluate financial statements and credit risks before committing to short- or long-term loans or extending credit for raw materials, parts, or finished goods the firm needs to operate.	Evaluate the financial health of the firm before making a decision to retain or purchase stocks or bonds issued by the firm.	Confirm tax liabilities, confirm payroll deductions, and approve new issues of stocks and bonds before they are issued.

In addition to proprietary information used inside the firm, certain financial information must be supplied to lenders, suppliers, stockholders and potential investors, and government agencies (see Table 15.1). An important function of accountants is to ensure that such information is accurate and thorough enough to satisfy these outside groups.

Different Types of Accounting

Many people think that all accountants do the same tasks, but there are special areas of expertise within the accounting industry. In fact, accounting usually is broken down into two broad categories: managerial and financial.

Managerial accounting provides managers and employees with the information needed to make decisions about a firm's financing, investing, and operating activities. By using managerial accounting information, both managers and employees can evaluate how well they have done in the past and what they can expect in the future. **Financial accounting**, on the other hand, generates financial statements and reports for interested people outside of an organization. Typically, stockholders, financial analysts, bankers, lenders, suppliers, government agencies, and other interested groups use the information provided by financial accounting to determine how close a business has come to achieving its goals. In addition to managerial and financial accounting, special areas of accounting include the following:

* *Cost accounting*—determining the cost of producing specific products or services.

* *Government accounting*—providing basic accounting services to ensure that tax revenues are collected and used to meet the goals of municipal, provincial, and federal agencies.

* *Not-for-profit accounting*—helping not-for-profit organizations to account for all donations and expenditures.

* *Tax accounting*—planning tax strategy and preparing tax returns for the firm or organization.

Many people have the idea that accountants spend their days working with endless columns of numbers in a small office locked away from other people. In fact, accountants do spend a lot of time at their desks, but their job entails far more than just add-

managerial accounting provides managers and employees with the information needed to make decisions about a firm's financing, investing, and operating activities

financial accounting generates financial statements and reports for interested people outside an organization

ing or subtracting numbers. Accountants are expected to share their ideas and the information they possess with people who need the information. Accounting can be an exciting and rewarding career—one that offers higher-than-average starting salaries. To be successful in the accounting industry, employees must

* Be responsible, honest, and ethical.
* Have a strong background in financial management.
* Know how to use a computer and software to process data into accounting information.
* Be able to communicate with people who need accounting information.

Today, accountants generally are classified as either private accountants or public accountants. A *private accountant* is employed by a specific organization. A medium-sized or large firm might employ one or more private accountants to design its accounting information system, manage its accounting department, and provide managers with advice and assistance.

Individuals, self-employed business owners, and smaller firms that do not require their own full-time private accountants can hire the services of public accountants. A *public accountant* works on a fee basis for clients and can be self-employed or be the employee of an accounting firm. Accounting firms range in size from one-person operations to huge international firms with hundreds of accounting partners and thousands of employees. Today, the largest accounting firms, sometimes referred to as the "Big Four," are PricewaterhouseCoopers, Ernst & Young, KPMG, and Deloitte Touche Tohmatsu.

Typically, public accounting firms include on their staffs at least one **chartered accountant (CA),** an individual who has met the industry requirements for accounting education and experience and has passed a rigorous accounting examination prepared by the CICA. The CICA uniform CA examination covers four areas:

* ethics, taxation, business law, and professional responsibilities,
* auditing
* business environment and concepts
* financial accounting and reporting.

More information about general requirements and the CA profession can be obtained by contacting the CICA at www.cica.ca.[7] Industry requirements usually include a university degree or a specified number of hours of college coursework and, generally, from one to three years of on-the-job experience.

Once an individual becomes a CA, he or she must participate in continuing-education programs to maintain their certification. These specialized programs are designed to provide the training needed in today's changing business environment. CAs also must take an ethics course to satisfy the continuing-education requirement.

Certification as a CA brings both status and responsibility. Depending on the province, only an independent CA can audit the financial statements contained in a corporation's annual report and express an opinion—as required by law—regarding the acceptability of the corporation's accounting practices. In addition to auditing a corporation's financial statements, typical services performed by CAs include planning and preparing tax returns, determining the true cost of producing and marketing a

chartered accountant (CA) an individual who has met the industry requirements for accounting education and experience and has passed a rigorous accounting examination prepared by the CICA

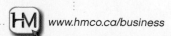

firm's goods or services, and compiling the financial information needed to make major management decisions.

In addition to certified accountants, there are also certified management accountants. A **certified management accountant (CMA)** is an accountant who has met the requirements for education and experience, passed a rigorous exam, and is certified by the Certified Management Accountants Canada. The CMA exam is designed to develop and measure not only accounting skills but also decision-making and critical-thinking skills. For more information about the CMA exam, visit the Certified Management Accountants Canada website at www.cma-canada.org. While both CAs and CMAs can work for the public, a CMA is more likely to work within a large organization. Both types of accountants are excellent career choices.

In Canada we also have Certified General Accountants. As the name suggests, these accountants provide a broad range of services to both public, private, and not-for-profit organizations. For more information about CGAs, visit their website at www.thinkcga.org.

The Accounting Process

Learning Objective 3

Discuss the accounting process.

In Chapter 4, *information* was defined as data presented in a form that is useful for a specific purpose. In this section we examine accounting as the system for transforming raw financial *data* into useful financial *information*. Then, in the next sections we describe the three most important financial statements provided by the accounting process.

The Accounting Equation

The accounting equation is a simple statement that forms the basis for the accounting process. This important equation shows the relationship between a firm's assets, liabilities, and owners' equity.

* **Assets** are the resources a business owns—cash, inventory, equipment, and real estate.
* **Liabilities** are the firm's debts—what it owes to others.
* **Owners' equity** is the difference between total assets and total liabilities—what would be left for the owners if the firm's assets were sold and the money used to pay off its liabilities.

The relationship between assets, liabilities, and owners' equity is shown by the following **accounting equation:**

$$\text{Assets} = \text{liabilities} + \text{owners' equity}$$

Whether a business is a small corner grocery store or a giant corporation such as Bombardier, its assets must equal the sum of its liabilities and owners' equity. To use this equation, a firm's accountants must record raw data—that is, the firm's day-to-

---

certified management accountant (CMA) an accountant who has met the requirements for education and experience, passed a rigorous exam, and is certified by the Certified Management Accountants of Canada

assets the resources that a business owns

liabilities a firm's debts and obligations

owners' equity the difference between a firm's assets and its liabilities

accounting equation the basis for the accounting process: *assets = liabilities + owners' equity*

day financial transactions—using the double-entry system of bookkeeping. The **double-entry bookkeeping system** is a system in which each financial transaction is recorded as two separate accounting entries to maintain the balance shown in the accounting equation. With the double-entry system, an accountant can use the steps in the accounting cycle to generate accounting information and financial statements.

The Accounting Cycle

In the typical accounting system, raw data are transformed into financial statements in five steps. The first three—analyzing, recording, and posting—are performed on a regular basis throughout the accounting period. The last two—preparation of the trial balance and of the financial statements and closing the books—are performed at the end of the accounting period.

Analyzing Source Documents Basic accounting data are contained in *source documents*, the receipts, invoices, sales slips, and other documents that show the dollar amounts of day-to-day business transactions. The accounting cycle begins with the analysis of each of these documents. The purpose of the analysis is to determine which accounts are affected by the documents and how they are affected.

Recording Transactions Every financial transaction then is recorded in a journal—a process called *journalizing*. Transactions must be recorded in the firm's general journal or in specialized journals. The *general journal* is a book of original entry in which typical transactions are recorded in order of their occurrence. An accounting system also can include *specialized journals* for specific types of transactions that occur frequently. Thus a retail store might have journals for cash receipts, cash disbursements, purchases, and sales, in addition to its general journal.

Posting Transactions After the information is recorded in the general journal and specialized journals, it is transferred to the general ledger. The *general ledger* is a book of accounts containing a separate sheet or section for each account. Today, most businesses use a computer and software to post accounting entries from the general journal or specialized journals to the general ledger.

Preparing the Trial Balance A **trial balance** is a summary of the balances of all general ledger accounts at the end of the accounting period. To prepare a trial balance, the accountant determines and lists the balances for all ledger accounts. If the trial balance totals are correct and the accounting equation is still in balance, the accountant can prepare the financial statements. If not, a mistake has occurred somewhere, and the accountant must find it and correct it before proceeding.

Preparing Financial Statements and Closing the Books The firm's financial statements are prepared from the information contained in the trial balance. This information is presented in a standardized format to make the statements as accessible as possible to the various people who may be interested in the firm's financial affairs—managers, employees, lenders, suppliers, stockholders, potential investors, and government agencies. A firm's financial statements are prepared at least once a year and included in the firm's annual report. An **annual report** is a report distributed to stockholders and other interested parties that describes a firm's operating activities and its financial condition. Most firms also have financial statements prepared semiannually, quarterly, or monthly.

double-entry bookkeeping system a system in which each financial transaction is recorded as two separate accounting entries to maintain the balance shown in the accounting equation

trial balance a summary of the balances of all general ledger accounts at the end of the accounting period

annual report a report distributed to stockholders and other interested parties that describes a firm's operating activities and its financial condition

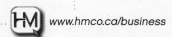

Once these statements have been prepared and checked, the firm's books are "closed" for the accounting period, and a *postclosing* trial balance is prepared, although, like the trial balance just described, the postclosing trial balance generally is prepared after *all* accounting work is completed for one accounting period. If the postclosing trial balance totals agree, the accounting equation is still in balance at the end of the cycle. Only then can a new accounting cycle begin for the next accounting period.

With this brief information about the steps of the accounting cycle in mind, let's now examine the three most important financial statements generated by the accounting process: the balance sheet, the income statement, and the statement of cash flows.

The Balance Sheet

Learning Objective ❹

Read and interpret a balance sheet.

balance sheet (or **statement of financial position**) a summary of the dollar amounts of a firm's assets, liabilities, and owners' equity accounts at the end of a specific accounting period

Question: *Where could you find the total amount of assets, liabilities, and owners' equity for Research in Motion?*

Answer: The firm's balance sheet.

A **balance sheet** (sometimes referred to as a **statement of financial position**) is a summary of the dollar amounts of a firm's assets, liabilities, and owners' equity ac-

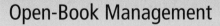

ENTREPRENEURIAL CHALLENGE

Open-Book Management

Why would an entrepreneur consider opening the company's financial details to all employees, a practice known as open-book management? Proponents say it's a good way to show employees how their activities actually affect profit performance. However, not everyone is open to open-book management. Here are some of the advantages and disadvantages:

Advantages. Helping employees understand the company's finances can involve them more deeply in their jobs, encourage initiative, and foster closer cooperation. Key financial data (except salaries) is available to employees as well as to other stakeholders.

Disadvantages. "Full disclosure has its own degree of misunderstanding," notes the founder of a restaurant design firm, who believes that employees need education and training to understand a company's accounting data. Another potential problem: employees may become overwhelmed by all the details or discouraged when they see profits dropping. Therefore, entrepreneurs should explain exactly what the numbers mean and what makes profits go up and down.

Sources: Based on information in Rachel Long, "Owner's Inc.," *Hospitality Design,* April 2006, p. 54; David Drickhamer, "By the Numbers," *Material Handling Management,* January 2006, pp. 29+.

Marty Campbell
Personal Balance Sheet
December 31, 2008

ASSETS
Cash	$ 2,500
Savings account	5,000
Automobile	15,000
Stereo	1,000
Television	500
Furniture	2,500

TOTAL ASSETS — $26,500

LIABILITIES
Automobile loan	$ 9,500
Credit card balance	500

TOTAL LIABILITIES — $10,000

NET WORTH (Owner's Equity) — 16,500

TOTAL LIABILITIES AND NET WORTH — $26,500

Figure 15.1

Personal Balance Sheet

Even individuals can determine their net worth, or owner's equity, by subtracting the value of their debts from the value of their assets.

counts at the end of a specific accounting period. The balance sheet must demonstrate that assets are equal to liabilities plus owners' equity. Most people think of a balance sheet as a statement that reports the financial condition of a business firm such as RIM, but balance sheets apply to individuals, too. For example, Marty Campbell graduated from college three years ago and obtained a position as a sales representative for an office supply firm. After going to work, he established a chequing and a savings account and purchased an automobile, stereo, television, and a few pieces of furniture. Marty paid cash for some purchases, but he had to borrow money to pay for the larger ones. Figure 15.1 shows Marty's current personal balance sheet.

Marty Campbell's assets total $26,500, and his liabilities amount to $10,000. While the difference between total assets and total liabilities is referred to as *owners' equity* or *stockholders' equity* for a business, it is normally called *net worth* for an individual. As reported on Marty's personal balance sheet, net worth is $16,500. The total assets ($26,500) and the total liabilities *plus* net worth ($26,500) are equal.

Figure 15.2 shows the balance sheet for Northeast Art Supply, a small corporation that sells picture frames, paints, canvases, and other artists' supplies to retailers. Note that assets are reported at the top of the statement, followed by liabilities and stockholders' equity. Let's work through the different accounts in Figure 15.2 from top to bottom.

Figure 15.2

Business Balance Sheet

A balance sheet summarizes a firm's accounts at the end of an accounting period, showing the various dollar amounts that enter into the accounting equation. Note that assets ($340,000) equal liabilities plus owners' equity ($340,000).

NORTHEAST ART SUPPLY, INC.

Balance Sheet
December 31, 2008

ASSETS

Current assets

Cash		$ 59,000	
Marketable securities		10,000	
Accounts receivable	$ 40,000		
Less allowance for doubtful accounts	2,000	38,000	
Notes receivable		32,000	
Merchandise inventory		41,000	
Prepaid expenses		2,000	
Total current assets			$182,000

Fixed assets

Delivery equipment	$110,000		
Less accumulated depreciation	20,000	$ 90,000	
Furniture and store equipment	62,000		
Less accumulated depreciation	15,000	47,000	
Total fixed assets			137,000

Intangible assets

Patents		$ 6,000	
Goodwill		15,000	
Total intangible assets			21,000
TOTAL ASSETS			$340,000

LIABILITIES AND STOCKHOLDERSí EQUITY

Current liabilities

Accounts payable	$ 35,000		
Notes payable	25,675		
Salaries payable	4,000		
Taxes payable	5,325		
Total current liabilities		$ 70,000	

Long-term liabilities

Mortgage payable on store equipment	$ 40,000		
Total long-term liabilities		$ 40,000	
TOTAL LIABILITIES			$110,00

Stockholders' equity

Common stock		$150,000	
Retained earnings		80,000	
TOTAL OWNERS' EQUITY			$230,000
TOTAL LIABILITIES AND OWNERS' EQUITY			$340,000

Assets

On a balance sheet, assets are listed in order from the *most liquid* to the *least liquid*. The **liquidity** of an asset is the ease with which it can be converted into cash.

Current Assets Current assets are assets that can be converted quickly into cash or that will be used in one year or less. Because cash is the most liquid asset, it is listed first. Next are *marketable securities*—stocks, bonds, and other investments—that can be converted into cash in a matter of days.

Next are the firm's receivables. Its *accounts receivables*, which result from allowing customers to make credit purchases, generally are paid within thirty to sixty days. However, the firm expects that some of these debts will not be collected. Thus it has reduced its accounts receivables by a 5 percent *allowance for doubtful accounts*. The firm's *notes receivables* are receivables for which customers have signed promissory notes. They generally are repaid over a longer period of time than the firm's accounts receivables.

Northeast's *merchandise inventory* represents the value of goods on hand for sale to customers. Since Northeast Art Supply is a wholesale operation, the inventory listed in Figure 15.2 represents finished goods ready for sale to retailers. For a manufacturing firm, merchandise inventory also may represent raw materials that will become part of a finished product or work that has been partially completed but requires further processing.

Northeast's last current asset is *prepaid expenses*, which are assets that have been paid for in advance but have not yet been used. An example is insurance premiums. They are usually paid at the beginning of the policy year. The unused portion (say, for the last four months of the time period covered by the policy) is a prepaid expense. For Northeast Art, all current assets total $182,000.

Fixed Assets Fixed assets are assets that will be held or used for a period longer than one year. They generally include land, buildings, and equipment used in the continuing operation of the business. Although Northeast owns no land or buildings, it does own *delivery equipment* that originally cost $110,000. It also owns *furniture* and *store equipment* that originally cost $62,000.

Note that the values of both fixed assets are decreased by their *accumulated depreciation*. **Depreciation** is the process of apportioning the cost of a fixed asset over the period during which it will be used, that is, its useful life. The depreciation amount allotted to each year is an expense for that year, and the value of the asset must be reduced by the amount of depreciation expense. Although the actual method used to calculate the dollar amounts for depreciation expense reported on a firm's financial statements are beyond the scope of this text, you should know that there are a number of methods that can be used. In the case of Northeast's delivery equipment, $20,000 of its value has been depreciated (or used up) since it was purchased. Its value at this time is thus $110,000 less $20,000, or $90,000. In a similar fashion, the original value of furniture and store equipment ($62,000) has been reduced by depreciation totalling $15,000. The furniture and store equipment now has a reported value of $47,000. All Northeast Art's fixed assets total $137,000.

Intangible Assets Intangible assets are assets that do not exist physically but that have a value based on the rights or privileges they confer on a firm. They include

liquidity the ease with which an asset can be converted into cash

current assets assets that can be converted quickly into cash or that will be used in one year or less

fixed assets assets that will be held or used for a period longer than one year

depreciation the process of apportioning the cost of a fixed asset over the period during which it will be used

intangible assets assets that do not exist physically but that have a value based on the rights or privileges they confer on a firm

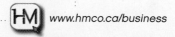

patents, copyrights, trademarks, franchises, and goodwill. By their nature, intangible assets are of value to the firm for a number of years.

Northeast Art Supply lists two intangible assets. The first is a *patent* for a special oil paint that the company purchased from the inventor. The firm's accountants estimate that the patent has a current market value of $6,000. The second intangible asset, *goodwill*, is the value of a firm's reputation, location, earning capacity, and other intangibles that make the business a profitable concern. Goodwill normally is not listed on a balance sheet unless the firm has been purchased from previous owners. In such a case, the new owners actually have paid an additional amount over and above the fair market value of the firm's assets for goodwill. Goodwill exists because most businesses are worth more as going concerns than as a collection of assets. Northeast Art's accountants included a $15,000 amount for goodwill. The firm's intangible assets total $21,000. Now it is possible to total all three types of assets for Northeast Art. As calculated in Figure 15.2, total assets are $340,000.

Liabilities and Owners' Equity

The liabilities and the owners' equity accounts complete the balance sheet. The firm's liabilities are separated into two categories—current and long term.

Current Liabilities A firm's **current liabilities** are debts that will be repaid in one year or less. For Northeast Art Supply, current liabilities include:

- *Accounts payable*—short-term obligations that result from a firm making credit purchases.
- *Notes payable*—obligations that have been secured with promissory notes. Only the obligations that must be paid within the year are listed under current liabilities.
- *Salaries payable*—payroll expense that has been incurred during the current accounting period but will be paid in the next accounting period.
- *Taxes payable*—tax obligations that have been incurred during the current accounting period but will be paid in the next accounting period.

As shown in Figure 15.2, current liabilities for Northeast Art Supply total $70,000.

Long-Term Liabilities **Long-term liabilities** are debts that need not be repaid for at least one year. Northeast lists only one long-term liability—a $40,000 *mortgage payable* for store equipment. Loans and other long-term obligations would be included here as well, if they existed. As you can see in Figure 15.2, Northeast's current and long-term liabilities total $110,000.

Owners' or Stockholders' Equity For a sole proprietorship or partnership, the owners' equity is shown as the difference between assets and liabilities. In a partnership, each partner's share of the ownership is reported separately in each owner's name. For a corporation, the owners' equity usually is referred to as *stockholders' equity*. The dollar amount reported on the balance sheet is the total value of stock plus retained earnings that have accumulated to date. **Retained earnings** are the portion of a business's profits not distributed to stockholders.

The original investment by the owners of Northeast Art Supply was $150,000. In addition, $80,000 of Northeast's earnings have been reinvested in the business since it was founded. Thus owners' equity totals $230,000.

current liabilities debts that will be repaid in one year or less

long-term liabilities debts that need not be repaid for at least one year

retained earnings the portion of a business's profits not distributed to stockholders

As the two grand totals in Figure 15.2 show, Northeast's assets and the sum of its liabilities and owners' equity are equal—at $340,000. The accounting equation (assets = liabilities + owners' equity) is still in balance.

The Income Statement

Learning Objective ⑤

Read and interpret an income statement.

Question: *Where can you find the profit or loss amount for Loblaw Inc.?*

Answer: The firm's income statement.

An **income statement** is a summary of a firm's revenues and expenses during a specified accounting period—one month, three months, six months, or a year. The income statement is sometimes called the *earnings statement* or the *statement of income and expenses*. Let's begin our discussion by constructing a personal income statement for Marty Campbell. Having worked as a sales representative for an office supply firm for the past three years, Marty now earns $33,600 a year, or $2,800 a month. After deductions, his take-home pay is $1,900 a month. As illustrated in Figure 15.3, Marty's typical monthly expenses include payments for an automobile loan, credit-card purchases, apartment rent, utilities, food, clothing, and recreation and entertainment.

While the difference between income and expenses is referred to as *profit* or *loss* for a business, it is normally referred to as a *cash surplus* or *cash deficit* for an individual.

income statement a summary of a firm's revenues and expenses during a specified accounting period

---

Marty Campbell
Personal Income Statement
For the month ended December 31, 2008

INCOME (Take-home pay)		$1,900
LESS MONTHLY EXPENSES		
Automobile loan	$ 250	
Credit card payment	100	
Apartment rent	500	
Utilities	200	
Food	250	
Clothing	100	
Recreation & entertainment	250	
TOTAL MONTHLY EXPENSES		1,650
CASH SURPLUS (or profit)		$ 250

Figure 15.3

Personal Income Statement

By subtracting expenses from income, anyone can construct a personal income statement and determine if he or she has a surplus or deficit at the end of the month.

Fortunately for Marty, he has a surplus of $250 at the end of each month. He can use this surplus for savings, investing, or paying off debts.

Figure 15.4 shows the income statement for Northeast Art Supply. Generally, revenues *less* cost of goods sold *less* operating expenses equals net income.

Figure 15.4

Business Income Statement

An income statement summarizes a firm's revenues and expenses during a specified accounting period. For Northeast Art, net income after taxes is $30,175.

NORTHEAST ART SUPPLY, INC.

Income Statement
For the Year Ended
December 31, 2008

Revenues			
Gross sales		$465,000	
Less sales returns and allowances	$ 9,500		
Less sales discounts	4,500	14,000	
Net sales			$451,000
Cost of goods sold			
Beginning inventory, January 1, 20XX		$ 40,000	
Purchases	$346,000		
Less purchase discounts	11,000		
Net purchases		335,000	
Cost of goods available for sale		$375,000	
Less ending inventory December 31, 20XX		41,000	
Cost of goods sold			334,000
Gross profit			$117,000
Operating expenses			
Selling expenses			
Sales salaries	$ 22,000		
Advertising	4,000		
Sales promotion	2,500		
Depreciation—store equipment	3,000		
Depreciation—delivery equipment	4,000		
Miscellaneous selling expenses	1,500		
Total selling expenses		$ 37,000	
General expenses			
Office salaries	$ 28,500		
Rent	8,500		
Depreciation—office furniture	1,500		
Utilities expense	2,500		
Insurance expense	1,000		
Miscellaneous expense	500		
Total general expense		42,500	
Total operating expenses			$ 79,500
Net income from operations			$ 37,500
Less interest expense			2,000
NET INCOME BEFORE TAXES			$ 35,500
Less federal income taxes			5,325
NET INCOME AFTER TAXES			$ 30,175

Revenues

Revenues are the dollar amounts earned by a firm from selling goods, providing services, or performing business activities. Like most businesses, Northeast Art obtains its revenues solely from the sale of its products or services. The revenues section of its income statement begins with gross sales. **Gross sales** are the total dollar amount of all goods and services sold during the accounting period. From this amount are deducted the dollar amounts of

* *Sales returns*—merchandise returned to the firm by its customers

* *Sales allowances*—price reductions offered to customers who accept slightly damaged or soiled merchandise

* *Sales discounts*—price reductions offered to customers who pay their bills promptly

The remainder is the firm's net sales. **Net sales** are the actual dollar amounts received by the firm for the goods and services it has sold after adjustment for returns, allowances, and discounts. For Northeast Art, net sales are $451,000.

Cost of Goods Sold

The standard method of determining the **cost of goods sold** by a retailing or wholesaling firm can be summarized as follows:

Cost of goods sold = beginning inventory + net purchases − ending inventory

A manufacturer must include raw materials inventories, work in progress, and direct manufacturing costs in this computation.

According to Figure 15.4, Northeast began its accounting period on January 1 with a merchandise inventory that cost $40,000. During the next twelve months, the firm purchased merchandise valued at $346,000. After taking advantage of *purchase discounts*, however, it paid only $335,000 for this merchandise. Thus, during the year, Northeast had total *goods available for sale* valued at $40,000 plus $335,000, or $375,000.

Twelve months later, at the end of the accounting period on December 31, Northeast had sold all but $41,000 worth of the available goods. The cost of goods sold by Northeast was therefore $375,000 less ending inventory of $41,000, or $334,000. It is now possible to calculate gross profit. A firm's **gross profit** is its net sales *less* the cost of goods sold. For Northeast, gross profit was $117,000.

Operating Expenses

A firm's **operating expenses** are all business costs other than the cost of goods sold. Total operating expenses generally are divided into two categories: selling expenses or general expenses.

Selling expenses are costs related to the firm's marketing activities. For Northeast Art, selling expenses total $37,000. *General expenses* are costs incurred in managing a business. For Northeast Art, general expenses total $42,500. Now it is possible to total both selling and general expenses. As Figure 15.4 shows, total operating expenses for the accounting period are $79,500.

revenues the dollar amounts earned by a firm from selling goods, providing services, or performing business activities

gross sales the total dollar amount of all goods and services sold during the accounting period

net sales the actual dollar amounts received by a firm for the goods and services it has sold after adjustment for returns, allowances, and discounts

cost of goods sold the dollar amount equal to beginning inventory *plus* net purchases *less* ending inventory

gross profit a firm's net sales *less* the cost of goods sold

operating expenses all business costs other than the cost of goods sold

Net Income

When revenues exceed expenses, the difference is called **net income**. When expenses exceed revenues, the difference is called **net loss**. As Figure 15.4 shows, Northeast Art's *net income from operations* is computed as gross profit ($117,000) *less* total operating expenses ($79,500). For Northeast Art, net income from operations is $37,500. From this amount, *interest expense* of $2,000 is deducted to obtain a *net income before taxes* of $35,500. The interest expense is deducted in this section of the income statement because it is not an operating expense. Rather, it is an expense that results from financing the business.

Northeast's *income taxes* are $5,325. Although these taxes may or may not be payable immediately, they are definitely an expense that must be deducted from income. This leaves Northeast Art with a *net income after taxes* of $30,175. This amount may be used to pay a dividend to stockholders, it may be retained or reinvested in the firm, it may be used to reduce the firm's debts, or all three.

The Statement of Cash Flows

 Learning Objective 6

Describe business activities that affect a firm's cash flow.

Cash is the lifeblood of any business. The **statement of cash flows** illustrates how the operating, investing, and financing activities of a company affect cash during an accounting period. A statement of cash flows for Northeast Art Supply is illustrated in Figure 15.5. It provides information concerning the company's cash receipts and cash payments and is organized around three different activities: operations, investing, and financing.

* *Cash flows from operating activities.* This is the first section of a statement of cash flows. It addresses the firm's primary revenue source—providing goods and services. The amounts paid to suppliers, employees, interest, taxes, and other expenses are deducted from the amount received from customers. Finally, the interest and dividends received by the firm are added to determine the total. After all adjustments are made, the total represents a true picture of cash flows from operating activities.

* *Cash flows from investing activities.* The second section of the statement is concerned with cash flow from investments. This includes the purchase and sale of land, equipment, and other assets and investments.

* *Cash flows from financing activities.* The third and final section deals with the cash flow from all financing activities. It reports changes in debt obligation and owners' equity accounts. This includes loans and repayments, the sale and repurchase of the company's own stock, and cash dividends.

The totals of all three activities are added to the beginning cash balance to determine the ending cash balance. For Northeast Art Supply, the ending cash balance is $59,000. Note that this is the same dollar amount reported for the cash account on the firm's balance sheet. Together the cash flow statement, balance sheet, and income

NORTHEAST ART SUPPLY, INC.

Statement of Cash Flows
For the Year Ended
December 31, 2008

Cash flows from operating activities

Cash received from customers	$ 451,000	
Cash paid to suppliers and employees	(385,500)	
Interest paid	(2,000)	
Income taxes paid	(5,325)	
Net cash provided by operating activities		$ 58,175

Cash flows from investing activities

Purchase of equipment	$(2,000)	
Purchase of investments	(10,000)	
Sale of investments	10,000	
Net cash provided by investing activities		$(2,000)

Cash flows from financing activities

Payment of short-term debt	$(9,000)	
Payment of long-term debt	(17,000)	
Payment of dividends	(15,000)	
Net cash provided by financing activities		$(41,000)

NET INCREASE (DECREASE) IN CASH	$ 15,175
Cash at beginning of year	43,825
CASH AT END OF YEAR	$ 59,000

Figure 15.5

Statement of Cash Flows

A statement of cash flows summarizes how a firm's operating, investing, and financing activities affect its cash during a specified period—one month, three months, six months, or a year. For Northeast Art, the amount of cash at the end of the year reported on the statement of cash flows is $59,000—the same amount reported for the cash account on the firm's balance sheet.

statement illustrate the results of past business decisions and reflect the firm's ability to pay debts and dividends and to finance new growth.

Evaluating Financial Statements

Learning Objective 7

Summarize how managers evaluate the financial health of a business.

All three financial statements—the balance sheet, the income statement, and the statement of cash flows—can provide answers to a variety of questions about a firm's ability to do business and stay in business, its profitability, its value as an investment, and its ability to repay its debts. Even more information can be obtained by comparing present financial statements with those prepared for past accounting periods.

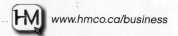 www.hmco.ca/business

Using Annual Reports to Compare Data For Different Accounting Periods

In addition to providing printed annual reports to stockholders and other interested parties, it is possible to view a firm's annual report by accessing the company's website. Typically, an annual report contains a great deal of information about the company, its operations, current financial statements, and its past and current financial health. The following five suggestions can help you get to the "bottom line" of a corporation's annual report.

1. Look at the firm's income statement to determine whether the company is profitable or not.

2. Read the letters from the chairman of the board and chief executive officer (CEO) that describe the corporation's operations, prospects for the future, new products or services, financial strengths, *and* any potential problems.

3. Compare the corporation's current income statement and balance sheet with previous financial statements. Look at trends for sales, expenses, profits or losses, assets, liabilities, and owners' equity.

4. Examine the footnotes closely, and look for red flags that may be in the fine print. Often the footnotes contain (and sometimes hide) important information about the company and its finances.

5. Learn how to calculate financial ratios, and determine how they may change a firm's financial condition. Some of the most important financial ratios are discussed in the last part of this section.

Most corporations include in their annual reports comparisons of the important elements of their financial statements for recent years. Figure 15.6 shows such comparisons—of revenue, research and development (R&D), operating income, and sales and marketing expenses—for Microsoft Corporation, a world leader in the computer software industry. By examining these data, an operating manager can tell whether R&D expenditures are increasing or decreasing over the past three years. The vice president of marketing can determine if the total amount of sales and marketing expenses is changing. Stockholders and potential investors, on the other hand, may be more concerned with increases or decreases in Microsoft's revenues and operating income over the same time period.

Annual Report

Financial statements are publicized quarterly and included in a public company's annual report as a record for shareholders and other stakeholders. Here, Darren Entwistle, President and CEO of Telus presents the report at the Telus AGM in Vancouver in 2006.

Comparing Data with Other Firms' Data

Many firms also compare their financial results with those of competing firms and with industry averages. Comparisons are possible as long as accountants follow generally accepted accounting principles.

Except for minor differences in format and terms, the balance sheet and income statement of the Royal Bank of Canada and the Bank of Montreal for example, will be similar. Comparisons among firms give managers a general idea of a firm's relative effectiveness and its standing within their industry. Competitors' financial statements can be obtained from their annual reports—if they are public corporations. Industry averages are published by reporting services such as D&B (formerly Dun & Bradstreet) and Standard & Poor's, as well as by some industry trade associations.

Still another type of analysis of a firm's financial health involves computation of financial ratios. A **financial ratio** is a number that shows the relationship between two elements of a firm's financial statements. Among the most useful ratios are profitability ratios, short-term financial ratios, activity ratios, and the debt-to-owners'-equity ratio. Like the individual elements in financial statements, these ratios can be compared with the firm's past ratios, with those of competitors, and with industry averages. The information required to form these ratios is found in a firm's balance sheet and income statement (in our examples for Northeast Art Supply, Figures 15.2 and 15.4).

REVENUE

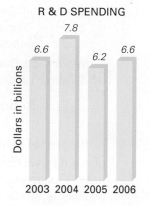

R & D SPENDING

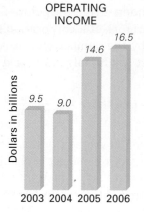

OPERATING INCOME

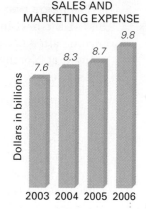

SALES AND MARKETING EXPENSE

Figure 15.6

Comparisons of Present and Past Financial Statements for Microsoft Corporation

Most corporations include in their annual reports comparisons of the important elements of their financial statements for recent years.

Source: Adapted From the Microsoft Corporation 2006 and 2005 Annual Reports, www.microsoft.com, November 14, 2006. December 3, 2005.

financial ratio a number that shows the relationship between two elements of a firm's financial statements

Profitability Ratios

A firm's net income after taxes indicates whether the firm is profitable. It does not, however, indicate how effectively the firm's resources are being used. For the latter purpose, three ratios can be computed.

Return on Sales *Return on sales*, sometimes called *profit margin*, is a financial ratio calculated by dividing net income after taxes by net sales. For Northeast Art Supply,

$$\text{Return on sales} = \frac{\text{net income after taxes}}{\text{net sales}} = \frac{\$30,175}{\$451,000}$$
$$= 0.067, \text{ or } 6.7 \text{ percent}$$

The return on sales indicates how effectively the firm is transforming sales into profits. A higher return on sales is better than a low one. Today, the average return

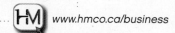

on sales for all business firms is between 4 and 5 percent. With a return on sales of 6.7 percent, Northeast Art Supply is above average. A low return on sales can be increased by reducing expenses, increasing sales, or both.

Return on Owners' Equity *Return on owners' equity* is a financial ratio calculated by dividing net income after taxes by owners' equity. For Northeast Art Supply,

$$\text{Return on owners' equity} = \frac{\text{net income after taxes}}{\text{owners' equity}} = \frac{\$30,175}{\$230,000}$$
$$= 0.13, \text{ or } 13 \text{ percent}$$

Return on owners' equity indicates how much income is generated by each dollar of equity. Northeast is providing income of 13 cents per dollar invested in the business. The average for all businesses is between 12 and 15 cents. A higher return on owners' equity is better than a low one, and the only practical ways to increase return on owners' equity is to reduce expenses, increase sales, or both.

Earnings per Share From the point of view of stockholders, *earnings per share* is one of the best indicators of a corporation's success. It is calculated by dividing net income after taxes by the number of shares of common stock outstanding. If we assume that Northeast Art Supply has issued 25,000 shares of stock, then its earnings per share are

$$\text{Earnings per share} = \frac{\text{net income after taxes}}{\text{common stock shares outstanding}} = \frac{\$30,175}{\$25,000}$$
$$= \$1.21 \text{ per share}$$

There is no meaningful average for this ratio mainly because the number of outstanding shares of a firm's stock is subject to change as a result of stock splits and stock dividends. Also, some corporations choose to issue more stock than others. As a general rule, however, an increase in earnings per share is a healthy sign for any corporation.

Short-Term Financial Ratios

Two short-term financial ratios permit managers (and lenders) to evaluate the ability of a firm to pay its current liabilities. Before we discuss these ratios, we should examine one other easily determined measure: working capital.

Working Capital *Working capital* is the difference between current assets and current liabilities. For Northeast Art,

Current assets	$182,000
Less current liabilities	$ 70,000
Equals working capital	$112,000

Working capital indicates how much would remain if a firm paid off all current liabilities with cash and other current assets. The "proper" amount of working capital depends on the type of firm, its past experience, and its particular industry. A firm with too little working capital may have to borrow money to finance its operations.

Current Ratio A firm's *current ratio* is computed by dividing current assets by current liabilities. For Northeast Art Supply,

$$\text{Current ratio} = \frac{\text{current assets}}{\text{current liabilities}} = \frac{\$182,000}{\$70,000} = 2.6$$

This means that Northeast Art Supply has $2.60 of current assets for every $1 of current liabilities. The average current ratio for all industries is 2.0, but it varies greatly from industry to industry. A high current ratio indicates that a firm can pay its current liabilities. A low current ratio can be improved by repaying current liabilities, by reducing dividend payments to increase the firm's cash balance, or by obtaining additional cash from investors.

Acid-Test Ratio This ratio, sometimes called the *quick ratio*, is a measure of the firm's ability to pay current liabilities *quickly*—with its cash, marketable securities, and receivables. The *acid-test ratio* is calculated by adding cash, marketable securities, and receivables and dividing the total by current liabilities. The value of inventory and other current assets are "removed" from current assets because these assets are not converted into cash as easily as cash, marketable securities, and receivables. For Northeast Art Supply,

$$\text{Acid-test ratio} = \frac{\text{cash + marketable securities + receivables}}{\text{current liabilities}} = \frac{\$139,000}{\$70,000} = 1.99$$

For all businesses, the desired acid-test ratio is 1.0. Northeast Art Supply is above average with a ratio of 1.99, and the firm should be well able to pay its current liabilities. To increase a low acid-test ratio, a firm would have to repay current liabilities, reduce dividend payments to increase the firm's cash balance, or obtain additional cash from investors.

Activity Ratios

Two activity ratios permit managers to measure how many times each year a company collects its accounts receivables or sells its inventory.

Accounts Receivable Turnover A firm's *accounts receivable turnover* is the number of times the firm collects its accounts receivable in one year. If the data are available, this ratio should be calculated using a firm's net credit sales. Since data for Northeast Art Supply's credit sales are unavailable, this ratio can be calculated by dividing net sales by accounts receivable. For Northeast Art,

$$\text{Accounts receivable turnover} = \frac{\text{net sales}}{\text{accounts receivable}} = \frac{\$451,000}{\$38,000}$$
$$= 11.9 \text{ times per year}$$

Northeast Art Supply collects its accounts receivables 11.9 times each year, or about every thirty days. If a firm's credit terms require customers to pay in twenty-five days, a collection period of thirty days is considered acceptable. There is no meaningful average for this measure mainly because credit terms differ among companies. A high accounts receivable turnover is better than a low one. As a general rule, a low accounts receivable turnover ratio can be improved by pressing for payment of past-due accounts and by tightening requirements for prospective credit customers.

Inventory Turnover A firm's *inventory turnover* is the number of times the firm sells its merchandise inventory in one year. It is approximated by dividing the cost of goods sold in one year by the average value of the inventory.

The average value of the inventory can be found by adding the beginning inventory value and the ending inventory value (given on the income statement) and dividing the sum by 2. For Northeast Art Supply, average inventory is $40,500. Thus

$$\text{Inventory turnover} = \frac{\text{cost of goods sold}}{\text{average inventory}} = \frac{\$334,000}{\$40,500}$$
$$= 8.2 \text{ times per year}$$

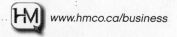

Northeast Art Supply sells its merchandise inventory 8.2 times each year, or about once every forty-five days. The average inventory turnover for all firms is about 9 times per year, but turnover rates vary widely from industry to industry. For example, supermarkets may have turnover rates of 20 or higher, whereas turnover rates for furniture stores are generally well below the national average. The quickest way to improve inventory turnover is to order merchandise in smaller quantities at more frequent intervals.

Debt-to-Owners'-Equity Ratio

Our final category of financial ratios indicates the degree to which a firm's operations are financed through borrowing. Although other ratios can be calculated, the debt-to-owners'-equity ratio is used often to determine whether a firm has too much debt. The debt-to-owners'-equity ratio is calculated by dividing total liabilities by owners' equity. For Northeast Art Supply,

$$\text{Debt-to-owners' equity ratio} = \frac{\text{total liabilities}}{\text{owners' equity}} = \frac{\$110,000}{\$230,000}$$
$$= 0.48, \text{ or } 48 \text{ percent}$$

A debt-to-owners'-equity ratio of 48 percent means that creditors have provided about 48 cents of financing for every dollar provided by the owners. The higher this ratio, the riskier the situation is for lenders. A high debt-to-owners'-equity ratio may make borrowing additional money from lenders difficult. It can be reduced by paying off debts or by increasing the owners' investment in the firm.

Northeast's Financial Ratios: A Summary

Table 15.2 compares the financial ratios of Northeast Art Supply with the average financial ratios for all businesses. It also lists the formulas we used to calculate Northeast's ratios. Northeast seems to be in good financial shape. Its return on sales,

Table 15.2

Financial Ratios of Northeast Art Supply Compared with Average Ratios for All Businesses

RATIO	FORMULA	NORTHEAST RATIO	AVERAGE BUSINESS RATIO	DIRECTION FOR IMPROVEMENT
PROFITABILITY RATIOS				
Return on sales	net income after taxes / net sales	6.7 percent	4–5 percent	Higher
Return on owners' equity	net income after taxes / owners' equity	13 percent	12–15 percent	Higher
Earnings per share	net income after taxes / common stock shares outstanding	$1.21 per share	—	Higher
SHORT-TERM FINANCIAL RATIOS				
Working capital	current assets—current liabilities	$112,000	—	Higher
Current ratio	current assets / current liabilities	2.6	2.0	Higher
Acid-test ratio	cash + marketable securities + receivables / current liabilities	1.99	1.0	Higher

ACTIVITY RATIOS				
Accounts receivable turnover	net sales / accounts receivable	11.9	—	Higher
Inventory turnover	cost of goods sold / average inventory	8.2	9	Higher
Debt-to-owners'-equity ratio	total liabilities / owners' equity	48 percent	—	Lower

current ratio, and acid-test ratio are all above average. Its other ratios are about average, although its inventory turnover and debt-to-equity ratio could be improved.

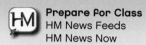

Prepare for Class
HM News Feeds
HM News Now

→ **RETURN TO INSIDE BUSINESS**

New reporting requirements require both the CEO and CFO (Chief Financial Officer) to personally certify that the data in the company's financial reports are accurate and complete. Although this should provide some comfort to the investment community, is it enough? What sort of penalties should be levied against corporate officers when inaccurate or fraudulent statements are made public?

Canada is experiencing an increasing level of white-collar crime. Experts suggest that this is due to ineffective and lax penalties imposed by the various governing bodies. They also point to the lack of a federal regulator to enforce the various securities and accounting laws across the country.

Questions

1. Which are more effective in curbing accounting fraud—fines, jail or both?
2. Who should be held responsible—the company, auditors or both?

CHAPTER REVIEW

1 Explain why accurate accounting information and audited financial statements are important.

Accounting is the process of systematically collecting, analyzing, and reporting financial information. It can be used to answer questions about what has happened in the past.

It also can be used to help make decisions about the future. The purpose of an audit is to make sure that a firm's financial statements have been prepared in accordance with generally accepted accounting principles (GAAPs).

Identify the people who use accounting information and possible careers in the accounting industry.

Primarily management uses accounting information, but it is also demanded by lenders, suppliers, stockholders, potential investors, and government agencies. A private accountant is employed by a specific organization to operate its accounting system. A public accountant performs these functions for various individuals or firms on a fee basis. Most accounting firms include on their staffs at least one chartered accountant (CA). In addition to CAs, there are also certified management accountants (CMAs) and certified general accountants (CGAs).

3 Discuss the accounting process.

The accounting process is based on the accounting equation: Assets = liabilities + owners' equity. The accounting process involves five steps: (1) source documents are analyzed, (2) each transaction is recorded in a journal, (3) each journal entry is posted in the appropriate general ledger accounts, (4) at the end of each accounting period, a trial balance is prepared to make sure that the accounting equation is in balance, and (5) financial statements are prepared from the trial balance.

4 Read and interpret a balance sheet.

A balance sheet is a summary of a firm's assets, liabilities, and owners' equity accounts at the end of an accounting period. On the balance sheet, assets are categorized as current, fixed, or intangible. Similarly, liabilities can be divided into current liabilities and long-term ones. For a sole proprietorship or partnership, owners' equity is shown as the difference between assets and liabilities. For corporations, the owners' equity section reports the values of stock and retained earnings.

5 Read and interpret an income statement.

An income statement is a summary of a firm's financial operations during the specified accounting period. On the income statement, the company's gross profit is computed by subtracting the cost of goods sold from net sales.

Operating expenses and interest expense then are deducted to compute net income before taxes. Finally, income taxes are deducted to obtain the firm's net income after taxes.

6 Describe business activities that affect a firm's cash flow.

This statement illustrates how the operating, investing, and financing activities of a company affect cash during an accounting period. Together the cash flow statement, balance sheet, and income statement illustrate the results of past decisions and the business's ability to pay debts and dividends and to finance new growth.

7 Summarize how managers evaluate the financial health of a business.

The firm's financial statements and its accounting information become more meaningful when compared with corresponding information for previous years, for competitors, and for the industry in which the firm operates. Such comparisons permit managers and other interested people to pick out trends in growth, borrowing, income, and other business variables and to determine whether the firm is on the way to accomplishing its long-term goals. A number of financial ratios can be computed from the information in a firm's financial statements. Like the information on the firm's financial statements, these ratios can and should be compared with those of past accounting periods, those of competitors, and those representing the average of the industry as a whole.

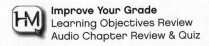
Improve Your Grade
Learning Objectives Review
Audio Chapter Review & Quiz

Review Questions

1. What purpose do audits and generally accepted accounting principles (GAAPs) serve in today's business world?

2. List four groups that use accounting information, and briefly explain why each group has an interest in this information.

3. What is the difference between a private accountant and a public accountant? What are chartered accountants, certified management accountants, and certified general accountants?

4. State the accounting equation, and list two specific examples of each term in the equation.

5. What is the principal difference between a balance sheet and an income statement?

6. How are current assets distinguished from fixed assets? Why are fixed assets depreciated on a balance sheet?

7. Explain how a retailing firm would determine the cost of goods sold during an accounting period.

8. How does a firm determine its net income after taxes?

9. What is the purpose of a statement of cash flows?

10. For each of the accounts listed below, indicate if the account should be included on a firm's balance sheet, income statement, or statement of cash flows.

Type of Account	Statement Where Reported
Assets	_____
Income	_____
Expenses	_____
Operating activities	_____
Liabilities	_____
Investing activities	_____
Owners' equity	_____

11. What type of information is contained in an annual report? How does the information help to identify financial trends?

12. Explain the calculation procedure for and significance of each of the following:
    a. One of the profitability ratios
    b. A short-term financial ratio
    c. An activity ratio
    d. Debt-to-owners'-equity ratio

Discussion Questions

1. Why do you think there have been so many accounting scandals involving public companies in recent years?

2. Bankers usually insist that prospective borrowers submit audited financial statements along with a loan application. Why should financial statements be audited by a CA?

3. What can be said about a firm whose owners' equity is a negative amount? How could such a situation come about?

4. Do the balance sheet, income statement, and statement of cash flows contain all the information you might want as a potential lender or stockholder? What other information would you like to examine?

5. Why is it so important to compare a firm's current financial statements and financial ratios with those of previous years, those of competitors, and the average of all firms in the industry in which the firm operates?

CASE STUDY

The Ethics of "Making the Numbers"

Will sales and profits meet the expectations of investors and Wall Street analysts? Managers at public corporations must answer this vitally important question quarter after quarter, year after year. In an ideal world—one in which the economy never contracts, expenses never go up, and customers never buy competing products—the corporation's share price would soar, and investors would cheer as every financial report showed ever-higher sales revenues, profit margins, and earnings.

In the real world, however, many uncontrollable and unpredictable factors can affect a corporation's performance. Customers buy fewer units or postpone purchases, competitors introduce superior products, energy costs and other expenses rise, interest rates climb, and buying power plummets. Faced with the prospect of releasing financial results that fall short of Bay Street's expectations, managers may feel intense pressure to "make the numbers" using a variety of accounting techniques.

Because accounting rules are open to interpretation, managers sometimes find themselves facing ethical dilemmas when a corporation feels pressure to live up to Bay Street's expectations. Consider the hypothetical situation at Commodore Appliances, a fictional company that sells to Home Depot, Canadian Tire, and other major retail chains. Margaret, the vice president of sales, has told Rob, a district manager, that the company's sales are down 10 percent in the current quarter. She points out that sales in Rob's district are down 20 percent and states that higher-level managers want him to improve this month's figures using "book and hold," which means recording future sales transactions in the current period.

Rob hesitates, saying that the company is gaining market share and that he needs more time to get sales momentum going. He thinks "book and hold" is not good business practice, even if it is legal. Margaret hints that Rob will lose his job if his sales figures don't look better and stresses that he will need the book-and-hold approach for one month only. Rob realizes that if he doesn't go along, he won't be working at Commodore for very much longer.

Meeting with Kevin, one of Commodore's auditors, Rob learns that book and hold meets generally accepted accounting principles. Kevin emphasizes that customers must be willing to take title to the goods before they're delivered or billed. Any book-and-hold sales must be real, backed by documentation such as e-mails to and from buyers, and the transactions must be completed in the near future.

Rob is at a crossroads: his sales figures must be higher if Commodore is to achieve its performance targets, yet he doesn't know exactly when (or if) he actually would complete any book-and-hold sales he might report this month. He doesn't want to mislead anyone, but he also doesn't want to lose his job or put other people's jobs in jeopardy by refusing to do what he is being asked to do. Rob is confident that he can improve his district's sales over the long term. On the other hand, Commodore's executives can't wait—they are pressuring Rob to make the sales figures look better right now. What should he do?

For more information about the Sarbanes-Oxley Act, go to www.aicpa.org. This is the website for the American Institute of Certified Public Accountants and is a good source of information about the act.

Questions:

1. What are the ethical and legal implications of using accounting practices such as the book-and-hold technique to inflate corporate earnings?

2. Why would Commodore's auditor insist that Rob document any sales booked under the book-and-hold technique?

3. If you were in Rob's situation, would you agree to use the book-and-hold technique this month? Justify your decision.

4. Imagine that Commodore has taken out a multi-million-dollar loan that must be repaid next year. How might the lender react if it learned that Commodore was using the book-and-hold method to make revenues look higher than they really are?

BUILDING SKILLS FOR CAREER SUCCESS

1. Exploring the Internet

To those unacquainted with current activities and practices in larger accounting firms, there is often some surprise at just how varied the accounting work involved actually is. Although setting up and maintaining accounting software for clients are standard, accounting firms also can provide a wide range of specialized services. For example, research into mergers or acquisitions of other firms, investment advice, and solutions to financial problems are now common strategies for revenue growth within accounting firms. Most websites for large accounting firms also will post information about current employment opportunities.

Assignment

1. Visit the website of a major accounting firm such as Deloitte Touche Tohmatsu (www .deloitte.com), KPMG (www.kpmg.com), PricewaterhouseCoopers (www.pwc.com), or Ernst & Young (www.ey.com). Describe in general terms how the website is used to communicate with clients and prospective clients. Visit the text website for updates to this exercise.

2. What are some of the content items presented on the site? What do these tell you about the firm and its clients?

3. Search the site for career information. Often the firm will post descriptions of employment opportunities along with educational and experience requirements. Describe what you find.

2. Building Team Skills

This has been a bad year for Park Avenue Furniture. The firm increased sales revenues to $1,400,000, but total expenses ballooned to $1,750,000. Although management realized that some of the firm's expenses were out of its control, including cost of goods sold ($700,000), salaries ($450,000), and advertising costs ($140,000), it could not contain expenses. As a result, the furniture retailer lost $350,000. To make matters worse, the retailer applied for a $350,000 loan at the Bank of Nova Scotia and was turned down. The bank officer, Mike Nettles, said that the firm already had too much debt. At that time, liabilities totaled $420,000; owners' equity was $600,000.

Assignment

1. In groups of three or four, analyze the financial condition of Park Avenue Furniture.

2. Discuss why you think the bank officer turned down Park Avenue's loan request.

3. Prepare a detailed plan of action to improve the financial health of Park Avenue Furniture over the next twelve months.

3. Researching Different Careers

As pointed out in this chapter, job opportunities for accountants and managers in the accounting area are expected to experience average growth between now and the year 2014. Employment opportunities range from entry-level positions for clerical workers and technicians to professional positions that require a university or college degree in accounting, management consulting, or computer technology. Typical job titles in the accounting field include bookkeeper, corporate accountant, public accountant, auditor, managerial accountant, and controller.

Assignment

1. Answer the following questions based on information obtained from interviews with people employed in accounting, from research in the library or by using the Internet, or from information gained from your university or college's career center.

   a. What types of activities would a person employed in one of the accounting positions listed above perform on a daily basis?

   b. Would you choose this career? Why or why not?

2. Summarize your findings in a report.

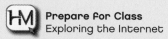

Prepare for Class
Exploring the Internet

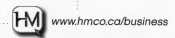

CHAPTER 16

Mastering Financial Management

Your Guide to Success in Business

Why this chapter matters
The old saying goes, "Money makes the world go around." For both individuals and business firms, the saying is true. The fact is that it's hard to live in this world or operate a business without money.

Mighty Microfinance Goes Multinational

Muhammad Yunus won the 2006 Nobel Peace Prize for pioneering a revolutionary financing concept: Microfinance, lending entrepreneurs a little *(micro)* money *(finance)* to start or expand a small business. Traditionally, banks have been reluctant to lend money to people who have no inventory, no credit history, no equipment, and little (if anything) of value to back up their repayment promises.

In contrast, microfinance helps even poor entrepreneurs over that high hurdle. What's really revolutionary about microfinance is that it offers would-be business owners the opportunity to borrow in the first place, on the assumption that they'll ultimately become self-supporting. Borrowers who use microfinance to fuel a business are expected to repay every loan, with interest, no matter how small—and well over 95 percent do.

Over the years, Yunus's Grameen Bank, based in Bangladesh, has loaned more than $5 billion to seven million borrowers who could pledge nothing but their personal promise to repay the money. In addition to Grameen Bank, 7,000 microfinance institutions worldwide now lend small amounts to small business borrowers. These include nonprofit organizations like the Gates Foundation (created by Microsoft's founder) and the Omidyar Network (created by eBay's founder). Increasingly, commercial banks such as BancoSol in Bolivia and even the New York–based banking giant Citigroup are getting involved.

In all, more than 100 million people each year borrow an average of $50 to $150 to start or grow a wide variety of small businesses. Most of these entrepreneurs are women with business ideas such as making tortillas to sell on market day or buying a cell phone and charging villagers to use it. Even a tiny loan can make a big difference. In Africa, a woman who was reselling fish bought from a local distributor borrowed money for a bus trip to the Nile River where she could buy directly from fishermen

continued on next page

● ● ●

> **DID YOU KNOW?**
>
> Through microfinance, more than 100 million people each year borrow an average of $50 to $150 to start or grow their small businesses.

KEY TERMS

financial management (488)
short-term financing (488)
cash flow (488)
speculative production (489)
long-term financing (490)
risk-return ratio (490)
chief financial officer (CFO) (491)
financial plan (492)
budget (493)
cash budget (493)
zero-base budgeting (494)

capital budget (494)
equity capital (494)
debt capital (494)
certificate of deposit (495)
cheque (495)
line of credit (496)
revolving credit agreement (496)
collateral (496)
debit card (496)
electronic funds transfer (EFT) system (497)

letter of credit (497)
banker's acceptance (497)
unsecured financing (498)
trade credit (499)
promissory note (499)
prime interest rate (499)
commercial paper (500)
factor (501)
initial public offering (IPO) (503)
investment banking firm (503)
convertible preferred stock (504)

retained earnings (504)
private placement (506)
financial leverage (506)
term-loan agreement (507)
corporate bond (508)
maturity date (508)
registered bond (508)
bond indenture (509)
serial bonds (509)
sinking fund (509)
trustee (509)

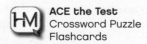

and pay far less for her merchandise. "A $10 bus ticket separated her from vastly expanding her profit," says Jessica Flannery, co-founder of the web-based nonprofit Kiva.org, which arranged the loan.

Based on information in Jay Greene, "Taking Tiny Loans to the Next Level," *BusinessWeek*, November 27, 2006, pp. 76+; Jay Greene, "A Big Stage for Small Loans," *BusinessWeek*, November 27, 2006, p. 82; Connie Bruck, "Millions for Millions," *New Yorker*, October 30, 2006, pp. 62+; Sonia Narang, "Sixth Annual Year of Ideas: Web-Based Microfinancing," *New York Times Magazine*, December 10, 2006, p. 84; Joseph P. Fried, "From a Small Loan, a Jewelry Business Grows," *New York Times*, November 12, 2006, sec. 10, p. 1; "Face Value: Macro Credit," *The Economist*, October 21, 2006, p. 78.

In this chapter we focus on how firms find the financing required to meet two needs of all business organizations: first, the need for money to start a business and keep it going and, second, the need to manage that money effectively. We also look at how firms develop financial plans and evaluate financial performance. Next, we look at the services provided by banks and other financial institutions for their business customers. Then we compare various methods of obtaining short-term financing. We also examine sources of long-term financing.

What Is Financial Management?

Learning Objective ❶
Explain the need for financial management in business.

financial management all the activities concerned with obtaining money and using it effectively

Financial management consists of all the activities concerned with obtaining money and using it effectively. Within a business organization, the financial manager not only must determine the best way (or ways) to raise money, but he or she also must ensure that projected uses are in keeping with the organization's goals.

The Need for Financing

Money is needed both to start a business and to keep it going. The original investment of the owners, along with money they may have borrowed, should be enough to open the doors. After that, it would seem that sales revenues could be used to pay the firm's expenses and to provide a profit as well.

This is exactly what happens in a successful firm—over the long run. However, income and expenses may vary from month to month or from year to year. Temporary financing may be needed when expenses are high or sales are low. Then, too, situations such as the opportunity to purchase a new facility or expand an existing plant may require more money than is currently available within a firm. In either case, the firm must look for outside sources of financing.

short-term financing money that will be used for one year or less

cash flow the movement of money into and out of an organization

Short-Term Financing Short-term financing is money that will be used for one year or less. As illustrated in Table 16.1, there are many short-term financing needs, but two deserve special attention. First, certain business practices can affect a firm's cash flow and create a need for short-term financing. **Cash flow** is the movement of

Whether a business seeks short- or long-term financing depends on what the money will be used for.

Table 16.1

Comparison of Short- and Long-Term Financing

CORPORATE CASH NEEDS	
SHORT-TERM FINANCING NEEDS	**LONG-TERM FINANCING NEEDS**
Cash-flow problems	Business start-up costs
Current inventory needs	Mergers and acquisitions
Speculative production	New product development
Monthly expenses	Long-term marketing activities
Short-term promotional needs	Replacement of equipment
Unexpected emergencies	Expansion of facilities

money into and out of an organization. The ideal is to have sufficient money coming into the firm in any period to cover the firm's expenses during that period. The ideal, however, is not always achieved. For example, New Brunswick–based Irving Oil offers credit to retailers and wholesalers who purchase gasoline and other related products. Credit purchases made by Irving's retailers generally are not paid until thirty to sixty days (or more) after the transaction. Irving therefore may need short-term financing to pay its bills until its customers have paid theirs.

A second major need for short-term financing is inventory. Most manufacturers, wholesalers, and retailers invest a considerable amount in inventory. Moreover, most goods are manufactured four to nine months before they are actually sold to the ulti-

speculative production the time lag between the actual production of goods and when the goods are sold

mate customer. This type of manufacturing is often referred to as *speculative production*. **Speculative production** refers to the time lag between the actual production of goods and when the goods are sold. Consider what happens when a firm such as Black & Decker begins to manufacture electric tools and small appliances for sale during the Christmas season. Manufacturing begins in February, March, and April. Black & Decker negotiates short-term financing to buy materials and supplies, to pay wages and rent, and to cover inventory costs until its products eventually are sold to wholesalers and retailers later in the year. Take a look at Figure 16.1. Although Black & Decker manufactures and sells finished products all during the year, expenses peak during the first part of the year. During this same period, sales revenues are low. Once the firm's finished products are shipped to retailers and wholesalers and payment is received (usually within thirty to sixty days), sales revenues are used to repay short-term financing.

Short-term financing

In granting customers credit terms, Irving Oil may resort to short-term financing options to meet its cash flow obligations.

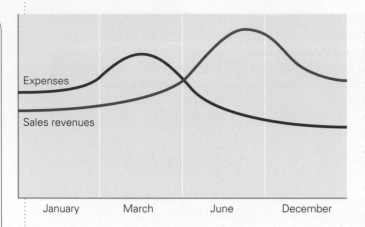

Figure 16.1

Cash Flow for a Manufacturing Business

Manufacturers such as Black & Decker often use short-term financing to pay expenses during the production process. Once goods are shipped to retailers and wholesalers and payment is received, sales revenues are used to repay short-term financing.

long-term financing money that will be used for longer than one year

risk-return ratio a ratio based on the principle that a high-risk decision should generate higher financial returns for a business and more conservative decisions often generate lesser returns

Retailers that range in size from Wal-Mart to the neighbourhood drugstore also need short-term financing to build up their inventories before peak selling periods. For example, Calgary, Alberta–based Sunnyside Greenhouses Ltd. must increase the number of shrubs, trees, and flowering plants that it makes available for sale during the spring and summer growing seasons. To obtain this merchandise inventory from growers or wholesalers, it uses short-term financing and repays the loans when the merchandise is sold.

Long-Term Financing Long-term financing is money that will be used for longer than one year. Long-term financing obviously is needed to start a new business. As Table 16.1 shows, it is also needed for business mergers and acquisitions, new product development, long-term marketing activities, replacement of equipment, and expansion of facilities.

Firms investing in research and development (pharmaceutical companies) and exploration (Barrick Gold Corporation) must expend large amounts of money without knowing if they will develop a new drug or find a gold deposit. In these cases, their financing options must allow flexibility in the payment terms or they could default on the repayment plan.

The Need for Financial Management

To some extent, financial management can be viewed as a two-sided problem. On one side, the uses of funds often dictate the type or types of financing needed by a business. On the other side, the activities a business can undertake are determined by the types of financing available. Financial managers must ensure that funds are available when needed, that they are obtained at the lowest possible cost, and that they are used as efficiently as possible. Financial managers also must consider the risk-return ratio when making decisions. The risk-return ratio is based on the principle that a high-risk decision should generate higher financial returns for a business. On the other hand, more conservative decisions (with less risk) often generate lesser returns. While financial managers want higher returns, they often must strive for a balance between risk and return. For example, WSE Technologies, a Saskatoon, Saskatchewan, solar power company might consider investing millions of dollars to fund research into new solar technology that would enable the company to use the sun to generate electrical power. And yet, financial managers must determine the potential return before committing to such a costly research project. And finally, financial managers must ensure that funds are available for the repayment of debts in accordance with lenders' financing terms. Prompt repayment is essential to protect the firm's credit rating and its ability to obtain financing in the future.

Many firms have failed because their managers did not pay enough attention to finances. In fact, poor financial management was one of the major reasons why an average of 10,000 businesses filed for bankruptcy in each of the last twenty-five years in Canada.[1] In addition, many fairly successful firms could be highly successful if they managed their finances more carefully. However, many people often take finances for granted. Their first focus may be on production or marketing. As long as there is sufficient financing today, they don't worry about how well it is used or whether it will be there tomorrow. Proper financial management can ensure that

* Financing priorities are established in line with organizational goals and objectives.

* Spending is planned and controlled.

* Bills are paid promptly to protect the firm's credit rating.

* Excess cash is invested in certificates of deposit (CDs), government securities, or conservative, marketable securities.

These functions define effective management as applied to a particular resource—money. And like all effective management, financial management begins with people who must set goals and plan for the future.

Careers in Finance

When you hear the word *finance*, you may think of highly paid executives who determine what a corporation can afford to do and what it can't. At the executive level, most large business firms have a chief financial officer for financial management. A **chief financial officer (CFO)** is a high-level corporate executive who manages a firm's finances and reports directly to the company's chief executive officer or president. Some firms prefer to use the titles vice president of financial management, treasurer, or controller instead of CFO for executive-level positions in the finance area.

Although some finance executives do make $300,000 a year or more, many entry-level and lower-level positions that pay quite a bit less are available. Banks, insurance companies, and investment firms obviously have a need for workers who can manage and analyze financial data. So do businesses involved in manufacturing, services, and marketing. Colleges and universities, not-for-profit organizations, and government entities at all levels also need finance workers.

People in finance must have certain traits and skills. In addition to honesty, managers and employees in the finance area must

1. Have a strong background in accounting or mathematics.

2. Know how to use a computer to analyze data.

3. Be an expert at both written and oral communication.

chief financial officer (CFO) a high-level corporate executive who manages a firm's finances and reports directly to the company's chief executive officer or president

Planning

Scotiabank provides a variety of products to customers including loans, electronic banking, and credit/debit card services.

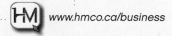

Typical job titles in finance include bank officer, consumer credit officer, financial analyst, financial planner, loan officer, insurance analyst, and investment account executive. Depending on qualifications, work experience, and education, starting salaries generally begin at $35,000 to $40,000 a year, but it is not uncommon for new university graduates to earn $50,000 a year or more.

Planning—The Basis of Sound Financial Management

Learning Objective 2

Summarize the process of planning for financial management.

In Chapter 7 we defined a *plan* as an outline of the actions by which an organization intends to accomplish its goals. A **financial plan,** then, is a plan for obtaining and using the money needed to implement an organization's goals.

Developing the Financial Plan

Financial planning (like all planning) begins with establishing a set of valid goals and objectives. Financial managers next must determine how much money is needed to accomplish each goal and objective. Finally, financial managers must identify available sources of financing and decide which to use. The three steps involved in financial planning are illustrated in Figure 16.2.

financial plan a plan for obtaining and using the money needed to implement an organization's goals

Figure 16.2

The Three Steps of Financial Planning

After a financial plan has been developed, it must be monitored continually to ensure that it actually fulfills the firm's goals and objectives.

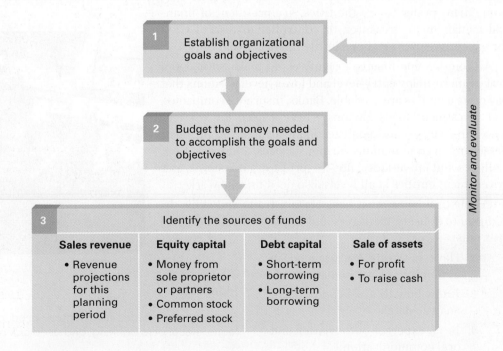

Establishing Organizational Goals and Objectives As pointed out in Chapter 7, a *goal* is an end state that an organization expects to achieve over a one- to ten-year period. *Objectives* are specific statements detailing what the organization intends to accomplish within a certain period of time. If goals and objectives are not specific and measurable, they cannot be translated into dollar costs and financial planning cannot proceed. Goals and objectives also must be realistic. Otherwise, they may be impossible to finance or achieve.

Budgeting for Financial Needs Once planners know what the firm's goals and objectives are for a specific period—say, the next calendar year—they can budget the costs the firm will incur and the sales revenues it will receive. Specifically, a **budget** is a financial statement that projects income and/or expenditures over a specified future period.

Usually the budgeting process begins with the construction of budgets for sales and various types of expenses. (A typical sales budget for Leaves and Trees Clothing is shown in Figure 16.3.) Financial managers can easily combine each department's budget for sales and expenses into a company-wide cash budget. A **cash budget** estimates cash receipts and cash expenditures over a specified period. Notice in the cash budget for Leaves and Trees Clothing, shown in Figure 16.4, that cash sales and collections are listed at the top for each calendar quarter. Payments for purchases and routine expenses are listed in the middle section. Using this information, it is possible to calculate the anticipated cash gain or loss at the end of each quarter.

budget a financial statement that projects income and/or expenditures over a specified future period

cash budget a financial statement that projects cash receipts and cash expenditures over a specified period

LEAVES AND TREES CLOTHING
Sales Budget   For January 1, 2008 to December 31, 2008

Department	First Quarter	Second Quarter	Third Quarter	Fourth Quarter	Totals
Infants'	$ 50,000	$ 55,000	$ 60,000	$ 70,000	$235,000
Children's	45,000	45,000	40,000	40,000	170,000
Women's	35,000	40,000	35,000	50,000	160,000
Men's	20,000	20,000	15,000	25,000	80,000
Totals	$150,000	$160,000	$150,000	$185,000	$645,000

Figure 16.3

Sales Budget for Leaves and Trees Clothing

Usually the budgeting process begins with the construction of departmental budgets for sales.

LEAVES AND TREES CLOTHING
Cash Budget   For January 1, 2008 to December 31, 2008

	First Quarter	Second Quarter	Third Quarter	Fourth Quarter	Totals
Cash sales and collections	$150,000	$160,000	$150,000	$185,000	$645,000
Less payments					
Purchases	$110,000	$ 80,000	$ 90,000	$ 60,000	$340,000
Wages/salaries	25,000	20,000	25,000	30,000	100,000
Rent	10,000	10,000	12,000	12,000	44,000
Other expenses	4,000	4,000	5,000	6,000	19,000
Taxes	8,000	8,000	10,000	10,000	36,000
Total payments	$157,000	$122,000	$142,000	$118,000	$539,000
Cash gain or (loss)	$ (7,000)	$ 38,000	$ 8,000	$ 67,000	$106,000

Figure 16.4

Cash Budget for Leaves and Trees Clothing

A company-wide cash budget projects sales, collections, purchases, and expenses over a specified period to anticipate cash surpluses and deficits.

Most firms today use one of two approaches to budgeting. In the *traditional* approach, each new budget is based on the dollar amounts contained in the budget for the preceding year. These amounts are modified to reflect any revised goals and objectives, and managers are required to justify only new expenditures. The problem with this approach is that it leaves room for padding budget items to protect the (sometimes selfish) interests of the manager or his or her department.

This problem is essentially eliminated through zero-base budgeting. **Zero-base budgeting** is a budgeting approach in which every expense in every budget must be justified. It can reduce unnecessary spending dramatically because every budget item must stand on its own merit. However, some managers oppose zero-base budgeting because it requires too much time-consuming paperwork.

To develop a plan for long-term financing needs, managers often construct a capital budget. A **capital budget** estimates a firm's expenditures for major assets, including new product development, expansion of facilities, replacement of obsolete equipment, and mergers and acquisitions

Identifying Sources of Funds The four primary sources of funds, listed in Figure 16.2, are sales revenue, equity capital, debt capital, and proceeds from the sale of assets. Future sales revenue generally provides the greatest part of a firm's financing. Figure 16.4 shows that for Leaves and Trees Clothing, sales for the year are expected to cover all expenses and to provide a cash gain of $106,000, or about 16 percent of sales. However, Leaves and Trees has a problem in the first quarter, when sales are expected to fall short of expenses by $7,000. In fact, one of the primary reasons for financial planning is to provide management with adequate lead time to solve this type of cash-flow problem.

A second type of funding is **equity capital.** Equity capital is provided by the owner or owners of a sole proprietorship or partnership. In a corporation, equity capital is money obtained from the sale of shares of ownership in the business. Equity capital is used almost exclusively for long-term financing. Thus it would not be considered for short-term financing needs, such as Leaves and Trees Clothing's first-quarter $7,000 shortfall.

A third type of funding is **debt capital,** which is borrowed money. Debt capital can be borrowed for either short- or long-term use—and a short-term loan seems made to order for Leaves and Trees Clothing's shortfall problem. The firm probably would borrow the needed $7,000 (or perhaps a bit more) at some point during the first quarter and repay it from second-quarter sales revenue.

Proceeds from the sale of assets are the fourth type of funding. Selling assets is a drastic step. However, it may be a reasonable last resort when neither equity capital nor debt capital can be found. Assets also might be sold when they are no longer needed or do not "fit" with the company's core business. To concentrate on its core business and to raise financing, General Motors sold its 8.7 percent stake in Japan's Fuji Heavy Industries, the maker of Subaru cars, to Toyota Motor Corporation for $315 million. General Motors also sold its remaining 11.4 percent in Fuji on the open market raising an additional $800 million.[2]

---

zero-base budgeting a budgeting approach in which every expense in every budget must be justified

capital budget a financial statement that estimates a firm's expenditures for major assets and its long-term financing needs

equity capital money received from the owners or from the sale of shares of ownership in a business

debt capital borrowed money obtained through loans of various types

Monitoring and Evaluating Financial Performance

It is important to ensure that financial plans are implemented properly and to catch potential problems before they become major ones. To prevent problems, financial managers should establish a means of monitoring financial performance. Interim budgets (weekly, monthly, or quarterly) can be prepared for comparison purposes. These comparisons point up areas that require additional or revised planning—or at least areas calling for a more careful investigation.

Financial Services Provided by Banks and Other Financial Institutions

> **Learning Objective** 3
>
> Identify the services provided by banks and financial institutions for their business customers.

It helps a business owner to know his or her banker. Banking services can be divided into three broad categories: traditional services, electronic banking services, and international services.

Traditional Banking Services for Business Clients

Traditional services provided by banks and other financial institutions include savings and chequing accounts, loans, processing credit and debit card transactions, and providing professional advice.

Savings and Chequing Accounts Savings accounts provide a safe place to store money and a very conservative means of investing. The usual *passbook savings account* earns between 0.50 and 2 percent in banks and slightly more in credit unions. A business with excess cash and that is willing to leave money on deposit with a bank for a set period of time can earn a higher rate of interest. To do so, the business firm buys a certificate of deposit. A **certificate of deposit (CD)** (also known as guaranteed income certificate, GIC) is a document stating that the bank will pay the depositor a guaranteed interest rate on money left on deposit for a specified period of time.

Businesses (and individuals) also deposit money in chequing accounts so that they can write cheques to pay for purchases. A **cheque** is a written order for a bank or other financial institution to pay a stated dollar amount to the business or person indicated on the face of the cheque. Monthly charges to businesses are based on the average daily balance in the chequing account and/or the number of cheques written.

Business Loans Banks and other financial institutions provide short- and long-term loans to both businesses. *Short-term business loans* must be repaid within one year or less. Typical uses for the money obtained through short-term loans include solving cash-flow problems, purchasing inventory, financing promotional needs, and meeting

certificate of deposit (CD) (also known as guaranteed income certificate, GIC) a document stating that the bank will pay the depositor a guaranteed interest rate on money left on deposit for a specified period of time

cheque a written order for a bank or other financial institution to pay a stated dollar amount to the business or person indicated on the face of the cheque

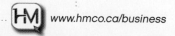

line of credit a loan that is approved before the money is actually needed

revolving credit agreement a guaranteed line of credit

collateral real estate or property pledged as security for a loan

unexpected emergencies. To help ensure that short-term money will be available when needed, many firms establish a line of credit. A **line of credit** is a loan that is approved before the money is actually needed. Because all the necessary paperwork is already completed and the loan is preapproved, the business can obtain the money later without delay, as soon as it is required. Even with a line of credit, a firm may not be able to borrow money if the bank does not have sufficient funds available. For this reason, some firms prefer a **revolving credit agreement**, which is a guaranteed line of credit. Under this type of agreement, the bank guarantees that the money will be available when the borrower needs it. In return for the guarantee, the bank charges a commitment fee ranging from 0.25 to 1.0 percent of the *unused* portion of the revolving credit agreement. The usual interest is charged for the portion that *is* borrowed.

Long-term business loans are repaid over a period of years. The average length of a long-term business loan is generally three to seven years but sometimes as long as fifteen to twenty years. Long-term loans are used most often to finance the expansion of buildings and retail facilities, mergers and acquisitions, replacement of equipment, or product development. Most lenders require some type of collateral for long-term loans. **Collateral** is real estate or property (stocks, bonds, equipment, or any other asset of value) pledged as security for a loan.

Repayment terms and interest rates for both short- and long-term loans are arranged between the lender and the borrower. For businesses, repayment terms may include monthly, quarterly, semiannual, or annual payments.

Credit-Card and Debit-Card Transactions Why has the use of credit transactions increased? For a merchant, the answer is obvious. By depositing charge slips in a bank or other financial institution, the merchant can convert credit-card sales into cash. In return for processing the merchant's credit-card transactions, the bank charges a fee that generally ranges between 1.5 and 5 percent. Typically, small, independent businesses pay more than larger stores or chain stores. Let's assume that you use a VISA credit card to purchase a microwave oven for $300 from Future Shop. At the end of the day, the retailer deposits your charge slip, along with other charge slips, cheques, and currency collected during the day, at its bank. If the bank charges Future Shop 5 percent to process each credit-card transaction, the bank deducts a processing fee of $15 ($300 × 0.05 = $15) for your credit-card transaction and immediately deposits the remainder ($285) in Future Shop's account. The number of credit-card transactions, the total dollar amount of credit sales, and how well the merchant can negotiate the fees the bank charges determine actual fees.

Do not confuse debit cards with credit cards. Although they may look alike, there are important differences. A **debit card** electronically subtracts the amount of the customer's purchase from her or his bank account at the moment the purchase is made. (By contrast, when you use your credit card, the credit-card company extends short-term financing, and you do not pay for your purchase until you receive your next statement.) Debit cards are used most commonly to obtain cash at ATMs and to purchase products and services from retailers.

debit card a card that electronically subtracts the amount of the customer's purchase from her or his bank account at the moment the purchase is made

Electronic Banking Services

An **electronic funds transfer (EFT) system** is a means of performing financial transactions through a computer terminal or telephone hookup. The following three EFT applications are changing how banks help firms do business:

1. *Automated clearinghouses (ACHs).* Designed to reduce the number of paper cheques, automated clearinghouses process cheques, recurring bill payments, government benefits, and employee salaries. For example, large companies use ACHs to transfer wages and salaries directly into their employees' bank accounts, thus eliminating the need to make out individual paycheques.

2. *Point-of-sale (POS) terminals.* A POS terminal is a computerized cash register located in a retail store and connected to a bank's computer. At the cash register, you pull your bank credit or debit card through a magnetic card reader. A central processing centre notifies a computer at your bank that you want to make a purchase. The bank's computer immediately adds the amount to your account for a credit-card transaction. In a similar process, the bank's computer deducts the amount of the purchase from your bank account if you use a debit card. Finally, the amount of your purchase is added to the store's account. The store then is notified that the transaction is complete, and the cash register prints out your receipt.

3. *Electronic cheque conversion (ECC).* Electronic cheque conversion is a process used to convert information from a paper cheque into an electronic payment for merchandise, services, or bills. Here's how ECC works. When you give your completed cheque to a store cashier, the cheque is processed through an electronic system that captures your banking information and the dollar amount of the cheque. Once the cheque is processed, you are asked to sign a receipt, and you get a voided (canceled) cheque back for your records. Finally, the funds to pay for your transaction are transferred into the business firm's account. ECC also can be used for cheques you mail to pay for a purchase or to pay on an account.

Bankers and business owners generally are pleased with EFT systems. EFTs are fast, and they eliminate the costly processing of cheques. However, many customers are reluctant to use online banking or EFT systems. Some simply do not like "the technology," whereas others fear that the computer will garble their accounts.

International Banking Services

Banking services are extremely important for international businesses. Depending on the needs of an international firm, a bank can help by providing a letter of credit or a banker's acceptance.

A **letter of credit** is a legal document issued by a bank or other financial institution guaranteeing to pay a seller a stated amount for a specified period of time—usually thirty to sixty days. Certain conditions, such as delivery of the merchandise, may be specified before payment is made.

A **banker's acceptance** is a written order for a bank to pay a third party a stated amount of money on a specific date. In this case, no conditions are specified. It is simply an order to pay without any strings attached.

electronic funds transfer (EFT) system a means of performing financial transactions through a computer terminal or telephone hookup

letter of credit a legal document issued by a bank or other financial institution guaranteeing to pay a seller a stated amount for a specified period of time

banker's acceptance a written order for a bank to pay a third party a stated amount of money on a specific date

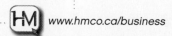

Both a letter of credit and a banker's acceptance are popular methods of paying for import and export transactions. For example, imagine that you are a business owner in Canada who wants to purchase some leather products from a small business in Florence, Italy. You offer to pay for the merchandise with your company's cheque drawn on a Canadian bank, but the Italian business owner is worried about payment. To solve the problem, your bank can issue either a letter of credit or a banker's acceptance to guarantee that payment will be made. In addition to a letter of credit and a banker's acceptance, banks also can use EFT technology to speed international banking transactions.

One other international banking service should be noted. Banks and other financial institutions provide currency exchange. If you place an order for Japanese merchandise valued at $50,000, how do you pay for the order? Do you use Canadian dollars or Japanese yen? To solve this problem, you can use a bank's currency-exchange service. To make payment, you can use either currency and, if necessary, the bank will exchange one currency for the other to complete your transaction.

Sources of Short-Term Debt Financing

Learning Objective ❹

Describe the advantages and disadvantages of different methods of short-term debt financing.

The decision to borrow money does not necessarily mean that a firm is in financial trouble. On the contrary, astute financial management often means regular, responsible borrowing of many different kinds to meet different needs. In this section we examine the sources of *short-term debt financing* available to businesses. In the next two sections we look at long-term financing options: equity capital and debt capital.

Sources of Unsecured Short-Term Financing

Short-term debt financing (money repaid in one year or less) is usually easier to obtain than long-term debt financing for three reasons:

1. For the lender, the shorter repayment period means less risk of nonpayment.
2. The dollar amounts of short-term loans usually are smaller than those of long-term loans.
3. A close working relationship normally exists between the short-term borrower and the lender.

Most lenders do not require collateral for short-term financing. When they do, it is usually because they are concerned about the size of a particular loan, the borrowing firm's poor credit rating, or the general prospects of repayment. **Unsecured financing** is financing that is not backed by collateral. A company seeking unsecured short-term financing has several options.

unsecured financing financing that is not backed by collateral

Trade Credit Manufacturers and wholesalers often provide financial aid to retailers by allowing them thirty to sixty days (or more) in which to pay for merchandise. This delayed payment, known as **trade credit,** is a type of short-term financing extended by a seller who does not require immediate payment after delivery of merchandise. It is the most popular form of short-term financing; 70 to 90 percent of all transactions between businesses involve some trade credit.

Let's assume that a McNally Robinson bookstore receives a shipment of books from a publisher. Along with the merchandise, the publisher sends an invoice that states the terms of payment. McNally Robinson now has two options for payment. First, the book retailer might pay the invoice promptly and take advantage of any cash discount the publisher offers. Cash-discount terms are specified on the invoice. For instance, "2/10, net 30" means that the customer—Indicgo—can take a 2 percent discount if it pays the invoice within ten days of the invoice date. Let's assume that the dollar amount of the invoice is $140,000. In this case, the cash discount is $2,800 ($140,000 × 0.02 = $2,800).

A second option is to wait until the end of the credit period before making payment. If payment is made between eleven and thirty days after the date of the invoice, the customer must pay the entire amount. As long as payment is made before the end of the credit period, the customer maintains the ability to purchase additional merchandise using the trade-credit arrangement.

Promissory Notes Issued to Suppliers A **promissory note** is a written pledge by a borrower to pay a certain sum of money to a creditor at a specified future date. Suppliers uneasy about extending trade credit may be less reluctant to offer credit to customers who sign promissory notes. Unlike trade credit, however, promissory notes usually require the borrower to pay interest. Although repayment periods can extend to one year, most short-term promissory notes are repaid in 60 to 180 days.

A promissory note offers two additional advantages to the firm extending the credit. First, a promissory note is a legally binding and enforceable document that has been signed by the individual or business borrowing the money. Second, most promissory notes are negotiable instruments and the supplier (or company extending credit) may be able to discount, or sell, the note to its own bank. If the note is discounted, the dollar amount the supplier would receive is slightly less than the maturity value because the bank charges a fee for the service. The supplier recoups most of its money immediately and the bank collects the maturity value when the note matures.

Unsecured Bank Loans Banks and other financial institutions offer unsecured short-term loans to businesses at interest rates that vary with each borrower's credit rating. The **prime interest rate** is the lowest rate charged by a bank for a short-term loan. This lowest rate generally is reserved for large corporations with excellent credit ratings. Organizations with good to high credit ratings might pay the prime rate plus 2 percent. Firms with questionable credit ratings might have to pay the prime rate plus 4 percent. (The fact that a banker charges a higher interest rate for a higher-risk loan is a practical application of the risk-return ratio discussed earlier in this chapter.) Of course, if the banker believes that loan repayment may be a problem, the borrower's loan application may well be rejected.

Banks generally offer unsecured short-term loans through promissory notes, a line of credit, or a revolving credit agreement. A bank promissory note is similar to the

trade credit a type of short-term financing extended by a seller who does not require immediate payment after delivery of merchandise

promissory note a written pledge by a borrower to pay a certain sum of money to a creditor at a specified future date

prime interest rate the lowest rate charged by a bank for a short-term loan

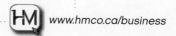

SPOTLIGHT

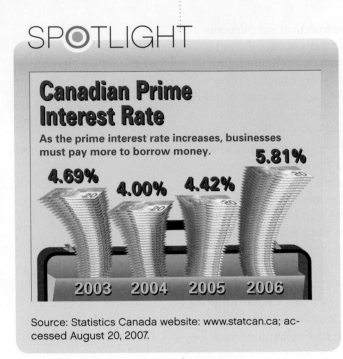

Canadian Prime Interest Rate

As the prime interest rate increases, businesses must pay more to borrow money.

4.69% — 2003
4.00% — 2004
4.42% — 2005
5.81% — 2006

Source: Statistics Canada website: www.statcan.ca; accessed August 20, 2007.

commercial paper a short-term promissory note issued by a large corporation

promissory note issued by suppliers described in the preceding section. For both types of promissory notes, interest rates and repayment terms can be negotiated between the borrower and a bank or supplier. A bank that offers a promissory note or line of credit might require that a *compensating balance* be kept on deposit at the bank. This balance can be as much as 20 percent of the borrowed funds. Assume that the Canadian Imperial Bank of Commerce (CIBC) requires a 20 percent compensating balance on a short-term promissory note or a line of credit. If you borrow $50,000, at least $10,000 ($50,000 × 0.20 = $10,000) of the loan amount must be kept on deposit at the bank. In this situation, the actual interest rate you must pay on the original $50,000 loan increases because you have the use of only $40,000. The bank also might require that every commercial borrower *clean up* (pay off completely) its short-term promissory note or line of credit at least once each year and not use it again for a period of thirty to sixty days.

Commercial Paper Commercial paper is a short-term promissory note issued by a large corporation. Commercial paper is secured only by the reputation of the issuing firm; no collateral is involved. It is usually issued in large denominations, ranging from $5,000 to $100,000. Corporations issuing commercial paper pay interest rates slightly below the interest rates charged by banks for short-term loans. Thus, issuing commercial paper is cheaper than getting short-term financing from a bank. The interest rate a corporation pays when it issues commercial paper is tied to its credit rating and its ability to repay the commercial paper. Large firms with excellent credit reputations can raise large sums of money quickly by issuing commercial paper. GE Capital in the United States, for example, might issue commercial paper totalling millions of dollars. However, commercial paper is not without risk. If a corporation has severe financial problems, it may not be able to repay commercial paper. Enron Corporation, for instance, had issued commercial paper worth millions of dollars at the time of its bankruptcy.[3]

Sources of Secured Short-Term Financing

If a business cannot obtain enough capital through unsecured financing, it must put up collateral to obtain additional short-term financing. Almost any asset can serve as collateral. However, *inventories* and *accounts receivable* are the assets most commonly pledged for short-term financing. Even when it is willing to pledge collateral to back up a loan, a firm that is financially weak may have difficulty obtaining short-term financing.

Loans Secured by Inventory Normally, manufacturers, wholesalers, and retailers have large amounts of money invested in finished goods. In addition, manufacturers carry raw materials and work-in-process inventories. All three types of inventory may be pledged as collateral for short-term loans. However, lenders prefer the much more saleable finished merchandise to raw materials or work-in-process inventories.

A lender may insist that inventory used as collateral be stored in a public warehouse. In such a case, the receipt issued by the warehouse is retained by the lender. Without this receipt, the public warehouse will not release the merchandise. The lender releases the warehouse receipt—and the merchandise—to the borrower when the borrowed money is repaid. In addition to paying the interest on the loan, the borrower must pay for storage in the public warehouse. As a result, this type of loan is more expensive than an unsecured short-term loan.

Loans Secured by Receivables As defined in Chapter 15, *accounts receivable* are amounts owed to a firm by its customers. They are created when trade credit is given to customers and usually are due within thirty to sixty days. A firm can pledge its accounts receivable as collateral to obtain short-term financing. A lender may advance 70 to 80 percent of the dollar amount of the receivables. First, however, it conducts a thorough investigation to determine the *quality* of the receivables. (The quality of the receivables is the credit standing of the firm's customers, coupled with the customers' ability to repay their credit obligations.) If a favourable determination is made, the loan is approved. When the borrowing firm collects from a customer whose account has been pledged as collateral, it must turn the money over to the lender as partial repayment of the loan. An alternative approach is to notify the borrower's credit customers to make their payments directly to the lender.

Factoring Accounts Receivable

Accounts receivable can be used in one other way to help raise short-term financing: They can be sold to a factoring company (or factor). A **factor** is a firm that specializes in buying other firms' accounts receivable. The factor buys the accounts receivable for less than their face value, but it collects the full dollar amount when each account is due. The factor's profit thus is the difference between the face value of the accounts receivable and the amount the factor has paid for them. Generally, the amount of profit the factor receives is based on the risk the factor assumes. Risk, in this case, is the probability that the accounts receivable will not be repaid when they mature.

Even though the firm selling its accounts receivable gets less than face value, it receives needed cash immediately. Moreover, it has shifted both the task of collecting and the risk of nonpayment to the factor, which now owns the accounts receivable. In many cases, the firm selling its accounts receivable must obtain approval from the factor *before* selling merchandise to a credit customer. Thus the firm receives instant feedback on whether the factor will purchase the credit customer's account. Generally, customers whose accounts receivable have been factored are given instructions to make their payments directly to the factor.

factor a firm that specializes in buying other firms' accounts receivable

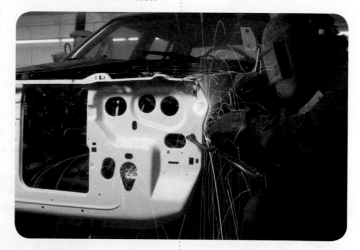

Factoring accounts receivable

An auto body repair shop may factor its accounts receivable because of the delay between performing repairs, thus incurring expenses, and receiving payment from insurance companies.

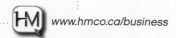

www.hmco.ca/business

Table 16.2

Comparison of Short-Term Financing Methods

TYPE OF FINANCING	COST	REPAYMENT PERIOD	BUSINESSES THAT MIGHT USE IT	COMMENTS
Trade credit	Low, if any	30–60 days	All businesses	Usually no finance charge
Promissory note issued to suppliers	Moderate	1 year or less	All businesses	Usually unsecured but requires legal document
Unsecured bank loan	Moderate	1 year or less	All businesses	Promissory note, a line of credit, or revolving credit agreement generally required
Commercial paper	Moderate	1 year or less	Large corporations with high credit ratings	Available only to large firms
Secured loan	High	1 year or less	Firms with questionable credit ratings	Inventory or accounts receivable often used as collateral
Factoring	High	None	Firms that have large numbers of credit customers	Accounts receivable sold to a factor

Cost Comparisons

Table 16.2 compares the various types of short-term financing. As you can see, trade credit is the least expensive. Factoring of accounts receivable is typically the highest-cost method shown.

For many purposes, short-term financing suits a firm's needs perfectly. At other times, however, long-term financing may be more appropriate. In this case, a business might try to raise equity capital or long-term debt capital.

Sources of Equity Financing

Learning Objective 5

Evaluate the advantages and disadvantages of equity financing.

Sources of long-term equity financing vary with the size and type of business. As mentioned earlier, a sole proprietorship or partnership acquires equity capital (sometimes referred to as *owner's equity*) when the owner or owners invest money in the business. Equity-financing options for corporations include the sale of stock and the use of profits not distributed to owners. All three types of businesses also can obtain venture capital.

Selling Stock

Some equity capital is used to start every business—sole proprietorship, partnership, or corporation. In the case of corporations, stockholders who buy shares in the company provide the equity capital.

Initial Public Offerings An **initial public offering (IPO)** occurs when a corporation sells common stock to the general public for the first time. One of the largest IPOs in recent history was for the search engine Google, which raised over $2.7 billion that it could use to fund expansion and other business activities.[4] Established companies that plan to raise capital by selling subsidiaries to the public also can use IPOs. For example, McDonald's sold a part of its stake in its Chipotle casual restaurant subsidiary. McDonald's will use the money it receives from the IPO to fund capital expenditures and expansion of its current business activities.[5] Generally, corporations sell off subsidiaries for two reasons. First, the sale of a subsidiary can boost the value of the firm's core business. Second, the sale of a subsidiary also can bolster corporate finances and improve the parent company's balance sheet if the money is used to reduce corporate debt.

A corporation selling stock often will use an **investment banking firm**—an organization that assists corporations in raising funds, usually by helping to sell new issues of stocks, bonds, or other financial securities. The investment banking firm generally charges a fee of 2 to 20 percent of the proceeds received by the corporation issuing the securities. The size of the commission depends on the financial health of the corporation issuing the new securities and the size of the new security issue.

Although a corporation can have only one IPO, it can sell additional stock after the IPO, assuming that there is a market for the company's stock. Even though the cost of selling stock (often referred to as *flotation costs*) is high, the *ongoing* costs associated with this type of equity financing are low for two reasons. First, the corporation does not have to repay money obtained from the sale of stock because the corporation is under no legal obligation to do so. If you purchase corporate stock and later decide to sell your stock, you can sell it to another investor—not the corporation.

A second advantage of selling stock is that a corporation is under no legal obligation to pay dividends to stockholders. As noted in Chapter 5, a *dividend* is a distribution of earnings to the stockholders of a corporation. For any reason (if a company has a bad year, for example), the board of directors can vote to omit dividend payments. Earnings then are retained for use in funding business operations. Of course, corporate management will probably hear from unhappy stockholders if expected dividends are omitted too frequently.

There are two types of stock: common and preferred. Each type has advantages and drawbacks as a means of long-term financing.

Common Stock In Chapter 5, common stock was described as the most basic form of corporate ownership whose owners may vote on corporate matters but whose claims on profits and assets are subordinate to the claims of others. In return for the financing provided by selling common stock, management must make certain concessions to stockholders that may restrict or change corporate policies. By law, every corporation must hold an annual meeting, at which the holders of common stock vote

initial public offering (IPO) when a corporation sells common stock to the general public for the first time

investment banking firm an organization that assists corporations in raising funds, usually by helping to sell new issues of stocks, bonds, or other financial securities

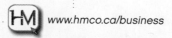

for the board of directors and approve or disapprove major corporate actions. Among such actions are

1. Amendments to the corporate charter or by-laws
2. Sale of certain assets
3. Mergers and acquisitions
4. New issues of preferred stock or bonds
5. Changes in the amount of common stock issued

Few investors will buy common stock unless they believe that their investment will increase in value. There are three basic ways to profit from stock investments: from dividend payments, from an increase in the value of the stock, or because of stock splits. One of the primary reasons many stockholders invest in common stock is *dividend income*. Generally, dividends are paid quarterly. Another way to profit on stock investments is to sell the stock when the market value of the stock is higher than the original purchase price. Finally, directors of many corporations feel that there is an optimal price range within which their firm's stock is most attractive to investors. When the market value increases beyond that price range, they may declare a *stock split* to bring the price down to the ideal range. Although there are *no guarantees that the stock will increase in value after a split*, the stock is more attractive to the investing public because of the potential for a rapid increase in dollar value.

Preferred Stock As noted in Chapter 5, the owners of *preferred stock* must receive their dividends before holders of common stock receive theirs. Moreover, the preferred-stock dividend amount is specified on the stock certificate. And the owners of preferred stock have first claim, after bond owners and general creditors, on corporate assets if the firm is dissolved or enters bankruptcy. These features make preferred stock a more conservative investment with an added degree of safety and a more predictable source of income when compared with common stock. Even so, as with common stock, the board of directors must approve dividends on preferred stock and this type of financing does not represent a debt that must be legally repaid. In return for preferential treatment, preferred stockholders generally give up the right to vote at a corporation's annual meeting.

To make preferred stock more attractive to investors, some corporations include a conversion feature. **Convertible preferred stock** is preferred stock that an owner can exchange for a specified number of shares of common stock. This conversion feature provides the investor with the safety of preferred stock and the hope of greater speculative gain through conversion to common stock.

Retained Earnings

Most large corporations distribute only a portion of their after-tax earnings to stockholders. The portion of a corporation's profits not distributed to stockholders is called **retained earnings.** Because they are undistributed profits, retained earnings are considered a form of equity financing.

The amount of retained earnings in any year is determined by corporate management and approved by the board of directors. Most small and growing corporations pay no cash dividend—or a very small dividend—to their stockholders. All or most

convertible preferred stock preferred stock that an owner may exchange for a specified number of shares of common stock

retained earnings the portion of a corporation's profits not distributed to stockholders

earnings are reinvested in the business for R&D, expansion, or the funding of major projects. Reinvestment tends to increase the value of the firm's stock while it provides essentially cost-free financing for the business. More mature corporations may distribute 40 to 60 percent of their after-tax profits as dividends. Utility companies and other corporations with very stable earnings often pay out as much as 80 to 90 percent of what they earn. Retained earnings can amount to a hefty bit of financing for a large corporation.

Venture Capital and Private Placements

To establish a new business or expand an existing one, an entrepreneur may try to obtain venture capital. In Chapter 6 we defined *venture capital* as money invested in small (and sometimes struggling) firms that have the potential to become very successful. Most venture capital firms do not invest in the typical small business—a neighbourhood convenience store or a local dry cleaner—but in firms that have the potential to become extremely profitable. And while venture capital firms are willing to take chances, they are also more selective about where they invest their money after the high-tech bust that occurred in the last part of the 1990s and first few years of the twenty-first century. Generally, a venture capital firm consists of a pool of investors, a traditional partnership established by a wealthy family, or a joint venture formed by corporations with money to invest. In return for financing, these investors generally receive an equity position in the business and share in its profits.

ENTREPRENEURIAL CHALLENGE

Finding the Money

How can an entrepreneur find the money for expansion, an important acquisition, or a new R&D initiative? Obtaining financing from a boutique private equity group can be a good alternative. Boutique private equity groups are like venture capital firms but much, much smaller. They often provide financing for companies too small to go public or attract the interest of the large venture capital firms.

Advantages

- The owner gets an infusion of funding without selling the business or going into debt.

- The owner benefits from the boutique's specialization, expertise, and advice.

- The boutique can provide a reality check on the owner's financial management skills.

Disadvantages

- Some boutiques insist on a majority interest in exchange for a sizable investment.

- The owner may chafe at the boutique's close scrutiny of company affairs.

- The owner may have to give control to the boutique if the investment doesn't achieve a specified rate of return.

private placement occurs when stock and other corporate securities are sold directly to insurance companies, pension funds, or large institutional or wealthy investors

Another method of raising capital is through a private placement. A **private placement** occurs when stock and other corporate securities are sold directly to insurance companies, pension funds, large institutional, or wealthy investors. When compared with selling stocks and other corporate securities to the public, there are often fewer government regulations and the cost is generally less when the securities are sold through a private placement. Typically, terms between the buyer and seller are negotiated when a private placement is used to raise capital.

Sources of Long-Term Debt Financing

Learning Objective 6

Evaluate the advantages and disadvantages of long-term debt financing.

As we pointed out earlier in this chapter, businesses borrow money on a short-term basis for many valid reasons other than desperation. There are equally valid reasons for long-term borrowing. In addition to using borrowed money to meet the long-term needs listed in Table 16.1, successful businesses often use the financial leverage it creates to improve their financial performance. **Financial leverage** is the use of borrowed funds to increase the return on owners' equity. The principle of financial leverage works as long as a firm's earnings are larger than the interest charged for the borrowed money.

financial leverage the use of borrowed funds to increase the return on owners' equity

To understand how financial leverage can increase a firm's return on owners' equity, study the information for Cypress Springs Plastics presented in Table 16.3. Pete Johnston, the owner of the firm, is trying to decide how best to finance a $100,000

Table 16.3

Analysis of the Effect of Additional Capital from Debt or Equity for Cypress Springs Plastics, Inc.

ADDITIONAL DEBT		ADDITIONAL EQUITY	
Owners' equity	$500,000	Owners' equity	$500,000
Additional equity	+0	Additional equity	+100,000
Total equity	$500,000	Total equity	$600,000
Loan (at 10 percent)	+100,000	No loan	+0
Total capital	$600,000	Total capital	$600,000
YEAR-END EARNINGS			
Gross profit	$95,000	Gross profit	$95,000
Less loan interest	−10,000	No interest	−0
Operating profit	$85,000	Operating profit	$95,000
Return on owners' equity	17 percent	Return on owners' equity	15.8 percent
($85,000 ÷ $500,000 = 17 percent)		($95,000 ÷ $600,000 = 15.8 percent)	

purchase of new high-tech manufacturing equipment. He could borrow the money and pay 10 percent annual interest. As a second option, Johnston could invest an additional $100,000 in the firm. Assuming that the firm earns $95,000 a year and that annual interest for this loan totals $10,000 ($100,000 × 0.10 = $10,000), the return on owners' equity for Cypress Springs Plastics would be higher if the firm borrowed the additional financing. Return on owners' equity—a topic covered in Chapter 15—is determined by dividing a firm's net income by the dollar amount of owners' equity. The return on the owners of Cypress Springs Plastics equity equals 17 percent ($85,000 ÷ $500,000 = 0.17, or 17 percent) if Johnston borrows the additional $100,000. The firm's return on owners' equity would decrease to 15.8 percent ($95,000 ÷ $600,000 = 0.158, or 15.8 percent) if Johnston invests an additional $100,000 in the business.

The most obvious danger when using financial leverage is that the firm's earnings may be less than expected. If this situation occurs, the fixed interest charge actually works to reduce or eliminate the return on owners' equity. Of course, borrowed money eventually must be repaid. Finally, because lenders always have the option to turn down a loan request, many managers are reluctant to rely on borrowed money.

For a small business, long-term debt financing generally is limited to loans. Large corporations have the additional option of issuing corporate bonds.

Long-Term Loans

Many businesses finance their long-range activities such as those listed in Table 16.1 with loans from banks and other financial institutions. Manufacturers and suppliers of heavy machinery also may provide long-term debt financing by granting extended credit to their customers.

Term-Loan Agreements When the loan repayment period is longer than one year, the borrower must sign a term-loan agreement. A **term-loan agreement** is a promissory note that requires a borrower to repay a loan in monthly, quarterly, semiannual, or annual installments. Although repayment may be as long as fifteen to twenty years, long-term business loans normally are repaid in three to seven years.

Assume that Pete Johnson, the owner of Cypress Springs Plastics, decides to borrow $100,000 and take advantage of the principle of financial leverage illustrated in Table 16.3. Although the firm's return on owners' equity does increase, interest must be paid each year, and eventually, the loan must be repaid. To pay off a $100,000 loan over a three-year period with annual payments, Cypress Springs Plastics must pay $33,333 on the loan balance plus $10,000 annual interest, or a total of $43,333 the first year. While the amount of interest decreases each year because of the previous year's payment on the loan balance, annual payments of this amount are still a large commitment for a small firm such as Cypress Springs Plastics.

The interest rate and repayment terms for term loans often are based on such factors as the reasons for borrowing, the borrowing firm's credit rating, and the value of collateral. Acceptable collateral includes real estate, machinery, and equipment. Lenders also may require that borrowers maintain a minimum amount of working capital.

The Basics of Getting a Loan Preparation is the key when applying for a business loan. To begin the process, you should get to know potential lenders before requesting debt financing. While there may be many potential lenders that can provide

term-loan agreement a promissory note that requires a borrower to repay a loan in monthly, quarterly, semiannual, or annual installments

the money you need, the logical place to borrow money is where your business does its banking. This fact underscores the importance of maintaining adequate balances in the firm's bank accounts. Before applying for a loan, you also may want to check your firm's credit rating with a national credit bureau such as D&B (formerly known as Dun & Bradstreet).

Typically, you will be asked to fill out a loan application. In addition to the loan application, the lender also will want to see your current business plan. Be sure to explain what your business is, how much funding you require to accomplish your goals and objectives, and how the loan will be repaid. Most lenders insist that you submit current financial statements that have been prepared by a chartered accountant (CA). Then compile a list of references that includes your suppliers, other lenders, or the professionals with whom you are associated. Once you submit your application, business plan, supporting financial documents, and list of references, a bank officer or a loan committee will examine the loan application and supporting documentation. You also may be asked to discuss your request with a loan officer. Your loan probably will be approved. If not, try to determine why your loan request was rejected.

Corporate Bonds

In addition to loans, large corporations can choose to issue bonds in denominations of $1,000 to $50,000. Although the usual face value for corporate bonds is $1,000, the total face value of all the bonds in an issue usually amounts to millions of dollars. In fact, one of the reasons why corporations sell bonds is that they can borrow a lot of money from a lot of bondholders and raise larger amounts of money than could be borrowed from one lender. A **corporate bond** is a corporation's written pledge that it will repay a specified amount of money with interest. The **maturity date** is the date on which the corporation is to repay the borrowed money.

corporate bond a corporation's written pledge that it will repay a specified amount of money with interest

maturity date the date on which a corporation is to repay borrowed money

registered bond a bond registered in the owner's name by the issuing company

Until a bond's maturity, a corporation pays interest to the bond owner at the stated rate. For example, assume that you purchase a $1000 bond issued by Air Canada and the interest rate is 5 percent. In this situation, you receive interest of $50 ($1000 × .05 = $50) a year. Because interest for corporate bonds in usually paid semiannually, Air Canada pays the interest every six months in $25 installments.

Types of Bonds Today, most corporate bonds are registered bonds. A **registered bond** is a bond registered in the owner's name by the issuing company. Until the maturity date, the registered owner receives periodic interest payments. On the maturity date, the owner returns a registered bond to the corporation and receives cash equaling the face value.

Corporate bonds generally are classified as debentures, mortgage bonds, or convertible bonds.

* *Debenture bonds* are backed only by the reputation of the issuing corporation.
* *Mortgage bonds* are secured by various assets of the issuing firm.
* *Convertible bonds* can be exchanged, at the owner's option, for a specified number of shares of the corporation's common stock.

Repayment Provisions for Corporate Bonds Maturity dates for bonds generally range from ten to thirty years after the date of issue. If the interest is not paid or the firm becomes insolvent, bond owners' claims on the assets of the corporation take precedence over the claims of both common and preferred stockholders. Some bonds are callable before the maturity date; that is, a corporation can buy back, or redeem, them. The corporation might pay the bond owner a call premium for these bonds. The amount of the call premium is specified, along with other provisions, in the bond indenture. The **bond indenture** is a legal document that details all the conditions relating to a bond issue.

Before deciding if bonds are the best way to obtain corporate financing, managers must determine if the company can afford to pay the interest on the corporate bonds. It should be obvious that the larger the bond issue, the higher the dollar amount of interest will be. For example, assume that Air Canada issues bonds with a face value of $100 million to finance the purchase of new airplanes. If the interest rate is 4.875 percent, the interest on this bond issue is $4,875,000 ($100 million × 0.04875 = $4,875,000) each year until the bonds are repaid. In addition, corporate bonds must be redeemed for their face value at maturity. If the corporation defaults on (does not pay) either interest payments or repayment of the bond at maturity, owners of bonds can force the firm into bankruptcy.

A corporation can use one of three methods to ensure that it has sufficient funds available to redeem a bond issue. First, it can issue the bonds as **serial bonds,** which are bonds of a single issue that mature on different dates. For example, a company can use a twenty-five-year $50 million bond issue to finance its expansion. None of the bonds mature during the first fifteen years. Thereafter, 10 percent of the bonds mature each year until all the bonds are retired at the end of the twenty-fifth year. Second, the corporation can establish a sinking fund. A **sinking fund** is a sum of money to which deposits are made each year for the purpose of redeeming a bond issue. When Pacific Gas & Electric Company sold a $200 million bond issue, the company agreed to contribute to a sinking fund twice a year until the bond's maturity in the year 2024. Third, a corporation can pay off an old bond issue by selling new bonds. Although this may appear to perpetuate the corporation's long-term debt, a number of utility companies and railroads use this repayment method.

A corporation that issues bonds also must appoint a **trustee,** an individual or an independent firm that acts as the bond owners' representative. A trustee's duties are handled most often by a commercial bank or other large financial institution. The corporation must report to the trustee periodically regarding its ability to make interest payments and eventually redeem the bonds. In turn, the trustee transmits this information to the bond owners, along with its own evaluation of the corporation's ability to pay.

Cost Comparisons

Table 16.4 compares some of the methods that can be used to obtain long-term equity and debt financing. Although the initial cost of issuing stock is high, selling common stock generally is the first choice for most financial managers. Once the stock is sold and upfront costs are paid, the *ongoing* costs of using stock to finance a business are low. The type of long-term financing that generally has the highest *ongoing* costs is a long-term loan (debt).

bond indenture a legal document that details all the conditions relating to a bond issue

serial bonds bonds of a single issue that mature on different dates

sinking fund a sum of money to which deposits are made each year for the purpose of redeeming a bond issue

trustee an individual or an independent firm that acts as the bond owners' representative

Table 16.4

Comparison of Long-Term Financing Methods

TYPE OF FINANCING	REPAYMENT	REPAYMENT PERIOD	COST/DIVIDENDS INTEREST	BUSINESSES THAT USE IT
EQUITY				
Common stock	No	None	High initial flotation cost; low ongoing costs because dividends and repayment not required	All corporations that sell stock to investors
Preferred stock	No	None	Dividends not required but must be paid before common stockholders receive any dividends	Large corporations that have an established investor base of common stockholders
DEBT				
Long-term loan	Yes	Usually 3–7 years	Interest rates between 7 and 13 percent depending on economic conditions and the financial stability of the company requesting the loan	All firms that can meet the lender's repayment and collateral requirements
Corporate bond	Yes	Usually 10–30 years	Interest rates between 5 and 10 percent depending on economic conditions and the financial stability of the company issuing the bonds	Large corporations that investors trust

As you complete this course, you must decide if you want to continue your education and obtain more university credits or a degree or begin your career.

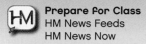

➜ **RETURN TO INSIDE BUSINESS**

Often budding entrepreneurs in developing countries are located many miles from the nearest bank branch or lack the official identification documents that banks usually require. As microfinancing becomes more common, institutions are finding ways around these barriers. Some institutions send representatives to villages every week to meet borrowers and collect payments. Others are taking a more high-tech approach. In India, some banks are installing automated teller machines that use customers' fingerprints as identification.

Microfinance is also opening business doors for Canadian entrepreneurs who need money for equipment or marketing. However, these loans can run to $10,000 or higher because the cost of starting and running a business in the Canada can be more, and often considerably so, than in developing countries.

Questions

1. Why would a financial institution choose not to engage in microfinance?

2. If you were a banker deciding whether to approve a microfinance loan, what would you ask the business borrower before you make your decision?

CHAPTER REVIEW

1 Explain the need for financial management in business.

Financial management consists of all activities concerned with obtaining money and using it effectively. Short-term financing is money that will be used for one year or less. There are many short-term needs, but cash flow and inventory are two for which financing is often required. Long-term financing is money that will be used for more than one year. Such financing may be required for a business start-up, for a merger or acquisition, for new product development, for long-term marketing activities, for replacement of equipment, or for expansion of facilities. Financial management can be viewed as a two-sided problem. On one side, the uses of funds often dictate the type or types of financing needed by a business. On the other side, the activities a business can undertake are determined by the types of financing available. Financial managers also must consider the risk-return ratio when making decisions.

2 Summarize the process of planning for financial management.

A financial plan begins with an organization's goals and objectives. Next, these goals and objectives are "translated" into departmental budgets that detail expected income and expenses. From these budgets, which may be combined into an overall cash budget, the financial manager determines what funding will be needed and where it may be obtained. Whereas departmental and cash budgets emphasize short-term financing needs, a capital budget can be used to estimate a firm's expenditures for major assets and its long-term financing needs. The four principal sources of financing are sales revenues, equity capital, debt capital, and proceeds from the sale of assets. Once the needed funds have been obtained, the financial manager is responsible for monitoring and evaluating the firm's financial activities.

Identify the services provided by banks and financial institutions for their business customers.

Most business firms would find it hard to operate without the services provided by banks and other financial institutions. To meet the needs of their business customers, banks and other financial institutions offer a tempting array of services. Among the most important and attractive banking services for businesses are savings and chequing accounts, loans, and processing credit-card and debit-card transactions. Increased use of electronic banking services (automated clearinghouses, point-of-sale terminals, and electronic cheque conversion) is also changing how banks help firms do business. A bank can provide letters of credit and banker's acceptances for firms in the global marketplace that will reduce the risk of nonpayment for sellers. Banks and financial institutions also can provide currency exchange to reduce payment problems for import or export transactions.

4 **Describe the advantages and disadvantages of different methods of short-term debt financing.**

Most short-term financing is unsecured; that is, no collateral is required. Sources of unsecured short-term financing include trade credit, promissory notes issued to suppliers, unsecured bank loans, and commercial paper. Sources of secured short-term financing include loans secured by inventory and accounts receivable. A firm also can sell its receivables to factors. Trade credit is the least expensive source of short-term financing. The cost of financing through other sources generally depends on the source and on the credit rating of the firm that requires the financing. Factoring generally is the most expensive approach.

5 **Evaluate the advantages and disadvantages of equity financing.**

A corporation can raise equity capital by selling either common or preferred stock. Common stock is voting stock; holders of common stock elect the corporation's directors and must approve changes to the corporate charter. Holders of preferred stock must be paid dividends before holders of common stock are paid any dividends. Another source of equity funding is retained earnings, which is the portion of a business's profits not distributed to stockholders. Venture capital—money invested in small (and sometimes struggling) firms that have the potential to become very successful—is yet another source of equity funding. Generally, the venture capital is provided by investors, partnerships established by wealthy families, or a joint venture formed by corporations with money to invest. In return, they receive an equity position in the firm and share in the profits of the business. Finally, a private placement can be used to sell stocks and other corporate securities.

6 **Evaluate the advantages and disadvantages of long-term debt financing.**

For a small business, debt financing generally is limited to loans. Large corporations have the additional option of selling corporate bonds. Regardless of whether the business is small or large, it can take advantage of financial leverage. Financial leverage is the use of borrowed funds to increase the return on owners' equity. The rate of interest for long-term loans usually depends on the financial status of the borrower, the reason for borrowing, the borrowing firm's credit rating, and the kind of collateral pledged to back up the loan. Acceptable collateral includes real estate, machinery, and equipment. Long-term business loans normally are repaid in three to seven years but can be as long as fifteen to twenty years. Term loan agreements usually require a business to repay borrowed money in monthly, quarterly, semiannual, or annual installments. Money realized from the sale of corporate bonds must be repaid when the bonds mature. In addition, the corporation must pay interest—usually every six months—on the borrowed money from the time the bonds are sold until maturity. Maturity dates for bonds generally range from ten to thirty years after the date of issue. Three types of bonds—debentures, mortgage bonds, and convertible bonds—are sold to raise debt capital. When comparing the cost of equity and debt long-term financing, the ongoing costs of using stock (equity) to finance a business are low. The most expensive is a long-term loan (debt).

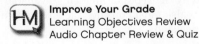
Improve Your Grade
Learning Objectives Review
Audio Chapter Review & Quiz

Review Questions

1. How does short-term financing differ from long-term financing? Give two business uses for each type of financing.
2. In your own words, describe the risk-return ratio.
3. What is the function of a cash budget? A capital budget?
4. How does a financial manager monitor and evaluate a firm's financing?
5. What is the difference between a line of credit and a revolving credit agreement?
6. How do automated clearinghouses, point-of-sale terminals, and electronic cheque conversion affect how a business firm operates?
7. How can a bank or other financial institution help Canadian businesses to compete in the global marketplace?
8. How important is trade credit as a source of short-term financing?
9. Why would a supplier require a customer to sign a promissory note?
10. What is the prime rate? Who gets the prime rate?
11. Explain how factoring works. Of what benefit is factoring to a firm that sells its receivables?
12. What are the advantages of financing through the sale of common stock? Preferred stock?
13. Where do a corporation's retained earnings come from? What are the advantages of this type of financing?
14. What is venture capital? What is a private placement?
15. Describe how financial leverage can increase return on owners' equity.
16. For a corporation, what are the advantages of corporate bonds over long-term loans?

Discussion Questions

1. What does a financial manager do? How can he or she monitor a firm's financial success?
2. If you were the financial manager for Leaves and Trees Clothing, what would you do with the excess cash that the firm expects in the second and fourth quarters? (See Figure 16.4.)
3. Assume that you are a business owner who needs to borrow $60,000. What can you do to convince the loan officer that you are a good credit risk?
4. Why would a supplier offer both trade credit and cash discounts to its customers?
5. How can a small-business owner or corporate manager use financial leverage to improve the firm's profits and return on owners' equity?
6. In what circumstances might a large corporation sell stock rather than bonds to obtain long-term financing? In what circumstances would it sell bonds rather than stock?

Mountain Thyme Takes Time to Plan Financing

Mike and Rhonda Hicks dreamed of opening their own bed-and-breakfast business after vacationing in cozy New England inns during one colourful fall season. The would-be entrepreneurs lived in Dallas, where Mike worked in the software industry. Although the two talked and talked about running a bed-and-breakfast, they didn't actually pursue the idea until pushed by Polly Felker, Rhonda's mother.

Felker had retired to Hot Springs, Arkansas, and was working on an herb farm twenty miles out of town in rural Jessieville, at the edge of the Ouachita National Forest. After listening to her daughter and son-in-law kick around the bed-and-breakfast concept any number of times, Felker told them to get down to business. The couple sought permission to buy nine scenic acres from the herb farm. Then they hired an architect to design an attractive country inn with eight spacious guest rooms, an old-fashioned wraparound porch, and private quarters for the owners. The Hickses estimated that purchasing the land, building the inn, buying furniture, and landscaping the property would cost nearly $600,000.

The next step was to get financing for what would be called the Mountain Thyme Bed & Breakfast Inn. The entrepreneurs approached bank after bank, explaining their idea and showing their plans, but could not get their loan application past worried bankers. Was the inn located too far from the well-known spa town of Hot Springs? Would guests find their way through the back roads and down the secluded gravel driveway to the inn? What about the size of the loan? "When you're used to doing simple little home mortgages, funding a project with that kind of price tag was indeed a scary thing," Mike Hicks observes.

After eighteen months of searching, the couple located a financial institution in California that agreed to approve part of the funding as a Small Business Administration loan. The couple also was introduced to the Arkansas Certified Development Corp. (ACDC), part of the nonprofit Arkansas Capital Corporation Group, which specializes in financing small businesses within the state. When an ACDC loan officer drove to Jessieville to see the site of the proposed inn, "he thought it was a little slice of heaven and fell in love with it," Rhonda Hicks remembers. The ACDC al-

lowed the Hickses to borrow the money they needed at a good rate—and construction on the inn could finally begin.

Polly Felker joined her daughter and son-in-law as a partner in the inn. Chef Felker has been cooking up gourmet breakfasts and late-night treats since Mountain Thyme opened in 1998. The inn's comfortable rooms, beautiful surroundings, and delectable food have brought it nationwide acclaim. Moreover, the owners have been listed among the Top 10 Friendliest Innkeepers in the United States.

Now that their dream of operating an inn has come true, the owners host seminars so that others can learn all about the business of inn ownership. They're always improving the inn with new snacks, new services, new gift items, and more. Although the inn isn't always full, its occupancy rate is high enough to make Mountain Thyme a financial success—and to allow the three partners to take a little time off now and then. Despite the years of planning and hard work, Mike Hicks says, "There'd be no bed-and-breakfast" without the funding approved by the ACDC. "But other than the trouble we had finding some money in the beginning, it'd be hard for this to be working out any better."

For more information about this company, go to www .mountainthyme.com.

Questions:

1. If you were a banker, would you have approved the loan the Hickses needed to build their bed-and-breakfast? Explain your answer.

2. How can establishing realistic goals and objectives, budgeting, and monitoring and evaluating financial performance help the Hickses to manage the Mountain Thyme Inn?

3. Why would the owners need a capital budget for Mountain Thyme years after its opening?

4. After reading this case and seeing how difficult it was for the Hickses to obtain financing, were the benefits of a small business such as this bed-and-breakfast worth the effort? Justify your answer.

BUILDING SKILLS FOR CAREER SUCCESS

1. Exploring the Internet

Finding capital for new business start-ups is never an easy task. Besides a good business plan, those seeking investor funds must be convincing and clear about how their business activities will provide sufficient revenue to pay back investors who help to get them going in the first place. To find out what others have done, it is useful to read histories of successful start-ups as well as failures in journals that specialize in this area. Visit the text website for updates to this exercise.

Assignment

1. Examine articles that profile at least three successes or failures in the following publications and highlight the main points that led to either result.

   Canadian Business Magazine (www .canadianbusiness.com

   Globe and Mail (www.globeandmail.com)

   National Post (www.canada.com/ nationalpost)

   Fast Company (www.fastcompany.com)
2. What are the shared similarities?
3. What advice would you give to a start-up venture after reading these stories?

2. Building Team Skills

Suppose that for the past three years you have been repairing lawn mowers in your garage. Your business has grown steadily and, recently, you hired two part-time workers. Your garage is no longer adequate for your business; it is also in violation of the city code, and you have been fined twice for noncompliance. You have decided that it is time to find another location for your shop and that it also would be a good time to expand your business. If the business continues to grow in the new location, you plan to hire a full-time employee to repair small appliances. You are concerned, however, about how you will get the money to move your shop and get it established in a new location.

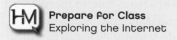

Prepare for Class
Exploring the Internet

Assignment

1. With all class members participating, use brainstorming to identify the following:
   a. The funds you will need to accomplish your business goals
   b. The sources of short-term financing available to you
   c. Problems that might prevent you from getting a short-term loan
   d. How you will repay the money if you get a loan
2. Have a classmate write the ideas on the board.
3. Discuss how you can overcome any problems that might hamper your current chances of getting a loan and how your business can improve its chances of securing short-term loans in the future.
4. Summarize what you learned from participating in this exercise.

3. Researching Different Careers

Financial managers are responsible for determining the best way to raise funds, for ensuring that the funds are used to accomplish their firm's goals and objectives, and for developing and implementing their firm's financial plan. Their decisions have a direct impact on the firm's level of success. When managers do not pay enough attention to finances, a firm is likely to fail.

Assignment

1. Investigate the job of financial manager by searching the library or Internet and/or by interviewing a financial manager.
2. Find answers to the following questions:
   a. What skills do financial managers need?
   b. What opportunities are available?
   c. What types of firms are most likely to hire financial managers? What is the employment potential?
3. Prepare a report on your findings.

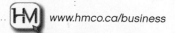

RUNNING A BUSINESS PART VI
Information Systems and Accounting at Finagle A Bagel

Like the hole in a bagel, any hole in Finagle A Bagel's information and accounting systems means less dough for the company. Co-presidents Alan Litchman and Laura Trust and their management team could not make timely, informed decisions to build the business profitably without reliable systems for collecting data, processing them, and presenting the results in a meaningful way.

Putting Technology to Work

Regina Jerome is Finagle A Bagel's director of information systems. She and her assistant are responsible for running the computerized accounting system in the company support centre, as well as the management information and marketing information systems. As a small business, Finagle A Bagel can't afford to spend money for the sake of having the fastest computer equipment or the flashiest software. Having a limited budget means that "it's absolutely imperative that every piece of technology that we invest in directly supports our business," she says.

One of Jerome's biggest challenges has been implementing a point-of-sale system that supports the information needs of the stores as well as of the senior managers. Unlike restaurant chains that sell standard menu items, Finagle A Bagel customizes everything to the individual customer's taste. Thus store employees must be able to record, prepare, and serve complicated orders. "We designed our point-of-sale system so that when a customer orders, the system follows our menu and enables our cashiers to deliver exactly what the customer ordered," Jerome says. "At the same time, the system collects all the pertinent financial information. Every transaction is recorded and can be retrieved by minute, by day, by store, by cashier, and by terminal." With information from the point-of-sale system, general managers can analyze detailed sales patterns before making decisions about store staffing levels, food orders, and other day-to-day operational issues.

Tracking Cash, Calculating Profits

The co-presidents use the financial data drawn from every cash register connected to this point-of-sale system to reconcile daily store sales with daily bank deposits. As a result, co-president Litchman knows by 7:30 each morning how much money was deposited on the previous day and the total amount the company has to cover payroll, food purchases, and other expenses. He also knows if a store's reported sales match its bank deposit. If not, a senior manager immediately looks into the discrepancy, which usually turns out to be some kind of error. Once in a while, however, the discrepancy is a sign of store-level theft that requires further investigation and—when warranted—legal action.

Finagle A Bagel's managers use the company's accounting system to make other important decisions. For every dollar of sales, a food service business makes only a few cents in profit. Finagle A Bagel makes about 8 cents in profit from every sales dollar, but Litchman is aiming to make a profit of 10 cents per dollar. He and his team need timely reports showing retailing and wholesaling revenues, the cost of goods sold, and operating expenses to calculate the company's pretax profit and measure progress toward this profit goal. Food and labour costs constitute more than two-thirds of Finagle A Bagel's costs—so the faster managers can see these numbers, the faster they can act if expenses are higher than expected.

Technology Drives the Frequent Finagler Card

Thanks to new software running on the point-of-sale system, Finagle A Bagel has been able to introduce a new and improved Frequent Finagler customer loyalty card.

Customers pay $1 to buy this card, which is activated immediately at the store. From that point on, the cardholder receives one point for every dollar spent in any Finagle A Bagel store. Points can be redeemed for free food, such as a cup of coffee, a bagel sandwich, or a bottle of fruit juice.

The Frequent Finagler card is an excellent way for the company to learn more about the buying habits of its most valuable customers. Managers can see which menu items loyal customers buy, in which store, and at what time of day. Going a step further, Finagle A Bagel is using the card to start a dialogue with loyal customers. The company's website (www .finagleabagel.com) plays a key role in this initiative. When cardholders log on and register personal data such as address, phone number, and e-mail address, they receive five points on their new Frequent Finagler card. Finagle A Bagel receives a wealth of customer data to analyze and use in targeting its marketing efforts more precisely.

Add a Product, Drop a Product

The technologies driving the Frequent Finagler card and the point-of-sale system help Finagle A Bagel to gather sufficient data to support decisions about changing the product line. "We add products to categories that are doing well, we eliminate things that are not selling, and we bring back products that have done well," says Trust. "Being able to know that a product isn't selling so we can get it off the menu and try something new is a vital piece of information."

For example, says Trust, "We just introduced a new sausage bagel pizza based on the fact that our pepperoni pizza sells very well—better than our veggie pizza." When sales data confirmed the popularity of sausage, Finagle A Bagel began introducing it in a breakfast bagel sandwich. Now the company is looking at incorporating sausage into other menu items to delight customers' taste buds and boost sales. However, Trust and her management team won't make any

product decisions without first consulting reports based on data collected by the Frequent Finagler card and the point-of-sale system.

Questions

1. Is Finagle A Bagel collecting data from internal sources, external sources, or both? What cautions apply to the sources of its data?

2. Finagle A Bagel uses information to track cash, sales revenues, and expenses on a daily basis. How does this type of accounting system encourage effective decision making and discourage store-level theft?

3. As a small business, which of the financial ratios might Finagle A Bagel want to track especially closely? Why?

4. Do you think the Frequent Finagler card has any effect on Finagle A Bagel's customer loyalty? What are the benefits to the firm of the loyalty program?

Notes

Chapter 1

1. Statistics Canada website, accessed October 5, 2006, http://www41.statcan.ca/1741/ceb1741_000_e.htm.
2. David Ebner, *Globe and Mail*, October 05, 2006, http://www.globeinvestor.com/servlet/story/RTGAM.20061005.wencana1005/GIStory/.
3. CIA World Factbook, accessed online October 5, 2006, https://www.cia.gov/cia/publications/factbook/rankorder/2173rank.html.
4. Wal-Mart Canada website accessed October 9, 2006, http://www.walmart.ca/wps-portal/storelocator/Canada-About_Walmart.jsp.
5. Statistics Canada website accessed October 9, 2006, http://www40.statcan.ca/l01/cst01/econ04.htm?sdi=gross%20domestic%20product%20expenditure%20based.
6. Statistics Canada, *Labour productivity, hourly compensation and unit labour cost*, Second quarter 2006, *The Daily*, September 13, 2006, http://www.statcan.ca/Daily/English/060913/d060913a.htm.
7. Statistics Canada, *Canadian Economic Accounts Quarterly Review*, catalogue number 13-010-XWE, accessed on October 13, 2006, http://www.statcan.ca/english/freepub/13-010-XIE/2006002/tables/table02.htm.
8. U.S. Bureau of Economic Analysis, *News Release: Gross Domestic Product and Corporate Profits*, September 28, 2006, http://www.bea.gov/bea/newsrel/gdpnewsrelease.htm.
9. Statistics Canada, Real gross domestic product, expenditure-based, website accessed October 19, 2006, http://www40.statcan.ca/l01/cst01/econ05.htm.
10. Statistics Canada, Federal Government Net Financial Debt , accessed October 15, 2006, http://www40.statcan.ca/l01/cst01/govt03a.htm.
11. For a good examination of early colonial and Canadian economic history, see W.T. Easterbrook and H. Aitkin, *Canadian Economic History* (Toronto: Macmillan, 1956).
12. Bill Weir, "Made in China: Your Job, You Future, Your Fortune," ABC News website at www.abcnews.com, September 20, 2005.

Chapter 2

1. Rita Trichur, "Conrad Black says he's feeling 'very optimistic' about upcoming U.S. trial," Canadian Press, CBC News Online, October 12, 2006, http://www.cbc.ca/cp/business/061012/b101292.html; http://www.cbc.ca/news/background/black_conrad/ accessed November 26, 2007.
2. Government of Canada, Department of Justice, Press Release, "GOVERNMENT OF CANADA ANNOUNCES LEGAL ACTION AGAINST TOBACCO COMPANIES," August 13, 2003, website accessed October 26, 2006, http://www.justice.gc.ca/en/news/nr/2003/doc_30962.html.
3. Anthony Bianco, William Symonds, and Nanette Byrnes, "The Rise and Fall of Dennis Kozlowski, *BusinessWeek*, December 23, 2002, pp. 64-77.
4. Tom Blackwell, "Distorted claims feared if remedy ads allowed," *National Post*, March 3, 2006, http://www.canada.com/nationalpost/news/story.html?id=07efed2a-2bae-47e5-9f7e-2d04460b4b7f&k=73111.
5. James Underwood, "Should You Watch Them on the Web," CIO, www.cio.com/archive/051500_face.html; accessed May 15, 2000.
6. Kristen Hays, Canadian Press, *National Post*, "Enron CEO Skilling and founder Lay convicted of conspiracy to commit fraud," May 25, 2006, http://www.canada.com/nationalpost/financialpost/story.html?id=5f2e1702-a550-478f-8e3e-d9fc665d1adf&k=1308&p=1.
7. Paula Dwyer et al., "Year of the Whistleblower," *BusinessWeek*, December 16, 2002, pp. 107-110.
8. *Victoria Times Colonist*, "General Mills joins CanWest literacy program," August 29, 2006, http://www.canada.com/victoriatimescolonist/news/story.html?id=f885e55a-d847-44e0-a0ab-56f7ab32393a&k=94772.
9. W. T. Easterbrook and H. Aitkin, *Canadian Economic History* (Toronto: Macmillan, 1956), pp. 492-93.
10. E. McInnis, *Canada: A Political and Social History*, 3rd edition (Toronto: Holt Rinehart and Winston, 1969), pp. 518-20.

11. Reuters staff, "Damages US$51M in Vioxx lawsuit," *National Post*, August 18, 2006, http://www.canada.com/nationalpost/financialpost/story.html?id=934f80e7-a222-422a-ab11-f7ddf6756048; Linda Johnson, Canadian Press, "Jury absolves Merck & Co. in New Jersey woman's heart attack, *Edmonton Journal*, July 14, 2006, http://www.canada.com/edmontonjournal/news/story.html?id=5ef42153-fcea-48f0-8516-ccc55023b9de&k=39149.

Chapter 3

1. The White House, Office of the Press Secretary, Press Release, August 6, 2002.

2. Seventh Annual Report on Canada's State of Trade, Update June 2006, http://www.dfait-maeci.gc.ca/eet/trade/sot_2006/sot-2006-en.asp#ai2.

3 *Business Review*, Federal Reserve Bank of Philadelphia, Second Quarter 2005, p. 70.

4. Seventh Annual Report on Canada's State of Trade, Update June 2006.

5. Seventh Annual Report on Canada's State of Trade, Update June 2006.

6. Central Intelligence Agency, *The World Factbook*, accessed online on November 18, 2006, https://www.cia.gov/cia/publications/factbook/index.html.

7. Seventh Annual Report on Canada's State of Trade, Update June 2006.

8. "The Global Economic Outlook and Risks from Global Imbalances," remarks by Rodrigo de Rato, managing director of International Monetary Fund, September 30, 2005.

9. William R. Cline, "Doha Can Achieve Much More than Skeptics Expect," *Finance and Development*, March 2005, p. 22.

10. Jesus Cañas and Roberto Coronado, "U.S.–Mexico Trade: Are We Still Connected?" *El Paso Business Frontier* (Federal Reserve Bank of Dallas), Issue 3, 2004, p. 2.

11. www.whitehouse.gov/news/releases/2005/08/print/20050803-1.html, September 21, 2005.

12. William M. Pride and O. C. Ferrell, *Marketing*, 12th ed. (Boston: Houghton Mifflin, 2003), p. 122.

13. The U.S. Agency for International Development, "7 More West African Countries Cut Tariffs, Boost Trade Pact," *Frontlines*, September 2005, p. 13.

14. Pride and Ferrell, *Marketing*, p. 127.

15. News release, New wind power project sends electricity to Alberta grid, CNW, November 17, 2006, http://www.cnw.ca/fr/releases/archive/November2006/17/c5943.html.

16. Based on information on the Bombardier website, www.bombardier.com, accessed November 18, 2006.

17. Nortel News Release, "Nortel and Microsoft Form Strategic Alliance to Accelerate Transformation of Business Communications," July 18, 2006, http://www2.nortel.com/go/news_detail.jsp?cat_id=-8055&oid=100203722.

18. www.iadb.org; accessed November 2, 2005.

19. ADB Operations, www.adb.org, November 2, 2005.

20. www.ebrd.com; accessed October 29, 2005.

21. Based on information from "IDG: Ten Years in China," *Asia Africa Intelligence Wire*, September 23, 2005, n.p.; "IDG Develops Partnerships in Vietnam to Expand Its Activities," *Tradeshow Week*, July 18, 2005, p. 5; Sean Callahan, "Publishers Explore Vast Chinese Market," *B to B*, December 9, 2002, p. 3; "'Let Many Gardens Bloom': IDG's Pat Kenealy Sees the Future Everywhere," *Min's B to B*, April 11, 2005, n.p.; www.idg.com.

Chapter 4

1. Based on information available at www.rogers.ca and http://www.tetesaclaques.tv/ accessed March 02, 2007; Patricia Bailey, "Quebec loves clay cartoons," *PlayBack*, February 5, 2007, http://www.playbackmag.com/articles/magazine/20070205/claque.html.

2. "The Web at Your Service," *BusinessWeek Online*, www.businessweek.com, March 18, 2002.

3. Knowledge Planet corporate website, Case study entitled "Firefly and Custom Content Dramatically Improve Productivity and Learning Quality at Bank of Montreal", accessed February 26, 2007, http://www.knowledgeplanet.com/customers/casestudies.asp?pagen=10.

4. Charlene Li, Shar VanBoskirk, "U.S. Online Marketing Forecast: 2005 to 2010," Forrester Research, Inc., website: www.forrester.com/Research/Document/Excerpt/0,7211,36546,00.html, May 2, 2005.

5. "Worldwide Internet Users Will Top 1 Billion in 2005. USA Remains #1 with 185M Internet Users," *Computer Industry Almanac* website: www.c-i-a.com/pr0904.htm, September 3, 2004.

6. Nielsen//NetRatings, "Two Out of Every Five Americans Have Broadband Access at Home," Nielsen//NetRatings website: www.nielsen-netratings.com/pr/pr_050928.pdf, September 28, 2005.

7. Based on information in Dennis Schaal, "Satisfaction 'Guaranteed' by Travelocity," *Travel Weekly*, May 2, 2005, pp. 1+; Suzanne Marta, "Travelocity Trying to Expand Services beyond Lower Prices," *Dallas Morning*

News, March 1, 2005, dallasnews.com; Avery Johnson, "Booking a $51 Flight to Fiji Online," The Flyertalk website: www.flyertalk.com, April 26, 2005; www.travelocity.com.

Chapter 5

1. Statistics Canada, *Self-Employment, historical summary*, accessed online December 07, 2006, http://www40.statcan.ca/l01/cst01/labor64.htm?searchstrdisabled=self%20employment&filename=labor64.htm&lan=eng; Statistics Canada, *Employment by industry and sex*, accessed online December 07, 2006, http://www40.statcan.ca/l01/cst01/labor10a.htm; Statistics Canada, *The 1997 Canada Yearbook*, edited by Jonina Wood, (Ottawa: Industry Canada), p. 191.
2. MSN Money website, "Wal-Mart Stores, Inc.: Financial Statement, accessed December 10, 2006, http://moneycentral.msn.com/investor/invsub/results/statemnt.aspx?symbol=WMT.
3. The Sony Ericsson Mobile Communications website: www.sonyericsson.com; accessed October 19, 2006.
4. The Wal-Mart website: www.walmart.com; accessed October 19, 2006.
5. The Oracle website: www.oracle.com; accessed October 18, 2006.
6. The Internet Security Systems website: www.iss.net; accessed October 18, 2006.
7. The Procter & Gamble website: www.pg.com; accessed October 18, 2006.
8. Boyd Erman, *National Post*, "Toronto companies at centre of merger bids," July 25, 2006, http://www.canada.com/nationalpost/news/artslife/story.html?id=3970a24e-5a97-482e-b187-0a314d068b55&k=44262.
9. Press release "Cerberus Takes Over Majority Interest in Chrysler Group and Related Financial Services Business for $7.4 Billion from DaimlerChrysler," May 14, 2007, Cerberus Capital website, accessed December 05, 2007, http://www.cerberuscapital.com/news_press_release_07132007.html.
10. Onex Corp. website, accessed December 10, 2006, http://www.onex.com/.

Chapter 6

1. Based on references from Statistics Canada Web Page, http://www.statcan.ca/.
2. Statistics Canada, "People," *The 2001 Canada Yearbook* Online Edition, Jonina Wood (ed.), Ottawa: Minister of Industry, http://142.206.72.67/02/02e/02e_007_e.htm.
3. Ibid.
4. Ibid.
5. Statistics Canada, BUSINESS AND PERSONAL SERVICES, *The 2001 Canada Yearbook* Online Edition, Jonina Wood (ed.), Ottawa: Minister of Industry, http://142.206.72.67/03/03e/03e_002_e.htm.
6. CIBC Small Business Report, "Women Entrepreneurs: Leading the Charge," 2005, accessed online December 21, http://www.cibc.com/ca/pdf/women-entrepreneurs-en.pdf.
7. U.S. Small Business Administration, *Small Business's Vital Statistics*.
8. Kim Girard and Sean Donahue, "Crash and Learn: A Field Manual for E-Business Survival," *Business2.0*, http//www.business2.com/content/magazine/indepth/2000/06/28/13700, June 11, 2000.
9. Industry Canada-Strategis, Small Business Research and Policy, Key Small Business Statistics—July 2006, "How many businesses appear and disappear each year?" http://strategis.ic.gc.ca/epic/internet/insbrp-rppe.nsf/en/rd02028e.html.
10. www.sba.gov/advo/, October 5, 2005.
11. Industry Canada-Strategis, Small Business Research and Policy, Key Small Business Statistics, July 2006, "How many jobs do small businesses create?" http://strategis.ic.gc.ca/epic/internet/insbrp-rppe.nsf/en/rd02031e.html.
12. U.S. Small Business Administration, "Small Business by the Numbers," www.sba.gov, January 11, 2003.
13. Charles Crawford, ed. *Montreal Entrepreneur's Guidebook*; Youth Employment Services Foundation, Montreal, 1997, pp. 7-34.

Chapter 7

1. Geoff Armstrong, "People Strategies Are Key to Future Success," *Personnel Today*, January 7, 2003, p. 2.
2. Stephanie Mehta and Fred Vogelstein, "AOL: The Relaunch," *Fortune*, November 14, 2005, pp. 78-84.
3. WestJet website accessed August 9, 2007, http://c1dsp.westjet.com/guest/about/westJetMissionTemplate.jsp.
4. William Diem, "Competitors Look at Nissan's Leadership," *Detroit Free Press Knight Ridder/Tribune Business News*, January 6, 2003, p. 9.
5. Christine Tierney, "Nissan CEO: The Making of a Superstar," *The Detroit News*, February 27, 2005, www.detnews.com/2005/autosinsider/0502/27/A01-101491.htm.
6. Scott Morrison, "From Tactics to Strategy," *Financial Times*, January 24, 2003, p. 8.

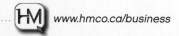

7. Henry Mintzberg, "The Manager's Job: Folklore and Fact," *Harvard Business Review*, July-August 1975, pp. 49-61.
8. Robert Kreitner, *Management*, 9th ed. (Boston: Houghton Mifflin, 2004), p. 505.
9. Ricky W. Griffin, *Fundamentals of Management*, 3d ed. (Boston: Houghton Mifflin, 2003), p. 96.
10. "IBM Announces PC Division's 2005 Plan," *SinoCast China Business Daily News*, London (UK), January 24, 2005, p. 1.
11. Paul R. La Monica, "After Carly, Is HP a Bargain?" *Money*, April 2005, p. 108.

Chapter 8

1. Bill Saporito, "Can Wal-Mart Get Any Bigger? (Yes, a lot Bigger . . . Here's How)," *Time*, January 13, 2003, p. 38.
2. Robert Kreitner, *Foundations of Management: Basics and Best Practices* (Boston: Houghton Mifflin, 2005), pp. 186-187.
3. Stephanie Thompson, "'God Is in the Details': Campbell Soup Chief Energizes Marketing; Fingerman Pushes Innovation Agenda to Stimulate Sleepy Sales," *Advertising Age*, January 27, 2003, p. 3.
4. Kreitner, *Management*, p. 192.
5. Rob Goffee and Gareth Jones, "The Character of a Corporation: How Your Company's Culture Can Make or Break Your Business," *Jones Harper Business*, p. 182.
6. Paul Sloan, "Dell's Man on Deck," *Business 2.0*, February 2003.
7. "Mergers' Missing Link: Cultural Integration," *PR Newswire*, January 23, 2003.
8. Kreitner, *Management*, p. 49.

Chapter 9

1. Robert Kreitner, *Management*, 9th ed. (Boston: Houghton Mifflin, 2004), pp. 577-578.
2. The 3M website: www.3m.com; accessed October 31, 2005.
3. The Campbell Soup website: www.campbellsoup.com; accesed October 31, 2005.
4. Kim Niles, "What Makes Six Sigma Work?" iSixSigma website: www.isixsigma.com.
5. The Maxager Technology website: www.maxager.com; accessed November 6, 2005.
6. The Dell website: www.dell.com; accessed November 6, 2005.

Chapter 10

1. Statistics Canada website: www.statcan.ca; accessed August 19, 2007; Vicki Lee Parker, "Workers at North Carolina Companies Undergo Diversity Training," *News and Observer*, Raleigh, January 13, 2003.
2. www.rbc.ca, accessed August 19, 2007.
3. Ibid.
4. Linnea Anderson, "Monster Worldwide, Inc.," Hoovers .com, http://cobrands.hoovers.com/global/cobrands/proquest/factsheet.xhtml?COID=41617.
5. Harry Wessel, "Jobs Column," *The Orlando Sentinel*, January 15, 2003.
6. www.edwardjones.com, accessed December 4, 2007.
7. www.robertjones.com, accessed August 19, 2007.
8. Ibid., pp. 521-523.
9. Cynthia D. Fisher, Lyle F. Schoenfeldt, and James B. Shaw, *Human Resource Management* (Boston: Houghton Mifflin, 2003), p. 527.

Chapter 11

1. Douglas McGregor, *The Human Side of the Enterprise* (New York: McGraw-Hill, 1960).
2. William Ouchi, *Theory Z* (Reading, MA: Addison-Wesley, 1981).
3. Ricky W. Griffin, *Fundamentals of Management*, 3d ed. (Boston: Houghton Mifflin, 2006), p. 334.
4. Alison Overholt, "Power up the People: Economy Stuck in the Doldrums? Morale Stuck There Too? Here Are a Few Things That You Can Do to Jazz Things up in 2003," *Fast Company*, January 2003, p. 50.
5. "Is Job Stress Taking Its Toll in Your Facility," *Safety Management*, February 2003, p. 3.
6. Alan Deutschman, "Making Change," *Fast Company*, May 2005, pp. 52+.
7. Nanette Byrnes, "Star Search," *BusinessWeek*, October 10, 2005, p. 78.
8. www.starbucks.com/job center.
9. "Boston College Report Presents Challenges and Advantages of Telework," *Work & Family Newsbrief*, January 2003, p. 8.
10. Arif Mohamed, "Bosses Split Over Productivity of Teleworkers," *Computer Weekly*, March 29, 2005, p. 55.
11. Ricky W, Griffin, *Fundamentals of Management* (Boston: Houghton Mifflin, 2006), pp. 428-447.
12. Barry L. Reece and Rhonda Brandt, *Effective Human Relations: Personal and Organizational Applications* (Boston: Houghton Mifflin, 2005), pp. 280-285.

13. "Case Study: Using the Right Incentive Can Improve Cooperation Among Departments," *Report on Customer Relationship Management*, September 2003, p. 5.

14. Bill Fischer and Andy Boynton, "Virtuoso Teams" *Harvard Business Review*, July-August 2005, pp. 116-123.

15. Milton Moskowitz and Robert Levering, "10 Great companies to Work For," *Fortune International*, January 20, 2003, p. 26.

16. Jens Meiners, "M-B Changes Product Development," *Automotive News*, September 12, 2005, p.18.

Chapter 12

1. Based on information from Julie Bosman, "What's Cool Online? Teenagers Render Verdict," *New York Times*, September 29, 2005, p. C14; Mae Anderson, "On the Crest of the Wave," *Adweek*, September 13, 2004, www.adweek.com; Matt DeMazza, "Teen Magnets," *Footwear News*, November 17, 2003, p. 15; Lev Grossman, "The Quest for Cool," *Time*, September 8, 2003, pp. 48-54; Irma Zandl, "B-T-S: Anything Hot?" *Marketing Insight from the Zandl Group*, August 2003, (n.p.); Barbara White-Sax, "Teens Become Price Savvy in Search for What's Cool," *Drug Store News*, March 23, 2003, pp. 17+.

2. *Marketing News*, September 15, 2004, p. 1.

3. Jagdish N. Sheth and Rajendras Sisodia, "More than Ever Before, Marketing Is under Fire to Account for What It Spends," *Marketing Management*, Fall 1995, pp. 13-14.

4. Coca-Cola 2004 Annual Report, www2.coca-cola.com/investors/annualandotherreports/2004/pdf/Coca-Cola _10-K_Item_01.pdf; accessed January 6, 2006.

5. Lynette Ryals and Adrian Payne, "Customer Relationship Management in Financial Services: Towards Information-Enabled Relationship Marketing," *Journal of Strategic Marketing*, March 2001, p. 3.

6. Werner J. Reinartz and V. Kumark, "On the Profitability of Long-Life Customers in a Noncontractual Setting: an Empirical Investigation and Implications for Marketing," *Journal of Marketing*, October 2000, pp. 17-35.

7. Roland T. Rust, Katherine N. Lemon, and Valarie A. Zeithaml, "Return on Marketing: Using Customer Equity to Focus Marketing Strategy," *Journal of Marketing* 68 (January 2004), pp. 109-127.

8. Rajkumar Venkatesan and V. Kumar, "A Customer Lifetime Value Framework for Customer Selection and Resource Allocation Strategy," *Journal of Marketing* 68 (October 2004), pp. 106-125.

9. Gina Chon, "Toyota's Marketers Get Respect—Now They Want Love," *Wall Street Journal*, January 11, 2006, p. B1.

10. Megan E. Mulligan, "Wireless for the Well Off," *Forbes.com*, http://forbes.com/2003/01/21/cz_mm _0121tentech_ print.html; accessed January 21, 2003.

11. Michael J. Weiss, "To Be About to Be," *American Demographics*, September 2003, pp. 29-36.

12. Cliff Edwards, "Inside Intel," *BusinessWeek*, January 9, 2006, p. 46.

13. Kenneth Hein, "Disney Puts Pooh, Power Rangers, Princess under Wing with $500M," *Brandweek*, January 27, 2003, p. 6.

14. Mark Jewell, "Dunkin' Donuts Eyes Turn Westward: Chain Evolves from No Frills," *The Coloradoan*, January 17, 2005, p. E1.

15. William M. Pride and O. C. Ferrell, *Marketing: Concepts and Strategies* (Boston: Houghton Mifflin, 2006), p. 233.

16. Chad Kaydo, "A Position of Power," *Sales and Marketing Management*, June 2000, p. 106.

Chapter 13

1. Peter Lewis, "Play That Funky Music, White Toy," *Fortune*, February 7, 2005, pp. 38-39.

2. William Hall, "Logitech Proves No Mouse Among Men," *Financial Times*, January 6, 2003, p. 15.

3. Procter & Gamble, www.pg.com (accessed April 27, 2006). Chennai, *Businessline*, February 6, 2005, p. 1; www.pg.com/common/sitemap.jhtml.

4. www.gefn.com/search/index; accessed January 24, 2003.

5. Kate MacArthur, "Drink Your Fruits, Veggies: Water's the New Fitness Fad," *Advertising Age*, January 3, 2005, p. 4.

6. Joseph B. White and Norihiko Shirouzu, "Ford Gambles in Rolling Out New F-150," *Wall Street Journal*, January 6, 2003, p. A15.

7. "10 Worst Strategy Changes," *Advertising Age*, December 19, 2005, p. 10.

8. Mike Beirne, "Hershey Gets Sweet with Sugarfree," *Brandweek*, January 20, 2003, p. 4.

9. Peter D. Bennett (ed.), *Dictionary of Marketing Terms* (Chicago: American Marketing Association and NTC Publishing Group, 1995), p. 27.

10. "Market Profile," www.plma.com; accessed January 23, 2006.

11. Deborah Ball and Sarah Ellison. "Two Shampoos Lather Up for Duel," *Wall Street Journal*, January 28, 2003, p. B7.

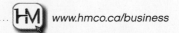

12. World's Most Valuable Brands," Interbrand, www .interbrand.com, July 2005.

13. Gabriel Kahn, "Still Going for the Gold," *Wall Street Journal*, January 28, 2003, pp. B1 and B4.

14. www.amazon.com; accessed January 23, 2006.

15. Emily Lambert, "The Buck Stops Here," *Forbes.com*, www.forbes.com/forbes/2003/0106/052.html; accessed January 6, 2003.

16. Alex Taylor III, "Porsche's Risky Recipe," *Fortune*, www.fortune.com/fortune/print/0,15935,418670,00 .html; accessed February 3, 2003.

17. www.netzero.com.

Chapter 14

1. "Industry Report 2005," *Convenience Store News*, April 18, 2005.

2. Statistics Canada, *The Daily*, March 27, 2006, http:// www.statcan.ca/Daily/English/060327/d060327a .htm

3. Michael Barbaro, "Readings," *Washington Post*, January 23, 2005, p. F3; David Moin, "Category Killers' Concerns: Overgrowth and Extinction," *WWD*, January 6, 2005, p. 17.

4. www.dsa.org; accessed January 28, 2006.

5. www.donotcall.gov/FAQ; accessed January 27, 2006.

6. John Eggerton, "DirecTV Settles $10 Million in Complaints," *Broadcasting & Cable*, December 19, 2005, pp. 4, 30.

7. Nicole Urso, "HSN Viewers Shop with Their Remotes," *Response*, May 2005, p. 8.

8. www.netflix.com; accessed January 30, 2006.

9. Robert McMillan, "Got 796 Quarters Handy? Get Yourself an iPod," *PC World*, January 2006, p. 54.

10. Sandra O'Loughlin, "Out with the Old: Malls versus centres," *Brandweek*, May 9, 2005, p. 30.

11. Statistics Canada, "Annual Survey of Advertising and Related Services—2004," posted May 2, 2006, http:// 222.statcan.ca/Daily/English/060502/d060502c.htm.

12. Canadian Newspapers Association, "A profile of the Canadian daily newspaper industry and its association," revised November 2005, http://www.cna-acj.ca/ Client/CNA/cna.nsf/object/Profile2006/$file/CNA per cent 20 English per cent 20Profile.pdf.

13. Paul Sloan, "The Sales Force that Rocks," *Business 2.0*, July 1, 2005, cnnmoney.com

14. Terence Shimp, *Advertising, Promotion, and Supplemental Aspects of Integrated Marketing Communications*, 2006, Mason, Ohio: Southwestern, pp. 476, 527.

15. Berry & Homer Wraps Bus Leading Lance Armstrong and Tour of Hope Team on Cross-Country Trek, *Business Wire*.

Chapter 15

1. Arthur Andersen, The Wikipedia website: www .wikipedia.org; accessed November 14, 2006.

2. American Institute of Certified Public Accountants (AICPA) website: www.aicpa.org; accessed November 14, 2006.

3. Nanette Byrnes and William Symonds, "Is the Avalanche Headed for Pricewaterhouse?" *BusinessWeek*, October 14, 2002, pp. 45-46.

4. Steve Rosenbush, "The Message in Ebbers' Sentence," *BusinessWeek Online*, www.businessweek.com, July 14, 2005.

5. "Ex-Tyco CEO Dennis Kozlowski Found Guilty," MSNBC, www.msnbc.msn.com, June 17, 2005.

6. Wendhy Grossman/Houston "The Enron Case Drags On," Time, www.time.com, October 24, 2006.

7. Canadian Institute of Chartered Accountants, www .cica.ca; accessed August 19, 2007.

Chapter 16

1. Statcan website www.statcan.ca: Cindy Lecavalier, *National and Regional Trends in Business Bankruptcies, 1980 to 2005*, (electronic resource). Ottawa: Statistics Canada, 2006.

2. Ian Rowley, "Fuji Heavy Trades GM for Toyota," *BusinessWeek Online*, www.businessweek.com, October 6, 2005; http://www.gm.com/corporate/investor _information/earnings/hist_earnings/05_q3/print .jsp, accessed December 18, 2007.

3. "Amicus Briefs in Enron Bankruptcy Litigation, BondMarkets.com website, www.bondmarkets.com, March 18, 2004.

4. Paul R. LaMonica "Google Sets $2.7 Billion IPO," CNN/Money website, http://money.cnn.com; accessed November 30, 2006.

5. Yahoo! Finance website: http://finance.yahoo.com; accessed November 29, 2006.

Sources

Chapter 1: Based on information from Steve Ham, "How This Tiger Got Its Roar," *BusinessWeek*, October 30, 2006, pp. 92–100; "Wipro to Open First Software Development Centre in Beijing," *Asia Africa Intelligence Wire*, September 12, 2005, n.p.; Steve Hamm, "Taking a Page from Toyota's Playbook," *BusinessWeek*, August 22–29, 2005, pp. 69–72; "Wipro to Invest More in Core Outsourcing," *Asia Africa Intelligence Wire*, September 7, 2005, n.p.; Wipro Quarterly Profit Rises 41% on Outsourcing," *InformationWeek*, July 22, 2005, n.p.; "Wipro, Ltd.," *Wall Street Journal*, July 25, 2005, p. C12; Terry Atlas, "Bangalore's Big Dreams," *U.S. News & World Report*, May 2, 2005, pp. 50+.

Chapter 2: Based on information from "New Belgium Brewing Wins Ethics Award," *Denver Business Journal*, January 2, 2003, Denver.bizjournals.com/Denver/stories/2002/12/30/daily21.html; Richard Brandes, "Beer Growth Brands," *Beverage Dynamics*, September–October 2002, pp. 37ff; www.newbelgium.com.

Chapter 5: Based on information from Laura M. Holson, "Former P&G Chief Names Disney Chairman," *New York Times*, June 29, 2006, p. C13; Ronald Grover, "How Eisner Saved the Magic Kingdom," *BusinessWeek Online*, September 30, 2005, www.businessweek.com; Ben Fritz, "Mouse Plays Board Games," *Daily Variety*, August 19, 2005, p. 1; Kim Christensen, "Disney Board Gives Shareholders More Clout," *Los Angeles Times*, August 19, 2005, p. C2; Gary Gentile, "Roy Disney, Company Resolve Their Disputes," *Washington Post*, July 9, 2005, p. D1; Merissa Marr, "One Year Later, Disney Attempts Smoother Ride," *Wall Street Journal*, February 7, 2005, pp. B1+; Joann S. Lublin and Bruce Orwall, "Funds Press Disney for Timeline to Replace Eisner," *Wall Street Journal*, May 21, 2004, p. B2.

Chapter 6: Based on information from Ed Christman, "Newbury Comics Cuts Staff," *Billboard*, September 10, 2005, p. 8; Wendy Wilson, "Newbury Comics," *Video Business*, December 20, 2004, p. 18; Ed Christman, "'We Have All Had to Grow Up a Little,'" *Billboard*, September 27, 2003, pp. N3ff; www.newburycomics.com.

Chapter 7: Based on information from Kristen Bellstrom, "Can Mark Hurd Reinvent Hewlett Packard?" *Smart Money*, October 2005, p. 33; "HP Chief Hurd Sees 'Lots of Work' to Change Company," *eWeek*, September 7, 2005, n.p.; Pui-Wing Tam, "Boss Talk," *Wall Street Journal*, April 4, 2005, pp. B1+; Peter Burrows and Ben Elgin, "Memo to HP's Mark Hurd," *BusinessWeek Online*, April 4, 2005, www.businessweek.com; "The Word from Hurd," *BusinessWeek Online*, September 1, 2005, www.businessweek.com; www.hp.com.

Chapter 8: Based on information from Lindsay Chappell, "GM Just Didn't Get the Magic of Spring Hill," *Automotive News*, July 25, 2005, pp. 14+; Dave Guilford, "Once Different Saturn Looks More Like GM," *Automotive News*, June 14, 2004, p. 30V; Lindsay Chappell, "GM's Saturn Plant May Lose Its Saturns," *Automotive News*, June 27, 2005, pp 1+; Lee Hawkins, Jr., and Joann S. Lublin, "Emergency Repairman," *Wall Street Journal*, April 6, 2005, pp. B1+; www.gm.com.

Chapter 9: Based on information in "Spectrum Brands Names David R. Lumley President, North America," *Business Wire*, January 16, 2006, www.spectrumbrands.com; Dick Ahles, "Remington Leaves Bridgeport Site," *New York Times*, January 9, 2005, p. 14CN-2; "Rayovac Corp.: Battery Maker to Change Name and Boost Its Earnings Target," *Wall Street Journal*, February 15, 2005, p. 1; "Remington Seeks Sexy Image after Court Win," *Marketing*, June 27, 2002, p. 1; "Analysis: What Remington's Ruling Means for Brands," *Marketing*, June 27, 2002, p. 15; www.remington-products.com and www.spectrumbrands.com.

Chapter 10: Based on information from Geoff Edgers, "With Eye on Growth, Aquarium Names New Chief," *Boston Globe*, June 15, 2005, www.bostonglobe.com; Stephanie Vosk, "It's February, But on Summer Jobs, Hope Springs Eternal," *Boston Globe*, February 20, 2005, p. 3; Jeffrey Krasner, "New England Aquarium Plunges into Financial Turmoil," *Boston Globe*, December 13, 2002, www.boston.com/global; www.neaq.org.

Chapter 11: Based on information from *Pioneering American Flatbread* video by Houghton Mifflin; Andrew Nemethy, "Waitsfield: American Flatbread," *See Vermont*, February 21, 2001, seevermont.nybor.com/dining/story/20722.html; www.americanflatbread.com.

Chapter 12: Sources: Based on information from Kerry Capell, Ariane Sains, and Cristina Lindblad, "IKEA: How the Swedish Retailer Became a Global Cult Brand," *BusinessWeek,* November 14, 2005, pp. 96+; "IKEA's Growth Limited by Style Issues, Says CEO," *Nordic Business Report,* January 21, 2004, www .nordicbusinessreport.com; "IKEA Sets New Heights with Cat," *Printing World,* August 21, 2003, p. 3; www.ikea-usa.com.

Chapter 13: Based on information from Adam Aston, "All Bruce, All the Time," *BusinessWeek,* November 7, 2005, p. 92; "Sirius Revenues Soar, But Losses Widen," *InternetWeek,* November 1, 2005, www.internetweek.com; Brad Stone, "Greetings, Earthlings: Satellite Radio for Cars Is Taking Off and Adding New Features—Now Broadcasters Are Starting to Fight Back," *Newsweek,* January 26, 2003, p. 55; "In Brief, Radio: XM Radio Ends '03 with 1.36 Million Users," *Los Angeles Times,* January 8, 2004, p. C3; Stephen Holden, "High-Tech Quirkiness Restores Radio's Magic," *New York Times,* December 26, 2003, pp. E1+; David Pogue, "Satellite Radio Extends Its Orbit," *New York Times,* December 18, 2003, p. G1.

Chapter 14: Sources: Elsa McLaren, "Harry Potter's final adventure to get record print run," Times Online, March 15, 2007, http://entertainment.timesonline.co.uk/ tol/arts_and_entertainment/books/article1521607.ece; and based on information from Sean Smith, "Movies: Who's That Guy with Harry Potter?" *Newsweek,* December 18, 2006, p. 22; Vicky Hallett, "The Power of Potter," *U.S. News & World Report,* July 25, 2005, p. 44; Jonathan Landreth, "Harry's Flame Heats Up China," *Washington Post,* November 26, 2005, p. C3; "Latest 'Potter' Spells Magic at Holiday Weekend Box Office," *Wall Street Journal,* November 28, 2005, p. B4; Jeffrey A. Trachtenberg and Deborah Ball, "A Magical Moment for Publishing," *Wall Street Journal,* July 18, 2005, p. B3.

Chapter 16: Based on information from Nate Hinkel, "Couple's Bed-and-Breakfast Benefits from SBA Loan," *Arkansas Business,* May 16, 2005, p. 22; Farrah Austin, "Thyme Out in Arkansas," *Southern Living,* April 2003, p. 33; www.mountainthyme.com.

Photo Credits

Chapter 1: Page 2: The Canadian Press (Larry MacDougal); Page 11: AP/Wide World; Page 12: Top: PRNewswire/eBay, Inc.; Bottom: AP/Wide World/Michael Probst; Page 16: AP/Wide World; Page 28: © Bettman/Corbis; Page 32: The Canadian Press (Larry MacDougal). **Chapter 2:** Page 38: © Royalty Free/Corbis; Page 50: The Canadian Press (Don Denton); Page 55: © Shawn Thew/epa/Corbis; Page 60: The Canadian Press (Sherbrooke La Tribune); Page 65: © Royalty Free/Corbis. **Chapter 3:** Page 70: The Canadian Press (Jonathan Hayward); Page 80: © Royalty Free/Corbis; Page 82: The Canadian Press (Rex); Page 91: The Canadian Press (St. John's Telegram/Rhonda Hayward); Page 94: © Royalty Free/Corbis; Page 98: The Canadian Press (Jonathan Hayward). **Chapter 4:** Page 104: Canadian Press; Page 123: AP/Wide World/Ben Curtis; Page 124: Courtesy Sprint PCS; Page 129: AP/Wide World/Gautam Singh; Page 131: Canadian Press.

Chapter 5: Page 136: The Canadian Press (Steve White); Page 140: AP/Wide World/The Daily Record, Heather Marcus; Page 148: AP/Wide World/Greg Baker; Page 150: © Royalty Free/Corbis; Page 157: © Rudy Sulgan/Corbis; Page 160: The Canadian Press (Steve White). **Chapter 6:** Page 164: The Canadian Press (Ryan Remiorz); Page 169: The Canadian Press/Toronto Star; Page 170: AP Photo/ Jae C. Hong; Page 173: © Royalty Free/Corbis; Page 174: Courtesy, Robeez Footwear; Page 182: © Bettman/Corbis; Page 186: The Canadian Press (Ryan Remiorz). **Chapter 7:** Page 194: Brad Barket/Getty Images; Page 199: CP/Larry MacDougal; Page 204: AP/Wide World/Koji Sasahara; Page 206: Toronto Star/Ken Faught; Page 210: © Royalty Free/Corbis; Page 214: Brad Barket/Getty Images. **Chapter 8:** Page 222: Rex/Paul Cooper; Page 227: CP/Larry MacDougal; Page 231: © Adrian Bradshaw/epa/Corbis; Page 236: AP/Mel Evans; Page 242: © Randy Faris/Corbis; Page 243: Rex/Paul Cooper. **Chapter 9:** Page 250: © Paul Benedict/Transtock/Corbis; Page 254: CP/Jeff McIntosh; Page 259: © Kate Mitchell/zefa/Corbis; Page 262: CP/Ryan Remiorz; Page 272: CP Photo/ Whitehorse Star/Vince Federoff; Page 275: © Paul Benedict/Transtock/Corbis.

Chapter 10: Darren McCollester/Getty Images; Page 288: © Jason Horowitz/ zefa/Corbis; Page 290: © Royalty Free/Digital Vision/Getty; Page 294: © Jack Hollingsworth/Corbis; Page 298: © Helen King/Corbis; Page 301: Courtesy HazMat Hotzone; Page 305: Darren McCollester/Getty Images. **Chapter 11:** Page 312: © David Vintiner/zefa/Corbis; Page 318: AP/Wide World; Page 327: AP/Wide World/Robert F. Bukaty; Page 329: AP/Wide World/Ted S. Warren; Page 332: AP/Wide World; Page 336: © David Vintiner/zefa/Corbis. **Chapter 12:** Page 344: CP/Don Denton; Page 352: PRNewswire/The Reader's Digest; Page 357: Courtesy RoC® Retinol Correxion®; Page 366: Courtesy Uni-Ball; Page 367: CP/Don Denton. **Chapter 13:** Page 372: Justin Sullivan/Getty Images; Page 375: PRNewswire/Tissot Watches; Page 381: PRNewswire/Gatorade; Page 388: CP/ Marianne Helm; Page 395: ©2005 GlaxoSmithKline; Page 398: CP/Jonathan Hayward; Page 405: Justin Sullivan/Getty Images. **Chapter 14:** Page 410: © Gregor Schuster/zefa/Corbis; Page 414: AP/Wide World/Paul Sancya; Page 421: CP/Steve White; Page 426: CP/Jonathan Hayward; Page 427: AP/Wide World/ Kevin Rivoli; Page 430: CP/Richard Buchan; Page 442: PRNewswire/The Merchandise Mart; Page 444: © Gregor Schuster/zefa/Corbis. **Chapter 15:** Page 454: © Ferruccio/Alamy; Page 458: AP/Louis Lanzano; Page 461: AP/Wide World; Page 476: CP/Adrian Lam; Page 481: © Ferruccio/Alamy. **Chapter 16:** Page 486: © Getty Images; Page 489: Brian Atkinson/Alamy; Page 491: Canadian Press; Page 501: © Richard Hamilton Smith/Corbis; Page 511: © Getty Images.

Name Index

Organization Index

Subject Index

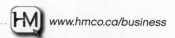

www.hmco.ca/business